The Emotions

The Emotions
A Cultural Reader

Edited by Helena Wulff

Oxford • New York

English edition
First published in 2007 by
Berg
Editorial offices:
First Floor, Angel Court, 81 St Clements Street, Oxford OX4 1AW, UK
175 Fifth Avenue, New York, NY 10010, USA

Berg is the imprint of Oxford International Publishers Ltd.

Library of Congress Cataloging-in-Publication Data

A catalogue record for this book is available from the Library of Congress.

British Library Cataloguing-in-Publication Data

A catalogue record for this book is available from the British Library.

ISBN 978 1 84520 367 2 (Cloth)
ISBN 978 1 84520 368 9 (Paper)

Typeset by Apex Publishing, LLC, Madison, WI, USA
Printed in the United Kingdom by Biddles Ltd, King's Lynn.

www.bergpublishers.com

In memory of Eduardo P. Archetti
a much loved and admired teacher, colleague and friend

Contents

PART II: LOVE AND HATE

PART III: ANGER, SHAME AND GRIEF

PART IV: DESIRE AND EXPECTATIONS

Acknowledgements

This work, *The Emotions: A Cultural Reader* is dedicated to the memory of Eduardo Archetti, who died prematurely in June 2005. When I, as a Swede, say that Eduardo, the Argentine, was emotionally expressive, radiating warmth and energy, this may be seen as an example of a cross-cultural difference between Latin Americans and Scandinavians, probably not in how we experience emotions but perhaps in how we express them—at least contextually. There is no doubt that Eduardo, who lived and worked in Oslo during the last decades of his life, put a lot of personal and intellectual vivacity into Scandinavian as well as European anthropology. Among many other pursuits, he was an early proponent of a literary anthropology and took an informed interest in the anthropology of performance, dance and sport. Sadly, Eduardo Archetti was supposed to write a chapter for *The Emotions,* a chapter on emotions, sport and identity. As late as two months before his death I was still in communication with him about this chapter. Now we are grappling with the grief, which incidentally is one of the emotions discussed in what follows here.

The Emotions has benefited from discussions during a one-day workshop titled 'Emotions Day' at the Department of Social Anthropology, Stockholm University, which was organized by Galina Lindquist and myself in February 2006. I appreciate the detailed and generous comments by two anonymous readers on the proposal and later on the full manuscript. Combining teaching, administrative duties, research and writing is often a tricky task, which requires precise planning. I am grateful for a part-time grant from the Social Science Faculty at Stockholm University during the final, but demanding, period of work on *The Emotions.* I also wish to thank The Academy for Irish Cultural Heritages, AICH, University of Ulster, and especially its director Máiréad Nic Craith, and Ulrich Kockel. Being able to devote my first visit as a research scholar at AICH in 2006–07 to *The Emotions* was a crucial step to its completion. Susann Ullberg deserves special thanks for compiling the Index.

I was very pleased when Kathryn Earle commissioned *The Emotions.* With her intuition and eye for character, she hit right on an old interest of mine: psychological anthropology. Both Kathryn Earle and Hannah Shakespeare, who took over as Berg's anthropology editor after a while, should be applauded for compassionate, yet firm, monitoring of this project. Even before I met Hannah, it was clear from her friendly and fun e-mail style that I would greatly enjoy working with her.

Helena Wulff

Introduction
The Cultural Study of Mood and Meaning

Helena Wulff

Emotions are vital to all of us. From love and hate to grief, fear and envy, emotions are increasingly understood as driving forces in social life. *The Emotions: A Cultural Reader* applies a cross-cultural perspective on emotions, which accentuates an awareness of emotions in social and cultural context. This also points to problems of comparison and translation of local terms and emotional experiences, and to what extent there are culturally distinct emotions. Are emotions cultural or universal? Emotions theory early identified the importance of the person, as collectively constructed, but also the individual, the self and subjectivity in emotional experiences. Recent social science work on emotions has incorporated ideas from neuroscience, such as the finding that emotions are central in rational choice making and social adjustment, as well as the fact that emotions influence thought. Emotions weave into cognition and biology. Importantly, this cross-disciplinary approach closes the traditional Western gap in which emotions are separated from rationality and thought: the heart versus mind debate.

The Emotions is organized in five sections beginning with a general studies section on Exploring Emotions in relation to culture, biology and ecology. Then we move on to investigations into Love and Hate; Anger, Shame and Grief; Desire and Expectations; as well as The Emotional Self and Identity. The Reader concludes with an Afterword by Robert LeVine in which he points out that: "I have hopes that in the area of emotion it will be evident even to the white-coated tribe that contexts beyond the laboratory are critical to their science. In their ethnographic investigations of emotions in context, anthropologists are natural historians of diversity". And he cautions, "the studies reported and reviewed in this volume illustrate how mistaken it would be to assume that emotions are unproblematically translated from one culture or historical period to another". The chapters relate to each other theoretically and thematically, especially in the five sections, sometimes in debate. This Introduction offers a synthesis of the panorama of the study of emotions, mostly anthropological, by tracing the development of this kind of research while appreciating both the theoretical and the empirical diversity that characterize these studies. It is an account of the significance of scholarship on the emotions at this moment in time.

Supported by theoretical and ethnographic extracts from powerful classic essays in anthropology, sociology and psychology as well as philosophy, this Cultural Reader reveals a whole range of new issues in the study of emotions from academia and nationalism, adoption, performance and advertising to tourism and migration, which are brought out in commissioned chapters. Theoretical and ethnographic references to the classic articles run through many of the new chapters, as a web of ideas. Most of the new chapters are written by anthropologists, but there is also a frontline chapter from neuroscience on emotions in the human brain. By including a variety of ethnographic examples from Europe, Russia, the United States, Latin America, Africa, Asia, and Australia, this Reader shows the force, richness and omnipresence of emotions in modern social life across the globe.

This Reader seeks to fuse not only different disciplinary traditions, but also different national traditions in the cultural study of emotions by putting together anthropological treatment of the emotions mainly emanating from the so-called American and British Schools of anthropology. The American Culture and Personality Studies which focussed on cross-cultural variation in socialization, personality and child-rearing practices developed into psychological anthropology, which on the whole is the current term (LeVine 1982; Schwartz, White, and Lutz 1992). In Britain, Needham (1962) and Lienhardt (1961) can be said to have made early contributions to the anthropology of the emotions, and more recently the British School has played up the notion of 'sensibility' as exemplified by Stewart and Strathern (2002). The French School has also dealt with emotions, such as in Maurice Leenhardt's (1947) *Do Kamo,* which has been brought back by Alexandre Surralés (2003). Presented as an interdisciplinary approach, Milton's (2002) argument for an ecology of emotions is elaborated in *Loving Nature,* which sheds light on the fact that environments, landscapes, places, buildings etc. are often inscribed with absent people and past events, stories and classifications by humans, as well as anticipations of future social relations to these places. A recent important addition to the anthropology of emotions is the volume *Mixed Emotions: Anthropological Studies of Feeling* edited by Milton and Svašek (2005). It suggests that the traditional contradictory views on emotions as either universalist biological phenomena or culturally constructed should be combined. As Svašek (2005: 2) notes, the 1970s saw the beginning of more systematic reflection on the role of emotions ranging from 'cultural relativism and constructionism, which lead to an emphasis on discourse (as distinct from culture) as the main object of analysis, followed by a counter-emphasis on embodiment, sensory experience, and renewed interest in naturalistic approaches to emotion and critical psychoanalysis'. As a part of the increasing interest in social relationships between humans and animals, John Knight (2005) writes about the human-monkey interface at monkey parks in Japan, discussing maternal feelings among monkeys and the visitors who watch them.

In research, especially when it involves first-hand data collection with people during participant observation or interviews, emotions matter. With Malinowski's (1967) controversial diary anthropologists have long been aware of the potential implications of this, not least as it was followed by the reflexive turn (Clifford and Marcus 1986; Marcus and Fischer 1986). Svašek (2005) considers emotions in anthropological fieldwork, especially the idea of empathy, central and distinct to ethnography and by extension to theoretical work in the discipline of anthropology. Wikan (1992) discusses this process of understanding in the field in terms of resonance.

Access to the field usually involves an emotional event 'pushing the fieldworker deeper into the setting' (Wulff 2000: 152; see also Wulff 1998). This happened to me in the beginning of my fieldwork in the transnational ballet world at the Stockholm Opera. I found myself in a confrontation with the ballet director in a corridor, which might have put my fieldwork in jeopardy. But he sent a dancer to calm me down, and later the ballet director became the single most important informant in my study. As the ballet world is characterized by expressions of strong emotions in the everyday life backstage, I had confirmed that I was just like the dance people I was studying. Steven Feld (1990) had a similar breakthrough in his fieldwork among the Kaluli in Papua New Guinea when he received a letter from home which touched him so much that he wept out of sheer happiness. That was when the Kaluli realized that he was just like them, another human being. Exiting the field often also evokes strong emotions, which already Evans-Pritchard (1956: 79) commented on (in the parlance of his time): 'an anthropologist has failed unless, when he says goodbye to the natives, there is on both sides the sorrow of parting' (see also Abu-Lughod this Reader.) Some ethnographers seem to be better at spending more time on empathy or resonance than others. Elizabeth Tonkin's (2005) call to take informants' emotions into account in the emotional process in the field is easy to agree with. Not only fieldworkers have feelings, so do the people we study.

Classic Studies of Emotion

The last section of *The Emotions* starts with a an extract from a chapter by Clifford Geertz, 'Person, Time and Conduct in Bali' from his *The Interpretation of Cultures,* a collection of essays which changed the discipline of anthropology and had a major impact on neighbouring disciplines by arguing for an interpretive approach to culture in social life. The chapter explores how the people of Bali define, perceive, and react to, that is, think about, individual persons. This article was also a seminal provocation over the question of the cultural construction of emotions, just as the groundbreaking article, 'The Shame of Headhunters and the Autonomy of Self' by Michelle Rosaldo (who died tragically in an accident in her field in the Philippines) offers an ethnographic extract here. Focussing on the notion of shame among Ilongot headhunters and separating it from that of shame in our culture, Rosaldo discusses shame and sex. She looks at whether shame entails that men or women should be restrained or not, issues of who feels shame, and when, and the relationships between the senses of 'having shame' and 'being shamed'; all are, according to Rosaldo, cultural variables shaped by social form. In 'Grief and a Headhunter's Rage: On the Cultural Force of Emotions', Renato Rosaldo (1989) weaves an ethnographic story about why an Ilongot man cut off human heads: 'He says that rage, born of grief, impels him to kill his fellow human beings. He claims that he needs a place "to carry his anger"'. By throwing away the victim's head, he is also hoping to throw away the anger caused by his grief. This classic chapter in the anthropology of emotions examines the cultural force of emotions. (It is also an account of how the author, the husband of Michelle Rosaldo, see above, experienced the death of his wife.)

In 'Emotion, Thought, and Estrangement: Emotion as a Cultural Category', Catherine Lutz (1986) examines the concept of emotion as a master Western cultural category, which has often obscured the process of anthropological translation between two cultural systems. It is crucial to understand both sides from a meaning point of view. As Lutz puts forward, the concept of emotions has been left out because emotions have been regarded as having an inherent essence, being universal and disconnected from context. The introductory essay to *Language and the Politics of Emotion,* by Abu-Lughod and Lutz (1990) is a strong proconstructionist pronouncement. It was followed by Leavitt's (1996) statement on meaning and feeling often referred to by anthropologists. The chapters by Milton, Lindquist, Svašek and Skinner are all influenced by Leavitt's ideas.

'Exploring the Managed Heart' is the title of the ethnographic extract by Hochschild, which was first published in one of the early collections in the sociology of emotions. The extract looks at power and emotional practices of service workers such as airline stewardesses in the United States. 'Emotional labour is potentially good. No customer wants to deal with a surly waitress, a crabby bank clerk, or a flight attendant who avoids eye contact in order to avoid getting a request. Lapses in courtesy by those paid to be courteous are very real and fairly common', says Hochschild (1983: 9). This raises questions about the impact of emotions on careers, as well as what is actually happening when we manage emotions, in private and public life. Although Hochschild is a sociologist, she uses ethnographic method and her work has had an impact among anthropologists.

The second section of *The Emotions* joins the opposite emotions of love and hate by starting with an ethnographic extract on love by Lila Abu-Lughod titled 'Shifting Politics in Bedouin Love Poetry' from the volume *Language and the Politics of Emotion* edited by Lutz and Abu-Lughod. The volume makes the case for 'emotion as discursive practice' (Abu-Lughod and Lutz 1990: 10). In the ethnographic extract, Abu-Lughod explores a changing social structure and relations between men and women in a Bedouin community in Egypt's Western Desert. We are told a dramatic Bedouin love story which involved a cassette with a love poem and herself as a fieldworker. An extract from another milestone in the early anthropology of emotions is 'Emotions and the Self: A Theory of Personhood and Political Order among Pintupi Aborigines' by Fred Myers. He examines ideas of the self and personhood that emerged in anthropology and other social and human sciences in the 1970s and soon became a major theoretical approach. By way of ethnography on how Pintupi Aborigines in Australia talk about the 'private self', Myers shows that this in fact reflects the cultural system

Ethnographies of Emotion

Fear is included in the seven emotions that often are referred to as basic emotions, the other ones being: anger, disgust, sadness, joy, shame and guilt, as Kringelbach points out in his contribution to *The Emotions*. Here we get an ethnography of fear in the extract from 'Catholics, Protestants and Office Workers from the Town: The Experience and Negotiation of Fear in Northern Ireland,' by Karen Lysaght, which, just like the chapters by Milton and Kringelbach, is informed by neuroscientific evidence on the relationship between emotions and human consciousness. This is applied to ethnographic data on how fear is experienced by individuals in segregated and conflict-ridden districts of Belfast. Lysaght shows how fear functions in a circular way: bodily manifestations of fear influence thoughts that are formed by social events that then alert the body to feared situations. In the article 'Whatever You Say Say Nothing', Finlay (1999) discusses fear and conceptions of shame and morality in Protestant-Catholic relations in Derry/Londonderry in Northern Ireland.

Just like Abu-Lughod's extract, Galina Lindquist's chapter 'Perilous Passions: Romantic Love and Love Magic in Russia' is about dramatic love stories. In the study of emotions, the controversy between constructionists and universalists seems to be over. It is generally recognized that emotions are both feelings and meanings, both universally shared, culturally shaped and individually unique, Lindquist argues. To understand emotions, some middle way is needed between unreflexive empathy, naïve imputation of 'what natives feel', and impassionate mapping of native categories, offered by linguistic studies of emotions. This chapter proceeds through semiotic analysis of the feeling-meaning complexes that involve logics of engagement with certain situations, prescribed orientations of the self in the world, and cultural practices, linguistic discourses and shared understanding around emotional complexes. This approach is applied to understanding the emotion of romantic love in the Russian context, based on ethnography of love magic in contemporary urban Russia. The chapter analyzes texts of love magic spells, and the narrative of a user of love magic, against the background of shared discourse of romantic love, ontologies of the person, and ideas about marriage, friendship, and sexuality.

It is suggested that an understanding of this emotion, central to human action and motivation cross-culturally, is best achieved by considering culturally specific practices, discourses, and symbols. In the ethnographic extract 'Knowledge and the

Practice of Love and Hate among the Enxet of Paraguay', Stephen Kidd points out that the Enxet see daily social practice in terms of notions of personhood. According to the Enxet, it is in an organ called *wáxok* that the cognitive and affective core of the person is constituted. This is also a person's social centre. The extract details how the *wáxok* is constructed and how the person becomes knowledgeable in the process. Knowledgeable people behave in a socially acceptable way. Certain behaviour is associated with those who are knowledgeable, while other behaviour is attributed to those without knowledge. This is conceptualized along the opposition of love and hate. Yet Enxet understand parts of people's behaviour as outside influences, in particular related to alcohol consumption. In the end, what matters is individual responsibility and knowledgeable people's control of their behaviour.

Howell's contribution, 'Relations with the Imagined Child: The Emotionality of Becoming an Adoptive Parent in Norway', brings up another type of love, parental love. Based on her study of involuntarily childless couples in Norway who adopt a child from a country far away, Howell shows how the adoptive process is highly charged emotionally, especially because this goal-oriented activity is filled with uncertainty. This is, for one thing, a process of procreation which is private by nature, but in an adoption it is moved to the public sphere and the unpredictable management of authorities. Many couples who adopt transnationally get together with other couples around the adoption. The adoption process contains a number of different emotions including desire, hope, frustration, joy and, probably the most difficult to handle, ambivalence and uncertainty. Howell explains the emotional journey of adoptive parents by change in the meaning of family, motherhood, fatherhood and childhood which leads to expectations that then make the feelings of parents as well as adoptive parents more forceful.

In 'Moving Corpses: Emotions and Subject-Object Ambiguity', Maruška Svašek investigates artefact production and emotional agency in terms of grief, anger, and outrage provoked by human body parts and casts of human body parts. Using Alfred Gell's notion of 'secondary agency', Svašek argues that these artefacts stir up strong emotions and influence social life because of their object/subject ambiguity. The analysis defines emotions as discursive practice and embodied experience, and demonstrates that subject/object-artefacts are powerful material presences that generate meanings and feelings. Furthermore, as emotionally evocative signifiers, they are incorporated into moral and political discourses that have a clear social relevance.

In precolonial Senegambia, women routinely organized themselves into groups along the lines of age, kinship, friendship, or residential proximity. These groups performed collective work for the community, and importantly, they served as networks of solidarity in times of hardship. Much of the postcolonial literature on the demise of collective values and the increasing individualism fostered by urbanization in Africa has neglected the world of women. In urban Senegal today, women do not passively accept exclusion from formal structures of power. They have revived traditional forms of association and quietly transformed them into powerful sites where unrealised potentialities may be explored. Women's groups, such as the rotating credit associations known as 'tontines', hold dance gatherings on a regular basis. There, they all enjoy themselves while conducting serious business away from the masculine gaze. This chapter '"Cool Play": Emotionality in Dance as a Resource in Senegalese Urban Women's Associations' by Hélène Neveu Kringelbach suggests that in urban Senegal, women's energetic and sensuous dances provide powerful counterpoints to everyday life, thereby relieving their anxieties as well as allowing them to explore emotions deemed inappropriate in other contexts, to consider an alternative sexuality, to compete for status and to gain confidence in order to act upon their lives.

In Moshe Shokeid's chapter 'The Emotional Life of Gay Men: Observations from New York', sexual desire is prominent. This chapter deals with this major facet of personal and social experience in contemporary Western society. Common perception and moral education suggests that sexual interaction in mainstream heterosexual society is strongly interwoven with expectations of emotional gratification and social obligations. In contrast, sexual interaction in gay society has often been presented in the literature and public discourse as free of emotional involvement and social obligation. In particular, anonymous sex, available in a wide spectrum of institutions, has been considered an important expression of this ethos. Based on ethnographic research in various gay organizations in New York—religious congregations, support groups and social clubs—this chapter explores that assumed ethos from the point of view of the participants themselves.

Expectation is key to tourism, which Jonathan Skinner elaborates in his chapter 'Emotional Baggage: The Meaning/Feeling Debate amongst Tourists'. While there have recently been many studies of emotions in cultural situ, or emotions amongst migrants and the displaced, this chapter turns a fresh look on emotions amongst those who are out of their culture for a short period of time as tourists. Tourism is a pleasure-seeking activity, one in which expectations, anticipations and motivations attract tourists to partake in experiences and liminal rituals which change their physiological states and heighten and exaggerate their emotions. By presenting an ethnography of several holiday groups—tourists to Cuba and Southport, England—this chapter appraises the cultural meaning/bodily feeling debate in the anthropology of emotions. By so doing, the chapter draws together the anthropology of emotions with the anthropology of tourism, suggesting that the meaning/feeling debate is a blend rather than a dichotomy, and that not only do individuals share emotions, but that tourists run through phases of emotions before, during and after their vacation.

This cultural approach of *The Emotions* also includes the existential individualism in Nigel Rapport's new contribution 'Rachel's Emotional Life: Movement and Identity'. This chapter takes, as a case-study, aspects of the life course of Rachel Silberstein, in order to offer a consideration of the relationship between emotion and identity. Rachel is a new immigrant to Israel from the United States. She is to be found making decisions on who to be in her new country, where to live, how to earn a livelihood, with whom to be friends and politically allied. Emotion is approached in the chapter as referring to those aspects of an individual's constitution that concern fluidity and movement ('emotion' from the Latin 'emovere', to stir up, ultimately from 'movere', to move). 'Emotion' denotes a stirring up of feeling, an agitation of mind. What can an anthropologist say about such emotion in the experience and the decision making of the individual, in the career of an individual life? What can the anthropologist add to the philosophical debate, current since the exchanges of Hume and Kant, on the question of how the emotional, the movemental, relates to both the fixing qualities of intellectual model building and the driving qualities of will that give onto action? This chapter offers an analysis largely based on ethnography. It is an account of the way in which Rachel Silberstein accrued experiences in Israel, the cultural context here, which she found to be 'schizo'—neither absolutely one thing nor another and of the way in which she found herself, her new Israeli identity, by travelling physically, sentimentally and intellectually between one experiential landmark and another. Rachel, it will be argued, settled herself into the Negev town of Mitzpe Ramon, and into Israel more generally, by emotional means.

Emotions as a central part of career and professional life is an area treated not only in the classic extract by Hochschild in this Reader (see also Hochschild 2003), but also by Ehn and Löfgren. They write about 'Emotions in Academia' and the idea that passion for science is supposed to be the sole emotion allowed in academia. Emotionality, by contrast with rationality, should be controlled. Yet academic settings feature many strong emotions. Ehn and Löfgren apply Raymond Williams's concept and investigate a specific 'structure of feelings' in the university world which is loaded with envy, admiration, irony and bitterness. They also explore what emotions are kept at bay or expressed in subtle ways. In line with psychologist James Hillman's ideas, this chapter presents emotions as a mediating process, linking body and mind, the personal and the collective, action and thought. The ethnography includes the lecture hall, but also coffee break conversations, ranking routines, and the daily struggle in front of the computer.

Creating desire and expectations is the agenda of advertising, which is evident in the chapter 'From Rational Calculation to Sensual Experience: The Marketing of Emotions in Advertising' by Timothy Malefyt, who uses a sociological method to examine shifting treatment of emotions among advertisers in the United States. Marketing strategies from many current advertising campaigns to consumers tend to divide product and brand benefits into emotional and rational dimensions. Appealing to consumers 'emotionally' is considered more desirable since marketers believe that consumer emotions drive purchase motivations and brand loyalty. By examining how marketers attempt to objectify consumer emotions and into what types of categories they objectify emotions, this chapter offers an understanding of the way in which advertisers operate. From detailing a case study of marketing chicken home delivery to consumers, the chapter explains that in the process of objectifying consumer motivations into rational and emotional models, marketers, in turn, create models for and of themselves.

Emotion and Nationalism

The last chapter in the first section investigates 'The Cartesian Divide of the Nation-State: Emotion and Bureaucratic Logic'. Written by Don Handelman, it shows how nationalism dominates the social horizons of state formations in modernity. The existence of states demands two major foci of organization: one, bureaucratic infra-structures that shape polities (and often organized religions), and two, the cathecting of state structures with emotions, galvanizing personal and group commitment to the national. Without both of these foci, modern states exist with difficulty. Bureaucracy produces systems of classification, and nationalism, the emotions that make these systems of classification come alive with the passions. Nationalism is the feeling for the national within and among its adherents. Nationalism generates the emotional commitments of persons to states. How emotions are aroused and channeled into the national, and from the national into the state, is the general problematic of this chapter. In this process, bureaucratic infrastructures have a major role, one that usually is ignored. The specific context of the problematic is Israel, providing an excellent state venue within which to discuss emotions of nationhood and ethnicity, shaped by systems of classification, and discussed through themes of time and history, trauma, territory, ritual, national symbols and sacrifice.

Nationalism is certainly emotional, not least in transnational and global processes. As Tom Boellstorff and Johan Lindquist (2004: 439) suggest, 'nationalism is perhaps the most obvious example of how affect is organized within decidedly non-local communities'. This is what Irish expatriates experience when they look back to Ireland for identity and belonging from the diaspora across the globe. Longing for the Irish land, they form a global imagined community of Irish expatriates as analyzed in Wulff (2007a, 2007b) in relation to emotions, memory and nature in Irish travel advertisements. Another instance of visual imagery evoking emotions of Irish nationalism is the paintings of Paul Henry, 'the best-known Irish artist of the period between the wars' (Arnold 1997: 140–41). Born in Belfast in 1876, Henry studied art in Paris and lived for a long time in Connemara in the west of Ireland. Henry's paintings are characterized by a hazy light and subtle colours of the Irish landscape: 'Many of these have an extreme simplicity, just the careful composition of water and headlands, of turf-stacks against the grey-blue hills along the horizon'. Henry's work has also appeared as illustrations in newspapers and books and, as a woman key informant in an anthropological study of dance and culture in Ireland (see mainly Wulff 2007b, but also for example 2005), told me: 'Some of Paul Henry's paintings were printed as tourist posters advertising Ireland during the post-war era. They are also collectors' items and appear in museums from time to time'. The fact that Henry's paintings do not address political agitation and land reform that took place in the west of Ireland when he was living there was in accordance with his post-impressionist style of 'formal autonomy'. It was the mastering of this style which had been 'the means at his disposal to give form to the emotion aroused by the landscape' (Cosgrove 1995: 96, 115).

This was the time of the establishment of the Irish Free State, which was prefigured by a cultivating of Irish nationalism in the cultural revival movement originating in the late nineteenth century. As a part of this movement, the west of Ireland was seen as the repository of authentic Irish culture (see O'Giolláin 2000). Writing about the construction of the west of Ireland, Catherine Nash (1997 [1993]: 87, 108) exemplifies this movement with Paul Henry and his artist wife Grace Henry, who settled in Achill island in 1912 after having read J. M. Synge's *Riders to the Sea* (see also Cosgrove 1995). Nash positions Henry's work as a contribution to the construction of the west of Ireland and suggests that this was both an Irish and an European endeavour in that he was a part of a group of artists in Brittany who headed for the peripheries. Yet the west symbolized Irishness; 'its uniqueness was utilised in promoting its suitability as a tourist destination. Experience of the West meant and continues to mean contact with Irish landscape and life'. Marianne Hartigan (2000: 54, 62) remarks that the 'thatched cottages' that Henry typically painted in 'dramatic mountainous landscapes' might be regarded as kitsch by people who do not know the area, and as reminders of primitive life in the past by people who knew about it. Now these paintings appear 'quaint and nostalgic' or are accepted as 'an acknowledged part of our history'. Hartigan also considers how Henry's 'reputation, and to some extent his work, suffered from success' when the London, Midland and Scottish (LMS) Railway Company reproduced his painting titled 'In Connemara' on travel posters. They were circulated transnationally, and this recognition led to a demand which had Henry making technically competent work which however was not always as empathetic and delicate as before. Yet these posters became highly popular: they seem to have hit a chord among many people both in Ireland and abroad, and still do. The fact that they were mass-produced posters and thus affordable to buy for people who normally would not have been able to buy a painting by a famous artist was surely important for their global fame.

Theories of Emotion

The theoretical or philosophical, even neurophysiological, pieces in *The Emotions* open the first of the five sections, Exploring Emotions. In an extract from an article titled 'Emotion Talk across Cultures' Paul Heelas (1986: 234) suggests that emotion talk differs a great deal when it comes to 'the number of emotions clearly identified; what emotions mean; how they are classified and evaluated'. Other points of divergence are the kind of environmental occurrences which are held to generate particular emotions, as well as 'management techniques'. Emotions are not experienced in the same way, according to Heelas. Providing a fine array of emotion talk, the article is informed by Robert Levy's (1973, 1984) influential work on Tahitians and their special way of classifiying emotions as exemplified by 'not suiting Tahitian values, "sadness" and "guilt" receive little conceptual attention'. 'Sadness' can then be explained by 'the effects of spirits' rather than by a loss. There is a tendency to prioritize certain emotions culturally (Levy 1984: 219, 223). Heelas brings up '"fear" and "shame" for the Tahitian' and '"love" and "guilt" for us' (Heelas 1986: 240).

Like several of the chapters in *The Emotions*, the first two new chapters discuss neurobiologist Antonio Damasio's work on body theory of emotions. In his chapter, 'Emotion, Feelings and Hedonics in the Human Brain', neuroscientist Kringelbach takes Damasio's ideas as a point of departure for a critique of bodily theories of emotions as 'underspecified with regard to what constitutes emotional stimuli'. Kringelbach connects emotions with consciousness and subjective experience. Based on neuroimaging experiments, he points at possible exploration of the brain systems involved in the conscious experience of pleasure and reward, which might provide a unique method for studying the hedonic quality of human experience. This is followed by a discussion of the novel insights into the importance of emotion and non-conscious processes in decision making. Finally, a model is proposed for the role of the various brain regions involved in emotional and hedonic networks. The chapter by Milton, titled 'Emotion (or Life, the Universe, Everything)' also develops Damasio's ideas about bodily reactions, emotions and stimuli to support an argument about emotions as ecological: such ecological mechanisms are seen to operate in relationships between individual organisms and their environment. Milton argues that this approach does not contradict the view that emotions are social, but encompasses it. By drawing on ideas from psychology and neuroscience, an ecology of emotions is positioned as an interdisciplinary model of emotion.

One hedonic quality which Kringelbach investigates is happiness, an obvious emotion to discuss in a Reader like this. 'Can Happiness be Taught?' asks psychologist Martin E. P. Seligman (2004: 80), in the next extract. As Seligman points out, the discipline of psychology has been oriented towards suffering in the form of notions such as 'depression, schizophrenia, and anger'. Seligman set out to study the idea of Positive Psychology in an annual undergraduate seminar he taught at the University of Pennsylvania. The study focussed on the Pleasant Life (positive emotions), the Good Life (positive traits such as virtues, talents, intelligence) and the Meaningful Life (positive institutions such as democracy, strong families, free inquiry). And the approach worked, the students did become happier.

Never in Anger is the suggestive title of Jean Briggs's (1970) book on the Utka Eskimos (Utkuhiksaklingmiut) in the Central Canadian Arctic. Just like the Tahitians, which Levy (1973: 214) writes about, these Eskimos do not get angry. But Tahitians spend a lot of time talking about anger, saying things such as 'my intestines were angry'. Known to be a gentle people, they have 47 terms for anger and a number of models for managing anger. From this it seems that Tahitians feel angry, but do not express it. The Utka Eskimos, on the other hand, are said not to express anger, feel anger or refer to it in conversation. The Jamesian theory of emotion from the nineteenth century (which was developed at the same time by C. Lange) recurs in the new chapters by Kringelbach and Milton. *The Emotions* includes an ethnographic and theoretical extract from 'Getting Angry: The Jamesian Theory of Emotion in Anthropology' by philosopher Robert Solomon (1984: 238, 240). The Jamesian theory claims that 'an emotion is an "inner experience", a "feeling" based on a physiological disturbance of a (now) easily specifiable kind plus ... the perception of a visceral disturbance brought about by a traumatic perception'. Like many contemporary emotions scholars, Solomon aims to connect intellect and emotion. With 'anger' as an ethnographic example, the Jamesian theory is rejected in this article, which argues that 'emotions are to be construed as cultural acquisitions, determined by the circumstances and concepts of a particular culture as well as, or rather much more than, by the functions of biology and, more specifically neurology'. This critique of neurology is, of course, a point of debate between Solomon and Kringelbach, whose emphasis is on brain function.

William Beeman's contribution, 'The Performance Hypothesis: Practicing Emotion in Protected Frames', states that performance has a unique ability to affect its audience emotionally. Moreover, it appears to be a uniquely human form of behaviour. This chapter proposes a hypothesis to explain both how this is accomplished, and why performance developed as a human behavioural institution. Emotions serve to warn humans of dangerous circumstances and reinforce pleasurable ones. Advances in the study of the structures of the human prefrontal cortex suggest that performance may provide a means for humans to experience and learn about emotional states in a protected environment.

Emotion and Culture

This is thus an ethnographically grounded cultural account of emotions, which hopes to help challenge the current dominance of psychological (laboratory, behaviourist) approaches to the study of the emotions. Seventeen of the 25 chapters and extracts can be categorized as anthropology of emotions. Yet the intention is to keep psychology in there. There is, among many other examples, recent important work by Luhrman (2000) on American psychiatric practice and by psychiatrists Margulies (1989) on the empathic imagination and Kirmayer (1992) on the body and meaning. There is also cultural psychology, the interdisciplinary orientation combining anthropology, psychology and linguistics launched by Stigler, Shweder and Herdt (1990), as well as ethnopsychology (Levy 1984; White 1981). Emotions and culture are discussed in relation to language (modes of speech) by Wierzbicka (1999) as an instance of her impact in this area, especially facial and bodily expressions of emotions. Paul Ekman's famous findings that facial expressions of emotions are universally understood, and the idea of basic emotions, have also been challenged among psychologists, which is evident in a review essay by Russell, Bachorowski and Fernández-Dols (2003).

Combining previously published articles with newly commissioned ones, *The Emotions* displays many different approaches to the study of emotions. Some of the previously published articles are classic, and others are more recent and are included because they exemplify a new development. Having pitched *The Emotions* as cultural, with anthropology as the defining discipline, I want to acknowledge that history, in particular eighteenth-century history, has had significant things to say about the emotions as evidenced in Barker-Benfield (1992), Riskin (2002), Vila (2001) and the review by Pinch (1995). Like most other fields, the cultural study of emotions owes much to philosophy, which the recent survey by Hatzimoysis (2003) confirms. In emphasizing context, anthropology's cultural and cross-cultural perspective comes in handy. Context tends to imply cultural context, which might well be multicultural. Many places and people are bi- or multicultural. The point is that culture is processual and nowadays often transnational, even global. It is crucial that culture is 'socially organized meaning', which yet gives space for the individual 'at least in part as a product of cultural organization' (Hannerz 1996: 39; see also Hannerz 1992).

Anthropologists have long been well aware that the West does not represent humanity. With an increasing number of ethnographic examples from different places we early knew that human nature is culturally shaped, as pointed out by Clifford Geertz (1973), and no less importantly that human nature also shapes culture. Going back to the evolution of *Homo Sapiens,* Geertz said that 'culture, rather than being added on, so to speak, to a finished or virtually finished animal, was ingredient, and centrally ingredient, in the production of that animal itself' (Geertz 1973: 47). And that 'we are, in sum, incomplete or unfinished animals who complete or finish ourselves through culture—and not through culture in general but through highly particular forms of it: Dobuan and Javanese, Hopi and Italian, upper-class and lower-class, academic and commercial' (Geertz 1973: 49). Culture as a concept and an analytical tool is included on different levels in *The Emotions*. There is academic culture in the chapter by Ehn and Löfgren and commercial culture in the chapter by Malefyt. Geertz's own chapter discusses Balinese character and culture, an influential regional culture, while other contributions develop ideas on the culture of a people ranging from the Enxet of Paraguay to the Pintupi Aborigines, let alone the two chapters by Michelle Rosaldo and Renato Rosaldo on the Ilongots, headhunters in the Philippines. Yet there are most likely aspects of the culture of these different peoples that on an analytical level would be a part of a national culture (cf. Hannerz 1992). *The Emotions* includes chapters on emotional expressions of national culture such as Israeli, Russian, Norwegian and Senegalese. There are also occupational cultures exemplified by the culture of flight attendants, as well as women's culture in Senegal. Gay organizations in New York are other subcultures. And when Catherine Lutz set out to 'explore the concept of emotion as a master Western cultural category', her area was Western or Euroamerican culture. Whatever level we focus on, it is clear that the cultural study of emotions is crucial for an understanding of the nature of emotions.

References

Abu-Lughod, L., and Lutz, C. (1990), 'Introduction: Emotion, Discourse, and the Politics of Everyday Life', in C. A. Lutz and L. Abu-Lughod (eds), *Language and the Politics of Emotion,* Cambridge: Cambridge University Press.

Arnold, B. (1997[1969]), *Irish Art: A Concise History,* London: Thames and Hudson.

Barker-Benfield, G. J. (1992), *The Culture of Sensibility: Sex and Society in Eighteenth Century Britain,* Chicago: University of Chicago Press.

Boellstorff, T., and Lindquist, J. (2004), 'Bodies of Emotion: Rethinking Culture and Emotion through Southeast Asia', *Ethnos* 69(4): 437–44.

Briggs, J. L. (1970), *Never in Anger: Portrait of an Eskimo Family,* Cambridge, MA: Harvard University Press.

Clifford J., and Marcus, G. E., eds. (1986), *Writing Culture: The Poetics and Politics of Ethnography,* Berkeley: University of California Press.

Cosgrove, M. (1995). 'Paul Henry and Achill Island', in U. Kockel (ed.), *Landscape, Heritage and Identity: Case Studies in Irish Ethnography,* Liverpool: Liverpool University Press.

Evans-Pritchard, E. E. (1956), 'Fieldwork under the Empirical Tradition', in *Social Anthropology,* London: Cohen and West Ltd.

Feld, S. (1990), *Sound and Sentiment: Birds, Weeping, Poetics, and Song in Kaluli-Expression,* Philadelphia: University of Pennsylvania Press.

Finlay, A. (1999), '"Whatever You Say Say Nothing": An Ethnographic Encounter in Northern Ireland and its Sequel', *Sociological Research Online,* 4(3).

Geertz, C. (1973), *The Interpretation of Cultures,* New York: Basic Books.

Hannerz, U. (1992), *Cultural Complexity: Studies in the Social Organization of Meaning,* New York: Columbia University Press.

Hannerz, U. (1996), 'When Culture Is Everywhere: Reflections on a Favourite Concept', in *Transnational Connections: Culture, People, Places,* London: Routledge.

Hartigan, M. (2000), 'History and Perception: The Art of Paul and Grace Henry', *Cara,* November/December, 33: 50–62.

Hatzimoysis. A., ed. (2003), *Philosophy and the Emotions,* Cambridge: Cambridge University Press.

Heelas, R. (1986), 'Emotion Talk across Cultures', in Rom Harré (ed.), *The Social construction of Emotions,* Oxford: Basil Blackwell.

Hochschild, A. (1983), 'Exploring the Managed Heart', in *The Managed Heart: Commercialization of Human Feeling*, Berkeley: University of California Press.

Hochschild, A. (2003), *The Commercialization of Intimate Life: Notes from Home and Work,* Berkeley: University of California Press.

Kirmayer, L. (1992), 'The Body's Insistence on Meaning', *Medical Anthropological Quarterly,* 6(4): 323–46.

Knight, J. (2005), 'Maternal Feelings on Monkey Mountains: Cross-species Emotional Affinity in Japan,' in K. Milton and M. Svašek (eds), *Mixed Emotions: Anthropological Studies of Feelings,* Oxford: Berg.

Leavitt, J. (1996), 'Meaning and Feeling in the Anthropology of Emotion', *American Ethnologist,* 23(3): 514–35.

Leenhardt, M. (1947), *Do Kamo,* Paris: PUF.

LeVine, R. A. (1982[1973]), *Culture, Behavior, and Personality,* New York: Aldine.

Levy, R. I. (1973), *Tahitians: Mind and Experience in the Society Islands,* Chicago: University of Chicago Press.

Levy, R. I. (1984), 'Emotion, Knowing, and Culture', in R. A. Shweder and R. A. LeVine (eds), *Culture Theory: Essays on Mind, Self and Emotion,* Cambridge: Cambridge University Press.

Lienhardt, G. (1961), *Divinity and Experience: The Religion of the Dinka,* Oxford: Clarendon.

Luhrmann, T. (2000), *Of Two Minds: An Anthropologist Looks at American Psychiatry,* New York: Alfred A. Knopf.

Malinowski, B. (1967), *A Diary in the Strict Sense of the Term,* London: Routledge and Kegan Paul.

Marcus G. E., and Fischer, M. J. (1986), *Anthropology As Cultural Critique: An Experimental Moment in the Human Sciences,* Chicago: University of Chicago Press.

Margulies, A. (1989), *The Empathic Imagination,* New York: W.W. Norton.

Milton, K. (2002), *Loving Nature: Towards an Ecology of Emotions,* London: Routledge.

Milton, K., and M. Svašek (eds.) (2005), *Mixed Emotions: Anthropological Studies of Feeling,* Oxford: Berg.

Nash, C. (1997[1993]), 'Embodying the Nation—The West of Ireland Landscape and Irish Identity,' in B. O'Connor and M. Cronin (eds), *Tourism in Ireland: A Critical Analysis,* Cork: Cork University Press.

Needham, R. (1962), *Structure and Sentiment: A Test Case in Social Anthropology,* Chicago: University of Chicago Press.

O'Giolláin, D. (2000), *Locating Irish Folklore: Tradition, Modernity, Identity,* Cork: Cork University Press.

Pinch, A. (1995), 'Emotion and History: A Review Article', *Comparative Studies in Society and History,* 37(1): 100–109.

Riskin, J. (2002), *Science in the Age of Sensibility: The Sentimental Empiricists of the French Enlightenment,* Chicago: University of Chicago Press.

Russell, J. A., Bachorowski, J.-A., and Fernández-Dols, J.-M. (2003), 'Facial and Vocal Expression of Emotion', *Annual Review of Psychology,* 54: 329–49.

Schwartz, T., White, G. M., and Lutz, C. A., eds. (1992), *New Directions in Psychological Anthropology,* Cambridge: Cambridge University Press.

Seligman, M.E.P. (2004), 'Can Happiness be Taught?', *Daedalus,* Spring: 80–87.

Solomon, R. S. (1984), 'Getting Angry: The Jamesian Theory of Emotion in Anthropology', in R. A. Shweder and R. A. LeVine (eds), *Culture Theory,* Cambridge: Cambridge University Press.

Stewart, P. J., and Strathern, A. (2002), *Gender, Song and Sensibility,* Westport: Praeger.

Stigler, J. W., Shweder, R. A., and Herdt, G. (1990), *Cultural Psychology: Essays on Comparative Human Development,* Cambridge: Cambridge University Press.

Surralés, A. (2003), *Au coeur du sens: Perception, affectivité, action chez les Candoshi,* Paris: CNRS.

Svašek, M. (2005), 'Introduction: Emotions in Anthropology', in K. Milton and M. Svašek (eds), *Mixed Emotions: Anthropological Studies of Feelings,* Oxford: Berg.

Tonkin, E. (2005), 'Being There: Emotion and Imagination in Anthropologists' Encounters', in K. Milton and M. Svašek (eds), *Mixed Emotions: Anthropological Studies of Feelings,* Oxford: Berg.

Vila, A. (2001), *Enlightenment and Pathology,* Baltimore, Md.: Johns Hopkins University Press.

White, G. (1981), '"Person" and "Emotion" in A'ara Ethnopsychology', paper for the 10th Annual Meeting of the Association for Social Anthropology in Oceania.

Wierzbicka, A. (1999), *Emotions across Languages and Cultures: Diversity and Universals,* Cambridge: Cambridge University Press.

Wikan, U. (1992), 'Beyond the Words: The Power of Resonance', *American Ethnologist,* 19(3): 460–82.

Wulff, H. (1998), *Ballet across Borders: Career and Culture in the World of Dancers,* Oxford: Berg.

Wulff, H. (2000), 'Access to a Closed World: Methods for a Multi-Locale Study of Ballet as a Career', in V. Amit (ed.), *Constructing the Field: Ethnographic Fieldwork in the Contemporary World,* London: Routledge.

Wulff, H. (2005), 'Memories in Motion: The Irish Dancing Body', *Body & Society,* issue on 'The Dancing Body', ed. Bryan S. Turner, 11(4): 45–62.

Wulff, H. (2007a), 'Longing for the Land: Emotions, Memory and Nature in Irish Travel Advertisements', *Identities,* 14: 1–18.

Wulff, H. (2007b), *Dancing at the Crossroads: Memory and Mobility in Ireland,* Oxford: Berghahn Books.

I
Exploring Emotions

Emotion, Thought, and Estrangement
Emotion as a Cultural Category

Catherine A. Lutz

The extensive discussions of the concept of the emotions that have occurred in the West for at least the last two thousand years have generally proceeded with either philosophical, religious, moral, or, more recently, scientific psychological purposes in mind. This discourse includes Plato's concern with the relation between pleasure and the good; the Stoic doctrine that the passions are naturally evil; early Christian attempts to distinguish the emotions of human frailty from the emotions of God; Hobbes's view that the passions are the primary source of action, naturally prompting both war and peace; the argument of Rousseau that natural feelings are of great value and ought to be separated from the "factitious" or sham feelings produced by civilization; the 19th-century psychologists' move to view emotions as psychophysiological in nature, with consciousness seen less and less as an important component of the emotions.[1] One of the notable aspects of this discourse is its concern with emotion as essence; whether the passions are portrayed as aspects of a divinely inspired human nature or as genetically encoded biological fact, they remain, to varying degrees, things that have an inherent and unchanging nature. With the exceptions of Rousseau, to some extent, and of Wittgenstein more recently, emotions have been sought in the supposedly more permanent structures of human existence—in spleens, souls, genes, human nature, and individual psychology, rather than in history, culture, ideology, and temporary human purposes.

In this article, I explore the concept of emotion as a master Western cultural category. An examination of the unspoken assumptions embedded in the concept of emotion is important for several reasons. In the first instance, those assumptions guide the investigation of people's lives in social science, including anthropology. Exploration of the cultural schema with which any anthropological observer begins fieldwork provides a methodological key, as translating between two cultural systems requires explication of the relevant meaning systems on both sides of the cultural divide. The cultural meaning system that constitutes the concept of emotion has been invisible because we have assumed that it is possible to identify the essence of emotion, that the emotions are universal, and that they are separable from both their personal and social contexts.

Secondly, to look at the Euroamerican construction of emotion is to unmask the ways in which that schema unconsciously serves as a normative device for judging the mental health of culturally different peoples. Despite an assiduous rejection within anthropology of explicit value judgments in the description of other cultural systems, we necessarily import a variety of Western value orientations towards emotions (as good or bad things to have in particular quantities, shapes, and sizes) whenever we use that concept without alerting the reader to the attitudes toward it that have developed in the West, attitudes that are necessarily invoked in the anthropological audience when the claim is made that "the Xeno people are prone to anger" or that they recognize fewer emotions than do we.

The concept of emotion has this and other sorts of ideological functions, that is, it exists within a system of power relations which the concept's use has played a role in maintaining. As we will see, emotion occupies an important place in Western gender ideologies; in identifying emotion primarily with irrationality, subjectivity, the chaotic and other negative characteristics, and in subsequently labeling women as the emotional gender, cultural belief reinforces the ideological subordination of women. The more general ideological role that the concept has played consists in reinforcing the split between facts and values as cognition, which can theoretically achieve knowledge of facts, is dichotomized in relation to emotion, which is "only" an index of value and personal interest.

The importance of the concept of emotion to Western thinking about self, consciousness, and society is evidenced by the dense network of cultural theories or assumptions that participate in everyday understanding and use of the word "emotion" and of the terms for the emotions, such as "love," "anger," and "boredom." These assumptions are evident in the number of sources of talk about emotion that the following discussion draws on, including both the everyday and the academic. In examining the cultural foundations of thinking about emotions, I will point particularly to the shared cultural assumptions that unite disputing academic theorists of emotion with each other and with everyday thought. While there are some significant ways in which those latter two types of discourse vary, the more important similarities between them justify treating them equally as products of contemporary social conditions and of the long history of Western thought on the subject. And while class and ethnicity are no doubt the source of important variation within the contemporary West in conceptions of emotion, the focus here will be on what I take to be a middle class Euroamerican model.

In this and further references to Western or Euroamerican culture, I am speaking about an amalgam of distinct cultural and subcultural traditions whose "unpacking" would allow for a better understanding of diversity in beliefs about emotion. Gaines (1982), for example, has identified one important source of variation in theories of the person which is potentially very relevant to cultural beliefs about emotion; he notes two different kinds of understandings of the self and mental disorder, one of which he terms Protestant European and other, Latin European. Where I do not specify a more precise locus for emotion beliefs (for example, everyday thought, American academic ideas, etc.), I am hypothesizing a widely shared American ethnotheory of basically Protestant European, middle class background, which is evident in social science theorizing, everyday discourse, and clinical psychological practice.

Emotion stands in important and primary contrast relationship to two somewhat contradictory notions: it is opposed, on the one hand, to the positively evaluated process of thought and, on the other, to a negatively evaluated estrangement from the world. To say that someone is "unemotional" is either to claim that that person is calm, rational and deliberate or that he or she is withdrawn or uninvolved, alienated or even catatonic. Although each of these two senses of the emotional has played an important role in discourse, the contrast to rationality and thought is currently by far the more dominant and common use of the concept.

Emotion Against Thought

The contrast between emotion and thought goes under several other rubrics, including the more academic and psychological affect and cognition, the more romantic and philosophical passion and reason, and the more prosaic feeling and thinking.[2] The distinction between them takes as central a place in Western psychological theory as do those between mind and body, behavior and intention, the individual and the social or the conscious and the unconscious, structuring (as do those latter contrasts) innumerable aspects of experience and discourse. Encoded in or related to that contrast is an immense portion of the Western world view of the person, of social life, and of morality.

It is first important to note, however that emotion shares a fundamental characteristic with thought in this ethnopsychological view, which is that both are internal characteristics of persons. The essence of both emotion and thought are to be found within the boundaries of the person; they are features of individuals rather than of situations, relationships, or moral positions. In other words, they are construed as psychological rather than social phenomena. Although social, historical and interpersonal processes are seen as correlated with these psychic events, thought and emotion are taken to be the property of individuals. Thought and emotion also share the quality of being viewed as more authentic realities and more truly the repository of the self in comparison with the relative inauthenticity of speaking and other forms of interaction.[3]

The contrast that has been culturally drawn between emotion and thought can be outlined initially by looking at the large set of paired concepts associated with the two terms and likewise set in contrast to each other. Thus, emotion is to thought as energy is to information; as heart is to head and as the irrational is to the rational; as preference is to inference; as impulse is to intention; as vulnerability is to control; and as chaos is to order. Emotion is to thought as knowing something is good is to knowing something is true, that is, as value is to fact or knowledge; as the relatively unconscious is to the relatively conscious; as the subjective is to the objective; as the physical is to the mental; as the natural is to the cultural; as the expressive is to the instrumental or practical; as the morally suspect is to the ethically mature; as the lower classes are to the upper; as the child is to the adult; and as the female is to the male. Although individuals in the West of course vary in the extent to which they would emphasize the connection between emotion and thought and any of these other paired associations, each appears as a cultural theme underlying much academic and everyday discussion of the nature of emotion. What is clear is that the evaluative bias in each of the associated pairs follows that bias evident in the distinction of emotion to thought itself, that is, as the inferior is to the superior, the relatively bad to the relatively good.

Emotion as Physicality

The concept of emotion bears a somewhat paradoxical relationship to the physical. Drawing, in the first instance, on the mind-body dichotomy that pervades Western thought, emotion is identified with physical feeling and the body in contrast with thought, which is seen as purely mental. This cultural view is evident in the predominance of physical images in talk about emotions (his stomach knotted up, she was fuming, his eyes popped out of his head); in the emphasis on the link between emotions and hormones; and in the linked contrasts of emotion and energy with thought and information. Images of emotions as so many B.T.U.s (and hence of an earlier, more primitive industrial age) contrast with images of thought as computer processing (and the more contemporary and advanced information age).[4] Although both sets of images can be seen as reifying, thought is viewed overall less physically than emotion. When combined with the idea that it is via the mental that we have distinguished ourselves from lower forms of life, this factor represents another route by which emotion is devalued.

The emphasis on this association between the emotional and the physical is especially strong within 20th-century academic psychology. Take, for example, the definition given by Tomkins, whose view of emotion is one of the most influential of the contemporary psychological theories; "Affects are sets of muscular and glandular responses located in the face and also widely distributed throughout the body, which generate sensory feedback that is either inherently 'acceptable' or 'unacceptable'" (1980:142). Although cognitive theories of emotion have been developed more recently (for example, Beck 1967; Lazarus 1977; Mandler 1975) in an attempt to balance the former view with a concern for the ways in which cognition regulates emotion, feelings or perceived physiological state, changes remain central to the definition of emotion in these latter theories as well. An example of this is found in the work of Kleinman who defines two types of emotion including "primary" affects, or "uncognized universal psychobiological experiences" (1980:3) which are transformed into "secondary" (and culturally specific) affects via cognitive processes of perception, labeling, and evaluation.[5]

Although this way of looking at the relationship between the emotions and the physical dominates in American culture, emotions are associated, in their positive but secondary sense of the engaged, with the spiritual and the sublime. To have feelings is to be truly human, which is to say, transcendent of the purely physical. Whereas emotions stand in close relationship to the instinctual when contrasted with cognition, they emerge as opposed to the animalistic and physical connotations of the instinctual when contrasted with what can be called the spiritual death of estrangement.

Emotion as Natural Fact

Closely related to the Euroamerican view of emotion as a physical event is the notion that emotions are more natural, and hence less cultural than thought. This view of emotion is obviously dependent first upon the nonuniversal distinction, elaborated in particular forms in the West, between nature and culture (Wagner 1981; MacCormack and Strathern 1980). Culture or civilization is seen predominantly as a conscious, cognitive process; emotion then takes its place as the natural complement to cultural processing—as material which culture may operate upon, but which is not culture. We speak of emotions as raw, as wild, and as primitive forces; they are the natural, aboriginally untouched by the cooking, taming, and civilizing of culture. Needham, for example, sees the diverse vocabularies of emotion developed in many societies as necessarily wrong about the feelings they purport to describe; this is so, he claims, because feelings, being natural and universal, exist at a level that is unaffected by the cultural modes of thought expressed in those vocabularies (Needham 1981:23). The emphasis on emotion as physical feeling means that the transformations wrought by culture on the affective base (as on the physical base) become secondary as in Kleinman's formulation (see also Levy 1984). An interest in the emotional aspects of culture—in raising the (for us, paradoxical) association of the two concepts—has necessitated the introduction by some anthropologists of the idea of sentiment or culturalized emotion, and the sharp distinction between it and private, natural feeling or emotion (see, for example, Fajans 1985).[6]

The ambivalent or multivalent stances taken toward emotion in the West result in part from variation across individuals and across time in the conceptualized relationship between and evaluation of nature and culture. Strathern has noted about this variability that at one point culture is a creative, active force which produces form and structure out of a passive, given nature. At another, culture is the end product of a process, tamed and refined, and dependent for energy upon resources outside itself. Culture is both the creative subject and the finished object; nature both resource and limitation, amenable to alteration and operating under laws of its own. [1980:178]

Emotions are seen in fundamentally the same way. Thus, emotions are alternately the pliant material upon which acculturative and cognitive forces have their way (for example, in the theories of Beck [1967] and Hochschild [1983])[7] or they are, quite literally in many theories of emotion (as Zajonc 1980), the energy which animates otherwise lifeless cultural forms.

It is the latter view of emotion that is particularly drawn upon when it is being discussed in contrast with alienation. Here the unemotional or disengaged is seen as an unnatural or cultural mode of being. While emotional response is still taken to be natural, the evaluations of the natural have a much more positive tone. Following the Romantic tradition, the natural (including emotion) is depicted as synonymous with the uncorrupted, the pure, the honest, the original. Culture, conscious thought, and disengagement are all viewed as disguise, artifice, or vise—as themselves the limitations which are more commonly seen as characteristic of nature and emotion. When emotion is seen as natural in this positive sense, thought and its offshoot, social speech, become seen as less authentic and less "really real"; it is only uncognized, unexpressed emotion that is truly natural, then, as it has not been reached and disturbed or warped by cultural conventions for the conscious experience or display of emotion.

This cultural view is evident in the speech presidential candidate Jesse Jackson made at the 1984 Democratic National Convention. Attempting to apologize for remarks insulting to Jewish voters, he asked that the public "Charge it [the mistake] to my head, not to my heart." Jackson was saying not only that he "thought" rather than "felt" the insult, but that the attitude revealed by the remark was not his "real" attitude, not his natural way of approaching the world. His apologetic appeal could only be sensibly made if things of the heart (the emotions) are commonly seen as the true, real seat of the individual self and things of the head (thoughts) as relatively superficial, socially influenced aspects of the self.

It is important to add a secondary proviso to this characterization of Jackson's apology. While his statement is consistent with and revealing of these American cultural views of emotion as the site of the true self, the appeal that it entailed may have had limited success in convincing his audience given some other aspects of those cultural views. In particular, Jackson may have disregarded the fact that such positive views about emotion and the implied denigration of thought are not appropriate for males in this society. A failure of the appeal to convince most Americans is probably likely, as well, given the dominance of the more negative model for understanding the emotion-thought relationship.[8]

The view of the naturalness of emotions is evident in psychological theory where, for example, Tomkins defines as "pseudo-emotion" any emotion which is at all socially constrained or suppressed, which is not "unconditionally free[ly] vocalized" (Tomkins 1979:208). Elsewhere, in Freud's theories, emotion play the role of the natural counterpart to the civilization of thought; for him, emotion is generated within its own domain, and thought (like culture) emerges, in Strathern's terms, as "finished object."

The culturally constructed naturalness of emotion has also had the effect of making Westerners less reticent about imputing universal emotional abilities to others than they have been about projecting particular cognitive abilities to all humans. This tendency to more readily infer what non-Westerners are really feeling than to claim that they are really thinking something other than what they claim to think is in part the result of the belief that natural processes are more invariant than cultural ones and, therefore, that emotions are both more uniform, cross-culturally, and less culturally malleable, than thought. This view is developed most fully by those universalists for whom emotion's naturalness has been further confirmed by such theories as the sociobiological or psychodynamic. Spiro (1953), for example, claims that the Ifaluk really feel anger or hostility though they mask it with fear. Freeman (1983) sees the occasional angry displays of Samoan orators at the island's competitive speaking events as demonstrations of the natural rage that any creature feels after dominance attempts by others. Freeman's analysis of Samoan behavior makes use not only of this assumption of the invariance of the natural features of humanness but of the notion that emotion is both natural and ultimately uncontrollable. In speaking of Samoan aggression in warfare, Freeman approvingly quotes from the ethnologist Kramer who, at the turn of the century, described how the "violent passions" of the Samoans were "set recklessly free" in wartime (Kramer 1903 cited in Freeman 1983:166). These turns of phrase obviously imply the naturalness— weakly controlled—of emotions. For Freeman, the natural (as the emotional) is the more active member of the nature-culture set; the following quote makes evident his implicit use of the cultural idea that nature's emotions are also a dark, animalistic force.[9]

On some occasions the chiefs I was observing would, when contending over some burning issue, become annoyed and then angry with one another. By intently observing their physiological states ... I was able, as their anger mounted, to monitor the behavior of these chiefs in relation to their use of respect language. From repeated observations it became evident that as chiefs became angry they tended to become *more and more polite* ... Occasionally, however, the conventions of culture would fail completely, and incensed chiefs, having attained to pinnacles of elaborately patterned politeness, would suddenly lapse into violent aggression ... [T]he conventional behavior is replaced, in an instant, by highly emotional and impulsive behavior that is animal-like in its ferocity. [Freeman 1983:300–301, emphasis in original]

In sum, emotions are primarily conceived of as pre-cultural facts, as features of our biological heritage that can be identified independently of our cultural heritage. Although there is variation in the evaluation of the impact of culture and the natural substrate of our emotions on each other, the element of natural emotion counterposes itself to either the civilization of thought or the social disease of alienation and forms the basis for much everyday and academic talk about emotions. The questions that are then asked concern the relationship between a natural fact—the affective response—and the cultural facts, including cultural beliefs and social institutions.

Emotions as Subjectivity

Emotions are viewed as constituting subjectivity in several of the senses in which the term subjective is used.[10] In the first instance, they are subjective in the sense of biased. To say of individuals that they are acting emotionally is to say that they are acting on the basis of a personal interest which is inconsistent with the wider interest they ought to consider. From this perspective, emotion necessarily creates bias in a way that thought does not; while thought may be subjective in the sense of consisting of individual and unique perceptions, it does not by its nature distort judgment as emotion does. Emotion, as we have noted, blinds the individual to judgments that she or he ought to make, causing thereby both a failure of perception and potential social disruption. As bias pushes individuals to pursue goals that accord only with their own view, the emotional/subjective person can potentially thwart the attainment of more global, social, objectively determined and valid goals.

The second sense in which the emotions are subjective consists of the notion that emotions constitute the perspective of the individual on events. This notion has several implications which are more positive than those associated with bias. In particular, the subjectivity of emotions in this sense gives them a fundamental—even sacred—role in individuating the person. Given the importance, in the American value system, of the individual personality, this aspect of emotion elevates them to a special place.

The emotions create the possibility for this individuality in at least two senses. First, they constitute individual opinion. It is only I who have these particular emotions, opinions, and values. From this perspective, emotions are Me in a way that thoughts are not. As thoughts may be objective, they will be the same in whatever mind they appear. Feelings, however, are subjective; they therefore are not completely communicable, and very possibly are uniquely my own. It is, then, impossible, in the parlance of this culture, to speak literally about *our* emotions or, conversely, to speak of someone as an individual who is not unique, a uniqueness which is achieved in part through one's emotions.

Secondly, the emotions stand for individual privacy or inviolability. Feelings, it is thought, cannot truly or absolutely be known except through self-revelation, that is, except through a decision on the part of the individual who experiences the emotion to discuss it. It is not possible to ascertain conclusively what someone else is feeling solely on the basis of observation.[11] Americans will in fact often react vehemently to any attempt that is construed as "telling me what I feel"; only the subject can truly know his or her own emotions. Self-revelation of emotion is made necessary and problematic, first, by the fact that it is considered much more difficult to accurately communicate one's feelings than one's thoughts (since thoughts can be objective) and, second, by the fact that the emotions are treated as the private property of the self. Individuals are sacred only insofar as each of them own their particular and distinct set of emotions.

References

Beck, Aaron (1967). Depression: Clinical, Experimental and Theoretical Aspects, New York: Harper and Row.

Comaroff, Jean (1983). The Defectiveness of Symbols or the Symbols of Defectiveness? On the Cultural Analysis of Medical Systems. Culture, Medicine, and Psychiatry 7:47–64.

Fajans, Jane (1984). The Person in Social Context: The Social Character of Baining "Psychology." *In* Person, Self, and Experience: Exploring Pacific Ethnopsychologies. Geoffrey White and John Kirkpatrick, eds. Berkeley: University of California Press.

Freeman, Derek (1983). Margaret Mead and Samoa: The Making and Unmaking of an Anthropological Myth. Cambridge: Harvard University Press.

Gaines, Atwood D. (1982). Culture Definition, Behavior and the Person in American Psychology. *In* Cultural Conceptions of Mental Health and Therapy. Anthony Marsella and Geoffrey White, eds. Dordrecht, The Netherlands: D. Reidel.

Goffman, Erving (1959). The Presentation of Self in Everyday Life. New York: Doubleday / Anchor.

Hochschild, Arlie R. (1983). The Managed Heart: Commercialization of Human Feeling. Berkeley: University of California Press.

Kleinman, Arthur (1980). Patients and Healers in the Context of Culture: An Exploration of the Borderland between Anthropology, Medicine, and Psychiatry. Berkeley: University of California Press.

Lazarus, R. S. (1977). Cognitive and Coping Processes in Emotion. *In* Stress and Coping. A. Monat and R. Lazarus, eds. New York: Columbia University Press.

Levy, Robert (1984). Emotion, Knowing, and Culture. *In* Culture Theory: Essays on Mind, Self, and Emotion. Robert LeVine and Richard Shweder, eds. Cambridge: Cambridge University Press.

MacCormack, Carol, and Marilyn Strathern, eds. (1980). Nature, Culture and Gender. Cambridge: Cambridge University Press.

Mandler, George (1975). Mind and Emotion. New York: Wiley.

Needham, Rodney (1981). Circumstantial Deliveries. Berkeley: University of California Press.

Sabini, John, and Maury Silver (1982). Moralities of Everyday Life. Oxford: Oxford University Press.

Spiro, Melford E. (1953). Ghosts, Ifaluk, and Teleological Functionalism. American Anthropologist 54:497–503.

Strathern, Marilyn (1980). No Nature, No Culture: The Hagen Case. *In* Nature, Culture and Gender. C. MacCormack and M. Strathern, eds. Cambridge: Cambridge University Press.

Tomkins, S. S. (1979). Script Theory: Differential Magnification of Affects. *In* Nebraska Symposium on Motivation. Vol. 26. H. E. Howe and R. A. Dientsbier, eds. Pp. 201–236. Lincoln: University of Nebraska Press.

Tomkins, S. S. (1980). Affect as Amplificaton: Some Modifications in Theory. *In* Emotion: Theory, Research, and Experience. R. Plutchik and H. Kellerman, eds. New York: Academic Press.

Toulmin, Stephen (1979). The Inwardness of Mental Life. Critical Inquiry 6(1):1–16.

Wagner, Roy (1981). The Invention of Culture. 2nd edition. Chicago: University of Chicago Press.

Zajonc, Robert B. (1980). Feeling and Thinking: Preferences Need No Inferences. American Psychologist 35:151–175.

Notes

Acknowledgements. I would like to thank Lila Abu-Lughod and John Kirkpatrick for their extensive and helpful comments on an earlier version of this paper, which expands on ideas first set out in "Depression and the Translation of Emotional Worlds" (Depression and Culture, A. Kleinman and B. Good, eds. Berkley: University of California Press, 1985.)

1. It is somewhat misleading to speak of a two thousand-year-long discourse on "emotion" when in fact that latter category bears only a family resemblance to the variety of related Greek, Latin, and other concepts which have occupied Western thinkers. Each historical period has also seen the use of a set of related terms to talk about the domain—such as the contemporary set of "feeling," "emotion," "affect," and (somewhat archaic) "passion"—each of which were used in varying and ambiguous ways in virtually all periods.

2. There are other subtle differences in historical and cultural source and connotation between emotion, affect, feeling, and passion. Feeling, for example, tends to be used to talk about internal body sensations more exclusively than do the other terms. Passion may be used synonymously with emotion but tends to more often refer specifically to love or sexual desire, or to enthusiasms, while affect is now rarely heard outside of academic discourse.

3. See, for example, the portrayal of persons in the popular theories of Goffman (1959).

4. As Toulmin (1979) and others have pointed out, there are two traditions of thought in the West as to the nature of cognition, one of which identifies it as a brain, or physical function, and the other of which locates it in the mind, which is defined as a nonphysical entity.

5. This perspective on the relationship between the emotional-qua-the-physical and the mental has a clear parallel with the culturally common view of the relationship between disease and mental processes. The idea that sickness is rooted squarely in the body, and is influenced by the mental only secondarily and less genuinely, is evident in the suspicion Americans hold for those who claim to be sick when no physical cause can be found. The distinction between disease (as underlying physical process) and illness (as the socially elaborated response to and cognitive experience of disease), which is common in the medical anthropological literature, draws on the same belief in "a stable and universal core of biophysical realities" (Comaroff 1983).

6. Sentiment is defined in the dictionary as "an attitude, thought, or judgment prompted by feeling; refined feeling, delicate sensibility, emotional idealism, a romantic or nostalgic feeling verging on sentimentality." Although it is not a term used in everyday talk, these anthropological uses intend to draw on the notion that it is only thought (including "thought ... prompted by feeling") that bears the impress of culture, while pure, pre-conscious emotion does not.

7. In Beck's view, certain types of premises, representations, or silent assumptions held by individuals intervene between an event and depressive feelings, and create the possibility for the emotion. Here cognition is the "creative subject" and affect the "resource" in Strathern's terms. Hochschild, in examining the social organization of emotional expression among airline stewardesses, critiques the process whereby the women's natural feelings are warped by the social pressures exerted by their bosses. Again, natural emotion is molded by the active pressure exerted by social expectations.

8. I am thankful to Jane Collins for this latter observation.

9. Freeman also talks about emotions in the positive sense which nature can have in his mention of the love which Samoans feel for each other, but this is certainly a minor theme.

10. See Sabini and Silver (1982) for a wonderful exposition of the various ways (they find eight) in which the term "subjective" is commonly used in everyday discourse. If, as Sabini and Silver point out, "notions of subjectivity are individually harmless, but dangerous in a mob" (1982: 183), it is important to distinguish these distinct senses for our purposes.

11. This cultural belief is somewhat mitigated by the fact that other cultural ideas exist which outline the ways in which it is possible to know what someone else is feeling without the other telling us, or even wishing us to know. Faces, body gestures, and tone of voice are all seen as relatively involuntary indices, or "leakages," of the person's internal states.

–2–

Emotion Talk across Cultures

Paul Heelas

Emotional life has sparked the human imagination. Members of different societies talk about their emotions in a wide variety of ways, many of which strike us as distinctly imaginative. The Javanese of Ponorogo, for example, employ liver talk: 'it is the liver *(ati)* that appears in idiomatic expressions indicating emotion'; and 'the role of the liver is not altogether just a metaphor' (Weiss, 1983, p. 72).

There are very considerable differences in the number of emotions clearly identi-fied; what emotions mean; how they are classified and evaluated; how the nature of emotions is considered with regard to locus, aetiology and dynamics; the kind of en-vironmental occurrences which are held to generate particular emotions; the powers ascribed to emotions; and management techniques. I hope I am justified in assuming that the relative inaccessibility of much of the ethnography means that many read-ers will not be aware of the extent to which emotion talk can diverge from our own. But what exactly has this to do with the social construction of emotions? Why do I plunge the reader into an assortment of ethnographic 'curiosities'?

By way of introduction, I shall indicate why I regard emotion talk to be of very considerable constructivist importance. I want to give some idea of the significance of the strange varieties of emotion talk to be encountered. For reasons which will become more apparent later, I shall indicate why emotion talk—clearly a product of the human imagination—does not have imaginary consequences. It in fact has great bearing on the nature of emotional life.

To argue this first means arguing against those who hold that emotions are en-dogenous. For, if emotions are part of our biological inheritance, emotion talk is ad-ventitious. Just as the stars are impervious to cross-cultural differences in how they are conceptualized, so too are the emotions—at least, in their core properties. I must thus side with Geertz (1980), the constructivist, against Leach, who has written that Geertz's approach is 'complete rubbish' because it ignores 'genetic' factors (Leach, 1981, p. 32). This is not difficult to do. Perhaps the majority of those psycholo-gists who have found evidence supporting the endogenous approach have also found it necessary to introduce exogenous determinants. Thus Leventhal, distinguishing between 'emotional elements' and 'emotional experiences', argues that biologically generated elements have to be 'enriched' by meanings ('conceptualizations of affect') before becoming emotional experiences (Leventhal, 1980, p. 192). Incorporating constructivist theorizing, Leventhal accords ample scope for the sociocultural to make impact. Meanings bound up with emotion talk can get to work.[1]

Granted this, what of the importance of emotion talk within the general context of sociocultural determinants? A number of theorists have argued for constructivism without mentioning emotion talk, let alone treating it as important. Mandler (1980) writes of 'languages of emotion' in this fashion: 'The label that something is good or the cognate facial expression of acceptance or approval influences the quality of the emotional experience' (p. 231). Mandler would certainly not want to discount emotion talk, but its *particular* importance is clearly diminished in that moral judgements as a whole can apparently function in generative fashion.

The particular importance I want to attach to emotion talk is seen by what happens when it is ignored. According to Kemper (1984), 'A very large class of human emotions results from real, anticipated, recollected, or imagined outcomes of power and status relations' (p. 371). More specifically, consider his explanation of how status loss generates anger:

> When we believe the other is the agent of our status loss, whether by insult, intentional infliction of pain, ignoring us when we have a right to be attended to, or depriving us of goods, services, money, or approval that we have earned or deserve according to our understanding ... the immediate emotional outcome ... is *anger.* (Kemper, 1978, p. 128)

Emotion talk, enabling participants to understand the emotional significance of status loss, does not enter the picture. This is unfortunate. It is true that we have acquired a strong tendency to respond to insults and the like in terms of anger, but by no means do we always do so: my status is affected by a public insult and I feel shame; my status is affected when I do not get what I deserve and I feel inadequate; I am deprived of the attention of my wife and feel jealous. Events of the kind mentioned by Kemper, in other words, need not mean that we respond with *anger.* How we respond depends on how we use our knowledge of our emotional life, interpreting an episode as shaming, for example, because it accords with our understanding the episode as being bound up with what we take shame to mean. In short, the fact that we attribute emotion-specific meanings to those more general sociocultural varieties discussed by Kemper explains why the 'immediate emotional outcome' is not always anger.

I do not want to conclude that the meanings provided by emotion talk are the only ones which constructivists should attend to. One consideration is that emotion talk does not exist in isolation from other domains of knowledge. The meaning of 'anger', for example, is obviously bound up with how we have learnt to use this word in connection with the moral domain (cf. Kemper's 'insults'). The term enables us to know (and so have) the emotion in connection with particular moral events precisely because its meaning is not purely psychological. That emotion talk is often bound up with the moral domain is also clearly seen in Peter's (1974) observation: 'emotions, such as pride, ambition, guilt and remorse, imply a certain view of ourselves. They are probably not felt in cultures in which little importance is attached to individual effort and responsibility' (p. 402).

Other reasons for not limiting emotionally significant meanings to emotion talk are provided by all those psychologists who do not limit themselves to this domain (cf. Mandler, 1980; and Lazarus et al., 1980, who include all 'transactions that the person judges as having implications for her or his *well-being*' (p. 195)). One final consideration, to do with the fact that the constructivist cannot simply attend to emotion talk when exploring the management of emotions, concerns what social learning theorists such as Bandura (1965) call 'attentional shift'. Do we not often try to manage distressful emotions by thinking of something other than our emotional states?

Having said this, the fact remains that meanings are necessary for the construction of emotions and that particular meanings (of some kind) are necessary for the construction of particular emotions. In the absence of such particular meanings, we are left with those differentiations in experience which occur at the level of what Leventhal calls emotional 'elements'. And it is difficult not to conclude that these particular meanings have more to do with emotion talk than with anything else. Indeed, it might be possible to argue that meanings can constitute different emotions only if they involve emotion terms which provide knowledge of differences. This certainly is what is implied by Lazarus (1980) when he writes that 'each emotion quality and intensity—anxiety, guilt, jealousy, love, joy, or whatever—is generated and guided by its own particular cognitive theme' (p. 192). And is not the importance of emotion terms suggested by experimental research (e.g. Schachter and Singer, 1962) apparently showing that emotions are states of physiological arousal defined by the actor as emotionally induced? If, indeed, such research shows that differences in knowledge (this situation means 'anger', this 'euphoria') are crucial in determining which emotions are experienced, then emotion talk, providing the linguistic distinctions, lies at the heart of the matter. To an extent, these distinctions *are* the differences in experience.

It is considerations such as these which explain why Lewis and Saarni, for example, place emotion talk at the very heart of the constructivist enterprise. For them, 'emotional experience ... requires that organisms possess a language of emotion' (Lewis and Saarni, 1985, p. 8). Other theorists who have emphasized the importance of emotion talk include Malatesta and Haviland ('the emotion words of a culture exert a powerful influence on the actual experience of emotion': 1985, p. 110); Levy (who introduces 'the idea of emotion as involving information about the relations of a person to his socially constituted world': 1984, p. 222); Gordon ('Arousal is socially interpreted in terms of sentiment vocabularies, which are sets of meaningful categories that connect sensations, gestures, and social relationships': 1981, p. 577) and Lutz ('Emotions are culturally constructed concepts which point to clusters of situations typically calling for some kind of action': 1981, p. 84).

This ethnographic material is not merely of curiosity value. It concerns how people understand their emotional lives. Being those culturally provided forms of knowledge which are most explicitly focused on emotions, they are perhaps the first thing the constructivist should attend to. They involve the attribution of the kind of meaning which is of paramount significance to those interested in exploring how emotions are constructed in the everyday life of other cultures. We might even learn how other cultures so manage things as to diminish, even do away with, distressful emotions such as 'jealousy' or even 'anger.'

A number of cultures do not make distinctions of the 'mental-physical', 'body-mind' and 'emotion-cognition' variety. Ethnographers studying societies which do not employ the category 'emotion' clearly have not found it easy to identify what counts as emotion talk. It is difficult to elicit satisfactory replies to the question. 'Does "m" term refer to an emotion?' if respondents' replies could be referring, for example, to what we consider to be bodily states of affairs (such as physiological arousal). There are in fact many interpretative and linguistic problems to do with establishing what counts as emotion talk—and, for that matter, to do with establishing the nature of forms of emotion talk.

Just as emotion talk is of the utmost importance in our psychological culture, so is it important in many of these rituals (see, for example, Kapferer, 1979).[2] On more general ways in which emotions are taught by way of emotion talk, see Geertz (1959), Myers (1979), Lewis (1958), Levy (1973, 1984) and Gordon (1981). Rather than dwell on this relatively well discussed topic, I want to end by making the point that there is a considerable difference between the way in which emotion talk of the Western psychological subculture generates core emotions and the way in which a different kind of emotion talk, found in many other societies, generates emotions of a core or hypercognated variety.

Gordon (1981) points out that 'A vocabulary of sentiments is a linguistic expression of experiences shared by group members, and mirrors their interests and concerns' (p. 578). In many societies the 'self' is defined as a social being. This means that the 'interests and concerns' mirrored in emotion talk belong to the social or moral order. People thus define how and what they should feel in terms of externalized forms of emotion talk. In other words, since emotion talk articulates the moral order and defines what people should feel if they are to be 'themselves' as social beings, it is externalized in terms of that order.

References

Bandura, A. (1965) Vicarious processes: a case of no trial learning. In L. Berkowitz (ed.), *Advances in Experimental Social Psychology,* vol. 4. London: Academic Press (pp. 167–223).

—— (1980) *Negara: The Theatre State in Nineteenth-Century Bali.* Princeton: Princeton University Press.

Geertz, C. (1973) *The Interpretation of Cultures.* New York: Basic Books.

Geertz, C. (1980) *Negara: The Theatre State in Nineteenth-Century Bali.* Princeton: Princeton University Press.

Geertz, H. (1959) The vocabulary of emotion. *Psychiatry,* 22, 225–37.

Gordon, S. (1981) The sociology of sentiments and emotion. In M. Rosenberg and R. Turner (eds), *Social Psychology.* New York: Basic Books (pp. 562–92).

Heald, S. (1982) The making of men. *Africa,* 52(1), 15–36.

Heelas, P. (1983) Anthropological perspectives on violence: universals and particulars. *Zygon,* 18(4), 375–404.

Heelas, P. (1984) Emotions across cultures: objectivity and cultural divergence. In S. Brown (ed.), *Objectivity and Cultural Divergence.* Cambridge: Cambridge University Press (pp. 21–42).

Izard, C. (1971) *The Face of Emotion.* New York: Meredith.

Kapferer, B. (1979) Emotion and feeling in Sinhalese healing rites. *Social Analysis,* 1, 153–76.

Kemper. T. (1978) *A Social Interactional Theory of Emotions.* Chichester: John Wiley.

—— (1984) Power, status and emotions: a sociological contribution to a psychophysiological domain. In K. Scherer and P. Ekman (eds), *Approaches to Emotion.* Hillsdale, NJ: Lawrence Erlbaum (pp. 369–83).

Lazarus. R. (1980) Thoughts on the relations between cognition and emotion. *American Psychologist,* 37, 1019–24.

—— et al. (1980) Emotions: a cognitive-phenomenological analysis. In R. Plutchik and H. Kellerman (eds), *Emotion Theory, Research and Experience.* Vol. 1: *Theories of Emotion.* London: Academic Press (pp. 189–218).

Leach, E. (1981) A poetics of power. *The New Republic,* 4 April.

Leventhal. H. (1980) Toward a comprehensive theory of emotion. In L. Berkowitz (ed.), *Advances in Experimental Social Psychology.* London: Academic Press (pp. 149–207).

Levy, R. (1973) *Tahitians.* London: Chicago University Press.

—— (1984) Emotion, knowing, and culture. In R. Shweder and R. LeVine (eds), *Culture Theory. Essays on Mind, Self, and Emotion.* Cambridge: Cambridge University Press (pp. 214–37).

Lewis. C. (1958) *The Allegory of Love.* London: Oxford University Press.

Lewis, M. and Saarni, C. (1985) Culture and emotions. In M. Lewis and C. Saarni (eds), *The Socialization of Emotions.* London: Plenum Press (pp. 1–17).

Lutz, C. (1981) Situation-based emotion frames and the cultural construction of emotion. In *Proceedings of the Third Annual Conference of the Cognitive Science Society, Berkeley* (pp. 84–9).

Malatesta, C. and Haviland, J. (1985) Signals, symbols and socialization. In M. Lewis and C. Saarni (eds), *The Socialization of Emotions.* London: Plenum Press (pp. 89–116).

Mandler, G. (1980) The generation of emotion: a psychological theory. In R. Plutchik and H. Kellerman (eds), *Emotion Theory, Research and Experience.* Vol. 1: *Theories of Emotion.* London: Academic Press (pp. 219–42).

Marsella, A. and White, G. (eds) (1982) *General Conception of Mental Health and Therapy.* London: Reidel.

Munn, N. (1969) The effectiveness of symbols in Murngin rite and myth. In R. Spencer (ed.), *Forms of Symbolic Action.* New York and London: American Ethnological Society (pp. 178–207).

Myers, F. (1979) Emotions and the self. *Ethos,* 7 (4), 343–70.

Peters, R. (1974) *Psychology and Ethical Development.* London: George Allen and Unwin.

Schachter, S. and Singer, J. (1962) Cognitive, social, and physiological determinants of emotional state. *Psychological Review,* 69 (5), 379–99.

Weiss, J. (1983) *Folk Psychology of the Javanese of Ponorogo.* Ann Arbor, Mich.: University Microfilms International.

Notes

1. See Heelas (1983; 1984, pp. 33–9). The evidence strongly suggests that Izard's (1971, p. 267) claim that 'the subjective experience component of emotion determines Emotion Labeling' be reversed.

2. See also Heald (1982) and Munn (1969), the latter referring to Geertz's (1973) work on 'symbolic models of emotion'. Marsella and White (1982) present a number of articles bearing on the topic.

–3–

Emotion, Feelings and Hedonics in the Human Brain

Morten L. Kringelbach

Introduction

Emotions are ubiquitous, and many will agree that it is difficult to imagine our lives without them. Every experienced event—whether current, remembered or imagined—seems to have an emotional tone. We cannot help but attach emotional significance to the events that shape our lives—for better and sometimes for worse. Yet, exactly this subjective quality of the emotions is also what for many years made scientific investigation difficult. For if emotions are highly subjective and private experiences, how can we study them with objective means? Does the subjective quality of emotions mean that they are different for each of us, and does this mean that they are not to be found in other animals? Are emotions different cross-culturally?

This chapter reports on the ongoing scientific struggle with emotion on the edge of our uncertainty and ignorance. While we have been able to gain some important scientific insights into the nature of emotion from both other animals and humans, much remains to be discovered. Neuroimaging methods are now allowing us to begin to start probing the subjective aspects of emotion, including its hedonic aspects, but we are only beginning to understand how brains deal with the intricate social and emotional fabric of human societies.

Of Emotional States and Feelings

Emotion and motivation remained for many years elusive scientific topics and were generally defined, in opposition to cognition, as that which move us in some way, as implied by the Latin root (*movere,* to move). Owing primarily to its perceived subjective nature, the scientific study of emotion was stunted despite ideas put forward by pioneering individuals such as Charles Darwin, who examined the evolution of emotional responses and facial expressions and suggested that emotions allow an organism to make adaptive responses to salient stimuli in the environment, thus enhancing its chances of survival (Darwin 1872).

A highly successful scientific strategy has been to divide the concept of emotion into two parts: the *emotional state* that can be measured through physiological changes such as visceral and endocrine responses, and *feelings,* seen as the subjective experience of emotion (Kringelbach 2004a). This allows emotional states to be measured in animals using, for example, conditioning, and most subsequent research has regarded emotions as states elicited by rewards and punishments (which, of course, is a rather circular definition) (Weiskrantz 1968). Emotional stimuli (primary and secondary reinforcers) are represented by brain structures, depending on the kind of reinforcer. Reinforcers are defined such that positive reinforcers (rewards) increase the frequency of behaviour leading to their acquisition, while negative reinforcers (punishers) decrease the frequency of behaviour leading to their encounter and increase the frequency of behaviour leading to their avoidance.

The subsequent emotional processing is a multistage process mediated by networks of brain structures. The results of this processing influence which behaviour is selected, which autonomic responses are elicited and which conscious feelings are produced (at least in humans).

An early, contrasting, but still influential theory of emotion was proposed in the 1880s independently by William James and Carl Lange, who proposed that rather than emotional experience being a response to a stimulus, it is the perception of the ensuing physiological bodily changes (James 1890; Lange 1887). The James-Lange theory of emotion suggests that contrary to popular perception we do not run from the bear because we are afraid, but that we *become* afraid because we run.

Several scientists have remained sceptical of such bodily theories of emotion. One of the initial main proponents, William Cannon, offered a detailed critique of the James-Lange theory. He showed that surgical disruption of the peripheral nervous system in dogs did not eliminate emotional responses as would have been predicted by the theory (Cannon 1927). Further investigations by Schachter and Singer suggested that bodily states must be accompanied by cognitive appraisal for an emotion to occur (Schachter and Singer 1962). However, this research did not fully resolve the basic question of the extent to which bodily states influence emotion and feelings.

More recently, the James-Lange theory was resurrected, first by Walla Nauta with his 'interoceptive' markers (Nauta 1971), and since—to far more popular acclaim—by Antonio Damasio in the form of his somatic marker hypothesis, in which feedback from the peripheral nervous system controls the *decision* about the correct behavioural response rather than the *emotional feelings* as postulated in the James-Lange theory (Damasio 1994).

Among the objections to these and other bodily theories of emotion are that they are underspecified with regard to what constitute emotional stimuli; that signals from the body are noisy and it is not clear whether they can distinguish the different emotions; and that animals and humans with severe spinal cord damage appear to have normal emotions. Some of these objections are addressed in the 'somatic marker' theory, which includes an 'as-if' loop for those decision-making situations with relatively low uncertainty that allows the brain to bypass the role of body (Damasio 1996). It has also been argued that emotions are constituted in large measure by visceral and endocrine responses rather than through the spinal cord. The orbitofrontal cortex certainly has the connectivity to receive and integrate visceral sensory signals to influence ongoing behaviour, and although it is not clear how this information is integrated, it remains possible that these signals have a significant role in decision making and emotion (Craig 2002). It should also be noted that most primary reinforcers are signaled via an interoceptive route and that this is likely to be essential for hedonic experience.

At the same time it is clear from the evidence of e.g. successful use of various beta blockers in alleviating stage fright, anxiety and panic attacks in stage musicians and other world-class performers that the body clearly must play a role in the regulation of emotions. Some observers have therefore suggested that the role of the body in emotion is perhaps more akin to an amplifier than to a generator.

There are of course close links between body and brain, as was fully clear to even Descartes, who is otherwise widely seen as one of the main proponents for the mind-body split. It is at best misleading to give Descartes such a simple-minded dualistic position (Descartes 1649; Sutton 2001)—although he was clearly on the wrong track when he named the pineal gland as the seat of the soul. Later research has shown that this brain structure is a key structure in the control of hormones and thus an unlikely contributor to the metaphysical construction of the soul.

Investigating Emotional States

Although the theoretical debates over the conceptual framework for emotion research have been very important, the development of experimental paradigms for the reliable testing of emotion in animals and humans has had just as much influence on the field of emotion research. Given that consciousness in animals remains controversial, the presence of feelings in animals is also a contentious issue. Animals do, however, show the characteristic behavioural, autonomic and hormonal responses associated with emotional states when confronted with emotionally salient stimuli.

Neuroscientists have concentrated on understanding the brain structures mediating rewards and punishments elicited by operationally defined reinforcers. Positive primary reinforcers are naturally occurring stimuli (such as sugar) that animals will work to obtain. Negative primary reinforcers are stimuli that animals will work to avoid (such as salt—although only when not salt-deprived). These primary reinforcers can be associated with arbitrary secondary reinforcers, which can be anything from the sound of Pavlov's bell to abstract paper representations such as banknotes. The learning process is called *conditioning*, and much psychological research has been dedicated to understanding the underlying principles (Skinner 1938; Thorndike 1911).

For many years behaviourism as led by Burrhus Skinner saw the brain as an uninteresting black box where the behaviour of animals was the only interesting feature; where responses slavishly follow stimuli; where subjective experience can ultimately be described solely as patterns of stimuli and responses and where all behaviour is completely flexible given the right reward schedule. Much later research has shown that the main tenets of behaviourism were oversimplified if not plain wrong. The species-specific features of the brain do matter very much and are decisive for its learning potential. Subjective experience does not depend in any simple way on stimuli and responses, and there are species-specific behaviours that even the most cunning reward schedules cannot change. In addition, there are many behaviours where the motivating reward is very seldom external, and often natural as in children's play (Lepper and Greene 1978; Lepper, Greene and Nisbett 1973; McGraw 1978).

Conditioning experiments are nevertheless important as they offer insights into some of the fundamental forms of learning. Neuroscientists have learned a great deal by studying brain activity using experimental paradigms adapted from behaviourism. One of the most successful paradigms in emotion research has been fear conditioning, in which an auditory conditioned stimulus is paired with a foot shock. In other words, when the animal hears a tone, it is given a foot shock and it subsequently learns this association.

LeDoux and others have shown that for rats to learn the appropriate fear response depends crucially on the amygdala, which is a brain structure in the temporal lobes (LeDoux, Cicchetti, Xagoraris and Romanski 1990). Subsequently, much neuroscientific research has concentrated on elucidating the full role of the amygdala in fear, so that it has become popularly known as the fear centre in the brain. However, the amygdala is not a homogeneous brain structure, but rather a collection of at least 13 anatomically distinct nuclei (Swanson and Petrovich 1998). In addition, other research using appetitive conditioning has also implicated the amygdala, indicating that it can be activated by both positive and negative stimuli (Holland and Gallagher 2004). It is therefore unlikely that the amygdala is only concerned with fear. Nevertheless, the fear conditioning paradigm has been very successful in creating an adequate scientific model of emotion and firmly establishing the field of emotion research. It has also become clear that the amygdala might be very important for rodents, but much has happened to the structure of the brain on the evolutionary path to higher primates such as humans.

As an interesting aside, it has been proposed that the amygdala obtains information about significant stimuli in the environment earlier than other brain areas in the cortex (LeDoux 1996). This gives the brain the possibility to quickly send early warning signals via the amygdala to the rest of the brain and the body. If we were to suddenly notice something which at first glance looked like a snake, our brain and body would be able to react quickly but essentially nonconsciously. The emotional fear reactions are able to commence immediately via the quick route of the amygdala, and we become aware that we are fearful before we are aware of what made us fearful. Throughout evolution this has likely conferred an evolutionary advantage to have very fast reactions to certain dangerous stimuli. These essentially nonconscious reactions could be a possible explanation of why James and Lange fashioned the idea that it is the body that controls emotions. But note that this cannot be true in the above example with the snake, as the information is first processed in the brain with the amygdala alerting the body. The example is, however, a good illustration of how little insight we have into our own brain processing.

Emotion and Feelings in Humans

Initially most scientific research thus mostly investigated emotions in experimental animals using conditioning paradigms with negative reinforcers such as fear. However, it was not clear if and how this research transfers to humans, especially given the subjective nature of conscious feelings, which are not necessarily present in other animals. Until quite recently, human research was limited to patients with lesion sites established post-mortem. The recent advent of neuroimaging has afforded a unique window on the living human brain and has also allowed for investigations into positive emotions such as joy.

It was clear, however, even from early behavioural cross-cultural studies, that there might be an innate, biological basis for emotional experience. Paul Ekman demonstrated that facial emotions are universally recognized across cultures (Ekman and Friesen 1971). Furthermore, analyses of emotion terms in all of the world's major languages have led to discussions on the existence and enumeration of the fundamental emotions that can act as basic building blocks of our entire emotional repertoire. Based on such research, up to seven emotions have been proposed: anger, disgust, fear, sadness, joy, shame and guilt. It remains an open question whether these emotions are really distinct or whether they are found on a continuum produced by shared brain mechanisms.

The case of Phineas Gage was one of the first neurological cases to indicate some possible neural correlates of emotions in human (Harlow 1848). Gage was a young railway engineer who suffered a tragic accident in which his brain and more specifically his medial parts of the frontal lobes, including the orbitofrontal cortex, were penetrated by a tampering iron. Miraculously Gage survived, but his personality and emotional processing were changed completely (although care should be taken when extrapolating from this case as our information is rather sparse) (Macmillan 2000).

Later cases of damage to the frontal parts of the brain and in particular the orbitofrontal cortex have been shown to cause major changes in emotion, personality, behaviour, and social conduct. Patients often show lack of affect, social inappropriateness and irresponsibility. It has been shown that patients are impaired at correctly identifying social signals, including for example face and voice expression identification (Hornak, Bramham, Rolls, Morris, O'Doherty, Bullock and Polkey 2003; Hornak, Rolls and Wade 1996). There are even cases of patients who retain their high intellectual abilities but show a complete change in personality and general irresponsibility (Eslinger and Damasio 1985).

Analyses of the effects of lesions to the human orbitofrontal cortex show that lesions impair the patients in a variety of important ways related to emotion, reversal learning and decision making. The severity of these changes can be measured by the patients' performance on neuropsychological tests including gambling (Bechara, Damasio, Damasio and Anderson 1994), reversal learning (Hornak et al. 2003; Rolls, Hornak, Wade and McGrath 1994), and decision making (Rogers et al. 1999).

In summary, animal studies and lesion studies in humans have allowed scientists to outline some of the brain structures involved in emotion. The three key regions in the human brain are the orbitofrontal cortex, amygdala and cingulate cortex (see Figure 3.1). Other important brain structures for emotion include the hypothalamus, insula/operculum, nucleus accumbens, and various brainstem nuclei such as the periaqueductal grey.

However, until the advent of neuroimaging of the normal human brain, almost nothing was known about the neural correlates of the subjective and social aspects of emotion. The following will concentrate on describing some of the recent advances in understanding the neural correlates of subjective hedonic experience. In addition, some of the recent research on representing of the social aspects of emotions will be described.

Hedonic Experience

Part and parcel of all sensory stimuli is our hedonic experience of their pleasant and unpleasant aspects. These hedonic experiences help us decide on the best possible actions for navigating complex physical and social environments. Neuroscience has been successful in elucidating some of the neural correlates of hedonic experience by studying food intake (Kringelbach 2005).

To put hedonic behaviour in a historical context, early drive theories of motivation proposed that hedonic behaviour is controlled by need states (Hull 1951). But these early theories do not, for example, explain why people still continue to eat nice food when they feel full. This was addressed by incentive motivation theories, in which hedonic behaviour is mostly determined by the incentive value of a stimulus or its capacity to function as a reward (Bindra 1978). Need states such as hunger are still important but only work indirectly on the stimulus's incentive value. The principle of modulation of the hedonic value of a consummatory sensory stimulus by homeostatic factors was coined *alliesthesia* (from *allios,* changed, and *esthesia,*

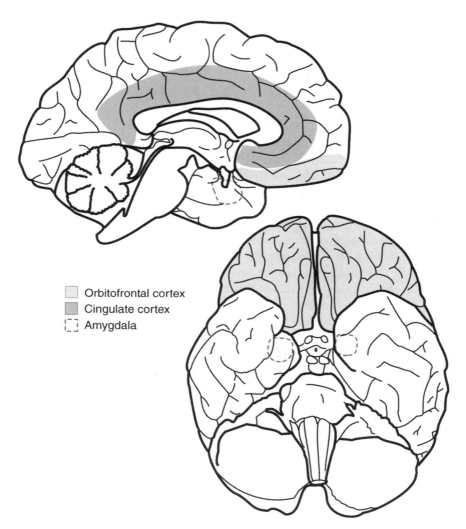

Figure 3.1 Emotion-related brain regions. The figure shows the approximate location of three key brain regions involved in emotion: the orbitofrontal cortex, cingulate cortex and amygdala. At the top is shown a mid-section of the human brain with the front of the brain facing right. At the bottom is shown the brain seen from below with the front facing upwards.

sensation) (Cabanac 1971). A useful distinction has been proposed between two aspects of reward: hedonic impact and incentive salience, in which the former refers to the liking or pleasure related to the reward, and the latter to the wanting or desire for the reward (Berridge 1996; Berridge and Robinson 1998).

Food intake is such a common act that most people rarely think about the complexities involved. Foremost, food intake is a precisely controlled act that can potentially be fatal if the wrong decision is taken to swallow toxins, microorganisms or nonfood objects on the basis of erroneously determining the sensory properties of the food. Humans and other animals have therefore developed elaborate food behaviours which are aimed at balancing conservative risk-minimizing and life-preserving strategies with occasional novelty seeking in the hope of discovering new sources of nutrients (Rozin 2001).

Importantly, food intake must also provide the right balance of carbohydrates, fats, amino acids, vitamins and minerals (apart from sodium) to sustain life. The neural mechanisms regulating food intake are complicated and must, like any regulatory system, include at least four features: system variables, detectors for the system variables, set points for these system variables and correctional mechanisms. A simple regulatory feedback system operates best with immediate changes, and it becomes significantly more complex when the feedback is not immediate. In the case of controlling food intake, there are significant delays in system changes caused by the relatively slow metabolic processes, and therefore the regulatory neural systems controlling food intake must include sophisticated mechanisms to learn to predict in advance when a meal should be initiated and terminated. Many of the basic components and principles of food intake have been elucidated in great detail and have been described in reviews elsewhere (LeMagnen 1985; Woods and Stricker 1999). Simple behaviours linked to food intake are controlled by homeostatic systems in the brainstem, as shown by the fact that even decerebrate animals are able to survive (Grill and Norgren 1978).

However, most of this research has been carried out in other animals, which has not helped to inform about the strong hedonic component of human food intake. Much complex human behaviour related to food intake must be linked to neural activity in the cerebral cortex, integrating the complex multitude of stimuli and situational variables. Important examples of complex behaviour include the decrease of the rated pleasantness of sweet tastes when subjects are sated relative to when they are hungry (alliesthesia) (Cabanac 1971) and satiation signals that selectively suppress further food intake of previously ingested foods, while other foods can still be readily ingested (selective satiety) (Rolls, Rolls, Rowe and Sweeney 1981).

In an aside, it should be noted that the relative sophistication of foraging in higher primates compared to other mammals indicates that significant parts of our large brains are dedicated to the required motivational, emotional and cognitive processing, and that mental processes related to food intake may indeed underlie other higher functions. The special importance of food in human life is underlined by the predominance of food symbols and metaphors in human expressions across cultures (Lévi-Strauss 1964) and the elaborate social constructions regarding purity and taboo of foods (Douglas 1966). Food intake and food choice constitute a fundamental and frequent part of human life and have played a major role in the cultural evolution of nonfood systems such as ritual, religion and social exchange as well as in the advancement of technology, development of cities, illnesses and warfare through agriculture and domestication (Diamond 1999).

Selective Satiety

Everyone is familiar with the important mechanisms for 'selective satiety' from the ability to still desire and have plenty of room for the dessert after feeling completely full from the main course. From an evolutionary perspective this has the clear advantage of allowing us and other animals to obtain a sufficiently wide variety of nutrients.

Selective satiety (or 'sensory-specific satiety' as it is also known) is a particularly useful phenomenon for studying affective representation in the brain, as it provides a means of altering the affective value of a stimulus, without modifying its physical attributes. As a consequence, any differences observed between the representation of a particular food stimulus in the brain before and after satiety can be attributed to the change in the impact of the reward, or the reward value. This controls for possible confounds such as increases in thirst, gastric distension and changes in blood glucose levels after feeding, by virtue of the fact that the neural response to another food which is not eaten in the meal is also measured. Selective satiety effects are strongest when using quite different foods such as e.g. tomato juice (savoury) and chocolate milk (sweet).

We investigated the neural mechanisms related to selective satiety with functional magnetic resonance imaging (fMRI), which in turn allowed us to identify the neural correlates of subjective pleasantness (Kringelbach, O'Doherty, Rolls and Andrews 2003). For those unfamiliar with neuroimaging I have included a detailed description of the experiment to provide a flavour for the steps involved.

The subjects refrained from eating for at least six hours prior to arriving at the imaging center on the day of the experiment in the late afternoon. Prior to participation in the experiment, the subjects were prescreened to ensure that they found both tomato juice and chocolate milk to be pleasant, and to ensure that they were not overweight or on a diet or planning to go on a diet. Both liquid foods are administrable in liquid form and palatable at room temperature, and the clear difference in their flavour and texture helps to facilitate sensory-specific satiety effects and minimizes the likelihood of the subjects developing a generalized satiety to both liquid foods.

Before feeding, the subjects were placed in the scanner, and scanned while being presented with each of the two liquid food stimuli, as well as a tasteless control solution which was delivered to the subject's mouth through three polythene tubes that were held between the lips. Each tube of approximately 1 meter in length was connected to a separate reservoir via a syringe and a one-way syringe valve. One reservoir contained the chocolate milk, another contained the tomato juice and a third reservoir contained a tasteless control solution (with the main ionic components of saliva). Note that water is not an appropriate control solution since it is rewarding to hungry subjects.

We used a block design with each epoch lasting 16 seconds. At the beginning of each epoch, 0.75 ml of one of the liquid foods (or the control solution) was delivered to the subject's mouth in under 0.5 seconds on average. The subject was then instructed to roll the stimulus around on the tongue and was then cued to swallow the stimulus (using a visual cue) after 10 seconds. The stimuli were delivered in an interleaved manner for each epoch, such that the subjects received tomato juice in one epoch, followed by the tasteless control solution, followed by the chocolate milk, and then followed again by the tasteless control solution. This cycle was repeated 16 times. At three points during the imaging run, there was an additional 16-second period following the presentation of each stimulus (at cycles 4, 8 and 12), during which no taste stimulus was delivered. Instead, subjects were presented with a visual rating scale ranging from +2 (very pleasant) to –2 (very unpleasant) in 0.25 increments, and had to rate the subjective pleasantness of the preceding liquid food stimulus by moving a vertical bar to the appropriate point on the scale through the use of a button box.

After the initial scanning run, the subjects were taken out of the scanner and fed to satiety on one of the liquid foods. The subjects were instructed to consume the liquid foods for their lunch and were asked to drink as much as they could until they absolutely did not want to have any more. The liquid food was poured into a 150 ml cup and offered to the subject. Once the subject had consumed the contents of the cup, it was then refilled. This was repeated a number of times until the subject was completely satiated and refused the offer of an additional cup. To achieve a balanced design, five subjects were fed to satiety on tomato juice and five subjects were fed to satiety on the chocolate milk. Each subject was randomly allocated one of the two liquid foods for their meal and the subjects were not informed in advance (until after the first imaging run) which liquid food they would be invited to consume.

Once the subjects had finished their meal, the most important part of the experiment took place. We put the subjects back into the scanner and repeated the exact same scanning procedure as before. Now, whether the subjects had been fed on chocolate milk or tomato juice, they reported not liking this stimulus and gave negative scores. But the same subjects still liked the other stimulus which they had not been fed. Importantly, it was only the subjects' subjective *pleasantness* ratings that had changed and not their intensity ratings.

We were then able to correlate the changes in brain activity over the course of the experiment with the subjective pleasantness ratings for all subjects. The statistical analysis found that a part of the anterior orbitofrontal cortex was correlated with the subjects' subjective pleasantness (see Figure 3.2). Since only the subjective pleasantness ratings had changed and not the intensity ratings, and since the experiment was counterbalanced in terms of stimuli, this means that the brain activity is not only related

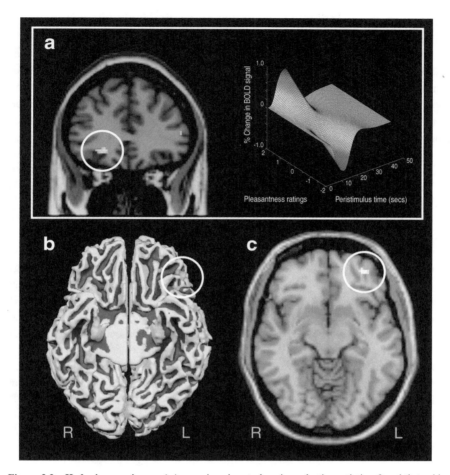

Figure 3.2 Hedonic experience. a) A neuroimaging study using selective satiation found that mid-anterior parts of the orbitofrontal cortex are correlated with the subjects' subjective pleasantness ratings of the foods throughout the experiment (Kringelbach et al. 2003). On the right is shown a plot of the magnitude of the fitted haemodynamic response from a representative single subject against the subjective pleasantness ratings (on a scale from –2 to +2) and peristimulus time in seconds. **b)** Additional evidence for the role of the orbitofrontal cortex in subjective experience comes from another neuroimaging experiment investigating the supra-additive effects of combining the umami tastants monosodium glutamate and inosine monophosphate (De Araujo et al. 2003a). The figure shows the region of mid-anterior orbitofrontal cortex showing synergistic effects (rendered on the ventral surface of human cortical areas with the cerebellum removed). The perceived synergy is unlikely to be expressed in the taste receptors themselves, and the activity in the orbitofrontal cortex may thus reflect the subjective enhancement of umami taste which must be closely linked to subjective experience. **c)** Adding strawberry odour to a sucrose taste solution makes the combination significantly more pleasant than the sum of each of the individual components. The supra-linear effects reflecting the subjective enhancement were found to significantly activate a lateral region of the left anterior orbitofrontal cortex, which is remarkably similar to that found in the other experiments (De Araujo et al. 2003b).

to the pleasantness of chocolate milk or to tomato juice but to both, and therefore to the pleasantness of the combination of taste, smell and structure of these foods.

Other subsequent neuroimaging experiments have also found that the orbitofrontal cortex appears to represent the subjective experience of pleasantness (De Araujo, Kringelbach, Rolls and Hobden 2003a; De Araujo, Rolls, Kringelbach, McGlone and Phillips 2003b; Gottfried, O'Doherty and Dolan 2003; Rolls, Kringelbach and de Araujo 2003a; Rolls et al. 2003b). More evidence to support this comes from studies that show the orbitofrontal cortex and other brain regions are active when representing the subjective effects of drugs such as amphetamine (Völlm et al. 2004) and cocaine (Breiter et al. 1997) as well as sex (Holstege et al. 2003). In addition, activation of the orbitofrontal cortex correlates with the negative dissonance (i.e. pleasantness) of musical chords (Blood, Zatorre, Bermudez and Evans 1999), and intensely pleasurable responses, or 'chills', that are elicited by music are correlated with activity in the orbitofrontal cortex, ventral striatum, cingulate and insula cortex (Blood and Zatorre 2001).

These potentially exciting findings from neuroimaging extend previous findings in nonhuman primates of reinforcer representations to representations of the *subjective affective value* of these reinforcers. One has to be careful not to overinterpret mere correlations with the elusive qualities of subjective experience, and it is unlikely that hedonic experience would depend on only one cortical region. Even so, it would be interesting to obtain more evidence on this issue by investigating patients with selective lesions to these areas to investigate whether their subjective affective experiences have changed. Some evidence has already been obtained to suggest that this is the case (Hornak et al. 2003).

Social Interactions

Humans are intensely sociable creatures and we spend an inordinate amount of time engaged in social interactions with others. The quest to understand intelligent social behaviour has taken many forms, and at least two distinct approaches with slightly different emphasis have led to interesting insights. One approach has emphasized the continuity with social behaviour in other animals, as studied for example by ethologists and zoologists, which points to the importance of environmental interactions in the development and exercise of intelligent behaviour. Other approaches traditionally taken by researchers in the social sciences have tended to emphasize the uniqueness of human behaviour and the uniqueness of the individual person, their environment and their social surroundings. These approaches are not mutually exclusive but complementary.

Most recently, the advances in neuroimaging have made it possible to forge a truce between these approaches and investigate the neural architecture underlying various forms of social behaviour by directly studying the brain mechanisms.

Although still in its innovative phase, these new experimental technologies are already providing insights into the brain activity which allows an individual to interact with others and how that behaviour becomes coordinated in an adaptive fashion over time.

One key aspect of human social interactions, and perhaps even a hallmark of human nature, is our remarkably flexible behaviour, especially in the social domain, which is perhaps also a major reason for our relative evolutionary success. Our social skills are already being honed as children and young adolescents, where we quickly become very adept at forming and breaking alliances within and between groups, and spend much of our time engaged in complex social interactions. At best these interactions enrich our society, at worst they become 'Machiavellian' and exploitative. In fact, while science might appear removed from such politics, many scientists would probably agree that science is in fact a social enterprise which shares many characteristics with other human pursuits, and that any claim to greater scientific truth can only be accorded over decades and even centuries.

Constituting flexible behaviour is the concept of *reversal learning*. While it is obviously important that we can learn arbitrary associations between stimuli and actions, it is also extremely important that we can relatively easily break these associations and relearn others. If we learn that choosing a certain object leads to a reward, it would be rather maladaptive to keep choosing this object when it was no longer associated with a reward but, say, instead a punishment. We need to be able to adapt or *reverse* the learning patterns when things change in order to accommodate complex behaviour.

For a long time it was thought that complex behaviour depends crucially on the prefrontal cortex, but it was not clear which parts were important for reversal learning. This was investigated in a classic paper (Iversen and Mishkin 1970). The authors lesioned discrete parts of the prefrontal cortex in different monkeys and showed convincingly that these lesions had differential effects on the ability of these animals to reverse rewarding associations in an object-reversal task. When the inferior prefrontal convexity and parts of the lateral orbitofrontal cortex were lesioned, these monkeys became significantly impaired on object-reversal learning. Specifically, the monkeys would continue to respond much longer than controls to the object that is no longer rewarded on the first reversal trial. This was not the case for monkeys who had the medial parts of the orbitofrontal cortex lesioned. These monkeys were not completely unaffected by the lesion but showed moderate impairment on all but the first of the object discrimination reversals and furthermore had moderate problems withholding response between trials on an auditory differentation task. This strongly suggested a differential role for the lateral and medial parts of the orbitofrontal cortex.

Iversen and Mishkin persuasively demonstrated the importance of the orbitofrontal cortex in reversal learning, and other studies have since extended this result in nonhuman primates. One study demonstrated that single neurons in the macaque orbitofrontal cortex change their responses to a visual cue after a single trial in which the reward association of the visual cue is reversed (Thorpe, Rolls and Maddison 1983). Another lesion study in marmosets by Dias, Robbins and Roberts (1996) found that the orbitofrontal cortex is essential for performing an emotion-related reversal learning task.

There is also some evidence that humans with lesions to the orbitofrontal cortex have problems with reversal learning, but in the experiments concerned, the lesions, caused by diffuse brain damage, were not very clean or focal (Rolls et al. 1994). In addition, lesions to the orbitofrontal cortex are associated with impairments in emotional and social behaviour characterized by disinhibition, social inappropriateness and irresponsibility (Anderson, Bechara, Damasio, Tranel and Damasio 1999).

However, it is not clear that these results necessarily transfer to humans, and we therefore decided to use neuroimaging of a probabilistic reversal-learning task. The subjects' task was, by trial and error, to determine which of two stimuli is the more profitable to choose, and to keep track of this—and reverse their choice when a reversal occurred. By design, the actual reversal event was not easy to determine since 'money' can be won or lost on both stimuli, but a choice of the rewarding stimulus would in general give larger rewards and smaller punishments, whereas the converse was true of the punishing stimulus, such that losing a large amount of money would often (but not always) signal that a reversal had occurred.

We used fMRI to show that dissociable activity in the medial orbitofrontal cortex was correlated with the magnitude of the monetary gains received, while activity in the lateral orbitofrontal cortex was correlated with the monetary losses received (O'Doherty, Kringelbach, Rolls, Hornak and Andrews 2001). This dissociation between the functions of medial and lateral orbitofrontal cortex mirrors Iversen and Mishkin's initial dissociation in monkeys, where the lateral orbitofrontal cortex in both cases is linked to the reversal trials.

However, our initial imaging study did not reveal the cortical localization of reversal trials due to the probabilistic nature of the task, where receiving a monetary punishment did not always signal reversal. In addition, our task used money as the secondary reinforcer that might be powerful in humans but have little biological relevance for other animals, and may not be linked directly to the interesting social domain.

Social Rewards from Faces

One way to solve these problems with localizing the neural correlates of reversal learning is to instead use facial expressions as the reinforcing stimuli. This makes sense given that the key to social intelligence is the ability to detect subtle changes in communication and act upon these changes rapidly as they occur. Such changes in social behaviour are often based on facial expression and come so naturally to humans (and are in place so early in child development) that some might argue that this functionality is essentially innate. However, human social behaviour is sufficiently flexible that we can easily learn to adapt our behaviour to most face expressions. For example, other people's neutral expressions do not normally indicate that our behaviour should change, but it is easy to think of social contexts where a neutral expression does indeed imply that our current behaviour is inappropriate and should change.

We designed a reversal task where the overall goal was for the subject to keep track of the mood of two people presented in a pair and as much as possible to select the image of a 'happy' person (who will then smile). Over time the person with the 'happy' mood (who will smile when selected), changes her mood to 'angry'. This person will thus no longer be smiling when selected but instead change to a facial expression that signals that this person should no longer be selected. In the main reversal task the facial expression used to cue reversal was an angry expression (the most natural facial expression to cue reversal), while in the second, control version of the reversal task, a neutral expression was used instead. By using two different reversal tasks where different facial expressions are signalling that behaviour must change, we were able to determine which brain areas are specific to general reversal learning rather than just to reversal following a particular expression such as anger.

We used fMRI to show that the ability to change behaviour based on someone else's facial expression is not reflected in the activity in the fusiform cortex (which invariantly appears to reflect only identity and not valence of faces), but that general reversal learning is specifically correlated with activity in the lateral orbitofrontal and anterior cingulate/paracingulate cortices (as well as other brain areas including the ventral striatum and the inferior precentral sulcus) (Kringelbach and Rolls 2003) (see Figure 3.3).

This result confirms and extends the results from the original Iversen and Mishkin paper. Further confirmation came from the neuropsychological testing carried out by Julia Hornak on human patients with surgical lesions to the orbitofrontal cortex, which showed that bilateral (but not unilateral) lesions to the lateral orbitofrontal cortex produce significant impairments in reversal learning (Hornak et al. 2004). Yet, as always, these results are not conclusive and raise many new issues. It is for instance unclear what other areas are necessary and sufficient for reversal learning. Among the other brain areas we found relating to general reversal learning in our study, the ventral striatum is an obvious candidate (Cools, Clark, Owen and Robbins 2002).

In addition, fMRI is essentially a correlative technique with poor temporal information, which makes it very difficult to infer causal relations between brain regions. It thus still awaits further investigations with e.g. magnetoencephalography (MEG) to gain temporal information on the milliseconds scale.

In his original masterpiece *The Prince*, Machiavelli offers a rather pessimistic view on human nature in which '... love is held by a chain of obligation which, since men are bad, is broken at every opportunity for personal gain'. Some of the

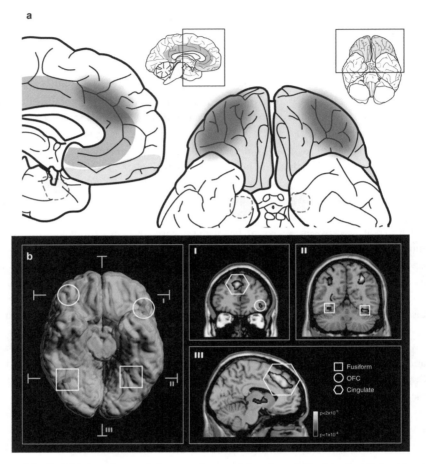

Figure 3.3   Social interactions and the case of reversal learning. a) The lateral orbitofrontal and parts of the anterior cingulate cortices in the rostral cingulate zone are often found to be coactivated in neuroimaging studies (with the regions superimposed in red). Most often this is found in tasks where the subjects have to evaluate negative stimuli which when detected may lead to a change in current behaviour. **b)** A recent neuroimaging study found that the lateral orbitofrontal and the anterior cingulate/ paracingulate cortices are together responsible for changing behaviour in an object-reversal task (Kringelbach and Rolls 2003). This task was set up to model aspects of human social interactions (see text for full description of the task). Subjects were required to keep track of the faces of two people and to select the 'happy' person, who would change mood after some time, and subjects had to learn to change, reverse, their behaviour to choose the other person. The most significant activity during the reversal phase was found in the lateral orbitofrontal and cingulate cortices (red and green circles), while the main effects of faces were found to elicit activity in the fusiform gyrus and intraparietal sulcus (blue circles).

challenges that await social neuroscience are to investigate how social interactions allow individuals to operate within a society. It may be that our ability for rapid reversal learning is sometimes used for less noble pursuits in both science and in interpersonal relations in general, but we would be in real trouble if we were not able to learn how to change.

Conclusions

The scientific study of emotion remains in its infancy, especially when it comes to understanding its hedonic aspects and the links to wider societal structures. Some progress has been made in understanding the putative brain structures involved in emotion, mostly based on animal models of emotion. This research has implicated the orbitofrontal cortex, amygdala and cingulate cortex as important for emotional processing. Other important brain structures include the hypothalamus, insula/operculum, nucleus accumbens and various brainstem nuclei such as the periaqueductal grey. These brain regions provide some of the necessary input and output systems for multimodal association regions such as the orbitofrontal cortex that are involved in representing and learning about the reinforcers that elicit emotions and conscious feelings (Kringelbach 2005).

This chapter has provided some of the novel findings from neuroimaging which have foremost demonstrated the importance of the orbitofrontal cortex in emotional processing. In particular, the recent convergence of findings from neuroimaging, neuropsychology and neurophysiology has demonstrated that the human orbitofrontal cortex is best thought of as an important nexus for sensory integration, emotional processing and hedonic experience. In terms of emotional processing, it has become clear that the orbitofrontal cortex plays an important role in emotional disorders such as depression (Drevets 2001) and addiction (Volkow and Li 2004), and it is now possible to offer a tentative model of the functional neuroanatomy of the orbitofrontal cortex (shown in Figure 3.4).

The posterior parts of the orbitofrontal cortex process the sensory information for further multimodal integration. The reward value of the reinforcer is assigned in more anterior parts of the orbitofrontal cortex, from where it can be modulated by hunger and other internal states and can be used to influence subsequent behaviour (in lateral parts of the anterior orbitofrontal cortex with connections to anterior cingulate cortex), stored for monitoring, learning and memory (in medial parts of the anterior orbitofrontal cortex) and made available for subjective hedonic experience (in mid-anterior orbitofrontal cortex). At all times, there is important reciprocal information flowing between the various regions of the orbitofrontal cortex and other brain regions including the anterior cingulate cortex and the amygdala.

At the present time, significant differences in terms of laterality have not been demonstrated in the orbitofrontal cortex (Kringelbach and Rolls 2004). However,

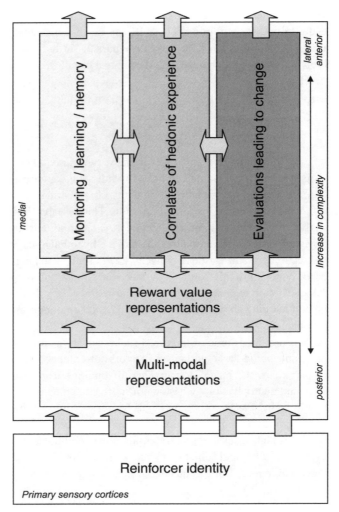

Figure 3.4 Model of the functions of the orbitofrontal cortex. The proposed model shows the interactions between sensory and hedonic systems in the orbitofrontal cortex using as an example one hemisphere of the orbitofrontal cortex (Kringelbach 2004b). Information is flowing from bottom to top on the figure. Sensory information arrives from the periphery to the primary sensory cortices, where the stimulus identity is decoded into stable cortical representations. This information is then conveyed for further multimodal integration in brain structures in the posterior parts of the orbitofrontal cortex. The reward value of the reinforcer is assigned in more anterior parts of the orbitofrontal cortex, from where it can then be used to influence subsequent behaviour (in lateral parts of the anterior orbitofrontal cortex with connections to anterior cingulate cortex), stored for learning/memory (in medial parts of the anterior orbitofrontal cortex) and made available for subjective hedonic experience (in mid-anterior orbitofrontal cortex). The reward value and the subjective hedonic experience can be modulated by hunger and other internal states. In addition, there is important reciprocal information flowing between the various regions of the orbitofrontal cortex and other brain regions.

in terms of neuroanatomy, the orbitofrontal cortex is a highly heterogeneous brain region, and future neuroimaging and neuropsychology studies are likely to find many more functional distinctions between its constituent parts.

The proposed link to subjective hedonic processing places the orbitofrontal cortex as an important gateway to subjective conscious experience. One possible way to conceptualize the role of the orbitofrontal and anterior cingulate cortices would be as part of a global workspace for access to consciousness with the specific role of evaluating the affective valence of stimuli (Dehaene, Kerszberg, and Changeux 1998). In this context it is interesting that the medial parts of the orbitofrontal cortex are part of a proposed network for the baseline activity of the human brain at rest (Gusnard and Raichle 2001), as this would place the orbitofrontal cortex as a key node in the network subserving consciousness. This could potentially explain why all experiences have an emotional tone.

There are many interesting and important issues in emotion research which are not yet fully understood. It is clear that personality and society play a significant role in shaping emotions, but we are a long way from understanding personality in neural terms. Studies in split-brain patients seem to suggest a hemispheric specialization of emotional processing, but the issue of lateralization is still much debated among researchers. It also clear that although conscious appraisal of emotion is important for emotional expression, many emotional stimuli appear to be processed on a non-conscious level, only later to become available for conscious introspection (or, as in the case of blindsight, not at all) (Naccache et al. 2005). Emotion helps to facilitate learning and memory adaptively, and so there are strong links between emotion, learning and memory, but their exact relationships are not yet fully understood.

The most difficult question facing emotion research remains the subjective experience of emotion, and while some progress has been made as described in this article, it is important not to overinterpret mere correlations from neuroimaging with the elusive qualities of subjective experience.

In summary, emotions are evolutionarily important for animals (including humans) in preparing for appropriate actions, and the evolution of conscious feelings in humans could be adaptive, because they allow us to consciously appraise our emotions and actions and subsequently to learn to manipulate these appropriately. Emotion may be one of evolution's most productive breakthroughs, constantly reminding us that we are still animals at heart, but endowed with the possibility of conscious appraisal and the enhanced control of our subjective experience that comes with it.

References

Anderson, S. W., Bechara, A., Damasio, H., Tranel, D., and Damasio, A. R. (1999), 'Impairment of Social and Moral Behavior Related to Early Damage in Human Prefrontal Cortex', *Nature Neuroscience,* 2: 1032–37.

Bechara, A., Damasio, A. R., Damasio, H., and Anderson, S. W. (1994), 'Insensitivity to Future Consequences Following Damage to Human Prefrontal Cortex', *Cognition*, 50: 7–15.

Berridge, K. C. (1996), 'Food Reward: Brain Substrates of Wanting and Liking', *Neuroscience and Biobehavioral Reviews*, 20: 1–25.

Berridge, K. C., and Robinson, T. E. (1998), 'What Is the Role of Dopamine in Reward: Hedonic Impact, Reward Learning, or Incentive Salience?' *Brain Research Reviews*, 28: 309–69.

Bindra, D. (1978), 'How Adaptive Behavior Is Produced: A Perceptual-motivational Alternative to Response-reinforcement', *Behavioral and Brain Sciences*, 1: 41–91.

Blood, A. J., and Zatorre, R. J. (2001), 'Intensely Pleasurable Responses to Music Correlate with Activity in Brain Regions Implicated in Reward and Emotion', *Proceedings of the National Academy of Sciences of the United States of America*, 98: 11818–23.

Blood, A. J., Zatorre, R. J., Bermudez, P., and Evans, A. C. (1999), 'Emotional Responses to Pleasant and Unpleasant Music Correlate with Activity in Paralimbic Brain Regions', *Nature Neuroscience*, 2: 382–7.

Breiter, H. C., Gollub, R. L., Weisskoff, R. M., Kennedy, D. N., Makris, N., Berke, J. D., Goodman, J. M., Kantor, H. L., Gastfriend, D. R., Riorden, J. P., Mathew, R. T., Rosen, B. R., and Hyman, S. E. (1997), 'Acute Effects of Cocaine on Human Brain Activity and Emotion', *Neuron*, 19: 591–611.

Cabanac, M. (1971), 'Physiological Role of Pleasure', *Science*, 173: 1103–7.

Cannon, W. B. (1927), 'The James-Lange Theory of Emotion', *American Journal of Psychology*, 39: 106–24.

Cools, R., Clark, L., Owen, A. M., and Robbins, T. W. (2002), 'Defining the Neural Mechanisms of Probabilistic Reversal Learning Using Event-related Functional Magnetic Resonance Imaging', *Journal of Neuroscience*, 22: 4563–7.

Craig, A. D. (2002), 'Opinion: How Do You Feel? Interoception: The Sense of the Physiological Condition of the Body', *Nature Reviews Neuroscience*, 3: 655–66.

Damasio, A. R. (1994), *Descartes' Error*, New York: Putnam.

Damasio, A. R. (1996), 'The Somatic Marker Hypothesis and the Possible Functions of the Prefrontal Cortex', *Philosophical Transactions of the Royal Society B: Biological Sciences*, 351: 1413–20.

Darwin, C. (1872), *The Expression of the Emotions in Man and Animals*, Chicago: University of Chicago Press.

De Araujo, I. E. T., Kringelbach, M. L., Rolls, E. T., and Hobden, P. (2003a), 'The Representation of Umami Taste in the Human Brain', *Journal of Neurophysiology*, 90: 313–19.

De Araujo, I. E. T., Rolls, E. T., Kringelbach, M. L., McGlone, F., and Phillips, N. (2003b), 'Taste-olfactory Convergence, and the Representation of the Pleasantness of Flavour, in the Human Brain', *European Journal of Neuroscience*, 18: 2059–68.

Dehaene, S., Kerszberg, M., and Changeux, J. P. (1998), 'A Neuronal Model of a Global Workspace in Effortful Cognitive Tasks', *Proceedings of the National Academy of Sciences of the United States of America,* 95: 14529–34.

Descartes, R. (1649), *Les Passions de l'Âme,* Paris: Henry LeGras.

Diamond, J. M. (1999), *Guns, Germs, and Steel: The Fates of Human Societies,* New York: Norton.

Dias, R., Robbins, T., and Roberts, A. (1996), 'Dissociation in Prefrontal Cortex of Affective and Attentional Shifts', *Nature,* 380: 69–72.

Douglas, M. (1966), *Purity and Danger: An Analysis of Concepts of Pollution and Taboo,* London: Routledge & Kegan Paul.

Drevets, W. C. (2001), 'Neuroimaging and Neuropathological Studies of Depression: Implications for the Cognitive-emotional Features of Mood Disorders', *Current Opinion in Neurobiology,* 11: 240–9.

Ekman, P., and Friesen, W.-V. (1971), 'Constants across Cultures in the Face and Emotion', *Journal of Personality and Social Psychology,* 17(2): 124–9.

Eslinger, P. J., and Damasio, A. R. (1985), 'Severe Disturbance of Higher Cognition after Bilateral Frontal Lobe Ablation: Patient EVR', *Neurology,* 35: 1731–41.

Gottfried, J. A., O'Doherty, J., and Dolan, R. J. (2003), 'Encoding Predictive Reward Value in Human Amygdala and Orbitofrontal Cortex', *Science,* 301: 1104–7.

Grill, H. J., and Norgren, R. (1978), 'The Taste Reactivity Test, II, Mimetic Responses to Gustatory Stimuli in Chronic Thalamic and Chronic Decerebrate Rats', *Brain Research,* 143: 281–97.

Gusnard, D. A., and Raichle, M. E. (2001), 'Searching for a Baseline: Functional Imaging and the Resting Human Brain', *Nature Reviews Neuroscience,* 2: 685–94.

Harlow, J. M. (1848), 'Passage of an Iron Rod through the Head', *Boston Medical and Surgical Journal,* 39: 389–93.

Holland, P. C., and Gallagher, M. (2004), 'Amygdala-frontal Interactions and Reward Expectancy', *Current Opinion in Neurobiology,* 14: 148–55.

Holstege, G., Georgiadis, J. R., Paans, A.M., Meiners, L. C., van der Graaf, F. H., and Reinders, A. A. (2003), 'Brain Activation during Human Male Ejaculation', *Journal of Neuroscience,* 23: 9185–93.

Hornak, J., Bramham, J., Rolls, E. T., Morris, R. G., O'Doherty, J., Bullock, P. R., and Polkey, C. E. (2003), 'Changes in Emotion after Circumscribed Surgical Lesions of the Orbitofrontal and Cingulate Cortices', *Brain,* 126: 1671–712.

Hornak, J., O'Doherty, J., Bramham, J., Rolls, E. T., Morris, R. G., Bullock, P. R., and Polkey, C. E. (2004), 'Reward-related Reversal Learning after Surgical Excisions in Orbitofrontal and Dorsolateral Prefrontal Cortex in Humans', *Journal of Cognitive Neuroscience,* 16: 463–78.

Hornak, J., Rolls, E. T., and Wade, D. (1996), 'Face and Voice Expression Identification in Patients with Emotional and Behavioural Changes Following Ventral Frontal Lobe Damage', *Neuropsychologia,* 34: 247–61.

Hull, C. L. (1951), *Essentials of Behavior,* New Haven, Conn.: Yale University Press.

Iversen, S. D., and Mishkin, M. (1970), 'Perseverative Interference in Monkeys Following Selective Lesions of the Inferior Prefrontal Convexity', *Experimental Brain Research,* 11: 376–86.

James, W. (1890), *The Principles of Psychology,* New York: Henry Holt.

Kringelbach, M. L. (2004a), 'Emotion', in R. L. Gregory (ed.), *The Oxford Companion to the Mind,* 2nd ed., Oxford: Oxford University Press.

Kringelbach, M. L. (2004b), 'Food for Thought: Hedonic Experience beyond Homeostasis in the Human Brain', *Neuroscience,* 126: 807–19.

Kringelbach, M. L. (2005), 'The Orbitofrontal Cortex: Linking Reward to Hedonic Experience', *Nature Reviews Neuroscience,* 6: 691–702.

Kringelbach, M. L., O'Doherty, J., Rolls, E. T., and Andrews, C. (2003), 'Activation of the Human Orbitofrontal Cortex to a Liquid Food Stimulus Is Correlated with Its Subjective Pleasantness', *Cerebral Cortex,* 13: 1064–71.

Kringelbach, M. L., and Rolls, E. T. (2003), 'Neural Correlates of Rapid Context-dependent Reversal Learning in a Simple Model of Human Social Interaction', *Neuroimage,* 20: 1371–83.

Kringelbach, M. L., and Rolls, E. T. (2004), 'The Functional Neuroanatomy of the Human Orbitofrontal Cortex: Evidence from Neuroimaging and Neuropsychology', *Progress in Neurobiology,* 72: 341–72.

Lange, C. G. (1887), *Über Gemütsbewegungen. (Org. Om Sindsbevægelser),* Leipzig: Thomas Theodor.

LeDoux, J. E. (1996), *The Emotional Brain,* New York: Simon and Schuster.

LeDoux, J. E., Cicchetti, P., Xagoraris, A., and Romanski, L. M. (1990), 'The Lateral Amygdaloid Nucleus: Sensory Interface of the Amygdala in Fear Conditioning', *Journal of Neuroscience,* 10: 1062–9.

LeMagnen, J. (1985), *Hunger,* London: Cambridge University Press.

Lepper, M. R., and Greene, D. (1978), *The Hidden Costs of Reward,* Morristown, N.J.: Lawrence Erlbaum.

Lepper, M. R., Greene, D., and Nisbett, R. E. (1973), 'Undermining Children's Intrinsic Interest with Extrinsic Reward: A Test of the Overjustification Hypothesis', *Journal of Personality and Social Psychology,* 28: 129–37.

Lévi-Strauss, C. (1964), *Le Cru et Le Cuit,* Paris: Librairie Plon [1969, *The Raw and the Cooked: Introduction to a Science of Mythology,* trans. J. Weightman and D. Weightman, Jonathan Cape, London].

Macmillan, M. (2000), *An Odd Kind of Fame: Stories of Phineas Gage,* Cambridge, Mass.: MIT Press.

McGraw, K. O. (1978), 'The Detrimental Effects of Reward on Performance: A Literature Review and a Prediction Model', in M. R. Lepper and D. Greene (eds), *The Hidden Costs of Reward,* Morristown, N.J.: Lawrence Erlbaum.

Naccache, L., Gaillard, R., Adam, C., Hasboun, D., Clemenceau, S., Baulac, M., Dehaene, S., and Cohen, L. (2005), 'A Direct Intracranial Record of Emotions

Evoked by Subliminal Words', *Proceedings of the National Academy of Sciences of the United States of America,* 102: 7713–7.

Nauta, W. J. (1971), 'The Problem of the Frontal Lobe: A Reinterpretation', *Journal of Psychiatric Research,* 8: 167–87.

O'Doherty, J., Kringelbach, M. L., Rolls, E. T., Hornak, J., and Andrews, C. (2001), 'Abstract Reward and Punishment Representations in the Human Orbitofrontal Cortex', *Nature Neuroscience,* 4: 95–102.

Rogers, R. D., Owen, A. M., Middleton, H. C., Williams, E. J., Pickard, J. D., Sahakian, B. J., and Robbins, T. W. (1999), 'Choosing between Small, Likely Rewards and Large, Unlikely Rewards Activates Inferior and Orbital Prefrontal Cortex', *Journal of Neuroscience,* 19: 9029–38.

Rolls, B. J., Rolls, E. T., Rowe, E. A., and Sweeney, K. (1981), 'Sensory Specific Satiety in Man', *Physiology and Behavior,* 27: 137–42.

Rolls, E. T., Hornak, J., Wade, D., and McGrath, J. (1994), 'Emotion-related Learning in Patients with Social and Emotional Changes Associated with Frontal Lobe Damage', *Journal of Neurology, Neurosurgery and Psychiatry,* 57: 1518–24.

Rolls, E. T., Kringelbach, M. L., and de Araujo, I. E. T. (2003a), 'Different Representations of Pleasant and Unpleasant Odors in the Human Brain', *European Journal of Neuroscience,* 18: 695–703.

Rolls, E. T., O'Doherty, J., Kringelbach, M. L., Francis, S., Bowtell, R., and McGlone, F. (2003b), 'Representations of Pleasant and Painful Touch in the Human Orbitofrontal and Cingulate Cortices', *Cerebral Cortex,* 13: 308–17.

Rozin, P. (2001), 'Food Preference', in N. J. Smelser and P. B. Baltes (eds), *International Encyclopedia of the Social & Behavioral Sciences,* Amsterdam: Elsevier.

Schachter, S., and Singer, J. (1962), 'Cognitive, Social and Physiological Determinants of Emotional State', *Psychological Review,* 69: 387–99.

Skinner, B. F. (1938), *The Behavior of Organisms: An Experimental Analysis,* New York: Appleton-Century.

Sutton, J. (2001), 'Descartes, René', in *Encyclopedia of Life Sciences,* Chichester: John Wiley and Sons.

Swanson, L. W., and Petrovich, G. D. (1998), 'What Is the Amygdala?' *Trends in Neurosciences,* 21: 323–31.

Thorndike, E. L. (1911), *Animal Intelligence: Experimental Studies,* New York: Macmillan.

Thorpe, S. J., Rolls, E. T., and Maddison, S. (1983), 'Neuronal Activity in the Orbitofrontal Cortex of the Behaving Monkey', *Experimental Brain Research,* 49: 93–115.

Volkow, N. D., and Li, T. K. (2004), 'Drug Addiction: The Neurobiology of Behaviour Gone Awry', *Nature Reviews Neuroscience,* 5: 963–70.

Völlm, B. A., de Araujo, I. E. T., Cowen, P. J., Rolls, E. T., Kringelbach, M. L., Smith, K. A., Jezzard, P., Heal, R. J., and Matthews, P. M. (2004),

'Methamphetamine Activates Reward Circuitry in Drug Naïve Human Subjects', *Neuropsychopharmacology,* 29: 1715–22.

Weiskrantz, L. (1968), 'Emotion', in L. Weiskrantz (ed.), *Analysis of Behavioural Change,* New York and London: Harper and Row.

Woods, S. C., and Stricker, E. M. (1999), 'Central Control of Food Intake', in M. J. Zigmond, F. E. Bloom, S. C. Landis, J. L. Roberts, and L. R. Squire (eds), *Fundamental Neuroscience,* San Diego, Calif.: Academic Press.

–4–

Emotion (or Life, The Universe, Everything)

Kay Milton

One of the most perceptive commentators on late twentieth-century Western culture was Douglas Adams, who created *The Hitchhikers' Guide to the Galaxy.* Connoisseurs of his work will recall that central to his story was the quest to find the answer to the big question—the question of life, the universe, everything (Adams 1979: 128). We might see this quest as a metaphor for any academic discipline whose practitioners define their work in terms of big questions. Anthropology is one such discipline, as it addresses questions central to the understanding of our species. How do human beings operate? How do we live together? What kinds of beings are we, or, to use a slightly controversial term, what *is* human nature? In this chapter I shall argue that the study of emotion can help us to address questions of this kind.

The route I took to reach this point resembles the travels of Douglas Adams's hitchhikers in another way. Like many researchers, they knew the answer before they knew what the question was. I knew that emotion was the key to understanding something fundamental about human beings, long before I was able to formulate a question that it might help to answer. It might be more accurate to say that I *felt* that emotion was the key, and this feeling came, not from any research I had done, but from the simple observation that emotions define the quality of my life. At any given moment, my feelings determine whether my life is good, bad or somewhere in between. They motivate me to act; a niggling unease tells me if I have done something wrong. Feelings of love, guilt, anxiety, envy, hope, desire, drive me to do what I do in my everyday life. I assumed, as we all must assume, however sensitive we might be to cultural diversity, that I resemble other human beings in fundamental ways, and that if my feelings are so central to my life, others' feelings must be central to their lives.

I came to the study of emotion through environmental (or ecological) anthropology, when I was doing research on the work of environmental protection groups and nature conservationists in Britain and Ireland. I wanted to understand why some people care enough about nature to want to protect it, while others appear indifferent or even hostile towards it. Because this was a question about emotional commitment—about why people feel as they do—it was clear that an understanding of emotion was going to be crucial. In this chapter I shall describe the kind of understanding of emotion that developed as a result of this research, and point to some of its implications for anthropology.

Models of Emotion

I shall begin by discussing briefly how emotions have been studied in anthropology and closely related disciplines. John Leavitt's (1996) article presented an insightful summary of the academic understanding of emotion at the time. He argued that the distinctions between nature and culture, body and mind, which seemed to pervade all the human sciences, had polarized the study of emotion, so that emotion was treated either as a biological phenomenon or as a cultural phenomenon. Biological approaches defined emotions as physical feelings and sought to explain them in biological terms, as innate and universal outcomes of human evolution. Cultural approaches defined emotions as cultural constructs, and therefore variable, and sought to show how they emerge out of social discourse. In these cultural approaches the emphasis was on meanings created and sustained through communication, rather than on physical feelings. Leavitt argued that neither approach is satisfactory because each fails to address the dual nature of emotion: that we tend to think of emotion as consisting of *both* feeling *and* meaning, as something that combines bodily processes and cultural interpretations. This model of emotion as a dual phenomenon is found in the work of several scholars including Rosaldo (1984), Wentworth and Yardley (1994) and Lupton (1998). The challenge for anthropology, Leavitt argued, was to find a way of understanding emotion that addresses both its physical and its cultural aspects.

Alongside and partly in response to the more polarized accounts of emotion, there have been studies which present emotion primarily as a *social* phenomenon, arguing that emotions arise and operate in social situations. Principle advocates of this approach have been Margot Lyon (1998), Arlie Hochschild (1998), Simon Williams (2001) and Brian Parkinson (1995). If I have understood these theorists correctly, they are not disagreeing with the view that emotion consists of both physical feeling and cultural meaning, but they are giving priority to the context in which emotions function, the context in which bodily feelings arise and acquire their cultural meanings, the context of social interaction and ongoing social relations. Lyon stated that 'Emotion has a social ontology ... a social-relational genesis' (1998: 55). Hochschild stated that, while emotions always have a biological component, 'it takes a social element to induce emotion' (1998: 6).

A variation on the social model of emotion is the view that emotions are mechanisms for communication. Wentworth and Yardley argued, from an evolutionary perspective, that displays of emotion were the mechanisms through which prelinguistic humans communicated. They wrote, 'Emotions may be private, self-feelings, but they are eminently social. They are about the social self that emerged from participation in the social world' (1994: 36). Parkinson argued that emotions find expression in interpersonal encounters, which are moments in evolving social relationships, and that 'getting emotional is primarily an interpersonal activity' (1995: 277), in which people present their own images of themselves to each other.

I would agree that emotions are crucially important in interpersonal situations, but it is clear that they operate and are expressed outside these contexts. I find, for instance, that I am more inclined to display some emotions more strongly when alone than when someone else is present. If I watch an emotionally moving film on my own, I cry freely and unselfconsciously, but if there is someone else present, even someone who knows me very well, I try to stifle such reactions. Emotions that are experienced and expressed outside interpersonal encounters are often, of course, socially informed, in the sense that they arise when we are thinking about (remembering, anticipating, imagining) social situations. And I would agree with Abu-Lughod and Lutz (1990) that emotions are often constituted and shaped by social discourse. But it is also the case that emotions are often induced by non-social things (cf. Ekman 1999). The nature conservationists whose work I studied get emotional about birds, insects and landscapes. I also get emotional about these things. Does this happen only because we have learned, through socialization, to feel strongly about such things? If so, it could reasonably be argued that our joy at the sight of a beautiful sunset or our sadness at the death of a wild animal are just as fundamentally social as our feelings for each other. But I shall argue that, in order for emotions to operate in and be shaped by social situations, they must have a presocial origin.

In addition, the focus on the social context of emotion fails to meet the challenge identified by Leavitt. It does not provide an alternative to the polarized models which treat emotion either as biological or as cultural. In fact it reproduces the cultural model. In the cultural constructionist perspective, cultural phenomena are understood as being generated in and sustained by social interaction. So the view that emotion has a social genesis is not significantly different from the view that emotions are cultural constructs whose meanings are generated and sustained through social discourse.

An Alternative Approach

In trying to develop a different approach to emotion, I found it helpful to draw on a model originally proposed by William James (1890) and taken up in recent decades by many theorists. James suggested that emotion is composed of two stages (see Fig. 4.1). There is the physical response (quickening heartbeat, muscle tension, sweating) that takes place when the body encounters a stimulus (which could be anything that causes a sensory reaction—a sight, a sound, a smell) and there is the subjective experience of that response—the feeling of fear or excitement which we get

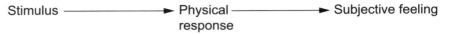

Figure 4.1   James's model of emotion.

when our bodies do these things. In James's model, this is the order in which things happen. The physical response comes first and the feeling follows and is caused by it, so we feel afraid because we tremble, we feel sad because we cry, rather than crying because we feel sad.

This seems to run counter to our common-sense understanding of emotion, according to which, we might insist, the feeling of sadness comes before the tears. But I would suggest that James's model reflects our experience quite accurately. Douglas Adams recognized this and used it in *The Hitchhikers' Guide to the Galaxy*. One of the principal characters, Arthur Dent, is trying to come to terms with the fact that his former home, the planet Earth, has just been demolished to make way for a hyperspace bypass:

> There was no way his imagination could feel the impact of the whole Earth having gone. He prodded his feelings by thinking that his parents and his sister had gone. No reaction. He thought of all the people he had been close to. No reaction. Then he thought of a complete stranger he had been standing behind in the queue at the supermarket two days before and felt a sudden stab—the supermarket was gone, everyone in it was gone. Nelson's Column had gone! ... From now on Nelson's Column only existed in his mind. England only existed in his mind—his mind, stuck here in this dank, smelly steel-lined spaceship. A wave of claustrophobia closed in on him.
>
> (Adams 1979: 51)

Having grasped that England no longer existed, Arthur focused on America:

> America, he thought, has gone. He couldn't grasp it. He decided to start smaller again. New York has gone. No reaction. He'd never seriously believed it existed anyway. The dollar, he thought, has sunk for ever. Slight tremor there. Every Bogart movie has been wiped, he said to himself, and that gave him a nasty knock. McDonald's, he thought. There is no longer any such thing as a McDonald's hamburger.
>
> He passed out. When he came round a second later he found he was sobbing for his mother.
>
> (Adams 1979: 51)

Although (thankfully) the circumstances in which Arthur found himself are unfamiliar to us, I suspect that many would recognize the emotional process described here. Arthur is thinking about things, seeing whether he gets any bodily reaction to those thoughts, in order to discover how he feels. The sequence is stimulus, bodily reaction, subjective feeling, just as in James's model. In the end, he 'finds' he is sobbing for his mother; the tears flow, and he discovers them flowing.

One of the recent theorists to have adopted and developed James's model is the neuroscientist Antonio Damasio (1999), who draws a distinction between emotions and feelings (see Fig. 4.2). An emotion is a physical response to a stimulus (the first part of James's model). Emotions are observable, either with or without the use of special instruments (we can see a blush, hear a trembling voice, measure a heartbeat or a glandular secretion). A feeling, in Damasio's model, is a *perception* of an emotion and is directly caused by it. When I perceive my heartbeat quickening I feel excited, when I perceive my tears I feel sad. Unlike emotions, feelings are always private and internal. When we think someone looks frightened, what we observe are the physical signs that make up the emotion that produces a feeling of fear. We assume, on the basis of what we observe, that the person feels fear, but we cannot observe that feeling directly (Damasio 1999: 42).

Damasio's terminology is slightly confusing in the context of the wider literature on emotions, because he reserves the term 'emotion' for the initial part of the two-stage process, while other theorists use it in a different or broader sense. But it is worth living with this confusion, because he has something valuable to contribute to the debate on how emotions can be understood.

So how does the kind of model proposed by James and Damasio lead to a different approach to emotion, an alternative to biological and sociocultural approaches? My response to this question has two stages. First, Damasio argued that emotions (and feelings) have had an important role to play in the evolution of consciousness. He argued that most, perhaps all, species of animals have emotions, in the sense that their bodies respond to environmental stimuli, while only some species are equipped to perceive those emotions, in his words, to have 'feelings'. But the ability to have feelings, in his view, does not equate with full self-consciousness. He went on to suggest that only some of those species that have feelings are equipped to know that they have feelings, to know that it is *they* who are having these feelings, and so develop a consciousness of self (Damasio 1999: 36).

Each stage in the process offers different possibilities for survival. An animal that has emotions (in that its body responds to environmental stimuli) but is unaware of them—unable to perceive them—has very limited possibilities for escaping danger. This is perhaps one reason why the so-called lower order animals reproduce in very large numbers, to increase the chances that some of them will survive. An animal

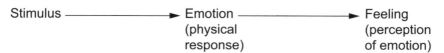

Stimulus ⟶ Emotion ⟶ Feeling
(physical (perception
response) of emotion)

Figure 4.2 Damasio's model of emotion.

that has emotions *and* feelings—an animal that feels afraid in the face of danger, for instance—has a better chance of responding appropriately, because it is motivated to escape. An animal with self-consciousness, an animal that not only has feelings but *knows* that it does, can actively plan its activities to avoid unpleasant feelings, such as fear, and to pursue pleasurable ones.

What all this amounts to is neither a biological nor a sociocultural understanding of emotions, but an *ecological* model. Emotions and feelings arise and operate, in Damasio's perspective, in the relationship between an organism and its environment.

The second stage in my argument draws on the work of psychologists who have argued that emotions (using that term now, not as Damasio uses it, but in its looser and more general sense) play an important role in learning. For example 'interest' (sometimes referred to as 'attention', 'expectancy' or 'anticipation') has been identified by some psychologists as a 'basic emotion' (see Kemper 1987), one assumed to be shared by all human beings. Ulrich Neisser (1976) argued that 'anticipation' is part of the normal process of perception, that an individual receives information from their environment by anticipating, being alert to, its possibilities. Izard wrote, 'Interest literally determines the content of our minds and memories, for it plays such a large part in determining what it is we actually perceive, attend to, and remember' (1991: 92–3). Lazarus (1991) argued that what we learn from a situation produces an emotional response which affects how we think about that and other situations we encounter, so in his view emotion engages dialectically with cognition in the process of learning. Other psychologists have argued that the emotional state we are in when we experience something will affect the ease with which we remember it (see Christiansen 1992; Rolls 1990). Harvey Whitehouse has incorporated this idea into his theory of religion and cultural transmission, arguing that rituals which occur only rarely (such as initiation rites) often involve highly emotional experiences which fix them in the memories of the participants (Whitehouse 2005).

I suggest that the idea that emotion plays a role in learning substantiates the view that emotion can be understood as an ecological phenomenon. Learning is a process that takes place between an individual organism and its environment, a process through which that individual receives and interprets information from their surroundings and becomes a skilled mover within their environment. This is what I propose as an alternative to the biological, cultural and social models of emotion—that emotion can be understood as an ecological mechanism. I am not suggesting that this is the only context in which emotion operates, but that this is perhaps its most important and fundamental role in the lives of human beings (and nonhuman animals as well).

To tidy up this argument, I want to clarify two points. First, given that the environment of human beings is predominantly social, that we interact primarily with our fellow human beings, we could question whether the ecological approach to emotion is significantly different from the social approach. I suggest that it is, because, although other human beings may be the most important things in most people's environments, this is not the case for everyone, and our environments contain many nonhuman things, some of which have very deep significance for us.

An ecological approach to emotion locates it in the relationship between an individual and their environment, *whatever* that environment may consist of; it does not privilege the social environment over the nonsocial. As we have seen, according to some psychologists, emotions, or certain kinds of emotion, are a part of what enables us to learn from our environment. The implication is that, without emotions, we would not learn. If emotions operated only in a social environment, the logical conclusion would be that human beings are capable of learning only from other human beings—which is manifestly not the case. Instead, I suggest that emotions are part of a general learning capacity that enables us to learn from any particular part of our environment, human or nonhuman. As such they must be presocial or precultural; they must operate in every 'normal' human being prior to and independently of that individual's involvement in social relationships.

The second point I want to clarify leads directly from this one and is slightly more complicated. It might appear, from what I have just written, that an ecological approach to emotion is similar to a biological approach. It might appear that emotion, as I have described it, is an innate mechanism, part of our genetically determined apparatus that enables us to live in the world. But there is a difference, in that biological models of emotion tend to create the impression that emotions are somehow fixed, not susceptible to change—so that, for instance, there is potentially an emotion in each of us which we call 'fear', which consists of a particular pattern of bodily reactions, and which springs into action when the situation demands. Some biological models of emotion have sought to fix the objects of emotion as well as its bodily mechanisms, to suggest that emotions are what cognitive psychologists might call 'domain-specific'. E. O. Wilson's (1984) 'biophilia hypothesis', for instance, seems to imply that we might have an inherent fear of snakes, or spiders, or thunderstorms, and that we might have an inherent preference for lush green landscapes over deserts (see Milton 2002: 60–2 for a more detailed discussion). This kind of impression is reinforced by the polarization identified by Leavitt, the assumption that all human phenomena are either biological (in which case they are innate, universal and more or less fixed) or cultural (in which case they are culture-specific, arise out of social interaction and are susceptible to change). My point is that we do not have to assume that emotion, or any other human phenomenon, is either biological or cultural. We can assume instead that there is no clear line between biology and culture, or at least that it is not useful to draw one.

In order to explain how I think an ecological approach to emotion can overcome the polarization between biological and cultural approaches, I shall look in more detail at the kind of process described by James and Damasio. As mentioned above, James described emotion as a two-stage process consisting of a bodily response and a subjective experience of that response, a feeling. But there is more to it than this. If we think of an emotional episode as beginning with a stimulus and ending with an action motivated by feeling, there are four elements involved (see Fig. 4.3). For instance, I might see a snake, which causes my stomach to tighten, my heart to beat more quickly, as a result of which I feel afraid, and I am motivated by this fear to take action—to throw a stone, or run away.

There are three points in this process at which learning can potentially play a role. First, our bodies can learn to respond differently to specific stimuli—so that we come to fear, or love, or get angry about different things. An ecological approach suggests that our bodies learn, through their engagement with their environment, how to respond to particular things—so that some people learn to fear snakes and spiders but others learn to love them, some people learn to love mountains while others learn to love flat open plains, and so on.

The second point at which learning might play a role is between the bodily response and the perception or subjective feeling of it. Is a particular set of bodily responses always and inevitably perceived, by those who experience them, as fear, and a different set inevitably perceived as anger, or can we learn to perceive what our bodies do in different ways? Psychologists and neuroscientists debate the extent to which the physiology of specific feelings might vary (see Ekman 1999). Even if it is going too far to suggest that the same bodily processes might produce different feelings as a result of learning, it seems reasonable to suggest that cultural or individual interpretations of emotions will vary in more subtle ways. For instance, a tightening of the stomach and a quickening heartbeat might amount to nervousness, but the feeling of nervousness in anticipation of meeting a lover is unlikely to be experienced in exactly the same way as the feeling of nervousness when about to give a public lecture.

The third point at which learning plays a role is between the subjective feeling and the action that follows. This is less contentious, because it is very well established that different societies, groups and individuals have different ways of displaying their feelings. In some cultures and contexts anger is expected to be expressed through shouting and physical violence; in others a tight-lipped silence is considered more appropriate. In some cultures, grief is expressed in apparently uncontrolled and potentially dangerous behaviour towards self and others; elsewhere it might be expressed through a withdrawal from the world, a refusal of food or company.

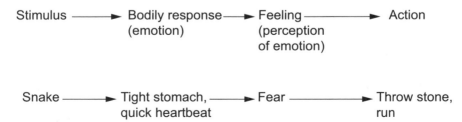

Figure 4.3 The emotional process, from stimulus to action.

All this implies that learning and emotion affect each other. Emotions shape learning in the ways suggested by psychologists, and what we learn, by interacting with our environment in everything we do, also shapes our emotions. There is no place in this model for a polarization between biology and culture (or society). There is no place for it because *neither* emotion *nor* learning can be allocated to one category or the other. We cannot say, according to this approach, that emotions belong to biology and learning belongs to culture.

It is now possible to formulate the 'big question' which I think the study of emotion helps us to answer. That question is, 'What connects us, as individual human beings, to our environment?' What enables me, as an individual, to engage with the world, to learn from it, to act in it, to change and be changed by it? I am suggesting that emotions play a central role in this relationship between ourselves, as individuals, and the world around us.

Emotions in Ecological Anthropology

I shall now consider the implications of this ecological understanding of emotions for anthropology and related disciplines. I shall begin by considering the field of ecological anthropology, because that is the area within which an ecological approach can be expected to have the most impact. It is also the area from which I started exploring ideas about emotion. A brief historical summary of this field will help to set the scene.

From its early development at the beginning of the twentieth century, ecological anthropology has shifted, from a crude form of environmental determinism, in which features such as climate and topography were thought, in a very general way, to shape human cultures, to a series of more refined models. Julian Steward's 'cultural ecology' of the 1950s still placed the environment in the determining role, but in a much more precise way than the earlier theories, arguing that particular environmental features gave rise to particular core cultural features (Steward 1955). In the 1960s came Marvin Harris's 'cultural materialism', in which the satisfaction of people's material needs within particular environments was seen as the driving force of cultural evolution (Harris 1968), and the 'ecosystem approach', of which the most often cited example is Roy Rappaport's study of the Tsembaga Maring ritual cycle (Rappaport 1968). In the ecosystem approach, it is not cultures and cultural features that are related to the environment, but human populations that are seen as interacting with environmental elements in a complex system in which energy and matter are exchanged. People are adapted to the environment through 'cybernetic loops and homeostasis' (Kalland 2003), and culture, rather than being seen as one side of the focal relationship, is the medium through which this adaptation takes place.

Alongside the ecosystem approach and more popular among British anthropologists, there emerged the cultural constructionist model, which was becoming dominant in other areas of anthropology, in which culture was seen as the ultimate determinant of the natural environment, not in a material sense, but in terms of how nature is defined and interpreted. A society's understanding of the natural world was assumed to be a product of the forms of social interaction in which its members engaged; meanings derived from social discourse were 'imposed' on nature; the implication was that, without cultural models through which it could be understood, nature was meaningless chaos (Ingold 1992). Probably the best-known example of this kind of interpretation was Mary Douglas's grid-group model. Understandings of nature as 'robust', 'fragile' or 'capricious' were shown as being determined by the underlying social structure (Douglas 1992). So, for instance, in a society characterized by individualistic networks in which the dominant ethos is entrepreneurial, nature will be thought of as robust. In a society characterized by groups rather than networks, and with an egalitarian ethos, nature will be thought of as fragile.

Cultural constructionism has come under attack in many areas of anthropology over the past fifteen years or so. Its principal critic in ecological anthropology has been Tim Ingold, who pointed out that an approach which treats the whole natural world as being defined by human culture seems to deny nature itself any role in our understanding. It is as if human cultures invent meanings and impose them on nature, as if nature is a blank slate upon which human cultures write their own interpretations. Ingold suggested that, instead of human cultures imposing meaning *on* the world, people, by engaging with their environment in various ways, *perceive* meaning *in* the world, and how they understand the world comes from this engagement. To illustrate this, Ingold suggested that hunters, who need to understand and predict the behaviour of their prey, are likely to perceive and respect animals as autonomous beings with thoughts, feelings and intentions whose behaviour is recognizably rational, because these are the characteristics of animals to which they will be most alert. Farmers, on the other hand, whose animals are much more under their domination and care, will perceive more vividly those characteristics of animals which make them seem dependent, like their tendency to become ill, their vulnerability to predators, and so on. As a result, farmers see animals as less autonomous, less intentional, less able to run their own lives (Ingold 1994). These ways of understanding animals grow out of the way hunters and farmers interact with them on a daily basis.

If we look back at the approaches which I have described briefly, we find that, for most of its history, ecological anthropology has studied the relationship between the nonhuman environment and collective human entities. In the earlier approaches, these entities were *cultures*. In the ecosystem approach it was human *populations* that were studied in their relation to the nonhuman world. But in Ingold's approach, the emphasis is on people as individuals interacting with their environments and, as a result, developing their understanding of the world.

An ecological approach to the study of emotion fits into this very well. It recognizes that the essential ecological relationship is that between the individual human being and their surroundings, and not between some kind of collective human entity and the environment. It has to be, for two main reasons. First, the individual is the only entity in human society capable of experiencing emotions and having feelings, the only seat of consciousness, and therefore the only entity capable of learning (cf. Rapport 1997; Hornborg 2003: 98). So if we are interested in how human beings come to understand the world around them, we have to focus first on individuals, because societies and cultures as whole entities do not learn—individuals do.

Second, the individual is the only entity sufficiently discrete to *have* an environment. An environment is, literally, 'that which surrounds' (Ingold 1993: 31). I suggest that entities like 'society', 'culture' and 'population' are too abstract to be surrounded by anything with which a substantive relationship is possible. They are not sufficiently corporate or self-contained. Even though it is possible to imagine extreme cases in which a society might be said to have 'an environment'—a small community living on an island, for instance—one would have to admit that different individuals within that society would have very different experiences of their environment. Some would travel across the sea while others would remain on land, some would experience danger while others would not, and so on. Different personal modes of engagement with 'the environment' would generate different emotions, feelings and knowledge. However discrete a society or population might appear, its environment will never be a single identifiable phenomenon, because the environment of each individual is unique. My environment contains the people with whom I associate. Their environments contain me and, in some cases, each other.

So, like Nigel Rapport (1997: 2), I consider a focus on the individual to be 'ontologically necessary'. This is, of course, a controversial and highly contested position, as it is located on one side of a very long-standing and possibly irresolvable debate in social science (see Rapport 2003: 56ff.), between those who understand social phenomena as emerging out of individual actions and those who treat individual actions as determined by social factors. For the reasons outlined above, a focus on the individual as the primary locus of social reality is a logical consequence of an ecological approach to emotion. I have suggested that the mode of an individual human being's engagement with their surroundings is essentially *emotional*—that emotions connect us with our surroundings, enabling us to learn from them, defining the quality of that engagement, shaping our memories and therefore our knowledge. A study of people's cultural understandings of nature thus begins with an analysis of how they, *as individuals*, engage with the nonhuman things in their environment, and of the emotional content of that engagement.

But the implications of an ecological model of emotion extend far beyond ecological anthropology. I argued earlier that emotions operate in the relationships between an individual and *all* the things in their environment—or at least all the things that impinge on them in some way. Emotions connect us to the things that surround us, whether those things are human or nonhuman. Ecological anthropology has traditionally been concerned with relations between the human and nonhuman worlds, but the rest of anthropology has been concerned primarily with relations among human beings.

Once we recognize that the only possible starting point for ecological anthropology is the individual rather than 'society' or 'culture', then *social* relations are encompassed and subsumed by *ecological* relations. An individual's environment includes their fellow human beings and all the institutions and cultural phenomena those human beings have created. So, social relations *are* ecological relations, social anthropology melts into ecological anthropology; or, to put it another way, all social and cultural anthropology, by virtue of the fact that it deals with relations, is ecological.

Ingold expressed this as follows:

> ... the single focus of enquiry will come to be the living organism-person in its environment. Such enquiry must by nature be fundamentally ecological. Thus conceived, the ecological anthropology of the future, far from remaining a narrow sub-discipline concerned with the material conditions of cultural adaptation, will become a fulcrum around which the science of human life in the world will revolve.
>
> (Ingold 2003: 54)

Emotions and the Boundaries of Anthropology

There are pointers, in this quotation, to the even wider implications of an ecological approach to emotion. As well as blurring the boundaries between ecological anthropology and other areas of the discipline, it also points to a blurring of interdisciplinary boundaries. As we have seen, one of the main ways in which emotion connects the individual to their environment is through the process of learning, and learning, like emotion, cannot be fully understood through either biological or cultural approaches. Clearly, there has to be a biological capacity to learn, and cognitive psychologists debate the nature of that capacity—how general or specific it is, for instance. But they also recognize the importance of the cultural context in which learning takes place.

And cultural anthropologists, many of whom used to regard physiology as outside their area of concern, now recognize that we learn with our bodies as well as our minds. A wealth of anthropological and philosophical literature in recent decades has encouraged us to treat experience, knowledge and thought as *embodied*. Our bodies learn responses to the world which we reflect on and interpret. The model of emotion proposed by James and Damasio, and on which I have drawn, reflects this point. Remember that the bodily response comes first. The tightening of the stomach when we encounter something we consider dangerous is a learned response (for detailed discussions on this point, see Milton 2002) and comes before the perception of it, which is the feeling of fear. So an ecological approach to emotion locates it at the point at which the traditional interests of biology, anthropology, psychology and philosophy meet.

What kind of anthropology is this leading to? One that is, in a sense, narrower than the discipline has often been in the past, in that it treats the individual, rather than groups, societies or cultures as its prime focus, but one that is also broader, in that it enters territories traditionally occupied by biology and psychology. But it does not end there. Because emotion is so central to human lives, its understanding is important in virtually every discipline whose focus is humanity. Let us consider the kinds of questions an ecological approach to emotion leads us to ask. Those I find most interesting and most compelling are those that relate to the first part of the process illustrated in Figure 4.3—questions about how people come to respond, emotionally, to different things. These questions lie at the root of understanding why people act as they do, because there is no action without motivation, and no motivation without emotion. So the key to understanding human action is to understand people's emotional commitments—what they care most about and why, how they come to care about particular things.

This is the area in which I was operating when I asked, in my own research, why some people care about nature and others do not (Milton 2002). This question is not only interesting, it is also urgent, given the damaging impact of human activities on the nonhuman world, and the potentially dangerous implications of that impact for the future of human and nonhuman life. Equally interesting and important, I suggest, are questions about the things many people take for granted as desirable: money, power, prestige, beauty, material comforts, knowledge, freedom, dignity. *Why* do these things matter? How do they *come* to matter in the lives of individuals? What kinds of personal experiences, patterns of personal engagement with human and nonhuman things, shape people's commitment to these values and lead them to spend their lives pursuing or protecting them? We are now in the realm of biography, examining an individual's past in order to understand the person they have become, an approach long-established in history, psychology, criminology, sociology and, of course, anthropology.

So I end this chapter with a feeling of unease. The argument seems to have reached a point at which the discipline in which I was trained and have spent my career threatens to dissolve and lose its identity. This was not my intention, but we may have to accept it as inevitable when we start, not with a particular disciplinary approach or perspective, but with an object of interest about which we ask questions and seek understanding. If we begin with the question of how people produce emotions as cultural constructs through their social discourses, we are almost bound to remain safely within the territory of anthropology or sociology. If we start with emotion itself, as an object of interest, and ask how it operates and what role it plays in human lives, we have to go wherever these questions take us. When the questions we ask are not confined by disciplinary boundaries, it would be foolish to expect the answers to be so confined.

But perhaps the unease is misplaced. Anthropology has always been the most interdisciplinary of disciplines. It has always drawn its insights from wherever it has found them; it has always entered territories that other disciplines claim as their own and, as a consequence, it has often experienced crises of identity. Its very breadth of vision is one of its distinguishing features and, in my view, its greatest strength. It is precisely what enables us to address the big questions of human existence.

Acknowledgements

This chapter is a revised version of an article published under the same title in *The Australian Journal of Anthropology*, 2005 (Vol. 16, no. 2). I am grateful to participants in the Australian Anthropological Society's conference at the University of Melbourne in September 2004, and to colleagues at the School of Anthropological Studies at Queen's University Belfast, for comments on earlier drafts.

References

Abu-Lughod, L., and Lutz, C. (1990), 'Introduction: Emotion, Discourse, and the Politics of Everyday Life', in C. Lutz and L. Abu-Lughod (eds.), *Language and the Politics of Emotion*, Cambridge: Cambridge University Press.

Adams, D. (1979), *The Hitchhiker's Guide to the Galaxy*, London and Sydney: Pan Books.

Christiansen, S. A. (1992), 'Emotional Stress and Eyewitness Memory: A Critical Review', *Psychological Bulletin*, 112: 284–309.

Damasio, A. R. (1999), *The Feeling of What Happens: Body and Emotion in the Making of Consciousness*, London: Heinemann.

Douglas, M. (1992), *Risk and Blame: Essays in Cultural Theory*, London: Routledge.

Ekman, P. (1999), 'Basic emotions', in T. Dalgleish and M. Power (eds), *Handbook of Cognition and Emotion*, Sussex: John Wiley & Sons.

Harris, M. (1968), *The Rise of Anthropological Theory: A History of Theories of Culture*, London: Routledge & Kegan Paul.

Hochschild, A. R. (1998), 'The Sociology of Emotion As a Way of Seeing', in G. Bendelow and S. J. Williams (eds), *Emotions in Social Life: Critical Themes and Contemporary Issues*, London: Routledge.

Hornborg, A. (2003), 'From Animal Masters to Ecosystem Services: Exchange, Personhood and Human Ecology', in A. Roepstorff, N. Bubandt, and K. Kull (eds), *Imagining Nature: Practices of Cosmology and Identity*, Aarhus: Aarhus University Press.

Ingold, T. (1992), 'Culture and the Perception of the Environment', in E. Croll and D. Parkin (eds), *Bush Base: Forest Farm*, London: Routledge.

Ingold, T. (1993), 'Globes and Spheres: The Topology of Environmentalism', in K. Milton (ed.), *Environmentalism: The View from Anthropology*, London: Routledge.

Ingold. T. (1994), 'From Trust to Domination: An Alternative History of Human–animal Relations', in A. Manning and J. Serpell (eds), *Animals and Human Society: Changing Perspectives*, London: Routledge.

Ingold, T. (2003), 'Three in One: How an Ecological Approach Can Obviate the Distinctions between Body, Mind and Culture', in A. Roepstorff, N. Bubandt, and K. Kull (eds), *Imagining Nature: Practices of Cosmology and Identity,* Aarhus: Aarhus University Press.

Izard, C. E. (1991), *The Psychology of Emotions,* New York and London: Plenum Press.

James, W. (1890), *Principles of Psychology,* New York: Holt.

Kalland, A. (2003), 'Anthropology and the Concept of "Sustainability": Some Reflections', in A. Roepstorff, N. Bubandt, and K. Kull (eds), *Imagining Nature: Practices of Cosmology and Identity,* Aarhus: Aarhus University Press.

Kemper, T. D. (1987), 'How Many Emotions Are There? Wedding the Social and Autonomic Components', *American Journal of Sociology,* 93: 263–89.

Lazarus, R. S. (1991), *Emotion and Adaptation,* Oxford: Oxford University Press.

Leavitt, J. (1996), 'Meaning and Feeling in the Anthropology of Emotions', *American Ethnologist,* 23(3): 514–39.

Lupton, D. (1998), *The Emotional Self: A Sociocultural Exploration,* London: Sage.

Lyon, M. (1998), 'The Limitations of Cultural Constructionism in the Study of Emotion', in G. Bendelow and S. J. Williams (eds), *Emotions in Social Life: Critical Themes and Contemporary Issues,* London: Routledge.

Milton, K. (2002), *Loving Nature: Towards an Ecology of Emotion,* London: Routledge.

Neisser, U. (1976), *Cognition and Reality: Principles and Implications of Cognitive Psychology,* San Francisco: W. H. Freeman and Co.

Parkinson, B. (1995), *Ideas and Realities of Emotion,* London and New York: Routledge.

Rappaport, R. (1968), *Pigs for the Ancestors,* New Haven, Conn.: Yale University Press.

Rapport, N. (1997), *Transcendent Individual: Towards a Literary and Liberal Anthropology,* London: Routledge.

Rapport, N. (2003), *I Am Dynamite: An Alternative Anthropology of Power,* London: Routledge.

Rolls, E. T. (1990), 'A Theory of Emotion and Its Application to Understanding the Neural Basis of Emotion', *Cognition and Emotion,* 4: 161–90.

Rosaldo, M. (1984), 'Towards an Anthropology of Self and Feeling', in R. A. Schweder and R. A. LeVine (eds), *Culture Theory,* Cambridge: Cambridge University Press.

Steward, J. (1955), *Theory of Culture Change.* Urbana: University of Illinois Press.

Wentworth, W. M., and Yardley, D. (1994), 'Deep Sociality: A Bioevolutionary Perspective on the Sociology of Human Emotions', in W. M. Wentworth and J. Ryan (eds), *Social Perspectives on Emotion,* vol. 2, Greenwich, Conn.: JAI Press Inc.

Whitehouse, H. (2005), 'Emotion, Memory and Religious Rituals: An Assessment of Two Theories', in K. Milton and M. Svašek (eds), *Mixed Emotions: Anthropological Studies of Feeling*, Oxford: Berg.

Williams, S. (2001), *Emotion and Social Theory*, London: Sage.

Wilson, E. O. (1984), *Biophilia: The Human Bond with Other Species*, Cambridge, MA: Harvard University Press.

–5–

Can Happiness Be Taught?

Martin E. P. Seligman

Since World War II, the field of psychology has largely focused on suffering. Psychologists now measure such formerly fuzzy concepts as depression, schizophrenia, and anger with respectable precision. We have discovered a fair amount about how these disorders develop across life, about their genetics, their neurochemistry, and their psychological underpinnings. Best of all, we can relieve some of the disorders. By my last count fourteen of the several dozen major mental illnesses could be effectively treated—and two of them cured—with medications or specific psychotherapies.[1]

Unfortunately, for many years interest in relieving the states that make life miserable has overshadowed efforts to enhance the states that make life worth living. This disciplinary bias has not preempted the public's concern with what is best in life, however. Most people want more positive emotion in their lives. Most people want to build their strengths, not just to minimize their weaknesses. Most people want lives imbued with meaning.

What I have called Positive Psychology concerns the scientific study of the three different happy lives that correspond to these three desires: the Pleasant Life, the Good Life, and the Meaningful Life. The Pleasant Life is about positive emotions. The Good Life is about positive traits—foremost among them the strengths and the virtues, but also the talents, such as intelligence and athleticism. The Meaningful Life is about positive institutions, such as democracy, strong families, and free inquiry. Positive institutions support the virtues, which in turn support the positive emotions.[2] In its scope, then, Positive Psychology diverges markedly from the traditional subject matter of psychology: mental disorders, developmental stunting, troubled lives, violence, criminality, prejudice, trauma, anger, depression, and therapy.

But can a science of Positive Psychology lead us to happiness? Five years ago, in an effort to answer that question, I started to teach an annual seminar to undergraduates at the University of Pennsylvania.

This seminar is similar to the other courses I have taught for the last forty years: we read and discuss the primary scientific literature in the field. It differs, however, in an important way: there is a real-world homework exercise to do and write up every week. When one teaches a traditional seminar on helplessness or on depression, there is no experiential homework to assign; students can't very well be told to be depressed or to be alcoholic for the week. But in Positive Psychology, students can be assigned to make a Gratitude Visit, or to transform a boring task by using a signature strength, or to give the gift of time to someone they care for. The workload is heavy: two essays per week, one on the extensive readings and the other on the homework exercises.

The course begins with personal introductions that are not perfunctory. I introduce myself by narrating an incident in which my then five-year-old daughter, Nikki, told me that she had given up whining and if she could do that ("It was the hardest thing I've ever done, Daddy"), I could "stop being such a grouch." I then ask all of the students to tell stories about themselves at their best, stories that display their highest virtues. The listening skills taught in traditional clinical psychology center around detecting hidden, underlying troubles, but here I encourage the opposite: listening for underlying positive motivations, strengths, and virtues. The introductions are moving and rapport building, and they easily fill the entire three hours.

The course then spends four meetings on what is scientifically documented about positive emotion: about the past (contentment, satisfaction, serenity), about the future (optimism, hope, trust, faith), and about the present (joy, ebullience, comfort, ecstasy, mirth, pleasure). We read and discuss the literature on depressive realism (happy people may be less accurate than miserable people[3]), on set ranges for weight and for positive emotion (lottery winners and paraplegics revert to their average preexisting level of happiness or misery within a year, because the capacity for pleasure, 'positive affectivity,' is about 50 percent heritable and therefore quite resistant to change[4]), on wealth and life satisfaction (the one hundred fifty richest Americans are no happier than the average American[5]), on education, climate, and life satisfaction (there is no impact[6]), on optimism and presidential elections (80 percent of the elections have been won by the more optimistic candidate—partialing out standing in the polls, vigor of the campaign, and funding[7]), on longevity and positive emotion (novitiates who at age twenty included positive-emotion words in their brief biographies live about a decade longer than more deadpan nuns[8]), and on the brain and positive emotion (positive emotion correlates well with activity in left-frontal regions of the cortex[9]).

This leads to my formulation of the Good Life: identifying one's signature strengths and virtues and using them in work, love, play, and parenting to produce abundant and authentic gratification.

To identify their signature strengths, the students take the VIA (Values-In-Action Institute of the Mayerson Foundation) questionnaire of strengths and virtues.[10] This instrument picks out the five highest self-rated strengths for each student from a classification (Psychology's UnDSM–1)[11] of twenty-four that includes love of learning, valor, perspective, kindness, optimism, capacity to love and be loved, humor, perseverance, spirituality, fairness, and the like.

The first time I taught my undergraduate seminar on the Good Life, I asked the students after they had identified their five highest strengths if they got to deploy at least one of these strengths every day at college. They all said no.

My class's homework assignments followed from this dismal statistic. We each chose an unavoidable task that we found tedious and invented a way to perform the task using one of our signature strengths. One student transformed data entry into flow. Using his strengths of curiosity and love of learning, he began to look for patterns in the mound of demographic data he had been entering for months as a research assistant. He discovered a pattern: the higher the family income, the more likely the parents remain married. Another student transformed his lonely midnight walk from the library to his apartment using his strength of playfulness by rollerblading home and trying to set a new Olympic record on each run. Another student used her strength of social intelligence to turn waitressing into gratification by setting the goal of making each customer's interaction with her the social highlight of his or her evening.

An assignment that contrasts fun with altruism makes the distinction between pleasure and gratification clearer to my students. We each select an activity that gives us pleasure, and we contrast this with doing something philanthropic that calls upon one of our strengths. There is quite a uniform emotional experience that ensues. The pleasurable activities—hanging out with friends, getting a scalp massage, going to the movies—have a square wave offset. When they are over, they leave almost no trace. The gratification of the altruistic activities, by contrast, lingers. One junior who spontaneously tutored her third-grade nephew in arithmetic on the phone for two hours wrote, "After that, the whole day went better, I could really listen and people liked me more. I was mellow all day." One Wharton student said, "I came to Wharton to make money because I thought money would bring me happiness. I was stunned to find out that I am happier helping another person than I am shopping."

This assignment is the transition to the final part of the course—the study of the third happy life, the Meaningful Life. From the perspective of Positive Psychology, meaning consists in attachment to something larger. So on this account, the Meaningful Life is similar to the Good Life, but with one further ingredient: identifying and using your highest strengths in order to belong to and serve something larger than you arc. We call these larger things Positive Institutions.

In this part of the course we read some of the primary literature on Positive Institutions (e.g. Robert Putnam's *Bowling Alone* and Viktor Frankl's *Man's Search for Meaning*) and we do a set of exercises designed to connect the students to things larger than their own successes and failures. In one exercise, they create a family tree of strengths and virtues by having their parents, grandparents, and siblings take the VIA test, and by interviewing their parents about dead relatives. In another, they mentor a younger student who is facing the specific issues they faced and solved in high school or college. In another, they write their vision of a positive human future and what their role in bringing it about might be. In another, they write their own obituary from the point of view of their grandchildren, emphasizing their own legacy.

We read George Vaillant's *Aging Well,* which seems to demonstrate that American higher education is not teaching its students the Good Life. In a sixty-year longitudinal study of the lives of 268 top members of the Harvard classes of 1939–1942 and 456 Core City men of Boston from the same era, Vaillant came up with a robust and disturbing finding: higher education made little or no difference for "success in life." (I hasten to add that Vaeillant, like I, means not champagne and Porsches, but a life well led, a eudaimonic life.) Looking at a panoply of indicators such as life satisfaction, marital happiness, physical vitality, freedom from depression, longevity, lack of alcoholism, job promotions, maturity, and enjoyment, Vaillant found that the Core City men did as well as the Harvard graduates, save for two variables: higher Harvard incomes and more Harvard entries in *Who's Who.* My students were not at all puzzled by this, although they were discomfited that their parents were paying six figures for such an education. "We are taught the wrong stuff at college," they said. "If college taught the material we've learned in this course, higher education would lead to success in life."

To end the course—having read the literature on memory and hedonics that shows that what people most remember about any endeavor is how it ends[12]—we parallel our serious introductions with serious farewells. Each of us picks our favorite ending—of a movie, poem, or piece of music—explains it and then presents it in a final all-day session.

All in all, teaching this subject has been the most gratifying teaching I have done in my forty years as an instructor. I have seen young lives change before my eyes, and more importantly, I have never before seen such engagement and such mature intellectual performances by undergraduates. So encouraged, I am now teaching this material both at the introductory level in college and at the professional level once a week on the telephone to a massive audience of clinical psychologists, social workers, executive coaches, and life coaches.[13]

Teaching about the Good Life is by no means the unique province of a psychology course. Indeed, if the pursuit of eudaimonia can be taught to psychology students steeped in a century of victimology and shallow hedonics, think how easily this lesson might be taught to students who have previously encountered the better examples of well-led lives found in the humanities. A stance, moreover, that gives the best in life equal footing with the worst, that is as concerned with flourishing as with surviving, that is as interested in building as in repairing, should find a comfortable home in most any discipline. In the end, I believe that we learn more when lighting candles than when cursing the darkness.

Notes

1. Marlin E. P. Seligman. *What You Can Change & What You Can't* (New York: Knof, 1993).
2. Martin E. P. Seligman. *Authentic Happiness* (New York: Free Press, 2002).

3. Lauren B. Alloy and Lyn Y. Abramson, "Judgment of Contingency in Depressed and Nondepressed Students: Sadder but Wiser," *Journal of Experimental Psychology: General* 108 (1979): 441–485.
4. Phil Brickman, D. Coates and Ronnie Janoff-Bulman. "Lottery Winners and Accident Victims: Is Happiness Relative?" *Journal of Personality and Social Psychology* 36 (1978): 917–927.
5. Ed Diener, Jeff Horwitz and Robert Emmons, "Happiness of the Very Wealthy," *Social Indicators* 16 (1985): 263–274.
6. Chapter 4 of my book *Authentic Happiness* reviews these data.
7. Harold Zullow and Martin E. P. Seligman, "Pessimistic Rumination Predicts Defeat of Presidential Candidates: 1900–1984." *Psychological Inquiry* 1: 51– 61.
8. Deborrah D. Danner, David A. Snowdon, and Wallace V. Friesen, "Positive Emotions in Early Life and Longevity: Findings from the Nun Study," *Journal of Personality and Social Psychology* 80 (5) (2001): 804–813.
9. Richard Davidson, "Biological Basics of Personality," in Valerian J. Derlega, Warren H. Jones, and Barbara A. Winstead, eds., *Personality: Contemporary Theory and Research* (Chicago: Nelson-Hall, 1999).
10. The VIA questionnaire is available at <www.authentichappiness.org>. This website contains all of the leading tests of positive emotion. As of this writing, two hundred thousand people have taken the VIA on this website. We have found the web collection of psychometric data vastly cheaper and faster than paper questionnaires, and the samples are more representative of our target populations than are college sophomores.
11. Christopher Peterson and Martin E. P. Seligman, *Classification of Strengths and Virtues* (New York: Oxford University Press: Washington. D.C.: American Psychological Association Press, 2004).
12. Daniel Kahneman, Barbara L. Fredrickson, Charles A. Schreiber, and Donald A. Redelmeier, "When More Pain is Preferred to Less: Adding a Better End," *Psychological Science* 4(6) (November 1993): 401–405.
13. <www.authentichappinesscoaching.com>

–6–

Exploring the Managed Heart

Arlie Russell Hochschild

In a section in *Das Kapital* entitled "The Working Day," Karl Marx examines depositions submitted in 1863 to the Children's Employment Commission in England. One deposition was given by the mother of a child laborer in a wallpaper factory: "When he was seven years old I used to carry him [to work] on my back to and fro through the snow, and he used to work 16 hours a day ... I have often knelt down to feed him, as he stood by the machine, for he could not leave it or stop." Fed meals as he worked, as a steam engine is fed coal and water, this child was "an instrument of labor."[1] Marx questioned how many hours a day it was fair to use a human being as an instrument, and how much pay for being an instrument was fair, considering the profits that factory owners made. But he was also concerned with something he thought more fundamental: the human cost of becoming an "instrument of labor" at all.

On another continent 117 years later, a twenty-year-old flight attendant trainee sat with 122 others listening to a pilot speak in the auditorium of the Delta Airlines Stewardess Training Center. Even by modern American standards, and certainly by standards for women's work, she had landed an excellent job. The 1980 pay scale began at $850 a month for the first six months and would increase within seven years to about $20,000 a year. Health and accident insurance is provided, and the hours are good.[2]

The young trainee sitting next to me wrote on her notepad, "Important to smile. Don't forget smile." The admonition came from the speaker in the front of the room, a crewcut pilot in his early fifties, speaking in a Southern drawl: "Now girls, I want you to go out there and really *smile*. Your smile is your biggest *asset*. I want you to go out there and use it. Smile. *Really* smile. Really *lay it on*."

The pilot spoke of the smile as the *flight attendant's* asset. But as novices like the one next to me move through training, the value of a personal smile is groomed to reflect the company's disposition—its confidence that its planes will not crash, its reassurance that departures and arrivals will be on time, its welcome and its invitation to return. Trainers take it as their job to attach to the trainee's smile an attitude, a viewpoint, a rhythm of feeling that is, as they often say, "professional." This deeper extension of the professional smile is not always easy to retract at the end of the workday, as one worker in her first year at World Airways noted: "Sometimes I come off a long trip in a state of utter exhaustion, but I find I can't relax. I giggle a lot, I chatter, I call friends. It's as if I can't release myself from an artificially created elation that kept me 'up' on the trip. I hope to be able to come down from it better as I get better at the job."

As the PSA jingle says, "Our smiles are not just painted on." Our flight attendants' smiles, the company emphasizes, will be more human than the phony smiles you're resigned to seeing on people who are paid to smile. There is a smile-like strip of paint on the nose of each PSA plane. Indeed, the plane and the flight attendant advertise each other. The radio advertisement goes on to promise not just smiles and service but a travel experience of real happiness and calm. Seen in one way, this is no more than delivering a service. Seen in another, it estranges workers from their own smiles and convinces customers that on-the-job behavior is calculated. Now that advertisements, training, notions of professionalism, and dollar bills have intervened between the smiler and the smiled upon, it takes an extra effort to imagine that spontaneous warmth can exist in uniform—because companies now advertise spontaneous warmth, too.

At first glance, it might seem that the circumstances of the nineteenth-century factory child and the twentieth-century flight attendant could not be more different. To the boy's mother, to Marx, to the members of the Children's Employment Commission, perhaps to the manager of the wallpaper factory, and almost certainly to the contemporary reader, the boy was a victim, even a symbol, of the brutalizing conditions of his time. We might imagine that he had an emotional half-life, conscious of little more than fatigue, hunger, and boredom. On the other hand, the flight attendant enjoys the upper-class freedom to travel, and she participates in the glamour she creates for others. She is the envy of clerks in duller, less well-paid jobs.

But a close examination of the differences between the two can lead us to some unexpected common ground. On the surface there is a difference in how we know what labor actually produces. How could the worker in the wallpaper factory tell when his job was done? Count the rolls of wallpaper; a good has been produced. How can the flight attendant tell when her job is done? A service has been produced; the customer seems content. In the case of the flight attendant, the *emotional style of offering the service is part of the service itself,* in a way that loving or hating wallpaper is not a part of producing wallpaper. Seeming to "love the job" becomes part of the job; and actually trying to love it, and to enjoy the customers, helps the worker in this effort.

In processing people, the product is a state of mind. Like firms in other industries, airline companies are ranked according to the quality of service their personnel offer. Egon Ronay's yearly *Lucas Guide* offers such a ranking; besides being sold in airports and drugstores and reported in newspapers, it is cited in management memoranda and passed down to those who train and supervise flight attendants. Because it influences consumers, airline companies use it in setting their criteria for successful job performance by a flight attendant. In 1980 the *Lucas Guide* ranked Delta Airlines first in service out of fourteen airlines that fly regularly between the United States and both Canada and the British Isles. Its report on Delta included passages like this:

> [Drinks were served] not only with a smile but with concerned enquiry such as, "Anything else I can get you, madam?" The atmosphere was that of a civilized party—with the passengers, in response, behaving like civilized guests ... Once or twice our inspectors tested stewardesses by being deliberately exacting, but they were never roused, and at the end of the flight they lined up to say farewell with undiminished brightness ...
>
> [Passengers are] quick to detect strained or forced smiles, and they come aboard wanting to enjoy the flight. One of us looked forward to his next trip on Delta "because it's fun." Surely that is how passengers ought to feel."[3]

The work done by the boy in the wallpaper factory called for a coordination of mind and arm, mind and finger, and mind and shoulder. We refer to it simply as physical labor. The flight attendant does physical labor when she pushes heavy meal carts through the aisles, and she does mental work when she prepares for and actually organizes emergency landings and evacuations. But in the course of doing this physical and mental labor, she is also doing something more, something I define as *emotional labor*.[4] This labor requires one to induce or suppress feeling in order to sustain the outward countenance that produces the proper state of mind in others—in this case, the sense of being cared for in a convivial and safe place. This kind of labor calls for a coordination of mind and feeling, and it sometimes draws on a source of self that we honor as deep and integral to our individuality.

Beneath the difference between physical and emotional labor there lies a similarity in the possible cost of doing the work: the worker can become estranged or alienated from an aspect of self—either the body or the margins of the soul—that is *used* to do the work. The factory boy's arm functioned like a piece of machinery used to produce wallpaper. His employer, regarding that arm as an instrument, claimed control over its speed and motions. In this situation, what was the relation between the boy's arm and his mind? Was his arm in any meaningful sense his *own?*[5]

This is an old issue, but as the comparison with airline attendants suggests, it is still very much alive. If we can become alienated from goods in a goods-producing society, we can become alienated from service in a service-producing society. This is what C. Wright Mills, one of our keenest social observers, meant when he wrote in 1956, "We need to characterize American society of the mid-twentieth century in more psychological terms, for now the problems that concern us most border on the psychiatric."[6]

When she came off the job, what relation had the flight attendant to the "artificial elation" she had induced on the job? In what sense was it her *own* elation on the job? The company lays claim not simply to her physical motions—how she handles food trays—but to her emotional actions and the way they show in the ease of a smile. The workers I talked to often spoke of their smiles as being *on* them but not *of* them. They were seen as an extension of the make-up, the uniform, the recorded music, the soothing pastel colors of the airplane decor, and the daytime drinks, which taken together orchestrate the mood of the passengers. The final commodity is not a certain number of smiles to be counted like rolls of wallpaper. For the flight attendant, the smiles are a *part of her work,* a part that requires her to coordinate self and feeling so that the work seems to be effortless. To show that the enjoyment takes effort is to do the job poorly. Similarly, part of the job is to disguise fatigue and irritation, for otherwise the labor would show in an unseemly way, and the product—passenger contentment—would be damaged.[7] Because it is easier to disguise fatigue and irritation if they can be banished altogether, at least for brief periods, this feat calls for emotional labor.

The reason for comparing these dissimilar jobs is that the modern assembly-line worker has for some time been an outmoded symbol of modern industrial labor; fewer than 6 percent of workers now work on assembly lines. Another kind of labor has now come into symbolic prominence—the voice-to-voice or face-to-face delivery of service—and the flight attendant is an appropriate model for it. There have always been public-service jobs, of course; what is new is that they are now socially engineered and thoroughly organized from the top. Though the flight attendant's job is no worse and in many ways better than other service jobs, it makes the worker more vulnerable to the social engineering of her emotional labor and reduces her control over that labor. Her problems, therefore, may be a sign of what is to come in other such jobs.

Emotional labor is potentially good. No customer wants to deal with a surly waitress, a crabby bank clerk, or a flight attendant who avoids eye contact in order to avoid getting a request. Lapses in courtesy by those paid to be courteous are very real and fairly common. What they show us is how fragile public civility really is. We are brought back to the question of what the social carpet actually consists of and what it requires of those who are supposed to keep it beautiful. The laggards and sluff-offs of emotional labor return us to the basic questions. What is emotional labor? What do we do when we manage emotion? What, in fact, is emotion? What are the costs and benefits of managing emotion, in private life and at work?

The Private and Public Faces of an Emotional System

Our search for answers to these questions leads to three separate but equally relevant discourses: one concerning labor, one concerning display, and one concerning emotion.

Those who discuss labor often comment that nowadays most jobs call for a capacity to deal with people rather than with things, for more interpersonal skills and fewer mechanical skills. In The *Coming of Post-Industrial Society* (1973), Daniel Bell argues that the growth of the service sector means that "communication" and "encounter"—"the response of ego to alter and back"—is the central work relationship today.[8] As he puts it, "The fact that individuals now talk to other individuals, rather than interact with a machine, is the fundamental fact about work in the post-industrial society."

Critics of labor studies, such as Harry Braverman in *Labor and Monopoly Capital* (1974), point out a continual subdivision of work in many branches of the economy. Complex tasks in which a craftsman used to take pride are divided into simpler, more repetitive segments, each more boring and less well paid than the original job. Work is deskilled and the worker belittled. But celebrants and critics alike have not inspected at close hand or with a social-psychological eye what it is that "people jobs" *actually require* of workers. They have not inquired into the actual nature of this labor. Some do not know exactly what, in the case of emotional labor, becomes deskilled.

A second discourse, closer to the person and more remote from the overall organization of work, concerns the display of feeling. The works of Erving Goffman introduce us to the many minor traffic rules of face-to-face interaction, as they emerge at a card game, in an elevator, on the street, or at the dining table of an insane asylum. He prevents us from dismissing the small as trivial by showing how small rules, transgressions, and punishments add up to form the longer strips of experience we call "work." At the same time, it is hard to use Goffman's focus to explain why companies train flight attendants in smiling, or how emotional tone is supervised, or what profit is ultimately tied to emotional labor. It is hard, in other words, to draw on this discourse alone and see how "display work" fits into the larger scheme of things.

The third discourse takes place in a quiet side street of American social science; it deals with the timeless issues of what an emotion is and how we can manage it.

To uncover the heart of emotional labor, to understand what it takes to do it and what it does to people, I have drawn on elements from all three discourses. Certain events in economic history cannot be fully understood unless we pay attention to the filigreed patterns of feeling and their management because the details of these patterns are an important part of what many men and women do for a living.

Because such different traditions are joined here, my inquiry will have a different relevance for different readers. Perhaps it will be most relevant for those who do the work it describes—the flight attendants. But most of us have jobs that require some handling of other people's feelings and our own, and in this sense we are all partly flight attendants. The secretary who creates a cheerful office that announces her company as "friendly and dependable" and her boss as "up-and-coming," the waitress or waiter who creates an "atmosphere of pleasant dining," the tour guide or hotel receptionist who makes us feel welcome, the social worker whose look of solicitous concern makes the client feel cared for, the salesman who creates the sense of a "hot commodity," the bill collector who inspires fear, the funeral parlor director who makes the bereaved feel understood, the minister who creates a sense of protective outreach but even-handed warmth—all of them must confront in some way or another the requirements of *emotional labor.*

Emotional labor does not observe conventional distinctions between types of jobs. By my estimate, roughly one-third of American workers today have jobs that subject them to substantial demands for emotional labor. Moreover, of all *women* working, roughly one-half have jobs that call for emotional labor. Thus this inquiry has special relevance for women, and it probably also describes more of their experience. As traditionally more accomplished managers of feeling in private life, women more than men have put emotional labor on the market, and they know more about its personal costs.

This inquiry might at first seem relevant only to workers living under capitalism, but the engineering of a managed heart is not unknown to socialism; the enthusiastic "hero of labor" bears the emotional standard for the socialist state as much as the Flight Attendant of the Year does for the capitalist airline industry. Any functioning society makes effective use of its members' emotional labor. We do not think twice about the use of feeling in the theater, or in psychotherapy, or in forms of group life that we admire. It is when we come to speak of the *exploitation* of the bottom by the top in any society that we become morally concerned. In any system, exploitation depends on the actual distribution of many kinds of profits—money, authority, status, honor, well-being. It is not emotional labor itself, therefore, but the underlying system of recompense that raises the question of what the cost of it is.

Private and Commercial Uses of Feeling

A nineteenth-century child working in a brutalizing English wallpaper factory and a well-paid twentieth-century American flight attendant have something in common: in order to survive in their jobs, they must mentally detach themselves—the factory worker from his own body and physical labor, and the flight attendant from her own feelings and emotional labor. Marx and many others have told us the factory worker's story. I am interested in telling the flight attendant's story in order to promote a fuller appreciation of the costs of what she does. And I want to base this appreciation on a prior demonstration of what can happen to any of us when we become estranged from our feelings and the management of them.

We feel. But what is a feeling? I would define feeling, like emotion, as a sense, like the sense of hearing or sight. In a general way, we experience it when bodily sensations are joined with what we see or imagine.[9] Like the sense of hearing, emotion communicates information. It has, as Freud said of anxiety, a "signal function." From feeling we discover our own viewpoint on the world.

We often say that we *try* to feel. But how can we do this? Feelings, I suggest, are not stored "inside" us, and they are not independent of acts of management.

Both the act of "getting in touch with" feeling and the act of "trying to" feel may become part of the process that makes the thing we get in touch with, or the thing we manage, *into* a feeling or emotion. In managing feeling, we contribute to the creation of it.

If this is so, what we think of as intrinsic to feeling or emotion may have always been shaped to social form and put to civic use. Consider what happens when young men roused to anger go willingly to war, or when followers rally enthusiastically around their king, or mullah, or football team. Private social life may always have called for the management of feeling. The party guest summons up a gaiety owed to the host, the mourner summons up a proper sadness for a funeral. Each offers up feeling as a momentary contribution to the collective good. In the absence of an English-language name for feelings-as-contribution-to-the-group (which the more group-centered Hopi culture called *arofa*), I shall offer the concept of a gift exchange.[10] Muted anger, conjured gratitude, and suppressed envy are offerings back and forth from parent to child, wife to husband, friend to friend, and lover to lover.

References

Bell, Daniel (1973). *The Coming of Post-Industrial Society*. New York: Basic Books.

Blauner, Robert (1964). *Alienation and Freedom*. Chicago: University of Chicago Press.

Braverman, Harry (1974). *Labor and Monopoly Capital*. New York and London: Monthly Review Press.

Etzioni, Amitai (1968). "Basic human needs, alienation and inauthenticity", *American Sociological Review* 33: 870-885.

Kohn, Melvin (1976). "Occupational structure and alienation", *American Journal of Sociology* 82: 111–130.

Lee, Dorothy (1959. *Freedom and Culture*. New York: Prentice-Hall.

Lifton, Robert (1970). *Boundaries: Psychological Man in Revolution*. New York: Random House.

Marx, Karl (1977). *Capital*. Vol. 1. Intro. By Ernest Mandel. Tr. Ben Fowkes. New York: Vintage.

Mills, C. Wright (1956). *White Collar*. New York: Oxford University Press.

Riesman, David (1953). *The Lonely Crowd: A Study of the Changing American Character*. New Haven: Yale University Press.

Seeman, Melvin (1967). "On the personal consequences of alienation in work", *American Sociological Review* 32: 273–285.

Tucker, Robert (ed.) (1972). *The Marx-Engels Reader*. New York: Norton.

Turner, Ralph (1976). "The real self: from institution to impulse", American Journal of Sociology 81: 989–1016.

Notes

1. Marx, *Capital* (1977), pp. 356–357, 358.
2. For stylistic convenience, I shall use the pronoun "she" when referring to a flight attendant, except when a specific male flight attendant is being discussed. Otherwise I shall try to avoid verbally excluding either gender.
3. *Lucas Guide 1980,* pp. 66, 76. Fourteen aspects of air travel at the stages of departure, arrival, and the flight itself are ranked. Each aspect is given one of sixteen differently weighted marks. For example, "The friendliness or efficiency of the staff is more important than the quality of the pilot's flight announcement or the selection of newspapers and magazines offered."
4. I use the term *emotional labor* to mean the management of feeling to create a publicly observable facial and bodily display; emotional labor is sold for a wage and therefore has *exchange value.* I use the synonymous terms *emotion work* or *emotion management* to refer to these same acts done in a private context where they have *use value.*
5. Marx, in his *Economic and Philosophic Manuscripts* (Tucker 1972), may have provided the last really basic idea on alienation. Among the recent useful works on the subject are Blauner (1964), Etzioni (1968), Kohn (1976), and Seeman (1967).
6. Mills (1956), p. xx.
7. Like a commodity, service that calls for emotional labor is subject to the laws of supply and demand. Recently the demand for this labor has increased and the supply of it drastically decreased. The airline industry speed-up since the 1970s has been followed by a worker slowdown. The slowdown reveals how much emotional labor the job required all along. It suggests what costs even happy workers under normal conditions pay for this labor without a name. The speed-up has sharpened the ambivalence many workers feel about how much of oneself to give over to the role and how much of oneself to protect from it.
8. Jobs that Bell includes in the service sector are those in transportation and utilities, distribution and trade, finance and insurance, professional and business services, jobs deriving from demands for leisure activities (recreation and travel), and jobs that deal with communal services (health, education, and government). Only some of these service-sector jobs call for much emotion management.
9. In general the term *feeling* connotes fewer or milder physical sensations—flushing, perspiring, trembling—than the term *emotion* does. Feeling, in this sense, is a milder emotion. For the purposes of this inquiry, the two terms are interchangeable.

    Let me briefly relate my model of the self as emotion manager to the work of Riesman (1953), Lifton (1970), and Turner (1976). Riesman's "other directed man" differs from the "inner directed man" with regard to where a person turns in search of social guidelines. The "other directed man" turns to peers, the "inner directed man" to internalized parents (superego). These can be seen in my framework as alternate ways of sensing feeling rules that apply to the narrower zone of self (the self as emotion manager) on which I focus. Lifton posits a new type of "protean" character structure, more elastic and more adaptive than previous ones. I share with Lifton an appreciation of the plastic, socially moldable aspect of human character and the social uses to which it may be put. But Lifton's focus is on the *passive* capacity to adapt, wrought of an absence of local attachments, whereas my focus is on the active component of our capacity to adapt. Turner contrasts an "institutional self" with an "impulse self" and notes a social trend from the first to the second. By the institutional self, Turner means the individual who believes that his "real" self resides in his behavior and feelings within institutional roles. The "impulse self" refers to the individual who locates his "real" self outside of institutional roles. I think the trend he spots is real, and the reason for it may lie in a contradiction between two trends, both related to individualism. On one hand, individualism as an idea implies a value on human feeling and will. Given this value, it comes to seem worthwhile to search out and locate one's "true" feelings. (People who do not entertain the idea of individualism do not take this as a worthwhile, or even thinkable, pursuit. It is a luxury of bourgeois life that only people not preoccupied with survival are able to think of doing.) On the other hand, job opportunities do not present a way of finding one's true self in work; work in which one has control and authority (that is, upper-class work) is not as plentiful as the demand for it. The supply of jobs with which one can identify has, as Braverman argues, declined. The two trends together lead to the spread of the "impulse self:" Turner implies that the impulse self is *less social,* less subject to the claims of others. In light of my thesis, the impulse self is not less social; rather, it is subject to different rules and controlled by a different sort of control system (feeling rules and the personal control system). It might be thought that the impulse self puts less premium on *managing* emotion (hence the term *impulse*). But there are for such individuals other rules. (For example, you can't be thinking about something else when you say your mantra; in Gestalt therapy, you shouldn't be "up in your head.") The "impulse self" is not more subject to impulse.

10. Lee (1959) discusses the concept of *arofa.*

Catholics, Protestants and Office Workers from the Town
The Experience and Negotiation of Fear in Northern Ireland

Karen D. Lysaght

Introduction

While violence and conflict have been dominant concerns for researchers on Northern Ireland for several decades, the closely allied theme of fear has remained largely absent from the academic debate. This chapter attempts to fill this gap by describing how residents in Northern Ireland live with and manage fear in their daily lives.

While Belfast is necessarily characterized by divided territories and regular acts of sectarian/political violence, it is equally a city typified by the dynamics of work, transport, schooling, social life and shopping, among other activities. Such mundane tasks take residents of these segregated residential districts over and across the seemingly set boundaries of the city in furtherance of their daily routines. While placing an emphasis upon everyday activities creates a more complex and nuanced picture of life in the divided city, it is important not to create a false sense of 'normality', which obscures the way in which the dividedness of the city proves a crucial aspect of the daily negotiation and management of life in these politicized urban spaces. It is necessary, therefore, to find the middle ground between a static sense of the city as violent and 'abnormal' and an equally skewed picture of the city typified by the 'normality' of everyday routines and untouched by the violence which necessarily exists.

This middle ground can be reached through the adoption of an ethnographic perspective to the issue of fear. This chapter presents a case study of the generation and management of fear in the divided city of Belfast. By focusing upon the actual experience of residents, it is possible to discern a highly attuned sense of fear which bears little relationship to the dualistic juxtaposition of 'real threat' against irrational groundless fear. Instead, fear is shown to be not merely individualized and personalized, but also intersubjectively shared, situationally specific, socially constituted and indeed socially constituting.

Fear and the Divided City: A Case Study of the Generation and Management of Fear

The way in which the experience of fear shapes the daily dynamic of life in Belfast has been overlooked, not merely as a result of the emphasis upon quantitative examinations, but also as a result of the relative invisibility of the topic to academic onlookers. The reason for this myopia is due in part to the rare self-conscious articulation of the topic by residents of districts characterized by division and boundary violence, where the issue is treated as a tacit unproblematic body of information. As one resident notes, it is the case that 'people are so used to living like that, that it seems normal to them and it's only when you jerk their memories that all of this starts coming out ... 'cause it's just your life'. It is precisely the 'normality' and casual mundanity of the topic which leads it to be overlooked by academic observers of Northern Ireland. In order to provide a context for the narratives presented in this chapter, I shall begin by illustrating the nature of the feared violence through a brief vignette which outlines a series of violent incidents which occurred over a twenty-four-hour period in the year 2000. The timing of these incidents is significant, occurring as they did six years after the initial paramilitary cease-fires of 1994, which led to reduced levels of violence twinned with a protracted period of political negotiations in search of a possible settlement to the conflict. Despite the cessation of hostilities, however, this period was not untouched by acts of violence, whether the result of sectarian or political attack or indeed internecine feuding between the illegal paramilitary groups.

> In December 2000, a 30-year-old Catholic builder, Gary Moore, from the small market town of Limavady, 58 miles north of Belfast, was employed on a building site in a local corporation housing estate with a near-exclusively Protestant population on the northern outskirts of Belfast. In the late afternoon of Wednesday 4 December he was approached by two men who shot him, wounding him fatally. Within hours of this shooting, another Catholic man, in his early twenties, Paul Scullion, was sitting in his taxi outside his depot on the Oldpark Road in North Belfast when he was shot several times by a pillion passenger on a motorcycle. The two shootings were determined to have been carried out by the Ulster Defence Association as revenge attacks for the killing the previous evening of a Protestant taxi driver: 35-year-old Trevor Kell was shot dead when he answered a bogus call to a house on the Hesketh Road, on the Protestant side of a highly tense interface in the north of the city. Initially the police blamed Republican elements for the shooting, but given their adamant denial, questions were raised as to whether the shootings might instead have been carried out by Loyalist paramilitaries in an attempt

to provide the justification for a series of revenge attacks. (From an interview in the research project)

This series of events raises several pertinent questions about the nature of fear experienced by individuals resident in communities where such violence is experienced. The three shootings appear to be merely the result of random, unpredictable and indiscriminate targeting of victims in tit-for-tat violent exchanges carried out during the course of the working day on individuals who are clearly noncombatant. The violence appears to be relatively chaotic and disorganized. Such a pattern of violence begs the question of how ordinary citizens live lives which are not entirely disabled and paralysed by fear of violent assault. As already mentioned, however, the city is characterized by those normal daily flows of employment, schooling, shopping and socializing which are common to all large urban spaces. Residents clearly do not live lives which are immobilized by fear of random acts of violence. Instead, they negotiate the city in a myriad of complex ways which are underpinned by a reading of the violence which attempts to find pattern, and by extension order, in the events which threaten to disrupt their lives.

Social Scripts of Fear in Belfast

As noted earlier, the residents of Belfast's inner-city districts live in residential areas characterized by high degrees of religious segregation. Movement outside of local residential areas therefore necessitates the navigation of a complex topography of politicized space. The following comments were made by two men who express some of the feelings triggered by engaging in such daily negotiations.

I honestly think fear is a factor ... there will be a fear factor, who I'm working with, there's a suspicion. Anybody, honestly, I really do think if you're born and bred in Belfast, I truly believe there's a suspicion. It's almost a gene! 'Right, you can't work in north Belfast', 'you can't work in west Belfast', 'you can't work in east Belfast'. It automatically clicks in and then the fear starts and you're sweating ... I remember going for an interview in the Upper Springfield, and Jesus, that was the worst day of my life ... I didn't feel safe ... it was the area ... I don't know that area, didn't know the people, didn't know the geography. You're going into somewhere strange, that's my opinion. (Jack, Protestant male, mid-twenties)

[That bus stop] is not that commonly used. A lot of people would walk into town first to get the bus [rather] than stand there on the road [an interface] [or] you'd find a lot of people they try to time it, so that they are only standing there maybe two or three minutes. They would hang about in [our community], maybe in the corner or they would stand on this side of the road where they feel safe and then move across [the road] when the bus is due to come around the corner. I mean, you look at who is passing. If there's two or three young men coming up, then you would feel threatened and your heart would start pumping a bit until they were eventually passed. (Gary, Protestant male, mid-thirties)

In their statements both Jack and Gary echo the paramilitary-associated interviewee above, in drawing upon a highly defined understanding of the threat of violence. This reading provides both known categories and known locations which trigger physical feelings of fear. Echoing the paramilitary script, Gary in particular speaks of a distinct social category, young men, as those most likely to trigger a sense of fear. As mentioned previously, young men represent the group who have suffered the highest number of deaths in the conflict, and, as demonstrated through this remark, the group who are seen by members of the local population as those who pose the greatest threat. The random targeting of young men from specific politicized districts has been a common feature of the conflict, regardless of whether or not these men were members of paramilitary groups. They are viewed by many in these localities as the social category most likely to be paramilitary members, to sympathize with the organizations or to engage, themselves, in politicized street violence.

Coming through in these scripts is a definite spatial locatedness of threat and a series of spatial practices designed to avoid becoming victims of attack, which depend upon the accurate interpretation of the situation. The spatial practices outlined by the young men above involve avoiding unknown spaces where the boundaries are unfamiliar and difficult to read, or using known dangerous spaces in ways which are highly defined. These practices necessitate the reading of space in highly intricate ways, in a situation in which all space is identified as either 'ours' or 'theirs' and given a sectarian complexion.

See that road there, well, the Catholics they walk on the other side of the road, they're the only ones that use that side, and then us Protestants use this side, and the office workers from the town. (George, Protestant man, mid-thirties)

While this remark illustrates the highly specific detailing of the spatial divisions, which divide streets into 'safe sides' and 'unsafe sides', it also illuminates an interesting feature of fear of sectarian violence. George points to the use of the Protestant side of the street by those invisible others whom he refers to as the 'office workers from the town'. These individuals do not come without their own religious identities, whether Catholic or Protestant, but for George, and indeed for the many others who echo his thoughts, they appear to exist outside the framework of fear and threat. Most city residents adopt spatial practices which avoid whole swathes of the city which they view as politicized residential territories with established negative reputations, but for the majority of people there is little reason to visit these residential communities.

Warnings, rumours and advice are a central part of local communication. In the following quotation, Terry outlines the best strategy for walking into or out of the city centre at night, a route which involves passing in the vicinity of a particularly volatile interface.

> The only problems that our people have had in the last while back is people going in or out of town late at night walking when the buses have not been on, and getting badly beaten going by Slatersville or coming back past it. Once they knew you weren't a Catholic, you'd run for your life. The way it is ... that's Slatersville [referring to a map], and see here, that brings you on up the Prendergast Road, and once you come past this point there's people watching. They see you coming up. Most of them know their own community down there because it's a very small community. We've always told our people, 'Come up Birchill Street', because Birchill Street goes up and brings you round this way. We always tell our people, 'If you're going into town go in that way if you want, and when you're coming home, try and come home the other way ... and cut across, because it means if you're walking down the far side you have a better chance of running up the bypass even, and round into Freyne Street if you see anything there'. (Terry, Protestant man, late forties)

Terry's remarks point to a highly intricate spatial detailing which is shared by those living in a particular locality, whether through direct instruction or merely through hearing numerous stories of local incidents of violence. Such stories provide local people with the knowledge of what it is that they should learn to fear. Knowing what to fear is critical to actually experiencing fear. While several of the respondents quoted detail the physical manifestations of fear, of sweating bodies and pumping hearts, what they relate is necessarily learnt and intersubjectively shaped. Cultural factors do play a role, and it is only through awareness that a particular thing represents a threat, that individuals actually experience fear.

These spaces have a long history of concentrated political and sectarian violence (Feldman 1991). This spatio-temporal emphasis is a common feature of the discussion of fear in Belfast. It is echoed clearly by Simon, a young Catholic man living directly on a volatile interface associated with recurrent violence and tension. Such violence is particularly intense during the summer months and the most controversial points in the marching season, such as the conflict over the right to march at Drumcree each July.[1] His narrative reveals how his community reads the potential threat in any given incident, and chooses either to ignore or to react on the basis of this reading.

> After dark ... any serious things that have happened within the district have happened three or four in the morning. I live beside one of the interfaces and I mean you get woke up and ... you're astonished at what time you hear people coming home drunk and wants to shout for his cause down the street. From both sides now you can hear people shouting, whether it's, 'you dirty Fenian B' or whatever, 'you dirty Orange B', you know, that type of thing. Whether they're standing in the street shouting 'Kill the Pope!', 'God save the Queen!' I've heard some mad obscenities being shouted, like.

Mostly it's down to drunkenness ... most of the time it's drunks and they're standing at the top of the street shouting, and a crowd comes out and off they go back up the road and it's all forgot about. Most of the times it's an individual just drunk ... no audience whatsoever and probably that's what the problem is ... once they get an audience ... But it's different when somebody is drunk ... I mean it's not as harmful as when it's the summer period whereby people only use alcohol to fire up their emotions. You know, people do come down and they're sober and they are fully conscious of what they're doing and they're causing trouble. Well, you always know ... Sometimes it could be orchestrated ... the likes of Drumcree over the summer marching season, things like that tend to be more orchestrated. 'If we want to do something we'll go down into the district, we'll go down into Clarence Road' [the interface], 'we'll do this or we'll do that'. But when you're talking drunks coming home, you know there isn't going to be a serious problem ... most people know that they are drunk and just let him go on up to where he belongs and it's the same up there. He'll go, he'll get tired of hearing himself shouting and away he'll go. (Simon, Catholic man, early twenties)

For residents like Simon, there is an interpretation of such situations, and the decision is made as to whether there is anything to fear, or whether they should merely remain in their beds and ignore the incident. The decision is based on the wider context within which the incident occurs, whether political or seasonal. Given the supposed predictability of violence, individuals can judge particular incidents as they arise. They judge these occurrences, and those which are deemed unusual are sometimes rejected as 'not sounding right', or 'making no sense', and dismissed as merely rumour or supposition. In addition to analyzing particular violent incidents, individuals also judge the spatial decisions of others.

The natural extension to such a judgement is made by the young Catholic man, Simon, who has very clear thoughts on safe spatial practice and on the judgement of those who do not act in ways which are fully cognizant of the fear of violence.

Driving and walking, you know, you wouldn't do the same thing at the same time every day, you know, people do have that mentality and it's because they saw how easy it is if you do something in a routine, you'll end up getting yourself shot. People in these areas do watch themselves more ... You do get people that say, 'Why would I get shot? I mean I don't do anybody any harm', and they're the ones that end up getting shot, because they go wherever they want. Well some people say, not that he deserved to be shot but he should have had more sense not to work in one of these types of places [employer in a Protestant district], or whatever. I know that's harsh to say, but when you go to work in one of these places you're taking a risk, and they're fully conscious of where they're going. (Simon, Catholic man, early twenties)

In his spatial practices, Simon mirrors the safety strategy of the leading Loyalists referred to in the interview extract above, in avoiding the formation of routine in his daily activities. For Simon, those who ignore the shared understanding that spatial freedoms need to be limited for the sake of safety, are foolish in the extreme. Thus, while negative assessments are made of those who are overly fearful, equally disapproving comments are directed at those who fail to live their everyday lives in ways that are fully cognizant of the very real dangers which exist.

Conclusion

From the comparison of the combatant and noncombatant scripts, it is clear that both are echoing the same overriding themes. From the ethnographic detail presented, it is possible to see that both categories have very definite patterns to their reading of the violence of the Northern Irish conflict. Order and predictability are credited to the violence in terms of victim-choice, spatial, temporal, seasonal and political influences. Tacit agreement exists on the nature of the violence and on the relative threat posed by various situations. Just as violence and threat are read intersubjectively, so too a variety of spatial strategies are shared, which offset potential danger. These strategies involve complex mapping processes, whereby space is carved into safe and unsafe zones, where both macro- and micro-territorial considerations exist, involving respectively the 'other side of town' or the 'other side of the street'.

Predictability ensures that palpable fear levels are reduced, and events are catalogued under merely 'normal' for this time of year, as no cause for undue concern or indeed as just cause for worry, distress and action. Just as specific violent incidents are interpreted by local onlookers, so too the spatial choices of others are examined and judged by community members, who view unsafe movements negatively, and often credit the individual with naivety, stupidity or foolishness. Fear is shown to be normalized and routinized in a range of daily practices. This is not an articulation of fear as neurotic, paranoid or immobilized. It is rather the complex appreciation of the very real dangers in the local environment and the development and sharing of a range of practices designed to offset the possibility of victimization.

This case study directly challenges an overly personalized and individualized reading of fear. The categories of 'real' as opposed to 'unreal' or irrational fears are shown to have little use within a case study which examines the practical impact of fear of violent assault in the daily negotiation of the mundane acts of shopping, working or socializing. Ultimately, fear is shown to be highly spatialized, with the sense of both threat and fear related to the occupation and use of space. In fact, in both combatant and noncombatant scripts there is a clear spatialization of identity, where there is an acute blurring of the individual into place. The quantitative appreciation of distinct social categories and the measurement of their respective level of risk would be difficult to ground in the realities of these blurred politicized readings, where presence in space and place can come to be a more important factor than an individual's political affiliation or sympathies. There is a blurring of the categories of the political and the nonpolitical, and space comes to define the person moving through it.

Reference

Feldman, A. (1991), *Formations of Violence: The Narrative of the Body and Political Terror in Northern Ireland,* Chicago: University of Chicago Press.

Note

1. Marches by Loyalist organizations take place regularly throughout the summer; one, at Drumcree in Portadown (thirty miles southwest of Belfast), became particularly controversial during the 1990s.

–8–

Emotions in Academia

Billy Ehn and Orvar Löfgren

An old building belonging to the Royal Netherlands Academy of Arts and Sciences, situated on the bank of Amsterdam's Kaisergracht canal, formed the home of a small research department specializing in the study of dialects and Dutch folk culture up until 1988. Excerpts, records, photos and drawings were collected here in these run-down premises. It was a relatively closed setting, not highly ranked by neighbouring disciplines or within the other departments of European ethnology. When one of the researchers, J. J. Voskuil, retired after thirty years of working in the very same place, he energetically and secretly set his hand to writing a 'roman à clef' of seven volumes of more than five thousand pages in the space of five years. His writings were based on an infinitesimal number of diary notes. Neither he nor the publishing company ever imagined that this would be a marketable product, and certainly never a best-seller.

When the first volume of *Het Bureau,* translated as *The Office,* came out in 1996, the book proved to be a sensation. Circulation quickly reached 35,000 copies and readers impatiently waited for the follow-up. Critics praised it to the skies as 'the brilliant Dutch novel' and made comparisons with Kafka's portrayals of hell. The seventh and final part reached the bookshops in 2000. In total, several hundreds of thousands of volumes have been sold (see Rooijakkers and Meurkens 2000).

The names of the 400 scholars and colleagues that feature under alias in the novel can be deciphered via a popular Internet homepage. Many have searched the site with trepidation to check whether their names are included in the cast, and under which name they appear. The books do not give a particularly flattering picture of the world of academic research, as we repeatedly encounter never-ending intrigue and power struggles over the most futile things. The portraits are often maliciously revealing. One critic described it as a compelling academic soap opera.

You get the same feeling of unreality as in the BBC's successful TV series, 'The Office' of 2002, where folk sit and stare at computer screens, rummage in files, wander in and out of the hopeless and self-important manager's office, and engage in surrealistic conversations with colleagues without the viewer having the faintest notion of what is actually being produced. Everybody seems to be fully occupied—but with what?

Hidden Emotions

It is striking that workplaces are not well-frequented ethnographic sites in studies of emotions, although it is obvious that work is emotionally driven and that every workplace produces a lot of emotional energies (see for example Fineman, 2000 and Barbalet, 2002). Both *Het Bureau* and 'The Office' seethe with emotions, although they are often concealed in the seemingly trivial routines and reactions of a nervous giggle, a bored look, an unconscious body movement or a sudden yawn.

While 'The Office' and *Het Bureau* look rather similar on the surface, they aren't. *Het Bureau* belongs to the world of academia, a world that is defined by another set of priorities, emotions and practices. It is not only populated by clerks, but also by scholars. That makes a difference.

Life at *Het Bureau* was one of our starting points for a book on the everyday culture of Academia (Ehn & Löfgren, 2004). Using a wide variety of sources—everything from autobiographies, academic reports and the rich interdisciplinary literature on university life, to interviews and observations—we set out to capture some of the basic themes encapsulated in university life. During the past year we have used the book as a platform for discussions with different groups of university people, exchanges that have given us further insights.

At a meeting with fifty administrative assistants, the opening question came from a woman who had spent all her working life in the private sector but who now experienced a cultural shock as a university department secretary: 'How come professors are so emotional?' she asked. That same question also struck us when we started collecting our material. The importance of emotions in university everyday life surprised us. Here was a world in which feelings are either denied or denigrated. In the academic mode of producing knowledge, emphasis is put on rationality, scientific objectivity and a constant rhetoric about keeping 'person and thing' separate. Emotionality, it would appear, should not be allowed to inhabit this world.

At the same time as matter-of-factness and emotional control are revered, university life is steered by strong feelings that often are camouflaged. In order to understand what it is that happens in university life it is important to analyze how researchers and teachers talk about and in different ways express their feelings, both in each other's presence and in the workplace.

In this essay we would like to discuss how the specific world of academic emotions can contribute to an understanding of the cultural organization and expression of complex feelings. The fact that this field is defined as emotionally neutral makes it an especially interesting study. Here the expressions of feelings are often organized and transformed in unexpected ways, given complicated forms or coloured with seemingly insignificant detail. The taboo of certain feelings at the same time results in a tendency to indirectness, the appearance of emotions in disguised forms or in surprising contexts. The way in which the sensitive and impassioned interact with the intellectual leads us to ask the question of how it might be possible to understand the university as an emotion-controlled and contradictory organization.

In researching emotions, a lot of energy has been put into trying to define them. Not only have polarities such as common sense and feelings been discussed, but also contrasts such as body and mind, interior and exterior, or individual and collective (see for example Dixon, 2004, and Hillman, 1991). Our starting point as cultural researchers is a different one in that we view feelings as a dimension that constantly colour our ideas, actions and social existence. They can focus, strengthen or form barriers. Emotions create a special form of presence in that they can sensitize or desensitize situations and impressions.

We see emotions as a cultural dimension of everyday life that cannot be separated from thought, cognition and bodily reactions. They are physical as well as complicated. Feelings aren't only conjured up by the eye or the mind but also by the whole body in some situations. In our analysis, feelings therefore appear more as an analytical tool rather than as a specific phenomenon (for a further discussion of this approach see Frykman and Löfgren, 2005). It's not just a question of understanding how moods and sensations colour situations, but also the problem of interpreting elusive and complex manifestations of feelings. Some situations and arenas become more like seismographic surfaces that make it possible to interpret different tensions. We are looking to capture some of those evasive overtones that form part of what Raymond Williams once called 'structures of feeling' (Williams, 1977) and, in doing this, we will talk of 'academia' rather than the many subcultures hidden in this generalizing concept.

Mixed Feelings

The emotional life of academia is full of contradictions. Memoirs and investigations reveal that researchers and teachers react strongly to each other, their work assignments and the organization itself. Some thrive and others don't, some idolize the university, while others—and here we are talking about extremes—are affected by what Bourdieu (1984/1996:57) calls 'academic hatred'. Scholars are, as Charlotte Bloch (2002a, 2002b, 2003) shows in her research, fully occupied in dealing with feelings of pride and joy, anger and shame.

The emotional charging of this milieu contrasts with intellectual aspirations towards logic and analytical distance. Scholars often talk about their pleasurable labours, the delight of formulating problems and the discovery of new ideas. But they also describe anxiety, envy and bitterness in 'the narrow-minded valley'—something that also applies to the most successful in 'the intellectual paradise'. (Academics love to use colourful metaphors, such as when they describe university life in terms of backwaters, ivory towers and tribal customs, see for example Becher, 1989.)

Strong criticism, as well as idolization, is incorporated into the descriptions of academia. Such ambivalence seems to be a general feature. Many scholars and teachers obviously love their jobs and are convinced that they have landed feet first in the best of all worlds. They identify themselves with both the freedom and the hunger for knowledge they find there and, in the main, are loyal to the system—at least as long as they are successful and acknowledged by their colleagues.

Others are less enthusiastic; they either find it difficult to adapt, don't assert themselves in competitive struggles, or collapse under the heavy weight of the teaching load. The experience of university shifts according to what you want to get out of it and what you are prepared to contribute. In this sense it resembles a very ordinary workplace, with a varying proportion of heaven and hell stirred into the mix. One thing that differentiates the Swedish university, however, is a relatively lower mobility, in that people often remain faithful to the same department for the whole of their working life. Many see themselves as unlikely candidates for other workplaces, or 'out there in reality', as is sometimes expressed with an ironic shrug of the shoulders.

When you analyze the rich autobiographical literature of academia, you find that it is often affectionate, humorous and perhaps somewhat (self-)ironic, although it also contains a fair amount of pain and discomfort. Not surprisingly success stories form the clear majority. It is mostly professors who write their memoirs. A sense of pride in one's own achievements glares through a desire to appear humble, while at the same time, stories about jealously guarding one's own interests, a sharp needling of elbows and scientific battles are recounted with some distaste.

The stars' love–hate relationship is perhaps not so illogical when all is said and done. There's nothing strange in having conflicting feelings towards an occupation if it is perceived as being the only mission in life—a kind of calling into which you put your heart and soul. Research is described as something more than just an ordinary job. High expectations increase the risk of disappointment, particularly in a situation where the fight for positions and research resources has become increasingly tougher.

Envy and Admiration

There is a constant battle for acknowledgement in a milieu that, to a great extent, puts performance on a par with personal value. The competitive mentality is strongly manifested in the everyday life of a university. The risk of exclusion makes people more aware of their position in the ranking, and thus even more prepared to exploit every opportunity to advance their position (and their value). The success of others can therefore lead to problems. If the rewards don't stretch to include everyone, it doesn't feel right if others are given what you yourself are striving for.

In academic autobiographies, envy is named as a special affliction, a kind of occupational hazard. The writers themselves do not see themselves as affected by it, however. It is others that are envious and grudging—those forbidden emotions that are both difficult to acknowledge and to disguise. There is always reason to be envious, both within and outside the university world. However, as it is considered an unpleasant emotion, the majority try not to let it show and instead invent counter-strategies. A furtive, sideways and secret comparison hides itself behind envy and is sometimes accompanied by a desperate desire to be somebody else. Envy results when you compare yourself with others and experience that you are less worthy. People suffer when a colleague writes yet another good book or is awarded a research grant or a scientific prize. It is not the case that just anyone can arouse a sense of envy, however, as for most people it is bound up with the equally good competitor. The abilities and competence of the other person threaten one's own sense of worth and diminish the significance of personal achievement.

Is there anything special about academic envy? That emotion exists in every context where people are assessed by what they achieve. One distinctive characteristic is that academic life, to an exceptionally high degree, is about people attaining their worth and rank as a result of achievements that take years to realize. It involves investing in a creative activity where you have to work with people who, in other contexts, are your competitors, critics and judges, on a daily basis. Perhaps envy is just as corrosive in other creative occupations, but it may find a different expression. The question is whether others outshine scholars in finding each other's shortcomings, doubting another's competence and accusing them of being a phoney—or even pointing the same finger at yourself.

Envy and gnashing your teeth are, however, not entirely negative, in that these feelings have also led to constructive rivalry and a number of epoch-making studies. A desire to write and publish treatises that might lead to a professorship or enhance your curriculum vitae (CV)—the shop-window of capability—is everyday grist in the scholar's mill. Arrogance and envy in the face of other people's success can, rather like the desire for revenge, sometimes be underestimated as productive forces. By envying another person you actually reveal your own longings.

Sometimes envy bears the disguise of one of its closest relatives in the world of emotions: admiration. Those of us who can't bear to feel ourselves inferior or less worthy can convert the emotion to flattery. Having a generous attitude towards those who seem to be more competent is a way of trying to disarm a destructive reactive pattern. In this context, the expression 'to praise someone to death' becomes actualized. Lavishing praise and idealizing the qualities of other people is akin to putting them on a dangerously high pedestal from which they can easily fall. The idealized person has to live up to those high demands that admiration craves. Exaggerated admiration and merciless belittlement are, to some people, as closely related as breathing out and breathing in, as many scholars, from Kierkegaard to Freud, have pointed out. Envy can be the result of a misplaced idealization or identification (see the discussion in Garber 2001: 53 ff).

Even if envy is not an acceptable reaction—one that you would rather not own up to—it can be that colleagues recognize and acknowledge it in each other. 'You are so talented! You have written precisely the kind of book I would have written myself.' They feel both delight and envy; appreciation makes the success of the other seem less painful. Everybody knows that academia is driven by a craving for success. They are also very aware of what it is like to succeed and to fail. The academic competitive system leads to people becoming single-minded and isolated in their desire to achieve, while at the same time forming a silent community against the curse of comparison and competition. Praising others to the skies is actually also a way of adjusting to the university's domineering scale of values, that which since time immemorial has meant that glory and fame are mostly earned through scholarly achievement.

In the university world, envy is an inheritance from the past that has been re-produced over and over again in new forms. It is a force that both steals and feeds energy in those who are preoccupied with a need to prove their worthiness and emerge as victors in the competitive struggle. But what kind of routines, traditions and thought patterns make envy and admiration such central emotions in the world of academia?

Competing Colleagues

On Christmas Eve 2003, readers of Sweden's most circulated daily newspaper (*Dagens Nyheter*) were surprised by a long polemic article in which a political science professor demonstrated, with the help of wide-ranging measuring apparatus, that colleagues who appeared most often in the press were not those who enjoyed the greatest international scholarly prestige. His own name was not to be found among the list of the ten most media-reported (men), but could be found, however, as the number two rating in the more important listing concerning international reputation. Several of his colleagues spent their Christmas holidays trying to refute his rankings. Another professor constructed a new list, this time based on the number of hits in the Social Science Citation Index. The previously mentioned number two was nowhere to be found, while the new ranker had himself sailed up the list to assume second place.

Academicians are obsessed with ranking, measuring and weighing as energy-creating activities. You meet this right at the beginning of your academic career, as a student, starting with the constant round of examinations and terminating with an obituary published in the professional journals. You can never relax. You are constantly being evaluated. Do you come up to scratch as scholar, teacher and colleague? 'You are always fair game', a senior professor complained. Even to the bitter end. Following a lengthy battle between two history professors, one of the antagonists had the task of giving a commemorative speech in honour of his deceased colleague. A listener recalls the atmosphere of that occasion. The deceased person's entire clan were on tenterhooks as they listened for any undertones in the competitor's homage. Which insinuations were bound up in this ritual extolment?

The constant measuring and weighing up is often internalized as one's own uncertainty, a nagging doubt. How do you know that you are a proper researcher? How is your position at the university legitimized? Many postgraduates carry a constant feeling of insecurity and sometimes feel themselves to be phoneys pretending to carry out research work. Is what I'm doing serious scientific work, or am I just a charlatan?

These same painful thoughts affect a surprising number of established scholars, whose belief in themselves is easily shaken by something as simple as a critical review or a stray comment in a seminar. In the same way we constantly struggle with oblivion—both as postgraduates and professors. How do we make an impression, how do we gain attention and repute, how are we read, heard and seen? The academic ego is fragile and swings easily between self-esteem and self-contempt.

The perpetual ranking—both in formal and informal guises—creates a fertile breeding ground for envy and admiration, as well as specific patterns of reaction. A special appeals tradition has been created in academic life that seemingly has no counterpart in other workplaces. Written complaints are not really always about getting a ranking changed (which seldom happens) but are rather an institutionalized form of expressing emotions like disappointment and anger. But there are also other ways of dealing with such feelings.

Irony—Betwixt Fun and Sarcasm

In a world where vanity, bitterness and insecurity about one's own position go hand in glove with more positive energies, techniques have been created that transform and conceal emotions. It is no coincidence that irony (including the more sophisticated self-irony) and sarcasm take up strong positions in the academic tradition. Irony becomes the technique used to deal with, as well as distance oneself from, uncomfortable emotions that form part of an academic 'habitus'.

To an outsider, visiting at the time of a departmental coffee break, an academicians' dinner or chatting during a pause in the conference, the sarcasm and jokes that fly through the air can seem very trying. The favourite target for humorous distancing is 'the others', stick-in-the-mud scholars, stupid administrators or the unsophisticated world of nonacademics.

Why this academic obsession with irony? Stories about the old masters of sarcasm abound in academic folklore. A teacher remembers what it was like to listen to one of its masters, a literature professor, talking to a group of colleagues during the 1940s:

> 'Every intelligent person with ulcers gets duodenal ulcers.' He then pauses and turns to one of his less bright professor colleagues: 'But I bet you don't have any duodenal ulcers.' (Villius 1991: 397)

Sometimes the ironist is regarded as the rational sceptic; someone who is prepared to live with uncertainty and who has the ability to critically relativize most things. Distancing becomes a virtue and an academic defence strategy. If you wish to understand the long tradition of the ironic attitude, and that includes the high-spirited jesting, you can usefully begin with how the university milieu once cultivated a bourgeois Bohemianism. Students, teachers and research scholars belonged to the establishment while at the same time finding themselves outside it. They were aloof in ways that could be perilous. Irony, especially towards nonacademics, communicated an ambiguous position in the social structure.

When we look back and see how students have acclimatized to this attitude, we realize that a sense of impotence in the face of formal hierarchy was also involved. The experience was one of being at the mercy of the teacher's whims and wielding of power. At the same time as representing role models, they also became objects of ridicule. They had to be parodied and rendered harmless. We come across them in countless diaries filled with anecdotes of absurd examinations, absent-minded docents and dotty professors. This high-spirited student tradition has, however, produced a number of great comedians, from Monty Python to Mr Bean.

In the transformation from student to lecturer to professor, this humoristic capital can be used as an effective power strategy to both create uncertainty in others and conceal it in yourself. In psychological terms, humour is often a technique of deflection, a way of masking problems and emotions. In such cases, irony can become indirect aggression's protective casing, indirectness that means putting on a brave face. A history professor, who for many years chaired one of the Swedish research councils, was feared for his cutting irony. Once at a meeting he said of a research applicant: 'Professor Andersson is probably the most stupid professor of language studies in the whole of Sweden'. He then paused and took a long searching look at the gathering of other language professors that surrounded him and added: 'but, gentlemen, in the face of extremely tough competition'. The laughter was nervous, and everybody left the meeting wondering which position they occupied in this ranking.

It should be added that such academic venom holds its own fascination. In the depictions of life at *Het Bureau,* we are confronted with both malice and full frontal attack. Many readers are witness to the relief this brings. That which is forbidden can be given expression. What others try to mask with contained aggression, can here be recognized as the interest (or need?) to talk badly about people.

Irony is certainly not neutral with respect to gender. In her discussion on humour and irony in the university, Charlotte Bloch (2003) indicates how, for example, some women can quickly and efficiently be branded as humourless. She shows how masculine norms reign with regard to expression and pitch. Class travellers in academia also witness the power with which irony marginalizes those who haven't grown up in an academic setting and have thus never learnt the art of elegant irony at home. They have not mastered this verbal balancing act and feel insecure about how to react to the sarcasm of others. If they protest instead of laughing, they are told 'Can't you take a simple joke?' Irrespective of the conscious or unconscious intention of irony, it is based on a competence that demands considerable practice. Above all it's a matter of 'timing', and choosing the right situation and the right audience. By going too far, however, irony can suddenly be revealed as perfidy and reflect back on the narrator.

At the same time, the joke and the lavish narration are resources that make it possible to breathe and enable a sense of solidarity to be maintained. People often talk about how nice it is to be in one's own department, in an atmosphere where laughter, parody and irony are used to combat the tendency of taking yourself too seriously. Charlotte Bloch (2003) has also discussed the importance of self-irony in downplaying your own achievements to avoid appearing pompous or bragging (a deadly academic sin). Joking about your own work is a way of avoiding the forces of envy.

The Deepening of Disappointment

Some time ago, at a university course on leadership, one of us asked the participants about their best and worst experiences of university life. Positive memories were not difficult to account for. One man mentioned the fascination of launching research projects and new courses. Others lit up when they talked about job satisfaction, well-being, the hungering after knowledge and the feeling of being accepted. When a woman talked about the praise that she had received for an article or a course, many nodded in confirmation. A newly appointed pro-vice chancellor radiated when she said that it was flattering to be made visible and to be esteemed for doing a good job. Everyone unanimously agreed that recognition was among the best things they had experienced at university.

When it came to the other part of the question, the atmosphere became more strained. How could you tell colleagues about the unpleasant experiences? Some found it traumatic to recall old injustices or occasions when they had made fools of themselves or felt isolated. One man recollected the time he received blistering criticism of his scientific paper at a seminar. A woman described in detail how badly she was treated after writing an article that criticized the approach taken within her particular field and how colleagues had completely deserted her as a result. Another woman was close to tears at the memory of how, for a number of years, she had been harassed by her 'psychopathic' head of department. All the bitterness over old, half-forgotten injustices suddenly welled up.

One person after another around the table described the darker sides of a workplace that they otherwise held in high esteem. The atmosphere in the room changed when they dared to trust and listen to each other without raising any objections or making any defences. That didn't happen very often, they said. Someone said that there was a fear of talking about personal defeats at university due to the risk of being branded by them; they become rather like the signature tune of a failed academic. For those who have already suffered in this way, however, recovery is difficult; a negative judgement sticks fast in the world of academic intrigue.

Despite the job satisfaction and intellectual appetite, the university sometimes sounds like a tearful place. Dissatisfaction is greatest amongst those who, rightly or otherwise, feel themselves to have been trampled on, steamrollered or overlooked—especially when it comes to those who have applied for, but not been awarded, a professorship, other positions or a research grant or, even worse, have been declared incompetent. That is a fate worse than death. It might also be tied up with not having been invited to a conference, not having been asked to be one of the keynote speakers, receiving negative reviews or no review at all, being wrongly quoted or not even quoted, being robbed of one's ideas and scientific results, having one's article refused or that one's material isn't used as course literature. It might also be connected to having one's contribution to seminars and conferences ignored, or not being acknowledged, seen or recognized. There are a hundred and one ways of being disappointed. The university is indifferent to those who don't live up to expectations and who therefore are destined to suffer from feelings of unrequited love.

One reason for dissatisfaction might be that scholars put a lot of time and energy into telling colleagues and rivals that their way of doing things is wrong. While it seems to go with the profession, the impersonal scrutinizing of scientific achievements comes dangerously close to an evaluation of personal merits. Sensitive people take it to heart when their ideas are questioned. Differentiating between person and thing becomes difficult.

Error detecting has an inherent polemic force that can give rise to new ways of thinking and interesting debates. But it can also cause a fair amount of grief to be harboured in the optimistic world of university. Even professors and others who outwardly seem to have been successful in their careers (still) bear the scars resulting from the critique of colleagues. The lack of recompense also poisons the most brilliant of minds. The occasions of being left out in the cold, or being affected by negative opinions, become distressingly pockmarked into the soul. The desire for revenge is therefore not an unusual source of motivation.

Bitterness is a special form of emotion that can undergo a number of transformations. Its starting point is often contained anger that either has a long or a short shelf-life. That which for some was just a fleeting word, a shrug of the shoulders, a few lines in a review (and immediately forgotten), are etched into the minds and hearts of others. Cultural organization and manifestations of bitterness remind us of how we talk of emotions in terms of intensity, using metaphors of depth and longevity, levels like conscious and unconscious as well as the gliding process through which an emotion can turn into a mood.

An irritation can be a continuous chafing, while a sudden disappointment may turn into 'a deep disappointment'. It can get stuck in one's memory in the form of a cultural cicatrization in a bitterness that is not an emotion as such, but rather a frame of mind that colours everything else. In bitterness anger is not only turned inwards but also becomes a filter through which the everyday is experienced and interpreted, expressed as cynicism and sarcasm, or in feelings of worthlessness or injustice. Many of us have also experienced how injustices that we regarded as being dead and buried suddenly come to life and are again activated.

As with most moods, bitterness can be both protracted and unfocussed. We can gradually find ourselves having a particular frame of mind without really noticing what is happening. In linguistics, this is often emphasized in that we finds ourselves 'in' a mood, whereas we 'have' a feeling. Moods act as filters that can colour our entire surroundings a rosy pink, black as night or a dull shade of grey.

As a mood, bitterness is one of the driving forces in the narratives of *Het Bureau,* where this form of sarcasm becomes a weapon of revenge. This becomes all the more evident in another academic ethnographic account. In 1993, the book written by American author Melvin D. Williams, *An Academic Village. The Ethnography of an Anthropology Department 1959–1979,* was published. Here he gives a detailed and critical account of the institutional milieu where he took his doctoral degree and later worked as a teacher. His ethnography is filtered through his personal bitterness; an emotion that also makes him very observant of how seemingly trivial situations are charged with elements of power and hierarchy. He charts the sociometry of inclusion and exclusion in the movements of people gathering to talk in the corridor or popping in for a chat with the chairman. He shows how the allotment of offices is seen by some as a ranking device. If you are out of favour, you can find yourself at the end of a corridor or occupying a room without windows.

Williams describes the atmosphere of the post-room, where emotions were choreographed in many different ways. The post arrived twice a day and gave the working day a special rhythm of anticipation. Collecting the post developed into a daily ritual and charged the department with nervous energy, as he puts it. Although the casual meetings in front of the postal pigeon holes seemed relaxed, tension was always in the air. Receiving letters was a confirmation of your position, and getting lots of letters was even better. A ceremonial waste-paper basket was placed in the corner, where people could throw away unimportant post with a nonchalant gesture. People kept an eye on the volume of post in the pigeon holes of their colleagues, some even leaving their post for days to make the collection look thicker. Some secretly leafed through the envelopes of colleagues to try to get an overview of their academic network. Did they get books for review, invitations to conferences or letters from Important Academics?

In many departments, the fact that you are assigned a pigeon hole is an important ritual of recognition for students. A young graduate student can never forget when she was refused such a pigeon hole. For the director of graduate studies it was just a formality, but for her it was a definite sign of exclusion and another example of being the lowest in the hierarchy. Her bitterness still lives on.

Seminar Emotions

Emotions act like feelers and orientation tools in academic life, where moving between different departments and arenas can mean encountering quite diverse emotional microclimates. How do you read the mood of a meeting, a lecture or a coffee break? Who decides the tone of the gathering and how can one and the same situation be given completely different emotional perspectives by the participants?

A research seminar is one of the most highly charged academic events. It's an intellectual high-water mark, brimming with conflicting feelings and emotions— especially a sense of nervousness and thrill at the discussion itself. Five female political science postgraduates (Henriksson, Jansson, Thomsson, Wendt Höjer and Åse, 2000) have described their seminar experiences of competition and hierarchies, and of male dominance and achievement demands that tie their stomachs in knots. There is a distinct boundary between the abstract scholarly world of university and existence beyond the academic walls, they write. The periods before and after a seminar are experienced as sensual. In those moments, say the postgraduates, we eat something, drink coffee and perhaps feel a strand of hair brush across our face. Things seem to have a kind of sensuality about them—their dresses, the coffee cups and the sunshine.

In the actual seminar, however, this sensual dimension is absent. During the seminar you can 'lose your body' and become victim to a feeling of emptiness, or of not being there. This fits with the female body being perceived as 'unscientific'. There is an antagonism between being both scholar and female, say the postgraduates, and they refer to the way in which science is developed around a masculine norm. In order to be acknowledged as a scholar you have to avoid being regarded as a woman, and in that way, connected to your body.

They are not alone in experiencing this strong feeling of lack of clarity in the seminar situation. The idea that it is connected to an understanding of others, and getting them to understand you, can dissolve into feelings of uncertainty. Seminars have a different set of rules in that they follow their own course of events that are characterized by something other than scholarly acumen. Rules and values are indirectly communicated via irony, parody, smiles, a shaking of the head and significant glances. (Seminars are important arenas for the constant negotiation of positions within the department and the discipline as a whole).

In a study of different seminar cultures, Lena Gerholm and Tomas Gerholm (1992) show how the order and structure of a seminar can be implicit to some and over-explicit to others. 'Here we try to be more informal and open', the professor might say, without observing that there is a definite pecking order in which people are allowed to speak—and as to who can say what. In a study into the working situation of postgraduate students, Fredrik Schoug (2004) highlights that, for many postgraduates, the seminar is not the arena for intellectual exchange that they had expected, but is instead a continuous rivalry for prestige and acknowledgement. A man who had recently gained his PhD degree called his own departmental seminar 'a closed discussion where the Society for Mutual Admiration met once a week', whereas a female postgraduate student from the same department felt that her questions seemed silly in an atmosphere that is 'so incredibly pretentious'. It begs the question of what exactly can be said at a seminar—how and by whom?

Different kinds of laughter can be an attempt to conceal the system of rules when it manifests itself. Over-explicit norm declarations are experienced as an embarrassment by some and have to be laughed off, whereas those who openly attack the system are regarded as deviants. Some find it hard to keep a straight poker face and thus unconsciously affect the climate of discussion with their mannerisms, while others manage to communicate their feelings and thoughts with the minimum of gestures. In the seminar room, a giggle, the clearing of one's throat, or a glazed look can be terrible weapons to use against those who are terrified of what others might think. Postgraduates described how such things affected both their bodies and their thoughts. But what sort of kind of emotional field is this?

Seminars are places where you can practice techniques of argument and the art of debate, and the giving and receiving of criticism. This is something that students have been doing since time immemorial. In the eighteenth century students were taught the art of opposition and defence, but it is only later that this came to mean that you defended your own thesis. The dictionary weaves an association-web of fighting, struggling or contesting, quarrelling or overthrowing someone around the phenomenon, disputation. Walter Ong (1982) has described this battle training as an important part of traditional masculinity at university. Masculinity is strengthened by public shows of the disputation battle. For or against! This was a proficiency that easily turned into the capacity to shine at someone else's expense. In effect, people were smitten by what was termed 'disputation disease', characterized by a focus on fault finding and self-assertion. It is a disease that still survives in many settings.

You only need to read the body language of the participants as they emerge from a seminar. Their eyes sometimes sparkle after these magical moments. Ideas flowed freely, people talked eagerly and straight from the heart. A feeling of scholarly euphoria permeated the air and the seminar became a collective journey into something new. On other occasions, it is the boredom, frustration and sense of what hasn't been aired that sit tight in the seminar-bound bodies after two dreary hours. More often than not, the reactions are mixed, depending on whether the participants felt themselves to be active or passive members. In these cases, a combination of feelings might be visible: openness and anxiety, laughter and boredom, bubbly talkativeness and obstinate silence.

Structures of Feeling

Our starting point was not the traditional juxtaposition of reason and emotion—a favourite element in academic rhetoric—but rather the fact that emotions are always part and parcel of people's thoughts and actions. This made it especially interesting to explore academic fields that are often regarded as being emotion-free, from the rankings of researchers to seminar discussions. We have not only focused on some of the stronger emotions, such as envy and bitterness, but also on the ways in which more low-key feelings are organized and expressed. What is it that makes some situations and settings so strongly charged with emotional energy? Who sets the tone or the emotional mood, and how is an emotional atmosphere created or challenged?

This reminds us that feelings are not just interior processes, but something created in a social context, and something that can be manipulated for certain ends. In some situations, feelings are internalized and privatized into experiences of personal failure, while in others they are projected into the social environment and colour social relationships.

Another aspect concerns the intensity of emotions. The joy of a scientific discovery may surface as a surprising euphoria, disappearing almost as quickly as it appeared, or it might remain as a silent feeling of contentment. The anger towards a peer reviewer can be transformed into tears, changed into self-contempt or hardened into an unforgiving bitterness. Such transformations show that the traditional obsession of delineating emotions into categories and taxonomies can lead to a simplification of more complex processes. This becomes obvious when dealing with the kinds of 'mixed feelings' we have explored: the love-hate relationship to the academic institutions, admiration expressed as envy, or the longing for change as a mix of anxiety and desire.

The power of ambivalence in scientific settings should not be underestimated. Some emotions are rapidly changed into other moods. In some cases they can result in pathological blockings, while in other instances they may rapidly fade into something else after having directed the interpretation of the situation. Everyday sensations of discomfort or invisibility during seminar discussions and coffee breaks, or in the scrutiny of footnotes, can either lead to bitterness or the relief of laughter. What appear to be trivial phenomena are imbued with emotional attitudes and evaluations.

We have found Raymond Williams's (1977) vague but evocative concept, 'structures of feeling', helpful in this context, because it not only points to the emotional tone of a specific setting, but also to how a certain emotional 'habitus' is anchored in institutions, routines and frameworks. In academia there is, as we have found, continuity in the ways that feelings are structured by the specific political and cultural organization of its everyday life.

As we try to point out, a number of dogged structures are involved in the repro-duction of the university's emotional climate, such as disputation disease, ranking obsession, irony and evasive indirectness. The point is that many of the fundamental rules and regulations and emotions of university life are embedded in the tools, the aesthetics and the mundane practices, in lab work, blackboard drawings, the corridor chit-chat or the order in which gratitude is expressed in the preface. All these operations and routines are charged with emotions, not least in relationships between people and things: the unpleasant red-pen corrections, the expectations resting in the welcoming light of the computer screen every morning, the feeling of inquisitively leafing through a new thesis, the tedium of yet another workday, and the pride felt when leaving a newly published essay on the desk of a colleague.

The microphysics of the working day is connected to feelings of acceptance and isolation, of either being a success or a failure, satisfied or dissatisfied. In order to deepen the study of such phenomena we need to develop ethnographic tools to capture what George Downing (2000: vii) called 'body micropractises'. By that he refers to our capacity to recognize an emotion, allow it to develop or be converted, using it as a lens to investigate the actual situation, and perhaps later being able to put what is happening into words. This competence—a kind of social capital—can not only vary according to different feelings, but also between individuals and cul-tural contexts. When expectations are vague in an otherwise regulation-controlled organization, it's a matter of being sensitive as to how behaviour and situations can be interpreted. Intuition is not only an underrated ability, but is also a useful resource in acclimatizing to university life.

The specific academic structure of feelings also functions as a subtle mechanism of exclusion. The female political science PhD students did not feel at home with the male and self-assured style of seminar discussions, but instead felt marginalized and silenced, in the same way as many working-class students find it hard to cope with the power play of irony.

The indirectness of emotions can also be especially problematic for many women who have been socialized into the sharing of emotions as a way of creating intimacy and trust in social relations. At university, they are told that 'this is not the way we do it here'. Don't be emotional.

We have argued that emotions characterize university life in two major ways. The first is the connection between person and achievement. Ardent inquisitiveness is sublimated in scientific work and explains much of the enthusiasm that is released in research. Commitment promotes job satisfaction but can also lead to vulnerability and disappointment when people don't feel that they have been adequately recognized or recompensed. We were already aware of the significance that scholarly achievement has for an individual's personal sense of worth, but our study has made this even more evident. The important role played by prestige and esteem is another case in point, as is the fear of being forgotten.

The second way is that we move in a world where people are constantly being ranked and scrutinized. The longing for public recognition in a system where colleagues both compete and judge each other can create dangerous situations in a workplace that many do not even think about. The idealism and joy of what is being undertaken makes research into something other than an ordinary job. The freedom to decide your own working tasks and pace are exceptional, although this same freedom carries with it a heavy responsibility to be innovative and creative. Many have high ambitions in an occupation that demands self-government, and the risk of failure in the face of continuous competitiveness is great. It is not only about science. The slightest routine is governed by a variety of diffuse achievement demands.

To survive and cope in an organization with such a high status in society as a university, it is important to understand the role that emotions play in that context and how the everyday paradoxes are dealt with. The gap between the openness that should characterize academic activity and the indirectness and vagueness that also exist in the encounter between colleagues hinders the realization of academia's more grandiose aims. Wrong gender or social background may make you feel ill at ease in the world of university and may also be an obstacle in correctly interpreting other people's expectations, or prevent you from being a fully fledged member of that community. There is therefore every reason to allow emotional life to be a central aspect in the analysis of how academic culture is both upheld and transformed.

References

Barbalet, J., ed. (2002), *Emotions and Sociology,* Oxford: Blackwell Publishing.

Becher, T. (1989), *Academic Tribes and Territories: Intellectual Enquiry and the Cultures of Disciplines,* Milton Keyes, UK: Open University Press.

Bloch, C. (2002a), Følelser og sociale bånd i Akademia, *Dansk sociologi,* 4: 43–61.

Bloch, C. (2002b), 'Managing the Emotions of Competition and Recognition in Academia', in J. Barbalet, (ed.), *Emotions and Sociology,* Oxford: Blackwell Publishing.

Bloch, C. (2003), 'Følelsernes skjulte spil i Akademia', in L. Højgård and D. M. Søndergård (eds), *Akademisk tilblivelse. Akademia og dens kønnede befolkning,* Copenhagen: Akademisk Forlag, pp. 121–59.

Bourdieu, P. (1984/1996), *Homo Academicus,* Stockholm: Symposion.

Dixon, T. (2004), *From Passions to Emotions. The Creation of a Secular Psychological Category,* Cambridge: Cambridge University Press.

Downing, G. (2000), 'Emotion Theory Reconsidered', in M. Wrathall and J. Malpas (eds), *Heidegger, Coping and Cognitive Science,* Cambridge, Mass.: The MIT Press.

Ehn, B., and Löfgren, O. (2004), *Hur blir man klok på universitetet?* Lund: Studentlitteratur.

Fineman, S., ed. (2000), *Emotion in Organizations,* London: Sage.

Frykman, J., and Löfgren, O. (2005), 'Känsla och kultur', *Sosiologi idag* 35(1):7–34.

Garber, M. (2001), *Academic Instincts,* Princeton, N.J.: Princeton University Press.

Gerholm, L., and Gerholm, T. (1992), *Doktorshatten. En studie av forskarutbildningen inom sex discipliner vid Stockholms universitet,* Stockholm: Carlssons.

Henriksson, M., Jansson, M., Thomsson, U., Wendt Höjer, M., and Åse, C. (2000), 'I vetenskapens namn: Ett minnesarbete', *Kvinnovetenskaplig Tidskrift,* 1: 5–25.

Hillman, J. (1991), *Emotion. A Comprehensive Phenomenology of Theories and Their Meanings for Therapy,* Evanston, Ill.: Northwestern University Press.

Ong, W. J. (1982), *Orality and Literacy. The Technologizing of the Word,* London: Routledge.

Rooijakkers, G., and Meurkens, P. (2000), 'Struggling with the European Atlas. Voskuil's Portrait of European Ethnology', *Ethnologia Europea,* 30(1):75–95.

Schoug, F. (2004), *På trappans första steg. Doktoranders och nydisputerade forskares erfarenheter av akademin,* Lund: Studentlitteratur.

Williams, M. D. (1993), *An Academic Village. The Ethnography of an Anthropology Department,* Ann Arbor, Mich.: Privately published.

Williams, R. (1977), *Marxism and Literature,* London: Oxford University Press.

Villius, H. (1991), 'En enkel Uppsala-Lund', in G. Blomqvist (ed.), *Under Lundagårds kronor. Femte samlingen,* vol. 2, pp. 394–405, Lund: Lund University Press.

Voskuil, J. J. (1996–2000), *Het Bureau,* vols 1–7, Amsterdam: G. A. van Oorshot.

The Cartesian Divide of the Nation-State
Emotion and Bureaucratic Logic

Don Handelman

Prologue: May 1967, On the edge of the town of Netanya, Israel

After breakfast in the institute where I am living and studying Hebrew, I board the crowded, clanking bus to the bank, to change British pounds into Israeli lirot. The excitable to the stolid. Three clerks, a line of metal folding chairs, and forms, many of them. As the first client moves over to the second clerk, the first sitting in line goes to the first clerk and the rest of us stand, almost synchronized, and move over one seat. From clerk to clerk, each with mounds of paper and a host of stamps standing like chessmen, to be moved strategically from form to form, adding, deducting, checking, checkmating the client over to the next clerk. From seat to seat we stand, move over, sit. Endgame, toppling under paper, spewed onto the pavement melting in the sun. Where in heaven's name do they keep all that paper, tripled, quadrupled, stacked in packets, packed in racks, racked on shelves, shelved ... somewhere, more likely under the earth. Huge underground storage vaults crowded to their metal ceilings with paper, silent, orderly, stamped into submission. The paper substrate of the Zionist State, the textual foundations of its pioneering subjects.

During the afternoon at the institute we dig trenches. When are we? Some ten days from the sixth of June, the outbreak of the 1967 Israeli-Arab War. Where? One kilometer from the sea, eight kilometers from the Jordanian town of Tulkarem. Trenches are our shelters if we are caught outside during an air attack. Holes in the ground. The Straits of Tiran are closed. Arab armies are massing on all the borders. Nearby, earth-moving machines are excavating a large open-air pit, the air-raid shelter of the neighborhood. My parents in Canada mail, call, telegram. Come home. War is coming. Please. Never, I reply, so long as my people, the Jewish people who have endured so much, are under dire threat in their homeland, the only place on the face of the earth that takes them in without question. The Jewish State must survive. Amazing. I've never been a Zionist. Israel is not an ideal. I'm here to collect material for my PhD thesis in Social Anthropology at the University of Manchester.

The institute is three-quarters empty; and we, a small motley crew, dig trenches that afternoon in a land besieged.[1] A couple of families who somehow managed to leave the Soviet Union. A British batchelor come to join his sister. The British bride of a Yemenite Jew, an officer in the standing army. A family from South Africa and another from Zimbabwe. A few American families, including one of evangelical Christians from the Ozarks, come to farm the desert and await the Second Coming. Their son has brought his prized possession, a Harley-Davidson 1000 cc., whose roar is a match for any two local buses in tandem, a messiah trumpet on wheels. And Rachel and David, American flower children of the 1960s, and their two small children. Sweet, easy people. Rachel is a child-survivor of Auschwitz. Digging, Rachel begins weeping. Weeping, keening, inconsolably. Sitting on the ground, crouched over, body heaving. Sobbing, crying that she can't go through this again, not again, can't put her children through this, again the Holocaust about to rend Jews to shreds, even here, here in the defended land. Between trench and terror, where to run? David is beside himself, utterly embarrassed. Yet we all feel the poignant edge of the precipice as we scrabble for footholds on the suddenly uncertain national surface that promises Zionist redemption to the Jewish few. As we open the earthen flesh of the motherland that may well enfold us. Sooner than expected. Inevitably, of course. Naturally.

I, all of us, I believe, were moved deep within ourselves, full of fellow feeling for one another and for the Jews we met, full of desire to do (something), our feelings bubbling now and then onto our surfaces, and, so, emotional encounters with others, knowing somehow that we were connected to each other through our insides, from deep (again!) within ourselves. These feelings and emotions are easy to summate and label (as patriotism, as nationalism, as love of country, as the readiness for self-sacrifice, as fear and hatred of the enemy, as feelings of togetherness), but not easy to delineate from one another (while it is not clear that they should be categorized, classified, catalogued). They were inside and outside the embodied self, transcendent in their embrace, yet stringing embodiment with thrumming rhythms that came from within, yet resonating between persons, amplifying, even beyond bearing. Each of us enfolded within ourselves, each of us enfolded within one another. Feelings and emotions larger than life, dominating, tiny, cuddly, needing to be caressed, protected, lest they flee—where throat catches, where breath stops, where tears come from, where eyes see themselves seeing. Above all (yet interior to all), fuzzy in their penumbras (and perhaps in their cores), and, so, filling space-time, itself ambiguous.

A day in May, in a miniscule corner of a modern nation-state, where I cross back and forth between an institution epitomizing and exuding the machinic assemblages of bureaucratic logic and a setting pervaded by a sense of coming war in which emotions of the national are embodied by and envelop all. *Ratio* is external, external to the body, natural to the mind; emotion is interior to the body, indeed natural to it. Bureaucratic logic and national emotion are so distant from one other in their epistemic premises, indeed antagonistic, yet each is crucial to the existence of the

State, depending on them both. So different, yet their copresence is utterly taken for granted by denizens of nation-states, without questioning how they coexist. Their split is consequential for how the modern state survives and problematic in how it tries to join this dualism of *ratio* and feeling. The problematic is ontological for the modern state, and this needs foregrounding and explication through Descartes, Durkheim, Weber, before turning to Israel, and to macro-level and micro-level attempts to generate the solidariness of this nation-state.

In the genealogy of the modern European state the ideas of Thomas Hobbes are often discussed as seminal to the creation of the monolithic state, the *Leviathan* (1968 [1651]). The formulations of Rene Descartes, by contrast, are seminal for European thinking on cognition and personhood but usually are not discussed as significant for modern state formation and politics (cf. Jenkins 2005). Nonetheless, I want to suggest that the European nation-state refracts Descartes' ideas that were not overtly political, yet that have had a profound influence on the ethos of modern times and modern state.[2]

Cartesian Dualism and the Nation-State

Cartesian dualism refers to the deep split in Being, which he wrote of as that of mind and body, of mind governing body, of body subjected to mind. It is this split in Being and its historical consequences that are crucial, rather than whether Descartes himself was a political thinker (the common view, cf. Skinner 2001). Skinner finds in Descartes' thought the 'birthpangs of the modern,' with its tensions and contradictions (Skinner 2001: 77–78). The split in Being should be recognized in the modern nation-state in which it is so deeply embedded, divided within itself between governance and administration on the one hand and nationhood and nationalism on the other. The split is experienced as one between Reason and Passion: such that governance and administration are analogous to the Reason of the Cartesian mind and nationalism to the Passion of the Cartesian body. The ontology of the split itself endures, with concomitant difficulties of organizing and integrating its dividedness.

Descartes and other adherents of Mechanical Philosophy understood the body as a machine, dehumanized, an automaton devoid of mentation and identified with nature and therefore with the instincts and their emotion. As Federici (2002: 15–16) points out, 'in the Cartesian model of the person is the same centralization of the functions of command that, starting from the 17th century, increasingly characterized the new form of the state. As the task of the state was to govern the social body, so the mind became sovereign in the new personality.' In my understanding, the ontic divide of Human Being came more and more to split the State in the era of Enlightenment, reaching its apex in the formation of nation-states in the eighteenth and nineteenth centuries. This split cuts through a variety of states, totalitarian and liberal alike, though they relate differently to it. European nation-states of the modern era were formed with the ethos of Cartesian division within them. In a sense these states formed around the divide, which became sewn within their modes of organization.[3]

In the modern era, machines (in factories, in armies) and machine-like social organization (in bureaucracies, factories, educational institutions, armies) increasingly make order (see Kern 1983; Rabinbach 1992). The (Deleuzian) machinic qualities of Reason (divorced from Passion) inform what I am calling bureaucratic logic and drive the infrastructures and governmentalities of the modern state. The Passions nevertheless are essential to the holistic integrity of the nation-state, not only through conflict with other states but also in relation to itself. (These problematics were recognized with clarity by Louis Dumont 1986). If anything, the divide between Reason and Passion in European states deepened during the vicious years of the twentieth century. Israel, founded in 1948, is a lineal descendant of the catastrophes of this divide, and undoubtedly a child (albeit a bastard one) of Europe.

Effervescent Emotion and Bureaucratic Logic in the Cartesian Divide

Durkheim and Weber, themselves citizens of nation-states whose members lived the divide between Reason and Passion, contribute to our understanding of this split, without quite relating to it. Instead each brings to the fore one or the other side of the divide. In *The Elementary Forms of Religious Life,* Durkheim (2001 [1912]) put forward the idea of (social) effervescence, central to the emotions of nationalism. In the *Theory of Social Organization* (1964: 329–340), Weber put forward the idea of rational-legal authority, which became a cornerstone of theorizing bureaucratic organization. In terms of the Cartesian divide, effervescent emotions are the Passions of the national in the nation-state, while rational-legal authority goes hand in hand with bureaucratic logic, the Reason of state infrastructure. The difficulties of joining and articulating these sides of the divide can produce either or both as extreme and out-of-control.

One of Durkheim's great concerns was how the French State, with its variety of cultural groups, with peasants being made into Frenchman (Weber 1976), could be held together. In no small way he projected his worries onto far-away so-called primitive societies, like that of Australian Aborigines (Richman 2002: 63). Through this trajectory he developed his theory of religion with its sacralization of the profane, and the *conscience collective,* given force especially through ritual, with its especial capacities for representations of the social whole, including its distinctions of sameness and difference (Ramp 1998: 140). Ritual generates *effervescence,* itself crucial to the strengthening of group boundaries and to the forming of group solidarity through the arousal and cathection of emotion. Without collective emotion, without this Durkheimian collective transcendence, there is no group-ness and therefore no group—in European terms, there is no nation and no national.

In Durkheim's usage, effervescence refers to passionate energies that may well produce exaltation, transporting persons outside themselves. Each person becomes 'the group incarnate' (a potential of *representation,* in the French sense of the term), and 'the most mediocre and inoffensive burgher is transformed into a hero or an executioner' (Durkheim 2001: 158; see also 163–4, 285). Effervescence enables 'society to become conscious of itself and sustain its feeling of itself with the necessary degree of intensity,' as a natural product of social life (Durkheim 2001: 317). Effervescence *is* emotion, such that each person incarnates the group, and therefore persons together are the group, incarnated in each and in all together. Durkheim thought of effervescence as transcendent and encompassing.[4] Within the Cartesian divide, effervescence is Passion, not Reason.

In my terms, collective effervescence *totalizes* the emotions, enabling them to swell and fill space/time. Jean-Paul Sartre (1948: 52) argues that 'emotion is a certain way of apprehending the world.' It is 'human reality itself in the form of emotion' (1948: 17), and so, human reality directed towards, into, the world, through (I add) vectors that totalize all in their path. These vectors are transdimensional, permeating those parts of our selves that, as Katz (1999: 315) comments, are just beyond our reach or always behind ourselves.

Sartre contends that emotion transforms the world, reconstituting it, absolutely, massively (Sartre 1948: 58; see also Solomon 1981: 223–4).[5] In a Cartesian world, emotion in its totalizing destroys those structures that would reject it and thereby reduce it to the exactness of Reason. The connectivity forged by emotion is felt as organic, growing deep within and among selves, therefore as authentic and true, and so, perhaps primordial. Emotion turns the person inside-out, so that totalizing feeling-states are evident on persons' exteriors, yet felt as their interiors, such that it is their interiors that are totalized together, rather than their exteriors. Therefore collective effervescence is felt as intimate. This trajectory of emotion, no less Durkheimian than effervescence as transcendence, indexes the intimate sharing of solidarity.

Katz argues that emotions metamorphose narrative themes, giving them new visible forms, dramatically, emphatically. Emotions, then, turn back on the self, 'reflexively amplifying and giving added resonance to the transcendent meanings of situated action' (Katz 1999: 332), a kind of auto-affection (Terada 2001: 24–25). Well and good for the appearance of emotion in the kinds of face-to-face interaction Katz discusses. For our purposes here, I prefer to say that the effervescence of nationalism (like that generated by ritual and religion) fuses together the interiority of feeling-tones and textures, the exteriority of emotion, and transcendent meta-themes and narratives. The totalizing effervescence of emotion is crucial to ethnogenesis and to the ongoing renewal of the nation and the national. But totalizing emotion need not be wild, exhilarating, uplifting. In relation to the national, totalizing emotion may be suffused with suffering and sadness, especially when this is linked to sacrifice for the common good, especially self-sacrifice, the conscious preparedness to sacrifice oneself (see Handelman 2004; Marvin and Ingle 1999; Renan 1996 [1882]). Durkheimian effervescence amplifies and magnifies the fusing capacities of emotion. Yet the effervescence of the emotional is not a phenomenon to be defined precisely and exactly. It is deeply and broadly *sensuous,* and in a Cartesian world it does not exist through mind-work, but only through its own doing, its practice, *while* it is being done. Emotion may be reflected upon, but unless it is being done all over again, it is beyond the reach of mind-work.

The Cartesian divide between mind and body, the rational and the embodied, Reason and Passion, is reproduced powerfully in the modern State in the differences between nationalism and emotion on the one hand, and bureaucracy and rationality on the other. Modern European states could not have survived without attending assiduously to the nurturance of the national while depending ultimately on the functioning of bureaucratic infrastructure. The State itself is in a way the uneasy trade-off of the two sides of the Cartesian divide.

More than any scholar of his time, Max Weber developed the conceptual significance of modern bureaucracy. Through the rational-legal type of authority, Weber brought to state-formation the foundation of bureaucratic institution and infrastructure. Weber, a German nationalist and patriot, was impressed and more than a little worried by the modern bureaucratic form and its effecting capacities. Elsewhere (Handelman 2004: 19–42) I argue that rational-legal institutions organized through this depend for their qualities on the kind of logic I call 'bureaucratic'. Bureaucratic logic generates lineal classification. Weber's understanding of rational-legal authority implicitly depended on the premise of lineal classification.

Lineal classification is a highly prevalent mode of ordering by sorting any manner of contents into categories, and of relating categories to one another. This is a way of generating and organizing a classification of individuals, groups, or things. Here, it is sufficient to say that a given level of lineal classification is composed of n number of categories, each of which contrasts with and excludes all others on the same level. All of the categories on a given level of abstraction are the equivalents of one another. This logic does not produce dichotomous distinctions. A scheme of classification can have n number of categories on any given level. However the logic prefers that a given item be placed in one and only one of the existing categories on a given level of classification, and therefore that it be excluded from all other categories on that level.

Such classification discourages overlap and permeability. Its metier is precision in making distinctions of difference, of the tiniest and greatest of magnitudes. The classifications themselves are more mathematical-like in their interior connectivities and applications, than they are textural and sensuous. Bureaucratic logic generates lineal classifications that can be applied to and used to process and reshape any and all phenomena. Any social phenomenon can be taken apart, fragmented, reshaped, or changed in other ways, and reinserted into social life. In principle, bureaucratic logic need not respect the integrity of any social phenomenon, any group, any relationship. Bureaucratic logic creates through division, distinction, separation, specification.

The machinic qualities of bureaucratic logic are pervasive in state institutions that acutely compact and concentrate lineal classification—the bureaucratic, the legal and judicial, the police, the military, and most educational setups that are organized through categorical classes based on age and examination.

Modern bureaucracies produce and modify lineal classifications of this kind in numbers without number; classifications that impact mundanely on members of the State in the most ordinary and extraordinary of ways. The production and operation of such classifications are expected to be devoid of the influences of emotion and feeling; or to be managed with emotion that is even in tone and texture, and therefore compatible with mind-work (cf. Graham 1999: 149ff.). Those who make lineal classifications are expected to use rational criteria that can be explicated and enumerated. These criteria are transcendent, if not universal, uncontaminated as much as possible by Passion. In a nutshell, this is a profound dilemma of the modern State, stretched on tenterhooks over the disjunction between the totalizing emotionality of nationalism and the bureaucratic logic of governmentalities.

In the founding of Israel there is deep existential angst. The international legitimation for this state was given by the United Nations in a historic vote of the General Assembly in November 1947. The state officially appeared on the world horizon at that point. Yet just as the United Nations voted for the creation of the state, so in the future, hypothetically, it could withdraw its legitimization and receive backing for this decision from an international supreme tribunal of some sort. In other words, just as bureaucratic logic makes available a category of existence, so too this can be reshaped and withdrawn by acts of will, altogether an unstable base on which to rest the hopes and dreams not to speak of the lives of the Jewish people. It would be far more certain for Israeli Jews to depend on themselves, to root this dependence in the national, the primordial, and to infuse this with emotion, and at the same time, to modify and reduce the influence of bureaucratic logic in matters pertaining to the survival of the Jewish people in their land.[6] The presence of nationalism is desired, if not officially then in performance, in institutions and practices that are expected to function through rationality and objectivity in making and filling numerous social classifications.

Two phrases, ubiquitous in the language of Israel's legal, political, and educational establishments, and in its mass media, illustrate the divide between national emotion and bureaucratic logic. One is that Israel is 'a Jewish and democratic state'; and the other, that Israel is 'a state of law and order' (*medinat chok veseder*). Consider the first phrase. Given the linearity of language, the order of sequencing is significant. The sequence, Jewish and democratic, is not by happenstance. It is a statement of value, enshrined in Israel's Declaration of Independence. Israel is first and foremost a national entity, a Jewish State, one which the Nation of Israel (*am yisrael*), the Jewish People, makes its home. This is the emotional cathexis: Israeli Jews and the Jewish State. That some twenty per cent of Israel's citizens are not Jews, are mainly Palestinians, is an accident of history, a matter to be worked out through participation in Israel's democracy, in which every citizen is equally enfranchised. That some three and a half million Palestinians in the West Bank and Gaza have been occupied since 1967, have no civil rights to speak of, are usually under autarchic military administration, is treated largely as an epiphenomenon of history, to be righted (indeed, *righted*) either by unfathomable political processes or by Jewish religious messianism. Citizenship and its absence are perceived as legal and administrative matters which may have to be handled properly in a State of law and order, but which arouse little emotion. Emotionally, the Jewish People take precedence over democratic government in the Jewish State.

More than this, the term, Jewish, is not understood to include the term, democratic. In relation to the term, Jewish, democratic is closer to mind-work, to a lineal taxonomy of social order necessary to exist juridically in the wider world of Western states. By contrast, the term, Jewish, opens into Judaism, into historical consciousness, into mythical cultural topologies, into the depths of shared identity, and in religious terms, into shared blood, into essential bodily-spiritual substance.[7] In many respects, the term, Jewish, is closer to body-work; and the phrasing, a Jewish and democratic state, reproduces to no small degree the Cartesian divide within the State.

The second phrase, Israel as a state of law and order, invokes the bureaucratic infrastructures of the State, organized through rational, lineal classifications, in which every category and its contents are in their proper location. This side of the Cartesian divide is more austere, more an unemotional grid that imposes the order of social control on a wide variety of individuals and groups, pushing them in place and keeping them in their place.

The State administrates as 'a state of law and order', and commemorates and celebrates as 'a Jewish State'. 'Democracy' wanders between the two, somewhat homeless, sometimes taking on the coloration of the first, rarely of the second. No less, citizenship, the instantiation of democracy in the rights and obligations of the individual member of the State, is recognized in the first and virtually excluded from the second, unless citizenship is made national (Handelman 2004: 43–51). Yet citizenship is made national only through emotional cathexis.[8] Once this occurs, bureaucratic logic is infused with emotion, and citizenship shaped by passion.[9] But it is the bureaucratic/legal category, citizenship, that is shaped this way, still stringently and absolutely distinguishing between those who are in and those who are not, those who belong and those who do not. In this way, bureaucratic logic is imbued with emotion in its classifying practices, and these practices are infused with emotions of authenticity that feel primordial because they are felt from within. In such conditions, the generation of solidarity depends upon infusing categories that are products of bureaucratic logic with passions of the national and nationalism.[10]

I now discuss two ways of generating solidarity. The first addresses the accomplishment of solidarity on the macro-level of Israel, and the second, on that of the micro. Though the second is only in part directed towards national solidarity, its vector can be directed easily and fully in this direction. Both cases address the sub-texts of the Durkheimian/Weberian problematic: how a modern state holds together despite its in-sewn divide between the passionate and the dispassionate.

Macro-Solidarity: Emotion, National Days and Rhythms of Time

After independence, the state promulgated three Days to commemorate and cele-brate its existence. None of these Days heightened citizenship. Nor did they heighten the institutional infra-structure of the state, nor reason, nor mind.[11] The dates of the Days were according to the Hebrew calendar. This synchronized them with the an-nual cycle of Sabbaths and traditional holidays. The choice of the people who did this work was to heighten the emotions of Jews, who would be totalized in relation to nation, nationalism, body, national body, and the State as the Jewish State. The three Days were planned as annual occasions to generate emotional enthusiasm for the Jewish national. Caught in the Cartesian divide, the Days were largely separated from Reason and devoted to Passion.

The Days were connected to one another. Once Independence Day was promul-gated, Memorial Day for the war dead was made the day prior. The linkage between these two Days was made so tight, that the end of Memorial Day occurs during the ceremony that opens Independence Day. The third Day was devoted to remembering the Holocaust, today perceived as foundational to the creation of the state. Holocaust Martyrs and Heroes Remembrance Day was positioned seven days before Memorial Day. Seven days are the period of the *shivah,* the seven days of mourning following a death. Two of the three Days are devoted to mourning and commemoration, echo-ing Ernest Renan's (1882) comments that suffering and sacrifice unify the national more than does joy.

The sequence of the three days is one of historical narrative. The murder of the Jews of Europe during the Second World War was followed by Israel's War of Inde-pendence, understood by Israeli Jews as a great victory, hard-won at the cost of many lives. The Palestinians were left with the bitter taste of the *Naqba,* the Catastrophe. The Nazis undertook the extermination of all Jews. Within this deepest, dankest pit of the soul, all light and warmth were extinguished. This was the lowest point of Jew-ish existence. Yet even within this darkness there were lights here and there, sparks of armed Jewish resistance, the brightest of which was the Warsaw Ghetto Upris-ing. The official name of this Day reflects the sequencing within the Day itself and within the three Days: Martyrs and Heroes Remembrance Day—from martyrdom to heroism. As Jewish life and living were decimated in Europe, so the focus of the three Days shifts to Israel, to the heroic military struggle to defend the nascent state, to commemorating the loss of soldiers and other fighters in all of Israel's wars and innumerable military actions.

The temporal distance between Holocaust Remembrance Day and Memorial Day is that of the existential distance between Europe and Israel, at least in the Zionist vision of the new Jewish society that was to replace the desuetude of diaspora. So, too, there is no distance between Memorial Day for the war dead and Independence Day. The two Days whose locus is in Israel are mutually embedded, the sacrifices of the war dead directly enabling and accomplishing independence. The independence of the state is the apex of the sequence. But there is no apex without the struggle to clamber from the depths of the pit, out of the subterranean darkness into the light. The climb is historical; the historical here is metaphysical and cosmological. Despite Lyotard's (1984) and others' pronouncements that meta-narrative is dead, it continues to triumph in this region. The three Days enact the great meta-narrative of the Jewish State and People—from destruction to rebirth.

The sequence of the three Days is itself embedded in a spring sequence of Judaic holidays that practice emotionally the ancient salvational onset of Jewish history. Holocaust Remembrance Day is preceded by the holiday of Passover, celebrating the exodus of the Israelites from bondage in Egypt. From today's national perspective, the Exodus marked the beginning of freedom for the Israelite nation. Like the weekly Sabbath, all Jewish holidays begin with sundown and end with sundown. Movement during the twenty-four hour day is from darkness into light. Many holidays are narratives that begin with disaster or potential disaster for the Jewish people (marked, told, enacted on the holiday eve), ending triumphally or on a salvational note during daylight. On Passover Eve the story of the Exodus is narrated during a ritual meal, with each participant told to see himself coming out of Egypt. The narrative is one of maturation, and the same thematic is embedded in subtexts of the ritual meal.

At the beginning of the Passover meal, the head of the household divides the middle unleavened bread (*matzah*) of three into two unequal parts, and puts aside the larger of the two parts (the *afiqoman*). This will be the last food eaten in the meal, and it is necessary to conclude the ritual. Shortly after, the youngest child present recites the riddle-like 'four questions' that ask why this night (Passover Eve) is different from all other nights. Then follows the answer—in fact the entire narrative of the Exodus. During the reading the children 'steal' and hide the *afiqoman*. At the close of the meal, the head of household must bargain with the children over the ransom of the *afiqoman*. Just as the ritual unfolding of the answers to the riddle-like 'questions' tells of the maturation of the Israelites, so, too, this is evoked through the changing behavior of the children. The child who recites the 'questions' represents all children and is normatively bound in the immaturity of ignorance. In taking the *afiqoman,* the children demonstrate increasing autonomy, but without responsibility. Then, in reaching agreement on its return, the children show the sense of obligation of moral maturity in striking a contractual-like agreement with adults. Thus the ritual meal has a fractal-like structure, through which the structure of the whole is embedded in certain of its parts.[12]

The following seven weeks are in Judaism a period of mourning. This period is likened to the wanderings of the Israelites in the deserts of Sinai, without a home, rootless and imbalanced. These weeks of mourning are ended with the holiday of *Shavu'ot* (weeks), marking God's giving the Torah (the Ten Commandments) to the Israelites, who from then on are His people who follow His law.[13] The Israelites have matured together as a people. Their path is set towards the land of Canaan that God has promised to them—the uniting of people and place through time, the modern nationalist vision. Again a sense of the fractal, in how the national narrative of the Three Days, Holocaust to Heroism, Destruction to Redemption, is embedded in and synchronized with the ancient myth of the Exodus.

The temporal articulation among the three Days is laid out topologically. In 1949 the remains of Theodor Herzl, the visionary of the Jewish State, were brought from Vienna and reinterred in Jerusalem, on the summit of the mountain named in his memory. Downslope from Herzl's grave is a cluster of gravesites reserved for presidents of the state, prime ministers, and speakers of the Knesset. These graves are virtually continuous with the military cemetery, begun during the 1948 war, sloping down the northeastern side of the mountain towards urban neighborhoods. In 1953 a lower spur of Mount Herzl, jutting from the western slope of the massif, turning its face from the city towards the sea in the direction of Europe, was named the Mount of Remembrance (*Har HaZikaron*). On this more distant ridge, the national Holocaust memorial, Yad Vashem, was built. There the opening ceremony of Holocaust Remembrance Day takes place. Unlike the topographical continuity between the graves of Herzl, the presidents and prime ministers, and the military, until recently one had to leave this mount and take a circuitous route to enter Yad Vashem.

The temporal sequence of the three Days is embedded topologically in these spaces. Holocaust Remembrance Day, the first, is commemorated on a lower, more distant spur of the Zionist mountain, just as this Day is distanced temporally from those commemorating and celebrating the Jewish State. On the morning of Remembrance Day a commemoration for the war dead is held in the military cemetery, on the lower reaches of the main massif itself. That evening, as it has since 1950, the venue climbs to the summit to open Independence Day, with Herzl's tomb as the axial fulcrum of the ceremony. The heights are scaled spatially in the temporal order of Days, from destruction, through the struggle for renewal, to the pinnacle of triumph.

The three Days are the products of bureaucratic logic. So, too, the choice of each was the product of mind-work. The contents of each Day are planned by different state committees as lineal classifications whose categories are stuffed with relevant contents (Handelman 2004: 101–17). Yet taken together their sequencing has deeper national resonances, primarily emotional, generated through body-work.[14] This was not unexpected, but neither has it been fully understood through mind-work by Israeli Jews. The Zionist body responds to the order of the Days as to a disarmingly simple, yet moving musical composition of three notes, sounding from low to high (to which I return momentarily). But this resonating body is no less (perhaps more so) a Jewish one. The aesthetic is that of a Jewish 'natural' progression of emotion that is so intimately embedded in movement through myth, history, fragmentation, solidarity.[15] I am *not* saying that this progression is a metaphor for these movements and processes. *Nor* am I saying that it is an organizing trope. I am saying that it is a profound cultural impetus to the movement of time as *moral* progression, one sewing together time and the cohesion of the nation; and that in our time the Jewish State has tied the progression of time and the cohesion of the nation to the modern national, without understanding fully the implications of what was being done. This 'natural' progression of emotion is salvationist and redemptive, and easily tipped towards a vector of messianism (itself accentuated by the Cartesian divide).[16] In saying that this progression of emotion is 'natural', I emphasize that it indexes pain and suffering, sacrifice and transcendence, as integral to this movement from low to high. Though often diluted and side-tracked, living time in this way is imbued with a deep substrate of feeling, and feeling for the national. But this is minimally connected to mind-work.

The leadership of the state has insisted always that the national is rational, that the national is the means to the physical and spiritual unification of the people, the nation, and to their moral purification and renewal. Yet this attainment depends upon a metaphysic of Becoming—exile, return, redemption—and this temporal rhythm is akin to a musical scale of three ascending notes. The temporal rhythm, and so the narrative(s) it encodes, are felt first and foremost, existentially, emotionally, in the following ways.

The first note, Holocaust Remembrance Day, sounds the horrific destruction of European Jewry, the rupturing of Jewish humanity: the disconnection of all vital values, the uncoupling of all essential relationships, the dismemberment of all community and collectivity, of social body and human body leading inevitably to death. Through its absolute negation of the human, the Holocaust is ramified destruction on the cosmic scale, a huge death-world in Wyschogrod's (1985) phenomenology, organized teleologically to take all life deliberately from the living, and for Jewry, the experiencing of the primeval extinction of cosmos. Presence is exterminated, turned into absence; and the body-work of effervescent pain, sorrow, tears, pervades.

The second note, Memorial Day for the war dead, sounds the nullification of this chaos. Cosmogenesis remakes order, but through violence, primarily the violence of sacrifice, more specifically, that of self-sacrifice, the willingness to die so that someone or something else will live. The self-sacrifice is that of voluntary death in warfare against enemies who would rend the collectivity. Through self-sacrifice the national collectivity is reproduced in each of its members, in a whole/part relationship. The part dies in place of the whole, which lives on, indeed given new life. The collectivity lives through the *sparagmos,* the tearing apart, of its members. In principle, no modern nationalism has relinquished warfare. The national practices itself into presence through the memorializing of sacrifice. Absence is turned into presence through the body-work of memory and its effervescence, the pain of loss, yet ascending towards hope.

The third note, Independence Day, sounds the fruition of the living Zionist cosmos, the Jewish State. Presence fills the time/space of the collectivity with emotions of unity, solidarity, fellow-feeling. This practice of cosmogony echoes Zionist allegories of biblical and liturgical process, a story-line of Becoming, elemental to Zionist credo, taken for granted and practiced over and again in public and private acts, filling this world with meaning and significance whose in-forming is emotional. The rhythm is one of the maturation of the moral, through which the moral ordering of cosmos and emotion are linked intimately.

Though I cannot go into this here (see Handelman 2004: 136–142), this cosmological rhythm of the national is itself embedded in Judaic rhythm, through a variety of time units—in the biblical myth of Genesis, in the twenty-four hour day, in the duration of the week, in holidays like Passover and Shavu'ot, in the sequence of Torah commentaries during segments of the annual round of Sabbath prayer, and in other durations including the lengthiest, the eschatological. This ethno-rhythm of time in its secular and religious versions is pulsating and climactic, felt morally, moving continuously from low to high, and holding within itself impulsions from fragmentation to unification. The rhythm is lived existentially, is deeply felt as integral to being—the rhythm of sacrifice that embodies and revivifies the Jewish national. The existential rhythms of time, thrumming within the person at different levels and in different domains, make the attainment of the nation-state the high point of national narrative and history.

Micro-Solidarities: *Gibush* and Emotion

The level of primary groups in the nation-state is extremely important for the generation of nationalism. Primary groups are the building blocks of national solidarity. Intra-group solidarity within primary groups has been a prominent concern of Zionists since the early days of settlement in Palestine (see Katriel 2004). Youth movements, initially influenced by the German Blau-Weiss, the British Scouts, the Soviet Komsomol, and others, had by the 1930s developed their own ethos and style (Kahane 1997). The communal bonfire, circle dancing, group singing, heartfelt discussions, soul talk, the pre-state military organizations, and other modalities, wove young people together within the fabrics of communities. These groups were predominantly Eastern and Central European in origin and relatively homogeneous in terms of culture. They intensely prepared for and lived the national undertaking, not needing conscious concepts to describe just how group solidarity was generated. Comradeship and togetherness were come by common-sensically, as it were. This situation changed drastically with mass immigration from Muslim countries during the 1950s and 1960s, producing a much more heterogeneous Jewish population, with very mixed cultural premises.

From the perspective of the bureaucratic and political elites who ran the country, these newcomers had to be shaped into persons properly committed to the modern national of Israel. The two major domains through which this inculcation was done were education and the military. In the terms of this chapter, both domains were organized through bureaucratic logic and mind-work, and therefore it was doubly important to find matrices of organization that would systematically generate vectors of fellow-feeling and sentiment most amenable to be turned into ones of patriotism and nationalism. One of the strongest beliefs motivating Israeli educators has been that every child should be within frameworks (*misgerot,* sing. *misgeret*), and so, shaped by these framework until he is mature, mentally and emotionally (see Golden 2005). A child outside frameworks (like one who leaves school) is in danger of falling into wayward, deviant ways, of going astray and losing his or her patrimony and fruitful future.

Most Israeli Jewish children enter nurseries at age two or three, kindergartens at four, and remain in the school system in one or another stream until graduating at eighteen when, again, most are drafted into the army. Though educational frameworks limp in their effective inculcation of values, from their early ages children participate in numerous Judaic and national commemorations and celebrations that all in all have been effective in shaping them as proud nationalists in their feelings and outlook (see Handelman 2004: 55–90). Shaping children emotionally was done no less through inculcating groupness, so that the individual identified with the solidary group that, in a sense, encompasses him or her. More indirectly, on the micro-level of interpersonal behavior, this forming of groupness was no less significant for identifying with the nation as an imagined 'group' (in Anderson's [1983] sense of the idea), and so with the nation-state.[17] Shaping groupness overtly in terms of a particular conception seems to have begun during the late 1960s and early 1970s, primarily in schools but also in more select army units.

The conception is called *gibush,* translated as 'crystallization'. In select army units, *gibush* is a process of selecting new recruits by putting them through some days of trial and suffering together. Those who demonstrate desirable personal capacities, but no less who develop social relationships with one another, of cooperation, of willingness to sacrifice themselves, of putting the welfare of others above that of their own, crystallize together, and form the group. The others depart. The military educators who introduced the conception of *gibush* into the army were influenced by studies of primary groups in the Wehrmacht, by the writings of social psychologists like Janowitz and Stouffer, by the military historian, S.L.A. Marshall, and by the studies of the gestalt psychologist, Kurt Lewin (Levine).[18] When a crystallized group (*kvutza megubeshit*) emerged, it appeared as a *gestalt,* as the creation of a unified whole greater than the sum of its individual parts, such that the social entirety of the whole was grasped sensibly, sensuously, and simultaneously by all of its members.

As it occurs, gestalt has qualities of Durkheimian effervescence in that its occurrence is one of deeper feelings, of coming together, of holism. This may also include, interestingly enough, one of the ancient meanings of the Greek *katharsis*—a 'pruning' that is 'a *maturing* directed by channeling the motivations that cause *growth*' (Highland 2005: 155, my emphases), through which, one may argue, persons' feelings resonate with and modulate one another harmonically. As gestalt, *gibush* synthesizes emotion and cognition, so that the Cartesian divide is effaced, if momentarily, and neither mind nor emotion dominate or confound the other.[19] What seems impossible to accomplish at the level of modern nation and state, where either domination or confutation are pervasive, is accomplished at the level of primary groups. This seems to be the case in the widespread use of *gibush* in school classes.

Doing and practicing *gibush* in classes is intended to generate 'an emergent ... collective possessing properties that are not reducible to the properties of the individual students in it ...' (Katriel 1991: 13).[20] *Gibush* will be accomplished indirectly by a variety of activities done together, yet exactly *how* to do this is very difficult to specify— 'a state of *gibush* cannot be willed into existence' (Katriel 1991: 22). Crystallization can be encouraged, as a shaping of spontaneous life processes (1991: 28), but it cannot be invoked. Nonetheless, when crystallization is accomplished—togetherness, mutual involvement, caring, harmonization of difference—all the participants *feel* this. A class with a high degree of crystallization will have clearly demarcated boundaries, interior integration and inner strength (1991: 18) and so, more internal homogeneity. Katriel (1991: 29) argues that crystallization is a dynamic of solidification, of the ingathering of scattered, atomized particles that, in coming together, form interior relatedness and integration within which these particles become parts of the whole, the group.

Through crystallization the formation of the social person and the formation of society 'are spoken of in the same metaphorical language ... [suggesting] ... the possibility of the mutual articulation of the individual and the group as contrasted with the modern Western conception of the fundamental individual/society opposition ...' (Katriel 1991: 30). Crystallization is used also in describing the formation of togetherness in a wide variety of informal groupings. However, in the central domains of education and military, both foundational for the national projects of the nation-state, *gibush* is intended to form *within* bureaucratic infrastructures that are organized through bureaucratic logic. The positioning of this forming is then more at the service of the bureaucratic state as it nurtures the emotions of nationalism, while generally masking the fact that this takes place through the guidance of bureaucracies and their lineal logic. The dream of the politicians and bureaucrats who established the state was precisely the unity and solidarity that *gibush* can accomplish in practice, but that is so difficult to accomplish on the macro-level of the State, where the Cartesian divide institutionally alienates emotion and bureaucratic logic from one another, or confutes their relatedness.

On the other hand (if I may be permitted this dualism), the interior emotional textures of numerous small groups are formed through degrees of crystallization, and their emotional commitment to the nation-state is crucial to its survival. However, one of the grave threats to the State is that groups can and do crystallize in relation to the nation but not in relation to the State, shifting their emotional effervescence from the latter to the former.

Torquing Reason and Passion

The glories and tragedies of modernism are refracted through the Cartesian divide. The achievements of science, of mind untrammeled by emotion, is unquestioned. The tragedy of the modern nation-state, caught between reason and emotion, also is undeniable, though these are not the usual social-scientific terms of reference. There is no neat solution to the Durkheimian/Weberian problematic of how the modern nation-state holds together, so long as lineally organized infrastructures and national effervescence clash, subvert one another, or, as is often the case, hide behind one another, the one masking itself as the other.[21] During the twentieth century the Cartesian ravine between nationalism and its emotional effervescences and the bureaucratic logic that organizes state infrastructures has filled deeper and higher with the corpses of those who believed in the dominance of one or the other, those who failed to see how one masked itself and operated through the other, or how the uneven interaction between the two generated ongoing turbulence that continues to overwhelm ships of state,[22] while, of course, filling with the victims of all of these.

The modern State depends on *torquing* together the sides of this divide. The vector of bureaucratic logic shifts the State towards the mathematical, towards lineal topologies of separating and fitting together parts with the exactitude of sameness and difference, while governing these machinic processes through rationality, clarity, precision, control. By contrast, the vector of totalizing, effervescent emotion shifts the State towards the modern national, towards the romantic sublime (Weiskel 1976), combining a secular metaphysics of transcendence with nationalism, generating the intense arousing of emotion, their over-abundant penumbra of effervescence spilling over, uncontainable within lineal classification. The emotions of holism in the modern nation-state swell from within the bodies of people in place through time, deeply texturing the sensuous presence of the national through their dreaming. The State must join the two sides of the divide, yet does so without being able to predict emergent outcomes.

Torquing (Bunn 1981: 16–17) indexes the joining of phenomena where their jointure fits together only partially and therefore discontinuously. The result of torquing across the Cartesian divide is the opening of vortices of turbulence, uncertain, unpredictable in their consequences (cf. Cohn 1987). The separation of mind and emotion makes both potentially uncontrollable in relation to the other: the lineal, angular shaping of bureaucratic logic in torsion with the swerving, swirling, twirling wildness that is the 'machine' of desire generating emotions of the national, in their manifold textures of sameness and difference—race, ethnicity, identity, historicity. The modern State in search of cohesion and continuity survives its in-sewn Cartesian dualism through the anxious descent of its transcendent metaphysics, of the utopic imaginary of moral and social order, into the upsurging desire within synchronized bodies territorialized through time. Bureaucratic logic may constrict, strangle, choke off the emotionalism of the national, and the enthusiasm of the national may over-flow and swamp the neat borders and divisions made through bureaucratic logic. Driven into separation by Cartesian dualism, each vector grows through the adum-bration of its own poietic momentum.

The mind side insists that its doings (bureaucratic, juridicial, corporate, military) should be untrammelled by the body side, by emotion. Mind-work is the judge and brake of emotion. Nevertheless, emotion and nationalism cannot be separated, despite the claims of theorists of the liberal state. Therefore emotion is encouraged, to the point of common insistence in Israel that national emotion is undoubtedly rational at its core, since only the rationality of the modern (nation) state can protect and preserve the na-tion. The existential rhythms of time I have outlined, thrumming within the person, make the attainment of the nation-state the high point of national narrative and history, and bureaucratic logic routinely is put to work to accelerate nationalism, body-work and its emotions. In the modern nation-state there is no systemic auto-modulation of poiesis in the torquing together of Reason and Passion. Israel is a case in point.

As I write, emotional support for the Jewish settlers in Gaza and the West Bank grows and is energized by temporal rhythms, by the ethos of sacrifice for the collectiv-ity, and by messianic fervor that, given the Cartesian divide, is easily presented as the very heart, the emotional core, of the nation. And the army, the defender of the state and bureaucratic logic, is afraid of the army—its officer corps is filling with religious nationalists, who have their own grounds for crystallization. It is hardly coincidental that a recently published novel tells of a religious right-wing military coup, and that a religious right-wing Member of Knesset has asked that the book be banned ...

Epilogue: Late 1991, Jerusalem

Despite my wife's derision we sealed one room in our apartment, as the defence authorities instructed: thick plastic sheeting over the windows and door, the cracks caulked; a radio, water, dried fruit, gas mask kits. In the middle of the night when the keening of the neighborhood siren rose and fell and drilled us out of bed, we tumbled panic-stricken, hearts pounding, blood racing, into our protective enclave. Iraqi missiles were somewhere over Israel. The radio issued instructions.

Enter the sealed room. Close the door tightly. You are not to leave until instructed that it is safe to do so. Open your gas mask kit. Remove the gas mask. Fit the mask over your head. Do not remove the atropine injection unless instructed to do so.

Remain in the sealed room at all times. Leave your radio or TV in the sealed room on at all times. And some hours later, *Remove your gas mask. Return your gas mask to the gas mask kit. Close the gas mask kit. You may now leave the sealed room, but you are not to leave your dwelling. You may now leave your dwelling, but you are not to leave the building. You may now leave the building and enter the street.*

Effervescent fear, apprehension, solidarity, anger, pervading everyone, everywhere, the authorities orchestrating a symphony of movement within the deepest, intimate reaches of our homes. All, of course, for our own protection. Like ourselves, people in the city we knew obeyed these countrywide instructions for two or three days, before fully realizing, as my wife had predicted, that no missiles were to strike Jerusalem, for obvious reasons. Wittingly or not, the authorities had succeeded in deliberately synchronizing the movement of most of the population of the country, a rehearsing of simultaneous population control previously unknown. Bureaucratic logic amplifying and shaping emotion. One kind of torquing. One kind of shaping.

References

Anderson, B. (1983), *Imagined Communities: Reflections on the Origin and Spread of Nationalism,* London: Verso.

Aronoff, M. J. (1989), *Israeli Visions and Divisions: Cultural Change and Political Conflict,* New Brunswick, N.J.: Transaction Books.

Ben-Ari, E. (1998), *Mastering Soldiers: Conflict, Emotions, and the Enemy in an Israeli Military Unit,* New York: Berghahn Books.

Berezin, M. (1998), 'Enacting Political Identity: Public Rituals As Arenas of the National Self', *Rassegna Italiana di Sociologia,* 39(3): 359–86 (in Italian).

Berezin, M. (2001), 'Emotions and Political Identity: Mobilizing Affection for the Polity', in J. Jasper, J. Goodwin, and F. Polletta (eds), *Passionate Politics: Emotions and Social Movements,* pp. 83–89, Chicago: University of Chicago Press.

Biale, D. (1992), 'Zionism As an Erotic Revolution', in Howard Eilberg-Schwartz (ed.), *People of the Body: Jews and Judaism from an Embodied Perspective,* pp. 283–307, Albany: State University of New York Press.

Bunn, J. H. (1981), *The Dimensionality of Signs, Tools, and Models,* Bloomington: Indiana University Press.

Burkitt, I. (1998), 'Bodies of Knowledge: Beyond Cartesian Views of Persons, Selves and Mind', *Journal for the Theory of Social Behavior,* 28: 63–82.

Cohn, C. (1987), 'Sex and Death in the Rational World of Defense Intellectuals', *Signs,* 12: 687–718.

Connell, R. W. (1990), 'The State, Gender, and Sexual Politics', *Theory and Society,* 19: 507–44.

Csordas, T. (1993), 'Somatic Modes of Attention', *Cultural Anthropology,* 8: 135–56.

Dorries, M. (2001), 'Purity and Objectivity in Nineteenth-Century Metrology and Literature', *Perspectives on Science,* 9: 233–50.

Dumont, L. (1986), *Essays on Individualism: Modern Ideology in Anthropological Perspective,* Chicago: University of Chicago Press.

Durkheim, E. (2001), *The Elementary Forms of Religious Life,* Oxford: Oxford University Press.

Federici, S. (2002), 'The Great Caliban: The Struggle against the Rebel Body', *The Commoner,* 3: 1–29 <www.thecommoner.org> accessed 24 April 2005.

Fraenkel, E. (1969 [1941]), *The Dual State: A Contribution to the Theory of Dictatorship,* New York: Octagon Books.

Gavison, R. (1999), 'Jewish and Democratic?: A Rejoinder to the "Ethnic Democracy" Debate', *Israel Studies,* 4(1): 44–72.

Golden, D. (2001), 'Storytelling the Future: Israelis, Immigrants, and the Imagining of Community', *Anthropological Quarterly,* 75: 7–35.

Golden, D. (2005), 'Childhood As Protected Space? Vulnerable Bodies in an Israeli Kindergarten', *Ethnos,* 70: 79–100.

Graham, M. (1999), *Classifications, Persons and Policies: Refugees and Swedish Welfare Bureaucracy,* Stockholm: Department of Social Anthropology, Stockholm University.

Hacking, I. (2006), 'The Cartesian Body', *BioSocieties,* 1: 13–15.

Handelman, D. (1998), *Models and Mirrors: Towards an Anthropology of Public Events,* 2nd ed., New York: Berghahn Books.

Handelman, D. (2004), *Nationalism and the Israeli State: Bureaucratic Logic in Public Events,* Oxford: Berg Publishers.

Handelman, D., and Shamgar-Handelman, L. (1990), 'Shaping Time: The Choice of the National Emblem of Israel', in Emiko Ohnuki-Tierney (ed.), *Culture through Time: Anthropological Approaches,* pp. 193–226, Stanford, Calif.: Stanford University Press.

Handelman, D., and Shamgar-Handelman, L. (1993), 'Aesthetics versus Ideology in National Symbolism: The Creation of the Emblem of Israel,' *Public Culture,* 5: 431–49.

Herf, J. (1984), *Reactionary Modernism: Technology, Culture, and Politics in Weimar and the Third Reich,* Cambridge: Cambridge University Press.

Highland, J. (2005), 'Transformative Katharsis: The Significance of Theophrastus's Botanical Works for Interpretations of Dramatic Catharsis', *Journal of Aesthetics and Art Criticism,* 63: 155–63.

Hobbes, T. (1968 [1651]), *Leviathan,* Harmondsworth: Penguin Books.

Jenkins, L. (2005), 'Corporeal Ontology: Beyond Mind-body Dualism?', *Politics,* 25: 1–11.

Kahane, R. (1997), *The Origins of Postmodern Youth: Informal Youth Organizations in a Comparative Perspective,* New York: de Gruyter.

Katriel, T. (1991), 'Gibush: The Crystallization Metaphor in Israeli Cultural Semantics', in T. Katriel (ed.), *Communal Webs: Communication and Culture in Contemporary Israel,* pp. 11–34, Albany: State University of New York Press.

Katriel, T. (2004), *Dialogic Moments: From Soul Talks to Talk Radio in Israeli Culture,* Detroit, Mich.: Wayne State University Press.

Katz, J. (1999), *How Emotions Work,* Chicago: University of Chicago Press.

Kern, S. (1983). *The Culture of Time and Space, 1880–1918,* Cambridge, Mass.: Harvard University Press.

Lieblich, A. (1989), *Transition to Adulthood During Military Service: the Israeli Case,* Albany: State University of New York Press.

Linke, U. (2006), 'Contact Zones: Rethinking the Sensual Life of the State', *Anthropological Theory,* 6: 205–25.

Lyotard, J.-F. (1984), *The Postmodern Condition: A Report on Knowledge,* Manchester: Manchester University Press.

Marvin, C., and Ingle, D. W. (1999), *Blood Sacrifice and the Nation: Totem Rituals and the American Flag,* Cambridge: Cambridge University Press.

Rabinbach, A. (1992), *The Human Motor: Energy, Fatigue, and the Origins of Modernity,* Berkeley: University of California Press.

Ramp, W. (1998), 'Effervescence, Differentiation and Representation in *The Elementary Forms*', in N. J. Allen, W.S.F. Pickering, and W. Watts Miller (eds), *On Durkheim's Elementary Forms of Religious Life,* pp. 136–48, London: Routledge.

Renan, E. (1996 [1882]), 'What is a Nation?', in G. Eley and R. Grigor (eds), *Becoming National: A Reader,* pp. 41–55, New York: Oxford University Press.

Richman, M. H. (2002), *Sacred Revolutions: Durkheim and the College de Sociologie,* Minneapolis: University of Minneapolis Press.

Sartre, J.-P. (1948), *The Emotions: Outline of a Theory,* New York: Philosophical Library.

Shavit, Y., and Sitton, S. (2004), *Staging and Stagers in Modern Jewish Palestine: The Creation of Festive Lore in a New Culture,1882–1948,* Detroit, Mich.: Wayne State University Press.

Skinner, Q., (2001), 'Descartes's Paradoxical Politics', *Humanitas,* 14: 76–103.

Smooha, S. (1997), 'Ethnic Democracy: Israel As an Archetype', *Israel Studies,* 2(2): 198–241.

Solomon, R. C. (1981), 'Sartre on Emotions', in P. A. Schilpp (ed.), *The Philosophy of Jean-Paul Sartre,* pp. 211–28, La Salle, Ill.: Open Court.

Terada, R. (2001), *Feeling in Theory: Emotion after the 'Death of the Subject',* Cambridge, Mass.: Harvard University Press.

Walzer, M. (1985), *Exodus and Revolution,* New York: Basic Books.

Weber, E. (1976), *Peasants into Frenchmen: The Modernization of Rural France, 1870–1914,* Stanford, Calif.: Stanford University Press.

Weber, M. (1964), *Theory of Social and Economic Organization,* Glencoe, Ill.: Free Press.

Weiskel, T. (1976). *The Romantic Sublime: Studies in the Structure and Psychology of Transcendence,* Baltimore, Md.: Johns Hopkins University Press.

Wyschogrod, E. (1985), *Spirit from Ashes: Hegel, Heidegger, and Man-Made Mass Death,* New Haven, Conn.: Yale University Press.

Yiftachel, O. (1992), 'The Concept of "Ethnic Democracy" and Its Applicability to the Case of Israel,' *Ethnic and Racial Studies,* 15: 125–36.

Yuval-Davis, N. (1987), 'The Jewish Collectivity and National Reproduction in Israel', in M. Salman, H. Kazi, N. Yuval-Davis, L. al-Hamdani, S. Botman, and D. Lerman (eds), *Women in the Middle East,* pp. 61–93, London: Zed Books.

Notes

1. In Israeli Hebrew the Jewish immigrant is called *oleh,* one who ascends. One who emigrates is called *yored,* one who descends. At the time, one of economic depression, there were few new immigrants.

2. There is little point in arguing here that, after all, human being in reality is not constituted by nor practices living through dualism (e.g. Csordas 1993; Burkitt 1998; Linke 2006). My concern here is to point to just how deeply embedded is Cartesian dualism in selves, lives, and organizations in Western states, and how this dualism returns over and again in different domains of social living, despite the intellectual claims that dualism is truly, finally, dead (cf. Hacking 2006).

3. This is perhaps nowhere more present than in the passionate concern of nation-states with the reasoning of exactness in boundary-making and the moral expunging of impurities through science (on science, see Dorries 2001).

4. Durkheim considered the *conscience collective* to be 'the highest form of psychic life, the consciousness of consciousness'. As meta-consciousness, 'it encompasses all of known reality' (Durkheim 2001: 339–340).

5. Sartre understands this transformation as magical, irrational, when the road of reason is unalterably blocked. As Katz (1999: 346) comments, Sartre thereby reconstitutes the Cartesian dualism he purports to challenge.

6. Thus the Law of Return enables speedy citizenship for any and all Jews who emigrate to Israel, while making it extremely difficult for non-Jews to acquire citizenship. So, too, predictions of the future demographic ratio of Jews to Palestinians influences policy making and interpretations of rules. Numerous other examples could be adduced.

7. And into nationalism. See, for example, Biale (1992: 297); Yuval-Davis (1987).

8. See Connell (1990) on the 'structure of cathexis'.

9. Thus scholars debate whether Israel is a 'liberal democracy' or an 'ethnic democracy', and so forth. See Smooha (1997), Yiftachel (1992) and Gavison (1999).

10. See Berezin (1998). She (Berezin 2001) summarizes this as, 'Culture (nation) and rationality (state) fuse to create the nation-state.'

11. Each Day was entirely modular, a neat framework of ceremonies and other events, with exact beginnings and endings, units designed by bureaucratic logic.

The design of each Day and its prominent ceremonies was planned by committee. This had a lengthy history in the organized Jewish community of prestate Palestine (Shavit and Sitton 2004), and continued after the founding of the state, without altering the bureaucratic logic of planning. This was so for choices made about national symbols. See Handelman and Shamgar-Handelman (1990, 1993). For a brief discussion of the government's Ministerial Committee on Symbols and Ceremonies, relating to the early 1980s, see Aronoff (1989: 43–67).

12. Michael Walzer (1985) understands the narrative of the Exodus to be paradigmatic for revolutions of modernity.
13. This period of seven weeks of seven days each is 7 times 7 or 49, plus the first day of *Shavu'ot,* which equals 50, the number of the Jubilee and a formula of holistic completion in Judaism.
14. Every attempt to alter or change the order of the three Days has failed. The sequencing feels natural, and therefore right, and is profound in this respect.
15. This progression likely is a complex product of monotheism, becoming integral to Western theologies. Hence Walzer's argument, referred to earlier.
16. Thus, David Ben-Gurion, the first prime minister and guiding genius of statehood, made biblical prophets his guide towards secular, national redemption and utopic salvation.
17. Golden (2001: 28) points out, correctly, I think, that the Jewish nation is perceived not only as 'a deep, horizontal comradeship', in Anderson's terms, but as 'a deep, vertical comradeship, ordered through time.'
18. My thanks to Einat Bar-On Cohen for information from Ben Bar-On, Mordechai Bar-On, and Shaike Tadmor. There are numerous examples of military *gibush* in Leiblich (1989).
19. Crystallization does not refer to the self-formation of individual personalities, but it does index the formation of social personhood. So too, it does not refer to the emotions of the individual, but rather to 'social emotions' of togetherness (Katriel 1991: 28).
20. Katriel argues that *gibush* is a root metaphor, a metaphor to live by, in Lakoff and Johnson's terms. Ben-Ari (1998: 98), writing on the Israeli army, accepts the use of metaphor. I would consider this if metaphor were used here in a causal sense of generating connections through and in practice (Handelman 1998), rather than as value guidelines or models for living. Gestalt strikes me as more powerfully configuring the solidary social unit, simultaneously from its boundaries and its interior, its whole and its parts.
21. Thus, the National-Socialist efforts to shape a gemeinschaft state within one based on rational-legal values (see Fraenkel 1969 [1941]).
22. Cf. Herf (1984) on how Germans (whom he calls reactionary modernists) shifted technology from the realm of reason to that of emotional effervescence, contributing to the primacy of National-Socialist ideology and politics over rational means-ends calculations.

II
Love and Hate

–10–

Shifting Politics in Bedouin Love Poetry

Lila Abu-Lughod

I focus, in this chapter, on the emotions or sentiments associated with relations between men and women in a Bedouin community in Egypt's Western Desert, especially the discourses of "love." My argument proceeds by way of a Bedouin love story. The community of Bedouins about which I write are part of a group known as the Awlad 'Ali who inhabit the area along the Mediterranean coast of Egypt west of Alexandria into Libya.[1] I lived in this community from 1978 to 1980, visited once for a month five years later, and went back for five months of fieldwork in 1987. Until about thirty-five years ago, those still living in the Western Desert made a living mostly by herding sheep, growing barley, and organizing camel caravans to transport dates from the oases to the Nile Valley. Now they are involved in all sorts of activities, from the old one of raising sheep to the newer ones of tending orchards, smuggling, supplying construction materials, and speculating in real estate. They used to live in tents. Now most of them live in houses, although they still pitch their tents next to their houses and prefer sitting in the tents at least during the day. They used to ride on horses, camels, and donkeys; now they prefer Toyota trucks. Although sedentarizing, they still proudly distinguish themselves from the settled peasant and urban groups of the Nile Valley—the Egyptians—by their tribal organization and what they see as their superior morality. But, as I will discuss, even this is beginning to change.

Here is the love story. I was back in Egypt in 1985, visiting for the first time since my initial fieldwork the families I had lived with for almost two years. It was early in the morning of the last day I was there. My host, the head of the family, with whom I had lived as a sort of adopted daughter, was getting ready to drive me to Cairo to catch my plane. He rummaged around in the pockets of his various robes and vests, looked in his briefcase, and finally in exasperation asked his children, who were all standing around, if they knew what had happened to the cassette of Fathalla Aj-jbēhi. His eldest daughter sheepishly went and got it from the cassette player she and her sisters often secretly listened to when he was away. The kids put my suitcases in the trunk of his new Mercedes, I said my goodbyes, and we set off. As soon as we were on the desert highway, he turned on the tape deck and said that I had to listen to this tape. We listened. A man chanted, in a moving and pained voice, poem after poem of the type called the *ghinnāwa*.

My host listened raptly, interjected exclamations of sympathy at the end of some of the poems, and elaborated, with intense and obvious admiration, on some of the references in the poems. Among the poems were the following two:

> Patience is hard,
> for my heart, so freshly wounded ...

> wa'r 'alēh iṣ-ṣabr
> jarḥā jdīd māzāl khāṭrī ...'

> I'd figured, oh beloved, that distance
> would be a cure but it only made it worse ...

> niḥsāb yā 'azīz il-mōḥ yabgā lī dwā nādh zādni ...

My host explained that Fathalla, the young man reciting the poems (whose kinship relation to one of our neighbors he identified) had been in love with his paternal cousin and wanted to marry her. Their fathers had first agreed to it but then got into an argument with each other. The young woman's father decided to refuse to give his daughter to the young man. In despair and thinking that he might get over this more easily if he put distance between them, the man set off for Libya (where until recently many Bedouin men went looking for work). Some time afterward, the girl's father arranged to marry his daughter to someone else. When Fathalla heard the news, he composed and recorded these poems and sent the tape to the girl's brother, a cousin with whom he had grown up. Fifteen days after the wedding, when the bride came back to her family's household for the ritual postmarital visit, her brother played her the tape. She listened to it and when it was over, she gasped for air, fainted, and then fell over, dead.

This story tells us a great deal about the politics of emotion discourse in Bedouin society.

The Awlad 'Ali are tribally organized. For them, common descent through the male line and shared blood provide the primary and the only legitimate basis for binding people together. Paternal kin live together, share some property, pass it on, and go to social functions together. They are also expected to feel close. If blood bonds between paternal relatives, male or female, are privileged as the only basis of social relationships, then heterosexual or romantic love, even in its legitimate guise of marriage, although necessary for the reproduction of society and the perpetuation of lineages, is hard to deal with. It does not rest easily within this framework for social relations and is in fact a threat.

Love and the bonds it might establish between individuals are not just threats to the framework that orders social relations, but are also talked about as threats to the solidarity of the paternal kin group, something often noted in the literature on patricentered societies from traditional China to Zinacantan (Collier 1974; Wolf 1972). The Awlad 'Ali view sexual bonds and the bonds of agnation as competing. Even more importantly, sexual bonds are seen as threats to the authority and control of elder male relatives who represent the interests of the agnatic family group, control its resources, and make its decisions. At marriage, sons begin to have a small domain of authority of their own, and daughters leave the domain of authority of their father and kin.

The threat marriage represents is counteracted at every point by social and ideological strategies. The marital bond is undermined in numerous ways: Women retain close ties to their paternal relatives, senior male relatives control the choice of marriage partners, and sexual segregation ensures that husbands and wives spend little time together. Divorce is easy and polygyny possible. And the married couple is rarely economically independent. Love matches are actively discouraged. One man told me that the only way people who loved each other would be allowed to marry was if their elder male relatives or the girl's paternal cousins did not know. Women often told me that love matches always ended badly for the woman because she would not have the support of her male kin if her husband mistreated her.

I have argued that the cultural preference for patrilateral parallel cousin marriage is another such strategy (Abu-Lughod 1986). The Awlad 'Ali frequently marry first cousins or other cousins on the father's side and the male even has legal claim to his paternal uncle's daughter. This type of marriage may be upheld as the cultural ideal, because it provides a means of defusing the threat of the sexual bond in this social system; it *subsumes* the marital bond under the prior and more legitimate bond of kinship.

The moral code that prescribes modesty is the most effective means of undermining the sexual bond. If the threat to the social order can be made to seem a threat to the respectability or moral worth of the individual, then that order will be reproduced by the actions of individuals in everyday life. The modesty code ensures that even individuals who do not have as much stake in the system—like young men and especially women—will help perpetuate it, because their virtue or their standing as moral beings, as good persons, depends on denying their sexuality. As I hinted earlier, these sentiments of sexual modesty are situational. They are important to display only in front of certain people—the elder male agnates. So, sexual modesty must be seen as a form of deference to them. The moral sentiments of modesty are part of a discourse that sustains and perpetuates the particular social system and the power of certain groups within it.

Conversely, then, the immodest sentiments of "love" are subversive. To express them is subversive of the social order and defiant of those whose interests are served by this order. This element of defiance is made concrete in the story of Fathalla. In singing about his feelings of love, he was, in a sense, defying the authority of his paternal uncle, who had thwarted his desires and prevented him from marrying his cousin.

Because it carries subversive sentiments of love, one could consider the *ghinnāwa* the Bedouin discourse of defiance. There is plenty of evidence that poetry is in general associated with opposition to the ideals of normal social life. This type of poetry is considered un-Islamic. The pious shouldn't recite it or show any interest in it. It is also considered unrespectable. Even the term "to sing" can't be said in mixed-sex company without causing all-around embarrassment. People say that they are ashamed or embarrassed about singing in front of nonintimates, especially elders. Women told me never to share their poems with the men. And in the past, older men avoided public settings like weddings and sheep-shearing parties where young men usually recited this type of poetry. The most persuasive evidence of the oppositional character of poetry is who recites poetry and who avoids it. Although older men occasionally recite them, *ghinnāwas* are most closely associated with youths and women. These are the disadvantaged dependents who have least to gain in the system as structured.

The Cassette

One aspect of Fathalla's story I want to take up is the somewhat surprising fact that his love songs were on a cassette. I had thought, when I left Egypt after my first period of fieldwork in 1980, that the Bedouin *ghinnāwa* was dying out. The adolescents I knew did not sing or recite this type of poetry, nor did they seem particularly interested in it. They were beginning to listen to Egyptian radio, and it was from their mothers, aunts, and grandmothers, and sometimes from their fathers and a few young men, that I collected poetry. These adults offered one explanation for why poetry was dying out: They said that there were no longer any occasions for singing. There is a certain truth to their deceptively straightforward explanation to which I will return.

If, however, it was the ideology of the political system, with its value of autonomy, that lent positive valence to expressions of love as defiance, even when they came from below, then one would not be surprised to find such discourses dying as the Awlad 'Ali Bedouins' political autonomy was undermined. This has been going on for quite a while as the Egyptian state has sought, over the last 35 years, to introduce its authority into the Western Desert, a process that has been underway in Bedouin areas closer to the Nile Valley for 150 years or more. The Awlad 'Ali have developed an impressive array of strategies to resist, subvert, and circumvent the authority of the state, which they consider illegitimate. Since they are not fazed by guns, and prison sentences carry no stigma, it is even hard to intimidate them into good citizenship.

There is, however, one process that began in their region in the 1970s that, more effectively than government efforts to disarm them, school them, put them in the military, license and register them, is progressively undermining their resistance to the state: the gradual shift in their economic life from herding and commercial activities, including smuggling, to investment in land. Land reclamation efforts by the government are transforming some of their desert into agricultural land, which they are increasingly buying and relying on for a livelihood, if not actually farming themselves. Land along the coast, on the other hand, has become valuable for tourist development, and many of them are doing quite well selling beachfront property. They are also fighting with each other over this land, which was formerly tribally held rather than individually owned. With this involvement in land, the Bedouins have become enmeshed in the state's legal system, since they need to get titles and make claims through it.

This shift in the Bedouin political economy can be connected with what I see as a shift in the dialectic of deference and defiance in which love songs are deployed. As the economic basis of the tribal system erodes, and with it the political under-pinnings of the value of autonomy, the older reality of mutual responsibility within the family and lineage is changing. There used to be a complex division of labor, with resources managed by elders but not owned. Now private ownership puts tre-mendous control in the hands of patriarchs. Young men suffer, as I will discuss, but those most dramatically affected are women. They are now economically dependent on men, having little access to money, and their work is increasingly confined to housework. With the moral value of modesty still in force, these women who live in the new circumstances of sedentarized communities, where they are surrounded by neighbors most of whom are nonkin, must be *more* secluded, more often veiled, and less free to move around.

Older women comment on these changes, reminiscing about things they used to do that young women today cannot get away with—like having rendezvous with sweethearts and exchanging songs with men at weddings and sheep shearings.[2] But they are also convinced that they were more modest, a perception that I think relates to a sense that it was more self-imposed. They often complain that their sons, hus-bands, nephews, and grandsons harshly restrict the girls, not letting them go any-where. Girls, for their part, are beginning to complain that they feel imprisoned. The domestic political divide now runs along gender lines, whereas it used to be between elders on one side and women and young men on the other. All men have access to the market and increasing freedom of movement; all women do not.

This shift in political economy has implications for traditional love poems, which, as I have discovered, are not, after all, dying out. Bedouin love songs are taking on different meaning and force, having been given new life by the advent of the cassette. The Bedouins had said that songs were dying out because there were no occasions for singing. In a sense, they were right. By the time I first met them, in 1978, they were reciting love poems only in intimate social situations. As I later learned, how-ever, the most important forum for love songs had been weddings, at which young men and women had sung within earshot of and sometimes to each other.[3] Those kinds of celebrations had stopped by then, and the weddings I attended were sexually segregated. The women sang only songs of blessing, congratulation, and praise, and the men did nothing but sit around. Today, locally made cassettes—copied, re-copied, and sometimes sold for money—provide a new occasion for song, as does a new kind of wedding celebration coming into fashion. At this new wedding, attended by invited guests but also attracting a growing group of somewhat rowdy young men, the small-time stars of these low-budget commercial cassettes perform. Because of the public nature of these occasions, where, unlike in the past, "public" includes a wide range of nonkin and complete strangers, women are absent. They are also, out of modesty, absent from the recording sessions where tapes are made. They make no tapes and no longer sing in public. No longer having as much social and political support for defiance, the women also seem to be losing one of the means for it—love poetry.

The poems sung on cassettes and at *mīkrofōn* weddings seem now to be part of a discourse of defiance by young men against the more absolute authority and economic control of their fathers and paternal uncles. This is a period when, at the same time, young men are beginning to have more possibilities for independence from the kin group through wage labor and more knowledge than their fathers about the ways of the state through their experiences in the army and school. A new sort of generational conflict produced by these transitional circumstances is being played out partly in the language of love.

I had unexpected confirmation of the new use of "love" on my visit in January 1987, when I was listening with friends to one of the latest cassettes of popular Bedouin songs of a different genre. There was a long and somewhat humorous song about the tribulations of a young man whose father and uncle had arranged three terrible marriages for him with women he'd never met. The first woman turned out to be bald, the second dumb, and the third insane and violent to boot. In the final verse of his song the poet, speaking on behalf of all young men who have suffered the tyranny of such fathers and uncles, sings:[4]

> My warnings are to the old man
> who imprisons the freedom of youths
> who's forgotten a thing called love
> affection, desire, and burning flames
> who's forgotten how strong is the fire of lovers
> how strong the fire of lovers who long for one another
> What's exquisite is that they're afraid
> they say, any minute my prying guard will turn up
> oh my father's about to catch us

The relationship between love and freedom in this song is complex—because, although he does not want the elders to force loveless marriages on their children, the poet recognizes that what makes love exquisite is that it is stolen—it is against the authority of elder agnates. In other words, he wants the freedom to defy the elders a bit, a freedom he reminds them they used to want, but he does not reject the system as a whole or want to have love easy or open.

The continuity of form in love songs is consistent with this attitude. Unlike rock and roll, which some would argue played and plays a similar role in our society, the protests occur in an idiom that the elders can appreciate: the poetry they themselves love and must respect, given their own values. This is true even though they disapprove of the young men's bare heads, occasional long hair, experimentation with drugs and liquor, and general loss of *hasham*. Everyone comments on this now—the new brand of young men aren't modest in front of their fathers. According to the girls I talk with, in front of their fathers these young men not only smoke cigarettes but, worse, they shamelessly play love songs on their cassette recorders.

This is only a partial analysis of the shifting politics of Bedouin discourses on love, a complex subject on which I do not want to impose a false coherence. Yet it should be sufficient to make clear my larger analytical point regarding the anthropology of emotion. As long as emotions remain the object of study, we cannot break with the idealism and mentalism of the interpretive approach.[5] These assumptions keep making it difficult to see how, for us, emotions serve as tokens in the construction of our subjectivity, how they bolster our belief in the truth of our individuality, and how all of this might also be political and specific to our place and time—that is, something worth analyzing critically rather than universalizing.[6]

If instead we take discourses as the object of analysis, we can get at something more interesting. I am not making a narrow plea for sociolinguistics or the ethnography of communication, although they are also involved. "Discourse" is a concept that recognizes that what people say, generously defined (which is, after all, what anyone is dealing with in the anthropological study of emotions), is inseparable from and interpenetrated with changing power relations in social life. There is a double movement implied in this notion. First, social and political life is to be seen as the product of interactions among individuals whose practices are informed by available discourses; second, language and culture are understood pragmatically rather than referentially. They are understood as part of social and political life. Analyzing emotion discourses as discourses rather than as data for our own "scientific" discourses on emotion provides us with a technique for avoiding the false attribution of the project of psychologizing to others as it reminds us relentlessly of the social nature of emotional expression.[7]

A Discourse Redeployed

If any further evidence need be offered for the critical importance of retaining a sense of the always social character of emotion discourse, consider the final aspect of this Bedouin love story: the context in which it was told. Fathalla's story was told to me, as I recounted, by my host, the man whose household I had lived in for two years. He played me the tape of those poignant love songs as I was about to depart again for the United States. I had been absent for five years the first time, and they did not know when I would next return. I promised it would be soon.[8] Although my host and his family had begged me to stay, and my host had gone as far as to offer to set up a job for me directing a private school he would finance, I insisted that my life was in *amrīka* and that it was not likely that I would come to live permanently in Egypt. When he played this tape for me and told me its sad tale, he was not interested in explicating Bedouin emotion concepts or in understanding himself, but rather in impressing on me the force of poetry. Wasn't he, in a way, using the force of poetry on me? Of course, he knew I was writing a book about poetry, and we often discussed poems. Was there more? Did he wish to move me, to resist my departure by these songs and by telling me what effect they had had on another woman?

I sensed that this may have been part of his intent when, two years later, as I went over Fathalla's love poems with my host's wife, a woman I always talked with about poetry and who was good at explaining poems, I heard something surprising. She knew the poems and knew Fathalla's story, but said she had not heard that the girl had died. In fact, she was fairly certain that she was alive and living with the husband of her arranged marriage.

This incident can serve as a reminder that the emotional discourses we might want to use for our anthropological discourse on emotion are hardly inert. They may indeed have a cultural context, but the more important thing about them is that they participate in social projects—whether the larger ones of generational contests over power in an eroding tribal system or the local and particular ones of a conversation between a Bedouin man and a youngish female anthropologist driving to Cairo in a Mercedes.

References

Abu-Lughod, Lila. 1986. *Veiled Sentiments: Honor and Poetry in a Bedouin Society.* Berkeley: University of California Press.

Asad, Talal. 1983. Anthropological Conceptions of Religion: Reflections on Geertz. *Man* (n.s.) 18:237–59.

Collier, Jane. 1974. Women in Politics. In M. Z. Rosaldo and L. Lamphere, eds., *Women, Culture, and Society.* Stanford: Stanford University Press, pp.89–96.

LeVine, Robert. 1984. Properties of Culture: An Ethnographic View. In R. Shweder and R. A. LeVine, eds., *Culture Theory.* New York: Cambridge University Press, pp. 67–87.

Lutz, Catherine. 1986. Emotion, Thought, and Estrangement: Emotion as a Cultural Category. *Cultural Anthropology* 1:405–36.

Messick, Brinkley. 1987. Subordinate Discourse: Women, Weaving, and Gender Relations in North Africa. *American Ethnologist* 14:210–25.

Wolf, Margery. 1972. *Women and Family in Rural Taiwan.* Stanford: Stanford University Press.

Notes

This paper was completed while I was a member of the Institute for Advanced Study, a unique institution to which I am grateful for many things, including support, through the National Endowment for the Humanities, for writing. Earlier versions were presented at the Anthropology Department Colloquia at New York University and the City University of New York Graduate Center, where questions from the audience helped sharpen my arguments. Several people, including Timothy Mitchell, Catherine Lutz, and Buck Schieffelin, carefully read and commented on drafts, and their suggestions, sometimes taken, sometimes not, are gratefully acknowledged. As always, my greatest debt is to the Bedouin families in Egypt who let me participate in their lives and learn from them. Funding from NEH, Williams College, and the Fulbright Commission enabled me to spend more time with them in Egypt in 1985, 1986, and 1987.

1. For a fuller discussion of the Awlad 'Ali, see Abu-Lughod (1986).
2. They talk about an institution called the *mijlās,* in which a young unmarried: woman would entertain all the eligible young men in a tent, challenging them to respond to her songs.
3. Like the dissolution of the discourse of women's weaving in North Africa, 'argued by Messick (1987) to be related to the capitalist transformation of domestic weaving, with the disappearance of one occasion for song have died the songs appropriate to it among the Awlad 'Ali. Sheep shearings, which used to be occasions for groups of young men to go from household to household shearing the sheep, no longer occur, as professionals, mostly from Sinai, have taken over this work. The songs that accompanied sheep shearing were more explicitly sexual than the *ghinnāwa,* couching in innuendo their references to relations between men and women. These are no longer heard, and I heard of no equivalently sexual genres.
4. The Arabic original, as sung by 'Awadh al-Mālkī, is as follows:

> nṣūba minnī lish-shāyib
> > illī hābis hurrīt ish-shab
> > wnāsī hāja ismhā hub
> > w'atf wshōg wnār thib
> > yā magwā nār il-ghāwī
> > yā magwā nār il-'ajgīn
> > illī ba'dhun mishtāgīn
> > simāḥithā yagbō khāyfīn
> > ygūl in-nāgir sā'a yjī
> > ygūl in-nāgir sā'a ytūg

5. For a critique of the idealism implicit in interpretive anthropology, see Asad (1983).

6. Lutz (1986) makes some of these points, but I think that three further sets of questions about the Euro-American emotion concepts she outlines need to be researched. First, which cultural concepts are most salient, and does this pattern differ by subcultures? Second, when do certain ways of thinking about emotion historically come into view, and what institutions and practices are they tied to? Third, when do ways of conceptualizing emotion come into play rhetorically in conversation?

7. See also LeVine (1984:82–3) for a discussion of the relative absence of psychologizing among the Gusii in East Africa.

8. I returned a year and a half later.

–11–

Perilous Passions
Romantic Love and Love Magic in Russia

Galina Lindquist

In the study of emotions, the debates between the universalists and the constructionists seem to be over. Most scholars agree that what in English is called 'emotion' is a phenomenological state experienced uniquely by a human being, but accounted for in terms of the local culture. Emotion is both feeling and meaning, both physically felt and cognized, both socially and linguistically constructed and expressed in neurophysiological processes and bodily sensations. Fred Myers (1996) has suggested going beyond 'the referential view of emotions', when the emotion terms are seen as Saussurian linguistic signs whose fixed referents are psycho-biological states. Instead he proposed to see the emotion terms, linguistic signs infused by cultural meaning, in terms of Peircian semiotics, as Representamina, whose Objects are life situations in which they arise. In Shweder's (1991) terms, semiotic Objects of emotion terms account for the 'ecological' aspect of emotions, or the 'logics of engagement' with life situations mentioned above. Interpretants, 'further signs born in consciousness', are in this view complex chains of thoughts and actions that ensue, the semantic and the management aspects of emotions.

Ethnography, Semiotics and Epistemology of 'Love'

If we assume that some basic ways of 'emoting', either conceived 'logically', as Myers (1996) proposes, seen as configurations of the engagement between the self and the world, or 'biologically', as has been usual in the universalist approach to emotions, are encountered in most known societies, romantic love would be a prime candidate for universality (Jankowiak 1995). Scholars who study the neurochemical basis of emotions have demonstrated that the emotional state connected with 'love' is accompanied by increased levels of phenylethylamine, an amphetamine-related compound in the body (Fisher 1995). It is a commonplace that different cultures also treat this emotion differently, especially as a ground for a lasting social bond known as marriage. In some cultures 'love' is accepted as the primary rationale for marital relations, as in Malaysia (Karim 1990), or in the West. In others, as in China (if we believe Jankowiak 1995), it is considered to be too volatile and unstable to serve as a basis for more long-term arrangements. In some cultures it is viewed as madness to be contained or cured, in others it is hushed or concealed, but it does seem to exist everywhere, in some form or another. What varies is its centrality, its cultural elaboration, its salience, and its place in the moral domain. So do the criteria for choosing the objects of 'love': feminist scholars have long recognized that the 'head is our most erogenous zone', and our choice of the objects of passion is governed by the cultural ideas of the desirable (Bell, Caplan and Karim 1993).

While the semiotic Objects of romantic love are obscure, the Interpretants, the actions of love-stricken individuals, the situations these actions engender, the havoc sometime wreaked, are the stuff of life itself as well as of its endless reflections in popular and high culture. The Interpretants of 'love' will be explored through case studies, but in my explication of romantic love in Russia I resort to another, perhaps most murky and enigmatic term of Peircian semiotic: that of Ground. Peirce wrote that the sign (Repesentamen) stands for the Object 'not in all respects, but in reference to some sort of idea, the Ground of Representamen' (Peirce 1987). Peirce does not explain it any more than saying that 'idea is here in a Platonic sense, ... that one man catches another's idea'. Ground is thus a shared cultural knowledge from which the Object draws its meaning. It is the Ground of emotion terms that ethnographies explicate in the discursive approach to emotions advocated, e.g., by Lutz and Abu-Lughod (1990). It is the knowledge of the Ground that makes it possible to comprehend the logics of individual situations, for culture-bearers and ethnographers alike.

The Ground: Romantic Passion Russian Style

In a private conversation long ago, a Russian woman defined love as 'when you have no choice'. Love in Russia is conceived as a superhuman force, external to the two individuals, that attacks them unexpectedly and often brutally. The famous Russian writer Mikhail Bulgakov captured this in his 'Master and Margarita', in the description of the first meeting of the protagonists: 'Love struck them as a killer dashing from around the corner [and stabbing them in the back with his knife]'. The Russian word Bulgakov uses, *porazila*, means to strike or to stab, and the image of the killer turning up from nowhere evokes the same associations. Love strikes and stabs, ruthlessly and painfully, transforming its victims beyond recognition and allowing no return to the old life. Ideally, the two victims of this assault become one, fused together by the nuclear explosion of love into one totalized composite, inseparable, but separated from the rest of the world. The English colloquial term for this emotion is 'falling in love', which implies the loss of agency, inevitable when being exposed to the natural forces of gravity, stronger then the individual will. In the Russian equivalent *vliubit'sia*, this connotation of losing agency is even stronger, connoting the ego in the grips of some singular, specific, although faceless force, exerting its cruel dictatorship on the ego, drawing or sucking him or her into another microcosm. Falling, or 'being drawn into', love means to surrender to a higher power, in return receiving the experience of delirious intoxication that is a value entirely in own right. The lovers' lot, their morbid and painful delight is in abandoning their free will, in foregoing 'the choice' and rationality in surrendering to this brutal power. The force of love is imagined as elemental, as a storm, ruthless, merciless, trashing and tearing its victim, much like ocean waves batter the shipwreck against the rocks. The realm of love is a universe of its own; and the dark blessing of being drawn within its confines is considered as the most supreme fulfillment for those in its grips.

This (and the fuller explication below) may seem to be in contradiction with the accounts of the totalitarian Soviet state as puritanical and inimical to romantic love as a highly individualistic feeling that challenges the commitments to bigger collectivities and disrupts order. It has been suggested that love is related to personal freedom and respect for the individual (Collins and Gregor 1995). Therefore, tightly bonded love dyads are hardly tolerated in societies where other bonds are more valued, be they kinship ties in traditional societies (Hsu 1972), or those between the individual and the collective, as in the Soviet state (Timasheff 1968; Kharkhordin 2000).

It is certainly true that in the official Soviet discourse sexuality was nonexistent or presented as degrading (Kon 1995), and that the kind of love that was extolled was that of 'individual to the party', a fact that many jokes played on. However, the official discourse was not the only cultural discourse, and not even the most important one, that shaped individuals in Russia, even in the darkest Soviet times. Along with the official discourse, there was a dissenting intellectual discourse of tacit protest and resistance; and there was a popular discourse, derived from literature high and low, cinema, pop and folk songs, pulp fiction and trash poetry books and rural folk tradition (of which the love magic spells discussed below are part). In both of these spheres of Russian culture, romantic love was highly elaborated and valued as supreme. To an extent, romantic and erotic love, and sex as its expression, were practiced as a form of protest, even though the majority of people did not consciously spell it out that way. Moreover, love was the only form of protest that was politically harmless. It did not threaten the regime directly, and it was tolerated by it, unlike other forms of protest. To engage in romantic love (as well as in flirting and fornication, which could be preludes, substitutes or sincere illusions of love) in the Soviet times was the easiest (and most pleasurable) way to experience the illusion of freedom. For the working class and the social strata between the working class and intelligentsia, romantic love was by and large conceived as a joy of life, receiving its nourishment from cultural scripts, some of which are discussed below.

All these diverse discourses, appealing to different social strata, were and still are in agreement as to the cultural model or script of romantic love, the semiotic Ground for the linguistic sign *liubov'* shared across the culture. Love in Russia is formidable, creating its own totalized cosmos, and thus destructive of the everyday one. Therefore love is expected to imply suffering and to be connected with pain. The idea of the destructive force of love, to which it is a sweet pain to surrender, is in the air the Russian person breathes growing up, irrespective of one's social provenance. Russian youth is brought up on such lyrics as 'with you, I forget about everything in the world; I plunge headlong into the abyss of love'.

The next line of this same song, however, introduces the inevitable dimension of inequality into the tormenting bliss, further deepening its painful dimension: 'But you are cold as an iceberg in the ocean, and all your sorrows are under the dark water'. Sometimes, in real life if not in Bulgakov's book, the killer stabs one person but the other remains intact and has to be drawn into the microcosm of love, causing the afflicted one ever more suffering, and pressing him or her to turn to all means available to break the resistance. This situation is indeed not a case where free will of another individual is to be respected (as it is not respected in other contexts of Russian life). This is where love magic comes into play, as a means to bend the will of another and to draw her into the microcosm of love. Love magic is considered to be the last resource, a drastic medicine, a combat for life or death.

Soft patience, forgiveness, unassuming humility bordering on subservience—all accepted Russian Orthodox values—are considered to be the means for a female to win over her object of desire. Another song by the same, at one time immensely popular, pop singer Alla Pugacheva, tells the story of a man who at one point neglected his love, but is then suddenly gripped by its element and rushes to call his beloved: 'and then you will yearn for the warmth that you once rejected, so much that you won't be able to wait for a couple of people in line at the telephone box'. This old song, written well before the era of mobile telephones, is still often replayed now, twenty years later, showing that cultural models are alive and well, despite the deep transformations rocking the society. The female narrator, the 'I' of the song, continues that she so firmly believes that this is going to happen, that she is prepared to wait by the door night and day, for her beloved to ring the bell.

These lyrics reflect the understanding that women, as more emotional beings, are expected to give themselves to the element of love with a much more unrestrained abandon and are generally more likely to let themselves be governed by their emotions. The Russian word for 'emotions', *emotsii,* is partly synonymous with that for feelings, *chuvstva.* The latter, however, denotes also physical sensations such as cold, tiredness, hunger or dizziness, while *emotsii* refers mostly to tumultuous, positive and negative, perhaps undefined feelings within the province of love (but also to other strong 'focal emotions' like anger and joy, felt in inappropriate contexts and taking the better of the person). Women are understood to be more prone to *emotsii,* while men are expected to be more restrained, keeping their 'sorrows under the dark water' of the tough manly facade. However, the element of love is supposed to make no distinction between the sexes, sweeping both men and women into its fold, wrecking their lives and victimizing them in its name. Romantic love in Russia is to be distinguished from sexuality and sexual desire. There can be the former without the latter, especially in unilateral, unreciprocated loves, and in imaginary projections, like those of teenage girls to movie stars. Generally speaking, romantic love is expected to be consummated in the erotic fulfillment, and sexuality is expected to be given full sway in the storm of love, unleashing and satisfying deep desires that may very well challenge the rules of social propriety. But 'true love' is expected to change the lives of the protagonists beyond simple sexual encounters, as in the classic examples of Russian literature like Anna Karenina.

Bonds of Intimacy: Love, Marriage, Sexuality, and Friendship

Everyday life is known to kill love. The two natural elements, 'love' and 'life'—especially in the meaning of everyday routine, the resented *byt*—are seen to be distinct worlds, laying rivaling claims on the individual, and even clearly adverse to each other. 'The boat of love has crushed against the shore of everyday life' is a well-known dictum, coming from the Russian poet Mayakovski, himself a victim of love (as befits a poet). In the Russian version, the word used for the metaphysical rocks against which the boat of love has wrecked is *byt*. *Byt* is drab and suffocating everyday life with its chores, tribulations, efforts of overcoming its roughness, brutality and grossness. *Byt* is deadening for the soul and thus for love. Love is ideally expected to lead to marriage, and indeed does serve as a basis for many marriages (just as love leads to breaking old ones and making new marriages). Still, love and marriage in Russia form an uneasy alliance and are not necessarily compatible.

The acceptance of this fact is one trait that is different between the Russian and the Western romantic love. The institute of marriage in the West appears to be more morally sanctified than is the one in Russia. The high incidence of divorces in Russia is one of the sad sociological facts, taking its toll especially when people's means of existence are scarce, informal networks of kinship and friendship are unstable under the ongoing deep social and economic transformations, and more formal ones from the Soviet welfare state are demolished. One of the foremost tasks of the Russian Church is to restore the preeminence of sacredness of the institution of the family over the reign of romantic love. The dogmatic Orthodox discourse frames romantic passion as a dark, demonic force, one among many demons of desire, such as desires to possess the worldly or supernatural power, which is reflected in success, money or the healing gift. Love magic, as well as other sorts of magic, are therefore vehemently denounced by the Church. They thrive nevertheless.

The Platonic tale of the halves always in search of their second halves is well known in Russia; in fact, a colloquial term to refer to spouses is 'my [second] half'. A known maxim, dating back to the eighteenth century, is that 'marriages are made in heaven'. An alternative, cynical view is conveyed by a word pun playing on the two meanings of the word *brak*. The Russian word for marriage, *brak*, is also a word for failed work, defective product, reject or waste. Playing on this word pun, a popular, somewhat joking, saying states that a 'good thing can't be called brak'. To be sure, the cultural ideal of a life-long marriage built on love and nourished by love is still there, but the tacit understanding is that this ideal is not easily attainable. The worldly union immersed in the everyday *byt* is hard-pressed to sustain the force of love.

But, in terms of susceptibility to new loves, there is no finality to the Russian marriage. The element of passion can always sweep over persons, as the ninth wave, washing away the earthly structures of *byt* and marriage. Love might not survive the drabness of the everyday, but it can come back again, directed at other objects. For the abandoned party there is not much to do other than to turn to love magic.

Traditionally, Russian women are valued for their unselfish, sacrificial love, exemplified in the image of Natasha Rostova in Tolstoi's *War and Peace,* tending for Prince Andrei when he is sick and dying. This giving up of the self for the sake of the beloved may be a form of romantic love, expected almost exclusively of women, and providing more space where love and sexuality may be separate pursuits. This facet of love is reflected in the phrases like 'she has given him everything', 'she has given him the whole of herself', etc., encountered, for example, in the descriptions of backgrounds of the female users of love magic rendered briefly in advertisements of magic services. In a recent conversation in Moscow a woman said that 'love that expects reciprocity is not a real love'. As a contrast, there is an idea of man as a hunter, an erotic conqueror, of male 'sexual energy' feeding on the female one, replenished and confirmed by more erotic victories (cf. Birth and Freilich 1995, on similar views in Trinidad). Romantic love can be a part of it, but does not need to, especially when it comes to male sexuality and the satisfaction of male sexual appetites. Here, again, love and sexuality are seen to belong to different domains, even though erotic fulfillment is seen as an important element of romantic love.

People in Russia may retrospectively admit to having been love's fools; to accept that what they thought was romantic love/true love/the love of their life/their second half was in fact just a mistake or an illusion. As elsewhere, in Russia there is a tendency, especially by women, to clothe sexual attraction in the garments of romantic love. Love is a power that has a supreme value and rivals the divine, while sexuality in Soviet times was, perhaps by older people, tacitly equaled with looseness, with the lowly, beastly instincts. (This attitude has been partly replaced by a more Western view on, especially, female sexuality, as one's natural inclination and intrinsic right to pleasure, but has not disappeared entirely.) Men are considered to be pawns of their sexuality to a greater extent than women, although this is rapidly changing and perhaps is no longer true for the post-Soviet environment: especially in popular culture, women are sometimes figured as active and even aggressive sexual agents who come and take what they want. Romantic love, however, spares no one and does not make a distinction between the sexes.

The conception of romantic love in Russia comes out in sharp relief if compared with another type of deep human connectedness, also highly valued and salient in this culture, namely the institution of friendship. If love is defined as a bond that presupposes intimacy, exclusivity and commitment, friendship in Russia is indeed a kind of love. There are, however, crucial differences. They can be illustrated through the reference to the notion of the 'soul', *dusha*. The Russian soul, even though being a deep contained essence, is relational to the extreme. It is known through others; it thrives through connectedness with others. The hedonistic luxuries that are conducive to soothing the soul are only good when they are achieved through relations with others and can only be enjoyed when shared with others. Suffering and pain through close relatedness, especially the pains of love, are seen as 'good for *dusha*', causing it to deepen, develop, and to know itself. *Dusha* unfolds, and fulfills itself, through sociality and sociability. Friendship, a foremost Russian cultural value, maybe rivaling romantic love in its centrality (but enjoying different relationship to *byt*), is this interpenetration of the souls, with insistent practical claims on the individual time and space. Friends share everything in thick and thin, including a considerable part of *byt*. As a friend once said, when a friend stands before the abyss, the friend's responsibility is to warn her; but when the friend is falling down into the abyss, the friend's duty is to fall together with her.

However, if friendship marks the terrains of the social universe of the Russian person, romantic love transgresses the borders of this universe, because it insists on delimiting the good of the soul to the two people only. The microcosm of romantic love strives to contain within it all that the two souls need to be utterly complete within one another, all the horizons and parameters of being that one could ever want or need, thus transgressing the most basic cultural rule of personal open-endedness and interdependence of many. Love thus claims to construct its own microcosm that is at odds with the normal social everyday one, presenting a challenge to all the other moorings and responsibilities. It is the force beyond the bounds of the normative that tends to demolish all other bounds of the existing moral universe, itself knowing no bounds except for the totalization of the other as integral to oneself. In contrast to Western relatedness, constituted through self and other, ideally connected in loving intimacy, but with one's deep innerness that is inviolable, Russian relatedness is realized through souls that are entangled, becoming parts of each other, or deeply ingrained in one another. Russian friendship is an index of this, partaking of some of the qualities of romantic love. This is why childhood friendships have the quality, the intensity, the intimacy that is striking, maybe unhealthy for the Western observer; and this is why Russians in exile often complain about the impossibility of making new friendships. Romantic love grows from this emotional space and overlaps with or feeds on the ethos and meaning of friendship in terms of interpenetrating of the souls. However, it always threatens to invade the space of friendship, to undo it, in its claim on totalizing the social cosmos to the microcosm of the two.

The Magic Aggression: Love Magic and Love Spells

Magic in Russia is an important part of everyday life for many people, for solving everyday problems of health and relationships, especially those of love (Lindquist 2005). Both books and individual magi often admonish to the effect that, to attract someone, to arouse love against one's will, is an unnatural process, an act of violence, that disturbs and destroys the 'spiritual structures' of both the object and the subject of desire. But, when people are gripped by passion, they do not think about the consequences. They might know they should not; but here it is, the tool kit of spells, and, as practitioners say, the very fact that they survived through time testifies to the fact that they work as they did before.

There are divided opinions as to how the instruments of love magic should be used. One of my informants, who makes her living as a practitioner of magic, strongly discourages amateurs from engaging in this craft on their own. According to her, the spells work as 'energy vibrations', best applied by an impassionate professional. If the person is vehemently interested in the outcome of the process, her desire interferes with the subtle work of energies, and the result may be skewed or not forthcoming. Manuals of magic and amateur practitioners disagree. They maintain that, to work, the spell should become one with you. That is, it is not the words that effect change, but the human intentionality that, through these words, has taken shape, come out into the world. In the manuals, the users are instructed not to expect miraculous results, but to be stubborn and persevere, by repeating a spell many times, following instructions to the minute point, which sometimes takes considerable concentration of time and effort. Also, the recognition of the fact that spells are but vessels for passion is reflected in the injunction that spells are a strong weapon, and they should not be used just for nothing better to do, and not too frequently. Nor should they be shared with anyone; otherwise you risk diminishing their effect at best, incurring dire consequences at worst. In general, all magic, and especially love magic, loses its potency if drawn out of the dark of privacy, into public domains; all magical operations should be kept secret. It is also said to be dangerous to use love magic if your feeling for the person is not deep and intense enough. It is strongly recommended, before plunging into love magic, to analyze the situation thoroughly; love magic is believed to do any good only if the object of your desire is what fate has in store for you. All these caveats are designed as token, and ultimately futile, attempts to put back into the frames of morality and propriety that which, as everyone realizes, is utterly beyond it. After all, the spells of love magic are widely published, and the market abounds with practitioners who are prepared to give recipes to anyone who pays.

The ways in which bonds of love are conceived in Russian culture can be glimpsed already from the etiology of the key terms. The word *privorot,* which figures in the lists of services offered by most of the magi in Moscow, denotes a complex and protracted magical operation to secure attachment of another person.

It derives from the word *privorazhivat'*, meaning to magically bind someone to another person. An attractive woman can be called *obvorozhitel'naia*, enchanting, as if casting spells or charms on everyone around; this word is used colloquially outside magical contexts. Another, more archaic, and stronger word for attracting love is *prisushivat'*, to bind a person to another so strongly as if the two have dried together, forming a kind of hard crust that cannot be separated other than shattered into pieces. It is connected to the verb *sokhnut'*, generally meaning to dry up. Specifically in the matters of the heart *sokhnut'* for someone means to be drying up out of love, as if all the bodily fluids have evaporated, maybe after the boiling of passion, killing the life in the body.

Privoroty, magical operations to attract love, consist of the textual part, the spells, and the ritual actions designed not as intricate structured rituals, but, rather, as simple pragmatic actions meant to support the verbal part. Spells are read over a substrate that is somehow connected with the object of desire, directly or indirectly, or that can be somehow associated with him or her. These readings must be made at carefully designated times, at specific places that have ritual significance in the context of the *privorot*, but the agentive locus of magic is the text of the spell itself. These texts are structured in the form of supplication and reflect the form of Orthodox prayer, also using some of its components. The request is made to various agents of change: sometimes natural or elemental forces of movement and fluidity like water, wind, or smoke; sometimes supernatural figures of the religious imaginary like Christ, Mary, or various saints; and sometimes even Satan himself. Irrespective of the agent invoked, the object of desire, and the targeted substrate of the magical change, is always referred to as *rab bozhii*, slave, servant, or serf of God, a canonical Orthodox designation of the human being. All the spells have the same endings as do Orthodox prayers: 'For ever and ever, amen'.

Following are some examples of love spells (readily available in popular books) that engage several themes that are repeated over and again with different variations.

White smoke, curly smoke, go travel, my smoke, over all woods, over all rivers, over all cities. Go fall down on the heart of God's slave (the name of the beloved is given, say, Ivan). Whatever path my destiny takes, let it not miss God's slave Ivan. So that he would not forget God's slave Elena not while eating, not while sleeping, so that God's slave Elena would be in his heart, in his mind, in his thoughts. Let my words be firm and sticky to God's slave Ivan [so that they can stick firmly to him], now and forever. Amen.

The user of this spell is instructed to fill the stove with birch wood and add bird feathers found in the woods, as well as certain precisely specified plants. The stove is lit at midnight, the valve is opened to let out the smoke, and the spell is read over the smoke coming out.

Here we do not deal with tepid or temperate emotions, nor is it a question of wishing well to the object of desire. Love is war, where all weapons are allowed. Interestingly, the word 'happiness' is never encountered in love spells. This illustrates the point made previously, namely, that romantic passion in Russia is conceived as a complete loss of agency and is equated with pain rather than pleasure. In these spells, as well as in other textual representations, passion is figured as obsession, a totalized state of being when the person is hit or struck, and totally possessed by its obliterating forces: a sickness, a state of paralysis.

Indeed, in passion, borders between life and death are blurred; the power of desire is as uncurbed, and as intractable, as the force of death itself.

> Just as the God's slave Ivan, dead, would never more wear his hat, so God's slave Ivan, alive, would never live without me, God's slave Tatiana. Just as God's slave Ivan, alive, would never walk around, so God's slave Ivan, alive, will not stay alive without me. Amen. Amen. Amen.

This spell should be made on Monday, after sending a request in the church to pray for Ivan's health (a traditional Orthodox prayer made for the living) and for his life eternal after death (traditionally said for those dead), which is done in one day in three churches; three pinches of earth are brought from a cemetery, from three graves; the person goes to an open space and throws the earth against the wind, saying the spell, whose effect is supposed to hold until the death of both. Sometimes, co-opting the benevolent celestial powers, spells start with the opening 'I'm standing, blessed, I am walking having made the sign of the cross, out of the gates, down the main threshold, out into the open field'. Here, the agent undertakes to use socially acceptable, legitimate means to attain her goals, not needing to hide from people, attempting to remain within the boundaries of the moral. This is in line with white magic, where the agent appeals to the powers of good and light, the powers of God, but the result is understood to be limited by God's will. Black magic, though reprehensible, is understood to be much more potent in terms of attaining results wished for. It might have dire consequences, but passion is always in now, burning up in its flames both past and future.

It can happen that love is stated in terms of having, fulfillment, bringing joy, by invoking good things in life, and equating them with the state of passion. Such spells are rare, and even those tend to go over into invocations of lacking.

> In the name of the Father, the Son, and the Holy Spirit: Just as the evening sunset rejoices by the falling night, just as the dark night rejoices by the multitude of stars, just as the bright day rejoices by the sun, so God's slave Tatiana will rejoice by God's slave Ivan. So that she will look at him and rejoice as she would at seeing soul in the body, at seeing cross on the church. Just as a dead man cannot be without earth, just as fish cannot be without water, just as the infant cannot be without his mother, so God's slave

Tatiana would not be able to be without God's slave Ivan. Just as ashes have dried up, so God's slave Tatiana will dry up for longing to see God's slave Ivan; at any day, at any time.

Fear is the opposite side of passion, and passion is fearful (no wonder since it is deadly); and only she who is without fear may succeed in effectuating her passion, the spells seem to suggest, as in this one:

> Under the burning stars there is a mountain of white stone; three boiling springs stream from this mountain; Christ the true and only stands by these springs together with his archangels and all the heavenly army. Everybody is terrified by this sight. I, God's slave Tatiana, am the only one who is not terrified, who is not frightened, who does not shudder. I will turn to them and ask them for water from these three boiling springs, to ignite in God's slave Ivan his light liver, his hot blood, his restless heart, so that he will be boiling and burning for God's slave Tatiana for ever and ever, amen.

These spells demonstrate the traits of cultural ontology of romantic love that have been sketched previously in more general terms. Love delineated by these spells is not a nice and kind story of dancing in the rain holding hands and singing sweetly, the image that Western pop culture often brings to mind. Romantic passion at its purest, at its very extreme (and the traits and expectations of such passion are hidden, as fatal seeds, in a most banal love affair) is betwixt and between nature and society, animal and human being. It negates sociality, or, more exactly, makes it irrelevant, in that it claims to build its very own relational field, limited to only oneself and the other, setting up the vectors of passion that reverberate and are conserved only between the two. The world contracts to the two persons, both slaves to passion. The drama of this cosmogonic transformation is a function of the power struggle that unrequited love can be: the vector of desire is directed to penetrate the other's soul as deeply and totalistically as can possibly be. The Russian soul is one that seeks another that reciprocates these feelings. If this response is not forthcoming, the vector of desire takes cultural equipment to arm itself, to achieve forced penetration into the soul of the other, to pervade, totalize and transform this other.

I see this as a contrast with romantic passion in the Anglo-Saxon cultures (but maybe not in the Latin ones), where the interior interpenetration of the selves, losing oneself in the other, is conceived as only fleeting and is considered unhealthy if it occurs for a longer time. Romantic love in the Anglo-Saxon West is not an ominous alternative to general sociality but its basic unit. The romantic dyad in the West is what it was admonished to be in Russia by the Communist ideology: the two people united by romantic love are a cell of the society (the Soviet version posited the family as that cell). In Soviet Russia this latter dictum was never uttered in folk parole other than with mocking scorn; real sociality was a continuous tightly woven net or fabric, rather than consisting of 'cells'. Therefore, the morality of everyday reason and the

[a]morality of love in Russia are inimical to each other, and therefore love in Russia is war and suffering: the hated *byt* finally triumphs, and if love endures the grind, it takes forms other than romantic passion.

What are the structural conditions on which the spells can achieve their work of the magical transformation of the other, of ripping her out of the social universe and drawing her into the microcosm of romantic passion, shut off from the others and shared only with one other individual? In the spells, such microcosm is delineated, and they activate or present a force that moves through space, fluid or air-driven. The microcosm created is hierarchical, but its hierarchy is inverted—the Higher Powers of the ordinary universe are relegated to marginality on the borders of the microcosm of passion and to the service of the will and agency of the subject of desire. This microcosm works according to its own laws of causality that are thus postulated. Through the spells, a force is invoked, formulated, solidified, and directed towards a goal—the other, the object of desire who is thus drawn into this microcosm and caught inside it. For example, when the smoke travels, to fall on the heart of Ivan, it sticks to him, penetrating and invading all of his being, enwrapping and totalizing him. Through this condition, the man has been transformed into the denizen of this microcosm of desire.

Metaphor here is used causally: white birch is burned together with bird feathers, the smoke is given means of locomotion, given wings to travel; or, the smoke is let out of the stove and sent its way, with direction and goal. Other agents of transformation work their way by force of their physical qualities, like boiling water, and inflicting the subject with grief and melancholy, the collaterals of love. Body with its restless heart, with its seventy-seven sinews, is invoked as a medium the two will share, even as the two are transformed into sharing the same body, rendering them post-factum not fully alive before. The two become zombies driven by desire, slaves of love, not God. Together, they become the crust that cannot be separated without fragmenting the whole and destroying them both. The transformation thus is enacted in both, rendering them one. There are two orders of transformation: (a) changes in the object of desire, in line with the will of the agent, and (b) changing the subject, the agent, and thus their relationship to one another, so that they become one, complementing and harmonizing one another. The destructiveness of love lies in that neither of the two are fully individuated again, never independent individuals with full agency.

In these texts, romantic desire takes shape as physical force, without bounds, without mercy, animal and elemental. Strong feelings are clad with words that turn back on the body, effecting physical changes, causing blood to boil, heart to beat, ripping it open and accessible for the desiring subject. In passion, the boundary between nature and culture, between the human being and the animal and elemental world is erased. In conquering the will of another human being, superhuman is drawn upon: saints and principle figures of the established religion, but also its anti-forces, those of evil, of Satan and his ilk. In being spelled out, these elemental and supernatural forces gain presence in the shared world, sharpen the turmoiled consciousness, and become a social force, bent on affecting the consciousness of another human being. Unauthorized, underground, cursed and banned, condemned, warned against, spells of love magic have, however, been used with a vengeance through many centuries, by successive generations of men and women, irrespective of historical calamities, political regimes, social orders. Concealed under their layers, deep inside the structures of meaning, the passions of romantic desire animated in the love spells remain something like an immutable element of Russian culture. Modern men and women, coming back from their industrial and bureaucratic labor, overwhelmed by desperation and pain of passion, in powerlessness, touch upon these cultural underground springs of power. These springs, conceived as superhuman, are in fact made real by the deeply human tool of language ripened on 'the thousand plateaus' of culture.

Elsewhere (Lindquist 2005) I suggested seeing spells as 'icons of power', because the relational dynamics they convey are homologous with the pertaining structures of power, sociality and affect. Those dynamic structures are deeply ontological, forming the very core of people as cultural beings. They are difficult to verbalize or pinpoint discursively, but they shape the very grounds of discourse itself and so, if perceived, can be illuminating for understanding this discourse. In the terms of Peircian semiotics outlined at the outset of this chapter, they are Representamina of the diffuse Objects that they denote, the original emotions of what here was referred to as 'romantic love'. In this semiotic function they can be seen as alternative to the linguistic term *liubov'*, but well fit for conveying to the students of emotions the inimitable 'tone-feeling' that is culturally specific. This is because spells, love spells included, are not just denotations, but rather what Susanne Langer called 'significant forms'. Speaking about art forms, such as music and dance, Langer notes that they 'present' rather than 'represent' or 'stand for'; they are forms immediately given to perception, revealing nondiscursive content of feeling, its raw quality, perhaps too painful or too overwhelming to be spelled out in the subject's own words (Langer 1986[1942]). As Representamina they are more complex than conventional linguistic signs—such as emotion terms—because they have import outside a conventional reference, presenting to consciousness what was beyond it—a quality of feeling prior to objectification or cognition. Prior to the complex of 'feeling-meaning-action' exemplified below they lend texture to what is then shaped as 'feeling', socializing chaotic sensations engendered by passion and desire into culturally acceptable, and thus potentially manageable, form.

Feeling-meaning-action: The Stories of Using Love Magic

As indicated above, concrete stories can give more substance to the bare bones of 'feeling-meaning-action'. The actions of people in love illustrate the 'ecological' aspect of emotions, the peculiar logics of engagement that is permissible and think-able. These stories both illustrate and fine-tune what I sketched previously as the semiotic Ground of emotions—the generals of what is known about 'love', even though perhaps never spelled in so many words. As all life stories, these are unique as well as recognizable; the fact that an individual acted like this does not mean that all Russians do. It does mean, however, that this particular configuration of actions is possible—imaginable—within this particular cultural context, both recognizable and understandable to outside observers, and still uniquely keyed by culture. Thus, it gives us what we look for in anthropology of emotions: a particular 'tone-feeling' that reconciles the idea of emotions as universal human expressions with that of emotions as cultural constructions.

*

Andrei was a talented artist, underground during the Soviet times. After perestroika, he mastered computer graphics and found a job where he could use his talent to earn very good money. When he came to Katerina (the magus I worked with, described in Lindquist 2005), he was in his late thirties. He was a warm, positive, and good-looking man with soft manners and kind eyes. But when he turned to the magus's help, he was a wreck of a human being. He was losing his wife Valentina, a smashing beauty fifteen years his junior. She had been having lovers openly, and she was all the time threatening to leave Andrei. But Andrei did not even want to consider the possibility. He said that Valentina was a pure, sincere creature, whose judgement was confused by the turbulent life in the capital. Andrei wanted Katerina to make his wife love him again, as she did some years ago, when they first met and the fatal passion flamed between them.

Andrei's previous wife had also been an artist, and they had a daughter together. It all started as a fun relationship with a lot of camaraderie and common interests, but then she got heavily on drugs and alcohol. They continued to live together, and Andrei was taking care of their daughter, while the wife was lying on the sofa dishev-eled in her nightgown, chain-smoking. This was when he met Valentina at a crowded party. Valentina had just arrived from a provincial town, she was barely twenty, full of life and energy, flirty with men but in a tender and innocent way, playful like a child. She planned to conquer the capital by becoming a fashion model. Andrei, being an artist, had a soft spot for beauty, and he was determined to help Valentina to make it in a big way. Before long he rented a room for Valentina and was considering divorcing his wife. At some point, after a hysterical row, his wife screamed at him: 'I curse you and your new whore! Don't you think you can build a life with her!' With these words she ran out of the house, and threw herself under a passing car. She died on the spot, and Andrei married Valentina.

He earned good money, Valentina stayed home, totally neglecting the little daugh-ter, but sparing no effort to pursue her career as a model, as she saw it. Andrei took her pictures in the nude and half nude, and they sent them to agencies; Valentina got new acquaintances, she started to go out herself, and she was not interested in having

Andrei around. Men started to call at home, Valentina started to be missing in the evenings and sometimes through the nights. Her first steady lover, and Andrei's real rival, was a young man trying to get through in business. To give him a helping hand, Valentina took several hundred dollars from the home resources, to lend it to the new friend. This debt was never paid back, but Andrei was not able to fight with Valentina. Instead, he came to Katerina, to ask her for love magic, to keep his new wife with him.

Katerina was pessimistic about the situation. She told Andrei what she usually told me when we discussed love magic: love, according to Katerina, was a gift from God; no magic can change another person, no magic can force one human being to love another if this love is not already there. What magic could do, however, was to bind one person to another, to make one dependent on another, to make one come back once and again after having left. Many cases of love magic, according to Katerina, imply acting against God or nature, so the result cannot be good by definition. Your object of desire will come back to you, not for a happy and harmonious life, but to torture you more, to continue the war you have been engaged in. This is what Katerina says to people who come to her asking to make a *privorot,* a series of spells to attract the love of another person, and *otvorot,* a parallel set of measures to divert one's object of desire from other people.

Katerina tried to reorient Andrei's attention to his own needs, to make him realize that his life with Valentina was doomed to failure, that he was a captive of a delusion, that the person in front of him was not the one he saw. As with people in passion, Andrei did not want to hear; all he wanted was that Valentina would stay with him. He drove his daughter to the kindergarten, did groceries, drove Valentina to meet her lovers, and picked her up at restaurants at nights. Katerina did her love magic: Valentina stayed with Andrei for five more years, after which she did eventually leave him for a younger and much richer man.

Katerina considers this case a success story: Andrei recovered, he was not destroyed like many people in his situation are, and he was even capable of forming a new bond. Two years after Valentina finally left him, he came to Katerina with a photograph of a new girl, asking Katerina to 'examine' *(prosmotret')* if this new relationship had good prospects. Katerina looked at the picture and gave her ok: she said that the girl was devoted, modest, loving, and a good homemaker; that she will stay at home and spare no efforts to make him happy. She warned Andrei that maybe he will be a bit bored with his new partner, that she lacked initiative, and that he will have to shake and move her in order to lure her out of the kitchen and sofa. This was the last time she met Andrei; from the fact that he never came back to her, Katerina surmised that his problems were eventually solved, and he had found a peaceful harbor.

*

Ovanes and Nina were a happy couple. They lived together, although without being officially married, for five years. Ovanes's family was from some place in the Caucuses, he was attached to his parents and his birthplace, but he had a good job in Moscow and was quite content with visiting his kin once a year, coming back to Nina with wine, raisins and walnuts from his home town's open market. He never took Nina with him to visit his family; they both knew that the family would never accept Nina as one of them, and that the relatives would never endorse their union; but the relatives, even though well loved by Ovanes, did not have much say in his life anyway. At some point Ovanes received news from home that his mother was not feeling well, and he took time off from his job to go home and say goodbye to her. Nina did not hear from him for several weeks, and then she received a letter in which he told her that he was not coming back: his relatives had found him a wife, and he intended to marry her and to start a new life on his home turf.

This was when Nina was referred to Katerina. Katerina consulted her cards and told Nina: 'I do not see you apart. Don't worry, he will come back to you. Whether or not you decide to let him back is another thing.' Nina was definite that Ovanes was the only one she needed, and she was determined to fight to the end. Her worst problem was in fact that her beloved was too far away, and she was deprived of any possibility to fight other than through magic. In fact, Katerina's magic gave her the possibility to engage all her passion, longing, will, and creative potential into one goal: to bring back her man; and she plunged into the magic activities with all of the passion she had been previously giving to Ovanes. Katerina worked magically as well; giving spells to Nina and instructing her how to read them, instructions that Nina followed to the letter and with great fervour. Katerina told Nina that the love was there, but that Ovanes's discernment was blurred, partly by his mother's sickness and impending death, partly by some magic his kinsfolk back home were working on him. What she and Nina were doing was to restore justice, to help implement God's plan for the two of them, the design that was unsettled by some other people's mean designs. This was a situation where magic works, said Katerina, consoling Nina and convincing her that she should continue working and hoping, that everything would end well.

Katerina pointed out for Nina that the success of the operation only partly depended on magic, which, in turn, depended to a degree on how much Nina herself was working on reading the spells and exercising magical operations. It also depended a great deal on Nina's behavior should Ovanes eventually come back. Katerina instructed Nina not to ring him, not to write, not to make any signs of life; and also not to make quarrelsome scenes should he eventually appear on her doorstep. She would swallow her *obida,* not scold or reproach him, but embrace him as if showing that she understood his breakaway not as betrayal and cowardice but as a temporary confusion of the mind, caused by foreign and mean forces, of which both of them were unwitting victims.

And, indeed, Ovanes came back after a while. He turned up one evening, without prior notice, remorseful, saying that he just left his family and his hometown behind, without saying goodbye, and that he was back forever because he did not imagine his life without Nina. The couple is still together, and Nina is still Katerina's friend and client, calling her once in a while to ask for advice on one or another complication of life. Their life is far from blissfully happy, the passion is gone and the feeling of betrayal, *obida,* sits forever deep inside Nina; but the couple has formalized their union, Ovanes is registered in Nina's apartment, and he has a decent job. There are no storms, but, as Katerina says, family boredom is a plight of those happy ones who have managed to keep their family intact, defending it from the attacks of passions.

Coda

How do the terms like Object, Interpretant, and Ground give us better understanding of people torn apart by passions, grappling with failures and rejections, putting on the stake moral values and even turning to ruthless warfare to satisfy their desires? It seems to me that Peircian semiotics is a good tool, because it accounts for the processual and intersubjective character of human being as embodied consciousness. Emotions, passions and desires, and the actions they trigger, are the tumult of consciousness, but they are also factors that lie behind broader social and political processes. Microdynamics of individual lives help to account for macroprocesses of politics and economics. Therefore the investigation of emotions in cultures should go beyond the studies of discourse, into particularities of individual lives. Peircian semiotics offer a tool to analyze these particularities as worlds in their own right, but also as parts of a broader culture. In this chapter, exposing the cultural category of 'romantic love' as semiotic Ground, but also as a complex of Object-Representamen-Interpretant—another way of grasping feeling-meaning-action—I tried to explore some ethnographic material beyond the studies of discourse. Part of it is esoteric—an ordinary person in the street of Moscow might never have heard about love spells, much less used one. Another part is sensitive, since using the blood and tears of individual loves as ethnography may be considered as preying or trespassing. Altogether, this chapter points at the deeply determining nature of cultural ontologies for the finest nuances of feelings and the most whimsical contingencies of actions that we call our personal, inner and social lives.

References

Bell, D., Caplan, P., and Karim, W.-J., eds. (1993), *Gendered Fields: Women, Men and Ethography,* London: Routledge.

Birth, K., and Freilich, M. (1995), 'Putting Romance into Systems of Sexuality: Changing Smart Rules in a Trinidadian Village', in W. Jankowiak (ed.), *Romantic Passion: A Universal Experience?* New York: Columbia University Press.

Collins, J., and Gregor, T. (1995), 'Boundaries of Love', in W. Jankowiak (ed.), *Romantic Passion: A Universal Experience?* New York: Columbia University Press.

Fisher, H. (1995), 'The Nature and Evolution of Romantic Love', in W. Jankowiak, (ed.) *Romantic Passion: A Universal Experience?* New York: Columbia University Press.

Hsu, F.L.K. (1972), 'Kinship and Ways of Life: An Exploration', in F.L.K. Hsu (ed.), *Psychological Anthropology,* Cambridge: Schenkman.

Jankowiak, W., ed. (1995), *Romantic Passion: A Universal Experience?* New York: Columbia University Press.

Karim, W.-J. (1990), *Emotions of Culture: A Malay Perspective,* Singapore: Oxford University Press.

Kharkhordin, O. (2000), *The Individual and the Collective in the Soviet Union,* Chicago: University of Chicago Press.

Kon, I. (1995), *The Sexual Revolution in Russia: From the Age of the Tsars to Today*, trans. James Riorda, New York: Free Press.

Langer, Susanne (1986 [1942]), 'Discursive and Presentational Forms', in R. Innis (ed.), *Semiotics: An Anthology,* Bloomington: Indiana University Press.

Lindquist, G. (2005), *Conjuring Hope. Healing and Magic in Contemporary Russia,* Oxford and New York: Berghahn Books.

Lutz, C., and Abu-Lughod, L., eds. (1993), *Language and the Politics of Emotion*, Cambridge: Cambridge University Press.

Myers, F. (1996), 'The Logic and Meaning of Anger among Pintupi Aborigines', *Man* (NS) 23: 589–610.

Peirce, C. S. (1987), 'Logic as Semiotic: The Theory of Signs', in Robert Innis (ed.), *Semiotics: An Anthology,* Bloomington: Indiana University Press.

Shweder, R. (1991), *Thinking Through Cultures,* Cambridge, Mass.: Harvard University Press.

Timasheff, N. (1968), 'The Great Retreat', in N. W. Bell and E. F. Vogel (eds.), *A Modern Introduction to the Family,* New York: Free Press.

Knowledge and the Practice of Love and Hate Among the Enxet of Paraguay

Stephen W. Kidd

One day during my fieldwork in Paraguay,[1] Alejandro, a member of the community of San Carlos, began to dismantle his house so that he could move to the nearby community of Alegre. On bumping into him I asked him why he had decided to leave. He replied that the blame rested with his wife's brother and neighbour Miguel whom he accused of having attacked him with a knife. 'He became angry and hated me and now I want to live among those who love me so that I can once again be tranquil.' The image of Miguel as a knife-wielding maniac contrasted markedly with my own experience of him as both pleasant and friendly, though somewhat shy. I determined to find out his version of the story and later that day paid him a visit. As we sat by the fire chatting, he explained to me that, the previous evening, Alejandro had been drunk and had begun to beat his wife. On hearing the commotion, Miguel had picked up a knife and run next-door to protect his sister. 'It was Alejandro who caused me to be angry', he said, 'and he is leaving because he is ashamed of what he did.' He explained that no one in the community loved Alejandro anymore and that they were pleased that he was leaving so that tranquility would, once more, return to the village. Furthermore, he continued, if Alejandro did not leave then Miguel himself would move away since he no longer wanted to live where he could 'be caused to be angry'.

Alejandro and Miguel are members of the Enxet indigenous people, a group of some 12,000 individuals inhabiting the Chaco region of Paraguay. The above description is a typical example of the type of conversation I engaged in with the Enxet whenever they tried to explain to me aspects of their social behaviour. Such discussions were characterised by a stress on the use of emotion words and I gradually gained the impression that the Enxet understood daily social practice to be intimately tied in with notions of personhood. The aim of this chapter is to begin to explain this understanding by attempting to create a picture of how the Enxet themselves explain human behaviour. In particular, I will focus on an organ of the body known as the *wáxok* which, in Enxet philosophical thought, is recognized as the cognitive and affective centre of the person. In addition, it is also an individual's social centre and a salient feature of the Enxet explanation of their social relations. A central theme of this chapter will be to examine how the *wáxok* is constructed and to describe how its development is associated with becoming knowledgeable. Knowledgeable people possess the ability to act in a socially appropriate manner and specific behaviour is expected of those who are knowledgeable as well as of those who lack knowledge. This behaviour is understood around the opposition of love and hate which, as among the Amuesha people, is a meaningful paradigm in Enxet thought and practice (cf. Santos-Granero 1991: 45). However, Enxet discourse on appropriate and inappropriate behaviour is not without its ambiguities. It will be seen that the Enxet explain many aspects of people's behaviour by reference to extraneous influences, focusing especially on the consumption of alcohol. Nevertheless, such explanations need to be seen in context. Ultimately, the stress is upon the individual's personal responsibility and the ability of knowledgeable people to control their actions.

Defining the *Wáxok*

The *wáxok*[2] is both a physical and metaphysical organ of the body that is located in the region of the stomach. On one hand it is conceived of as hollow and as part of the digestive process; as such, it is the organ of the body most prone to invasion by malevolent spirits and other subjects that are sent by enemy shamans to make people ill. However, it is also the cognitive and the affective centre of the person, and the encapsulation of both cognitive and affective processes in the *wáxok* is illustrated by a series of linguistic expressions that make use of the term in their construction. For instance, affects are often expressed by reference to the physical states of the *wáxok:* such as: 'the *wáxok* spreads out' and 'the *wáxok* is sweet', which suggests happiness and contentment; 'the *wáxok* is heavy' and 'the *wáxok* really leans over', which indicate sadness; and the 'the *wáxok* shivers', which is one way of describing fear. In contrast, terms associated with cognition ascribe agency to the *wáxok*. For example, thought is expressed by terms such as 'the *wáxok* mentions', 'the *wáxok* searches' and 'the *wáxok* says', while other terms that indicate the agency of the *wáxok* include 'the *wáxok* despises', 'the *wáxok* makes fun of' and 'the *wáxok* turns around and goes back to where it came from' which suggests a change of mind.

However, despite its physical and metaphysical qualities, the *wáxok* cannot be fully appreciated outside the context of social relations. It is, essentially, a social concept, and by developing *wáxok* that are 'knowledgeable' and 'understanding'—both of which are expressed by the term—*ya ásekyak*[3]—people learn how to relate to others in an appropriate manner cf. Palmer 1997: 162. As I will show, each individual is taught how and when to practise both love and hate but, before discussing this in more detail, I will first of all describe how the Enxet conceive of the development of the *wáxok*.

Being Knowledgeable about Love

Knowledge is an eminently social attribute and knowledgeable people are those who know how to practise love appropriately or, as Overing (1996) puts it, possess the capabilities to live a harmonious life. 'Love'—*[-]ásekhayo*—is understood by the Enxet to be at the very heart of proper social relations. While, in 'Western' folk concepts, love is defined as an emotion or bodily feeling, the Enxet notion of love is much wider, going beyond a feeling to encompass both a moral principle and a mode of behaviour. In effect, love is associated with what Western moral philosophy defines as the 'other-regarding virtues' which are essentially those that express a concern for the well-being of others (cf. Overing 1988: 178). Therefore, when the Enxet exhort people to love others, they are talking about a way of living. 'Those who love should be generous and share their produce and possessions with others so that, in essence, those who love, give, while those who give, love (cf. Santos-Granero 1991: 202; Overing 1993; 54). Love also implies helping others and encapsulates a way of talking so that only 'good speech' is directed towards those who are loved. In effect, love is conceived of by the Enxet as something that is done—in other words, the practice of sociality—and, if it is not manifested in actions, it does not exist.[4]

As a moral value, love should characterise any interaction between those who consider themselves to be in a sociable relationship. Consequently, the concepts of kinship and love are mutually implicated so that kin can be defined as those we love, while those we love are often referred to as kin. Another expression that is commonly used to describe a loving relationship is the phrase 'to look at someone'. Those who 'look at us' are those who love us by, for example, sharing their property, spending time with us and being willing to eat and drink our food. In other words, they want to develop a sociable relationship with us.

Knowledgeable people are said to have good 'thoughts' and, as I illustrated earlier, 'thinking' itself is understood to be an action of the *wáxok* as an agent. The voluntary sharing of food with others is a clear expression of love and is, in fact, said to be a thought, in other words, 'a mentioning of one's *wáxok*' (Kidd 1999: 192ff). A greeting is expressed by the same term and, since greetings are manifestations of a person's desire to create or re-create a relationship, the description of them as thoughts it particularly pertinent. Furthermore, people who express a desire to help others can be said to have 'good thoughts' which is expressed by the term 'one's *wáxok*'s searching is good'.

A further key form of behaviour associated with being knowledgeable is to act with *[-]ennawagko,* a term that is somewhat ambiguous. On the one hand, it can mean 'timidity' or 'shyness' and is described by the Enxet as similar to 'fear'. Thus, for instance, if, in a game of football, the members of one team seem wary of tackling their opponents, they could be accused of being too timid. Similarly, someone who is reticent to speak in public could be said to be shy. However, the Enxet themselves often translate *[-]ennawagko* as 'respect', which suggests that it is much more than an emotion. In fact, as with love, it also implies a moral value and an other-regarding mode of behaviour. In this context, it can best be translated by the term 'restraint'. In normal daily life, unless a relationship is particularly close, such as between members of the same household, people should treat each other with restraint and, in this sense, it is regarded as a virtue. By acting with restraint, one avoids harming the *wáxok*s of others. One should not, therefore, ask others for food, disturb them if they are otherwise occupied, deny requests, abuse community property, nor do things that are against the will of others. Furthermore, 'bad speech'—which includes criticising people to their face or speaking when angry—should be avoided. Consequently, the practice of restraint is regarded as constitutive of love and as derived from a knowledgeable and 'soft/unlocked' *wáxok*.[5] It is, therefore, associated with an aesthetics of controlling one's emotions, especially the wild, antisocial impulses—such as anger—which are an integral part of being human (cf. Grubb 1911: 200; Alvarsson 1988: 135; Overing 1989: 91, Belaunde, op. cit., p. 104, Palmer, op. cit., p. 162).

Knowledge and the Ability to Hate

Although I have suggested that knowledge is associated with love and a lack of knowledge with hate, it would, in fact, be more accurate to say that being knowledgeable implies having an understanding of when and how to act appropriately. Therefore, the relationships between knowledge, love and hate are more ambiguous than I have hitherto suggested and, in contrast to the Amuesha, who 'see love as permeating every aspect of human interaction' (Santos-Granero 1991: 201), the Enxet conceive of the requirement to love as contextual. Although they stress practising love, this does not imply a blanket condemnation of hate and so people are taught not just who and how to love but also who and how to hate (cf. Overing 1989: 82f). While one should love those considered to be in the in-group, it is acceptable to hate those on the 'outside'.[6]

Therefore, although acting with a 'strong/locked' *wáxok* is usually condemned within one's own in-group—which the Enxet describe as comprising 'those of us who love each other'—when a leader meets with White people on behalf of the community he should have a strong *wáxok* and show no fear.[7] He need not show restraint but should be strong and prepared to use 'heavy' speech. A leader who, when dealing with outsiders, demonstrates a 'soft/weak' *wáxok* is regarded as useless since his *wáxok* would shiver and he would remain quiet, too scared to speak up for his community. Such leaders are accused of being too 'restrained/timid,' with the stress clearly placed on the side of timidity.

Anger can even be considered appropriate behaviour in the right circumstances. While it should never be expressed in a relationship predicated on love, it may be acceptable when the need to practise love is irrelevant. This is clearest in the action of the shaman who, to save a patient, must fight with malevolent shamans and other dangerous beings of the invisible world. It is anger that causes shamans to harm people and the healing shaman must meet anger with anger in the battlefields of the cosmos and try his best to kill the enemy shaman. The *meteymog* revenge magic is also provoked by a mixture of sorrow and anger at the loss of a loved one. If a person's death is thought to have been caused by a shaman, before burial a red-hot stone, known as a *meteymog,* can be placed into an incision in the cadaver (cf. Grubb 1904: 42ff. 128; 1911: 160ff; Susnik 1977: 22; Chase-Sardi 1981). The stone shoots off into the sky to seek out the murdering shaman and burn him to death, and his demise is a cause of rejoicing.

Leaders could also use anger to confront missionaries, politicians or government officials if, by doing so, they can acquire material advantages for their communities. Anger, therefore, when directed towards the outside, can be productive of social life.

The above examples indicate that many Enxet emotion words tend to have multiple meanings and can be used in apparently contradictory and creative ways depending on the context. While a 'soft/unlocked' *wáxok* can be used positively to praise a generous loving person, the same term can be used to condemn someone regarded as cowardly. And, although a person who refuses to share can be denounced as having a 'strong/locked' *wáxok,* in another context the same expression can indicate courage. Indeed, different people can use similar words in conversation but lend quite distinct meanings to them. For instance, if, in a meeting, someone takes the initiative to confront a wrongdoer to his face, those who support the speaker may speak favourably of his strong *wáxok*—in other words, his courage—while those on the side of the person attacked could use the same expression to criticise the speaker's lack of restraint. Although such apparent contradictions may be confusing to outsiders, the Enxet themselves experience no difficulty in understanding their meaning, interpreting them according to the specific context.

Indeed, individuals can even be said to exhibit two quite different characters and the term 'two *wáxoks*' can be used to describe such people. They may, for example, demonstrate knowledge by acting in a loving, responsible manner but, at times, could comport themselves as if they were without knowledge by becoming angry and fighting with others.

References

Alvarsson, J. (1988) *The Mataco of the Gran Chaco: An Ethnographic Account of Change and Continuity in Mataco Socio-economic Organization,* Uppsala Studies in Cultural Anthropology 11.

Belaunde, L. E. (1992) 'Gender, commensality and community among the Airo-Pai of West Amazonia (Secoya, Western-Tukanoan speaking), Ph.D dissertation, University of London.

Chase-Sardi, M. (1981) *Pequeño decameron Nivaklé: literature oral de una etnia del Chaco Paraguayo,* Asunción: Ediciones NAPA.

Forrest, L. A., (1987) 'Economics and the social organization of labour: a case study of a coastal Carib community in Surinam', unpublished Ph.D dissertation, University of London.

Grubb, W. B. (1904) *Among the Indians of the Paraguayan Chaco,* London: Charles Murray.

———— (1911) *An Unknown People in an Unknown Land: an account of the life and customs of the Lengua Indians of the Paraguayan Chaco, with adventures and experiences met with during twenty years' pioneering and exploration amongst them,* London: Seeley.

Henley, P. (1982) *The Panare: Tradition and Change on the Amazonian Frontier.* New Haven, Conn. and London: Yale University Press.

Kidd, S. W. (1999) 'Love and hate among the people without things: the social and economic relations of the Enxet people of Paraguay', unpublished Ph.D dissertation, University of St. Andrews.

McCallum, C. (1989) 'Gender, personhood and social organization amongst the Cashinahua of Western Amazonia', unpublished Ph.D dissertation, University of London.

Overing, J. (1988) 'Personal autonomy and the domestication of the self in Piaroa society', in I. M. Lewis and G. Jahoda (eds). *Acquiring Culture,* London: Croom Helm.

Overing, J. (1989) 'Styles of manhood: an Amazonian contrast in tranquility and violence', in S. Howell and R Willis (eds), *Societies at Peace,* London: Tavistock.

———— (1993) 'The anarchy and collectivism of the "primitive other": Marx and Sahline in the Amazon', in C. Hann (ed.), *Socialism: Ideals, Ideologies and Local Practice,* London: Routledge.

———— (1996) 'Under the sky of the domesticated: in praise of the everyday', Inaugural Lecture for the Professorship and Chair of Social Anthropology, University of St. Andrews, 4 December.

Palmer, J. (1997) 'Wichí goodwill: ethnographic allusions', unpublished Ph.D dissertation, University of Oxford.

Santos-Granero, F. (1991) *The Power of Love: The Moral Use of Knowledge amongst the Amuesha of Central Peru,* London: Athlone Press.

Susnik, B. J. (1977) *Lengua-Maskoy: su hablar, su pensar, su vivencia,* Lenguas Chaqueñas VI, Asunción: Museo Etnográfico 'Andres Barbero'.

Notes

1. Research for this paper was, in part, financed by research grants from the Economic and Social Research Council and the Emslie Horniman Fund of the Royal Anthropological Institute.
2. *[-]wáxok* is always used with the addition of a prefix to indicate the person, such as *éwáxok* which means 'my *wáxok*'. However, in this chapter I will use the shorthand form *wáxok*.
3. Although *[-]ya'ásekyak* encompasses both knowledge and understanding, in my discussion I will express them both by the shorthand term: knowledge.
4. Similar ideas about the relationship between knowledge and sociable behaviour are held by other Lowland South American peoples. See, for example, Overing (1988), Belaunde (1992: 94ff) and Palmer (1997: 161ff).
5. The restraint practiced by the Enxet is distinct from the 'restraint respect' reported for other indigenous peoples by Henley (1982: 131), Forrest (1987: 325) and Belaunde (1992: 128ff). In these examples 'restraint/respect' characterises the behaviour of younger people to older people. Among the Enxet, even parents should practise restraint with their children and this is one explanation for the aversion to corporal punishment. Cf. McCallum (1989: 209) who refers to reciprocal restraint between neighbours and kin.
6. See Kidd (1999: 225ff) for a discussion of the problematic concept of inside/ outside among indigenous American peoples.
7. A 'strong' *wáxok* is, therefore, associated with courage (cf. Palmer 1997: 160)

–13–

Relations with the Imagined Child
The Emotionality of Becoming
an AdoptiveParent in Norway

Signe Howell

'We are going to leave on Monday. It can't be true ...! The feelings at that moment cannot be described. All thoughts stand still. After three years of waiting, waiting, waiting and more waiting we are finally going to become parents—hopefully. The uncertainty and the doubts are not far away' (*Adopsjonsforum* (2) 2000: 4).

And, 'It was Friday afternoon and I was in the office. For once it was quiet and I was all alone when Kristin from The Children of the World [Norwegian adoption agency] rang. She told me that we had been allocated a small boy, one month old ... Having replaced the receiver I slowly began to take it in. It took a little while before I could ring Odd [her husband]. The tears just ran and ran' (*Verdens Barn* (1) 1998: 12).

These statements by two women describing their reactions upon being told that they are going to become mothers to adopted children, from Chile and Brazil respectively, are typical. They illustrate the powerful emotionality of a situation— involuntary childlessness—that is experienced as a profoundly unhappy one; and the intense happiness that accompanies the fulfillment of their longings. They also provide a graphic illustration of the issues I want to discuss in this paper.

Emotions: Nature in Culture and Culture in Nature

While it is notoriously difficult to define emotions in any absolute sense, for present purposes—a discussion of the emotionality of adoptive relationships—I find the following suggested definition by Oatley and Jenkins useful:

An emotion is usually caused by a person consciously or unconsciously evaluating an event as relevant to a concern (goal) that is important; the emotion is felt as positive when a concern is advanced and negative when a concern is impeded (1996: 96).

Using empirical material from my study of involuntary childless couples in Norway who, in order to become 'a normal family', decide to adopt a child from a distant and (usually) unknown land, I shall explore how emotions are variously activated as a result of numerous events that both advance and impede the goal of obtaining a child. I shall argue that the adoption process is one that is highly emotional and that the emotionality is enhanced because the desire to adopt is a goal-oriented activity which is riven with uncertainty. This uncertainty is exacerbated by the very openness about the endeavour that prospective adoptive parents of a child from overseas must live with. To engage oneself in an adoption process removes procreation from a purely private concern to one that is public, and involves the authorities in a number of direct and unpredictable ways. Further, it has become usual for couples who plan to adopt transnationally to engage actively with a number of others like themselves before, during and after the adoption. All these factors mean that, once it has been embarked upon, the adoption process has become a goal that profoundly affects the couple; it is invested with a range of emotions from desire, hope, frustration, joy and, perhaps most difficult of all to handle, ambivalence and uncertainty. I shall link this emotional journey that most adoptive parents today undergo to changes over the past hundred years in the meaning of the family, the meaning of motherhood, fatherhood and childhood, and argue that these social statuses have become imbued with increased psychological elaborations and expectations which, in turn, intensify the feelings of those concerned. Everyone who has been through the process of coming to terms with their infertility and has solved it by adopting a child from overseas has a tale to tell (Sandelsowski 1993, Volkman 2005).

For a variety of social, cultural and economic reasons (Howell 2003, 2006), in present-day Norway, virtually no Norwegian-born children are available for adoption. Thus, adoption means, in effect, that the child will come from abroad; from Asia, Africa, Latin America or the former Soviet empire. Consequently, ethnic Norwegian prospective adoptive parents must adjust their expectations to not only incorporate an unknown and unrelated child into their own family setting, but also to the fact that this child will come from an unknown country with alien social and cultural values and institutions, and that the child will, in most cases, look very different from themselves. Unlike adoption during earlier times when the child was born of ethnic Norwegians, the nature of the transnational adoptive relationship cannot be hidden from public gaze. This forces adoptive parents to deal with the fact of their biological childlessness openly, and to inform their adopted children from the start about the special nature of their relationship. Arguably, the situation of childlessness becomes doubly stressful. Prospective adoptive parents must not only come to terms with the grief of their own childlessness and get ready to welcome a stranger, but because their child will never be taken for their biological child, they must also prepare themselves to handle the added challenge of being confronted with the fact of their decision whenever they move outside their home turf. In the outside world they will have to face a steady stream of inquiry into their personal life by total strangers, inquiries that, at times, may display racist overtones. The incorporation and kinning (see below) of the transnationally adopted child thus present personal challenges which, in most cases, exceed that of giving birth to a biological child.

Having said that, I want to make the point that human procreation everywhere is a matter of profound human interest. It is an event that is enmeshed in symbolism and ritualized behaviour, which may, or may not, be emotional in character. To what extent, and in what ways, pregnancy and birth provoke emotions or not must, I argue, be an empirical, not an analytical question. Maternal love and an instinctive mother-child bonding are today thought of as natural and universal (Rogoff 2003). However, as I shall show, ethnographic and historical material amply demonstrate that the picture is highly complex, drawing our attention—yet again—to questions of the relationship between the biological and the cultural in the constitution of personhood and sociality. A useful overview of the various anthropological theories on that relationship is given by Milton and Svasek (2005). Briefly, my own position is that I take as my starting point a psychological, cognitive and physiological unity of humanity, but suggest that while this enables us to create and maintain meaningful relationships across sociocultural boundaries, we must also assume that the way that people process and make sense of experiences is, to a very large extent, shaped by the values and understandings of their community. In other words, emotions are best understood as resulting from an active interplay between innate proclivities and cultural elaborations; an interplay, moreover, that implies moral considerations. It is my argument that it is analytically impoverishing to exclude issues of morality from the study of emotions. What at any time are acknowledged as appropriate emotions carry moral connotations in the wider social world (Howell 1997).

Changing Moral Reasoning about Family and Childhood

Important changes have occurred in medicine, technology and social values and practices during the second half of the twentieth century that have affected family life in Norway and other western European countries. I have in mind the advances made in new reproductive technology which enable a number of infertile individuals to procreate biologically, and the rapidly increasing popularity of transnational adoption. As a result, procreation has taken on a new meaning that readdresses questions of relatedness, morality and emotionality in novel ways.

According to Gillis (1996: xv–xvii), the connection between giving birth and giving nurture, of equating maternity with motherhood, was not generally made in Europe until the nineteenth century. Informal adoption and fostering of children by relatives was quite common well into the century, but by the end of the century a new moral preoccupation with the quality of the family and family life could be discerned and it was a time 'when houses became homes'—a concept that was constituted through heavy moral injunctions. Accompanying this shift was a shift in thinking about children and childhood. During the twentieth century, children became increasingly perceived as emotionally as well as intellectually and physically vulnerable, in need of adult (preferably biological parental) care and guidance. Bringing up children became a matter that no longer could be left to the adults in a child's social environment, but one that required the education of parents. This found its most graphic expression in the numerous 'how to' books on good parenting, of which that by Dr. Spock was the most widely read. His *Common Sense Book of Baby and Child Care,* published originally in 1946, and other similar books on how to be good parents, sold in their millions during the twentieth century, constituting not only the meaning of 'the child', but demonstrating also important changes in the moral duties and social practice of parents—in particular the mother. From being taught about correct nutrition in the interwar period, mothers became required to provide psychological nurture in the postwar period (Haavind[1] personal communication). Motherhood became the ultimate purpose of women's lives, and infertility in marriage was blamed on the wife.

Motherhood became, during the 1950s in Norway, the manifestation of one's success as a woman. Indeed, psychological literature of the time explained childlessness in women as the result of psychological abnormality (Leira 1996: 133). As a result, infertility was shameful and attempts to recompense it through adoption were shrouded in secrecy. With the introduction of transnational adoption, secrecy about the relationship became a thing of the past because, in most cases, the children could not be passed off as their parents' biological children. The emotionality of adoptive parents became more openly acknowledged, especially as parenthood—most notably motherhood—became a status that increasingly was perceived as not only desirable, but as necessary for personal fulfillment (Howell 2001). Probably as a result of the women's movement, involuntary childlessness became a political as well as a personal issue. Notions of shame about one's infertility vanished, to be replaced by demands for public assistance to alleviate the condition. The Norwegian welfare state followed up with more and better provisions for parents, making child care one of the hottest political issues of the late twentieth and early twenty-first centuries.

These changes may be linked to the central position granted children and childhood during the twentieth century, fuelled by the rapid growth of psychologically informed expertise. Rose argues that what he calls the 'psy factor' of contemporary Western forms of life has acquired a particular significance, as we 'have come to celebrate values of autonomy and self-realizing that are essentially psychological in form and structure' (Rose 1999: xv). This led to a new scrutiny of one's psychological state and gave emotions a new and enhanced status in individual lives.

In such a cultural climate, those who were unable to produce their own children felt this as a major loss; not only were they deprived of the posited emotional satisfaction of being mothers (and fathers), but perhaps more importantly, as the century wore on, of actively participating in the social life of their peers—lives that increasingly have become focused on bringing up children. As most women joined the labour force, couples' spare time became increasingly devoted to child-related activities. Most adoptive parents that I have interviewed give as a reason for wanting to adopt that they felt themselves to fall outside the activities of their contemporaries and that they wanted to remedy this by becoming a 'normal family.' (Howell 2003, 2006). Women, and also more and more men, express a sense of loss through not experiencing motherhood and fatherhood. A demand to have infertility classified as a disease—and hence a right to receive treatment at the cost of the state[2]—is becoming more persistent.

What all this amounts to is that procreation as a personal goal-oriented activity is more culturally elaborated than probably has been the case at any other time, and as a result, invested with intense emotionality by those who fail. Involuntary childlessness is a condition that gives rise to a complex of emotions of the couple involved. It is from this perspective that I shall present my findings on adoptive parenthood and, because motherhood still holds a special position in public and private thinking about the family, I shall pay special attention to adoptive motherhood. With such heavy cultural and moral elaborations on mother-love and motherhood (and to a lesser extent father-love and fatherhood), it is not, I argue, surprising that unachieved parenthood is a state that provokes strong emotions and strong motivations to alleviate the condition. The following statement by an adoptive mother sums up, in my experience, a feeling shared by many in the same situation: 'To want but not to have, biological children is a crisis, albeit a drawn-out and unpredictable one. In my opinion it does not resemble any other crisis. How can you grieve over something that never existed? When should one start to grieve a pregnancy which still might occur?' (Weigel 1998: 32).

Becoming Adoptive Parents

Norwegian couples began to adopt children from overseas sporadically in the late 1960s. Many children were adopted for humanitarian reasons from Vietnam and South Korea by couples who might already have one or more biological children. However, as time passed, the primary reason for adopting became involuntary childlessness, and the motivation that of wishing to become a normal family. It is likely that with this shift in motivation, the emotionality of the enterprise increased, just as today the adoption of a second or third child provokes less strong emotions than does that of adopting the first child. The countries from which people adopt has expanded to Latin America, other Asian countries, Ethiopia and, after the fall of the Soviet Union, several previous communist countries opened up for adoption. From the mid 1990s onwards, China has become the largest supplier of children for overseas adoption. Today, Norway adopts from about twenty different countries and, in terms of per capita, more children are adopted here than in any other country except Spain (Howell and Marre 2006). This means that more than 700 children arrive every year to become part of Norwegian family life, kinship, and nationhood. In recent years, most couples[3] who adopt have been through one or more unsuccessful attempts at assisted conception through the use of new reproductive technology before they turn to adoption. They are thus determined not to be distracted from their goal of becoming a family; of becoming mothers and fathers. They invest a lot of effort in the quest, most of which is experienced as frustrating and, as such, involves a high degree of emotional fluctuations.

The human experience of love and loving are thought by many in the contemporary Western world to be what gives life its principle meaning (Oatley and Jenkins 1996: 288). Surveys conducted to discover what Norwegians value most highly demonstrate that it is not wealth, material goods, power or career that the majority desire, but a satisfactory family life and spare time (e.g. Barstad 1999: 1; Hellevik 1999: 2). Spare time is especially wanted by the 25–40 age group in order to spend more time with the family. In other words, the good life to many Norwegians is perceived as 'quality' time which they may spend with friends, family and kin or pursue their interests. This means that for this age group not having children is a distinct handicap, a handicap of the reproductive organs, that can cause depression and a sense of unfulfillment and which, as a social status, becomes detrimental to the quality of one's social as well as personal life.

From my studies of people who are in this situation and who go through the process that leads to obtaining an adopted child, a pattern has emerged which, I suggest, may be divided into several stages. What all the stages have in common is a heightened awareness of everything that has to do with reproduction, and a tendency to become rather single-minded about it as time passes. What is also apparent about involuntary childlessness is a more than average involvement of husbands—as prospective fathers—in the whole process. In fact, many couples have told me that one very positive aspect of the adoption process was how they shared equally in the quest. In a sense they were both 'pregnant' together and the 'birth' affected them both equally and, for those who survived the tribulations, most claim that the experience has strengthened their marriage. This means that adoptive parents have a self-image of being particularly equal with regard to the distribution of responsibility, care and love.

The road that leads to adoption is often a long and painful one. After the initial surprise that they do not have control over their own destiny, disappointment becomes an overarching feeling that most have to contend with. Learning to come to terms with one's infertility and deciding to adopt is a process that it is characterized by strong emotions, ranging from exaltation to hopelessness; from optimism to frustration. In an article entitled 'The Empty Children's Room', an adoptive father writes: 'We *should* have children. That was the basic premise. We never thought that we might not have our own. Not then. Childlessness was a statistic, a negative statistic that did not concern us ... But then no children arrived ...' (Queseth 1995: 25). The scene is set for emotions to enter the stage.

Adoption As Procreation

Prepregnancy

Elsewhere I have described the whole process of transnational adoption as one that may be broken down into three stages (Howell 2001, 2003, 2006). The first of these is what I call the prepregnancy stage. This is the time when a couple decides that the time has come for them to start a family. They expect this to happen the natural way, and when it fails, they embark upon a round of medical check-ups which may end up with the use of new reproductive technology. This is a process that all describe as extremely painful and demanding, as individuals and as a couple (physically for the woman, and emotionally for both). Those who admit to failure and turn to adoption start on a new round of applications. It will bring them to the scrutiny of social workers at local and national levels, to that of adoption agencies and to the authorities in the donor country. They will have to 'prove' their suitability as prospective adoptive parents in ways that many find intrusive; they will have to provide a vast array of documentation, and they will have to choose a country from which to adopt. This is a time of refocusing their expectations from producing a child from their own bodies to adopting a child born by alien bodies in an alien land. It is, however, also a time of uncertainty. It is not certain that they will be found acceptable, and the anxiety of being rejected is a very real one amongst most applicants. Depending upon the capacity of the local authority, the time may take anything from half a year (rarely) to two years. Throughout the whole period, prospective parents experience that they are under constant pressure to perform according to rules that they feel uncertain about. They dare not enquire too deeply or complain for fear of being thought 'difficult' or 'unsuitable'.

Pregnancy

Pregnancy starts when the couple has received official approval, and their application is sent to the country of their choice. Adoption agencies and couples alike employ the term of pregnancy for this period, thereby investing it with familiar feelings. The couple now know that they will, one day, be the parents of a child from that country, but they do not know how long their pregnancy will last. Depending on the country, this may take anything from eight months (China and Ethiopia) to three years (Brazil and other Latin American countries). Although they have checked the likely length of time, local conditions may alter and it may take longer or shorter. Like the prepregnancy stage, pregnancy is also a time of uncertainty, but now it is tinged with new impatience. They start to prepare for family life. They tell family and friends about their plans and they start to readjust their expectations. Prospective adoptive parents are often highly sensitive about their choice at this early stage. Later, once the child is allocated, and after arrival, they become assertively culturalist in their understanding of family life. 'Adoption is the natural way for us to have children,' a father of three adopted children told me. Pregnancy is also a time when many prospective parents begin to take an active interest in the country that will give them a child. Many develop a special attachment to it which they carry over in their family life, culminating in a return visit as a family once the child is reaching adulthood (Howell and Marre 2006, Howell 2006).

Whereas parenthood is now definite, the child is still unidentified, and his or her time of arrival is unknown. It is a period of impatient waiting, of hoping for news, and of preparation. During this time couples are strongly encouraged to participate in classes organized by the adoption agencies, which will prepare them for the forthcoming event. Such classes are arranged by local branches of the agency throughout the country. The agencies have collected course material on various aspects of transnational adoption and this is used as a basis for discussion. Parents are being prepared for possible medical problems in the child and, more importantly, for psychological effects of having been abandoned and institutionalized. They discuss questions of bonding, of language learning, developmental problems which may result in later difficulties at school, issues of race and racism, and are given advice on how to handle the fact of adoption in their relationship with their children. In addition, a number of practical matters are discussed concerning collecting the children in their country of origin. Parents who already have adopted children talk about their experiences, and show video films from the travel to collect the child. These classes are highly emotional events; the tears are never far away. The prospective parents are very eager to learn as much as possible. They are insatiable for information about the actual collecting, the first meeting and time with the child, and the early days back home. Everyone wants to be told about the positive and wonderful aspects of transnational adoption. Most seem deaf to information about possible detrimental aspects of the practice. During this time, it is common for prospective parents to form lasting relationships with others whom they meet at the course (I return to this below).

Birth

The adopted child's birth is a prolonged period which starts when the parents are informed that a particular child has been allocated to them and ends when the child is installed in his or her new home. The news that they have got a child is described by everyone I have talked with as momentous. What usually happens is that someone from the adoption agency rings the applicant at work or at home and informs them without any ado that a child of such and such sex and age has been allocated them, and that they have 24 hours to accept him or her. In my experience, no one has refused the child they are offered, even though the details regarding sex or age may not correspond to those stated as preferable. A scenario of fate and destiny circumscribes the event, and to question this is unthinkable. Similar reactions are found amongst Spanish adoptive parents (Howell and Marre 2006). The following description by an adoptive mother of being informed about her allocated son is typical: Tuesday September 8 1981 at nineteen hours the telephone call that we were waiting for came. I don't remember if I was sitting or standing but I do remember the overwhelming feeling of joy that filled me when x from Adopsjonsforum [the agency] told me that I had become the mother of a tiny little boy ... From that telephone conversion it was that boy, Shavran, who was our boy. We had not seen him, not even in a photo, not held him, but I felt so strongly that it was precisely he who was our son (Karlsen 2002: 15). The moment of being told is one that is cherished by adoptive parents and one that they like to bring up in conversation. It is a moment of untrammeled happiness.

Upon accepting the child, the parents are sent a photo which they immediately copy and distribute amongst friends and family; they begin to carry copies in their wallets to show anyone expressing an interest and place enlarged copies about the house. They engage in kinning (Howell 2003, 2006) their unknown child through numerous little acts and utterances, so that by the time of arrival, he or she will be an acknowledged integral part of the family. By kinning I mean the process by which a foetus or newborn child (or a previously unconnected person) is brought into a permanent relationship with a group of people, expressed in a kin idiom.[4] For most, this is a period of profound anticipation mixed with exasperation with what they regard as needless delays. Depending on requirements and infrastructure of each donor country, this birthing period may take anything from six to eighteen months. The time is experienced as particularly painful. The couples know the identity of their children and they are able, to some extent, to keep track of their condition and activities, yet they are prevented from being with them.

Most children adopted these days are infants between six and eighteen months old, and the parents are fretful about missing so much of their development. They know that in most cases the facilities at the orphanage are minimal and the food is far from adequate. This is felt to be highly aggravating. The immediate bonding that occurred between most prospective mothers and fathers upon receiving information about their child's identity is very profound, and it is being consolidated through the kinning activities performed during the birthing period. There is no doubt in parents' minds that the allocated child is somehow 'meant' for them. They scrutinize the photo and even look for resemblances between the child and themselves and/or their close kin (Howell and Marre 2006). They give the child a Norwegian name in addition to the local one and refer to him or her by that name. The child has become a person. To them, it is *their* child who is waiting to 'come home'.[5] So the child is in effect an imagined child, but no less loved for that. The following example demonstrates the strength of the attachment formed by the parents to their allocated child. An allocated daughter died at the orphanage before her parent had been given permission to collect her. The parents experienced a deep sense of grief. Their daughter had died. Like the death of any child, she had to be ritually released from them and they arranged a memorial service in the local church where they mourned their loss in the company of family and friends.

Despite never having set eyes on her, the couple had emotionally completely accepted her as their daughter. As an imagined person, she had been kinned into their own Norwegian set of kin. Her very existence had made the previously childless couple into a mother and a father and they had bonded with her as if she were their biological child. In their mind's eye she was as real to them as if she actually was with them.

Some Questions Regarding Parental Love

The previous example of parental bonding is an interesting phenomenon from several perspectives. The mother-child relationship has usually been studied from the perspective of the child; how the newborn child develops his or her attachment to the mother has been the subject of many psychological studies, mainly based on the work by Bowlby (1969, 1973, 1980). Most literature has emphasized innate mother love with an accompanying bond between infants and mothers. However, this innate bond has been criticized for being too narrowly Euro-American middle class (Rogoff 2003: 111). Not least has ethnographic information from other parts of the world challenged the model (e.g. Alber 2003, Le Vine 1982). But even so, little research has been undertaken on the effect of the cultural understanding concerning parents', and especially mothers', expectations and experiences. It is important to remember the European practice among the upper and upper-middle classes of sending newborn babies away for wet-nursing, and that child abandonment was very common during the seventeenth and eighteenth centuries in France and southern Europe (Sá 2000, Fuchs 1984), provoking no moral condemnation. If we consider some random examples from other parts of the world, we find that, in many societies, babies may have no status as persons (humans) at all before certain events have taken place which ensure them a place in the kin system and in society. This is the case amongst the people on the Indonesian island of Bonerate studied by Broch (1990). Here the newborn child is characterized as being in a stage of transition. It is extremely vulnerable to experiences and shock and may decide not to enter the world of humans, but return to the 'land of unborn'. Moreover, a newborn child's name is also temporary until it has proved its intention to remain with its parents (Brock 1990: 24). Because of this knowledge, the loss of a young infant is not as hard for the parents as is the loss of child who has settled in the human world (ibid. 15). Neither is such a death publicly mourned. From this it seems that Bonerate parents refrain from engaging themselves fully with a newborn child but await the course of events before committing themselves emotionally.

Another example of a (to the contemporary Western eye) distanced mother-baby relationship is given by Scheper-Hughes in her study from a shantytown in Brazil. She challenges what she calls 'a psychobiological script of innate or universal emotions such as has been suggested in the biomedical literature on "maternal bonding", and more recently, in the new feminist literature on maternal sentiments' (1985: 292). Her argument—which is further developed in her ethnographic monograph from

1992—is that maternal thinking and practices are *socially produced* (Scheper-Hughes 1992). My own position, mentioned above, is that a nature or nurture stance are both equally unproductive. While evidence seems to point towards certain innate proclivities in humans—maternal bonding being one of these—cultural scripts shape and direct these to quite a large extent. Human beings create relationships and meanings (including meaningful emotions) intersubjectively (Bråten 1998), implying that culture is in nature and nature is in culture. This point notwithstanding, Scheper-Hughes provides a detailed exposition of maternal detachment and indifference towards infants that the mothers judged to be too weak to survive the harsh conditions of their lives (Scheper-Hughes 1985, 1992).

What the mothers learn is 'to let go' of those children for whom they see no hope for survival (Scheper-Hughes 1985: 295). In an environment of extreme scarcity, mothers 'protect themselves from strong emotional attachment to their infants through a form of nurturance that is, from the start, somewhat "impersonal".' Again, like the people on Bonerate, but in stark contrast to Norwegian adoptive parents, mothers in the shantytown refrain from giving their children a name until they begin to walk and talk (ibid. 311)—when they show signs of surviving. Scheper-Hughes's study is an example of radical cultural relativism which, as an approach, I suggest is less commonly held today. Nevertheless, it can be read as an example of the mutual constitution of cultural and psychological factors. These shantytown mothers' treatment of their children show how social and cultural factors may influence maternal thinking so that it appears as a cultural pattern. It is useful to bear Scheper-Hughes's ethnographic example, and her interpretation of it, in mind when we turn to the Norwegian adoptive mothers and their maternal thinking. The contemporary Norwegian cultural value attached to motherhood is of such a high intensity that failure to become mothers is felt as a major personal, psychological and social failure. The reactions of most adoptive mothers (and fathers) to the news of their identified child-to-be is so intense that a strong bonding occurs immediately, accompanied by a scenario of fate and destiny. So when, as the earlier example shows, the child dies before meeting her new parents, the grief is not only personal but has to be marked socially. The girl had been made into a kinned person and, as such, had to be mourned by her family and kin. The contrast with the mothers in the shantytown could hardly be starker. In order to demonstrate the strength of adoptive parents' feelings, I turn now to a discussion of the moment of first meeting, the culmination of the birth.

The First Encounter

During the 1970s and 1980s most children who did not come from Latin America— where the laws required that adoptive parents appear in person—met their child at the Norwegian international airport. Since the 1990s it has become increasingly popular to travel to the children's country of origin and collect them themselves.

Whichever option is chosen, pregnant adoptive parents now know that it is only a question of time before they will hold their child in their arms. This is a time filled both with anticipation of a dream come true and frustration over still having to wait. The magazines published by the Norwegian adoption agencies regularly carry reports by adoptive mothers or fathers in which they describe the intensity of emotions while waiting at the airport for the child to be delivered by an escort, or the triumphs and tribulations of the journey to China, Colombia or wherever, that resulted in them bringing home the child of their imagination.

The fact of imagining looms large in adoptive parents' description of this last stage. The description by a mother on her way to Colombia to pick up her daughter is typical: 'It was all rather unreal. Finally, on our way to Colombia to experience an unknown country and to collect our beautiful little daughter Oda Silvia.[6] ...We just received a photo of her before having to get ready. Love at first sight! The protection instinct arrived immediately when I held the photo in my hands. We were so happy and excited. We could hardly believe that this lovely girl was ours' (Ranheim 1999: 4). And, having arrived and spent the first night at the hotel, they are on their way to the orphanage: 'Tears in the taxi. Tears while we were waiting. Tears when the family Norvik [another adoptive family who they had become acquainted with on the journey] was given their beautiful girl. A good, calm feeling of happiness when they brought me a small girl dressed in pink. The maternal feeling was immediately aroused' (Ranheim 1999: 4) Many similar accounts can be found in the media, and they conform to stories I have been told by numerous adoptive parents whom I have interviewed. Another couple, who was allocated a son from South Korea, chose that he be escorted to Norway. They explained that they did not wish to watch what they thought would be an upsetting scene of the rupture between the boy and his foster mother. 'This is a way of tackling the emotional part', the mother said (*Aftenposten* 12 December 2005: 16).

As I have shown, the period from when a couple decides to adopt until they have a child whom they may call their own is an emotional time. Emotions run the gamut from deep depression, frustration, irritation and anger to excitement, anticipation and finally happiness and a great sense of achievement. Prospective adoptive parents are extremely reflexive about every move they make on the long road towards obtaining a child. Nothing is left to chance. As so much in their lives is focused on the one clear objective, they continuously evaluate events that affect the proceedings, and thoughts about adoption constantly hover at the rim of consciousness, contributing to their emotional state at any given time.

Conclusion

To obtain a child through one's own body or through adoption are, of course, two very different procedures. However, many adoptive parents like to talk about the two processes as more similar than different. Listening to a mother of three adopted children, who is also a midwife, giving a talk to prospective adoptive parents, I was struck by the very deliberate way she likened adoption to birth. She did so less from a biological standpoint and more from an emotional and moralistic one. The expectations and anxieties about the future child are very similar in both kinds of parent, she said. Adoption and birth are two sides of the same coin. She went on to talk about post-partum depression, not uncommon amongst birth mothers, and said that this also happened to adoptive mothers—although it is not much talked about. In fact, according to her, it has been a taboo subject in adoption circles, just as used to be the case with birth mothers. 'You have waited so long before you finally have your child in your arms,' she said, 'you have gone through much more stress than an average biological mother, therefore it is not surprising that, when finally the day arrives and all your dreams are fulfilled, you may experience that your initial euphoria gives way to a sense of anticlimax, even disappointment. This is natural and you must not feel upset or guilty about this. I know that it will vanish after a few days or weeks. Just let the fact of being a family slowly settle in your consciousness. Don't fret, and you will soon recapture the joy that you had anticipated.'

If we return now to the definition of emotion given by Oatley and Jenkins at the outset of this chapter, I would argue that the process of becoming adoptive parents in contemporary Norway exemplifies it well. However, it must be borne in mind that this particular emotionality is the result of an interplay between innate potentiality and cultural elaborations. The cultural elaborations on parenthood are of such complexity that the emotions experienced by the involuntarily childless are also profound and complex. In order to bring the argument to a conclusion, let me break the definition up into its constituent parts. (1) 'An emotion is usually caused by a person consciously or unconsciously evaluating an event as relevant to a concern (goal) that is important' (Oatley and Jenkins 1996: 96). In the case of potential adoptive parents, they evaluate very consciously a number of events that are relevant to their ultimate aim of obtaining a child and becoming adoptive parents. As I have shown, these events—the decision to adopt, the application procedures, the evaluations by an outsider, the waiting, the allocation and, finally, the encounter—all emerge as a fairly standard process and series of events and they seem to trigger off fairly similar emotional responses in the persons concerned.

(2) 'The emotion is felt as positive when a concern is advanced and negative when a concern is impeded, (ibid.). As I stated above, the prepregnancy stage—waiting to be accepted by the authorities as worthy parent material—involves clear fluctuations in strong emotions, ranging from anxiety and frustration while undergoing the examination to exultation when final acceptance is given. The prospective parents experience deep depression when delays are encountered in the visits by the social worker or in the submission of the various reports. They are excited when they choose a country and prepare themselves to obtain a child from it. This pattern continues during the pregnancy and birth stages. The prospective parents feel themselves to be the playthings of circumstances. Excitement is experienced when

something positive occurs that brings the day of receiving a child closer (the high points are the actual allocation of a real child and being informed of the date for collection). Frustration and despondency are experienced when their aims are impeded, e.g. by slow bureaucratic handling of their application in Norway and in the donor country, or delays in the time identified for collection.

The ultimate high is the culmination of the whole process, when they meet their child for the first time and can bring him or her home. In an article in the journal of one of the adoption agencies in which she describes the journey to China to collect their daughter, the mother concludes her description of the numerous emotional ups and downs—on the journey, on the visit to the orphanage, during the early days with her daughter at the hotel before returning home—by saying, 'I was sweating [from all the anxieties in China] but happy beyond belief when we finally sat on the plane going back home. I sat and cried the whole way home—don't quite know why—but I guess it was slowly dawning on me that I had become a mummy' (Marthinsen 2005: 16).

Acknowledgements

The research on transnational adoption has been supported by the Norwegian Research Council and a European Commission project under the Quality of Life and Management of Living Resources Programme; contract number QLG 7—CT—2001—01668. I wish to thank Harald Beyer Broch for suggestions about literature and for several pertinent comments to an early draft.

References

Alber, E. (2003), 'Denying Biological Parenthood: Fosterage in Northern Benin', *Ethnos* 68(4): 487–506.

Barstad, A. (1999), 'Hva synes nordmann de behøver for å få det bedre?' *Samfunnsspeilet*, 4: 1–3.

Bowlby, J. (1969), *Attachment and Loss*, vol. 1, *Attachment*, London: Hogarth Press; New York: Basic Books.

Bowlby, J. (1973), *Attachment and Loss*, vol. 2, *Separation: Anxiety & Anger*, London: Hogarth Press; New York: Basic Books.

Bowlby, J. (1980), *Attachment and Loss*, vol. 3, *Loss: Sadness & Depression*, *Attachment and Loss*, London: Hogarth Press; New York: Basic Books.

Bråten, S., ed. (1998), *Intersubjective Communication and Emotion in Early Ontogeny*, Cambridge: Cambridge University Press.

Broch, H. B. (1990), *Growing Up Agreeably: Bonerate Childhood Observed*, Honolulu: University of Hawaii Press.

Fuchs, R. G. (1984), *Abandoned Children: Foundlings and Child Welfare in Nineteenth Century France*, Albany: State University of New York Press.

Gillis, J. (1996), *A World of their Own Making: Myths, Ritual and the Quest for Family,* Cambridge: Harvard University Press.

Hellevik, O. (1999), 'Hvorfor blir vi ikke Lykkeligere?' *Samfunnsspeilet,* 4: 1–4.

Howell, S., ed. (1997), *The Ethnography of Moralities,* London: Routledge.

Howell, S. (2001), "'Self-conscious Kinship: Some Contested Values in Norwegian Transnational Adoption'". In S. Franklin and S. McKinnon (eds.), *Relative Values: Reconfiguring Kinship Studies,* Durham: Duke University Press.

Howell, S. (2002), 'Community beyond Place: Adoptive families in Norway', in V. Amit (ed.), *Realizing Community: Concepts, Social Relationships and Sentiments,* London: Routledge.

Howell, S. (2003), 'Kinning: The Creation of Life Trajectories in Transnational Adoptive Families', *Journal of the Royal Anthropological Institute (incorporating Man),* 9(3): 465–84.

Howell, S. (2006), *The Kinning of Foreigners: Transnational Adoption in a Global Perspective,* Oxford and New York: Berghahn Books.

Howell, S., and Marre, D. (2006) 'To Kin a Foreign Child in Norway and Spain: Notions of Resemblances and the Achievement of Belonging', *Ethnos. 71:3 (293–316)*

Karlsen, K. Beheim. (2002), Arve-Sonen Min [Arve-my son]. Oslo: Gyldendal.

Leira, A. (1996), *Parents, Children and the State: Family Obligations in Norway,* Oslo: Institute for Social Research.

Levine, R. (1982), *Culture, Behavior and Personality: An Introduction to the Comparative Study of Psychosocial Adaptation,* New York: Aldine.

Marthinsen, K. (2005), 'Dagbok fra Kina' [Diary from China], *Verdens Barn* 17(1): 14–17.

Milton, K. and M. Svasek (2005), *Mixed Emotions: Anthropological Studies of Feeling,* Oxford: Berg.

Oatley, K., and Jenkins, J. M. (1996), *Understanding Emotions,* Oxford: Blackwell.

Queseth, H. (1995), Det tomme barnerommet [the empty children's room]. In *Adopsjon av Utenlandske Barn,* Oslo: Universitetsforlaget.

Ranheim, G. Ø. (1999), 'Livets reise' [Journey of Life], *Adopsjonsforum* 24(3): 4–5.

Rogoff, B. (2003), *The Cultural Nature of Human Development,* Oxford: Oxford University Press.

Rose, N. (1999), *Governing the Soul: The Shaping of the Private Self,* London: Free Association Books.

Sá, I. dos G. (2000), Circulation of Children in Eighteenth-century Portugal', in C. Panther-Brick and M. T. Smith (eds.), *Abandoned Children,* Cambridge: Cambridge University Press.

Sandelowski, M. (1993), *With Child in Mind: Studies of the Personal Encounter with Infertility,* Philadelphia: University of Pennsylvania Press.

Scheper-Hughes, N. (1985), 'Culture, Scarcity, and Maternal Thinking', *Ethos* 13: 291–317.

Scheper-Hughes, N. (1992), *Death without Weeping: The Violence of Everyday Life in Brazil,* Berkeley: University of California Press.

Volkman, T. A., ed. (2005), *Cultures of Transnational Adoption,* Durham, N.C.: Duke University Press.

Weigel, K. (1997), *Langtansbarned: adoptivforeldrar beratter,* Stockholm: Norsteds.

Notes

1. Hanne Haavind is professor of child psychology at the University of Oslo.
2. Successive governments refuse to regard infertility as a disease. At the moment, couples are entitled to three attempts at assisted conception at the state's expense and adoptive parents receive a grant upon successfully bringing a child home. However, pressure groups demand more.
3. I say couples, because, at time of writing, although Norwegian law does not forbid single individuals to adopt, this is very rarely granted. The ideal applicants should be a married couple in a stable relationship and a stable lifestyle. Only married couples may undergo medical treatment for infertility. Homosexuals, even those who live in legal partnerships, may not receive infertility treatment or adopt.
4. I have suggested that kinning is not confined to adoptive relationships but is probably a universal process, marked in all societies by various ritual acts that ensure kinned subjectivation (Howell 2003), but that it has not generally been recognized as such. Because transnational adoption in Norway is such a public event, taking place in a cultural climate that predicates kinship upon biological connectedness, and because adoptive parents engage so deliberately in transcending the fact that they are not biologically connected to their children, my attention was drawn to this previously 'hidden' aspect of kinship.
5. The expression 'come home' is used by the adoption agencies. For example, their annual statistics will state 'x number of children came home from China in 2002'. I have argued elsewhere (Howell 2001) that by employing such an emotionally loaded term, they are in effect denying any significance of the children's place of origin and rendering the biological parents into merely temporary child-minders.
6. The name is significant. It shows that the parents have given her a Norwegian name, Oda, but that they keep her Colombian name, Silvia, as a middle name. The point is that they have engaged actively with her from the moment of allocation by naming her themselves, making her into a relative.

III
Anger, Shame and Grief

–14–

Getting Angry
The Jamesian Theory of Emotion in Anthropology

Robert C. Solomon

The Tahitians say that an angry man is like a bottle. When he gets filled up he will begin to spill over. (Tavana, quoted in Levy 1973: 285)

The metaphor is so pervasive, it so dominates our thinking about our feelings, that we find ourselves unable to experience our emotions without it. We find it in philosophy and medicine as well as in our poetry, and we find it too in other cultures. Consequently, we believe what the metaphor tells us instead of recognizing it as a metaphor, a cultural artifact that systematically misleads us in our understanding of ourselves and, in anthropology, our understanding of other peoples.

The metaphor, captured succinctly in the Tahitian simile that an angry man is like a bottle, is the *hydraulic metaphor*. It presents the image of emotion as a force within us, filling up and spilling over. Rendered as science, the same metaphor is made respectable in physiological garb. The medieval physicians theorized at length on the various "humours" that determined the emotions. And in this century, the metaphor has been elegantly dressed in neurology and presented as a scientific theory—indeed, the only theory that has thoroughly dominated the subject over the past century. The theory is that an emotion is an "inner experience," a "feeling" based on a physiological disturbance of a (now) easily specifiable kind plus, perhaps, some outward manifestation and an interpretation according to which we identify this feeling as an emotion of a particular kind.

The theory received its classic formulation by William James (1884), in "What Is an Emotion?" James answered his question with his theory: An emotion is the perception of a visceral disturbance brought about by a traumatic perception, for example, seeing a bear leap out in front of you or coming across a bucket filled with blood. The theory (developed simultaneously by C. G. Lange in Europe) is now appropriately called the "Jamesian (James-Lange) theory of emotion." It is, I shall argue, as misleading as it is pervasive.

Emotions in Anthropology

> Emotions as biological events are the same the world over. (Lindzey 1954; also see 1961)

The Jamesian theory has special appeal, and is particularly damaging, in anthropology. There is an obvious problem, given the nature of the theory. An emotion as an "inner feeling" is unobservable and inaccessible to the anthropologist, thus leaving any attempt at describing emotion in other peoples at the mercy of obviously anthropocentric "empathy." And yet, the theory (scientific or not) has been accepted as apparently useful for interpreting not only the emotional life of other peoples but also the language used by other peoples to describe their own emotions, thus suggesting a kind of double confirmation. The theory—that emotions, as feelings based upon physiological disturbances, can be understood in strictly biological terms—results in this familiar but fallacious consequence: Emotions can therefore be taken to be more or less universal human phenomena, the same in everyone, making allowances for certain minimal differences in physiology and, consequently, temperament. (In fact, I would argue that there is little reason to suppose that such differences or their emotional consequences are minimal, but that is not the thesis I wish to pursue here: see, e.g., Freedman 1974.)

Even if the emotions were essentially the same in all people, however, it is evident that the language and interpretation of emotions, as well as their causes, expressions, and vicissitudes, vary widely from culture to culture. The effects of epinephrine may be identical in angry people from Borough Hall in Brooklyn to the beaches of Bora Bora, but there are, nevertheless, differences in the emotional lives of various peoples, and this is where anthropology enters the picture.

The anthropological appeal of the Jamesian theory is obvious: It divides the phenomenon of emotion into two comprehensive components, a physiological feeling component, which can be presumed a priori (and falsely) to be more or less the same in all human beings, and a cultural component, which can be described by the anthropologist, using the same techniques of observation and interview that are appropriate for almost any other cultural phenomenon. Any mystery surrounding emotion is thus dispelled: the difficulty of "getting inside another person's head," without which one cannot understand another's feelings, is rendered unnecessary. Emotions are to be understood in the realm of physiology, not phenomenology, thus circumventing the hard problem of "empathy." The interpretation of emotions (including the basic interpretive act of naming and identifying one's emotion) is quite distinct from the emotion itself, thus leaving the emotion proper outside the realm of anthropology.

My argument turns on two related objections to the Jamesian theory. First, that the theory is not only incomplete but wholly mistaken. It trivializes, rather than captures, the nature of emotions.[1] Second, the distinction between an emotion and its interpretation is faulty and misleading in a variety of ways. The consequence of these objections is to insist that emotions themselves are the proper province of anthropology. My thesis is that emotions are to be construed as cultural acquisitions, determined by the circumstances and concepts of a particular culture as well as, or rather much more than, by the functions of biology and, more specifically, neurology. There may be universal emotions, but this is a matter to be settled empirically, not by a priori pronouncement.

The Variability of Emotions

Take aggression as an example. A distinction must be made between the instrumental acts that are indices of aggression (e.g., hitting, insulting, noncooperating) and the hypothetical "goal response" of the aggression motive (perceiving another person's reactions to injury). It is the latter that one would expect to find transculturally. The aggressor's instrumental activities that serve to hurt someone else—and thus enable him to perceive reactions to injury in his victim—will differ from one culture to another. The form of an insult, for instance, depends on the values held by the insulted one. Or to take another example: automobile racing and football can be instrumental activities for competition only if the society has automobiles and knows how to play football. (Sears 1955)

The cultural specificity and variability of several dimensions of emotion are not in question. For instance, the various causes of emotion are clearly cultural in their specifics (whether or not there are also some causes of some emotions that might be argued to be universal or even "instinctual"). What makes a person angry depends upon those situations or events that are considered offensive or frustrating. A New Yorker will become infuriated on standing in a queue the length of which would make a Muscovite grateful. The same action will inspire outrage in some societies and not others; consider, as examples, failing to shake hands, kissing on the lips, killing a dog, not returning a phone call. The same objects will provoke fear in one culture but not in others, for example, snakes, bewitchment, being audited by the IRS, not getting tenure, and being too rich or too thin. Causes of emotion vary from culture to culture; it does not follow that emotions do, or do not, vary as well.

The *names* of emotions clearly vary from culture to culture, along with most vocabulary entries and names for virtually everything else. But this obvious point hides a subtle and troublesome one; how do we know whether it is *only* the names (i.e., phonetic sequences) that vary, rather than their reference? The problem here is what W. V. O. Quine calls "radical intranslatability"; do the words "anger" in English and "*riri*" in Tahitian refer to "the same" emotion? How would we tell? Even if the causes are commensurable and the behavior seems to be similar, how do we gauge the similarity of the emotions? Names of emotions are clearly cultural artifacts, even "arbitrary" in the sense that it is now said as a matter of Paris-inspired cant that "all signs are arbitrary." But the identities of the phenomena that those names name are yet an open question, not obviously the same references for quaintly different vocabularies but clearly not entirely different either. We are, after all, identifying a shared reference to *something*.

A similar point can be made about the various *expressions* of emotion. Clearly some expressions, at least, differ from culture to culture as learned gestures and more or less "spontaneous" actions. Clenched fists are expressions of anger in one culture, not in another. Banging one's head on the wall is an expression of grief in one society, not in others. And the *verbal* expressions of emotion vary not only along with the language (of course) but also according to the familiar images and metaphors of the culture. (Not everyone would understand what we so easily and now clumsily refer to as "heartbroken.") There may well be emotional expressions that vary very little from culture to culture, particularly certain minimal facial expressions, as Paul Ekman (1975) has recently demonstrated. But that there are such universal expressions, if there are any, no more demonstrates the universality or "nature" of emotions than the wide variety of more complex expressions proves the variability of emotions. Again, this must at least start as an open question, for which the observation of emotional expressions may serve at most as a preliminary. Indeed, the more fundamental question—of what are these expressions expressive?—will have to wait for an account of the emotions themselves.

Finally, there is the series of metaphors to be found in almost every culture with any vocabulary of psychological self-description that are essentially explanations and diagnoses of emotions, rather than merely names for them. The Tahitian gentleman quoted at the start of this essay, for example, is expressing a theory, the hydraulic theory, which has long been dominant in discussions of emotion in our culture, too, in part because of (but also culminating in) Freud's "dynamic" and "economic" models of the psyche in terms of various "forces" within. Metaphors and theories of emotion are often related and even interchangeable. They also influence the experience of the emotions themselves. To believe that anger is a force building up pressure is to experience the physiological symptoms of anger as a force "inside," just as believing that "falling in love" is bound to have a certain irresponsible influence on one's loving.

It is a matter of no small interest that the same metaphors—the hydraulic metaphor in particular—can be found in societies of very different temperaments. But such metaphors are by no means universal. Catherine Lutz (1982) describes an emotional vocabulary among the Ifaluk that is relatively devoid of references to the hydraulic metaphor or the Jamesian theory,[2] and the prevalence of the metaphor by no means proves the Jamesian theory to be true. Nevertheless, the variability of emotion metaphors and theories can be counted among the various dimensions of variability of emotion, if, that is, it is true that beliefs about emotions influence or determine the nature of the emotions themselves. (On the Jamesian theory, it is hard to see how or why this should be so; on the alternative view I shall propose at the end of this essay, the mutual influence of beliefs and emotions should be quite transparent.)

Names of emotions do not yet entail metaphors or theories, but even so rudimentary a psychological activity as "naming one's feelings" already stakes out a network of distinctions and foci that are well on their way to extended metaphors and crude theories. The fact that one language has a dozen words for sexual affection and another has fifty words for hostility already anticipates the kinds of models that will be appropriate. A culture that emphasizes what David Hume called "the violent passions" will be ripe for the Jamesian theory, but a culture that rather stresses the "calm" emotions (an appreciation of beauty, lifelong friendship, a sense of beneficence and justice) will find the Jamesian theory and the hydraulic model that underlies it patently absurd. A culture that bothers to name an emotion pays at least some attention to it, and it is hard to find a culture with named emotions that does not also have theories about them, however primitive. In some cases, the theory might consist simply of the warning "anger is dangerous." In theory-enthusiastic cultures such as our own, the theories surrounding an emotion might more resemble the theology of the druids, thus prompting more or less perennial cries about emotional: simplicity and "getting in touch with your feelings." But whether the theory at stake is the labyrinth of Jungian typologies or the homilies of Joyce Brothers, the beliefs people have *about* emotions vary considerably, and it remains to be seen just how this reflects—or doesn't reflect—the crosscultural (and intracultural) variability of the emotions themselves.

(Not) Getting Angry: Two Examples

"My intestines were angry." (quoted in Levy, 1973: 214)

Anger is an emotion that would seem to be universal and unlearned if any emotion is, however different its manifestations in various cultures. John Watson chose anger as one of his three "basic" emotions (fear and dependency were the other two). It is one of those emotions most evident even in infants, and Watson suggested that it is one of the building blocks for all other emotions. More recently, Robert Plutchik (1962) has developed an evolutionary model of emotions and emotional development in which anger, again, emerges as one of the (this time eight) basic building blocks of emotion. Anger is one of the most easily observable emotions; we might debate its nuances (outrage or indignation) and perhaps surmise its etiology (jealousy, frustration, or moral offense). The causes of anger might differ from culture to culture, and the expressions, at least the verbal expressions, might vary too. Bur it is too easy to assume that anger itself and its basic manifestations—the reddened face, visible irritability and what William James properly called "the tendency to vigorous action"—are much the same from the Philippines to the Lower East Side, from Bongo Bongo to the more boisterous committee meetings of the Social Science Research Council. Everyone gets angry—at least at some time and for some reason. Or so it would seem.

But let us consider two quite different accounts of anger, in two quite different societies. I want to discuss later in this chapter some of the methodological problems to which any such account is subject. But, as a first, superficial observation, let us make clear certain gross differences—or at least claims about certain gross differences—in two cultures: the Tahitian (Levy 1973) and the Utka (Utkuhikhalingmiut) Eskimos (Briggs 1970) in the Northwest Territories. In both cases, these people do not get angry. Some of this may be emphasis rather than substance, but that too constitutes a significant difference in emotional life. It might be argued, for instance, that Americans give far more importance to the emotions of anger and moral indignation than do the Russians or Japanese, for example, whether or not the emotions themselves are so significantly different. But having pointed out this difference in emphasis, have we not already indicated vast differences in temperament and emotional constitution as such? For both the Tahitians and the Utka, however, anger is as rare as it is feared.

The Tahitians, according to Levy, place an unusual amount of emphasis on anger. They talk about it and theorize about it extensively; it is "hypercognized," he tells us, in that "there are a large number of culturally provided schemata for interpreting and dealing with anger." (See Levy 1984.) Other emotions, sadness, for instance, are "hypocognized" and, Levy suggests, virtually unrecognized. Anger, however, is rare, no matter how much the object of concern. Does this mean, however, that it is indeed present but unaccounted for or, rather, that in circumstances in which *we* (for example) would most certainly have an emotion, they do not?

A partial answer to this crucial question can be couched in terms of the Tahitian theory of emotion, which is distinctively Jamesian. Emotions have a "place" in the body, the intestines, for example. Indeed, the language of emotion is often "it" rather than "I," although one must quickly add that this grammatical feature of the Tahitian language is not to be found only in the realm of emotions (Levy 1973:213). He quotes an informant:

> "In my youth, [it was] a powerful thing, very powerful, very powerful 'it' was [*sic*], when 'it' came, and I tried to hold it down there was something that was not right. That was the cause of a lot of bad anger inside one ... after a time ... that thing, 'it' would go away." (ibid., p. 212)

Levy adds that "people will say 'my intestines were angry'" (ibid., p. 213). This locution may seem slightly odd but certainly not unfamiliar; it indicates, however, a much deeper difference between our conception of anger and the Tahitian conception and, consequently and more important, a deep difference between Tahitian anger and our own.

Throughout the literature on Tahiti, Levy tells us, one message above all keeps repeating itself: "These are gentle people" and there are "extremely few reports of angry behavior." Morrison noted two centuries ago that the Tahitians are "slow to anger and soon appeased." (in Levy 1973:275). Levy quotes a contemporary policeman who talks of "the lack of a vengeful spirit" (ibid., p. 276), and though Levy reports some forty-seven terms referring to anger, he adds that the Tahitian concern with, and fear of, anger and its violent effects are "in the face of little experience of such anger" (ibid., p. 285). The pairing of so much attention and theorizing with so rare an emotion points to a curious relationship between the having of an emotion and the understanding of it, but it is clear from Levy's descriptions and reports that this relationship is *not* to be construed (as we might be likely to construe it in ourselves) as one of "suppression" or social "control" as such. It is the gentleness, the lack of anger itself that seems to be learned, not the inhibition or suppression of it. And part of this learning experience, ironically, is the acquisition of an enormous number of myths and metaphors about anger through which this rather rare emotion is explained—and feared.

In Jean Briggs's (1970) descriptions of the Utka Eskimos, they do not, as her title *Never in Anger* indicates, get angry. Not only do they not express anger: they do not "feel" angry, and, unlike the Tahitians, they do not talk about it. They do not get angry in circumstances that would surely incite us to outrage, and they do nor get angry in other circumstances either. The Utka do not have a word or set of graded distinctions for anger, as we do and as the Tahitians do; indeed the word with which they refer to angry behavior in foreigners and in children is also the word for "childish." There is no reason to suppose that, biologically, the Utka have any fewer or more impoverished epinephrine secretions than we do, and Dr. Briggs's descriptions show that, on occasion, they get just as "heated up" as we do. But they do not get angry, she assures us. They do feel annoyed, even hostile, and they can display raw violence, for example, the beating of their dogs (in the name of "discipline," of course). But is this to be considered merely a nuance of terminology? Or something more significant?

There have been some severe objections to the observations and conclusions of this research, but the central claim remains intact, at least by way of a plausible hypothesis not yet refuted. Michelle Rosaldo (1984), for instance, has argued that Briggs confuses lack of anger with fear of anger, the sense—to be found in Tahitian society as well as in Filipino society and in our own—that anger is dangerous and can even destroy a society. But here again, we meet that suspicious and too-neat distinction between the essence of the emotion itself and talk *about* emotion, as if it can be assumed that the emotion remains more or less constant while our thoughts and feelings about the emotion alter its expression and its representation. But even if Briggs is wrong about the absence of anger as such, the context of that emotion and the peculiar absence of (what we would consider) the usual expressions and manifestations of it would have to be explained.

References

Briggs, Jean L. 1970. *Never in Anger.* Cambridge, Mass.: Harvard University Press.

Ekman, Paul. 1975. *Unmasking the Face.* Englewood Cliffs, N.J.: Prentice-Hall.

Freedman, D. G. 1974. *Human Infancy.* Hillsdale, N.J.: Erlbaum.

James. William. 1884. What is an emotion? *Mind* 9: 188–205.

Levy, Robert I. 1973. *Tahitians.* University of Chicago Press.

Levy, Robert I. 1984. Emotion, Knowledge and Culture. In Richard A. Schweder and Robert A. LeVine, eds., *Culture Theory: Essays on Mind, Self and Emotion.* Cambridge: Cambridge University Press.

Lindzey, Gardner. 1954. *Psychology.* Cleveland: Worth.

—— 1961. *Projective Techniques and Cross-Cultural Research.* New York: Appleton-Century-Crofts.

Lutz, Catherine. 1982. The domain of emotion words in Ifaluk. *American Ethnologist* 9: 113–28.

Plutchik, Robert. 1962. *The Emotions.* New York: Random House.

Rosaldo, Michelle Z. 1984. Toward an Anthropology of Self and Feeling. In Richard A. Schweder and Robert A. LeVine, eds., *Culture Theory: Essays on Mind, Self and Emotion.* Cambridge: Cambridge University Press.

Sears. Robert R. 1955. Transcultural variables and conceptual equivalence. In Bert Kaplan, ed., *Studying Personality Cross-Culturally.* Evanston, Ill.: Row, Peterson.

Solomon, Robert C. 1976. *Passions.* New York: Doubleday.

1978. Emotions and anthropology. *Inquiry* 21: 181–99.

Notes

This chapter was stimulated by the Social Science Research Council meeting in May 1981 on Concepts of Culture and Its Acquisition. Special thanks to Richard A. Shweder for his helpful criticism and encouragement. A portion of the "methodology" section has been adapted from my "Emotions and Anthropology" (*Inquiry* 21 [1978]: 181–99), with the generous permission of the editors.

1. This has often been argued, and I shall not repeat the primary arguments here: see Solomon 1976, chap. 7: 1978.

2. It is worth noting, however, that the criterion used for distinguishing emotion words in Ifaluk was whether or not they were identified as "about our insides," despite the argument that "the Ifaluk see the emotions as evoked in, and inseparable from, social activity" rather than "internal feeling states" (Lutz 1982: 114, 124).

–15–

The Shame of Headhunters
and the Autonomy of Self

Michelle Z. Rosaldo

My point is simple. Psychological idioms that we use in offering accounts of the activities of our peers—or our companions in the field[1]—are at the same time "ideological" or "moral" notions. As ethnographers (and moral persons) we are compelled at once to use and to suspect them. The assumptions bound to our familiar forms of psychological explanation prove attractive yet inevitably problematic when confronted with a cultural account.

"Guilt" and "shame"[2] are, of course, the idioms to concern me. Paired by Western theorists[3] as complementary and/or alternative means for controlling selfish energies that we think belong to every human heart, these terms assume our faith that people everywhere are frustrated, repressed, rebellious, unfulfilled, or—at least—at odds with their society. Guilt and shame are seen, in short, as moral affects[4] necessary to constrain the individuated self from dangerous and asocial acts of impulse, lust, and violence. Surely, this is a vision most of us find as suspect as it seems difficult to reject. Guilt and shame may everywhere be linked to things like violence, sex, and strain, just as, in every case, they may concern the threat of circumstance or activity to undermine an ideal presentation of the self. And yet the "selves" that these, or other feelings, help defend—and so, the ways such feelings work—will differ with the culture and organization of particular societies. "Our" view of persons as embodiments of continuing and conflictual inner drives and needs is one which, in all likelihood, reflects important aspects of the "individualism" famous in the modern West, along with the experiences of Western "individual" suppressed by modern forms of social inequality. Considering data from the Ilongots,[5] a horticultural and hunting population of Northern Luzon, Philippines, my questions here concern alternatives that emerge among a people who assume that persons want to be not different but equivalent or "the same," and see in individuality not essential self, but a persona born of conflict.

To begin. Most adult Ilongot men at the time of my research were, or had been, headhunters. That is, most had at one time joined with fellows on a raid in which they had the opportunity to toss a newly severed human head upon the ground. In severing and tossing human heads, Ilongot men recount, they could relieve hearts burdened with the "weight" of insult, envy, pain, and grief; and in discarding "heavy" thoughts, they could achieve an "anger" that yields "energy," makes shy and burdened youths "the same" or equal to their peers, and "lightens" both their footsteps and the feelings in their hearts.

And yet occasionally, Ilongots say, some one among a group of raiders found himself immobilized by the "smell of blood." "Heaviness" would overwhelm his heart, so that he could not flee. When this happened, one of his fellows, generally an older man, would cut a lock of the afflicted's hair, hoot loudly, call for "lightness" and, in so doing, cause relief.

What is involved here? Kind and generous in their everyday affairs, Ilongot headhunters were not reluctant to admit that there is something wrong or bad about the act of killing. But none appeared to feel remorse for prior violent deeds, or speak of moral right and wrong when telling why they killed. Did they not, then, feel anything like shame or guilt about the violent impulse celebrated in their murders? Did they not see difficulty in reconciling gory violence and a cooperative mundane life?

With these questions in mind, let me consider three accounts for what we now might call the headhunter's paralysis. The first—the contribution, let us say, of a Naive Psychologist—holds that those Ilongots who claim that they are heavy with the smell of blood would speak more truly if they used the English metaphor instead and so described themselves, perhaps, as "frozen with fear." This translation, I suggest, can be discarded because it tells us nothing about why the stricken killers describe themselves the way they do, or why haircutting brings relief. Second, there is the Naive Culturalist's account. It argues simply that Ilongots speak the truth: The "smell of blood" goes to "the heart" and sickens it, evoking a subjective sense of weight and immobility. The cultural remedy is then explained by cultural belief: Paralysis is eliminated by removing heavy hair from off the head when raiders wish their bodies light and fleet.

I argue later that this cultural account may lend itself to less naive reflections. But a third and, initially, at least, much richer explanation must first be entertained. This third account is one that sees in men's paralysis a cultural symptom in response to culturally induced distress. It argues that occasional killers, when confronted by the gory evidence of wrong, aware that they need not have killed, perhaps perturbed by the great gap between their savage practice and the humanity that rules their daily world, are overwhelmed by sentiments of ambivalence, shame, and guilt. They hate their actions and the violence thus revealed within themselves. In such a story, paralysis marks the moral man. Haircutting is his purge.

For some time, I found this third alternative most attractive. Not only did it hint at an ambivalence and moral feeling that struck me as oddly lacking in most headhunters' reports, but it provided fertile ground for further musing. Surely, the fact that headhunters spoke of the "mark" caused by "the smell of blood" and sought to "beautify" themselves with a sweet-smelling fern suggests dynamics linked to things like guilt, shame, and denial. And if some killers were, in fact, distressed by what they did, it made good sense that they should "sacrifice" some of their beautiful and carefully tended hair. Furthermore, because Ilongots saw in headhunting a device for transferring the fading energy of old men to growing youths—and an activity that boys should best perform before they married—it would seem reasonable to assume that headhunting itself involved the guilt of Oedipal conflict. In this case, haircutting would be a punishment aptly suited to the crime, a "compromise" that managed simultaneously to "castrate" and to absolve the guilty psyche. Thus, although Ilongots never speak of guilt, require punishment for wrongs, or seek displays of suffering and remorse in making up for untoward violence, it might appear that they had managed to create symbolic forms designed to mediate, and thus help actors to resolve, inevitable tensions harbored deep within men's adolescent minds. Culture's wisdom, this sort of argument suggests, is as infallible as it is blind.

But is it? In what follows, I want to show why Ilongot talk of heaviness does not displace but qualifies our talk of guilt, because indigenous idioms help us grasp the ways Ilongot killers think about the things they feel and how their understandings figure both in social practice and in psychological process. My earlier question—do not killers suffer guilt?—is shown of questionable relevance to the Ilongot moral world, because it presupposes notions of a selfish and impulsive self requiring the constraints of its society. And "shame," which for the Ilongots operates as much as stimulus as constraint, emerges as a concept that can help us understand what is involved in "weight" and how subjective experiences of heaviness are related to their social context.

My argument proceeds as follows. First, I comment on my reasons for suspecting, if not discarding, the claim that Ilongot headhunters feel guilt. Second, I show that "shame" for Ilongot is less concerned with the control of a presocial self than with a set of feelings that relate to the conflicting claims of hierarchy and "sameness," or autonomy, in Ilongot social life. Third, I ask how "weight" and "lightness"—understood as concepts that link physical sensation to the experience of "shame" and its release— provide a reasonable and illuminating account of the paralysis that seems to interrupt headhunters' progress. And in conclusion, I discuss the ways that heaviness/lightness resembles and yet differs from accounts derived from our constraint-oriented psychology. What is at stake is an appreciation of the power, and limitations, of familiar ways of grasping psychic life, and the possibility of a more deeply cultural psychology.

The fact that Ilongots never speak of "guilt" in their reports of raids does not itself decide the cultural (or psychological) irrelevance of such things as self-recrimination and remorse in the experience of killers. More telling, I suggest, is the fact that Ilongots but rarely discuss actions with reference to established normative codes or formal rules of wrong and right. People do things, Ilongots say, because of kinship, because they "recognize" their "fellow humans," because they fear the consequences of acting otherwise, because of strength or weakness, "pity," "envy," or "desire."[6]

But notions of "ought" and obligation appear lacking,[7] as are ideas of punishment wherein wrong-doing children or adults are made to suffer for the untoward things that they have done.[8]

Thus, for example, rather than confess, and so be forced to pay for murder perpetrated by his kin upon a group of friends with whom he wanted to go fishing, an Ilongot leader, Tukbaw, lied, denying knowledge of the crime, in full awareness that his fellows stood in supernatural danger should they fish and share a meal with unrepentant "slashers" of their "body." Clearly, for Tukbaw, strength, not care, was what decided his denial. Because he knew the fearfulness of the group that "he" had "killed," he knew that they could not enforce demands for payment corresponding to their "anger" at the loss. He could, then let his fellows risk such suffering as might subsequently ensue,[9] in favor of the opportune and henceforth realized claim that as a distant kinsman of his friends, he had no plans (nor had he had them in the past) to act in any way but as a brother who, of course, abjures all violence. Since they were, Tukbaw insisted, kin, there was no cause to look for payments, because kinfolk do not fight.

My point is not (of course) that Ilongots take advantage of their fellows when, and insofar as, they see benefit in doing wrong: in fact, the evidence of "criminal" acts like theft, adultery, or physical abuse is very small. Instead, I would suggest that if and when Ilongots see their interests as potentially opposed, issues of forcefulness and strength (Dare you confront me with a threat? Can I, through strength alone, insist that we construe ourselves as blood relations?) and not guilt, or personal desire and restraint, are likely to determine moral choice. "Punishment," when it occurs, is not for Ilongots a thing concerned with a wrong-doer's "paying back" or suffering for past wrongs. Instead, it is a gift to soothe offended parties who are "angered" and perceived as volatile because of loss or slight. What matters to disputants in the end is not the kind of moral change we seek within the criminal or guilty human heart, but, much as with Tukbaw's lie discussed above, the establishment of bonds of kinship wherein all violent, selfish, and disruptive acts are seen as "shameful" and at odds with an assumption of cooperation, "sameness," and autonomy. For opposites to act as kinfolk what is needed is, in brief, the "abolition" (by fiat, dominance, or gift exchange) of such grievances and fears as could be cause for untoward "anger." And for cooperation to proceed, no more is necessary than the correction of imbalances by which men are divided.

Let us now go one step further. I have hinted as to why the concept "guilt" appears at odds with Ilongot understandings, actions, and so, I hazard, their subjective feelings bound to deeds of wrong, abuse, or violence. But is not "shame"—the sanction of tradition, the acknowledgement of authority, the fear of mockery, or the anxiety associated with inadequate or morally unacceptable performance—in some sense an "equivalent" Ilongot device in attuning individuals to the demands of social order? Surely, Ilongots have a word—a set of words[10] for "shame," embracing notions of timidity, embarrassment, awe, obedience, and respect. And they associate these words with prohibitions and constraints of real significance in their daily lives.

Thus, for kin to fight, engage in contest, or pursue demands for payments in response to wrong or loss are all, Ilongots say, things to avoid for fear that "others" will "belittle" us or "shame" us.[11] "Shame" keeps in-married men from naming kin of wives; it silences sexual allusions and innuendos among sisters and brothers. "Shame" is what quiets noisy children in a household full of guests; it teaches youths to follow the directions of adults and leads women to obey commands by husbands.[12] Is not Ilongot "shame," then, an equivalent to our guilt, an affect through which individuals are attuned to their society's controls—controls appropriate, perhaps, to a "traditional" and collectively oriented form of society? Ilongots may not feel any guilt for taking heads. Headhunters' paralysis stands unexplained. But maybe, this line of questioning suggests, it is a sense of shame that keeps Ilongot violence from erupting in more mundane kin-based contexts.

Perhaps. As is the case with guilt, the argument that shame effects emotionally meaningful social control has evidence to recommend it. Given what I take to be a popular Western view, which holds that impulse harbored deep "inside" ourselves will ultimately be reflected in our acts, it would appear that Ilongot individuals need strong constraints if they are both to celebrate, and yet in daily life avoid, displays of violence. And yet I suggest, albeit quickly, that seeing shame essentially as a mechanism of control is to miscast its place in Ilongot social life and psychology.

Briefly, if guilt and shame are both, for us, affects designed to regulate a problematic inner self, Ilongot shame involves an "anger" born not in a hidden and asocial sphere but in the confrontation of a would-be peer with facts of weakness and social inferiority. Striving for parity with their equals among men, Ilongots are aware as well that preservation of ongoing bonds requires "shame" and the acceptance of occasional forms of social hierarchy. Thus, shame for Ilongots, as for ourselves, Involves a set of feelings tied to threatening sociality and threatened boundaries of the self. And yet, for them, it is concerned much less with hiding or constraint than with addressing, or redressing, situations where the fact of hierarchy provides a challenge to ideals of "sameness" and autonomy. Our inner truths are things for shame to mask, whereas for Ilongots "shame" speaks more of reserve than of disguise. The thoughts they harbor deep inside their hearts are more like plans than impulses repressed. And hidden thoughts do not contrast with spoken words as things more vital, true, or rich in inner conflict.

In short, Ilongot "shame" is not a sentinel assigned to keep insides from coming out. It is, instead, a feeling of considered weight that can look forward to, inhibit, or replace displays of "anger" and activity characteristically born at times of conflict and perceived inequality. At times, "shame" is a thing that leads to striving and the shows of "anger" through which unacceptable imbalances are eventually overcome.[13] At others, "shame" names the stasis born in the acknowledgment of asymmetry, and recognition that one's challenges, in everyday relations among kin, are apt to yield defeat, tense isolation, or destructive violence.

Thus, if we examine situations in which Ilongots speak of feeling "shame," they seem to fall into two sorts of contexts.[14] First, there are the times when "shame" involves awareness of deficiency or slight, a weight one is enjoined to overcome in subsequent displays of one's capacity and "anger." Infants who, Ilongots say, begin their lives in vulnerability and "fear," are in their early lives constrained by the related affects of "shame," "fear," and shyness.[15] And yet, as children learn to speak, the verbal challenges of adults are seen to "shame" them in a way that motivates the acquisition of new skill and knowledge. Verbal wit, fine dress, productive skill are all, Ilongots claim, things that the young acquire because they envy the accomplishments of peers and would not have their fellows' excellence stand to "shame" them. Growing up and learning to behave with competence and poise requires casting off youthful vulnerability to one's fellows' taunts, and doing this means one redresses "weighty" shame with "light" displays of energy and force. In fact, headhunting, as I suggest below, is in large part an angry answer to the distressing "shame" of childhood.

But if at times the weight of "shame" is lifted through a passionate display, at other times (and especially, I would argue, among already-equal adult men),[16] "shame" is accepted as a necessary constraint in order to avoid acknowledgment of conflict-breeding inequalities. Adult varieties of "shame" involve restraint and caution—much as the "shame" of youth—and yet where youthful "shame" inclines toward "anger" as the self transcends its "weight," "shame" in adults is characteristically concerned not with an ego but some other (a superior, or "equal" friend or kin) who one hopes to keep in a cooperative relationship with oneself. Thus, two men who fought when they were drunk in ways that seemed to me to show dissension building in their everyday affairs, could, when sober, seriously declare that they were "ashamed" that the alcohol (and it alone!) had led them to forget their bond as "brothers." Subsequently, these men in fact behaved as "equal" kin, and to my knowledge, neither ever spoke again of what appeared the underlying cause of conflict.

Ilongot children learn from youth that "knowing" kinship means one does not argue with one's kin, for fear that "someone else" will mock or "shame" them. And similarly, most Ilongot adults confronted with dissension in their homes will move or flee instead of speaking out because the "anger" likely to emerge is dangerous, a cause for both anxiety and "shame," and, it would seem, best left to die in silence.[17] Furthermore, in those relationships where structural inequalities in fact exist, clear expectations of obedience (in "shame," most women will heed men's commands), taboos on naming (between a spouse and spouse's kin), and prohibitions on obscenity in speech (when sisters are in the company of brothers) at once depend upon and highlight "shameful" attitudes that, in turn, acknowledge and restrain conflicts associated with a volatile sexual politics.

In summary, "shame" is, like childhood fear, a weight that can, in angry acts, be overcome. A cause for action, "shame" of this sort is as inevitable as it seems undesirable. But equally, "shame" is associated with autonomy and respect: Constraints one learns for fear of others' laughter become constraints that one accepts in situations where there is good cause at once to fear, and to abjure, displays of violence. Quests for parity, and a refusal to be "shamed," are necessary, in the Ilongot view, to children moving toward the status of adults. But married people (and in particular, of course, men) are seen as able freely to forget distressing differences among themselves, and in constructing a cooperative life in which conflicting and unequal interests are suppressed, to show that they are party to a "shame" that grows not from the fear/inadequacy of youth, but from the knowledge of mature, already proved, adults. Thus, accomplished adult men, no longer fearful that they will be "shamed," can demonstrate consideration, pity, and an exemplary "humility/shame/ respect" that serves in fact to guarantee that everyday cooperation is not experienced as weight, and that most Ilongots, most of the time, construe their social bonds as the creation of autonomous and equal hearts.[18]

How does all of this relate to headhunting? Again, I must be far too brief. Feelings of "weight"—whether one's grief at loss, or shame at insult, or envy at the headhunting accomplishments of peers—are what make all men think of killing. Killing is the casting off of weight, an act designed to make the awkward and distracted heart a light and energetic source of joy. And in particular, it is through headhunting that "shamed" and "clouded" youths begin to be like married men, who, proved in "anger," show themselves in everyday relations among kin as kind and generous as they are socially secure and capable of avoiding mundane conflict. Headhunting transforms the "shameful" weight of childhood into the ease and the respectful "shame" appropriate to adults.

Most youths declare that they are loathe to marry until they have taken heads for fear others will "shame" them. As novices, their hearts are burdened by a readiness to take offense. They cannot work dependably, think clearly, or enjoy the company of kin because their "shame" brings sullenness, distraction, and ill-ease. But then, Ilongots claim, headhunting cures this. When on a raid, young killers who set out with sullen hearts, slow movements, heaviness, and fear, will slowly learn from older men to "focus" thought until they literally can toss and thus discard a heavy head and heartfelt weight. And if intent and slow in their approach, successful killers shout and run with feelings of expansive ease that come from "casting of" accumulated burdens. Victorious, they ornament themselves with reeds and feathers that make their hearts and limbs as light and graceful as the wings of birds. The imagery of the headhunting raid, in short, appeals consistently to oppositions like motion/stasis, lightness/heaviness, ease/constraint. And these, I am suggesting, are consistent with the way in which raids are designed to turn the vulnerable, subordinate, and awkward youth into an adult peer. The heavy "shame" of youth becomes, through raiding, something more like "shame/humility/respect," made possible by the realization of new poise and "anger" in a boy who can accept his fellows' subsequent demands without fear of being vulnerable to "shame."[19]

Killing, however, is not really enough. Occasional raiders, as we have seen, are paralyzed by "the smell of blood." And yet more frequently, experienced headhunters report that they did not, on killing, feel a loss of weight and heightening of ease. In fact, their symptoms seem most clearly to suggest a brief identification between still "heavy" killers and the victims of their raid, as both are, first, immobile, and then "lightened" through the shouts and gestures that accompany a severance of head or hair.

For some, perhaps, identification of this sort reveals unconscious feelings of ambivalence or guilt, to be resolved by sacrificing themselves in expiation. And yet my hunch is that, for most, paralysis has its source less in unspoken penitence for wrongs than in the "shame" which comes with recognition of the fact that not all men are equally involved in the collective celebration of lightness, parity, and well-being. Haircutting, then, might best be seen less as a personal sacrifice than as a reenact-ment of the crime—a new attempt to "lighten" hearts that are still burdened with a sense of "shamefulness," social impotence, and ill-ease. Whether initially distressed by fear, remorse, or memory of tensions unresolved in mundane lie, paralyzed killers are, I would suggest, men stricken with awareness of the ways that they are not "the same" as happy peers.

In fact, my evidence on those who have experienced this paralysis in the past suggests that sufferers are all individuals who have previously taken heads, and yet (with one exception out of six), that all continue to be bachelors or otherwise marginal social figures.[20] Their heaviness may be related, then, less to consideration for the dead, than to a felt inadequacy in their relationships with would-be equals. Certainly, the symptom is not a moral judgment on the act of headhunting per se. If anything, it is a considered statement of the raid as a transformer of relationships defined by "shame," and the creator of important moral and affective meanings.

References

Barth, F. 1975. *Ritual and Knowledge Among the Baktaman of New Guinea.* New Haven: Yale University Press.

Benedict, R. 1946. *The Chrysanthemum and the Sword.* Boston: Houghton Mifflin.

Dodds, E. R. 1951. *The Greeks and the Irrational.* Berkeley: University of California Press.

Doi, T. 1973. *The Anatomy of Dependence.* Tokyo: Kodansha International.

Ekman, P. 1974. Universal Facial Expressions of Emotion. *Culture and Personality* (R. Levine, ed.), pp. 8–15. Chicago: Aldine.

Geertz, C. 1973. Person, Time and Conduct in Bali. *The Interpretation of Cultures,* pp. 364–411. New York: Basic Books.

Geertz, H. 1959. The Vocabulary of Emotion: A study of Javanese Socialization Processes. *Psychiatry* 22: 225–237.

Harris, G. 1978. *Casting Out Anger.* Cambridge: Cambridge University Press.

Levy, R. 1973. *Tahitians.* Chicago: University of Chicago Press.

Lynd, H. 1958. *On Shame and the Search for Identity.* New York: Harcourt, Brace.

Marx, K. 1963. On the Jewish Question. *Karl Marx: Early Writings* (T. B. Bottomore, ed.), pp. 3–40.

Macpherson, C. B. 1962. *The Political Theory of Possessive Individualism.* Oxford: Oxford University Press.

Murdoch, I. 1970. *The Sovereignty of Good.* London: Routledge & Kegan Paul.

Myers, F. 1979. Emotion and The Self: A Theory of Personhood and Political Order Among Pintupi Aborigines. *Ethos* 7: 343–370.

Neu, J. 1972. *Emotion, Thought and Therapy.* London: Routledge & Kegan Paul.

Piers, G., and M. Singer. 1953. *Shame and Guilt.* New York: Charles C. Thomas.

Rosaldo, M. 1980. *Knowledge and Passion: Ilongot Notions of Self and Social Life.* Cambridge: Cambridge University Press.

———. 1982. The Things We Do With Words: Ilongot Speech Acts and Speech Act Theory in Philosophy. *Language in Society* 11: 203–238.

Rosaldo, R. 1976. The Story of Tukbaw. *The Biographical Process* (F. Reynolds and D. Capps, eds.), pp. 121–151. The Hague: Mouton.

———. 1980. *Ilongot Headhunting, 1883-1979.* Stanford: Stanford University Press.

———. n.d. Red Hornbill Earrings. Ms. in author's possession.

Rorty, A. 1980. *Explaining Emotions.* Berkeley: University of California Press.

Solomon, R. 1976. *The Passions: The Myth and Nature of Human Emotions.* New York: Anchor/Doubleday.

Strathern, A. 1975. Why is Shame on the Skin? *Ethnology* 14:347–356.

Williams, B. 1973. *Problems of the Self.* Cambridge: Cambridge University Press.

Notes

1. Thanks to Jane Collier, Ward Keeler, Robert Levy, Sherry Ortner, and Renato Rosaldo for their comments.

2. After this point, I use quotations around "guilt" and, in particular, "shame" only when referring to Ilongot linguistic concepts. When the terms are used without quotations I am speaking both of "the real feelings" and "our" culturally organized understandings of these feelings; such a move seems justified by my conviction that knowledge about feeling is always, and necessarily, mediated by some cultural/linguistic frame.

3. Of all themes in the literature on culture and personality the opposition between guilt and shame has probably proven most resilient (e.g., Benedict 1946: Doi 1975; Dodds 1951; Levy 1973; Lynd 1958; Piers and Singer 1953), at least in part because guilt and shame are affects concerned at once with psychological state and social context, thus providing a significant terrain for culturally oriented social scientists; and in part because the opposition is consistent with numerous others in our psychological and sociological vocabularies (inner/ outer; Oedipal/ pre-Oedipal; The West/The Rest; modern/ primitive; individual/

communal; egalitarian/hierarchical). One of my purposes here is to join those few (e.g., C. Geertz 1973) who have been concerned to go beyond dichotomizing accounts and provide a vocabulary for *differentiating among* alien systems of affective orientation. What this requires is appreciation, not simply of the imagery of particular emotional states (e.g., shame as the "stage fright" of Geertz's Balinese), but relationships among affective states and between affectives states and social process. So, for example, my discussion of the workings of Ilongot "shame" is informed by considerations like the following: for Ilongots and Javanese (H. Geertz 1959) "shame" is associated with "fear," but among Javanese (and many other peasant groups), shame is acquired in establishing a relationship with a relatively distant father; for Ilongots and Hageners (Strathern 1975), "shame" and "anger" are related, and yet for Hageners (unlike Ilongots) shame is "on the skin" and anger festers deep within the heart, whereas for Ilongots shame and anger contrast more as stasis/motion (in a context of ill-ease) than as outer/inner forms of conflict.

4. Insofar as all emotional states involve a mix of intimate, even physical experience, and a more or less conscious apprehension of, or "judgment" concerning, self-and-situation, one might argue that emotions are, by definition, not passive "states" but *moral* "acts" (see, e.g., Solomon [1976]). Surely, affective life has more to do with social morality (and rationality) and less with (passive) irrationality than has often been assumed (see e.g. Williams [1973]). But the matter is complicated; how one transcends an opposition between an unsatisfactory physical determinism and an equally problematic model of free, existential consciousness seems to me the crucial philosophical and empirical issue in discussions of this topic (see e.g., Neu [1972], Murdoch [1970], and Rorty [1980]. By discussing guilt and shame as "moral affects" (and refusing to distinguish "affect," "emotion," "feeling," "sentiment," and the like), I have a dual purpose: first, to sidestep some of these difficulties by dealing with emotions that involve clear conscious, social, and cultural components (and attendant questions of judgment and morality), and second, to suggest that, as anthropologists interested in affect, we might do well to work *from* instances like these, where the relevance of culture is clear, *towards* cases where it is more problematic, instead of starting (à la Ekman [1974]) with presumed physiological universals and then "adding culture on."

5. For more materials on Ilongot, and in particular, their conceptions of the self, affect, and headhunting, see M. Rosaldo (1980, 1982) and R. Rosaldo (1976, 1980, n.d.).

6. Here, as elsewhere, my use of quotations indicates rough glosses on Ilongot words. "Desire" or "liking" *(ramak)* figures in accounts of action (like Tukbaw's below) in which actors perceive no reason not to "follow" the "direction" of their "hearts"; strength, autonomy, and lack of fear are all, thus,

relevant to acts motivated by "desire." "Pity" *(diri)* is recognized by Ilongots as a good reason for suspending privileges of strength and putting another's interest first; adults who receive "shame/respect" from youths are apt to "care for" them because of "pity." Tukbaw's endangered friends in the anecdote below might have succeeded had they adopted a more humble stance and asked him to "pity" them.

7. There is no obligatory modal in Ilongot, and the word they use to speak of "obligation" or "necessity" *(kailangan)* is borrowed from Tagalog. In addition (see M. Rosaldo [1982]), Ilongots have neither a word for, nor conception of, anything like our "contract" or "promise."

8. Wrong-doers may be required to make presentations to their victims, but this is not an "apology" so much as an "exchange" for volatile "anger" in their opposites (see Barth [1975] for a similar phenomenon). Similarly, Ilongot children are not "punished" for misbehaving or "rewarded" for acting considerate or mature. Physical threats to naughty children are understood more as an expression of the anger that their actions caused adults than as a method of instruction.

9. If the fishing partners had subsequently gotten ill and interpreted this illness as a result of eating with Tukbaw's company, Tukbaw might then have been asked to "pay" not simply for the murder but for the illness his deceit had caused. Tukbaw, however, was willing to take this risk, counting on the relative strength of his kin to keep the issue from arising. He imagined that at some future time he would be called upon to "pay," but he was willing to win time by promulgating deceit because he knew that time "lowers" the anger in men's hearts, that illness in his opposites need not necessarily occur, and furthermore, that Ilongots are never called to task for lying.

10. *Betang,* "shame, humility, respect" (and derivatives, *'ubētang* "shameful, shy"; *'embētang,* "to be ashamed, be shameful, humble"; *pabētang,* "cause shame") is probably most common. As indicated, it alternates in some contexts with *kayub,* "fear" (as when Ilongots say they do things out of "fear" or "shame" before the wishes of fathers or brothers). Elsewhere, it alternates with *tu'gnan,* "humility, respect, obedience" and *ege,* "awe, humility, respect, dizziness, as from a height." In addition. Ilongots sometimes use the Ilocano *galang,* "to honor, respect" in place of *tu'ngan* (see also M. Rosaldo [1980])

11. There is an interesting Ilongot contrast between "others," *sita tu'u* ("other person") and "equals" *anurutkun tu'u* ("people like me"). The former are construed, contrastively, as non-relations and/or relative "outsiders" who can laugh, mock, and gossip about one's behavior; they act *upon* the speaker. The latter are seen as fellows (whether enemies or friends) *towards whom* one orients one's actions.

12. See M. Rosaldo (1980 and 1982) for a fuller discussion of the relationship between commands, respect, and hierarchy.

13. "Anger" for *liget* is a concept far too rich and complex for exegesis here (see M. Rosaldo [1980]). All that matters for our purposes is that in the Ilongot view, *liget* can be as creative and energizing as it can be destructive.

14. Here, as elsewhere, the dichotomy is too simple. "Being shamed" (as a child who is fearful and constrained) and "feeling shame" (as an adult who knows shame in the form of *tu'ngan,* "humility/respect") does not, for instance, adequately account for the fact that women and children are not seen as having more adult shame than men although they have more people to respect and are more likely to receive, and to obey, commands.

15. These relationships are explored in M. Rosaldo (1980). See also H. Geertz (1959) for illuminating similarities and contrasts.

16. There is an ambiguity throughout this text as to whether my object is all Ilongot adults or Ilongot men. The ambiguity obtains because, in many contexts, Ilongots understand and explain men's and women's actions in related terms. At the same time, Ilongots assume that women are more fearful and less angry than most men, and since, in many contexts anger/strength is what determines moral/social dominance, Ilongot men and women see nothing odd in linking the moral prerogatives of men to their "higher" anger. For a fuller discussion, see M. Rosaldo (1980).

17. An interesting contrast between Ilongots and such peoples as the Hageners of New Guinea (Srathern 1975) or African Taita (Harris 1978) is that they see no particular danger in a failure to express one's anger. Anger for Ilongots is dangerous largely insofar as it is apt to lead to violent *acts;* it does not acquire added force through being hidden, leading to illness, witchcraft, or the like. In subsequent writings I will argue that these differences in the ordering of "anger" reflect consistent differences in the organization of social life.

18. "Equal," or more properly, "the same" (*'anurut*) in Ilongot does not have the connotations of "equality" associated with "abstract" and "possessive" individualism in modern Western thought (see e.g., Marx [1963]; Macpherson [1962]). This point is touched on briefly in my last pages, but it clearly deserves more careful work.

19. The realization of "anger" through headhunting is often confirmed by the fact that men who go headhunting together coin reciprocal names to commemorate their experience. In a large number of cases, youths go on headhunting raids with future affines, persons they will be forced to "respect" by avoiding their proper names throughout life. The fact that these persons can, through joint raiding, establish reciprocal names for one another is yet another evidence of the way in which headhunting makes equals of otherwise unequal men.

20. Haircutting as a response to paralysis on a raid is familiar to all Ilongots, but it in fact occurs very rarely, possibly on no more than one raid out of ten or fifteen. Of six cases reported in our data, five victims were aging bachelors who had already taken heads. The sixth was a man who joined a raid in order to assist

his son's headtaking: A member of a largely missionized community, he himself was considering conversion. Furthermore, he was forced to rely on quite distant kin to join with him on the raid. In terms of character and kinship relations he was, then, a marginal man in the raiding party, although it is possible in his case that paralysis had less to do with marginality than with feelings of guilt, remorse, or ambivalence in the context of new Christian ideals.

–16–

Grief and a Headhunter's Rage
On the Cultural Force of Emotions

Renato Rosaldo

If you ask an older Ilongot man of northern Luzon, Philippines, why he cuts off human heads, his answer is brief, and one on which no anthropologist can readily elaborate: He says that rage, born of grief, impels him to kill his fellow human beings. He claims that he needs a place "to carry his anger." The act of severing and tossing away the victim's head enables him, he says, to vent and, he hopes, throw away the anger of his bereavement. Although the anthropologist's job is to make other cultures intelligible, more questions fail to reveal any further explanation of this man's pithy statement. To him, grief, rage, and headhunting go together in a self-evident manner. Either you understand it or you don't. And, in fact, for the longest time I simply did not.

In what follows, I want to talk about how to talk about the cultural force of emotions.[1] The *emotional force* of a death, for example, derives less from an abstract brute fact than from a particular intimate relation's permanent rupture. It refers to the kinds of feelings one experiences on learning, for example, that the child just run over by a car is one's own and not a stranger's. Rather than speaking of death in general, one must consider the subject's position within a field of social relations in order to grasp one's emotional experience.[2]

My effort to show the force of a simple statement taken literally goes against anthropology's classic norms, which prefer to explicate culture through the gradual thickening of symbolic webs of meaning. By and large cultural analysts use not force but such terms as *thick description, multi-vocality, polysemy, richness,* and *texture.* The notion of force, among other things, opens to question the common anthropological assumption that the greatest human import resides in the densest forest of symbols and that analytical detail, or "cultural depth," equals enhanced explanation of a culture or "cultural elaboration." Do people always in fact describe most thickly what matters most to them?

The Rage in Ilongot Grief

Let me pause a moment to introduce the Ilongots, among whom my wife, Michelle Rosaldo, and I lived and conducted field research for thirty months (1967–69, 1974). They number about 3,500 and reside in an upland area some 90 miles northeast of Manila, Philippines.[3] They subsist by hunting deer and wild pig and by cultivating rain-fed gardens (swiddens) with rice, sweet potatoes, manioc, and vegetables. Their (bilateral) kin relations are reckoned through men and women. After marriage, parents and their married daughters live in the same or adjacent households. The largest unit within the society, a largely territorial descent group called the *bertan,* becomes manifest primarily in the context of feuding. For themselves, their neighbors, and their ethnographers, headhunting stands out as the Ilongots' most salient cultural practice.

When Ilongots told me, as they often did, how the rage in bereavement could impel men to headhunt, I brushed aside their one-line accounts as too simple, thin, opaque, implausible, stereotypical, or otherwise unsatisfying. Probably I naively equated grief with sadness. Certainly no personal experience allowed me to imagine the powerful rage Ilongots claimed to find in bereavement. My own inability to conceive the force of anger in grief led me to seek out another level of analysis that could provide a deeper explanation for older men's desire to headhunt.

Not until some fourteen years after first recording the terse Ilongot statement about grief and a headhunter's rage did I begin to grasp its overwhelming force. For years I thought that more verbal elaboration (which was not forthcoming) or another analytical level (which remained elusive) could better explain older men's motives for headhunting. Only after being repositioned through a devastating loss of my own could I better grasp that Ilongot older men mean precisely what they say when they describe the anger in bereavement as the source of their desire to cut off human heads. Taken at face value and granted its full weight, their statement reveals much about what compels these older men to headhunt.

In my efforts to find a "deeper" explanation for headhunting, I explored exchange theory, perhaps because it had informed so many classic ethnographies. One day in 1974, I explained the anthropologist's exchange model to an older Ilongot man named Insan. What did he think, I asked of the idea that headhunting resulted from the way that one death (the beheaded victim's) cancelled another (the next of kin). He looked puzzled, so I went on to say that the victim of a beheading was exchanged for the death of one's own kin, thereby balancing the books, so to speak. Insan reflected a moment and replied that he imagined somebody could think such a thing (a safe bet, since I just had), but that he and other Ilongots did not think any such thing. Nor was there any indirect evidence for my exchange theory in ritual, boast, song, or casual conversation.[4]

In retrospect, then, these efforts to impose exchange theory on one aspect of Ilongot behavior appear feeble. Suppose I had discovered what I sought? Although the notion of balancing the ledger does have a certain elegant coherence, one wonders how such bookish dogma could inspire any man to take another man's life at the risk of his own.

My life experience had not as yet provided the means to imagine the rage that can come with devastating loss. Nor could I, therefore, fully appreciate the acute problem of meaning that Ilongots faced in 1974. Shortly after Ferdinand Marcos declared martial law in 1972, rumors that firing squads had become the new punishment for headhunting reached the Ilongot hills. The men therefore decided to call a moratorium on taking heads. In past epochs, when headhunting had become impossible, Ilongot had allowed their rage to dissipate, as best it could, in the course of everyday life. In 1974, they had another option; they began to consider conversion to evangelical Christianity as a means of coping with their grief. Accepting the new religion, people said, implied abandoning their old ways, including headhunting. It also made coping with bereavement less agonizing because they could believe that the deceased had departed for a better world. No longer did they have to confront the awful finality of death.

The force of the dilemma faced by the Ilongot eluded me at the time. Even when I correctly recorded their statements about grieving and the need to throw away their anger, I simply did not grasp the weight of their words. In 1974, for example, while Michelle Rosaldo and I were living among the Ilongots, a six-month-old baby died, probably of pneumonia. That afternoon we visited the father and found him terribly stricken. "He was sobbing and staring through glazed and bloodshot eyes at the cotton blanket covering his baby."[5] The man suffered intensely, for this was the seventh child he had lost. Just a few years before, three of his children had died, one after the other, in a matter of days. At the time, the situation was murky as people present talked both about evangelical Christianity (the possible renunciation of taking heads) and their grudges against lowlanders (the contemplation of headhunting forays into the surrounding valleys).

Through subsequent days and weeks, the man's grief moved him in a way I had not anticipated. Shortly after the baby's death, the father converted to evangelical Christianity. Altogether too quick on the inference, I immediately concluded that the man believed that the new religion could somehow prevent further deaths in his family. When I spoke my mind to an Ilongot friend, he snapped at me, saying that "I had missed the point: what the man in fact sought in the new religion was not the denial of our inevitable deaths but a means of coping with his grief. With the advent of martial law, headhunting was out of the question as a means of venting his wrath and thereby lessening his grief. Were he to remain in his Ilongot way of life, the pain of his sorrow would simply be too much to bear."[6] My description from 1980 now seems so apt that I wonder how I could have written the words and nonetheless failed to appreciate the force of the grieving man's desire to vent his rage.

Another representative anecdote makes my failure to imagine the rage possible in Ilongot bereavement all the more remarkable. On this occasion, Michelle Rosaldo and I were urged by Ilongot friends to play the tape of a headhunting celebration we had witnessed some five years before. No sooner had we turned on the tape and heard the boast of a man who had died in the intervening years than did people abruptly tell us to shut off the recorder. Michelle Rosaldo reported on the tense conversation that ensued:

> As Insan braced himself to speak, the room again became almost uncannily electric. Backs straightened and my anger turned to nervousness and something more like fear as I saw that Insan's eyes were red. Tukbaw, Renato's Ilongot "brother," then broke into what was a brittle silence, saying he could make things clear. He told us that it hurt to listen to a headhunting celebration when people knew that there would never be another. As he put it: "The song pulls at us, drags our hearts, it makes us think of our dead uncle." And again: "It would be better if I had accepted God, but I still am an Ilongot at heart; and when I hear the song, my heart aches as it does when I must look upon unfinished bachelors whom I know that I will never lead to take a head." Then Wagat, Tukbaw's wife, said with her eyes that all my questions gave her pain and told me: "Leave off now, isn't that enough? Even I, a woman, cannot stand the way it feels inside my heart."[7]

From my present position, it is evident that the tape recording of the dead man's boast evoked powerful feelings of bereavement, particularly rage and the impulse to headhunt. At the time I could only feel apprehensive and diffusely sense the force of the emotions experienced by Insan, Tukbaw, Wagat, and the others present.

The dilemma for the Ilongots grew out of a set of cultural practices that, when blocked, were agonizing to live with. The cessation of headhunting called for painful adjustments to other modes of coping with the rage they found in bereavement. One could compare their dilemma with the notion that the failure to perform rituals can create anxiety.[8] In the Ilongot case, the cultural notion that throwing away a human head also casts away the anger creates a problem of meaning when the headhunting ritual cannot be performed. Indeed, Max Weber's classic problem of meaning in *The Protestant Ethic and the Spirit of Capitalism* is precisely of this kind.[9] On a logical plane, the Calvinist doctrine of predestination seems flawless: God has chosen the elect, but his decision can never be known by mortals. Among those whose ultimate concern is salvation, the doctrine of predestination is as easy to grasp conceptually as it is impossible to endure in everyday life (unless one happens to be a "religious virtuoso"). For Calvinists and Ilongots alike, the problem of meaning resides in practice, not theory. The dilemma for both groups involves the practical matter of how to live with one's beliefs, rather than the logical puzzlement produced by abstruse doctrine.

How I Found the Rage in Grief

One burden of this introduction concerns the claim that it took some fourteen years for me to grasp what Ilongots had told me about grief, rage, and headhunting. During all those years I was not yet in a position to comprehend the force of anger possible in bereavement, and now I am. Introducing myself into this account requires a certain hesitation both because of the discipline's taboo and because of its increasingly frequent violation by essays laced with trendy amalgams of continental philosophy and autobiographical snippets. If classic ethnography's vice was the slippage from the ideal of detachment to actual indifference, that of present-day reflexivity is the tendency for the self-absorbed Self to lose sight altogether of the culturally different Other. Despite the risks involved, as the ethnographer I must enter the discussion at this point to elucidate certain issues of method.

The key concept in what follows is that of the positioned (and repositioned) subject.[10] In routine interpretive procedure, according to the methodology of hermeneutics, one can say that ethnographers reposition themselves as they go about understanding other cultures. Ethnographers begin research with a set of questions, revise them throughout the course of inquiry, and in the end emerge with different questions than they started with. One's surprise at the answer to a question, in other words, requires one to revise the question until lessening surprises or diminishing returns indicate a stopping point. This interpretive approach has been most influentially articulated within anthropology by Clifford Geertz.[11]

Interpretive method usually rests on the axiom that gifted ethnographers learn their trade by preparing themselves as broadly as possible. To follow the meandering course of ethnographic inquiry, field-workers require wide-ranging theoretical capacities and finely tuned sensibilities. After all, one cannot predict beforehand what one will encounter in the field. One influential anthropologist, Clyde Kluckhohn, even went so far as to recommend a double initiation: first, the ordeal of psychoanalysis, and then that of fieldwork. All too often, however, this view is extended until certain prerequisites of field research appear to guarantee an authoritative ethnography. Eclectic book knowledge and a range of life experiences, along with edifying reading and self-awareness, supposedly vanquish the twin vices of ignorance and insensitivity.

Although the doctrine of preparation, knowledge and sensibility contains much to admire, one should work to undermine the false comfort that it can convey. At what point can people say that they have completed their learning or their life experience? The problem with taking this mode of preparing the ethnographer too much to heart is that it can lend a false air of security, an authoritative claim to certitude and finality that our analyses cannot have. All interpretations are provisional; they are made by positioned subjects who are prepared to know certain things and not others. Even when knowledgeable, sensitive, fluent in the language, and able to move easily in an alien cultural world, good ethnographers still have their limits, and their analyses always are incomplete. Thus, I began to fathom the force of what Ilongots had been telling me about their losses through my own loss, and not through any systematic preparation for field research.

My preparation for understanding serious loss began in 1970 with the death of my brother, shortly after his twenty-seventh birthday. By experiencing this ordeal with my mother and father, I gained a measure of insight into the trauma of a parent's losing a child. This insight informed my account, partially described earlier, of an Ilongot man's reactions to the death of his seventh child. At the same time, my bereavement was so much less than that of my parents that I could not then imagine the overwhelming force of rage possible in such grief. My former position is probably similar to that of many in the discipline. One should recognize that ethnographic knowledge tends to have the strengths and limitations given by the relative youth of field-workers who, for the most part, have not suffered serious losses and could have, for example, no personal knowledge of how devastating the loss of a long-term partner can be for the survivor.

In 1981 Michelle Rosaldo and I began field research among the Ifugaos of northern Luzon, Philippines. On October 11 of that year, she was walking along a trail with two Ifugao companions when she lost her footing and fell to her death some 65 feet down a sheer precipice into a swollen river below. Immediately on finding her body I became enraged. How could she abandon me? How could she have been so stupid as to fall? I tried to cry. I sobbed, but rage blocked the tears. Less than a month later I described this moment in my journal: "I felt like in a nightmare, the whole world around me expanding and contracting, visually and viscerally heaving. Going down I find a group of men, maybe seven or eight, standing still, silent, and I heave and sob, but no tears." An earlier experience, on the fourth anniversary of my brother's death, had taught me to recognize heaving sobs without tears as a form of anger. This anger, in a number of forms, has swept over me on many occasions since then, lasting hours and even days at a time. Such feelings can be aroused by rituals, but more often they emerge from unexpected reminders (not unlike the Ilongots' unnerving encounter with their dead uncle's voice on the tape recorder).

Lest there be any misunderstanding, bereavement should not be reduced to anger, neither for myself nor for anyone else.[12] Powerful visceral emotional states swept over me, at times separately and at other times together. I experienced the deep cutting pain of sorrow almost beyond endurance, the cadaverous cold of realizing the finality of death, the trembling beginning in my abdomen and spreading through my body, the mournful keening that started without my willing, and frequent tearful sobbing. My present purpose of revising earlier understandings of Ilongot headhunting, and not a general view of bereavement, thus focuses on anger rather than on other emotions in grief.

Writings in English especially need to emphasize the rage in grief. Although grief therapists routinely encourage awareness of anger among the bereaved, upper-middle-class Anglo-American culture tends to ignore the rage devastating losses can bring. Paradoxically, this culture's conventional wisdom usually denies the anger in grief at the same time that therapists encourage members of the invisible community of the bereaved to talk in detail about how angry their losses make them feel. My brother's death in combination with what I learned about anger from Ilongots (for them, an emotional state more publicly celebrated than denied) allowed me immediately to recognize the experience of rage.[13]

Ilongot anger and my own overlap, rather like two circles, partially overlaid and partially separate. They are not identical. Alongside striking similarities, significant differences in tone, cultural form, and human consequences distinguish the "anger" animating our respective ways of grieving. My vivid fantasies, for example, about a life insurance agent who refused to recognize Michelle's death as job-related did not lead me to kill him, cut off his head, and celebrate afterward. In so speaking, I am illustrating the discipline's methodological caution against the reckless attribution of one's own categories and experiences to members of another culture. Such warnings against facile notions of universal human nature can, however, be carried too far and harden into the equally pernicious doctrine that, my own group aside, everything human is alien to me. One hopes to achieve a balance between recognizing wide-ranging human differences and the modest truism that any two human groups must have certain things in common.

Only a week before completing the initial draft of an earlier version of this introduction, I rediscovered my journal entry, written some six weeks after Michelle's death, in which I made a vow to myself about how I would return to writing anthropology, if I ever did so, "by writing Grief and a Headhunter's Rage ..." My journal went on to reflect more broadly on death, rage, and headhunting by speaking of my "wish for the Ilongot solution; they are much more in touch with reality than Christians. So, I need a place to carry my anger—and can we say a solution of the imagination is better than theirs? And can we condemn them when we napalm villages? Is our rationale so much sounder than theirs?" All this was written in despair and rage.

Not until some fifteen months after Michelle's death was I again able to begin writing anthropology. Writing the initial version of "Grief and a Headhunter's Rage" was in fact cathartic, though perhaps not in the way one would imagine. Rather than following after the completed composition, the catharsis occurred be-forehand. When the initial version of this introduction was most acutely on my mind, during the month before actually beginning to write, I felt diffusely depressed and ill with a fever. Then one day an almost literal fog lifted and words began to flow. It seemed less as if I were doing the writing than that the words were writing themselves through me.

My use of personal experience serves as a vehicle for making the quality and intensity of the rage in Ilongot grief more readily accessible to readers than certain more detached modes of composition. At the same time, by invoking personal experi-ence as an analytical category one risks easy dismissal. Unsympathetic readers could reduce this introduction to an act of mounting or a mere report on my discovery of the anger possible in bereavement. Frankly, this introduction is both and more. An act of mourning, a personal report, *and* a critical analysis of anthropological method, it simultaneously encompasses a number of distinguishable processes, no one of which cancels out the others. Similarly, I argue in what follows that ritual in general and Ilongot headhunting in particular form the intersection of multiple coexisting social processes. Aside from revising the ethnographic record, the paramount claim made here concerns how my own mourning and consequent reflection on Ilongot bereavement, rage, and headhunting raise methodological issues of general concern in anthropology and the human sciences.

Notes

An earlier version of this chapter appeared as "Grief and a Headhunter's Rage: On the Cultural Force of Emotions," in *Text, Play, and Story: The Construction and Reconstruction of Self and Society,* ed. Edward M. Bruner (Washington, D.C.: American Ethnological Society, 1984), pp. 178–95.

1. In contrasting Moroccan and Javanese forms of mysticism, Clifford Geertz found it necessary to distinguish the "force" of cultural patterning from its "scope" (Clifford Geertz, *Islam Observed* [New Haven, Conn.: Yale University Press, 1968]). He distinguished force from scope in this manner: "By 'force' I mean the thoroughness with which such a pattern is internalized in the personalities of the individuals who adopt it, its centrality or marginality in their lives" (p. 111). "By 'scope,' on the other hand, I mean the range of social contexts within which religious considerations are regarded as having more or less direct relevance" (p. 112). In his later works, Geertz developed the notion of scope more than that of force. Unlike Geertz, who emphasizes processes of internalization within individual personalities, my use of the term *force* stresses the concept of the positioned subject.

2. Anthropologists have long studied the vocabulary of the emotions in other cultures (see, e.g., Hildred Geertz, "The Vocabulary of Emotion: A Study of Javanese Socialization Processes," *Psychiatry* 22 (1959): 225–37). For a recent review essay on anthropological writings on emotions, see Catherine Lutz and Geoffrey M. White, "The Anthropology of Emotion," *Annual Review of Anthropology* 15 (1986): 405–36.

3. The two ethnographies on the Ilongots are Michelle Rosaldo, *Knowledge and Passion: Ilongot Notions of Self and Social Life* (New York: Cambridge University Press, 1980), and Renato Rosaldo, *Ilongot Headhunting, 1883–1974: A Study in Society and History* (Stanford, Calif.: Stanford University Press, 1980). Our field research among the Ilongots was financed by a National Science Foundation predoctoral fellowship, National Science Foundation Research Grants GS-1509 and GS-40788, and a Mellon Award for junior faculty from Stanford University. A Fulbright Grant financed a two-month stay in the Philippines during 1981.

4. Lest the hypothesis Insan rejected appear utterly implausible, one should mention that at least one group does link a version of exchange theory to headhunting. Peter Metcalf reports that, among the Berawan of Borneo,

"Death has a chain reaction quality to it. There is a considerable anxiety that, unless something is done to break the chain, death will follow upon death. The logic of this is now plain: The unquiet soul kills, and so creates more unquiet souls" (Peter Metcalf, *A Borneo Journey into Death: Berawan Eschatology from Its Rituals* [Philadelphia: University of Pennsylvania Press, 1982], p. 127).

5. R. Rosaldo, Ilongot Headhunting, 1883–1974, p. 286.

6. Ibid., p. 288.

7. M. Rosaldo, *Knowledge and Passion,* p. 33.

8. See A. R. Radcliffe-Brown, *Structure and Function in Primitive Society* (London: Cohen and West, Ltd., 1952), pp. 133–52. For a broader debate on the "functions" of ritual, see the essays by Bronislaw Malinowski, A. R. Radcliffe-Brown, and George C. Homans, in *Reader in Comparative Religion:An Anthropological Approach* (4th ed.), ed. William A. Lessa and Evon Z. Vogt (New York: Harper and Row, 1979), pp. 37–62.

9. Max Weber, *The Protestant Ethic and the Spirit of Capitalism* (New York: Charles Scribner's Sons, 1958).

10. A key antecedent to what I have called the "positioned subject" is Alfred Schutz, *Collected Papers,* vol. 1, *The Problem of Social Reality,* ed. and intro. Maurice Natanson (The Hague: Martinus Nijhoff, 1971). See also, e.g., Aaron Cicourel, *Method and Measurement in Sociology* (Glencoe, Ill.: The Free Press, 1964) and Gerald Berreman, *Behind Many Masks: Ethnography and Impression Management in a Himalayan Village,* Monograph No. 4 (Ithaca, N.Y.: Society for Applied Anthropology, 1962). For an early anthropological article on how differently positioned subjects interpret the "same" culture in different ways, see John W. Bennett, "The Interpretation of Pueblo Culture," *Southwestern Journal of Anthropology* 2 (1946): 361–74.

11. Clifford Geertz, *The Interpretation of Cultures* (New York: Basic Books, 1974) and *Local Knowledge: Further Essays in Interpretive Anthropology* (New York: Basic Books, 1983).

12. Although anger appears so often in bereavement as to be virtually universal, certain notable exceptions do occur. Clifford Geertz, for example, depicts Javanese funerals as follows: "The mood of a Javanese funeral is not one of hysterical bereavement, unrestrained sobbing, or even of formalized cries of grief for the deceased's departure. Rather, it is a calm, undemonstrative, almost languid letting go, a brief ritualized relinquishment of a relationship no longer possible" (Geertz, *The Interpretation of Cultures,* p. 153). In cross-cultural perspective, the anger in grief presents itself in different degrees (including zero), in different forms, and with different consequences.

13. The Ilongot notion of anger (*liget*) is regarded as dangerous in its violent excesses, but also as life-enhancing in that, for example, it provides energy for work. See the extensive discussion in M. Rosaldo, *Knowledge and Passion.*

–17–

Moving Corpses
Emotions and Subject-Object Ambiguity

Maruška Svašek

Introduction

In this chapter, I shall explore the emotional agency of material objects that consist of human remains, or that are casts of human body parts. Analyzing a number of cases, I shall argue that such objects are able to evoke strong and often contradictory emotions, partly because they problematize the 'subject-object' divide—the idea that humans are radically different from lifeless matter. The latter perspective implies, amongst other things, that material objects lack social and emotional agency—properties which are commonly regarded as distinguishing features of the human species. I shall argue, instead, that artefacts can actively trigger emotions and cause social action. The ability to move people to tears, evoke anger, or generate other emotions is particularly strong when material entities consist of human remains. This is not surprising, because encounters with lifeless beings confront subjects with their own postmortum object-status.

But what are emotions? In the last decades, anthropological theories of emotions have argued that emotions should neither be regarded as evolutionary bodily processes, a common biological approach, nor as intrapersonal mental states, a perspective that has long dominated psychology.[1] Even though particular individuals may experience emotional processes as 'forces beyond their control', or as 'highly personal feelings', these explanations are limited and reflect dominant Western assumptions which reinforce the Cartesian split between body and mind (cf. Lutz and White 1986). By contrast, as Csordas (1990, 1992), Leavitt (1996) and others have convincingly argued, emotional dynamics involve both physical and mental processes, and connect the individual and the social. People selectively interpret certain (and not other) bodily feelings as emotional states. How they objectify their sensations is shaped by both sociohistorical and cultural dynamics, and by individual idiosyncrasies (Svašek 2005a).

This implies that emotions are complex experiential and discursive processes that often function as moral judgements—prescribing how one should (or should not) behave in specific situations. In the words of Michelle Rosaldo (1983: 136):

> Insofar as all emotional states involve a mix of intimate, even physical experience, and a more or less conscious apprehension of, or 'judgement' concerning, self-and-situation, one might argue that emotions are, by definition, not passive 'states' but *moral* 'acts'. (italics in original).

The social embeddedness and moral imperative of many emotional processes does not, of course, imply that people can only experience emotions when surrounded by other people, but rather, that 'frequent social interaction is vital to the process of embodiment in which emotions are learned, felt and interpreted, and in which emotional ties are formed with relevant others' (Svašek 2005b: 201). Relevant others who act as emotional agents are not only other human beings, but also include nonhuman phenomena such as animals, landscapes, artefacts and works of art (cf. Knight 2005; Milton 2005; Svašek 2005c, 2007). Furthermore, people's emotional life is not only shaped by direct confrontations with human or nonhuman environments, but also by inner dialogues with internalized presences—embodied memories and imaginations of phenomena in these environments (cf. Casey 1987: 244; Svašek 2005b: 201).

But how are lifeless things able to affect emotional dynamics? How do objects actively generate emotional processes, and how do people respond to objects emotionally? In this chapter, I shall emphasize three processes in particular. First of all, people frequently experience and discursively construct the things that surround them as subject-like phenomena. They may, for example, swear at their old car when the engine fails to start, or stroke its dashboard in an act of encouragement. A positive 'response' from the car will evoke genuine feelings of relief, which may be communicated to the car through words of gratefulness and praise. In such cases, objects are clearly imagined and experienced as emotional agents that have the ability to challenge, anger and please. Their subject-like 'behaviour' has real emotional impact, even though the interacting person (in this particular example, the driver) remains conscious of their lifeless object status.

Secondly, the fact that people and objects often move together through space and time also stimulates people's experience of artefacts as active subject-like emotional agents. Imagine, for example, someone who has owned a bag for many years. The bag has accompanied this person frequently on different trips, to different locations, as no other person has done. It has held a variety of possessions, has been endlessly filled, emptied and refilled, thrown in corners, picked up with care, lost, found and cleaned, slowly becoming a personal item with a very familiar shape, touch, weight, colour and smell. From an experiential perspective, the value of the bag cannot, or can no longer, be measured in terms of its commodity value, as the bag has rather become a 'priceless' part of the multiple self, a subject-like emotional agent (cf. Svašek 2005b: 202), and an extension of one's body.

Thirdly, as memories of emotional encounters 'guide and motivate our continued exploration of our environment' (Milton 2005: 34), expectations vis-à-vis material realities influence the ways in which we respond to them emotionally. Think, for instance, of a Catholic person who has learnt to perceive a crucifix as a sacred sign of Christ and automatically respond to it through proper embodied engagement—feeling respect and making the sign of the cross. Such a person will instantly react with horror when he or she comes across a crucifix that has been sprayed with insulting graffiti. As will become clear throughout this analysis, the knowledge that the manipulation of matter may cause particular reactions in others is a powerful way in which people distribute their own emotional agency.

But what when objects consist of human remains? How are corpses or parts of corpses actively involved in emotional processes? Human remains—as former thinking and feeling bodies—possess a past of emotional subjectivity. As such, they are radically different from subject-like objects that have never cried, blushed or run away in fear (even though people in various contexts may of course imagine material realities as being bewitched or animated in other ways). At the same time, there is no doubt that human remains have object-like characteristics. Through death, they have transformed into lifeless matter, which can be moved around, taken to pieces and 'processed' in various ways. In this chapter, I shall discuss the emotional and moral dimensions of such transformative processes, and offer some initial thoughts about the emotional agency of human body parts and their casts. The discussion will focus on five rather different categories of objects: death masks, national monuments, works of art, anatomical specimens and ethnographic objects.

The Widow and the Death Mask: Grief and Mourning

On 6 September 2003 the German tabloid *Bild*[2] showed the photograph of an elderly women behind the wheel, leaning over to the seat next to her, caressing the death mask of her late husband, the famous actor Klaus Löwitz. The widow explained:

> To me, Klaus is not dead. I talk to him, and he is always with me. At first I put the mask in bed with me, but then Klaus remarked: 'I'd rather drive around in the car' ... Klaus loves to drive long stretches. When we are on the road, he always wears a warm hat ... I cannot touch him but I feel him. That's a big consolation. (*Bild* 1993: 4)[3]

The bronze cast did not mean to celebrate the actor's professional status, but rather helped the widow to actively engage with her own memories of her husband. The couple's lifetime emotional interaction and the sad experience of his death had anchored memories in the widow's body and mind. Active as internalized presences, these memories generated a range of feelings and meanings, including experiences of love and grief.

The externally present death mask played an important role in the mourning process. From the perspective of Peircean semiotics, the cast was both an iconic sign, sharing some of the characteristics with the person it represented, and an index, a '"natural sign" ... from which the observer can make a causal inference of some kind, or an inference about the intentions or capabilities of another person' (Gell 1998: 13). As such, it had 'secondary agency', the power to evoke emotions and cause social action, actively influencing the widow's experience.

Gell made a distinction between 'primary' and 'secondary' agents, and defined primary agents as 'intentional beings who, through their actions, produce causal reactions in others' (Gell 1998: 20). Primary agents, he noted, use secondary agents to 'distribute their [own primary] agency in the causal milieu, and thus render their agency effective'.[4] It is important to note that primary agents are not just those who produce objects, but also those who use and display them in different ways in different contexts. In the case of the actor's death mask, both the actor, who (I assume) had agreed to the making of the cast before his death, and the widow, who consciously used the cast to express her love and grief for her husband, were primary agents. The actor had extended his agency posthumously, as he had expected that his death mask would set in motion certain, to him desirable, emotional reactions in his wife. The widow distributed her agency through the mask as it actively identified herself as a 'mourning widow', a new status she herself had to get used to.

The widow's interaction with the mask reinforced her feelings of love for her deceased husband, but also (at least potentially) allowed her to slowly come to terms with her loss. Its material presence enabled her to create some sort of continuity with the past, allowing her to enact their relationship in real time and space. In the form of the death mask, her 'husband' was still there to see and touch. As an indexical sign, the object strengthened her husband's active presence in the widow's embodied thoughts. Her dealing with the death mask demonstrates that grief-related behaviour should thus not be understood as purely mentalist reliving of the past, but as a process of active imagination *and* embodied material engagement (cf. Seremetakis 1994: 9).[5] What is more, this embodied engagement with the object added another dimension to her relationship with her husband. She could now remember him (as she had done before) as an independent living human being, *and* as a willing object that could be handled according to her own wishes.

Several Germans I spoke with about the case[6] noted that they fully understood the widow's need for the death mask, as it obviously helped her to live with his absence. Yet some were shocked or angered by the fact that she had taken the mask out into the public realm, outside the personal space of her home, and outside spaces designed for public mourning that traditionally house material reminders of the deceased (graves, urns, portraits, and the like). As a fifty-year-old female nanny from Berlin noted: 'She must really love her husband, but this is insane'. This comment reminds us that, in the context of the wider public, the death mask gained new emotional agency, triggering negative, morally loaded responses. Numerous other people I spoke with about the case argued that the widow had overstepped certain ethical boundaries by disrespecting common practices concerning the treatment of the dead. A thirty-five-year-old shop keeper, also from Berlin, suggested that, maybe unintentionally, the widow had made a complete fool of her husband. He thought the mask looked ridiculous with its white cap on, hanging on a string on the front seat of the car. If the actor had known about it, the man argued, he would have been highly embarrassed, and would certainly have objected to his wife's handling of his image. He himself, he added, dreaded the thought that something similar would happen to him after his death. The latter comment shows again the ambiguous subject-object status of corpses and their casts. Thinking about the case, the speaker actively engaged both with the image of the death mask (as object) and the actor it represented (as subject). His comments also illustrate the uneasiness casts of corpses can create, confronting onlookers with their own mortality.

Death as Political Statement: Martyrdom and Nationalist Sentiments

It is interesting to compare the case of the actor's death mask with a second death mask that was produced in a rather different context, namely the death mask of the Czech student Jan Palach. Palach's death had not just been a personal tragedy, but more importantly, a conscious moral and political statement. The anger and despair, which led to his suicide, reflected the feelings of many Czechoslovak citizens when their country was invaded by Warsaw Pact forces in the late 1960s. The Soviet-led invasion put an end to Alexander Dubček's 'socialism with a human face', a liberating political movement which had diverted from hard-line Soviet-style state socialism. On 16 January 1969, in an extreme act of protest to the invasion, Palach burnt himself to death in Prague on Wenceslas Square. Shocked students organized meetings during which they raised 200,000 Czechoslovak crowns to build a memorial in Palach's honour, which would support his cause. The director of Charles University, who did not yet realize how drastically the invasion would change the political climate in the country, commissioned the official Union of Visual Artists to make a memorial plaque, which was to be mounted at the Philosophical Faculty where Palach had studied (Svašek 1996: 109).

During a meeting of the Art Union's central committee, committee members proposed to take a death mask from Palach's face. The art historian Jindřich Chalupecký stated in an interview with the art journal Vytvárná Práce (Creative Work): 'We recommend that a death mask be mounted on the memorial plaque. I think it is really the best solution, a direct cast of his face will remind the students of Jan Palach. Not a heroic portrait but a document; the injured and swollen face of a dead person' (Burda 1969: 10). Yet the plans to create a memorial for Palach were thwarted by the return of an oppressive, pro-Soviet regime. Dubček was sidelined and replaced by hard-line communists, such as President Svoboda and Gustav Husák. The sculptor Olbram Zoubek had, however, taken an imprint of Palach's burnt face, which he hid in a secret place (Svašek 1996: 111).

During the twenty years of political 'normalization' that followed, Palach's corpse was initially buried at the Olšanská Cemetery in Prague.[7] The grave became an emotionally loaded memorial site, which points out that corpses do not need to be actively *seen* to have an impact on people's feelings. Through memory and imagination, the dead continue to speak to our hearts. Visitors spoke back, expressing their admiration for Palach's heroic deed, by leaving candles, flowers and other symbolic objects.

In October 1973, in an attempt to stop the illegal pilgrimages, Palach's remains were exhumed and cremated and were moved to his home town of Všetat. Yet as a brave martyr who had died because of foreign oppression, Palach had become an emotionally evocative symbol of political resistance. As a powerful internalized presence, he continued to trigger antistate protests and spark off illegal commemorations of his suicidal act. On 15 January 1989, for example, the evening before the twentieth anniversary of Palach's suicidal act, the police prevented a demonstration during which the actress Vlasta Chadimová had planned to read a document written by Charter 77, entitled 'In Memory of Jan Palach'. Fourteen demonstrators, including the well-known dissident (and later president) Václav Havel, were detained when they tried to lay flowers on the site where Palach had set himself on fire.

Not surprisingly, after the collapse of Communism in 1989, 'Palach' became an official symbol of freedom and democracy. In 1990, he was given the T. G. Masaryk Order,[8] and his remains were returned to the Olšanská Cemetery. The square in front of the Philosophical Faculty of Charles University was officially renamed 'Jan Palach Square', and the sculptor Olbram Zoubek, who had secretly taken the imprint of Palach's burnt face in 1969, was commissioned to use the death mask to design a national memorial. Zoubek mounted the cast on a rectangular bronze plaque, which also showed his signature, and the date of his death.

The symbol 'Palach' was incorporated into a political narrative which imagined the Czechs as a nation of victims who had almost constantly struggled against different forms of oppression. Radio Prague *(Radio Praha)* claimed, for example, that Jan Palach's deed symbolized the Czech past, because

[t]hroughout history, there was hardly any time when Czechs didn't have to fight for their freedom. And throughout history, there were those who didn't hesitate to sacrifice their lives in order to encourage and unite the intimidated and resigned nation. (http//archiv. radio.cz/palach99/eng/ aktual3.html: 1)

In this narrative, three historical figures acted as freedom fighters and symbols of democracy. First, the Catholic Church reformer Jan Hus who was burnt at the stake in 1415; second, the student Jan Opletal who was shot in 1939 during the German occupation; and third, Jan Palach, who burnt himself to death in 1969. As the Web site notes:

> [f]or Czechs, [these] three names will always symbolise truth, freedom and democracy ... three names used to uplift the crushed spirits in times of oppression, and the very names used to trouble the authorities whose power was based on force rather than democracy.

The Palach memorial added a direct, physical presence to this nationalist understanding of Czech history. The fact that the cast showed the 'real' scars of a person who had died 'for the nation' turned it into an even more powerful and evocative artefact. A twenty-year-old female student told me in 2001: 'I normally don't really notice the monument because I'll just be rushing past it to our Faculty. But sometimes I stop and really look at his face. Then I admire Palach for his courage, and feel proud to be Czech'.

As with the actor's death mask in the previous example, this object was both an iconic sign and an index. As a 'secondary agent', it did not only distribute Palach's primary agency (whose main aim had been to discredit the communists and propagate democratic values), but also served as a proof of the 'collective' suffering of the Czech nation. It criticized foreign intervention and heroized public protest, actively reinforcing nationalist sentiments. This again shows that objects can function as active agents, generating emotions and moral judgements. In the Palach case, they had a clear political subtext.[9]

Body Parts as 'Art': Outrage over Anthony-Noel Kelly's Sculptures

In the case of Palach's death mask, no moral objections were made in relation to the fact that a Czech artist had secretly taken a cast of a dead face. As noted earlier, this is understandable, because the making of the mask and its subsequent transformation into a national monument was perceived to be in line with Palach's own political intentions. This public acceptance stands in sharp contrast with the moral outrage that flared up in Britain when it was revealed that the British artist Anthony-Noel Kelly had secretly used casts of human body parts in his sculptures. When Kelly displayed the works in an art exhibition in 1997, some viewers became suspicious and contacted the police. During the investigation, human remains were discovered on the grounds of Kelly's home in Kent, and in the basement of a flat in London. Officers discovered that, with the help of a laboratory technician, the artist had stolen around forty anatomical specimens from the Royal College of Surgeons. In 1998 he was convicted and sentenced to a nine-month jail term.

In an interview with Varsity, a Web journal published by Cambridge University, Kelly noted:

> I understand there's a reverence for dead bodies which I don't share. Working with dead things is therapeutic. It gives me pleasure and balance. (http://www.varsity.cam.ac.uk/ 802567B80049EF7D/Pages/932000_AnthonyNoelKelly: 1)

The main cause of anger was, however, not that the artist had simply 'worked with dead things', but rather that he had done this illegally, and without the consent of the deceased. The individuals whose body parts were cast by Kelly had donated their bodies 'to science'; they had not agreed to be turned into objects of art. Their surviving relatives had not given their consent either. Kelly's works thus evoked strong criticism because he had denied the last wishes of the deceased to distribute their own primary agency through the specimens. Instead he had used the corpses for his own artistic aims, turning them from scientifically relevant anatomical samples into objects of personal therapeutic and aesthetic value.

To gather some opinions about this case, I approached some of my friends, a number of anthropology students at Queen's University Belfast, and a few people I met in public places in England. 'I find this disgusting', a thirty-two-year-old hairdresser from London told me. 'It gives me the creeps, the thought of Kelly with these poor dead people, who thought they were helping medical science. A really scary body snatcher, you know, like straight from a horror movie'. The image of the evil body snatcher has been widely used in popular culture, especially in films. Drawing on the emotionally powerful narrative of 'mythical struggles between good and evil', the accusation marked Kelly as an utterly amoral being.

Some people's fury was also directed at Kelly's claim that the works had aesthetic value. As a thirty-three-year-old builder from the north of England whom I met in a pub in Lancashire said:

> I thought art had to aspire to try and recreate the best of the human body, like that's what the Greeks and Romans tried to do, but nicking a body and sticking it on a pedestal don't involve no skill, does it. I mean I could have done that and so could my grandma, and it wouldn't make us Michelangelo, and we wouldn't get paid millions for it either, and they expect us to think that this modern art stuff is great. They should learn to fucking paint a picture or something.

In fact, this angry reaction is what many postmodern artists like Kelly aim for, who intend to question the more established boundaries between 'art' and 'non-art' (Svašek 2007). They purposely break taboos, and many have tried to create shock effects through the use of cadavers and body fluids in their art. Damien Hirst, for example, has become famous for his pickled animals. Marc Quinn is known for his sculptural self-portraits, filled with his own blood, and Andreo Serrano created furore with 'Piss Christ', a crucifix submerged in the artist's own urine.

Closer to Kelly's case and the ethical concerns it raised was a statue by Rick Gibson, created in 1985. The work, entitled 'Human Earrings' showed a plastic hairdresser's model's head in a perspex case with two twelve-week-old dried human foetuses hanging from her ears. As Walker (1999) commented, the case revealed the public availability of dead body parts. Gibson told one newspaper that he was given them by a lecturer in pathology after placing an advert for 'legally preserved human limbs and foetuses' in a gallery window. Not surprisingly, 'Human Earrings' evoked angry responses. When it was exhibited in 1987 at an exhibition in the Young Unknowns Gallery, the police removed the statue and Gibson and the gallery owner were charged. In 1989, they were found guilty of committing 'an act of a disgusting nature outraging public decency' and were fined £500 and £350 respectively.

When I talked about the case with a number of anthropology students at Queen's University Belfast in 2002, some accused the artist of disrespecting human life. In the words of a mature female student and mother from Belfast: 'the fact that these foetuses have been exhibited as art makes me physically sick. I am an open-minded person, but I find this unacceptable. They are, after all, human life. Even though I approve of abortion and do not think that embryos have an automatic right to live, they do have the right to be treated respectfully'. Another student noted: 'It is awful, how can you do such a thing? Unborn life needs to be protected, these are small babies, you cannot treat them like dirt'. These views were close to the accusations expressed during the trial that Gibson had 'mutilated the foetuses' (Walker 1999: 152).

The comments show that the corpses of embryos have a rather special emotional agency. They are not only, like all corpses, ambiguous subject-object phenomena, but they also draw on emotional debates amongst prolife and proabortion activists that question the sometimes unclear boundaries between life and potential life. Anger and disgust, in this case, functioned as a moral judgement and as an attempt to set certain rules.

Interestingly, Rick Gibson claimed to have made the statue in order to address exactly such issues; to pose ethical questions about the use and misuse of human embryos. He proclaimed that he had intended 'not to offend visitors but to intrigue them, to make them think about what materials are suitable for art and adornment, and about the ethics of using such objects' (Walker 1999: 151–2). Whatever the artist's intentions, it is clear that he had deliberately called upon the emotional power of dead embryos to attract the attention of the wider public, thus distributing his own agency as a daring, provocative artist. His critics, by contrast, emphasized the subject status, the personhood of the foetuses, and the fact that neither they, nor their parents, had had a choice in the matter—whether or not to pose as earrings. Evidently, the critics also used the foetuses as secondary agents to communicate their own passionate opinions.

Displaying Anatomical Specimens: Art, Science or Embarrassment?

Lack of consent and dubious claims to beauty were also major reasons why the German anatomist Gunther von Hagen faced fierce protests after he had launched the exhibition 'Body Worlds: Fascination Beneath the Surface' in Mannheim in 1998. Like Hirst and Gibson, von Hagen displayed real corpses and body parts, but his exhibits were not dried or preserved in formaldehyde. Instead, the anatomist had developed the method of plastination in 1977, a technique which replaced bodily fluids in cadavers by reactive plastics in a special vacuum process. This method preserved the original colours of human tissue and allowed the anatomist to manipulate individual body parts in intricate ways.

In 1994, von Hagen established the Institut für Plastination in Heidelberg, which received specimens from various sources. Some came from existing anatomical collections, others from donors who had expressed the wish to be plastinated after their death, and other bodies had been bequeathed to the institute by their survivors. The remaining specimens were unclaimed corpses that had been purchased by von Hagen in China and Russia (http://www.channel4.com/science/microsites/A/anatomists/hagens1.html: 1–2).

For the 'Body Worlds' exhibition, von Hagen and his team processed human corpses in several ways and displayed them in various positions, playing on their subject-object ambiguity. In 'exploded-view' specimens, body parts were pulled in different directions to enable a good view of all the details. 'Open-door' specimens were hinged, allowing a closer look at the corpses' interiors, and 'open-drawer' specimens included movable parts. Other specimens consisted of thin slices, either of whole bodies or of particular body parts. These samples clearly dehumanized the human body as scientific *objects*—as artefact-like things that could be opened, closed or taken to pieces. At the same time, other exhibits emphasized the *subject* status of the samples, creating humorous or dramatic narratives. A male body, for example, was stripped of his skin, which was hung from one of his raised hands, so that it seemed as if he was hanging up his coat. Another skinned male was riding the corpse of a skinned horse, holding his own brain in one hand and the horse's in another. A third exhibit showed a pregnant woman, reclined on her side. She held her left arm up behind her head to enable a better view of the dead embryo inside her. Other samples showed the result of unhealthy lifestyles, such as the lungs of a heavy smoker. The latter triggered viewers to think about the possible consequences of their own behaviour, pushing them to make a connection between their own and the corpses' subject status.

Von Hagen's Web site noted that 'Body Worlds' was purposely made visually attractive in order to serve an important educational aim, offering the general public the enjoyment of 'fascinating insights into the human body', a privilege that had, so far, been 'confined to medicine students and anatomists'. On the Web site, visitors expressed strong admiration for von Hagen's hard and courageous work, and claimed to have learned a great deal (http://www.koerperwelten.com/en/pages/ausstellungsinhalte.asp: 1).

The controversial exhibition was, however, strongly criticized in German and international media. Religious leaders, philosophers, medics, artists, law specialists and many others participated in the ethical debate about the display of human corpses (cf. Rager and Rinsdorf 2001). This again demonstrates that objects, whether works of art or medical samples, can have consequential emotional agency. Some critics of 'Body Worlds' fiercely objected to the exhibition, claiming that it disturbed the peace of the dead, that it destroyed basic human rights and values, or that it was unethical to use corpses from people who had not given their consent. Several churches held services for the souls of the plastinated cadavers. Other critics argued that von Hagen had turned death into a mere spectacle, or that the exhibits were simply macabre kitsch objects that easily responded to the onlookers' sentimental and artistic expectations, but yet without any real aesthetic value. Furthermore, numerous anatomists pointed out that the display was scientifically worthless because it provided minimal new anatomical knowledge (Wetz and Tag 2001: 9–11). Interestingly, the debates either focused on the bodies' subject status, discursively constructing them as 'souls', or as 'people with certain rights', or stressed that they were worthless objects in terms of their scientific or aesthetic value.

Yet despite the widespread criticism, 'Body Worlds' was a highly successful exhibition. It attracted 550,000 visitors in Vienna, 600,000 in Basel, more than 1.5 million in Cologne and Oberhausen, and over 2.5 million in Japan. But what did the visitors expect, and how did their expectations shape their emotional experience of the display? The sociologist Ernst D. Lantermann (2001) interviewed around 3,200 visitors in Vienna, Basel and Cologne, and found that, before entering the exhibition, 82 per cent of those interviewed had been extremely curious, 25 per cent had felt fear, and 19 per cent had experienced mixed feelings. Most respondents expected to gain anatomical knowledge and to increase their respect for the wonder and beauty of human nature. Others thought the exhibition would urge them to become more reflexive about life and death, or to adopt a healthier life style.[10] Only five per cent feared that the display would offend their moral values. Evidently, these responses are far more positive than those expressed in the public debates, reflecting the fact that the respondents had chosen to visit the exhibition. After having visited the exhibition, 89 per cent noted that they had indeed learned a lot about human anatomy; 69 per cent had become more concerned about the vulnerability of their own bodies, and 39 per cent said they felt more respect for their own bodies. Three per cent of the visitors expressed outrage about the display, claiming that the exhibition makers disrespected basic human values.

The subject-object ambiguity of the exhibits—the fact that they were *real* bodies—whether positively or negatively experienced, clearly gave the samples a powerful aura. As a British journalistic report noted:

[p]eople who have seen the show have said that they were torn between being fascinated and incredibly frightened by what von Hagen had done. They say that if they hadn't known what they were about to see before they walked in, they would have just assumed they were extremely impressive anatomical models, and if we were all able to think of them as just that—models—we would also agree that they were fascinating. However, at the back of our minds we cannot escape from the fact that they were real people. (http://www.bbc.co.uk/dna/h2g2/alabaster/A804322, last accessed 14–11–2006)[11]

As with famous art works, the 'authenticity' of the corpses strongly increased their emotional force. In von Hagen's words: '[n]either illustrations nor models can convey the individual beauty of these structures to us, for the source of truth is in the originals' (http://www.koerperwelten.com/en/pages/ausstellungsinhalte.asp: 2). The anatomist made his aesthetic claims more emphatically by positioning some of the specimens in poses that reminded visitors of well-known art works.

Numerous critics strongly objected to the display of human remains as 'pieces of installation art'. The BBC Web site compared the aesthetic manipulation of body parts to infamous Nazi practices.[12] In Lantermann's study, 29 per cent of the respondents objected to von Hagen's 'artistic' presentation, arguing that anatomic specimens should not be displayed as aesthetic artefacts.[13] This reminds us of the furore around the art works by Kelly and Gibson, and the arguments about the disparity between artists' and dead subjects' desires. It also brings home that context and context-dependent expectations strongly influence people's perceptions and emotional judgements. The display of corpses may be acceptable to some viewers in scientific environments that breathe an atmosphere of cool rationality, while they would object to their incorporation into more joyful, playful settings that emphatically offer experiences of beauty.

In 'Body Worlds', the causal nature of lifeless matter was also obvious in other ways. Interviewed immediately after their visit to 'Body Worlds', 53 per cent of the visitors claimed that they planned to take better care of their health in the future. Six months later, some had reduced smoking (25 per cent), increased sport activities (18 per cent), or reduced their alcohol intake (11 per cent) (Lantermann 2001). Not surprisingly, the 'Body Worlds' exhibition also stimulated visitors to think about their own postmortum destination, and a number of visitors decided to donate their bodies for plastination to von Hagen's Institute.[14] Noting that over three thousand people had signed the consent forms, the BBC Web site questioned their motivations:

Are the three thousand simply looking for a route to immortality, or do they consider themselves worthy of becoming a 'cultural or educational asset?' If their reaction were the latter, surely it would be better to donate their bodies to science after their deaths, saving lives rather than becoming museum pieces to simply sit and gather dust? (http://www.bbc.co.uk/dna/h2g2/ alabaster/A804322)

This adds another dimension to the emotional agency of subject-objects—through plastinated body parts, deceased subjects may challenge ideas of the living about the postmortal distribution of human agency. And through public expressions of anger and concern, the latter may openly doubt the morality of the former.

Tsantsas: Exotic Human Remains As Ethnographic Objects

The 'Body Worlds' case showed that the scientific status of anatomical specimens can justify the appearance of human remains in the public realm (even though, as the case showed, it does not necessarily convince all members of the public). In my own discipline of anthropology, human remains have also been presented under the umbrella of science, discursively constructed and displayed as 'ethnographic objects' in ethnographic collections. This last section will analyze the changing emotional agency of Jivaro *tsantsas,* shrunken heads from the Amazon region, as they were moved from this region to changing museum settings in Europe.

Traditionally, the Jivaro regarded shrunken heads as powerful matter which possessed transferable human agency. Roughly until the second half of the twentieth century, Jivaro men had the obligation to avenge death within their own lineages through headhunting, killing a member of a rival lineage. The opponent's head was shrunken through a complex procedure, taking out the skull, boiling the remaining head, and filling it with hot stones or sand. The aim of the captor was to paralyze the spirit of the enemy, and take its power to please the ancestors and increase one's own status and well-being. By stealing the dead, Jivaro believed they diminished the capabilities for future existence of rival groups, and increased the chance for survival of their own lineage. As Anne Christine Taylor (1993: 671) has noted:

> The ritual of the *tsantsa* ... is built around the gradual transformation of an unknown foe first into an affine, and at a later stage into a foetus to be born of a woman in the captors' group. The purpose of head-hunting is not therefore merely to kill an antagonist and display him as a trophy, but rather to capture a dead enemy, and then operate on the elements that constitute him.

After the ritual transition of life potential, *tsantsas* were regarded as empty, powerless objects. They were tossed away or kept as harmless war trophies.

In the nineteenth century, European and American collectors of exotic artefacts became fascinated by the phenomenon of the *tsantsas.* The shrunken heads embodied everything they regarded as 'primitive'—lawless, uncontrolled fierceness—and they were therefore excellent ethnographic examples of the earlier stage of human progress. The so-called civilized nations thus utilized the *tsantsas* to evoke feelings of horror about the primitive bloodthirstiness of early man, and feelings of superiority about their own supposedly rational manners. The changed emotional agency of the *tsantsas* (from triggers of pride over victory to triggers of horror and self-righteousness) shows what was noted earlier, namely that objects can be used by different people to generate different types of emotional reactions. In the Western context, the subject status of the shrunken heads was emphasized in a particular way; the items were displayed as physical examples of people who belonged to a cruel and primitive race.

Not surprisingly, in the nineteenth and early twentieth centuries, many ethnographic museums that propagated the theory of social evolution acquired shrunken heads for their collections. The Jivaro were eager to exchange them for more useful goods, such as guns and bullets. From the 1850s onwards, the *tsantsas* trade grew steadily, and this stimulated the production of counterfeit shrunken heads. In the late nineteenth century, an adventurer reported that a counterfeiter in Panama had used the heads of unclaimed hospital corpses, 'white men, black men, Chinese men and natives', to meet the demand of interested tourists (http:/www.head-hunter.com/fakes.html:1, 2). The growing trade also increased Jivaro warfare, and the Peruvian and Ecuadorian governments passed severe laws to stop the traffic of human heads.

Between 1884 and 1936, the Pitt Rivers Museum in Oxford acquired ten *tsantsas*. For the biggest part of the nineteenth and twentieth centuries, the ownership and display of human remains, such as shrunken heads, was regarded as unproblematic. Of the over 275,000 objects collected, about 2,000 are human remains, or are artefacts made of human remains. This collection includes 300 skulls or parts of skulls, 600 bones or objects made of bones, 400 specimens of hair, 300 artefacts made out of hair, and several teeth and artefacts consisting of teeth (http://www.prm.ox.ac.uk/human.html).

In the 1990s, influenced by increasingly critical discussions amongst anthropologists about the ethics of displaying human remains and the issue of cultural ownership, staff from the Pitt Rivers Museum participated in a working group to discuss the ownership and display of human body parts. This led to the publication in 1994 of the UK Museum Ethnographers Group's 'Professional Guidelines Concerning the Storage, Display, Interpretation and Return of Human Remains'. On its Web site, the museum ensured 'the highest possible standard of care for human remains and artefacts made with human remains', and pointed out that it had introduced innovations in its exhibition practices, having 'begun to redisplay cases that include human remains to ensure that the intended educational and cultural information is communicated well and that the displays are respectful to both visitors and the dead'.

The artefacts were recontextualized through the explanation of their local significance in the region of origin and display of them amongst comparative material from around the world. The *tsantsas,* for example, appeared in a case that was rather neutrally entitled 'Treatment of Dead Enemies'. The Web site stressed that '[t]hese materials are interpreted in a respectful manner'. In other words, the new displays intended to prove and distribute the new moral claims of the museum staff. Instead of presenting the *tsantsas* as spectacular indices of primitive otherness and horror, as had happened earlier, the museum now aimed to spark interest in human diversity without evolutionary connotations. The museum also worked together with members of ethnic groups to whom the human remains had once belonged. As a result, Maori tattooed heads were removed from the permanent display in 1987, and skeletal remains were returned to Australian Aboriginal communities in 1990. The changed policy clearly showed how human body parts can evoke different emotional processes and cause distinct social actions throughout history. Even though the specimens remained constant in terms of their materiality, with regard to emotional dynamics, their symbolic and indexical impact varied considerably.

Conclusion: Subject/Object Ambiguity and Emotional Agency

In this chapter, I have demonstrated that matter has emotional efficacy, and that material objects distribute the primary agency of their producers and users who experience and construct them as mediators of their own desires, fears and convictions. Objects are thus often perceived as subject-like forces, which—like human subjects—exist in time and space. Experienced through the senses, they express and evoke emotions and make themselves 'known' as bodily felt and imaged internalized presences. Human body parts and their casts have a particularly strong emotional agency; they are ambiguous phenomena that problematize the subject-object divide more fundamentally. On the one hand, as lifeless substance, human remains and casts of human remains are 'things' that can be moved, displayed or manipulated by adding bits or taking bits away. On the other hand, they are clearly the remains of human individuals, who may be dead but who have a past of emotional sociality.

In the five cases discussed in this chapter, the emotional force of the ambiguous subject/objects depended on a number of factors. First of all, the material characteristics mattered. The actual presence of *real* human flesh added an authentic feel to the confrontation between the living and the dead, and this influenced the emotional impact on the onlookers. Even when viewers were presented with *casts* of human flesh, the knowledge that they bore an imprint of 'real people', and that the producers of the casts had touched and handled 'real' human corpses influenced their emotional efficacy. Not surprisingly, questions of authority were frequently asked about people's right to manipulate and display dead bodies and their casts.

This brings us to the second factor of context. In different types of contexts, different professional codes of conduct dominated that corresponded with distinct emotional responses and moral judgements. While the practice of studying and displaying corpses and their casts was generally regarded as an acceptable practice in medical and scientific settings (even though there have recently been numerous cases of misconduct in Britain), the outrage over the exhibition of anatomical specimens in the 'Body Worlds' exhibition clarified that human remains cannot, according to many critics, be studied by just anybody, and that there are different opinions as to how human remains should be presented to the wider public. As long as the corpses were displayed as 'scientific samples', and the scientific context was presented as a utilitarian realm of action, aiming to improve human well-being while respecting human rights and values (however defined), the display of human remains seemed more or less unproblematic to most people. When, however, aesthetic considerations came into play, many commentators thought that morality was at stake. With regard to aesthetic aims, the outrage was fiercest when body parts or their casts were presented as 'art' in artistic contexts, as clearly shown by the Kelly case.

The factor of consent—had the subject (or the subject's relatives) agreed with his or her postmortal transformation into a particular class of objects?—was vital to the debates, and emotional judgements (anger, outrage, disgust) were clear moral statements. Only in the case of Jan Palach's death mask, nobody doubted that the student would have agreed to the transformation of his facial imprint into a national monument. His primary agency was reinforced through the making of the monument. In all the other cases, critical questions were raised about the right of the living to manipulate or process human corpses. There were accusations of disrespect for the primary agency of the deceased, and of misusing the corpses for other people's own artistic, therapeutic, or political goals. In some of the cases, anxiety about the inability to control their own postmortem existence as lifeless matter strongly shaped negative emotional judgements. This is not surprising, as death awaits us all.

References

Bild (1993), 'So fährt Witwe Löwitsch ihren Klaus spazieren', 6 September 1993: 1, 2.

Burda, V. (1969), 'Pomnik pro J. Palacha?'. *Výtvarná Práce,* 3(4): 10.

Casey, E. S. (1987), *Remembering: A Phenomenological Study,* Bloomington: Indiana University Press.

Csordas, T. J. (1990), 'Embodiment As a Paradigm for Anthropology', *Ethos* 18(1): 5–47.

Csordas, T. J. ed., (1994), *Embodiment and Experience. The Existential Ground of Culture and Self,* Cambridge: Cambridge University Press.

Gell, A. (1998), *Art and Agency: An Anthropological Theory,* Oxford: Clarendon Press.

Hallam, E., and Hockey, J. (2001), *Death, Memory, and Material Culture,* Oxford: Berg.

Knight, J. (2005) 'Maternal Feelings on Monkey Mountain. Cross-Species Emotional Affinity in Japan', in K. Milton and M. Svašek (eds), *Mixed Emotions: Anthropological Studies of Feeling,* pp. 179–93, Oxford: Berg.

Lantermann, E. D. (2001) 'Der eigene Körper im Spiegel der Anatomie', in F. J. Wetz and B. Tag (eds), *Schöne Neue Körperwelten. Der Streit um die Ausstellung,* pp. 279–300, Stuttgart: Klett-Cotta.

Leavitt, J. (1996) 'Meaning and Feeling in the Anthropology of Emotions', *American Ethnologist* 23(3): 514–39.

Lutz, C. A., and White, G. M. (1986), 'The Anthropology of Emotions', *Annual Review of Anthropology* 15: 405–36.

Milton, K. (2005), 'Meanings, Feelings and Human Ecology', in K. Milton and M. Svašek (eds), *Mixed Emotions: Anthropological Studies of Feeling,* pp. 25–41, Oxford: Berg.

Parkinson, B. (1995), *Ideas and Realities of Emotion,* London: Routledge.

Rager, G., and Rinsdorf, L. (2001), 'Wenn die "Gruselleichen" kommen. Die "Körperwelten" in der Presse', in F. J. Wetz and B. Tag (eds), *Schöne Neue Körperwelten. Der Streit um die Ausstellung,* pp. 301–27, Stuttgart: Klett-Cotta.

Roach, M. (2003), *Stiff: The Curious Lives of Human Cadavers,* New York: Norton and Company.

Rosaldo, M. Z. (1983), 'Towards an Anthropology of Self and Feeling', in R. A. Schweder and R. A. LeVine (eds), *Culture Theory,* Cambridge: Cambridge University Press.

Seremetakis, C. N., ed. (1994), *The Senses Still: Perception and Memory As Material Culture in Modernity,* Chicago: University of Chicago Press.

Svašek, M. (1996), 'Styles, Struggles and Careers: An Ethnography of the Czech Art World, 1948–1992', Unpublished PhD thesis, University of Amsterdam.

Svašek, M. (2005a), 'Introduction: Emotions in Anthropology', in K. Milton and M. Svašek (eds), *Mixed Emotions: Anthropological Studies of Feeling,* pp. 1–23, Oxford: Berg.

Svašek, M. (2005b),'The Politics of Chosen Trauma. Expellee Memories, Emotions and Identities', in K. Milton and M. Svašek (eds), *Mixed Emotions: Anthropological Studies of Feeling,* pp. 195–214, Oxford: Berg.

Svašek, M. (2005c), 'Postsocialist Ownership. Emotions, Power and Morality in a Czech Village', in M. Svašek (ed.), *Postsocialism: Politics and Emotions in Central and Eastern Europe,* pp. 95–114, Oxford: Berghahn.

Svašek, M. (2007), *Anthropology, Art, and Cultural Production,* London: Pluto.

Taylor, A. C. (1993), 'Remembering to Forget: Identity, Mourning and Memory among the Jivaro', *Man* (N.S.) 28: 653–78.

Walker, J. A. (1999), *Art & Outrage: Provocation, Controversy and the Visual Arts,* London: Pluto.

Wetz, F. J., and Tag, B. (2001), '"Körperwelten". Die erfolgreichste Wanderausstellung unserer Zeit', in F. J. Wetz and B. Tag (eds), *Schöne Neue Körperwelten: Der Streit um die Ausstellung,* pp. 7–19, Stuttgart: Klett-Cotta.

http://archiv.radio.cz/palach99/eng/aktual3.html, last accessed 14/01/04.

http://www.bbc.co.uk/dna/h2g2/alabaster/A804322, last accessed 08/06/04.

http://www.head-hunter.com/fakes.html, last accessed 24/06/04.

http://www.koerperwelten.com/en.pages/ausstellungsinhalte.asp, last accessed 08/06/04.

http://www.prm.ox.ac.uk/human.html, entered 24/06/04.

http://www.varsity.cam.ac.uk/802567B80049EF7D/Pages/932000_AnthonyNoelKelly, last accessed 08/06/04

http://www.channel4.com/science/microsites/A/anatomists/hagens.html, last accessed 08/06/04.

Notes

1. But see, for example, Parkinson (1995) for an approach in psychology which focuses on the social dynamics of emotions.

2. The article was entitled: 'This is How the Widow Löwitz Takes her Klaus for a Drive' (*So fährt Witwe Löwitz ihren Klaus spazieren*).

3. 'Klaus ist für mich nicht tot. Ich rede mit ihm, und er ist immer bei mir. Die Maske habe ich erst zu mir ins Bett gelegt, aber da meinte Klaus: Ich fahre lieber Auto ... Klaus liebt weite Strecken. Wenn wir unterwegs sind, trägt er immer eine warme Mütze ... Ich kann ihn nicht greifen, aber fühlen. Das ist für mich Trost'.

4. Gell conceptualized subject-object relations as a dialectical process in which subjects produced objects, and vice versa. His theory of art and enchantment attacked semiotic and discursive views of artefacts as sign-vehicles with aesthetic properties. Gell noted that: 'The innumerable shades of social/emotional responses to artefacts (of terror, desire, awe, fascination, etc.) in the unfolding patterns of social life cannot be encompassed or reduced to aesthetic feelings; not without making the aesthetic response so generalized as to be altogether meaningless' (1998: 6). Gell claimed to be the first to have formulated a truly *anthropological* theory of art which refused to be lured by aesthetic arguments. He criticized the culturalist relativist aim to study indigenous aesthetic systems because 'such a programme is exclusively cultural, rather than social' (1998: 2).

5. 'Memory cannot be confined to a purely mentalist or subjective sphere. It is a culturally mediated material practice that is activated by embodied acts and semantically dense objects' (Seremetakis 1994: 9; quoted by Hallam and Hockey 2001: 11).

6. I spoke with eight of my German friends and acquaintances about the case, including five women and three men, all aged between thirty and fifty years old. The group included three nannies, one interpreter, one housewife, two journalists and one shopkeeper.

7. The Web site of Radio Praha noted that on 25 January 1969, Jan Palach was 'buried in Prague at the Olsany cemeteries; the funeral included a ceremony at the Karolinum organized by Petr Josef Vilimek, who was the state's witness

of Palach's deed; Zdenek Tous said farewell to Palach for the Prague studentry; the funeral became a large demonstration for freedom and democracy; the coffin with Palach's remains was displayed in the Karolinum as an act of last respects. Academic functionaries, artists, students, and several politicians took their turns at the coffin. The evening after the funeral, church dignitaries held a funeral mass for the deceased', <http://archiv.radio.cz/palach99/eng> accessed 14 November 2006.

8. Masaryk was the first president of the Czechoslovak state that was founded in 1918. He strongly defended democratic values and became a symbol of anticommunist struggle for those who opposed the state-socialist system.

9. Under Communism, 'suffering for the nation' had not been a common experience at all. To many, Palach's monument was therefore a more abstract symbol of shared nationhood, and a reminder of their own, less heroic political choices at the time of the invasion. It must also be noted that the sculptor Zoubek distributed his own, personal agency as 'dissident artist' through the monument. In numerous art catalogues, the monument was listed as one of his important artistic products.

10. Eighty-eight per cent of the visitors interviewed expected increased knowledge about the human body, 63 per cent expected to gain respect for the 'wonder' of the human body, 53 per cent hoped to be stimulated to adopt a healthier life style, and 41 per cent thought that the confrontation with the corpses would make them more reflexive about life and death. In addition, 41 per cent of the visitors hoped that the exhibition would offer them an aesthetically pleasing experience.

11. Mary Roach pointed out in a study of the handling of human cadavers by professionals (including medical anatomical specimens, human crash test dummies, bodies used for organ transplant and bodies used in forensic studies of human decay): 'The problem with cadavers is that they look so much like people. It's the reason most of us prefer a pork chop to a slice of whole suckling pig. It's the reason we say "pork" and "beef" instead of "pig" and "cow"' (Roach 2003: 21). She further noted that '[d]issection and surgical instruction, like meat-eating, require a carefully maintained set of illusions and denial. Physicians and anatomy students must learn to think of cadavers as wholly unrelated to the people they once were'. Subject-object ambiguity was, for example, clearly expressed at the medical faculty of the University of California in San Francisco, where corpses used for the instruction of medical students were emphatically presented as 'object' as 'the heads and hands are often left wrapped until their dissection comes up on the syllabus'. At the same university, after the corpses have been reduced to neatly sawed segments, a memorial service was held by the anatomy lab students. 'This is not a token ceremony. It is a sincere and voluntary attended event, lasting nearly three hours and featuring thirteen student tributes' (Roach 2003: 38–9).

12. 'Von Hagen considers his displays to be a combination of art, science, and education; however his activities have been compared to those in Nazi concentration camps during the Second World War, where people's teeth and hair were hoarded for money and even lampshades were made from skin' (http://www.bbc.co.uk/dna/h2g2/ alabaster/A804322).

13. In reaction to the accusations of false artistic pretense, von Hagen noted that: 'If, as many believe, this exhibition preaches science as art, I am for sure on the side of science. I see myself not as an artist but rather as an inventor and for this I need the creativity of an artist and even more, the scientific thinking' (www.channel4.com/science/microsites/A/anatomists/hagens.html: 2). He also stressed that the individuality and beauty of the specimen could not be reproduced by models.

14. In Lantermann's (2001: 294) study, while 18 per cent of those questioned immediately after their visit to the exhibition claimed to be more interested than before in donating their organs to science, another 18 per cent said that they 'could imagine that they would donate their body for plastination'.

IV
Desire and Expectations

–18–

'Cool Play'
Emotionality in Dance as a Resource in Senegalese Urban Women's Associations

Hélène Neveu Kringelbach

In Wolof-speaking Senegal, *àndal ak sa sago,* 'stay cold-blooded' or 'control yourself', is a common phrase thrown at someone whose emotions seem to be slipping out of control. This is a society in which emotional restraint is closely associated with a high social and moral status. Popular events such as *sabar* dances, however, provide a unique space in which respectable women may enact a wider range of emotions than in everyday life. Men, by contrast, risk being classified as homosexual, mad people or lower-status praise-singers (Griots in French, or *géwël* in Wolof) if they allow themselves to dance as expressively as some women do.

In this chapter, I suggest that Dakarois[1] women, therefore, have appropriated the dance circle as a space in which men are excluded from female sociality. This is where 'women's business' (*afééru jigéen*) takes place. As it becomes more difficult for male household heads to fulfil their 'traditional' role as breadwinners, in practice women's associations and similar mechanisms of solidarity, all facilitated by the dance events, quietly undermine the socioeconomic power of a growing proportion of Dakarois men. These developments are bound to affect gender relations in urban Senegal, but for now, most women seem to choose the route of outward compliance with their roles of good wives and good mothers. Yet the dance events they have come to dominate provide them with the emotional resources necessary to work out the tensions between dominant discourses on gender roles, 'caste' and class hierarchies and a contradictory everyday practice.

In their introduction to *Language and the Politics of Emotion,* Abu-Lughod and Lutz (1990: 1) argue that "the most productive analytical approach to the cross-cultural study of emotion is to examine discourses on emotion and emotional discourses as social practices within diverse ethnographic contexts". Over the past three decades or so, the anthropological study of emotion has placed a great deal of emphasis on verbal language. In their effort to disentangle the topic from the dominance of psychology and psychiatry, social scientists have argued that emotion should be studied as the outcome of sociological processes rather than as physiologically bounded phenomena. Emotion, they argued, is mediated by and constructed through language. Within the broader framework of European philosophical history, their work went against the conception held since the seventeenth century, that emotions were involuntary, noncognitive perturbations human beings must learn to transcend (Harré 1986b). Over time however, an exclusively language-focused approach has appeared to be problematic. Along with a growing interest in the body in the social sciences, it has now become obvious that "what can be said in language does not fully match all that is going on in life" (James 2003: 92). Rather than being exclusively concerned with discourse, in this paper I draw on ethnography of a Senegalese genre of performance, the *sabar,* to argue that bodily activities may help uncover aspects of the social elaboration of emotion that would remain hidden in the study of verbal language alone.

An important issue social studies of performance have addressed is that of whether bodily performance is akin to emotional expression, or whether emotions are generated by bodily activities and changing bodily states. Does moving in rhythm with others have the power to generate specific emotions, as argued early on by Durkheim (1912)? So far there has been no definite answer to this question, but the contribution of such disciplines as psychology and neuroscience may provide fresh insights. Rather than attempting to contribute to the debate with inappropriate tools, I argue for the role that the cross-cultural study of dance should play in illuminating the relationship between body and emotion. More specifically, I argue that part of the success of *sabar* performances lies in the intense stimulation of the senses that takes place amongst participants. The altered states these sensual experiences generate are very much the product of socialization from an early age. Thus the smells, colours, fabric textures, sounds and rhythms people respond to, are largely specific to Senegambia. Meanwhile these experiences are powerful enough to help momentarily invert the verbalized norms related to the display of emotions.

Before delving further into the subject, it might be useful to interrogate notions like 'emotions', 'feelings' or 'sentiments', which often escape the full grasp of verbal language. The social sciences have often made little distinction between these different concepts. The social constructionist school has sought to define itself in opposition to the experimental sciences, arguing that there was no single substance that might be isolated as emotion, but rather "the ordering, selecting and interpreting work upon which our acts of management of fragments of life depend" (Harré 1986a: 4). Apart from being fairly obscure, such definitions tend to reduce the world of emotions to an exclusively cognitive or linguistic domain. Alternatively, social scientists have made a distinction between "emotion, defined as private feelings that are usually not culturally motivated or socially articulated, and sentiment, defined as socially articulated symbols and behavioral expectations" (Lutz and White 1986: 409). The main concern with such dichotomies has been to distance the cultural study of emotion from earlier psychological approaches. In recent years however, anthropologists have increasingly recognized that insights might be gained from the experimental disciplines (see Leavitt 1996). Without borrowing from these fields, I attempt to promote a holistic view of emotion by purposefully using a single term to designate both the subjective experience of emotion and its social significance.

The Human Seriousness of Dance

Whereas recent approaches have become more diverse, early studies involving the emotional dimension of dance can be broadly divided into two strands. The first approach was heavily influenced by a strong version of the Cartesian mind/body dichotomy, with the reason/emotion divide as a corollary. In this view, dance was a 'primitive' form of expression pertaining to the domain of emotion. The second approach interpreted community-wide dances as the 'safety valve' necessary to resolve latent conflicts, and thus maintain social order. Although rephrased in less evolutionary terms, both approaches remain common in the scholarly study of dance.

According to the first approach, so-called primitive peoples were assumed to dance more than people from more sophisticated societies, because their lives were led by emotion rather than by reason. In a tautological argument well described by Castaldi (2000), the importance of dance in the social life of many African societies was thus used as evidence that Africans were indeed more 'primitive' than Europeans. Poet and first President of Senegal Léopold Sédar Senghor has been much criticized for "internalizing and even legitimizing the denigration implicit in the colonial and imperial enterprise" (Harney 2004: 41), in particular when he stated that "European reason [was] analytic and Negro reason intuitive" (Senghor 1964: 203). It is therefore no coincidence that Senghor also regarded dance as the most 'African' form of expression. Obviously, this school of thought is problematic in that it takes the reason/emotion dichotomy for granted, thereby failing to acknowledge its historical roots in European philosophy. Through a deceptive shortcut, dance is relegated to the domain of the irrational, but the case for its irrationality is never made. In this chapter, I attempt to demystify the notion that dance is a purely emotional activity; on the contrary, I argue, dance may well be one of the human activities in which the inseparable nature of reason and emotion becomes most evident.

With his ethnography of the rituals of the Andaman Islanders, Radcliffe-Brown (1922) was an early proponent of the second approach. He argued that music and dance played a functional role in bringing community members to a heightened state of shared emotional experience. In this view, the 'function' of dance is to regulate the feelings of the individual participants so that they conform to the collective interest. Writing a few years later on the Zande beer dance, the *gbere buda,* Evans-Pritchard (1928) criticized this radical form of functionalism, pointing out that Radcliffe-Brown had missed "the complexity of motives in the dance" (460) and the threat of chaos which inevitably followed the exacerbation of individualistic tendencies.

Turner's work on ritual (e.g. 1969), and later Cohen's writings on cultural performance (e.g. 1993) brought more substance to the interpretation of bodily performance as a potential site for either rebellion or the social control of dangerous emotions. At the other end of the spectrum, philosopher of the arts Susanne Langer (1953) challenged the idea that dance, as an art form, may involve genuine emotions. With classical ballet in mind, she argued that dance created a virtual rather than a real world of emotions. She acknowledged that this virtual world could be powerful enough to move audiences, but her reliance on a somewhat artificial dichotomy between dance as art and as nonart undermined her argument. It has since become obvious that the relationship between different dance forms is a complex one, and that the real and the virtual cannot be easily differentiated (James 2003: 78).

Since the 1970s, a growing body of studies has attempted to shift the focus away from functional explanations, towards the phenomenology of performance. If few have focused on dance, these studies are nevertheless useful as they help illuminate the emotional power of performance.[2] Schieffelin's work, in particular, emphasizes the emotional dimension of the performer-audience connection. He suggests that the Aristotelian divide between a "world of spectator which is real and a world conjured up by performers which is not" prevents us from fully grasping the relationship between performance and the "social construction of reality" (Schieffelin 1998: 200). In the Gisalo ceremony of the Kaluli in Papua New Guinea, Schieffelin (1976) describes how performers sing with nostalgia about the landscapes the audience is emotionally attached to. People may be so moved by the performance that they end up burning the dancers with torches. It is not that the Kaluli are unable to conceive of the performance as a virtual world, it is rather that they take it as a provocation. The fusion of realities in the participants' experience, Schieffelin suggests, may be one of the ways in which performance accomplishes something unique. Similarly in the Senegalese *sabar,* the emotional intensity of the interaction amongst participants, with its extraordinarily competitive dimension and enacted sexual suggestiveness, may well work as a unique opportunity for many women to experience an alternative reality. In order to convey the extent to which urban dance events in Senegal challenge the appropriate ways in which one is expected to express emotion, I will now turn to the relationship between emotionality and status in Wolof society.

Emotionality and Status in Wolof[3] Society

In today's Senegal, emotionality remains central in maintaining social hierarchies. Status is not only affected by such factors as age, gender, income or place of origin, but also by genealogy, which determines an individual's status within the hereditary ranks. Much as for the Haalpulaaren of the Fuuta Toro, 'traditional' stratification follows the lines of hereditary caste-like groups, or social ranks. The two main ranks are the *géér* majority[4] and the minority *ñeeño*. Whereas the *géér* are undetermined in terms of occupation, the *ñeeño* are further divided into occupational categories of performers ('Griots') and artisans. Nowadays the practice of the trade associated with one's rank has become less relevant, and *ñeeño* status is primarily determined by genealogy.[5] Artisan categories include Blacksmiths *(tëgg)*, Leatherworkers *(uude)*, Woodworkers *(lawbe or seeñ)* or Weavers *(ràbb)*.[6] Here I focus on the Griot, traditionally a performer, genealogist/praise-singer, ritual specialist and social intermediary. Griots epitomize the *ñeeño* categories widely regarded by the *géér* as of a lower social and moral status,[7] but in private people often acknowledge that Griots derive a significant power from their role in validating the status of others. Irvine (1990) gives an accurate description of the connection between rank and affectivity:

> Central to [the Wolof ideology of stratification] is the idea that people are inherently unequal, having different constitutions that govern their feelings and motivations and make them behave in different ways. These different behavioral dispositions incline their bearers to differing but complementary forms of action, whence arise the occupational specializations of the caste system ... One's constitution—the biological, emotional, and moral qualities one derives from ancestral inheritance and from childhood experience—is the source of one's *naw* "temperament" or "capacity for emotionality". (Irvine 1990: 133)

In other words, a person's status within Wolof stratification is very much associated with his or her ability for emotional display. Whereas the *géér* are expected to speak, move and more generally act with *kersa,* a mix of restraint and deference to others, the Griots in particular are assumed to lack the capacity for restraint and to be overtly expansive and emotional. More generally, emotional restraint is positively valued as the manifestation of a higher moral status.

Expectations of restraint spill out into all aspects of everyday life, from speech to movement style, dancing skills, dress and other forms of bodily expression. *Waxu géwël,* for example, the emphatic, rapid and metaphorical speech style of the Griots, is contrasted with the quieter and slower *waxu géér,* the speech style of the *géér.* When it comes to dancing, it is particularly for women that skills are taken to be differentiated: "Griot women are supposed ... to be the best dancers, since high-caste women are 'too stiff' and 'too ashamed' to perform in the sexually suggestive manner deemed the most skilful" (Irvine 1990: 134). Yet during *sabar* parties, women of all ranks indulge in short sequences of suggestive dancing, without their status being necessarily affected by such behaviour. Non-Griot men past their teenage years, on the other hand, risk being classified as homosexuals (*goorjigéen,* literally 'man-woman'), mad people or Griots if they allow themselves to dance in suggestive ways, with the exception of short sequences framed as a parody of women. The perception that suggestive, passionate dancing is the natural prerogative of Griots is not new.[8] According to older Dakarois informants, what is more recent, however, is the fact that *sabar* events have become the quasi-exclusive domain of women participants.

Verbal language reinforces the positive perception attached to emotional restraint. Affect is often expressed in terms of fluidity, weight or heat: whereas the cool, the solid and the heavy are positively valued, the hot, the fluid and the lightweight have negative, or at least ambiguous, connotations. 'To have a cool heart', for example, is 'to be happy'.[9] An excellent praise-oratory[10] performance by a Griot is said to make the blood of his or her patron 'boil' or 'run faster', with the implication that it is impossible for the patron to control his or her emotions.

These observations, however, must be tempered. In practice, status is contextual and relative: people manipulate their speech style, vocabulary, movement style and behaviour according to the context and according to the type of relationship they intend to establish. It is therefore common to see *géér* momentarily adopt the attitude of Griots in order to position themselves as 'clients' in a patron-client relationship. But it is particularly during dance events organized by women that the norms of restraint are visibly contested.

Sabar and Women's Associations

Sabar is an overarching Wolof term used to designate all elements in *sabar* performance: the drums, the rhythms, the dances and the events themselves. *Sabar* drums are beaten with one hand and a stick, and a complete ensemble includes at least six different drums. The popular *tama,* the small 'talking drum' strapped over the player's shoulder, may also be used intermittently. The *tama* is said to have the power to make women dance in sexually suggestive ways and is often described as an incarnation of the devil (*seytaan*). There is evidence that in a fairly recent past, *sabar* drums served a wide range of purposes, from intervillage communication to encouragement in warfare, in agricultural work or as musical support in the display of strength before wrestling competitions. But importantly, drumming remains the near-exclusive domain of men.[11]

The dances themselves are performed in infinite variations and with much individual creativity. Nevertheless, many Dakarois are able to classify the dances that belong to the older repertoire—such as *ceebu jën*[12] (pronounced 'tiebudien'), *Baara Mbaye* or *kaolack*—and those which have been more recently revived or created in the ever-changing fashion of popular dances. The more fashionable dances are usually 'launched' by the latest music videos from Senegalese pop stars. They spread from the TV to the city's streets and nightclubs like fire. Some dances are known to be particularly suggestive. The *lëmbël* for example—also called 'electric fan dance'—consists in rolling the hips in tune with the rhythm, including accelerations and sudden stops, with bent knees and the back turned to the drummers. Other *sabar* dances are more aerial, with movements of the legs alternately thrown high into the air, one arm lifting a top or a skirt while the other performs a distinctive 'waving' movement in tune with the rhythm.

At first it would seem as if the choice of rhythm is in the hands of the musicians. But as Castaldi (2000) has explained, in its best moments the interaction between dancers and musicians follows a thrilling call-and-response pattern. The best dancers will challenge the lead drummer to play more complex, faster rhythms and if inspired, he will in turn respond by initiating new challenges. A lead drummer I knew compared the *sabar* interaction to a conversation, adding that he simply needed to 'look at the leg' of a good dancer to 'know what it [was] going to do next'.

Sabar events are so common in Dakar's highly populated districts that it often feels as if the city's pulse is beating to their rhythm. *Sabar* parties take on different names depending on the time of the day; a *tannbeer,* for example, takes place in the evening, and at a *tannbeer* the dancing is expected to be more sexually suggestive than during an afternoon *sabar.* I have broadly identified three categories of events during which the genre is commonly performed: family ceremonies, the regular gatherings of women's associations, and the rallies organized by political parties or civic associations. Most women in Dakar belong to at least one, and often several associations of kin, friends, neighbours, or fellow members of a Sufi brotherhood.[13] Dance events in the context of political rallies have been discussed elsewhere (Heath 1990, 1994) and are beyond the scope of this chapter, but they are structured in a very similar way as the more private events I am focusing on. *Sabar*-like parties advertised as *soirées sénégalaises* on the radio also take place in Dakar's many nightclubs; these tend to have a *mbalax*[14] band with a lead singer performing, rather than a *sabar* ensemble. But the keenest organizers of *sabar* events remain the informal associations around which the social life of a great majority of 'Dakaroises' is structured. Some closely resemble the older age sets (*mbotaay*), and with the exception of the religious associations, most of them engage in dancing during their regular meetings.[15]

Many of these networks simultaneously serve as rotating credit associations or 'tontines' (*nat*). In Dakar the generic term *tur* is used to designate any association in which a fixed number of members take turn to organize the meetings, and therefore a tontine may also be designated as a *tur,* but not all *turs* involve a money-raising mechanism. These associations usually meet weekly, fortnightly or monthly. Although some are mixed, in practice few men feel welcome at the meetings, even when they contribute financially. Thus one of the family *turs* I came across in Dakar has three men out of a membership of forty-one, and although the men pay their contributions, none of them shows up to the meetings. Women in the group told me that the men would be 'ashamed' to take part in the dancing or be seen to watch openly. Indeed, whenever an association organizes a dance in the privacy of a house, there is an implicit understanding that the household's men ought to leave or make themselves inconspicuous. Those who admitted having caught glimpses of *turs* said that they just happened to be there and were not supposed to know what was going on. They commented on their feigned ignorance in such terms as 'even when we [men] are around, we must pretend we don't see anything'.

Money usually plays an important role in these meetings, and it could be said that the dances and the atmosphere they establish facilitate the circulation of cash, a point also made by Castaldi (2000). Contributions must be the same every time for the rotation to be fair, and their level depends on the resources of the members. As a consequence, women's associations rarely break class boundaries. Contributions may range from 500 to 50,000 F CFA[16], but most women raise between 500 and 5,000 F CFA per week.[17] Those who raise larger amounts often spend their payout on business activities rather than on household, ceremonial or health expenses, as many of the poorer women do. In some groups, the more 'business-minded' among the participants also use the meetings as opportunities to sell the goods they import from neighbouring countries: jewellery from Morocco and Mauritania, fabrics from Mali, shoes, underwear or watches from the Gambia.

Apart from the small trade aspect, many 'Dakaroises' regard these associations as essential to develop their social networks, and thereby build up social capital. Maintaining a regular face-to-face contact enables them to mobilize kin and friends in times of crisis, and to gather help with the extravagant expenses generated by family ceremonies. The meetings also provide opportunities to discuss family conflicts, initiate marriage negotiations and impose the authority of older over younger women, often under the guise of 'correcting deviant behaviour'. Because the explicit purpose is entertainment and money-raising, anything else that might take place during these events remains hidden to outsiders, and in particular to men.

Sensuality and 'Cool Play'

To render a sense of a *sabar* as an intensely sensual experience, I find it useful to consider the phase of preparation as an integral part of the event itself. There is an important collective component in the run-up to a dance event as the organizers must collect money for the musicians' fees (in the case of 'tontines' these are usually deducted from the payout), the rental of plastic chairs, sometimes lighting equipment, and occasionally the fee for a photographer or video-maker. But the preparation also involves an essential individual component: it has to do with transforming the body into a site of sensual excitement and an object of envy, and a great deal of time, effort and money may be devoted to this. In Dakar, dressing well (*sañse*) and grooming the body are indeed unavoidable means of gaining status in the female world.[18]

When preparing for a dance event, women must find money for a new outfit, hairstyle and the latest fashionable underwear. There is a clear hierarchy of events, and this is particularly important for weddings and name-giving ceremonies. Moreover, married women are expected to dress more expensively than younger, unmarried women, as their elegance is assumed to be, at least in part, a reflection of their husbands' status. Social expectations to look one's best are so high that I have often heard women comment on their anguish to be humiliated if they did not live up to the ideal of *sañse*. One woman in her early thirties confessed that she no longer went to the dances organized by her kinswomen, because she could not cope with the pressure to dress up. Married Dakarois women are expected to dress up in everyday life as well, and failure to do this may be condemned harshly by their peers. Friends and relatives may then, more or less intentionally, humiliate the woman concerned by offering her money to buy cosmetics and a few yards of cloth.

Preparations for a dance may also include an aggressive skin-bleaching treatment (*xeesal*[19]) to achieve the fair complexion many city-dwellers regard as attractive and as a sign of wealth, even though the *xeesal* is most widely practised in poorer neighbourhoods. There is a whole ethos of conspicuous consumption around the *xeesal*. Thus women who cannot afford to treat the whole body may choose to bleach parts of it, or only the face. Women I knew who no longer practised the *xeesal* made fun of this, calling partially bleached women '*taxis jaune et noir*' ('yellow and black cabs') in reference to the city's fast but rundown, bumpy cabs. A thick layer of make-up supplements the complexion. Beautifying is not always an individual affair, however. In the afternoon preceding a dance, those women who can afford it flock to hairdressers' and beauty parlours with friends and relatives. There, valuable hours are spent chatting, having the latest fashionable hairstyle done and makeup applied. An important element of dress is the underwear, which is particularly elaborate for dance events. The most important piece of underwear is the 'petit pagne' (*beeco*), a wrap-around skirt usually made of light cotton, either plain or with a netting forming fashionable patterns, and tied underneath the heavier 'pagne'. This is supplemented by several ranges of waist beads and for younger women, a thong in a fashionable design. In the privacy of the house, women carefully hang both underwear and waist beads over clay pots filled with ash and burning *curaay,* Senegalese women's 'secret' incense. The sensuality of this elaborate combination of elements resides in the fact that much is suggested rather than openly revealed: the slightest movement of the body gives off fragrant wafts, the waist beads can be heard in discreet *click-clicks* and the *beeco* can be glimpsed during the dance.

Finally, the outer outfit, which may be a 'boubou', a 'taille basse'[20] or a camisole with a 'pagne', will be carefully designed to make a striking impression. Whereas in the 1950s and 1960s, any woman who could afford it would wear a European-style dress to go to a dance, the 1970s saw a revival of the 'Senegalese' styles. Status has now become embodied in expensive, heavily embroidered damask cloths and in the matching head scarves, jewellery, bags and shoes.

As Beatty (2005) pointed out, ethnographers are not well-equipped to grasp emotional practices outside the context of specific social encounters. Drawing on a year of fieldwork in Dakar between May 2002 and February 2004, I will therefore describe two scenes from *turs* organized by neighbourhood women in the districts of Fass and

Fann Hock.[21] The third snapshot is drawn from an event organized by a Bollywood dance association, which shares a similar structure with the *turs*. Bollywood dances, routinely called 'danses indoues' in Dakar, have been hugely popular in the crowded suburban district of Pikine since the early 1970s at least. Although most aficionados are women, Bollywood associations also include men. When not gathered for rehearsals or evening dances, members spend a great deal of time watching the latest Bollywood films in the local cinemas or from videocassettes.

A Married Women's 'tur' in Fass

It is late afternoon on a tiled rooftop in the populous district of Fass, and the drummers are late. As they make their way up, the hostess is already greeting the first wave of guests. She snaps at the musicians for being late, as usual. As they take seats on the rooftop and begin playing *sabar* rhythms, the space fills up until some fifty women, accompanied by a few toddlers and teenage girls, are seated on a circle of plastic chairs rented for the occasion. They all wear colourful outfits in the fashionable light green, yellow, pink and two-colour combinations. The mix of strong *curaay* fragrances combined with the display of shiny fabrics, glossy make-up and glittering jewels is overwhelming. Small party bags and high heeled mules match the outfits. Headscarves are tied according to the latest *jalgáti* ('bend the rules') or *uppukaay* ('fan') fashion. Although the women are friends or neighbours, they obviously appraise each other with a sharpness of the eye which leaves little doubt that this is a highly competitive affair.

Having warmed up the atmosphere with nondance rhythms, the drummers slowly begin to play the rhythms that will initiate the dance. A young woman gets up, takes her shoes off and lifts her skirt up to the knee with one hand while stepping forward in rhythm; the other arm is waving back and forth in a continuous movement that seems to be carrying the upper body forward. One step opening the knee to one side, then to the other; the initial steps are meant to 'get into the rhythm' and attract the attention of the participants. The woman steps forward until she is a few steps away from the musicians, facing them; she jumps on the left foot while the right leg leaps forward and fends the air, landing on both feet at the same time. She jumps three more times, pushing the knees up, then pivots on the left leg, both arms folded and pointing upwards; finally she jumps on both feet to reestablish the balance, and starts again. She dances solo for half a minute and runs back to her chair, laughing heartily. Her friends laugh, congratulate her in high-pitched voices, and the atmosphere becomes increasingly electric. Gradually, more women get up and step into the central space, taking turns to dance solo or in pairs,[22] thus challenging each other playfully. Although this is a 'private' event, the open-air roof fills up with the sounds of loud drumming, laughing and chatting.

The group leader in charge of collecting the money from the participants and organizing the lottery, the *yaayu mbotaay* (literally 'mother of the age-set'), sits in a corner and plots the names and amounts collected in her notebook as the women turn in their contributions.[23] One of the high points of the evening, the lottery, will take place later: the names of the participants entitled to take their turn that week will be written down on small bits of paper, and a single name will be picked randomly from a small basket under the surveillance of the *yaayu mbotaay* and of three other women appointed for the occasion. It is of utmost importance that the 'ritual' be followed carefully so as to prevent cheating. As the name of the payout winner is announced, she lets out a loud cry, twirls and performs a few dance steps while her friends congratulate her.

Later in the evening, the energy level rises along with the sexual suggestiveness of the dances. Loud cheering resonates when the drummers initiate the rhythms associated with *Lawbe*[24] dances such as the *lëmbël*. With much laughter, the women encourage each other to be daring, to make generous use of the buttocks and to perform creative, sometimes acrobatic steps. In fact there is no evidence that the more provocative *sabar* dances were created by the *Lawbe,* but their reputation for sexual expertise makes the 'just-so' connection all too tempting. At this point there is much to-and-fro movement and brushing of fabrics. Chairs are taken and quickly left again. The few women who refuse to dance at least once are forced to pay a symbolic fine. Some walk across to their friends and playfully lift their skirt, revealing their underwear, and in a few cases, the full extent of their female anatomy. "You know what we Senegalese women say", a woman friend tells me, "the bigger, the better!" Others simply remove their outer skirt and go on dancing with bare legs showing through their *beeco,* some of which are made of plain white cotton covered with bawdy inscriptions—such as *Saf na,* 'it is deliciously spicy'—and erotic drawings. Most participants speak louder than usual, make wider gestures and their bodies feel stronger when we happen to brush against each other, as if they were 'charged' with a sudden flow of energy.

Meanwhile, the two *tama* players who had been playing alongside the *sabar* have started moving around the rooftop, acting as if they are aroused by the sight. They comment on the underwear; "It is Sotiba[25] that is teasing us", one of them shouts. He literally grabs a woman wearing a painted *beeco,* and for a few seconds thrusts his hips at her. She laughs and plays along while all the women gather in a commotion to take a look. A few seconds later the game is over, and so is the *tur.* The drummers stop playing and most women disappear from the rooftop as quickly as they had arrived. Later, on the way out, I ask the musicians whether they had been genuinely aroused by the women, or just pretending. They simply smile and reply ambiguously that this is their job, and that they are 'used to it'.

A Neighbourhood 'tannbeer' in Fann Hock

Sabar events that take place in a closed-off portion of a street or small sandy alley have a different flavour. There, the boundary between 'public' and 'private' space is deliberately kept fuzzy, as participants (mostly women) and onlookers alike (including men and young boys) feign to ignore each other. As usual that evening in Fann Hock, the awareness of being watched by neighbours and family members did not prevent some of the girls from rivalling in creativity and sexual suggestiveness. Most were unmarried girls in their late teens to early twenties, and while the majority lived in the vicinity, a few had come from neighbouring districts so as not to be seen dancing by male family members.

Once again the climax of the evening is reached when the so-called *Lawbe* dances are performed. On the edge of the *sabar* circle, away from the main focus of attention and yet very visible, a plump young woman dressed in a 'boubou' stands in front of a group of her friends, turning her back to the centre of the circle and to the drummers. With agile movements of the hips and loose knees, she reveals a satin-like, shiny *beeco* to her grinning friends. She is wearing the obligatory five rows of waist beads but has given them a bawdy twist: a kind of bracelet is dangling from one of the rows, moving in small circular movements in tune with her hips. As if to make the trick even more explicit, she lowers her hand in front of her, and follows the rotating movement of the bracelet with the index finger. She seems proud of her little trick, and she and her friends are obviously having a good laugh. No one around them seems to mind.

Not everybody is willing to dance however, and one of the organizers, striking in her pink damask *taay bas,* is walking around the circle holding a wooden stick which she uses to hit the legs of the recalcitrant girls. She is about ten years older than many of them. Occasionally, one or two young men in T-shirts, trousers and trainers throw themselves into the circle and perform a short *sabar* dance, accompanied by much laughter from the women. The men's dances look like parodies of the women's, as they exaggerate the hip movements, the athletic leaps with legs high in the air or the eyes rolling upwards in the manner of a trance, as the girls often do. Some blend in movements from the Wolof *kasag* dances performed during boys' circumcision ceremonies, grabbing their crotch and thrusting the hips forward. The more daring young girls respond and in turn parody the boys, grabbing their crotch too. But before long the cheering and clapping ceases, and there is a distinct feeling that the boys are no longer welcome.

Once the *tannbeer* is over, the participants quickly disperse into the nearby streets. Although the dancing has stopped, some of the girls still seemed 'charged' with the energy of the dancing. When two men who had been watching the dance pass by and make provocative comments, a couple of young girls respond by making scary faces and pretending to chase them. The men move on quickly and do not bother looking back.

A 'Hindu' Evening in Pikine

In a school courtyard, white plastic chairs have been set up in a 'U' shape, and the open end is occupied by a disc jockey and his equipment. Songs from older and newer Bollywood films are already playing loudly as about sixty elegantly dressed women, some with babies and toddlers, take their places on the chairs. The few men present are also dressed up for the occasion. Here the audience is even more numerous than the participants, and the aisles of the schoolyard are filled with onlookers of all ages. They have come to watch 'les Indous', and the children's faces in particular are filled with the tension of expectation. The women who will be performing are easily distinguishable from the association members who will simply watch: whereas the latter sit motionless and dignified in their 'boubous', the former walk around the space and chat, dressed in tight-fitting, sparkling two-piece 'made in Pikine' imitations of Bollywood costumes. The performers' bodies are freshly bleached, and faces are covered with a distinctive Bollywood-style makeup. As the event begins, sequences performed by a single performer (man or woman), a woman/man duet or a chorus of girls follow each other to the sound of film songs. The dancers act out the love scenes and move the lips as if singing in Hindi. Although none of them speaks Hindi, the keenest dancers know the words by heart. By contrast with an ordinary *sabar,* these dances are choreographed and have been rehearsed beforehand.

On several occasions, one young woman in her early twenties comes forward and starts twirling, abandoning herself to the pleasure of the dance. Each time she is grabbed forcefully and forced back into her chair. By the fourth time she is violently pushed back, and several association members admonish her loudly for interrupting the sequences. One of the men, a very keen and effeminate dancer, is so aggressive that it looks as if he is going to hit her. Eventually, she bursts into tears and runs out of the courtyard while the evening goes on as if nothing had happened. One of the two male informants with whom I have arrived comments on the incident: "Her husband doesn't want her to dance. Besides, she doesn't dance very well, and it isn't even good for her. Every time she dances, she gets a headache." In a contemptuous tone, he also adds that the male dancer who shooed her away, like many male members of the association, is a *goorjigéen.* Later, another Pikinois describes the 'Hindu' circles as prostitution networks, making widely uninformed and derogatory comments such as 'Don't you see? All these women are divorced, they are prostitutes!'

With these snapshots I have attempted to convey a sense of the heated atmosphere that is characteristic of many dance events in Dakar. These dances convey a sense of 'cool play' in that they are obviously playful, but they only become significant against the everyday backdrop of 'coolness'. Following dance events, women often gossip about each other's looks and skills as dancers, but no one ever comments on how it *feels* to dance. Asking people directly about it would probably not have elicited very deep introspective statements, not only because emotions are rarely discussed in Wolof sociality, but also because we, as human beings, often find it difficult to verbalize emotions. What are we then left with to interpret what is going on during events in which women are obviously more sensual and 'emotional' than they allow themselves to be in everyday life?

Emotionality as a Resource

As Beatty (2005) has argued, we cannot simply assume that we know what counts as 'emotion' in a different cultural setting. Despite feeling a great deal of empathy with the women I watched and danced with in Dakar, I am not in a position to make claims about the authenticity of people's emotions as expressed in this peculiar mix of sensuality and competitiveness displayed during the dances. Nevertheless it seems fair to say that dance events provide an opportunity for many Dakarois women in particular to enact a wider range of emotions than usual, or at least to enact them in a less restrained manner. Intuitively, it would seem that positive sentiments come through in the dances, such as 'strength', 'sexual confidence', 'togetherness' and 'playfulness', but also the more complex sentiments of 'jealousy' and 'fear' of gossip and social exclusion. Coming back to the questions raised at the beginning of this chapter, there are two issues I find worth addressing in conclusion. First, to what extent do the dances help generate altered emotional states? And second, why do many women choose to momentarily transgress the norms of restraint attached to their status?

As suggested earlier, the issue of whether it is the dancing that generates out-of-the-ordinary displays of emotion or whether people dance because they are in a particular emotional state is not an easy one to answer through analysis of ethnography. The fact that dance events are the only social moments during which many Dakarois behave in such expansive ways points towards the first option. This must be qualified however, because people's emotional display is not spontaneous and does not happen haphazardly as soon as they step into the dance circle. What takes place is still a highly codified inversion of the restraint displayed in most 'ordinary' situations. For example, many informants of both sexes associate the dances with moments for young women to enact a flourishing sexuality in which they are able to pursue selfish pleasure and no longer be available as mere sexual objects. The suggestiveness of some of the dances, the bawdy jokes and gestures, the way women 'toy' with the male drummers and the sensory set-up of the events are all part of this enactment. But rarely do people allow themselves to display sentiments of anger or sadness, for example, and when they do, they are quickly excluded. Thus, even when the usual norms seem to be suspended, a different set of 'rules' still prevails.

Emotionality is also highly dependent on the context, and particularly on who is watching the dances; it is obvious, therefore, that these are 'cultural performances', and not just individualized emotional states, even though the sensory stimulation of individual participants does shape what goes on. Women do not dress, behave or perform in the same ways whether the event takes places in the intimate setting of the house or in a closed-off portion of the street. There, participants remain very much aware of being watched, even though everyone feigns to ignore this. Also, not just any kind of dancing causes people to become 'charged' with extraordinary emotional energy; new dance styles and rhythms people are not used to produce a different effect altogether. This is evident among the professional dance troupes I spent much time with in Dakar. There people happily use breaks during training to re-create 'miniature' *sabars,* in which they perform in very similar ways as during events in their neighbourhoods. As soon as they revert back to choreographed movements, however, their attitude changes dramatically. They become more restrained, less playful, and the female dancers, in particular, seem to fall back into an attitude of submission to the dance master. I would therefore argue that it is only when a dance style has been repeated over and over again, thus 'growing into' the body, that we are able to reach this 'moving together' of reason, emotion and body (Parkin 1985) characteristic of altered emotional states. With the *sabar* many women seem to reach an altered emotional state—albeit not to the degree of a 'trance'—but this is in part because the *sabar* is part of their 'habitus' (Bourdieu 1972). In short, it is very likely that the dances described in this chapter contribute to generating altered emotional states, but this only happens in prescribed, almost ritualized, social contexts where the scene is set for participants to relive the sensory experiences they have been socialized into.

Finally, there is the question of why so many women choose to transgress the norms of *kersa* so explicit in everyday discourse. Following Deborah Heath's (1994) argument that some women's lack of restraint works as a 'foil', allowing their husbands or male relatives to maintain their reputations, one might argue that the dances ultimately serve to maintain the status quo of gender and 'caste' stratification. But I find it important to take people's experience into account, and few Dakarois seem to experience the social relations they are involved in as 'maintaining the status quo'. The responses one gets when asking women why they dance the way they do vary a great deal depending on the individual and on who is listening. In front of men, middle- to upper-class women, in particular, tend to deny taking part in *sabars* altogether, particularly in front of older family members. Some married women over the age of thirty-five to forty confess that they used to have fun dancing but that they have become too old to do so, thereby implying that it is no longer appropriate, even shameful (*rus*), for them to dance in public. Although some of those who deny dancing indeed refrain from doing so—in some cases for fear of exposing their lack of dancing skills!—others simply wish to conceal that they fully participate in the suggestive dancing that takes place during *turs*. I have come across women who claimed to have witnessed dances without ever taking part; yet in a number of these cases, I knew for certain that they occasionally joined in.

Those who admit to dancing rarely make the suggestive nature of their dancing explicit; rather, they speak in understated terms about 'having fun' amongst women, sometimes adding that the dances are the only time during which women are able to genuinely let off steam. There is obviously a genuine element of relief from the obligations of everyday life in the playfulness of these events. But I also want to suggest that there are two important dimensions which are rarely verbalized: rivalry and competition for status in the women's world on the one hand, and a complementary aspect of solidarity on the other hand.

Female rivalry is central to many social relations in Dakar. It is likely that this has long been the case in a polygamous society like the Muslim Senegalese. In Dakar, polygamy remains alive and well, with 40 per cent of women having lived in a polygamous union by the age of forty (Adjamagbo, Antoine, and Dial 2004). In addition, the depressed economic climate since the 1980s has rendered the competition for men with a stable income even fiercer. The complex sentiments this generates are rarely verbalized because this would be regarded as selfishness and as a lack of emotional control. Yet many women enjoy enacting the competitive dimension of their lives, and having a space in which to compete seems to help some build confidence in their ability to be independent from the tutelage of a husband or a father. Skilled and suggestive dancing allows some women to show themselves amongst their peers as sexually desirable to men, entertaining, and above all as socially active. Indeed, not only must one be socially active to keep up with the ever-changing fashion of popular dances, but also, the amount and style of dancing performed at a given event is an indication of the organizer's status among her peers. If she is well-liked and respected among her friends, people will dance a great deal more at her *tur* than if she is not. In Dakar, being able to display social status in this way forms an essential part of an ongoing competition which far exceeds the concern of finding a suitable partner. Social status amongst one's peers is so crucial that it is not always clear whether women actually compete for men, or whether men are simply pawns in women's competition for social recognition.

Unsurprisingly, solidarity is a more explicitly acknowledged value in Wolof social life. But dominant discourses emphasize solidarity amongst kin, rather than amongst women peers. Yet the sensuality and emotionality expressed in the dance events re-inforces a *de facto* exclusion of men. This was not always the case: according to older informants who grew up in Dakar, in the past young men routinely took part in the dances. Nowadays however, once on their own women are able to go about 'women's business' (*afééru jigéen*). Whereas 'women's business' used to refer to the sexual education of young girls, or sharing secrets on intimate matters and the best ways to 'tie'[26] a husband, the time women spend with their peers is increasingly de-voted to 'business' in the real sense of the term. Indeed, urban women's associations have multiplied since the early 1980s, and while the male-dominated formal sector of the economy is sinking into crisis,[27] they compete with the local chapters of reli-gious movements, youth movements, 'sports and culture' groups, migrants' associa-tions, professional organizations and trading communities, to harness the economic resources provided by the development sector among others (Dahou 2004). In ad-dition, a growing number of women coach each other in how to engage in inde-pendent business activities: small-scale trade, catering, tailoring, hairdressing and, for fishermen families, the transformation of fishing products are among the most common choices.

For this, 'tontine' meetings and *turs* have become the most widely used spaces to meet, raise money and provide each other with both moral and material support. This does not mean, of course, that all women succeed in compensating for their husbands' or fathers' decreasing capacity to provide for their families on a stable basis, but the success of a few is enough to entertain the hopes of many others. The networks facilitated by the dance events also form a formidable social capital on which Dakarois women are able to draw in times of need. This is not to say that they all seek to gnaw at men's economic power. Amongst the many married women I knew in Dakar, most were either working or looking for jobs, and although many were keen to retain some degree of financial independence, none ever phrased this in oppositional terms towards her husband's role as the main provider for the family. Rather, they either found themselves obliged to supplement their husband's income to cope with household and health-care expenses, or wished to earn money to sup-port their own relatives and spend on ceremonial expenses.[28] In a significant number of cases, what had started as a supplementary activity ended up making a more stable contribution to the household than the husband's income. Alcoholism and various health problems are rampant amongst husbands, who are on average 14 years older than their wives (Adjamagbo et al. 2004), and often unemployed.

But if more and more women find themselves having to take over the role of breadwinner, this is bound to affect the moral authority (*kilifteef*) of male house-hold heads as well as gender roles in the wider society. Meanwhile, *sabars* and similar urban dance events play an important role in these developments because they are among the few spaces from where women have managed to exclude men, even though they still need the tacit agreement of men to participate in or orga-nize the dances. When agreement fails, as was the case with the young woman at the 'Hindu' event, women too find themselves excluded. In addition, because the dances allow for an ambiguous mix of 'genuine' and 'enacted' emotionality, and because much of what goes on is never put into words, they are a particularly appropriate medium through which the class, 'caste', age and gender hierarchies which tend to dominate in everyday life can be quietly played with. Although I have argued elsewhere (Neveu Kringelbach 2005) that this is part of a wider process of change in gender relations in urban Senegal, more time and depth will be needed to evaluate the extent to which such renegotiation will extend further into other domains of social life.

It should also be said, as a final note, that many of the tensions and dilemmas urban Senegalese society is faced with are being crystallized around the dances. An increasing number of city dwellers of both sexes describe them as both a symptom and a cause of the moral decline of Senegalese society. The mass media are a widely used tribune for this.[29] This is not new of course, and indeed much 'popular culture' in twentieth-century Senegal has developed in a constant tension with the religious, political and economic elites. Meanwhile, without a word being uttered, the circle is reformed and the dance goes on in Dakar's 'quartiers'.

References

Abu-Lughod, L., and Lutz, C. A. (1990), 'Introduction: Emotion, Discourse, and the Politics of Everyday Life', in C. A. Lutz and L. Abu-Lughod (eds) *Language and the Politics of Emotion,* pp. 1–23, Cambridge: Cambridge University Press.

Acogny, G. (1994), *Danse Africaine,* 4th ed., Frankfurt: Weingarten.

Adjamagbo, A., Antoine, P., and Dial, F. B. (2004), 'Le dilemme des dakaroises: entre travailler et "bien travailler"', in M.-C. Diop (ed.), *Gouverner le Sénégal— Entre Ajustement Structurel et Développement Durable,* pp. 248–72, Paris: Karthala.

Beatty, A. (2005), 'Emotions in the Field: What Are We Talking About?', *Journal of the Royal Anthropological Institute,* 11(1): 17–37.

Boilat, A.P.-D. (1853), *Esquisses Sénégalaises,* Paris: Bertrand.

Bourdieu, P. (1972), *Esquisse d'une Théorie de la Pratique,* Geneva: Droz.

Castaldi, F. (2000), *Choreographing African Identities: Negritude and the National Ballet of Senegal,* unpublished PhD dissertation, Dance History and Theory Department, Riverside: University of California.

Chidzero, A.-M. (1996), 'Senegal' in P. Fidler and L. Webster (eds), *The Informal Sector and Microfinance Institutions in West Africa,* Washington, D.C.: The World Bank.

Cohen, A. (1993), *Masquerade Politics,* Oxford: Berg.

Cruise O'Brien, D. (1998), 'The Shadow-politics of Wolofisation', *Journal of Modern African Studies,* 36(1): 25–46.

Dahou, K. (2004), 'Les nouvelles formes de groupements en Afrique de l'Ouest: l'action collective en postcolonie,' in S. Mappa (ed.) *Forum de Delphes: les Métamorphoses du Politique au Nord et au Sud,* Paris: Karthala.

Dilley, R. (1999), 'Ways of Knowing, Forms of Power: Aspects of Apprenticeship among Tukulor Mabube Weavers', *Cultural Dynamics,* 11(1): 33–55.

Dilley, R. (2000), 'The Question of Caste in West Africa, with Special Reference to Tukulor Craftsmen, Senegal', *Anthropos,* 95(1): 149–65.

Dilley, R. (2004), *Islamic and Caste Knowledge Practices among Haalpulaar'en in Senegal: Between Mosque and Termite Mound,* Edinburgh: Edinburgh University Press/International African Institute.

Diop, A.-B. (1981), *La Société Wolof: Systèmes d'Inégalité et de Domination,* Paris: Karthala.

Durkheim, E. (1912), *Les Formes Elémentaires de la Vie Religieuse: Le Système Totémique en Australie,* Paris: F. Alcan.

Evans-Pritchard, E. E. (1928), 'The Dance', *Africa,* 1: 446–62.

Evers Rosander, E. (1997), 'Le dahira de Mam Diarra Bousso à Mbacké', in E. Evers Rosander (ed.), *Transforming Female Identities: Women's Organizational Forms in West Africa,* pp. 160–74, Uppsala: Nordiska Afrikainstitutet.

Goffman, E. (1959), *The Presentation of Self in Everyday Life,* Garden City, N.Y.: Doubleday Anchor.

Harney, E. (2004), *In Senghor's Shadow. Art, Politics and the Avant-Garde in Senegal, 1960–1995,* Durham, N.C. and London: Duke University Press.

Harré, R. (1986a), 'An Outline of the Social Constructionist Viewpoint', in R. Harré (ed.), *The Social Construction of Emotions,* pp. 2–14, Oxford: Blackwell.

Harré, R., ed. (1986b), *The Social Construction of Emotions,* Oxford: Blackwell.

Heath, D. (1990), 'Spatial Politics and Verbal Performance in Urban Senegal', *Ethnology,* 3: 209–23.

Heath, D. (1992), 'Fashion, Anti-fashion and Heteroglossia in Urban Senegal', *American Ethnologist,* 19(1): 19–33.

Heath, D. (1994), 'The Politics of Appropriateness and Appropriation: Recontextualizing Women's Dance in Urban Senegal', *American Ethnologist,* 21(1): 88–103.

Irvine, J. T. (1974), *Caste and Communication in a Wolof Village,* unpublished PhD dissertation, Anthropology Department, University of Pennsylvania.

Irvine, J. T. (1989), 'When Talk Isn't Cheap: Language and Political Economy', *American Ethnologist,* 16(2): 248–67.

Irvine, J. T. (1990), 'Registering Affect: Heteroglossia in the Linguistic Expression of Emotion', in C. A. Lutz and L. Abu-Lughod (eds), *Language and the Politics of Emotion,* pp. 126–61, Cambridge: Cambridge University Press.

James, W. (2003), *The Ceremonial Animal. A New Portrait of Anthropology,* Oxford: Oxford University Press.

Langer, S. K. (1953), *Feeling and Form: A Theory of Art,* London: Routledge and Kegan Paul.

Leavitt, J. (1996), 'Meaning and Feeling in the Anthropology of Emotions', *American Ethnologist,* 23(3): 514–39.

Lutz, C., and White, G. (1986), 'The Anthropology of Emotions', *Annual Review of Anthropology,* 15: 405–36.

Mbow, P. (1997), 'Les femmes, l'islam et les associations religieuses au Senegal: le dynamisme des femmes en milieu urbain', in E. Evers Rosander (ed.), *Transforming Female Identities: Women's Organizational Forms in West Africa,* pp. 148–59, Uppsala: Nordiska Afrikainstitutet.

Neveu Kringelbach, H. (2005), *Encircling the Dance: Social Mobility through the Transformation of Performance in Urban Senegal,* unpublished DPhil thesis, Institute of Social and Cultural Anthropology, Oxford: University of Oxford.

Parkin, D. (1985), 'Reason, Emotion and the Embodiment of Power', in J. Overing (ed.), *Reason and Morality,* ASA monograph no. 24, pp. 135–51, London: Tavistock.

Rabine, L. W. (2002), *The Global Circulation of African Fashion,* Oxford and New York: Berg.

Radcliffe-Brown, A. R. (1922), *The Andaman Islanders,* Cambridge: Cambridge University Press.

Schieffelin, E. (1976), *The Sorrow of the Lonely and the Burning of the Dancers,* New York: St Martin's Press.

Schieffelin, E. (1998), 'Problematizing performance', in F. Hughes-Freeland (ed.), *Ritual, Performance, Media,* ASA Monograph no. 35, pp. 194–207, London: Routledge.

Senghor, L. S. (1964), *Liberté I: Négritude et Humanisme,* Paris: Seuil.

Silla, O. (1966), 'Persistance des castes dans la société wolof contemporaine', *BIFAN(Bulletin de l'Institut Français de l'Afrique Noire),* 28(3–4): 731–70.

Sud Quotidien, (2002) 'Commentaire du jour: obscurantisme', 8 August: 1.

Swigart, L. (1992), *Practice and Perception: Language Use and Attitudes in Dakar,* unpublished PhD dissertation, Anthropology Department, Seattle: University of Washington.

Tamari, T. (1997), *Les Castes de l'Afrique Occidentale,* Nanterre: Société d'Ethnologie.

Turner, V. W. (1969), *The Ritual Process,* London: Routledge and Kegan Paul.

Wane, Y. (1969), *Les Toucouleũ du Fouta Tooro, stratification sociale et structure familiale*, Initiations et études africaines (IFAN), No. 25, Dakar: Institut fondamental d'Afrique noire.

World Bank (2004), *Senegal Data Profile,* <http://devdata.worldbank.org/external/CPProfile.asp?CCODE=sen&PTYPE=CP> accessed 26 August 2007.

Wright, B. (1989), 'The Power of Articulation', in W. Arens and I. Karp (eds), *Creativity of Power,* Washington, D.C.: Smithsonian Institution Press.

Notes

1. For reasons of convenience, I use the French term for an inhabitant of Dakar: 'Dakarois' (fem. 'Dakaroise').
2. The term 'performance' is used here in the sense of 'particular "symbolic" or "aesthetic" activities' (Schieffelin 1998: 195). It is not, therefore, in Goffman's (1959) sense of the performativity of everyday life.
3. Here the term 'Wolof' refers to people who identify themselves with the Wolof ethnic group—44% of the Senegalese in the early 1990s, up from 36% in 1970 (Swigart 1992: 80)—and whose first language at home is Wolof. According to Swigart (1992), as much as 71% of the population spoke Wolof as first or second language in the early 1990s. This is an indication of the increasing dominance of Wolof as a *lingua franca,* which also goes hand in hand with a significant degree of 'Wolofization' of Senegalese culture, especially in cities. In practice ethnic boundaries in contemporary Senegal are fuzzy, and Wolof self-identification could best be described as 'a process, one which relates to a range of subjects: urbanisation, migration, religion, statehood' (Cruise O'Brien 1998: 27).
4. Diop (1981) estimates the *géér* and similar higher ranks throughout the region to make up some 80% of the population.
5. Patri- or matrilineage may be equally invoked to classify an individual. Although status classification is partly contextual, the child of a *géér-ñeeño* union is likely to be considered as a *ñeeño,* a reason often invoked by *géér* families to prevent such marriages.
6. I was inspired by Dilley (e.g. 2004) to use capital letters for social categories; this indicates that the status associated with the category transcends the occupation itself.
7. Key works on caste-like models of stratification in Senegambia include Silla (1966), Wane (1969), Irvine (1974, 1989, 1990), Diop (1981), Wright (1989), Tamari (1997) and Dilley (e.g. 1999, 2000, 2004).
8. In his *Esquisses,* missionary Abbé Boilat commented on this in terms which obviously reflected the *géér* view: "Dance is the art at which they [the wives of the Griots] excel the most ... It is from the Griottes that young girls learn

these lascivious postures they are so good at performing in their dances" (Boilat 1853: 313–14, translated from French).

9. In Wolof 'sama xol dafa sedd', i.e. 'my heart is cool' means 'I am happy' or 'content'.

10. Following Irvine (1989), I often use 'praise-oratory' rather than 'praise-singing', as Griot performance is not characterized by singing as much as it is by emphatic speech.

11. Senegal's famous Master Drummer, Doudou Ndiaye Rose, has taught his daughters to play the *sabar* drums but this remains an exception, and the *Rosettes* perform during concerts rather than *sabar* parties.

12. Some of my informants in their mid-forties reported that the *ceebu jën* had not changed since their childhood and Acogny (1994) mentions that it was already known in 1928. *Ceebu jën* is also the name of a common Senegalese dish of fish and rice. The *ceebu jën* rhythm, which is extremely fast and demanding for the dancers, may be executed with sticks beaten on the bottom of a metallic dish turned upside-down.

13. Senegal is an overwhelmingly Muslim nation, and most Senegalese Muslims belong to one of the four main Sufi brotherhoods, or *tariqa:* the Muridiyya, the Tijaaniyya, the Qaddiriyya and the Laayenes.

14. *Mbalax* originally designated a series of *sabar* rhythms, but Senegalese singer Youssou Ndour coined the name to designate the urban music genre he helped popularize in the 1970s–1980s. *Mbalax,* the most popular music in much of urban Senegal today, mixes *sabar* rhythms with influences from funk, pop music, Cuban styles or even reggae.

15. The same women may dance during meetings with friends but refrain from dancing in their local religious association, or *daa'ira*. Women's *daa'ira* have been flourishing in the past two decades, particularly in Senegalese cities (see for example Evers Rosander 1997, Mbow 1997).

16. The F CFA, or 'Franc de la Communauté Financière d'Afrique' (XOF), is the common currency used in the former French colonies of West Africa, with the exception of Guinea Conakry, and in Guinea Bissau. Formerly linked to the French Franc, since 1999 it has been linked to the Euro through a fixed exchange rate: 1 € = 655,957 F CFA.

17. These amounts should be held against statistics (both official and empirical) on average incomes in Dakar. The World Bank (2004) estimated the average income per capita at $550 in 2003 (approximately 25,000 FCFA per month) for Senegal as a whole. Informal sources estimate that the figure should be doubled for Dakar, with great variations in the different parts of the capital.

18. For a fascinating study of *sañse*, see Heath (1992).

19. From the Wolof word *xees,* 'to have a fair skin'.

20. A 'taille basse' (*taay bas*) is a two-piece outfit which includes a long skirt and a tight-fitted top. Although perceived as traditional, the style was inspired by

European dress and became popular in the 1930s (Rabine 2002). An important element in Senegalese outfits is the matching head scarf tied in various fashionable ways, the *musoor.*

21. During fieldwork I attended *turs* and other dance events where *sabar* was performed in Fann Hock, Fass, Pikine and Dalifort.

22. There are three common patterns in *sabar* dancing, always facing the musicians or facing each other: solo, in a pair, or usually towards the end of the event, a group of participants dancing simultaneously and competing for audience attention.

23. In this case a fixed amount of 1,500 FCFA was collected every other week.

24. The *Lawbe* are an endogamous category of Woodworkers. The women are perceived as experts in sexual matters, and market vendors of waist beads, *beeco, curaay* or potency enhancers are assumed to be *Lawbe.*

25. Sotiba, with its large factory in the outskirts of Dakar, is the main industrial manufacturer of fabrics and clothing items in Senegal.

26. The Wolof verb *takk* means both 'to marry' and 'to tie'; in addition, in colloquial Wolof it refers to the magic practices some women resort to in order to keep their husbands.

27. The waged sector of the economy in which men had been taught to place their hopes has shrunk to the extent that it does not absorb more than 10% of employment in Dakar (Chidzero 1996, quoted in Rabine 2002).

28. The obligatory gift exchange between in-laws during weddings and name-giving ceremonies often involves staggering amounts when held against local income levels.

29. For example, according to several informants, former President Senghor deemed 'indecent' and banned a popular dance, the *arwatam,* from public performance in 1972. Also see the ban on public *sabar* performance which is regularly decreed in Dakar and other cities during years when the rainy season is late (Heath 1994, *Sud Quotidien* 2002). In addition, the hundreds of *mbalax* music videos in which some of the more suggestive popular dances are performed are copiously attacked for their 'indecency'.

–19–

The Performance Hypothesis
Practicing Emotions in Protected Frames

William O. Beeman

The Performance Hypothesis

If man is a sapient animal, a toolmaking animal, a self-making animal, a symbol-using animal, he is, no less, a performing animal, *Homo performans,* not in the sense, perhaps that a circus animal may be a performing animal, but in the sense that a man is a self-performing animal—his performances are, in a way, *reflexive,* in performing he reveals himself to himself. This can be in two ways: the actor may come to know himself better through acting or enactment; or one set of human beings may come to know themselves better through observing and/or participating in performances generated and presented by another set of human beings.

Victor Turner

Introduction: Performance and Its Purpose in Human Life

I was once singing in a production of Puccini's *La Bohème.* In the fourth act, the heroine, Mimi, dies of consumption. The last notes of the opera are delivered by her lover, the tenor Rudolfo, who bends over her lifeless body and sobs while singing her name four times on a high G. The effect is universally the same for the all audiences. Almost as if a button were pushed, the scene triggers an autonomic response. Grown men and women weep openly. There is rarely a dry eye in the house. During one rehearsal for this production, our director had a problem with the soprano portraying Mimi. 'My dear,' he said, 'you cannot cry when Rudolfo sings your name. You are already dead.' 'I know!' she wailed, 'but I can't help it. It's SO SAD!'[1]

It is events like this that point up the unique ability of performance to affect the cognitive and emotional[2] state of its audience. Determining the reasons why it does so is much more difficult. Human beings in every culture are so extraordinarily engaged with performance. Not only do they enjoy it immensely, they also expend an amazing amount of energy and material resources to arrange for it to happen, and for them to see it. Moreover, they never seem to tire of it. Specific performance experiences are revisited repeatedly—sometimes thousands of times over a lifetime, with no decrease in engagement or enthusiasm. Why this should be so defies logic, and cries out for an explanation.[3]

The two broad questions that I hope to elucidate are, then: 'Why do humans engage in performance activity?' and 'How does performance achieve its effects?'

In the last twenty years or so, astonishing advances have taken place along two fronts in the understanding of the human mind. The first of these developments is the progress made in understanding the neural structures that underlie the reception and generation of affective states in human beings. Work by several remarkable teams of scientists in England and the United States have moved toward resolving some age-old questions about the relationship between autonomic reactions in humans and the identification of those responses as 'emotion'. Whereas much of this work remains somewhat hypothetical, it has proved convincing enough to allow me to formulate an hypothesis about the evolutionary value of performance.

A second development has been advances in the philosophical and psychological problem known as 'Theory of Mind.' This refers to the ability of humans to understand (or to believe that they understand) the feelings and motivations of others—literally a theory that humans develop about the states of minds of people they deal with in social life. If humans do not have a Theory of Mind, they can neither perform for others with the hope of affecting their state of mind, nor can they become an audience for performance, understanding what they are seeing and hearing.

Eight Basic Concepts

It is important to begin this discussion with some clear working concepts about performance and its properties.[4] Unless otherwise specified, when I say 'performer', this term can interchangeably refer to one person, or many persons acting collectively (as an orchestra or dance troupe). When I say 'audience' this can interchangeably refer to a collective group of people or a single individual.[5]

Performance is Purposeful Enactment or Display Behaviour Carried out in Front of an Audience

Enactment and display are the basic materials of performance. This form of behaviour is one that humans share with probably every vertebrate animal species. The difference between mere display and enactment in fish, birds or mammals and performance is its purposefulness. The male peacock spreading his tail is genetically programmed to do so under specific circumstances. How *well* he is able to do it may make a difference in his life, but his behaviour is instinctual.

Humans, by contrast, are not only aware of their performative behaviour, they generally know for what purpose they are doing it, and they know clearly for whom they are doing it and why. I grant that some human performance we see every day is behaviour on autopilot. In these cases, however, it is rarely effective. Part of the purpose of performance, as I have already mentioned, is to change the cognitive states of others. Therefore a near-autonomic, zombie-like enactment or display comes close to lacking purposefulness, and therefore is, I would argue, barely performance.

It is the breadth of this definition that allows me to discuss used-car salesmen, speechmaking politicians, persons engaged in ordinary conversation, clever sycophantic social climbers, Olympic gymnasts, flamenco dancers, Kabuki actors and opera singers under the same rubric.

Performance Aims to Change the Cognitive State of Participants

I reiterate this point, stated earlier, because it is so essential. There is no reason for performance to endure as a human activity if the possibility of affecting an audience is not present.

It is important to add a dimension to this requirement, however. To change the cognitive state of the audience involves a whole range of consequences. First and foremost is the phatic dimension of engagement. The audience by *being* an audience undergoes a changed cognitive state. They are engaged in 'framed behaviour' with the performer, in which every communicative element of the event becomes performatively significant. Entering this state is largely a choice on the part of the audience, although the performer may try to influence that choice with a variety of enticements. These generally involve promises of benefits for the audience (social approbation, enjoyment, gain, safety, comfort), or promises of prophylaxis against unpleasant consequences (social sanctions, unhappiness, loss, danger, discomfort).

Second, audience members are subject to experiencing altered emotional states that they would not otherwise have, were they not engaged in a performance event. This does not mean that they will always have an emotional experience in performance, only that the performance event primes them for that possibility.[6]

Third, they are subject to experiencing altered dispositions to behaviour through performance. Whether they act on those dispositions involves a more complex set of personal decisions. The performer may wish to have the audience engaged in all sorts of behaviour—laughing, weeping, buying something, going to bed with them, fighting with them, etc. The cognitive disposition to this behaviour must precede the action, however.

Performance is an accomplishment. Through performance an audience is moved and transformed. They are made to laugh, to cry, to change their opinions, to take social action, to be surprised, to question their existence, to acquire a feeling of well-being and integration.

Some Performers are More Effective in this than Others

Even with all the desire in the world, however, some performers are ineffective. Because performance is an achievement, there is a degree of skill involved in it that differentiates members of society. This is why performance is virtually always extensively practiced before it takes place. This is as true for an opera diva preparing a role as for a stuttering swain trying to find the right words and bodily attitude to propose marriage successfully.

Language helps performers tremendously. It is the principal tool humans use to affect others. It is powerfully instrumental, having the power to transform human existence directly as Austin and Searle have shown, and as I have argued in previous writings (Beeman 1986). However, language alone is often not enough to guarantee success in performance. Physical movement, personal adornment, arrangements of the environment, music and every other conceivable human activity can be transformed and brought to bear in performance. Because curiosity and love of novelty are primal human behavioural traits, creativity and innovation are powerful tools in performance. Through them audiences are attracted, engaged and encouraged to participate in the performance process.

Ultimately, then, every performer creates a 'unique synthesis of contextual and textual realms' (Briggs 1988: 357; cf. Beeman 1986). The creation of an effective performance involves a calculus that includes taking account of past performances and their effects, the immediate performance situation, and the available repertoire of performance materials, harnessed to serve a particular goal.

Performance is Collaborative Behaviour

Both the performers and the audience participate in reinforced feedback, which I will term *the performance loop.* Performers attempt to change the state of consciousness of the audience; the audience evaluates the actions of the performers and manifests its own behavioural display. The actions of the performer are thereby affected and changed. One of the most important factors in the audience–performer connection is the regulation of *attention.* Schechner (1977) has dealt with this in an important essay on *selective inattentiveness,* emphasizing the fact that the audience directs attention to one or another aspect of performance as it is ongoing.[7] The performer likewise does his or her best to direct the audience to attend to specific aspects of the performance. An extreme example of this is the magician whose performative task is to direct the audience *away* from that which they are not supposed to see.[8]

Not all performers are in direct contact with their audience. Some enactment and display is done for the benefit of people who will not see it immediately. Artistic products may be thought of as 'frozen performance' by this formulation. Novels, sculptures, paintings, films and photographs are designed to change cognitive states of their consumers, but over time, and over diffuse space. The collaboration between performer and audience is nevertheless established when the art object is viewed.

It is for this reason that in the modern age, performers and those responsible for marketing performance are continually trying both to identify audiences and to monitor them. New magazines, books and television shows all have demographic profiles that predict specific groups of consumers for these products. Much effort is made to 'reach' these people and alert them to the fact that they *are* the audience for these communications. Then, since it is not possible in these instances for the performer to obtain an immediate reaction, the audience is surveyed independently to determine the effects of the performance, thus closing the feedback loop.

Performance is Iterative, Ongoing, and Ultimately Unpredictable in its Results

Performance is 'emergent', in Richard Bauman's terms (1977). Because it is co-created, the results always depend dynamically on the behavioural dispositions of the participants. The results of any given instance of performance are therefore unpredictable.

Any performer knows this unpredictability well. A politician does not realize that his audience is full of beekeepers and makes a disparaging remark about apiaries, getting an unanticipated negative reaction. A salesman inadvertently wears a particular cologne that reminds his customer of her father and predisposes her to a sale. The audience for a theatrical comedy consists largely of a theatre party from a particular industrial plant where hundreds of people were laid off the previous afternoon, and nothing can make them laugh, to the surprised dismay of the performers. (All of the above are true stories.)

Performance takes Place within Culturally Defined Cognitive Frames that have Identifiable Boundaries

The concept of the cognitive 'frame' is one of the most durable and useful in social science. The concept refers to the ability of human beings (and other higher animal species) to collaboratively 'bracket off' a spate of behaviour from the ongoing stream of social life for special treatment. Special rules for behaviour exist within the 'frame' to which participants adhere for its temporal and spatial duration. Examples of framed behaviour include games (cf. Caillois 1962), play sequences, ceremonies, rituals and sporting events (cf. MacAloon 1984). Multiple framing is common in human life. Frames within frames, overlapping frames, ongoing frames, and interrupted frames are some of the variants that researchers have analyzed over the years.

The frame concept has a long pedigree, going back in some respects to Hume and Heidegger. In recent times Alfred Schuetz is often credited with an important formulation of the notion in his influential essay 'On Multiple Realities' (1945). Equally important are Gregory Bateson's work on 'play' (1955), Goffman's *Frame Analysis* (1974) and Deborah Tannen's *Framing in Conversational Structures* (1993). For those who may be unfamiliar with the concept, I give a brief sketch of framed behaviour here.

The minimal performance frame is one in which an agreement exists between an audience and a performer whereby the audience will attend to the enactment and display behaviour of the performer. This frame can be as fleeting as an encounter between a passer-by and a street musician, or as elaborate as a lifelong role as a participant in the palace ritual of a royal court (cf. Geertz's *Negara* 1980).

Frames may arise spontaneously or be invoked through linguistic interchange ('Let's pretend you're the patient and I'm the doctor'). Many are predetermined through culturally specified custom. 'Toasting' at a Russian dinner is a fine, structured performance frame with a master of ceremonies, a protocol of toasting order, and expected drinking behaviour. That the frame holds even after everyone becomes very drunk is a tribute to its strength. 'Going to the theatre' in today's Western society is clearly framed behaviour, where audience members must refrain from loud noise and excessive movement at certain times and are allowed to make quite a lot of noise and move about at other times. Added to this is the framed behaviour of the actors, who themselves must deal with at least two cognitive frames, 'on stage' and 'off stage.' Their behaviour is, of course, markedly different in these two settings. Some very complicated framings occur when playwrights and directors begin to experiment artistically with the frames in the theatre. Some examples are 'breaking the fourth wall' (Pirandello, Thornton Wilder) and engaging or involving the audience in the action of the performance, establishing 'plays within a play' (*Pagliacci, Midsummer Night's Dream*) or exposing the offstage area to the view of the audience (cf. Schechner 1993).

The Most Effective Performances are Those in Which the Performers and Audience Achieve Full Engagement with the Performance Activity through 'Flow'

Goffman wrote in his classic work *The Presentation of Self in Everyday Life* (1959)'

> When an individual becomes engaged in an activity, whether shared or not, it is possible for him to become caught up by it, carried away by it, engrossed in it—to be, as we say, spontaneously involved in it. He finds it psychologically unnecessary to refrain from dwelling on it and psychologically unnecessary to dwell on anything else. A visual and

cognitive engrossment occurs, with an honest unawareness of matters other than the activity. (p. 38)

The psychologist Mihalyi Csikszentmihalyi discussed this concept in two important books, *Beyond Boredom and Anxiety* (1975) and the more popular *Flow* (1990). Flow is in fact the term that he uses to label the engagement experience Goffman mentions. According to Csikszentmihalyi, flow takes place when a person is engaged in an activity that is sufficiently challenging that they do not become bored, and sufficiently comfortable that they do not become anxious.

In daily life one typically 'rehearses' difficult tasks until they become routinized enough in the body so as to not require active attention to the physical details of executing them. This echoes Bourdieu's (1997) notion of *habitus*.

An experience of flow can take place outside of performative activity. Common examples are the loss of attention to the body one experiences when driving a car over familiar territory (Wallace 1965), or in achieving meditative states. Sports activity often results in flow. It may be that trance states are the result of a particularly strong sense of flow.

I would contend, along with Turner (1982: 55–58) that effective performance also involves a concomitant ability to enter 'flow'—to make that activity appear effortless and natural. The sense of 'truth' created during a performative activity is established on this bedrock. This is as essential for the most commonplace incidents of performance, such as when individuals are engaged in face-to-face interaction, as it is for highly structured, conscious performance, such as for stage actors, dancers and other entertainers.

Naturally a performer's ability to induce a feeling of flow in an audience is an exceptionally valuable skill. Audience members want to be carried along by the performance, since the flow experience is one of the most enjoyable of human feelings. I remarked to a theatre critic of my acquaintance that I thought he had a great job—being paid to go to the theatre. His reply was a derisive laugh, and the observation that when he was 'working' he never enjoyed a minute of his theatre experience, because he could never surrender to the action on stage. He was prevented from entering flow by the need to continually observe and make critical notes on the performance.

Performance has Broad Evolutionary Value for Human Beings

Many of the preceding points have been widely discussed by me in other works (Beeman 1986, 1993) and by other authors, but the study of the biological basis for performance is in its infancy. I note the exceptional pioneering work of d'Aquili, Laughlin, and McMannus (1979) and Lex (1979) in dealing with altered cognitive states[9] in ritual.

The argument depends on two important aspects of human behaviour: the function of emotion in decision making, and the importance of 'theory of mind' in human interaction, both of which, I maintain, are essential for human survival. Performance, I hypothesize, plays a crucial role in the maintenance of these two vital human bio-behavioural routines.

The Evolutionary Value of Performance

The Nature and Function of Emotion

Performers change the cognitive state of their audience in two principal ways. The first way is by arousing an emotional response. The second, by changing a disposition to action. These two responses are related, but I want to spend some time describing them. In particular, to reach my conclusion I need to review some recent developments in the investigation of emotion by psychologists and neurophysiologists.

Our view of emotions has changed tremendously in recent times. The Greeks referred to them as *pathe*—sufferings. It didn't matter whether it was love, anger or greed; these forces had to be countered and conquered by mastery of will to achieve wisdom and a balanced life. Romans translated *pathe* with several terms. One of them was *passiones,* from which we get the English word 'passion,' and from then on, the description of these emotional terms became a huge collection of imprecise metaphors—happy coming from *hap* meaning luck, glad from *glat,* meaning smooth or bright, and so on.

As philosopher Jonathan Ree notes in a recent review of several books on emotion:

> Then there was the rise of scientific medicine. If our bodily infections could be brought within the scope of physical laws, then perhaps our mental affections could as well. The word 'emotion' (which originally referred to civil unrest) was recruited to the cause of science and, with a little help from Charles Darwin and William James, pathe became a theme for physiologists and psychologists rather than moral philosophers. (Ree 2000: 1)

What is notable about the Greek and Roman formulations of what we today identify as emotion is the clear separation between the bodily sensations of emotion and awareness of them.

Today it often seems that individuals are powerless in the face of their emotions. When these sensations arise in an uncontrolled manner, one needs some medicament to quell the fires.

William James and indeed Freud slightly before him had a somewhat Greek notion about the nature of these emotions. In his article 'What Is an Emotion' (1884) James starts with a stimulus and ends with a feeling. In between is some kind of bodily response. The precise physiological mechanism that operates in the gap between initial stimulus and recognition of a feeling or emotion is still being debated and investigated. However, researchers in the field of emotion now recognize that, in Joseph LeDoux' words: 'emotions are things that happen to us rather than things we will to occur' (LeDoux 1996: 19).

LeDoux goes on to point out that:

> [O]nce emotions occur they become powerful motivators of future behaviors. They chart the course of moment-to-moment action as well as set the sails toward long-term achievements. But our emotions can also get us into trouble. When fear becomes anxiety, desire gives way to greed, or annoyance turns to anger, anger to hatred, friendship to envy, love to obsession, or pleasure to addiction, our emotions start working against us. Mental health is maintained by emotional hygiene, and mental problems to a large extent reflect the breakdown of emotional order. Emotions can have useful and pathological consequences. (LeDoux 1996: 19–20)

LeDoux (1996: 162–65) has demonstrated fairly conclusively that the generation of *fear* proceeds from outside stimulus—particularly auditory stimulus. Most of the action seems to take place in and around a central area of the brain, close to the juncture of the two hemispheres, and the prefrontal cortex. Much of the 'routing' of information takes place in this region. There are three bodies in particular that seem to have particularly important roles in the experience of emotion—the amygdala, the hippocampus and the thalamus. Signals pass through the auditory pathway to the thalamus (which relays information) in the lower forebrain and thence to the dorsal amygdala (which evaluates information). The hippocampus has a number of functions, but one seems to be the regulation of working memory.

Emotion activated by way of the thalamo-amygdala (subcortical) pathway results from rapid, minimal, automatic, evaluative processing. Emotion activated in this way need not involve the neocortex. Emotion activated by discrimination of stimulus features, thoughts, or memories requires that the information pass from the thalamus to the neocortex and then to the amygdala. LeDoux believes this to be the neural basis for cognitive appraisal and evaluation of events. These two routes—the direct route from the thalamus to the amygdala, and the thalamus-neocortex-amygdala route are termed the 'low road' and the 'high road' by LeDoux (1996: 164).

Researchers Ralph Adolphs, Antoine Bechara, Antonio Damasio, Hanna Damasio, Daniel Tranel and others in their research team at the University of Iowa have made exciting strides toward understanding both the mechanisms of the production of emotion, and the functionality of emotion in human life. Anthony Damasio has emerged as a public spokesman for this research group in two important semi-popular treatments of their research results, *Descartes' Error: Emotion, Reason and the Human Brain* (1994), and *The Feeling of What Happens, Body and Emotion in the Making of Consciousness* (1999).

As is typical with neurophysiologists, this group of researchers have hypothesized the functions of emotion through a study of pathology. It appears that a small nexus in the prefrontal cortex, the *amygdala,*[10] is the centre of a complex system whereby emotional stimulus is first evaluated, and then an appropriate emotional response is generated. Adolphs describes it simply:

> The amygdala plays an important role in emotion and social behavior. Its principal function appears to be the linking of perceptual representations to cognition and behavior on the basis of the emotional or social value of the stimuli. (Adolphs 2001: 232)

Individuals with damage to the amygdala, and surrounding ventromedial prefrontal cortex—the area of the brain right above the eyes—can perform well on intelligence-quotient and memory tests. However, these same individuals, when faced with real-life decisions, hesitate, equivocate, then make unwise choices. The same patients also display little emotion. The team wondered if emotional—rather than factual—memories might be missing.

They performed several gambling experiments with these individuals on the theory that gambling involves both rational decision making and emotional involvement (Bechara and Damasio 1997; see also Adolphs 1999). The individuals with damage to the prefrontal regions were hopeless losers in the games, even when the best strategies were revealed to them. The team's stated hypothesis is that rational decision making is dependent upon emotion. And emotion arises when an individual is neurologically capable of making a connection between *past experience* and *immediate experience.*

These developments are exciting particularly for those who have had some experience with pragmatic philosophy. Consider the famous statement made by the pragmatic philosopher Charles Sanders Peirce in his now classic article: 'How to Make our Ideas Clear':

> Consider what effects, that might conceivably have practical bearings, we conceive the object of our conception to have. Then our conception of these effects is the whole of our conception of the object (Peirce 1878).[11]

Damasio and company first posit that emotion 'is the combination of a *mental evaluative process,* simple or complex, with *dispositional responses to that process,* mostly *toward the body proper,* resulting in an emotional body state, but also *toward the brain itself,* resulting in mental changes (Damasio 1994: 139; see also Damasio et al. 2000).'

Next, they hypothesize that emotions are necessary for rational decision making. Individuals encounter new experience, and rather than carefully evaluating every aspect of this experience, they make decisions about future action based on emotional reactions—'gut reactions' if one will—to those experiences. This is termed the 'somatic marker hypothesis' (Damasio 1994: 165–222). The 'somatic markers', based on past experience, serve as filters for evaluating new experience. Presumably the somatic markers are linked with new sensory input through the thalamus-amygdala mechanism in the brain—a neurophysiological verification of Peirce's pragmatic formulation of 1878.

One other factor regarding emotion is important for this discussion. This is the concept of 'emotional contagion'. This refers to the tendency of humans when exposed to facial expressions and bodily reactions of others exhibiting an emotion to themselves manifest the same bodily reactions. Paul Ekman has investigated this phenomenon extensively[12] and Damasio and company deal extensively with this phenomenon in evaluating their patients. Those with damage to the pre-frontal portions of the brain do not exhibit this characteristic.[13]

Theory of Mind

I introduced the concept of Theory of Mind earlier and suggested that it was an essential human behavioural routine. The capacity to know or guess what others are thinking or feeling is crucial in human decision making. The pioneer in this line of research, George Herbert Mead, is rarely cited in contemporary studies of Theory of Mind.

Many of Mead's concepts, crucial for understanding of social behaviour, seem to have been forgotten by today's researchers. I provide here a brief synopsis of some of his central concepts crucial to this discussion.

Fundamental to Mead's (1934: 18) thinking is the notion that the 'mind' arises in social interaction. Although brains are essential for the development of mind, mind is essentially and fundamentally social. Indeed, for Mead there can be no mind at all without an interactive social environment.

> In defending a social theory of mind we are defending a functional, as opposed to any form of substantive or entitative, view as to its nature. And in particular we are opposing all intra-cranial or intra-epidermal views as to its character and locus. For it follows from our social theory of mind that the field of mind must be co-extensive with, and include all the components of, the field of the social process, or experience and behavior: i.e. the matrix of social relations and interactions among individuals, which is presupposed by it, and out of which it arises or comes into being. If mind is socially constituted, then the field, or locus of any given individual mind must extend as far as the social activity or apparatus of social relations which constitutes it, extends; and hence that field cannot be bounded by the skin of the organism to which it belongs. (Mead 1934: 223)

A second crucial element in Mead's formulation involves the view that incipient action is, neurophysiologically, a completed action. He illustrates this in a celebrated passage:

There is an organization of the various parts of the nervous system that are going to be responsible for acts, an organization that represents not only that which is immediately taking place but also the stages that are about to take place. If one approaches a distant object, he approaches it with reference to what he is going to do when he arrives there. If he approaches a hammer, he is muscularly ready to seize the handle of the hammer. The latter stages of the act are present in the early stages—not simply in the sense that they are ready to go off, but in the sense that they serve to control the process itself. They determine how we are going to control the object, and the steps in our early manipulation of it (Mead 1934: 11).

This prefigures the formulations of Damasio and LeDoux about the functioning of emotions. Attitudes and feelings about actions must be concomitants of those actions. The total act of picking up the hammer is a melding of present stimulus with past experience (routed through the amygdala). If Damasio is correct, Mead's total act has an emotional component governing its execution.

The second notion promulgated by Mead is an outgrowth of the first. This is that humans not only engage in physical actions, but also in verbal actions. This question was explored philosophically by Austin (1962) and Searle (1969, 1979, 1982, 1983) in their development of speech act theory later in the century. For Mead (1934: 131), verbal action became concretized in the *vocal gesture* which eventually may concretize into a 'significant symbol'. Thus in the development of language, Mead sees incipient action in every utterance.

The most crucial concept for understanding the notion of the Theory of Mind, however, comes from Mead's development of the concept of the 'generalized other'. For Mead, social action was impossible without the ability to posit and predict the actions of others, indeed, to experience the effects of one's actions on others in one's self. The individual in Mead's formulation is both subject and object in social encounters. What one does to others one does to one's self and meaning[14]

... arises in experience through the individual stimulating himself to take the action of the other in his reaction toward the object. Meaning is that which can be indicated to others while it is by the same process indicated to the indicating individual (Mead 1934: 89).

To summarize, the mind is by its nature collective, and individuals engaging in action in social space conceive of that action as complete from the very moment of their conception of the action. Verbal gestures have the force of action, and concretize into symbols. The meaning of any action, whether employing an object or a verbal gesture, inheres in the individual's knowledge of the effects of the action on others and the simultaneous knowledge of the effects of the action on him- or herself.

Theory of Mind (TOM) researchers are still puzzling over the mechanisms of the dynamic relationship posited by Mead.[15] In trying to understand how individuals come to an understanding of how other individuals feel and are likely to act, most do not follow his notion of the social mind; they still are looking for connections between two separate minds. The two dominant theories are simulation-theory, which is close to Mead's formulation, in that it assumes that

> one first recognizes one's own mental states under actual or imagined conditions and then infers on the basis of an assumed similarity or analogy, that the person simulated is in similar states. (Gordon 1996: 14)[16]

This is one of two simulation theory scenarios posited by Gordon, one of the leading proponents of this approach. The other formulation, which he prefers (1996: 15), emphasizes *imaginative transformation* of the individual into the other using one's motivational and emotional resources combined with practical reasoning.

> Theory-theory by contrast assumes that individuals are figuring out each others' motives, emotional states, and actions through a kind of mental calculation—a 'set of rules of symbol manipulation embodied, like a Chomskian universal grammar, in an innate module.' (Gordon 1996: 11)

To be fair, Gordon is an opponent of theory-theory, and therefore characterizes it somewhat narrowly. As one leading *proponent* of this theory, Carruthers, puts it:

> [O]ur understanding of mentalistic notions—of belief, desire, perception, intention and the rest—is largely given by the positions those notions occupy within a folk-psychological theory[17] of the structure and functioning of the mind. (Carruthers 1996: 22)

The debate rages on the merits of these formulations, but at this reading I am inclined to side with the simulation theorists, and George Herbert Mead. I do so because these proposals seem much more clearly in line with the earlier cited work on the generation of emotions. If emotional reactions arise as 'gut reactions' to external stimuli, there must be a large degree of autonomic response in the exercise of Theory of Mind. A solution depending entirely on rational processes seems not to be supported by current data.[18] Simulation-theory also accords more closely with the clinical work that most engages Theory of Mind researchers, namely studies of autism. It seems that autistic individuals lack the capacity to exhibit Theory of Mind (Carruthers and Smith 1996: 6). They also have difficulty perceiving and exhibiting emotion, making them seem close in their cognitive situation to the prefrontal brain-damaged individuals studied by Bechara, Damasio, Damasio, Tranel and their team.

Recent theoretical approaches to the study of autism suggest that the amygdala and related regions are crucial in generating Theory of Mind. Researchers such as Brothers go so far as to call this region of the mind the 'social brain' (Brothers 1990). The 'amygdala theory of autism' was put forward by a group of researchers at Cambridge University and has strong currency (Baron-Cohen et al. 2000).

Theory of Mind has also been raised as a question in one of the most fundamental anthropological problems, namely, the determination of the division between human and nonhuman animal species. Premack and Woodruff (1978), primate behavioural specialists, asked the question: 'Does the chimpanzee have a Theory of Mind?' and set many researchers on a search for an answer. Their question has not yet been answered definitively, but it points up the importance of the notion of a Theory of Mind as a defining human characteristic.[19] And for purposes of the set of problems I am exploring, the question itself is crucial.

To sum up, Theory of Mind represents a basic human capacity to understand and predict the mental states of others. Although a variety of theories abound to explain the mechanism of how this occurs, the brute fact of its existence seems not to be in question. This capacity is essential for the function of performance.

The Performance Hypothesis

I now wish to return to the two questions with which I started this discussion. To repeat: 'Why do humans engage in performance activity?' and 'How does performance achieve its effects?' I believe I can now state a tentative hypothesis concerning the first question. I will return to the second question later.

Performance is the arena of activity that allows humans to practice the display and reception of emotional states and the social transformation of individuals in a protected 'framed' environment. It has evolutionary value because accurate emotional sensitivity and socially sanctioned transformation are necessary for human survival. Its practice is psychologically reinforced; it is inherently enjoyable for both performer and audience.

I will now break this statement down into separate points and take each in turn, discussing their ramifications.

Performance is the Arena of Activity that Allows Humans to Practice the Display and Reception of Emotional States in a Protected 'Framed' Environment. In formulating this hypothesis, I am accepting the hypothesis reflected in the collective work of Adolphs, Bechara, A. Damasio, H. Damasio and Tranel as referenced in several papers by those authors earlier in this discussion, that emotional acuity is necessary for rational decision making. This alone would make any behavioural routine that would hone these skills valuable for human existence.

The warning from the Greeks down to LeDoux of both the positive and the negative aspects of emotion is the point at which anthropological analysis can enter the discussion of the function of emotion and performance. Assuming Damasio and company are right, then the capacity for emotion and the linkage of somatic markers to ongoing experience is essential for human decision making. One difficulty for human beings is that experience in confronting and practicing emotional states is hard to come by without subjecting oneself to danger. Therefore a protected arena in which one can be brought to feel love, fear, anger, despair, hilarity and other emotions both subtle and extreme is of high value. It is a safe practice arena.

Performance Facilitates the Social Transformation of Individuals in a Protected Environment. However, performance does much more than provide for emotional practice. It is also an arena of activity where individuals can undergo transformation. Performance is the behavioural routine that humans use to persuade, cajole, enlist support, solicit friendship and life partners, calm disturbed individuals and groups, treat behavioural disorders, delight others and present themselves to others. Performance achieves this by fostering the active collaborative engagement of performer and audience mentioned in the second section of this chapter. The audience willingly engages with the performer in the performance frame with the expectation of emerging from that frame in a different state than at the frame's inception.[20] Because performance is framed, it always protects the audience, since they can break the frame and leave if they are unhappy with the course of events.[21]

I view ritual and ceremony as the most serious form of performance, because the consequences for participants result in real and permanent changes to the human condition. The audience witnesses the transformation of the performers into something permanently different. The bride and groom can't walk out of their wedding like they walk out of the theatre, and slough off all that happened in the ceremony.[22]

Performance Has Evolutionary Value Because Accurate Emotional Sensitivity and Socially Sanctioned Transformation Are Necessary for Human Survival. Performance is one of the most sophisticated of human cultural activities. Therefore it is paradoxical that it may derive its power to engender emotional response from affective expressive urges that predate human emergence as homo sapiens. Yet, the ability to perform and react to performance may be one of the most uniquely human things we are able to do as a species.

Here we may question the link between expressive behaviour and performance. In the Pamir region of Central Asia there is a vocal musical form called *falak*. It is recognized as a distinct musical genre, but it is essentially seen as an artistic outpouring of emotion. It is very powerful for the hearer—a quality in popular Western music one calls 'edgy'. It can be carried out without an audience in the open air on a mountainside as well as in a closed room with a formal audience. It may be a lament, or an exuberant outpouring. Urban (1988), Feld (1982), and Wilce (1998a, 1998b) maintain that laments are at once personal expressions of grief and performative acts that demonstrate social and cultural solidarity. The Pamiri *falak* has some of the same quality but is cast within an artistic frame. This reinforces the idea that some of the emotional power in performance may be due to intersubjective emulation. The artist seems to be engaged in expressing emotion, and the audience is affected empathetically by the performance. This phenomenon is also seen in the powerful *ta'ziyeh* performances in Iran and other Shi'a Muslim countries. These epic theatrical depictions of the martyrdom of Imam Hussein, grandson of the prophet Muhammad, are designed to induce weeping and mourning in spectators (cf. Beeman 1979, 1981). As I will show later, vocal acoustic expression emulating emotion is one of the most powerful dimensions of performance.

Delineating those behavioural capacities which are uniquely human has been a venerable task for students of human biology and culture for most of this century. For a long time, tool making and linguistic communication were presented as the two activities that were the sole purview of humans.

In the last two decades, we have learned much more about the behavioural and cognitive capacities of other animal species, particularly our nearest species cousins, the great apes. The research of Jane Goodall and Sue Savage Rumbaugh among others has shown us that they have the capacity both for tool making and linguistic communication. Although the scientific community continues to split hairs evaluating the details, it is clear that human uniqueness is no longer defined unequivocally by these capacities. If we wish to understand human uniqueness, we may need to look to behavioural capacities that are still more complex than language and tool making. Performance is one of these capacities, as I have argued.

One of the principal functions of expressive behaviour would seem to be to encourage and facilitate bonding within human groups on a large scale. Over time, this leads to more effective social organization.

Language itself is good at communicating information, but it is deficient in conveying affective states to others. Humans are able to accomplish a great deal of affective communication through the use of tropes, such as metaphor, but even these structures lack immediacy. When humans really want to express interpersonal affect, language often breaks down. The deepest emotional expressions between two people, even hostile and violent ones, are usually tactile (perhaps also olfactory and gustatory) rather than linguistic, and this physical contact usually is a central component of bonding between individuals.

How do whole groups achieve bonding through sharing of inner states? Most human societies find orgiastic behaviour unpalatable or impractical. It is also problematic in terms of social organization. Untrammeled tactile intimacy leads to social disturbance due to another factor in human social behaviour: the need to establish hierarchies and the related competition for exclusive sexual partners.

One solution has been extensively explored by Victor Turner in a wide number of publications. Drawing on the classic work of Arnold Van Gennep (1960), Turner points out that performance frames allow members of society the freedom to suspend the normal structures of social life and enter into alternative 'subjunctive' structures. One feature of this can be a feeling of *communitas,* a state where members of society feel uniquely connected to each other. Reversals and other transformations of the social order are also possible. This is not only good for the individuals, but for the survival of society itself:

> [A]ny society which hopes to be imperishable must whittle out for itself a piece of space and a while of time, in which it can look honestly at itself. The supreme honesty of the creative artist who, in his presentations on the stage, in the book, on canvas, in marble, in music, or in towers and houses, reserves to himself the privilege of seeing straight what all cultures build crooked. (Turner 1986: 122)

Auditory and visual channels for communication have the advantage of being able to encompass and affect large numbers of individuals without the need to touch, smell or taste every other person in the group. Normal language is of course primarily conveyed through auditory and visual channels. It is then not surprising that forms of communication conveying affect in an immediate manner have language as a component but provide significant enhancements from other dimensions of communication.

To sum up, performance has both the strong utility functions associated with creating enhanced emotional acuity and social transformation, and the ideal mechanisms to accomplish these functions through symbolic elements conveyed through visual and auditory channels. I hypothesize that individuals with the capacity to engage in this kind of activity have many advantages in life over those that do not. They succeed in terms of enhanced decision making, better chances in establishing a functionally useful position in social hierarchies, and attracting allies and potential mates.

Performance is Inherently Enjoyable for Both Performer and Audience

Just as so many other functionally useful things in human life are reinforced by pleasurable feelings, performance generally 'feels good' for everyone involved. Humans genuinely enjoy performance both as performers and as audience, and this reduces inhibitions about participating in performance. I may be understating the case. Audience members go back repeatedly to experience it, as I mentioned at the beginning of this essay.

The 'flow' sensation arising from total engagement in performance is one of the reinforcing sensations, but not the only one. I have already invoked the fact that the cognitive frame is one of the most basic aspects of human behaviour. One of the most common forms of framed behaviour is 'play'. Performance shares so many features with play behaviour that it can be thought of in the same light.[23] The enjoyment humans derive from play has been extensively commented upon.

One source of pleasure in play and performance may be the ability of these routines to tap into some of the most basic human emotions. A number of researchers have posited a list of basic, innate emotions, among them McDougall (1908/1996), Tomkins (1962) Izard (1971), Plutchik (1994), Frijda (1986, 1994) and Ekman

(1992). All of these researchers vary both in the list of specific innate emotions they posit, and the ways that emotions that are more complex are derived. Tomkins's early list: surprise, interest, joy, rage, fear, disgust, shame and anguish, is typical. Such formulations are hardly new. The *Natyasastra,* an Indian treatise on dramatic arts complied between the second century BCE and the second century CE lists nine basic emotional states or *rasas:* love, mirth, sadness, anger, heroism, fear, disgust, surprise and peace.[24]

The intriguing possibility we find in performance is that emotions may be involved twice. First basic emotions such as interest, joy and surprise may be involved to encourage engagement in performance. Second, emotions are aroused during the course of performance. This *double emotional involvement* may be one of the strongest motivating factors for humans to seek out and repeat performance behaviour.

John Emigh suggests an additional source of enjoyment for performance: it allows humans to use all of their faculties in the exercise of exuberant play.

> The 'framing' of performance ... is both protective and liberating: Why the complex reworking of emotional states, the endless variations on and subversions of the 'who–done–it'? Why the manic persona shifting of a Robin Williams or the radical attack on social constructs of race and gender of an Anna Deavere Smith or a Kate Bornstein? To make the stone stony, as Shklovsky (*sic*). He needs to be introduced to reinvest the world with wonder, to move men and women to action, as Brecht hoped. No doubt. But most of all, I suspect, and as a prelude to all of these worthy aims, to exercise our sensory and cognitive faculties in a situation where we are freed from decisions that may affect lives and livelihoods, where nothing seems to be at stake, and, in that purchased or stolen time between times, to question our categorical precepts, and to keep our responses alert and working. To use all our mental capacities while monitoring the bodies of others in action. To do this for enjoyment, because, owing to sensory and cognitive systems that have evolved, no doubt, for very different purposes, this activity makes wonderful use of everything that the body-minded brain does best. (Emigh 2002: 262–3)

Finally, humans, like other primates, are fascinated by themselves. Many researchers have noted that performance holds up a 'mirror' to spectators.[25] Turner's epigram at the beginning of this chapter—'in performing [man] reveals himself to himself' (Turner 1987: 81)—reflects this truth. Schechner (1990: 43) has noted that performance is 'twice behaved behavior', since it derives from natural behavior, but is rehearsed and repeated for an audience. The human capacity to exhibit Theory of Mind as discussed above is a clear prerequisite for both performer and audience (Emigh 2002: 262–3).

It is noteworthy that humans especially enjoy seeing performance that emphasizes and underscores the limits of human behaviour. Exemplary goodness, badness, and extremes of physical skill are among the most popular themes of performance.[26] It also shows reversal and transformation. In this regard, the mirror of performance is a fun-house mirror. It exaggerates, simplifies, and distorts in the subjunctive mode examined by Turner as cited above. It holds the promise and wonder of witnessing things as they might be without the danger of the actual disruption that true change might bring.

References

Adolphs, R. (1999), 'Social Cognition and the Human Brain', *Trends in Cognitive Sciences* 3(12), December: 469–79.

Adolphs, R. (2001), 'The Neurobiology of Social Cognition', *Current Opinion in Neurobiology* 11(2), April: 231–39.

Austin, J. (1962), *How to Do Things with Words,* Oxford: Oxford University Press.

Baron-Cohen, S., Ring, H. A., Bullmore, E. T., Wheelwright, S., Ashwin, C., and Williams, S.C.R. (2000), 'The Amygdala Theory of Autism', *Neuroscience & Biobehavioral Reviews* 24(3): 355–64.

Bateson, G. (1955), 'A Theory of Play and Fantasy', *Psychiatric Research Reports* 2: 39–51.

Bauman, R. (1977), *Verbal Art As Performance,* Rowley, Mass.: Newbury House.

Bechara, A., and Damasio, H. (1997), 'Deciding Advantageously before Knowing the Advantageous Strategy', *Science,* 275(5304): 1293–95.

Beeman, W. O. (1979), 'Cultural Dimensions of Performance Conventions in Iranian Ta'ziyeh', in P. J. Chelkowski (ed.), *Ta'ziyeh: Ritual and Drama in Iran,* pp. 24–31, New York: New York University Press.

Beeman, W. O. (1981), 'A Full Arena: The Development and Meaning of Popular Performance Traditions in Iran', in M. Bonine and N. Keddie (eds), *Modern Iran: The Dialectics of Continuity and Change,* pp. 381–82, notes pp. 440–44, Albany: State University of New York Press.

Beeman, W. O. (1982), *Culture, Performance and Communication in Iran,* Tokyo: Institute for the Study of Languages and Cultures of Asia and Africa (ILCAA).

Beeman, W. O. (1986), *Language, Status and Power in Iran,* Bloomington: Indiana University Press.

Beeman, W. O. (1993), 'The Anthropology of Theater and Spectacle', *Annual Review of Anthropology* 22: 369–93.

Beeman, W. O. (2005), 'Making Grown Men Weep', in A. Hobart and B. Kapferer (eds), *Aesthetics and Performance: The Art of Rite,* New York: Berghahn Books.

Bennett, S. (1990), *Theatre Audiences,* London and New York: Routledge.

Bourdieu, P. (1997), *Outline of a Theory of Practice,* trans. R. Nice, Cambridge: Cambridge University Press.

Bråten, S. (1998), 'Infant Learning by Altercentric Participation: The Reverse of Ego-centric Observation in Autism', in S. Bråten (ed.), *Intersubjective Communication and Emotion in Early Ontogeny. Studies in Emotion and Social Interaction,* 2nd series, pp. 105–24, Cambridge: Cambridge University Press.

Briggs, C. (1988), *Competence in Performance: The Creativity of Tradition in Mexicano Verbal Art*, Philadelphia: University of Pennsylvania Press.

Brothers, L. (1990), 'The Social Brain: A Project for Integrating Primate Behaviour and Neuropsychology in a New Domain', *Concepts in Neuroscience*, 1: 27–51.

Caillois, R. (1961), *Man, Play and Games*, M. Barash, trans., New York: Free Press of Glencoe.

Carruthers, P. (1996), 'Simulation and Self-knowledge: A Defense of Theory-theory', in P. Carruthers and P. K. Smith (eds), *Theories of Theories of Mind*, pp. 22–38, Cambridge: Cambridge University Press.

Carruthers, P., and P. K. Smith (1996), 'Introduction', in P. Carruthers and P. K. Smith (eds), *Theories of Theories of Mind*, pp. 1–10, Cambridge: Cambridge University Press.

Carruthers, P., and P. K. Smith, eds. (1996), *Theories of Theories of Mind*, Cambridge: Cambridge University Press.

Csikszentmihalyi, M. (1975), *Beyond Boredom and Anxiety: The Experience of Play in Work and Games*, San Francisco: Jossey-Bass.

Csikszentmihalyi, M. (1990), *Flow: The Psychology of Optimal Experience*, New York: Harper and Row.

Damasio, A. R. (1994), *Descartes' Error: Emotion, Reason and the Human Brain*, New York: Grosset/Putnam.

Damasio, A. R. (1999), *The Feeling of What Happens, Body and Emotion in the Making of Consciousness*, New York: Harcourt Brace.

Damasio, A. R., Grabowski, T. J., Bechara, A., Damasio, H., Ponto, L.L.B., Parvizi, J., and Hichwa, R. D. (2000), 'Subcortical and Cortical Brain Activity during the Feeling of Self-Generated Emotions', *Nature Neuroscience* 3(10): 1049–56.

D'Aquili, E. G., Laughlin, C. D., and Mc Mannus, J., eds (1979), *The Spectrum of Ritual*, New York: Columbia University Press.

Dennett, D. (1969), *Content and Consciousness*, London: Routledge & Kegan Paul.

Dennett, D. (1987), *The Intentional Stance*, Cambridge, Mass.: MIT Press.

Dennett, D. (1988), 'The Intentional Stance in Theory and Practice', in R. W. Byrne and A. Whiten (eds), *Machiavellian Intelligence: Social Expertise and the Evolution of Intellect*, Oxford: Oxford University Press.

Duranti, A. (1986), 'The Audience As Co-author: An Introduction', *Text (Special Issue: The Audience as Co-Author)*, 6(3): 239–48.

Ekman, P. (1992), 'Facial Expressions of Emotions: New Findings, New Questions', *Psychological Science* 3: 34–8.

Ekman, P., Levenson, R. W., and Friesen, W. V. (1983), 'Autonomic Nervous System Activity Distinguishes among Emotions', *Science*, 221(4616), 1208–10.

Emigh, J. (2002), 'Performance Studies, Neuroscience, and the Limits of Culture', in Nathan Stucky and Cynthia Wimmer (eds), *Performance Studies As a Discipline*, Carbondale, Ill.: University of Southern Illinois Press.

Feld, S. (1982), *Sound and Sentiment: Birds, Weeping, Poetics and Song in Kaluli Expression,* Philadelphia: University of Pennsylvania Press.

Frijda, N. (1986), *The Emotions,* Cambridge: Cambridge University Press.

Fridja, N. (1994), *Emotions: Essays on Emotion Theory,* Hillsdale, N.J.: Lawrence Erlbaum.

Garfinkel, H. (1967), *Studies in Ethnomethodology,* Englewood Cliffs, N.J.: Prentice-Hall.

Geertz, C. (1980), *Negara: The Theater State in Nineteenth Century Bali,* Princeton, N.J.: Princeton University Press.

Goffman, E. (1959), *The Presentation of Self in Everyday Life,* New York: Doubleday Anchor.

Goffman, E. (1967), *Interaction Ritual,* Garden City, N.Y.: Doubleday.

Goffman, E. (1971), *Relations in Public,* New York: Basic Books.

Goffman, E. (1974), *Frame Analysis,* Cambridge, Mass.: Harvard University Press.

Goodall, J. (1986), *The Chimpanzees of Gombe: Patterns of Behavior,* Cambridge, Mass.: Harvard University Press.

Goodwin, C. (1986), 'Audience Diversity, Participation and Interpretation', *Text (Special Issue: The Audience as Co-Author)* ed. A. Duranti and D. Brenneis, 6 (3): 283–316.

Gordon, R. M. (1996), '"Radical" Simulationism', in P. Carruthers and P. K. Smith, *Theories of Theories of Mind,* pp. 11–21, Cambridge: Cambridge University Press.

Helfgot, D., and Beeman, W. O. (1993), *The Third Line: The Opera Performer As Interpreter,* New York: Schirmer Books.

Huizinga, J. (1955), *Homo Ludens: A Study of the Play Element in Culture,* Boston: Beacon Press.

Izard, C. E. (1971), *The Face of Emotion,* New York: Appleton-Century-Crofts.

James, W. (1884), 'What Is an Emotion', *Mind* 9: 188–205.

LeDoux, J. (1996), *The Emotional Brain,* New York: Simon and Schuster.

Lex, B. (1979), 'Neurobiology of Ritual Trance', in E. G. d'Aquili, C. D. Laughlin, and J. Mc Mannus, *The Spectrum of Ritual,* pp. 117–51, New York: Columbia University Press.

Lipps, T. (1903), 'Einfühlung, innere Nachahmung und Organempfindung', *Archiv für die gesamte Psychologie,* 1, 465–519.

MacAloon, J., ed. (1984), *Rite, Drama, Festival, Spectacle,* Philadelphia: Institute for the Study of Human Issues.

McDougall, W.F.R.S. (1908/1996), *An Introduction to Social Psychology,* 24th ed., London: Methuen & Co.

Mead, G. H. (1934), *Mind, Self and Society: From the Standpoint of a Social Behaviorist,* Chicago: University of Chicago Press.

Mills, C. W. (1964), *Sociology and Pragmatism,* New York: Paine-Whitman.

Peirce, C. S. (1878), *Popular Science Monthly,* 12 (January): 286–302.

Plutchik, R. (1994), *The Psychology and Biology of Emotion,* New York: Harper-Collins.

Povinelli, D. J., Nelson, K. E., Nelson, B., and Nelson, S. T. (1992), 'Comprehension of Role Reversal in Chimpanzees: Evidence of Empathy?', *Animal Behaviour,* 43(4), 633–40.

Premack, D., and Woodruff, G. (1978), 'Does the Chimpanzee Have a Theory of Mind?', *The Behavioral and Brain Sciences,* 1: 515–26.

Ree, J. (2000), Mixed Emotions: Keeping Them In and Getting Them Out, *Los Angeles Times* (Book Review Section), 7 May: 1 ff.

Schechner, R. (1973), *Environmental Theater,* New York: Hawthorn.

Schechner, R. (1977), *Essays on Performance Theory 1970–1976,* New York: Drama Book Specialists.

Schechner, R. 1988. *Performance Theory,* London and New York: Routledge.

Schechner, R. (1990), 'Magnitudes of Performance', in R. Schechner and W. Appel, *By Means of Performance,* Cambridge and New York: Cambridge University Press.

Schechner, R. (1993), *The Future of Ritual,* London and New York: Routledge.

Schechner, R., and Appel, W., eds (1990), *By Means of Performance,* Cambridge and New York: Cambridge University Press.

Schuetz, A. (1945), 'On Multiple Realities', *Philosophy and Phenomenological Research* 5(4): 533–76.

Searle, J. (1969), *Speech Acts: An Essay in the Philosophy of Language,* Cambridge: Cambridge University Press.

Searle, J. (1979), 'Intentionality and the Use of Language', in A. Margalit (ed.), *Meaning and Use,* Dordrecht: Reidel.

Searle, J. (1982), 'What Is an Intentional State?', in H. L. Dreyfus (ed.), *Husserl, Intentionality and Cognitive Science,* Cambridge, Mass.: MIT Press.

Searle, J. (1983), *Intentionality, an Essay on the Philosophy of Mind,* Cambridge: Cambridge University Press.

Singer, Milton. (1972), *When a Great Tradition Modernizes,* New York: Praeger.

Stich, S. (1981), 'Dennett on Intentional Systems', *Philosophical Topics* 12(1): 39–62.

Stich, S. (1983), *From Folk Psychology to Cognitive Science,* Cambridge, Mass. M.I.T. Press.

Tannen, D. (1993), *Framing in Conversational Structures,* Cambridge: Cambridge University Press.

Tomkins, S. (1962), *Affect, Imagery, Consciousness,* New York: Springer.

Turner, V. (1974), *Dramas, Fields and Metaphors,* Ithaca, N.Y.: Cornell University Press.

Turner, V. (1982), *From Ritual to Theater: The Human Seriousness of Play,* New York: PAJ Publications.

Turner, V. (1986), *The Anthropology of Performance,* New York: PAJ Publications.

Urban, G. (1988), 'Discourse, Affect and Social Order: Ritual Wailing in Amerindian Brazil', *American Anthropologist* 90: 385–400.

Van Gennep, A. (1960), *The Rites of Passage,* Chicago: University of Chicago Press (first published in 1908).

Wallace, A.F.C. (1965), 'Driving to Work', in M. Spiro, *Context and Meaning in Cultural Anthropology,* pp. 277–92, New York: The Free Press.

Wilce, J. (1998a), *Eloquence in Trouble: The Poetics and Politics of Complaint in Rural Bangladesh,* New York: Oxford University Press.

Wilce, J. (1998b), 'The Pragmatics of "Madness": Performance Analysis of a Bangladeshi Woman's "Aberrant" Lament', *Culture, Medicine, and Psychiatry* 22(1): 1–54.

Notes

1. I hope readers will forgive me citing this anecdote, which I have used in a previous publication on singing and emotion (Beeman 2005). The anecdote serves the purposes of both topics admirably.

2. I take the position that emotional states are cognitive states, as will be seen below, but include them both here given the commonly held view that they are distinct.

3. As will be seen below, I include under performance not just events that occur in formal performance settings, but also many of the routines of everyday life, and face-to-face behavior. This tradition dates back to Goffman (1959, 1967, 1971, 1974), Garfinkel (1967) and a long pedigree of ethnomethodologists and symbolic interactionists. (See Singer 1972 for an early application to Indian society.)

4. Much of this will be familiar ground for those with knowledge of the work of Turner, Schechner, Kirschenblatt-Gimblett, Myerhoff, Zarilli and other luminaries in the field of performance studies. I do not intend to take personal credit for these ideas, but rather to lay them out here as a foundation for subsequent discussion.

5. As will be seen below, the role of audience or performer is the result of an interactional dynamic relationship. Throughout a performance the roles may be fixed, as is usual in theatrical events, or as in the case of conversational interaction, may alternate or exist simultaneously with each other. They are, however, symbiotic. One role cannot exist without the other; they define each other.

6. Naturally, emotional reactions occur in all sorts of human situations, most of them outside of performance events. As I will argue, performance may have adaptive value precisely because it allows the experience of emotions one may not encounter in everyday life.

7. See also Goodwin (1986) for additional perspectives on the direction of attention in conversational performance.
8. See Duranti (1986) and Bennet (1990) for more perspectives on the audience as collaborator.
9. Again, I remind readers that cognitive state as I use the term in this discussion includes emotions and dispositions to action, or embodiment.
10. Literally 'almond' because of its shape.
11. C. Wright Mills points out that the initial formulation of the pragmatic position took place some years before in a paper Peirce wrote for a group of friends which included William James, whose position on this matter I have already alluded to (Mills: 1964: 86).
12. Cf. Ekman 1992, and Ekman, Levenson, and Friesen 1983.
13. Emotional contagion is the latest manifestation of an old concept in psychology, *Einfühlung* (Lipps 1903) whereby an individual is thought to project feelings onto an object of observation. McDougall describes emotional contagion as 'the primitive, passive sympathy', a nonspecific tendency for like emotions to be evoked in observers of emotional displays (1996: 78–82). He cites examples of children who smile in response to a smile from their mother, people who feel tenderness watching a mother-infant interaction, and chimpanzees that are aroused by the distress of a conspecific. Bråten (1998) posits an interesting concept, which he terms 'e-motion' noting that infants learn to develop an accord with adults by matching their bodily movements. He thus hypothesizes that infants exhibit an 'inherent self-other connectivity that enables infants unwittingly to feel a virtual moving with the movements of others' (1998: 105). If Bråten is correct, this 'e-motion' disposition would be the basis for the development of the intersubjectivity necessary for the development of Theory of Mind as described below. His theory gains plausibility when it is understood that autistic children also exhibit 'imitation errors' in early development to a greater degree than nonautistic children.
14. This echoes the developmental theory of Bråten cited in note 13. We might expect Mead's generalized other to have originally arisen from the infants' predisposition to physical imitation of other individuals in their social universe (Bråten 1998).
15. It is notable that a recent, celebrated volume on Theory of Mind (Carruthers and Smith 1996) does not reference Mead even once.
16. This is an almost perfect paraphrase of Mead's formulation.
17. The term folk-psychology is used in the sense of lay accounting procedures that people (nonscientists and nonphilosophers, one presumes) use to account for the mental states of others.
18. The question of Theory of Mind is closely allied to a long-standing philosophical question—that of *intentionality*. In recent years this problem has been approached by a number of philosophers, most notably Dan Dennett (1969, 1987, 1988), John Searle (1979, 1982, 1983) and Stephen Stich (1981, 1983). The problem

derives ultimately from the nineteenth-century philosopher Franz Brentano, who claimed to have made a clear distinction between mental phenomena and physical phenomena. Mental phenomena exhibit intentionality:

Every mental phenomenon is characterized by what the scholastics of the Middle Ages called the Intentional (and also mental) inexistence (Inexistenz) of an object (Gegenstand) and what we would call, although in not entirely unambiguous terms, the reference to a content, a direction upon an object. (quoted in Dennett 1969:20)

Dennett and others have taken this as a 'disposition toward an object'. Searle claims that "Intentional states represent objects and states of affairs in exactly the same sense that speech acts represent objects and states of affairs (Searle 1982: 260). While many philosophical questions about the nature of intentionality remain live, the aspects that concern performance for the purposes of this discussion have been subsumed under the discussion of emotion and Theory of Mind above. I have never seen George Herbert Mead discussed in conjunction with questions of intentionality, but his theory of action, discussed above, is clearly pertinent.

19. Of course, chimpanzees and other great apes do possess amygdalar structures. They also exhibit behavior that has been identified in humans as involving the amygdala in a central way, such as facial recognition (cf. Goodall, 1986; Povinelli, Nelson, K. E., Nelson, B., and Nelson, S. T. 1992).

20. It is possible for an audience to unwittingly be entrapped in a performance frame. This entrapment is a 'con', whether perpetrated by an individual or a group. Erving Goffman (1959) has written extensively about this kind of performance. Even when one becomes entrapped, at some point the performance frame is revealed, and at that juncture the audience chooses to continue to participate or to exit. Some audiences may continue to 'play along' even when the performance is revealed for a variety of reasons: politeness, curiosity, desire for revenge, embarrassment at having been entrapped or ineptitude at making an escape. Salesmen, seducers and thieves hope to entrap people so thoroughly that they are unable to leave the frame without carrying out some action desired by the performer. See Beeman (1982) for examples of how these dynamics play out in the cultural framework of Iranian society, and Helfgot and Beeman (1993) for their application in musical performance.

21. Schechner (1993: 27) referred to this as a 'safety net, or a chance to call time-out'. See also Schechner 1988.

22. Schechner (1993: 228–30) argues for subsuming performance under the rubric of ritual. I would subsume ritual under the rubric of performance. We have little argument here. Schechner unites performance and ritual in his way by focusing on acts and institutions (but his ground has shifted too; see Schechner 1990).

I unite the two in my way by focusing on behavioral capacities and functions. There is no doubt in either of our formulations about the essential unity of these human phenomena or their functions in human life. See Beeman (1982) for examples of how these dynamics play out in the cultural framework of Iranian society, and Helfgot and Beeman (1993) for their application in musical performance.

23. I have here to resist following this discussion of play further for fear of losing the main thread of my argument. Others have trod this ground extensively, and I refer readers to the numerous works written on the fascinating topic of human play, including some already mentioned: Bateson (1955), Turner (1974, 1982), Schechner (1988, 1993) and the classic work by Huizinga (1955). I am content here with the point that both play and performance are entered into willingly in part because they are so vastly enjoyed. See Goffman's essay on "Fun in Games" (1967) for one of the best discussions on this point. This is also extended in Goffman (1971).

24. The final *rasa,* peace, was added at a later date (cf. Schechner 1990: 32–6)

25. It noteworthy that the ability of a child (or a nonhuman primate) to recognize themselves in an *actual* mirror is used by child psychologists as a test of normal intellectual and emotional development.

26. Wise theatrical producers who want to attract the attention of young people put children in their productions. If they are used well, the children virtually guarantee the rapt attention of other children in their audience.

–20–

The Emotional Life of Gay Men
Observations from New York

Moshe Shokeid

One wonders, is there something unique about the emotional life of gay men? Is there a different sense of intentionality, of feelings and other types of patterned emotional responses when homosexuals meet their sexual partners? I plan to tackle the issue of the emotional template, its display and the self-awareness of the participants about that code.

However, when I came to analyze my observations in terms of the previous anthropological studies of emotions, I could not erase a few major dilemmas. In particular, what is the appropriate definition of emotions relevant to my subject? How would my ethnography and interpretation relate to other studies of emotions carried out by anthropologists?

In recent decades, notable ethnographic studies of emotions have emerged in the aftermath of Geertz's seminal portrait of the socially patterned, restrained reactions of Balinese to personal trauma, and the orchestrated manner of their presentation of self. Geertz had professed: 'but emotions too, are cultural artifacts' (1973: 81). And these subsequent studies presented evidence for the cultural construction of emotions, an idea developed about the same time by sociologists (e.g. Arlie Hochschild 2003, Rom Harre 1986). Though they often criticized his work, these anthropologists actually refined Geertz's insights while conducting their research with a more intensive, interactionist approach (e.g. Levy 1984, Lutz 1986, Lynch 1990, Myers 1979, 1988, Michelle Rosaldo 1984, Wikan 1990). The vocabulary of emotions reported in these studies related to the demonstration or the suppression of behavioural responses to powerful sensations, such as shame, anger, fear, compassion, grief, happiness, and kinship obligations. Much, if not most, of the ethnographic research on emotions has concentrated in India, Southeast Asia and other 'classical' fields (exemplified in a recent issue of *Ethnos,* 69(4), 2004).

My field of observation among gay men has been remote both from the ethnographic sites and the type of emotions addressed in previous anthropological discourses. Altogether, later generations of anthropologists have not followed the founders'—Malinowski and Mead—interest in the study of sexuality (e.g. Vance 1991). It seems particularly relevant to be reminded of Malinowski. When dealing, for example, with themes of sexuality such as the 'jealousy of passion' (1929: 322), he related directly to emotions. Of his theoretical premise, he wrote: 'The salient points which distinguish human attachments from animal instincts are the dominance of the object over the situation, the organization of emotional attitudes, the continuity of the building up of such attitudes and their crystallization into permanent adjustable systems' (1927: 240) , or, 'culture depends directly upon the degree to which the human emotions can be trained, adjusted, and organized into complex and plastic systems' (1927: 236).

The neglected field of sexuality has been reclaimed in recent years, in particular by the protagonists of gay and lesbian studies (e.g. Herdt 1981, Kulick 1998, Lancaster 1988). They have also gradually moved away from the old concentration on Third World 'other' societies (e.g. Leap 1999, Lewin 1993, Kennedy and Davis 1993, Newton 1993). However, emotions were not an initial focus. The first studies of gay men's behaviour in anonymous sex venues were dominated by Goffman's symbolic interaction methodology and interpretation, which left little space for an analysis of emotions in vivo (e.g. Humphreys 1970, Delph 1978, Style 1979). The anthropologists who became engaged in the study of homosexuality, both in Third World and Western societies, focused on the processes and the rituals of 'coming out' and identity formation, community development, and other types of social interaction in the gay milieu. The issue of emotions remained, for the most part, the domain of the psychologists who were studying and treating the population 'suffering' from the symptoms of homosexuality.

My own work for the last fifteen years has been principally devoted to study of gay and lesbian institutions in New York. My first research was conducted at Congregation Beth Simchat Torah (CBST), a gay and lesbian synagogue. I then observed the meetings of a number of groups at the Lesbian and Gay Community Services Center. Most recently, I have been observing gay churches: Metropolitan Community Church (MCC), Dignity NY, and Unity Church in Brooklyn. In the course of this research, however, I have had the opportunity to form close friendships with many single men and a few long-term couples. I have heard their life stories and was privy to their recent activities. I have also visited a variety of venues catering to gay men. These included bars as well as sites of 'anonymous sex.'

The subject of emotions seems particularly complex when considering a type of behaviour that is so closely if not inevitably associated with the physical domain. A thorough discussion would lead us back to Plato, who first introduced the distinction between erotic love and sexual desire, associated with the distinction between the animal and the rational motivation and demeanor (e.g. Scruton 2001). In simple terms, how separate is the sexual drive/instinct/libido and orgasm from the realm of emotions, feelings and affection? Not considering acts of rape, sexual abuse and paid sex, how remote is the 'pure' act of sexual intercourse from the Western concept of 'lovemaking' (Weitman 1998)? In sum, can we apply the term 'emotion' to the display of sexual attitudes, values and actual demeanor, with the same meaning as employed by anthropologists in other spheres of the manifestation of emotions? And last, our major research quest, can we identify a code of patterned verbal responses and of behavioural expressions in the landscape of gay men's mating interaction?

Among the sociologists, I suggest Hochschild's definition (2003: 88–89): 'The concept "emotions" refers mainly to strips of experience in which there is no conflict between one and another aspect of self: the individual "floods out," is "overcome" ... emotion differs from other adaptive mechanisms [such as shivering when cold or perspiring when hot] in that thinking, perceiving, and imagining—themselves subject to social influence—enter in.'

Among the various definitions of emotions suggested by anthropologists, I still favor Levy's (1973: 271) broad perspective: 'Emotions seem to be feelings which convey and represent information about one's mode of relationship as a total individual to the social and nonsocial environment: and they seem to involve sensations with essential autonomic nervous system components.'

I did not interview in any direct fashion or intentionally used the term 'emotion' as I listened to reports on contemporary experiences or stories about past events. I sometimes asked relevant questions of clarification, but as part of a natural discourse between close friends. Actually, during most of the time of my acquaintance with the people I write about, I was unaware that I would report specifically on the issue of emotions. After all, emotion is a term used and interpreted more often by the observers of individuals and their society, namely, social scientists, analysts and authors in particular. In real life, the daily vocabulary and behavioural signs of emotions are less specific and direct.

I intend to present in this chapter the detailed stories of two of my close, single friends, who were usually open, in my company, about their search of sex and love. For comparative illustrations, I will also introduce shorter descriptions of life experiences reported to me by a few other gay men. No doubt, I could employ a different strategy to introduce my data. Actually, in earlier publications, I presented gay men's attitudes on issues of sexual behaviour, affection and intimacy, as expressed during meetings of members of voluntary associations. These included congregants at a Jewish gay synagogue (Shokeid 1995/2003), a group of older men—members of SAGE (Shokeid 2001a), a group of bisexuals (Shokeid 2001b), participants in Sexually Compulsive Anonymous support groups (Shokeid 2002), and an interracial group of blacks and whites (Shokeid n.d.). I could assemble my observations and a number of the stories I collected from my informants in various locations. However, I thought I could better substantiate my views about gay men's modes of emotionality in their quest of sex and intimacy through the presentation of two full research personas. By no means do I consider these two men as representatives of the world of

American gay men. I follow, however, a long tradition in anthropology employed by ethnographers who introduced the life history of one or a few individuals to illuminate some major themes in the culture of their studied society (e.g. Crapanzano 1980, Eickelman 1985, Langness and Frank 1981, Lewis 1967, Myerhoff 1978, Rapport 2003, Shostack 1981).

It has been often assumed that gay men routinely tend to separate their experiences of sexual gratification from the socially sanctioned, emotional realm. As proof for that orientation has been introduced the history of the clandestine and quick rendezvous of gay men in a variety of public spaces (such as the cruising in parks, beaches, downtown streets) as well as in the more secluded institutions that also catered to their immediate sexual relief (back rooms in bars, video parlors, clubs, baths, sex parties, etc.). The spread of AIDS in recent decades among gay men helped to confirm the belief that they routinely engage in casual sex devoid of emotional obligations. These habits seem to represent, also in the reports of gay observers, an essential part of the culture of gay life (e.g. Adam 1992, Bronski 2000, Delany 1999, Forrest 1994, Newton 1993, Rechy 1977). In view of these prevalent assumptions, this chapter addresses, in particular, the question of what circumstances may induce gay men to engage in casual sex with other men. I will also inquire into the other facets of their relationships with their sexual partners.

I met Jeffrey through CBST, the gay synagogue, and Nigel in one of the groups I observed at the Lesbian and Gay Community Services Center, also in Greenwich Village. They came from very different social background and had different life experiences. My acquaintance with Jeff goes back for more than ten years, but I will relate, in this paper, mostly our meetings and conversations during the last three years. I met Nigel more recently, and I will explore, here, the two years since we incidentally attended the same social group at the Lesbian and Gay Community Center. I believe that my continuing communication with these two men reveals a reliable picture of their sexual and emotional life. I am convinced they treated me as a close friend and shared with me many details considered intimate and confidential. I was also open with them about myself as never before in my ordinary daily life with friends. I consider Jeff and Nigel among my closest friends. I had many opportunities to test the reliability of their stories as I came to know individuals that took part in their lives. I believe that I do not betray our friendship as I expose their intimate life and feelings before an audience of strangers. They knew all along that I am a 24-hour researcher and that our relationship was also part of my professional agenda. They both had read my CBST ethnography and relied on my code of confidentiality, which would never allow a disclosure of their identity. Jeff, in particular, had his experience with my publications. I quoted him in my ethnography, and he was pleased with his role in the text. 'Jeff,' the name I gave him, became our shared secret and a source of private jokes. Naturally I changed some personal details that might have easily revealed their identity and avoided reporting of some intimate issues that might embarrass or pain them.

Jeffrey

I first met Jeff in 1989 at a Yom Kippur breakfast following services at the gay synagogue. He was in his early forties. As we became acquainted, Jeff began to share his life history with me. He was raised in a lower-middle-class Jewish family. An only child, he had no close relatives growing up save for a loving mother and a forbidding stepfather. His memories of family and youth were not happy. A college graduate, he was comfortable, but not really content with his job in the New York State judicial bureaucracy. At the time of our first introduction, he was concluding a two-year relationship with a Jewish fellow of about his age. His only other relationship had been of the same duration with a younger, less well educated, and less economically secure Hispanic partner. This partner conformed better with his ideal physical type: slim, boyish and preferably, though not exclusively of Puerto Rican or similar Latino extraction. As Jeff described it, he was always first attracted to the physical and erotic appeal of a potential mate. Everything else came second. That ordering, however, was often a source of later disappointment when the sexual attraction of his partner was not matched with the personality and shared interests that could sustain a continuing relationship. This disparity, as well as his partner's later infidelities, ultimately doomed this first relationship.

As our friendship developed over the years, Jeff became more and more open about the intimate details of his life and his search for physical pleasure and emotional connection. In the summer of 2000, Jeff invited me to a sex party organized by the local Water Sport Association. He told me it had taken him a long time before he felt comfortable enough to be willing to let me observe him in a sex club 'like a specimen under a microscope.' It was equally embarrassing for me to accept an invitation to a site of 'kinky' behaviour. But the invitation and my acceptance of it promised to cement our relationship, and I agreed to attend.

Once inside the place, I was impressed by the friendly atmosphere and the affectionate behaviour displayed by the participants. I experienced a transformation of the mental image I came in with about its 'sleazy' activity, which was dominated by men urinating on each other as part of their sexual enjoyment. During that evening I met a few men who had known Jeff a long time. I saw that it was a place of sexual activity, but not of the 'anonymous sex' I had anticipated. Many in the crowd knew each other as members of the organization. They had met each other at other sites. On the whole, there was a sense of familiarity, a feeling of community. Jeff made clear to me afterwards that he did not consider the evening's events the quintessential aim of his sexual life. As much as he went there for sexual gratification and entertainment, he was hoping to meet someone at the event with whom he might pursue a continuing relationship.

In the summer of 2003, Jeff had just returned from a week-long retreat with the GNI, the Gay Naturists/Gay Nudist International Association, one of several organizations he had joined since we first met. As Jeff recounted, it was a great event of continuous entertainment and sexual activity, in which 800 to 1000 gay men of all ages and shapes got together to enjoy the pleasures of nature in a remote, forested site. They were housed in comfortable cabins shared by groups of friends. They participated in grand parties as well as smaller cabin events. Jeff had sex with attractive partners in various more or less secluded locations and recounted how once, when he was sexually engaged with a handsome young man, he suddenly heard applause and realized they were being watched by an admiring crowd. Jeff admitted that this was all mostly about fun and pleasure. It was like taking part in a performance. But he was open to the possibility of pursuing a relationship with some attractive man he might meet at the retreat. And, in fact, he had made a few trips to Boston over the last year to get together with a fellow he had met at the prior camp event. As often before, however, the attraction faded, in this case, when distance, as well as work and social obligations, made it too difficult to sustain a continuing relationship.

Sometime during 2003, Jeff started a part-time, after-hours job in a sex club he used to visit sometimes. Twice a week for a few hours, he worked an evening shift as cashier at the entry door. Although not supposed to get involved with customers during work, he sometimes had an opportunity to communicate with visitors who seemed interested in his company. When we met in February 2004, he told me that a few weeks earlier he had noticed a very handsome man who made a point of telling him that he liked his looks and attitude. At the end of Jeff's shift around 4 a.m., the man went home with him, and they enjoyed a great sexual rendezvous. Adding to his pleasure, Jeff discovered that they were both Jewish. His partner was the son of Israeli immigrants. That was the good part of the story. He soon learned to his disappointment that the handsome and pleasant man was HIV positive. Jeff was still attracted, however, when, on their second encounter, he discovered he was a drug addict who went hungry at times. Jeff now avoided this once promising partner. It was about this time that Jeff shared with me two failures in his life that made him feel 'incomplete': The first was his lack of a career distinguished by professional achievement; the second was his failure to develop a stable love relationship. He missed the experience of going to bed and starting the day stretched out next to a lover.

One evening in April, Jeff and I were having dinner when he noticed a group of men at a nearby table who were regulars at his club, some of whom he had had sex with. 'They come from a good stable,' he commented, appraising them neutrally as sexual merchandise. This prompted me to repeat a question I had asked Jeff on various occasions: 'Isn't there a show of feelings when gay men engage in casual sex?' He answered: 'Heterosexuals naturally combine sex with feelings, but gays don't mix sexual pleasure with feelings. It is a cultural construct for gays!' But he added: 'Sometimes following a sexual encounter, a conversation might develop that reveals shared interests and consequently an emotional relationship might follow.' On another occasion, however, he concluded that 'sex can never be completely devoid of emotions'.

Shortly after my dinner conversation with Jeff, I had a chance to take up its subject with an acquaintance from the Community Center, a professional in his late fifties. He was in a stable relationship of many years standing with a partner of similar age. They allowed each other to go out sometimes and have sex in their chosen venues. 'We have an open relationship', he explained. I asked him whether there was an emotional component in his sexual encounters at the gay bath he occasionally visited. Without hesitation, he responded: 'No! It's a fantasy of mutual attraction. Oh, sometimes a conversation may develop if you discover shared interests, but it all ends when you prepare to go home.'

Another frequent visitor to the same bath, a single man, added some supporting evidence for this attitude, though he himself seemed somewhat frustrated by it. On a few occasions, he had felt a great sense of pleasure and a rush of affection toward his sexual partner. When he asked if they wanted to meet again, they responded positively. But when he called them, they often apologized that they were busy and promised to call back, which they never did. When I told Jeff about that behaviour, he explained it as a symptom of 'a candy shop culture.' In the heat of the moment, the partner offers a positive reaction. But when he cools off, having consumed one sweet, he is looking for a new candy. In the rich market of New York's gay life, one can always look for another novelty.

Some years ago, I was surprised to learn about a couple I knew from the synagogue being spotted separately in anonymous sex venues. Their 'infidelity', as mainstream society would term it, however, did not appear to impact their relationship, which was marked by mutual support and affection. I later learned that another much admired couple, who were together for many years, had maintained an 'open relationship'. Their ultimate separation was not a direct consequence of their fleeting affairs. A number of gay men I was acquainted with confirmed that they too maintained open relationships with their partners. They were aware they were engaged in a type of behaviour apparently inadmissible in both heterosexual and lesbian society. I gradually concluded the open relationships pattern was a credible feature in the local gay lifestyle repertoire.

I mentioned to Jeff that when I had walked by the Citicorp building earlier in the day, it was surrounded by police. Jeff said he hoped it wasn't a target for a terrorist attack. Smiling, he explained it is close to a place he cherishes: a popular bathhouse, one of the few left in New York. For Jeff, the place held many pleasant memories. When I asked him why he continued to go to the bath since he had free admission to the sex club on his off days, he explained: 'In the club I already know most customers; there's more variety, more new faces in the bath'.

A month later, Jeff told me about a new affair he had recently begun with a younger Latino he met at a private party. They had spent 36 hours together over the weekend on sex, food, long hours of conversation, and trips around town. Jeff was attracted to the man's physical beauty and was pleased with his role advising the younger man on personal issues. He was aware, however, of the difficulties that might block the development of this relationship. His new lover had unresolved family problems, only a basic education and some traditional, conservative attitudes. His work schedule was also chaotic. Jeff explained to his new friend that they had very different lifestyles, but needed each other for sex and intimacy. But after about a month of failed efforts to stabilize their connection, Jeff decided to let it go. He believed he had no need to keep the relationship going only because he enjoyed the sexual part. He could find his sexual needs gratified elsewhere with less effort.

Later in July, Jeff was delighted when he was at last approached by a man he had been interested in since first meeting him at a GNI retreat a few years before. Steven was an extremely attractive, educated professional in his early forties, and physically Jeff's type. Until now, it had been a frustrating one-sided relationship with Jeff repeatedly failing in his attempts to transform casual sexual encounters into a more serious connection. On three occasions in recent years they had happened upon each other in various venues and had sex. But Jeff's suggestions that they get together for a date, and his flattering invitations and phone calls, had all been rebuffed. So it was a great surprise when Jeff, coming home very tired from a day of work preceded by a night of sexual activity, got a phone call from Steven suggesting they meet for dinner. Jeff forgot he was tired and immediately agreed to meet later at a popular Chinese restaurant in Chelsea. For years Jeff had been disturbed by Steven's attitude: did he consider Jeff only a nice piece of meat, only a body to use and discard? But dinner went well. They spent two hours in conversation and parted kissing in the rain and agreeing to call and make a date.

When Steven called, Jeff seemed elated. They arranged to meet the next week. Steven would come directly to Jeff's place from work and shower there before dinner. No doubt, I wrote in my notes, Jeff is in love. Jeff added that he had learned from Steven that he was still in a relationship, but his sex life was not satisfying. Jeff expressed excitement about the coming rendezvous. He hoped Steven would soon leave his rocky relationship. Then, he thought, the prospects for a new partnership with Steven were on his side.

But after a few weeks of sex and warm get-togethers, Jeff realized there was not much hope for developing a more serious relationship. Among the issues was the discovery that Steven was into S&M, an interest Jeff did not share. He described himself as attracted to pleasure, not to pain. He interpreted Steven's sexual inclination and inability to commit himself to a serious relationship as related to his history of child abuse. Nevertheless, they continued to meet occasionally and enjoy physical intimacy.

A year later, in the summer of 2005, Jeff seemed to have begun a new stage in life. He spoke of the preceding year as 'my annus horribilis,' quoting Queen Elizabeth's characterization of her own trying time. Not only had he been unlucky in love, he had fallen seriously ill, been hospitalized, and slipped into a severe depression. But out of this misfortune, he hoped, would come the seeds of a better future. He had begun therapy, which helped him cope with old demons. 'He saved my life,' Jeff told me, referring to his gay therapist. Jeff concluded it was probably childhood trauma and low self-esteem that handicapped his professional and intimate life. He could now better perceive how self-defeating was his choice of incompatible mates. And sure enough, shortly after beginning therapy, he met a man at the club, a few years his junior, who seemed to be the partner he had missed for so many years. They were spending four nights a week together, but they still retained the freedom to pursue sex with other mates. Jeff had no hesitation about that 'open relationship'. To my surprised reaction, he responded, 'Why not add some meat on the side?'

Jeffrey invited his 'boyfriend', as he termed him, to join us for dessert at a Village restaurant close to his mate's apartment. One could easily sense the strong sentiment and physical attraction between them. The boyfriend, however, was not the 'cute Latino' of Jeff's erstwhile erotic vision, but a blond 'WASP' (white Anglo-Saxon Protestant) with a small bulging belly. (Jeff had often told me a flat stomach is 'a must' in gay culture.) As I walked with Jeff to his bus stop, he commented that I might feel the earth rumbling the next evening: he was getting together with his lover. When we spoke a week later, Jeff told me about their most recent time together. Jeff was working at the club in the evening and let his boyfriend in. After the friend 'played' around a while, they left together for Jeff's apartment. 'I washed and disinfected him, and we had wonderful sex for a long time.' Jeff opened his eyes the next morning, his lover a few inches from him, with happy memories of the past night.

It is still too early to conclude whether Jeff has at last reached his land of happiness and is on track to a stable love partnership. In trying to predict his prospects, I was reminded of an Israeli man I met a few years ago at the Lesbian and Gay Community Center. A good-looking computer engineer in his late thirties, he had recently 'come out' in New York, leaving behind a wife and children. He was now on an aggressive and endless search for sex in a wide variety of anonymous venues, and I was worried he was risking his health in the process. When I met him two years later, with a younger man at his side, he was completely transformed. He had stopped altogether visiting his earlier haunts and seemed engaged in a homey domesticity. 'I've been married for the last two years', he told me, proudly introducing his partner.

Nigel

I first met Nigel in the summer of 2003 at a talk at the Lesbian and Gay Community Center in Greenwich Village. He was among the few blacks present, and we struck up a conversation debating the guest speaker's ideas. We discovered mutual interest in each other's life experiences: a visiting academic from an area of international conflict and a black American engineer with an interest in international affairs. I was impressed by his skill at interviewing me—a role reversal for an anthropologist and his potential subject. I realized I was open about myself in his company, as if with a therapist. I believe that candid first encounter set the tone for our continuing relationship, which has been one of confidences shared and intimate feelings revealed. We met regularly during my visits to New York, often for brunch on Sunday. I also met a few of his friends at various events. Nigel's world-view included a belief in God, in a very universal fashion, and in reincarnation. He suggested that my having been black in my previous life explained my easy chemistry with black people.

Nigel was raised in a lower-middle-class family by a mother and a supportive stepfather. He went to college and pursued a career as a structural engineer. He was comfortable and generally content with life and work. At an early stage of our acquaintance, Nigel told me he had had a few long-standing relationships with men. But they had all failed, including the most recent—the one to which he alluded—a strong bond that had lasted for nearly two years. Though he did not regret the inevitable breakups, he would have preferred to remain in a stable relationship. As we were strolling down Sixth Avenue one Sunday afternoon taking in the annual Brazilian street fair, Nigel pointed out a few men he considered his 'type'. They were slim, dark and masculine in appearance. He added that he liked men who looked and acted masculine, but were submissive in bed. Nigel believed that his taste in men was taken from the image of his stepfather. He had an early memory as a toddler of watching this man's naked body. He never complained about his mother's mate, who treated him decently. When I arrived back home, I had an e-mail from Nigel with a few Internet photos of men he found erotically appealing. They were of well-developed and well-endowed black male torsos.

When we met again in February 2004, Nigel was in the process of testing out a relationship with an attractive black man from Chicago, whose photo looked not unlike those Nigel had e-mailed me. He was now anxiously awaiting his friend's visit to New York. But Nigel's report of the visit was not positive: 'It was as expected, but not hopeful.' He concluded that the fellow was not interested in having sex with him. When they were in bed together, he allowed Nigel to hold and caress him, but he did not respond. In deep disappointment, all Nigel could do was roll over in frustration. It was a serious blow to his affections. Nevertheless, Nigel invited a few close friends to a Harlem restaurant for a farewell dinner with his Chicagoan friend.

About a month later, I got together with Peter, another acquaintance from the Community Center and the first black academic with whom I had close contact. I had not seen him in a long time. When I first met Peter in 1999, I was impressed by his political convictions. I was somewhat frustrated, however. He seemed interested in my company but was rather reserved and difficult to get to know. He seemed to be testing my sincerity as a white empathetic with the problems of blacks and other minorities. Nevertheless, we continued to communicate occasionally by e-mail.

At our get-together, I told Peter about my current research interest and the groups I was studying. He asked if I had come across a fellow whose description matched that of Nigel. To my great surprise, Peter turned out to be the boyfriend Nigel had separated from two years before. In appearance and outlook they were quite different. Nigel appeared like the corporate engineer he was, and he seemed content with his position in mainstream American society. In contrast, Peter's mode was that of a 1960s radical, and he often decried the treatment of blacks and other minorities in America. On learning of my friendship with Nigel, Peter immediately told me that he still lamented the breakup, which Nigel had initiated. And he remained deeply in love with him. He asked me not to tell Nigel about our renewed acquaintance, a promise I soon regretted having made. (I kept this promise for some time but eventually revealed to Nigel that I had met Peter years before. To my relief, Nigel responded equably.)

When I next met Nigel on our way out of a group meeting, we were stopped by a woman who asked 'How's Peter doing?' 'It's over', he responded tersely. Nigel explained that the woman had not seen him in a long time and naturally assumed he was still with Peter. I asked if Peter looked like the fellow from Chicago. No, he responded, he was an intellectual, older and skinnier. Nigel continued to recount the sad separation, although it was he himself who brought about the breakup. They used to spend a lot of time together, and Peter often stayed over in his apartment. When problems started to crop up in the relationship, they agreed to see a counselor. But Nigel felt Peter was not really responsive, and his close friends were convinced the relationship was doomed.

When I got together again with Peter, he soon returned to the subject of his life with Nigel. But first he argued that blacks have a problem with intimacy. They are unable to display feelings because they worry that any inner self-revelation might be used against them. He went on to suggest that black men are taught to cruise women, something that is also expressed analogously in their gay relationships. Black women are used to looking 'into the inside of their partners, but black men look to the outside appearance, and therefore they keep on changing their mates, women or men.' He concluded that Nigel, like many other blacks, was not prepared for a long-term relationship. Peter's sudden new openness and his reflective attitude, I soon learned, were the result of therapy he had undergone since the separation with Nigel. He wanted to overcome some personal problems he thought that might have contributed to their breakup. Peter invited me to join him at several support groups he was attending for both gays and straights who wanted to break their addiction to various self-destructive habits.

I soon realized that therapy had not assuaged Peter's feeling of loss. He asked me if Nigel was seeing someone. (I refrained from the role of an informer on Nigel's love life.) He complained that the breakup had been unwarranted, and that Nigel never explained why he wanted to end the relationship, asking only that he remove his stuff from the apartment. Peter phoned Nigel every day for a month pleading with him to resume their relationship. Looking for clues to Nigel's action, Peter reflected on Nigel's habits, which seemed to him selfish. Nigel was less accommodating sexually and less needy than Peter, who wanted to engage more frequently in sex with a loving partner. Peter's disconsolation at losing Nigel was compounded by a belief that there were not many gay black candidates who were healthy, highly educated, and well employed to replace him. Nevertheless, Peter had not given up the search for sex and love. He looked for prospects in various local support groups and social organizations. He also traveled out of town, attending conferences on gender issues and going on gay retreats.

Nigel had his own view of the breakup. He had lost his tolerance for Peter's demanding attitude and his careless household habits. He had become concerned about Peter's increasing obliviousness to the world around them. And he was particularly disappointed when Peter refused to consider the counselor's advice that he go to therapy—advice he only took after the separation. To Nigel, it all meant that Peter needed help to overcome some personal problems. Nigel had no wish to resume a relationship that could not be free of the pain and jealousy Peter displayed. And although he cherished the memories of his happy days with Peter, he would not consider reconciliation.

After the disappointment of his Chicago friendship, Nigel's search for a partner turned mainly to the Internet. He only rarely went to gay bars, usually in the company of out-of-town friends, and he had no interest in gay baths or other sites that offered the possibility of short-term gratification, but little real prospect for a long-term relationship. At our weekly get-togethers, Nigel informed me of his successes and failures on the Internet. He showed me his personal ad on the Manhunt Web site. It contained his picture, dressed, from the neck down, and listed his age, taste in sex, and other interests. It noted that Nigel was not interested in casual sex but was looking for a serious relationship.

The response was not overwhelming. Over ten months of this project, Nigel calculated he contacted about ten candidates a month and was approached by five. Of these, only about three reached the phone call stage, and only one or two resulted in a face-to-face meeting. Only once did that lead to a sexual contact. Even then, Nigel was not really excited: 'I went with the flow.' In June 2004, however, a more promising contact emerged on the horizon. Nigel received a positive response from a man whose profile seemed a match for Nigel's intellectual interests and sexual preference. Anthony was black, in his late forties, a teacher enrolled in graduate studies at New York University. They met for dinner and seemed to hit it off. When Nigel got home, he found an e-mail from Anthony mentioning their mutual interest in golf and adding what seemed a sexual innuendo: 'I have a club and balls.' Nigel responded: 'We can play with balls ...'

The relationship with Anthony took some time to develop. Nigel was careful to proceed slowly with the relationship. He was aware that the lack of a sexual 'tingle', as he defined the erotic chemistry between lovers, may ultimately lead to disappointment. But he had no wish to begin the relationship with the sexual test. He was aware that even when physical and social attraction exist, sexual incompatibility may be a stumbling block. But he felt that the 'tingle' could even overcome this. Both he and Peter had identified themselves as 'tops'. But they found a solution in switching roles, and their ultimate separation was not a result of the ostensible sexual incompatibility.

It took a few more dinners and films ending in hugs and kisses before Nigel invited Anthony over one night, and they had sex. Nigel told me it was 'okay'—expressing neither excitement nor disappointment. 'We have to wait and see how it develops', he concluded. They had many shared interests in sports and movies, and he enjoyed their developing friendship and intimacy. In the meantime, Nigel was pursuing an ongoing Internet relationship with an older white musician. They exchanged a few phone calls and eventually met at the musician's home, where they had a good time discussing music and other interests. They fondled affectionately, but Nigel was careful to stop before things went too far. Nigel now seemed more ambivalent about his conviction that the ideal relationship is one based on a spiritual communication that later leads to an erotic tingle. Would the tingle prove positive with Anthony? Ironically, it had already emerged during the first rendezvous with the musician, although he conformed less to Nigel's ideal of an attractive man. In any case, Nigel was not interested in 'recreational sex' with any of his Internet acquaintances.

The relationship with Anthony developed in the next few weeks. They enthusiastically shared sport activities and met each other's friends. A close friend of Nigel asked about the slow pace of the relationship: 'Are you officially dating Anthony, or only exploring the possibility of dating him?' Nigel replied: 'I am officially exploring dating Anthony.' Anthony was away on business for a while, and Nigel went to see the musician, who lived nearby. At last, Nigel could not resist his affectionate entreaty, and they had sex. When Anthony returned and he and Nigel started to meet more regularly, some minor problems emerged including an incompatible schedule of sexual desire. Anthony slept late on the weekends, while Nigel wished to start early and have sex. Anthony was willing to have sex in the afternoon when Nigel was ready to leave for home and other engagements.

Nigel told me that while they were happy socializing together, he rated his sexual satisfaction as 4 on a scale of 10. That compared with 8 or 9 during his happy days with Peter. He reminisced about those times—when he and Peter showered together, how good he felt and how relieved of all other problems. The sexual fulfillment they experienced from the very beginning of their relationship was the 'glue' that mended the minor difficulties that emerged. But then, he continued, more serious problems began that eventually ruined their happiness. That sexual bond seemed missing in the present connection with Anthony. In contrast, Nigel commented, the one full sexual encounter he had with the musician rated an 8. But he did not consider that a sufficient basis for a serious relationship. Nor did he consider it 'recreational sex'; instead he deemed it 'charity sex', an obligatory reciprocation of the musician's enthusiasm and affection.

Later in the summer, Nigel concluded that the relationship with Anthony could not lead to a satisfactory partnership. They remained in a friendly relationship but gave up sex. When I met Anthony about then for the first time, I discovered he did not fit Nigel's 'type'. He was tall, somewhat overweight, and had a large build—not the slim 'cute' men Nigel had often pointed out as we walked around New York. In any event, Nigel was again looking for new candidates on the Internet, although he considered it a difficult venue for men his age. Visitors to the sites, both young and old, seemed to prefer younger males.

Nigel's experience on the Internet differed from that of his friend George, whom he had introduced to the gay sites. Nigel described George as a good-looking black man in his forties, a successful, politically engaged professional. He told Nigel he averaged fifty replies a month, and met a number of them, on short notice, for sex. He attributed Nigel's poor showing to his insistence on a drawn-out process of getting to know the other party first. Most men answering an Internet ad, George claimed, wanted to connect right away, 'within 30 minutes'. (Gudelunas (2005: 29) reported: 'Advertisers were interested in interacting locally, eager to move from online to offline communication.') Nigel was puzzled that with all George's successful encounters, he had no desire to meet any of these attractive and willing partners again. His friend replied, echoing Jeff's 'candy shop' metaphor: 'There are so many new attractive men to meet.'

Nigel came to believe that this attitude is characteristic of many in the younger generation—both gay and straight—who feel less responsibility toward their relationships. Many on line already have partners but are looking for one-night stands. Interested in themselves and their careers, they take advantage of the growing availability of casual sex and neglect the obligations of fidelity and married life.

About the same time Nigel was experimenting with on-line dating, I learned that another close friend of mine, from the gay synagogue, was searching for partners on the Internet. A retired academic in his late sixties, Adam never had anyone to share a long-term relationship. He was closeted throughout his professional career and re-mained obligated to his former wife and children. During the pre-AIDS days, Adam often patronized anonymous-sex venues. He spoke of the emotional excitement, the feeling of adventure, the risks, the competition, the victories and embarrassments he encountered. But he gave it all up when the AIDS epidemic started to take its toll among his close friends. His focus turned to the many gay social organizations he was active in, and among whose members he often found partners for relationships of varying duration, none long-term.

When we got together during the summer of 2004, I told Adam about Nigel's experience with gay Web sites. To my surprise, he told me he was regularly search-ing the 'silver-daddies' Web sites, which connect young and older gay men. He also related a recent experience with a man his own age he found on the Web. For their first meeting, they chose a cafeteria close to Adam's apartment. Adam was a few minutes late and was embarrassed to see his partner waiting for him at the entrance. To break the ice, Adam held out his hand and said, kiddingly, 'I'm horny.' His new acquaintance responded in kind: 'Should we go back to your place now?' So the in-troductory phase in a neutral space was skipped over and they went directly to Sam's apartment. Once there, they lay back on the sofa, hugged, kissed, gradually stripped one other, and ended up in bed. Adam said it was just wonderful. Never before had he enjoyed a feeling of intimacy and sexual pleasure to such a degree. When they had a chance to learn about each other, they found they shared a similar professional and cultural background. Adam also learned, however, that his new friend was in a long-term relationship and his Web site wandering was unknown to his partner. Adam did not mind the clandestine nature of the relationship, and they continued to meet at his place. Naively, I had assumed that Adam had reached a stage of life and of health that put him beyond an adventurous search for sex and love on the Internet. His bold quest proved me wrong.

Jeffrey, Nigel, Peter, Adam, George and the Question of Emotions

Jeffrey, Nigel, Peter, Adam and George were all looking to connect with other men. But what was the aim of their search? Sexual gratification? An intimate relationship? Or a mix of both? If both, what was the interplay between the two? How did their behaviour comport with their ideology, their claims, about gay men's physical and social connection? Have they shared a vocabulary and a set of symbols for express-ing the existential position and expectations of gay men searching for mates? (Leap 1996, Shokeid 2002). The five men presented in this paper, apart from race, were of similar background. They were of the same socioeconomic status and roughly shared the same generational experience. However, they brought to their search for partners or connections a wide range of different attitudes and approaches. Which was more representative of the general gay society is difficult to assess. Nevertheless, they seemed to share an ethos about the habits and contradictions prevalent among gay men in their sexual and emotional life.

From our limited view of him, George, whose success online Nigel envied, ap-pears to most embody the paradigm expressed by Jeffrey and others that gay men separate sexual pleasure from feelings. His aim was solely physical, and to Nigel's puzzlement, he had no interest in pursuing any further involvement with the men he met for sex. George had age in his favor and perhaps other factors as well, but their comparative experience suggests that George's approach better conformed to the expectations of those looking to connect on-line than did Nigel's.

Nigel, by contrast, seems his friend's polar opposite. He was not looking for an encounter that was only sexual. Instead, he was looking exclusively for a long-term relationship. He was not indifferent to the sexual component, however. He had a deeply implanted ideal physical type, and he believed in the importance of erotic chemistry—'the tingle'—and sexual compatibility in a relationship. He hoped the sex would rate high on his 10-point scale, both for itself and the strength it gave the social bond. But he had a firm belief that the ideal relationship was one in which the erotic emerges from the spiritual connection between the parties. This convic-tion was concretized into a code that precluded his acting out his sexual urge when first meeting someone to whom he was physically drawn. Instead, he would delay materializing the erotic attraction until he had tested his potential partner's suitability in social, cultural and other personal terms. It was that incubation period, he believed, that allowed the emergence of the emotional bond. A partner who passed the first test but failed the later sexual test, however, would be relegated to the status of a friend.

Peter, I had the impression, was first and foremost looking for social, cultural and personal camaraderie. He was more accommodating in his sexual taste and expectations and, when partnered, had adjusted to Nigel's sexual preferences. Adam seemed to resemble Peter in his search for partners with whom, above all, he seemed socially and culturally compatible. He had long ago given up anonymous sex venues. His behaviour in recent years, I believe, reflected changes in his personal circumstances—family situation and age—as well as those of the gay scene.

Jeff's behaviour seemed more complex and more contradictory. Nevertheless, there is reason to believe he is not unique in this type of comportment. On the one hand, Jeff was clearly searching for a long-term partner. Like Nigel, he believed that sexual attraction and compatibility were a requirement for a durable emotional relationship. But their approach to achieving that end differed markedly. For Jeff, no prospective relationship of any duration could materialize without the immediate realization of an erotic attraction. He had to have sex with the partner before any other quality could be considered. It was only when compatibility in this arena was confirmed that Jeff would look to other issues that might sustain or doom the relationship. For Jeff, a lasting 'emotional' connection required 'good sex' substantiated by other criteria of personal compatibility. A good sexual mate would be discarded and the emotional connection halted if the mate was later discovered to be unsuitable in social, cultural or psychological terms.

On the other hand, Jeff was also a regular at sex venues, where, in his terms, he 'got his rocks off' with men he had no interest in forming a relationship with. He claimed—sincerely, I believe—that when he went to the bath or the club it was for an evening purely of sex. It was devoid of any emotional investment or expectation. In this regard, his behaviour conformed to the 'gay cultural construct', as he defined it, which separates sexual fun from 'serious feelings'. This division was borne out, in most instances, by the results of his and others' encounters in these sites. The statistics supported his analytical supposition. (That claim may also have served both him and others as a defence mechanism against the potential disappointment or humiliation of being unceremoniously deserted after a sexual encounter.)

Exceptions—and there were more than a few—however, sometimes prove rules. And Jeff's claims notwithstanding, all the relationships he pursued were with partners he had met in sex sites, venues that would seem to discourage, if not preclude, the emergence of lasting emotional bonds and the development of long-term, committed, partnerships. This is not surprising given Jeff's insistence that the sex test was the first and most basic criterion for pursuit of a relationship. But it is at odds with his categorical avowal that sexual pleasure and feelings were separate in these venues. He did occasionally qualify this claim, however, with the acknowledgement that post-sex conversation sometimes revealed shared background, interests, and temperament that might lead to a relationship.

It seems that much has changed in the role of the venues identified as 'anonymous sex' institutions. For many years, gay connections remained much invisible in the public domain. Anonymous sex venues, sleazy or more elegant in their decorum, functioned in Humphreys' conception (1970) as vending machines, providing quickly, safely (to an extent) and inexpensively (both in social and economic terms), a needed commodity. They 'saved' their clients from the risks, but also deprived them of the opportunities of developing emotional attachments. Many of the old establishments survived and many new ones have emerged since the days of gay liberation. The expansion of the commercial market of sexual gratification and the variety of new venues had a double meaning. The new liberation made it easier for these institutions to flourish with little public intervention and without the aura of stigma of its participants. But the expectations of its patrons were also undergoing an important change. The 'vending machine' economy of sexual release and fun did not exclude any longer the prospects of expanding the casual connections made on the premises of these sites into a new type of more stable relationship. The reputation and the symbolic position of theses sites, however, have not changed much in spite of the changing benefits of participation.

Of the gay male couples I knew from the various institutions I studied, many had first met in anonymous sex sites. These venues offered an opportunity to meet a wide variety of gay men, who could be pursued with little introduction and free of the ordinary rituals and rules of interaction expected not only in mainstream society, but in the more conventional gay social environments as well. But a long-term partnership was not the usual outcome from a sexual encounter there. As easy as they were to initiate, these encounters did not usually provide more personal sharing beyond the physical. Indeed, there was a deeply rooted belief there that sex and feelings would remain separate domains. This perception allowed them to even be treated as safe spaces for long-term partners to act out their sexuality without threatening the emotional bond between the mates.

From a heterosexual perspective, one might react in puzzlement (or perhaps, in admiration), in view of the transformation of the Judeo-Christian credo that sanctifies sex in marriage, as demonstrated in our observations. A number of couples I knew, or were acquainted with, maintained an 'open relationship' and, indeed, did take advantage of the presumed emotional neutrality of these places. Men in long-term relationships, with the consent of their partners or with uninformed liberty, occasionally visited anonymous sex sites. They claimed that the sexual connections made there were devoid of emotional involvement. They used various metaphors to express that idea, such as, 'these are fantasies', 'infatuations at the heat of the moment', harmless temptations of the 'candy shop society'. Jeff, as we have seen, took his then new boyfriend to the sex club while he worked. Even the scrupulous Nigel got together with his musician friend while Anthony, with whom he was developing a relationship, was out of town.

Among the men in the study, as well as others I have met, there appeared to dominate a complex of attitudes and emotions toward sexuality that differed from that considered normative in the heterosexual world. Whether this represented the majority of gay society is a question well beyond this study. But it seemed prevalent enough to constitute an ethos among the men I came to know. The men profiled here often spoke of a type of behaviour, in what they defined as the 'gay culture', that was carefree in its attitudes and activities in the sexual domain. This was not the heterosexual ethos, which in spite of its many transgressions—places sex within an emotional connection. That gay world view legitimated sex without an emotional involvement. Nigel, whose own behaviour conformed more to the heterosexual ideal, still recognized the prevalence of another ethos, one he decried.

But this did not mean they were not interested in sex with affectionate intimacy or a long-term relationship. In fact, they were engaged in a continual search for long-term partners. This effort was a permanent element in their daily life and was conducted in a variety of venues. These included social organizations, such as synagogues, churches, voluntary associations, and support groups of all type; commercial sites, such as bars and those offering 'anonymous sex'; and the new rich field for cruising and matchmaking, the Internet. The details of this quest were also a field of experience that was shared with friends and even former lovers. The men in my study were remarkably verbal about their feelings and were regularly analyzing and interpreting their fortunes in their quest for mates.

The eagerness with which they pursued this aim belied, at times, their allegiance to what they deemed the 'gay cultural' sexual ethos. Jeffrey, for instance, was concerned that he was being viewed as a piece of meat by his erstwhile partner, though he himself described others in those terms. Even seemingly carefree, unencumbered encounters—'getting your rocks off'—could be freighted with subtextual meanings, as well as hopes for emotional intimacy. This was also likely the case for the wider population of men with whom they interacted in their search. The continual 'trial and error' process they were engaged in reflected a yearning for a stable relationship.

In sum, can we designate a pattern that indicates a cultural construction of emotions apparent in the perspective and behaviours of the gay men presented in our ethnography? If there is a specific vocabulary for the culture of emotions in our observations, it made its impact in a set of symbols that projected first that gay men are necessarily and continuously on the search for partners for sex and intimacy. Under these premises it is also deemed that sexual compatibility is paramount whether it is tested at first meeting or later (nevertheless, serious relationships were not necessarily with men who suited a preconceived fantasy of the erotic male body). That vocabulary informed about the frequency of 'open relationships', it sustained the ability to talk about sex with friends, and it promoted the continuing of friendships with former sex partners. Differentiated from the code of heterosexual mating and bonding, the contract of gay coupled relationships does not seem to be universally threatened with the sanctioned mainstream society condemnation of extra-marital fornication. The pleasure of 'pure' sex, although indispensable for a continuing bonding, nevertheless did not appear in the narratives I collected a monopoly of the partners to a stable bond.

The mass media and some research indicate attitudes and behaviours apparently prevalent among heterosexuals that remind one of the narratives presented above. However, these are not expressed in terms of a cultural code and a vocabulary legitimate in mainstream society. It is tempting to close our presentation with another query: As Western culture changes with greater acceptance of homosexuality (gay marriage etc.), will the gay ethos of sex and emotions evolve and infiltrate toward the heterosexual? Will they converge somewhere in between?

Acknowledgements

I thank Edward Pass for his helpful comments and editorial suggestions (he also raised the closing query in my presentation). My deepest thanks go to the men who shared with me their experiences, their thoughts and feelings.

References

Adam, B. D. (1992), 'Sex and Caring among Men: Impact of AIDS on Gay People', in K. Plumer (ed.), *Modern Homosexualities,* pp. 175–83, London: Routledge.

Bronski, M. (2000), *The Pleasure Principle: Sex, Backlash, and the Struggle for Gay Freedom,* New York: St. Martin Press.

Crapanzano, V. (1980), *Tuami: Portrait of a Moroccan,* Chicago: University of Chicago Press.

Delany, S. R. (1999), *Time Square Red, Time Square Blue,* New York: New York University Press.

Delph, E. W. (1978), *The Silent Community: Public Homosexual Encounters,* Beverly Hills, Calif.: Sage.

Eickelman, D. F. (1985), *Knowledge and Power in Morocco: The Education of a Twentieth-Century Notable,* Princeton, N.J.: Princeton University Press.

Forrest, D. (1994), '"We're Here, We're Queer, and We're Not Going Shopping": Changing Gay Male Identities in Contemporary Britain', in A. Corrnwall and N. Lindisfarne (eds), *Dislocating Masculinities: Comparative Ethnographies,* pp. 97–110, London: Routledge.

Geertz, C. (1973), *The Interpretation of Cultures,* New York: Basic.

Gudelunas, D. (2005), 'Online Personal Ads: Community and Sex, Virtually', *Journal of Homosexuality,* 49: 1–34.

Harre, R. (1986), *The Social Construction of Emotions,* Oxford: Basil Blackwell.

Herdt, G. H. (1981), *Guardians of the Flutes: Idioms of Masculinity*, New York: McGraw-Hill.

Hochschild, A. R. (2003), *The Commercialization of Intimate Life*, Berkeley: University of California Press.

Humphreys, L. (1970), *Tearoom Trade: Impersonal Sex in Public Places*, Chicago: Aldine.

Kennedy, L. E., and Davis, M. D. (1993), *Boots of Leather, Slippers of Gold: The History of a Lesbian Community*, New York: Routledge.

Kulick, D. (1998), *Travesty: Sex, Gender and Culture among Brazilian Transgendered Prostitutes*, Chicago: University of Chicago Press.

Lancaster, R. N. (1988), 'Subject Honor and Object Shame: The Construction of Male Homosexuality and Stigma in Nicaragua', *Ethnology* 27: 111–26.

Langness, L. L., and Frank, G. (1981), *Lives: An Anthropological Approach*, Nevato, Calif.: Chandler & Sharp Publishers.

Leap, W. L. (1996), *Word's Out: Gay Men's English*, Minneapolis and London: University of Minnesota Press.

Leap, W. (1999), *Public Sex/Gay Space*, New York: Columbia University Press.

Levy, R. I. (1973), *Tahitians: Mind and Experience in the Society Islands*, Chicago: University of Chicago Press.

Levy, R. I. (1984), 'Emotion, Knowing, and Culture', in R. A. Shweder and R. A. Levine (eds), *Culture Theory: Essays on Mind, Self, and Emotion*, pp. 214–37, Cambridge: Cambridge University Press.

Lewin E. (1993), *Lesbian Mothers: Accounts of Gender in American Society*, Ithaca, N.Y.: Cornell University Press.

Lewis, O. (1967), *La Vida*, London: Martin Sacker & Warburg.

Lutz, C. (1986), 'Emotion, Thought, and Estrangement: Emotion as a Cultural Category', *Cultural Anthropology* 1: 287–309.

Lynch, O. M., ed. (1990), *Divine Passions: The Social Construction of Emotion in India*, Berkeley: University of California Press.

Malinowski, B. (1927), *Sex and Repression in Savage Society*, London: Routledge & Kegan Paul.

Malinowski, B. (1929), *The Sexual Life of Savages*, New York: Halcyon House.

Meyers, F. R. (1979), 'Emotions and the Self: A Theory of Personhood and Political Order among Pintupi Aborigines', *Ethos* 7: 343–70.

Myers, F. (1988), 'The Logic and Meaning of Anger among Pintupi Aborigines', *Man*, New Series, 23: 589–610.

Myerhoff, B. (1978), *Number Our Days*, New York: Simon and Schuster.

Newton, E. (1993), *Cherry Grove, Fire Island: Sixty Years in America's First Gay and Lesbian Town*, Boston: Beacon.

Rapport, N. (2003), *I Am Dynamite: An Alternative Anthropology of Power*, London and New York: Routledge.

Rechy, J. (1977), *The Sexual Outlaw*, New York: Grove.

Rosaldo, M. Z. (1984), 'Towards an Anthropology of Self and Feeling', in R. A. Shweder and R. A. Levine (eds), *Culture Theory: Essays on Mind, Self, and Emotion,* pp. 137–57, Cambridge: Cambridge University Press.

Scruton, R. (2001), *Sexual Desire: A Philosophical Investigation,* London: Phoenix Press.

Shokeid, M. (1995), *A Gay Synagogue in New York,* New York: Columbia University Press (an augmented edition, University of Pennsylvania Press, 2003).

Shokeid, M. (2001a), 'Our Group Has a Life of Its Own: An Affective Fellowship of Older Gay Men in New York City', *City & Society* 13: 5–30.

Shokeid, M. (2001b), 'You Don't Eat Indian and Chinese Food at the Same Meal: The Bisexual Quandary', *Anthropological Quarterly* 75: 63–90.

Shokeid, M. (2002), 'Sexual Addicts Together: Observing the Culture of SCA Gay Groups in New York', *Social Anthropology* 10: 189–210.

Shokeid, M. (n.d.), 'Erotics and Politics in the Agenda of an Interracial Gay Men's Association in New York', a paper prepared for a forthcoming festschrift in honor of Professor Georg Pfeffer at the Free University Berlin.

Shostak, M. (1981), *Nisa: The Life and Words of a Kung Woman,* Cambridge, Mass.: Harvard University Press.

Style, J. (1979), 'Outsider/Insider: Researching Gay Baths', *Urban Life* 8: 135–52.

Vance, C. S. (1991), 'Anthropology Rediscovers Sexuality: A Theoretical Comment', *Social Science and Medicine* 33: 875–84.

Weitman, S. (1998), 'On the Elementary Forms of the Socioerotic Life', *Theory Culture & Society* 15: 71–111.

Wikan, U. (1990), *Managing Turbulent Hearts: A Balinese Formula for Living,* Chicago: University of Chicago Press.

–21–

From Rational Calculation
to Sensual Experience
The Marketing of Emotions in Advertising

Timothy de Waal Malefyt

Over the last fifty years the economic base has shifted from production to consumption. It has gravitated from the sphere of rationality to the realm of desire: from the objective to the subjective; to the realm of psychology. (Muschamp, 1999: C2)

When a person buys a service, he purchases a set of intangible activities carried out on his behalf. But when he buys an experience, he pays to spend time enjoying a series of memorable events that a company stages—as a theatrical play—to engage him in a personal way. (Pine and Gilmore, 1999: 2)

This chapter discusses a current marketing trend[1] and concomitant new consumer model that reflect a major shift in the way advertisers market to consumers. The classic advertising view of marketing to consumers, I claim, no longer follows a rational choice model of consumer decision making, which has been based roughly on discourse and sign value (reading and writing) modes of communication but rather embraces an emotive sensory model based on marketers' notions of consumers' experience and emotions with brands. Advertisers now conceptualize and practise brand communication as a form of experiential exchange with consumers in their attempt to market directly to consumer emotions. The shift towards more engaging consumer advertising is most evident in the new media venues that advertisers use. Passive modes of television, radio and print, which are heavily image and language dependent, have dropped precipitously over the years in favor of more interactive modes of marketing, including the Internet, in-store displays, public relations marketing, direct mail, trade promotions, product placement, event sponsorships, and viral marketing.

New York Times writer Stuart Elliot, reports that ad agencies such as BBDO Worldwide Advertising increasingly devote more attention and resources to various media markets to spread ads from big budget television ads to more interactive campaigns. General Electric, one of BBDO's largest clients, boasts that on-line marketing is the fastest growing part of its overall advertising budget, along with viral marketing and advertising through cell phones and online games (Elliot 2005b). Even traditional television advertisements have become more experientially focused. For instance, McCann Erickson's present campaign for MasterCard provides no information about the card's features, but rather attempts to evoke sentimental support in using the card for 'priceless' moments such as in one execution where a grandmother and a granddaughter cook together after having purchased ingredients with MasterCard. To put this change in perspective, US advertisers in 1965 could reach 80 per cent of the most coveted viewers (audiences aged 18 to 49) through the three existing major television networks of CBS, NBC and ABC. Today, more than one hundred television channels and six major networks compete for only 30 per cent of the same target audience (Auletta 2005). I claim that as advertisers are using more sensory stimulating forms of media and more emotional marketing messages they have also created a different kind of awareness of the consumer, one that makes product choices with emotions rather reason. In advertising terms, this shift in marketing messages and media outlets reflects the reprioritized importance of experiential and emotional approaches to consumer marketing over those deemed functional and rational.

While the literature on consumption in culture has raised our awareness to the dynamics of local and global forces in producing and consuming advertising, most critiques have created advertising mainly for its discursive nature or sign value. From Williamson's (1978) textual analysis of advertising's structures, and Jhally's (1987) and Marchand's (1985) 'decoding' of advertising's social messages, adverts have been labeled an empire of signs, a discourse of persuasion, and a system of symbols, among other terms. Lash and Urry assert that advertising promotes a global culture industry of image and discourse production, which is 'supremely visual' (1994: 138). Goldman and Papson claim Nike speaks to the 'penetration of more and more social spaces through the discourse of signs and logos' (1998: 18). For Perry, the object of Benetton's United Colors campaign is to 'cannibalize existent cultural meaning' in order to construct 'signs of distinction' (Perry 1998: 37). Mazzarella's recent ethnographic study on advertising in India describes brand advertising as 'a process of commodity image production' (2003a:202). Moreover, while these views treat advertising largely as a production of signs and symbols, they also assume that the effects of advertising can be 'read' and discussed from a general, public point of view. Williamson's seminal work (1978) informs readers about the codes of advertisements, which to her are readable texts about production and consumption, and whose effects create desires in a consumer society seeking to sell what is produced. Marchand (1985) also assumes a certain 'read' on advertising and society, especially from the era of the 1920s and 1930s when mass media helped shape ideas for many new immigrants arriving to the US. O'Barr likewise follows this line of analysis, when he claims that the larger flows of 'advertising discourse' and 'public ideology' operate to 'support and buttress the social order of a society based on mass production and consumption' (1994: 2–3).

Lacking in these critiques is any embodied sense of consumers' sentiments or personal experiences with brands, especially through the many interactive modes of media they encounter. Beyond the generalized 30-second spot or the printed page, what are the different effects, real or imagined, of individualized and directed marketing approaches to consumers which are customized to a user's style of consumption? Other ethnographic studies, such as Kemper (2001), Lien (1997), Malefyt and Moeran (2003), Miller (1997), and Moeran (1996, 2005) attempt to integrate the effects of consumer experience with advertised messages. Taking Appaudari's observation that advertising inculcates a sentimental nostalgia for commodities, albeit vacant of associated consumer experience (1996: 77–8), this chapter explores the ways in which advertisers attempt to use various media channels and marketing methods to incorporate back into commodity production those very sentiments and individual sensations consumers experience in consumption. Rather than view advertising as public discourse or a text to be read, this chapter holds that ads are directed increasingly to embody personal and private meaning for consumers, as marketers strive for more customized ways to create individualized experiences for their brands.

On one level, this chapter claims that while visual auditory messages of advertising have been associated with rationality and reason and their importance through traditional media has waned, experience-based notions of advertising are associated with consumers' embodied senses and emotions, and their significance through new media has waxed prolifically. This redirection of advertising to consumers' emotions isn't a mere passing phase. Rather, this shift heralds the new reign of emotional over rational marketing approaches. As forecasted in the introduction to *Advertising Cultures,* it speaks to a new mode of human enquiry that anthropologists once held: 'the kind of study of emotion in culture that began in American anthropology, and was highlighted in the work of Ruth Benedict, has come to be almost fetishized in marketing' (Malefyt and Moeran, 2003: 24). Since corporate clients increasingly hold their agencies accountable for advertising's effectiveness, advertisers have responded by placing greater emphasis on consumer research that elicits emotions to determine the best return on investment (Elliot 2005a: C10). Citing a recent Annual Advertising Research Foundation conference in New York City, *New York Times* writer Stuart Elliot notes that marketing to emotions is suddenly popular in an industry that historically snubbed research. Elliot quotes Bruce Hall, a partner and research director of Howard, Merrell & Partners, who states: 'You can ask people what they think about an ad, but until you move them on an emotional level, their behavior will not change' (C10). The following discussion on marketing a brand of prepared chicken for home delivery shows that selling to consumers' emotions is not only about a new direction in marketing consumption, but also about adding strategic value to an ad agency by maximizing a client's return on investment: the embodied consumer emotion.

On another level, I claim that this shift from the marketing of information and reason to the marketing of sensation and emotion has an added benefit for advertisers. This benefit centers on customizing the value of the brand to the consumer. Because brands are so amorphous and ambiguous, and yet so central to advertising's strategic development, marketing activities and client relations, they have come to represent highly charged conceptual forces that can be bent to suit particular ends. Just as brand advertising has evolved from promoting a product's functional features to its sensory experience to be more effective, I argue that advertising's priorities have also shifted from promoting straightforward general information to consumers—which is subject to public scrutiny—to producing messages that are more private, individually interpretive, and thus less open to criticism.

This shift from marketing to the public sphere of commodities, to the private sphere of embodied experiences importantly allows advertisers to tailor consumer, brand and ultimately client relations along strategic lines. Advertisers can develop a range of marketing activities labeled as 'emotional' or 'experiential' for their client's consumer, not only to gain more corporate business and secure a longer-term investment with their client, but to reduce public scrutiny that has thwarted advertising campaigns in the past. Thus by revealing the way marketers load messages into consumer sensations in various media modalities I will show that advertisers gain in two strategic ways. First, marketing to consumers through an extended range of media modalities lets advertisers, in a sense, expand the value of the consumer. Such interactive methods let the advertiser make more out of the consumer-brand interaction, hence securing current and potential opportunities for advertisers to serve their corporate client. Second, marketing to the ambiguous nature of 'embodied consumer experiences' lets advertisers make more of the private relationship consumers have with brands, and from their interpretation of that ambiguity, claim more effective ad response while reducing public accountability. This shift from reason to emotions becomes clear when we examine how advertising is intended to work.

From Rational Commodity Images to Branded Emotional Experiences

According to advertising communication theory, the notion of consumer persuasion is based on appealing to a prospective buyer's sense of choice (Beeman 1986). For advertisers, this means crafting messages that let the consumer distinguish one product from another through a benefit that adds real or perceived value (Davidson 1994). Apparent product differentiation isn't new since, as Douglas and Isherwood (1979) posit, in a world of goods, items always exist relative to other goods through positions that signify relations of difference. Moeran (1996) notes that relations of contrast and difference are how Levi-Strauss alleged 'primitive cultures' classified and understood their world. In the world of marketing, perceived difference is the central principle by which advertisers produce brand messages for consumers in the first place.

The traditional marketing model of differentiation is predicated on a consumer who distinguishes one brand from another by factual information and 'common-sense' reason. In the 1960s advertising legend David Ogilvy evidenced this approach with ads that were copy-heavy and singular in image. He inveterately maintained that effective ads should let the 'facts' speak for themselves, and declared, 'If your advertising is going to be successful, if it is going to stand out from the clutter, you must be objective about the benefits of your product' (1985:109). He famously stated that more facts are better:

> The consumer isn't a moron; she is your wife. You insult her intelligence if you assume that a mere slogan and a few vapid adjectives will persuade her to buy anything. She wants all the information you can give her. (Ogilvy 1971:96)

Following his 'factual' line of reasoning, a product of better quality should apparently, that is, rationally stand out from its competitors. This orientation not only favors a visual modality of attention but also informs a rational hierarchy of messaging communication by which advertisers rank and order human sensibilities as well as understand the consumer process of commodity selection. According to the timely volume, *Empire of the Senses* (2005), David Howes notes that Western culture customarily associates discursive reason with rational thinking and planning aspects of culture and civilization. Beginning with the ancient Greeks, Plato and Aristotle respectively ranked vision and audition as the higher senses of rational perception, while relegating tactile, taste and smell to the realm of unruly base emotions (Synnott 1991:62).

Nonetheless, if vision and audition rank higher as perceptual means for differentiating a product, would advertisers prioritize another consumer approach that markets to all the senses, including the unruly base emotions? Indeed, at the fifty-first annual advertising research foundation convention in New York City, author Martin Lindstrom, reiterates that marketers are recognizing the importance of selling to 'all the senses'. He claims that Ford automobiles focuses on the sound of its doors closing; Singapore Airlines has patented their 'warm towel' smell; and counterfeit Crayola brand crayons were detected because they didn't have the identifiable Crayola scent. To be sure, as Howes aptly points out in his chapter on Hyperaesthesia (2005: 288), marketers and advertisers are now producing messages with sensations in every media modality, thereby attempting to blitz or otherwise bypass reason by means of emotions. I would add that, since the sensory realm of vision and audition are still largely marketed to in emotionally stimulating ways, the issue for marketers is not whether vision and audition are 'dated' channels for consumer marketing, but rather, that they are largely associated with reason in the public sphere, and advertising to a general 'rational' public has been the bane of advertisers.

For over a century, US advertisers produced advertisements biased towards a generalized population. In fact, early ad images were conspicuously absent of ethnic differences or gender equalities and reflected instead the self-restrained order of dominant white Protestant males (O'Barr 1994). O'Barr continues, stating that advertising 'has tended throughout the twentieth century to treat the American public as a colourless, English-speaking mass audience of rather uniform tastes, preferences, and sensibilities (1994: ix). Along these lines, historian Daniel Boorstin, in *The Americans,* notes: 'Advertising has done far more than persuade, state, or convey information. It is a kind of declaration of equality. It assumes a mass market. It thrives on tastes that are completely average. It serves the desires of the largest possible number. It certainly attempts to reflect the hopes and fears of the majority, and cannot escape identifying itself with them' (1965: 88–89). To be sure, advertisers in the past not only undifferentiated their audience as a uniform white target, but broadly (mis)directed their messages towards the general visual media of television, radio and print, for which they received much criticism.[2] Indeed, the increased individuality of our society, the proliferation of multiethnic groups, the advancement of affirmative action, and women's prominence in economics and politics, as well as other specialized social categories, have necessitated a change in the mode and channels of advertising, against any type of generalized message.

As a consequence, advertisers have begun to take a less general 'rational' approach by marketing to consumers with targeted messages through specific media that are more personalized, customized and sensory-engaging. As marketing expert Richard Levey states at the Annual Advertising Research Foundation conference in New York City, traditional 'rational' marketing approaches have failed because 'they overestimate the reasoning power of consumers, and ignore the way people actually think and make decisions' (Levey 2004: 22). Businesses currently attempt to bypass reason by directing multimedia campaigns directly to consumer experiences and internal sensations, an approach that Howes terms 'the new sensual logic of late capitalism' (2005: 281). This new mode of marketing not only reflects a belief that brand selection and consumer loyalty can link directly to consumer emotions and sensual experience, but also engenders a way for marketers to eschew public rejection by focusing on the individual.

Customized Marketing: Targeting Emotions in Consumer Experience

Faced with a deluge of similar products and services competing across audio and visual channels, marketers realize that the sign image and authoritative voice of brands in the public commodity market is overwhelmed. Marketing experts Ries and Trout exhort that we live in an age of 'too many products, too many companies, and too much marketing noise' (1986: 5). The contemporary consumer is simply too overtaxed with myriad choices to make a sound 'rational' decision. Marc Gobe, an expert on 'emotionalizing' brands, claims that consumers are introduced to over three thousand new brands each year and so cannot distinguish between one cola and another, one sneaker and its competitor, or the many different kinds of jeans, coffees or gas stations. Amid this 'ocean of offerings, all fighting for the same consumer dollar,' he claims, 'the emotional connection is what makes that all-important, essential difference' (2001: xxvi).

The recent 'discovery' of emotions and experience-based marketing has no immediate architect but is likely attributed to the successful publication of *The Experience Economy* (1999). In their work, Pine and Gilmore detail the way progressive companies have moved beyond rational branding approaches, which treat their goods as commodities, to more experiential approaches, which stage their brands as personalized experiences. Disney, Starbucks and Harley Davidson are held as examples of successful experiential brands which continuously improve their product offerings, by making them more emotionally engaging and sensorily stimulating for consumers. Writer Jeanette McMurtry claims that Harley Davidson taps experientially into an emotional connection with its consumers. She cites the passionate consumer who, for instance, not only brandishes Harley tattoos and wears distinctive Harley clothing, but belongs to one of over 1,200 Harley Owners Group (HOG) chapters that hold rallies nationwide, where 650,000 Harley customers 'ride together, bond together, and speak passionately about their Harleys, thus strengthening their brand commitment' (McMurtry, 2004).

Consumer trends writer Virginia Postrel details how Starbucks became a successful experiential brand. Beyond serving coffee, it offers an environment abundant in rich textures, colours, aromas, taste treats, and music, which induces a respite from the busy world. She claims, 'Starbucks is to the age of sensory aesthetics what McDonalds was to the age of convenience or Ford was to the age of mass production' (2003: 20). In another book on experiential marketing, Dan Hill in *Body of Truth* advocates marketing products directly to consumers' bodies—through their senses—claiming that 'below the surface of rational thought, the five senses interpret the world, and they dictate emotional responses to the environment and different stimuli' (2003: 2). Harvard marketing guru, Gerald Zaltman, likewise, asserts that, while consumer decision making involves rational consideration, consumer choice is emotionally driven. He claims that sensations influence emotions and cognition to affect overall behaviour, such that, 'a Nestle crunch bar has immediate sensory benefits such as taste, texture, and sound. But these benefits also evoke powerful emotional benefits, such as fond memories of childhood and feelings of security' (2003: 19).

Indeed, the proliferation of personally engaging marketing approaches has launched what Howes calls, 'the progressive privatization of sensation' (Howes 2005: 287). This trend of marketing directly to consumer sentiments through sensations has gained rapid ascension perhaps because it closely accords with Western assumptions about emotional embodiment. According to Lutz (1998), Western belief holds that human emotions link directly to physical feelings and sensations of the body and lie in direct contrast to thought and reason, which are viewed as purely mental phenomena. For marketers, this sort of assumption fuels the drive towards more privatization of sensation and emotions, since producing brands that are personally meaningful to consumers moves the focus of brand messages and consumer research away from the public realm of visual and auditory channels, to the private realm of feelings, tastes and emotional responses. Advertising research now depends on personalized consumer feedback for developing its communications. Jon Steel, a leading figure in account planning, advocates that advertising is only effective when it involves consumers in intimate 'dialogue'.

> First, [advertising] needs to involve [people] in the process of developing the communication. Their feelings, habits, motivations, insecurities, prejudices, and desires all have to be explored to understand both how the product fits into their lives and how they might respond to different advertising messages The second way that consumers need to be involved in advertising is in the communication itself. In other words, advertising works better when it does not tell people what to think, but rather allows them to make up their own minds about its meaning. They participate by figuring it out for themselves. (Steel 1998: 5–6)

For advertisers, the appeal that sensory messages speak directly to consumers' emotions is compelling. Such an idea not only imparts the notion of an exclusive relationship with the individual's private 'inner' world over the public 'outer' world, a division that accords with the western worldview (Ryle 2002: 83), but also invokes the myth of the authentic self versus the disingenuous public world. Along these lines, Lutz informs us that in the West, emotions and sensations not only unequivocally identify the private self in opposition to public reason and intellect, but that 'emotion is held as a sole essential aspect of the individual, the seat of the true and glorified self' (1998: 56). According to Lutz, 'things of the heart (the emotions) are commonly seen as the true, real seat of the individual self, and things of the head (thoughts) as relatively superficial, socially influenced aspects of the self' (1998: 68). Dan Hill reiterates this distrust of 'superficial' rational thought by advising marketers to 'deeply' pursue 'the (emotive) hearts and (sensory) bones' of consumers (2003: 134). Increasingly apparent about marketing interest in the consumer's embodied experience is not what is 'shallowly' thought about a brand, but what is 'deeply' felt towards it.

> Experiences that trigger the senses entertain, though the effects fade as new stimuli arrive. Experiences that engage the mind inform and satisfy, but their impact diminishes as thoughts move on to something else. The most compelling experiences though are emotionally affective—they may pause at the sensory and rational levels. But they eventually touch the heart and linger there. (Robinette, Brand, and Lenz 2001: 76)

Evoked in this passage is the metaphor of the 'inside', which not only assumes that the true essence of consumer motivation and brand loyalty lie deep within the individual, but also conceptually allows marketers to direct their messages to a place concealed from public scrutiny. By selling consumers private (emotional) experiences over public (rational) commodities, advertisers are assured that, if what counts for advertising can be challenged, what counts for the way people feel about it cannot.

The emotional-experiential marketing framework has another implication for advertisers. It also indicates a way for marketers to esteem their client's consumers and brand through directed market research. As marketing to consumers aims to be more sensory, personal and immune to attacks from the outside public realm, the consumer–brand experience has become more idealized from within advertising agencies. In the following case study, I trace how market research of the consumer experience with home-delivered chicken allows advertisers to expand the consumer–brand relationship for their corporate client. Such apparent regard and pursuit of the consumer's emotional experience leads to an idealization, even fetishization of their consumer (see Miller 1997, Moeran 1996). The terms and marketing methods advertisers use among themselves and their corporate clients to describe consumer experience and consumer emotive states facilitates a greater sense of affinity between agency and client through a mutual understanding of their subject.[3] As such, the marketing dimensions of the consumer–brand experience offer a framework for a new type of 'deep' relationship between ad agency and client.

Case Study: Marketing Prepared Chicken for Home Delivery

When strategizing plans for marketing ready-to-eat chicken for home delivery, advertisers used a systematic process to map out consumer–brand interactions along the lines of experience and emotions. The marketing process is outlined here during an encounter between an advertising agency and its corporate client. Before delving into the study, a brief background is necessary to explain the expanded role of agency relations with clients.

As Brian Moeran nicely details, ad agencies serve many obligations of their clients' needs beyond making advertisements. Most full-service ad agencies tout their own research and marketing departments, which include account planning, public relations, product and design development, promotional service and product placement, event planning, store distribution and sales development, as well as media and Internet divisions. This level of service is required because the client often expects the agency to fully manage or at least equally partner their brand. Full-service agencies also develop the appropriate marketing tools, either in house or through vendor relations, to provide added value for their client's brand. These tools are branded as proprietary to keep the client's brand on the edge of consumer trends, market changes, competitor breakthroughs or recalls, consumer alerts or science advances (Moeran 1996: 105).[4] The agency in this capacity not only shows itself responsible and proactive on the clients' behalf, but also is obliged to fully implement its resources and continuously develop new ones to maintain an active partnership with its clients. As Moeran puts it, agencies are always 'trying to meet [the clients'] various demands by providing a total marketing service which both gauges social changes and is thoroughly conversant with present consumer patterns' (1996: 105).

A recent tool to emerge among experiential approaches is the 'touch point' model (see Figure 21.1). This framework classifies and orders the most salient consumer–brand interactions in terms of the particular experiences a consumer has with a brand, and add up to an overall attitude towards the brand.[5] This sequence also demonstrates the way in which marketers interpret consumer experience for purposes of shaping customized media and marketing messages. Each touch point represents a strategic opportunity for marketers to explore and develop a consumer brand interaction along behavioural and emotional constructs. As such, consumer experiences and emotional needs are 'discovered' to form the basis for a marketing mix of brand messages, product placement and other marketing plans.

Advertisers of Fresh Chicken Express (a pseudonym) use the touch point model to move beyond a general consumer target: a white American mother aged thirty-five, with three plus people living at home, supported by an annual household income of $52,000, and ordering home delivered food with the frequency of 1.6 times a month.[6] While a rational approach to customer research might end at this generalized demographic profile, an experiential model looks to customize the approach on more specific consumer features.

From previous market research on mothers who routinely plan for family dinners, the advertising research team arrives at a consumer 'problem'. This mother's dinner dilemma not only must contend with what to serve her family for dinner that evening, but her problem offers fast food manufacturers, such as Fresh Chicken Express, an emotive

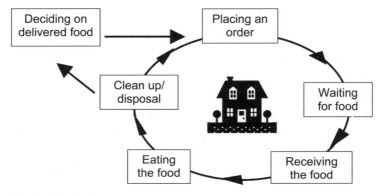

Figure 21.1 Touch point chart.

crisis they can respond to. The mother in 'crisis' is then segmented into two distinct emotional predispositions that inform a unique set of 'need states' that marketers can work with: either mothers are motivated by pressures of the day, and simply want a quick, inexpensive dinner solution; or they are motivated by a planned occasion and want an enjoyable, relaxed family dinner experience. Indeed, as Mazzarella notes, consumer need states are not 'found' in the consumer, but rather, are invented for purposes of the marketer's design (Mazzarella 2003b: 62). In this case, the construction of two distinct need states has practical implications for marketing plans. Rather than accept that consumer choice is mediated by rational thought which can be reduced or simplified to a few marketing options, an emotional need state approach explores a range of potential consumer behaviour that increases an array of marketing options. The experiential dimension of consumption is thus as much about expanding an understanding of consumer behaviour as it is about increasing the range of controllable marketing opportunities. In this way, each emotional consumer type presumes a particular relationship with the brand, which necessitates a separate media and advertising plan for an ad agency department to carry out. Each touch point scenario calls for advertisers to segment and manage the consumer–brand experience along distinct communication and media lines, which involves greater roles from the various agency departments and services. So, from the consumer touch points of deciding on delivered food, placing an order, waiting for food, getting the food, eating the food, to cleaning up, each consumer–brand experience presents an opportunity for the agency to increase its value by linking a consumer emotion to a particular marketing or media method.

From the touch point framework, the two consumer types relate experientially and emotionally to delivered chicken in distinct ways that marketers build upon. 'Hurried' mothers, the account team decides, are driven by life's daily demands, and their emotional need state is concerned with minimizing dinner preparation time and food costs. In our meeting, an agency account executive asserts that by ordering chicken for home, 'these moms are open to suggestions about trying additional menu items, or are more likely to try a new item altogether'. He continues, 'Above all, the hurried mom wants food delivered that is fast, predicable, inexpensive and satisfying'. As this construction makes clear, the service dimension of Fresh Chicken Express most immediately fulfills the consumer's anxious emotional state regarding saving time and money. And to satisfy this need state, the agency is ready to develop a specific course of action.

On the other hand, the mother who plans for a more relaxed dinner occasion invokes a different emotional state and, accordingly, calls for another marketing plan. The 'planned' mother anticipates a festive mood in serving her family chicken that may accompany watching a rented movie or inviting friends over. The construction goes further; the 'planned' mom is more likely to consult family members for menu preferences so that the physical properties of the brand's product line matter more. So, whereas the 'hurried' occasion focuses on the brand's service attributes, the 'planned' occasion centers on the brand's product attributes. The experiential dimensions of the consumer–brand interaction thus provide two distinct lines of marketing and media opportunities, out of which additional opportunities arise.

In agency–client discussions about the first touch point, of deciding to order chicken, an agency account supervisor states that the hurried mother is predisposed to feed her family quickly and affordably, with little thought of seeking consensus. Since fast service is held as the primary need, this mother, he claims, seeks prepackaged offers and whole meal specials over configuring a meal herself. In this regard, he states, 'We can respond to her needs by developing communication that is simple and clear, and offer her specials and value priced deals'. The agency media planner then recommends a tactic to reach the hurried mom by airing heavily on radio during prime drive-time occasions, such as on her way home from work or on picking her children up from school. The agency promotion manager then responds by recommending a branded placement of 'meal deal' displays in out-of-home locations, such as on billboards, banners, and stand-ups near family destinations and associations. Specifically she calls out locations of Little League parks, school cafeterias, and Girl Scout centres. In this way, the agency's branding actions can build on local community presence through targeted media placement and direct a more customized brand experience to the consumer.

The agency account team then identifies a different emotional need state for the planned mother in how she decides to order chicken, which yields yet another marketing opportunity. This planned mother, the team maintains, is less pressured by time and value constraints than the hurried mother, and instead seeks an optimum brand experience for her family. This ostensibly means that she is more open to suggestions which frame the dinner experience around the mood of 'family fun'. The account team further claims that as she seeks family consensus in deciding what side dishes to order, the agency can provide its media department with additional marketing opportunities by exploring ways to promote the brand's variety, specialty and quality of food offerings. A media executive then claims that the agency can reach the planned mother though television spots aired during afternoon programmes (soaps) as well as by offering her interactive promotional tie-ins with video rental stores, theme park giveaways, and sponsorship programming, which leverage the idea of 'family fun'. In this way, media options are coordinated with marketing messages to help the consumer experience align with the brand value of 'family fun'.

Our meeting discussion then turns to the next touch point: ordering the meal. The hurried mother is framed as being highly anxious and seeking assurance for a dinner solution. An agency account executive responds by stating: 'Her anxiety is an opportunity for us to improve our brand's phone-in response, so that food options can be immediately available to her and ease her stress'. The client agrees. Shortly after the meeting, a deal is planned with the phone company to expedite calls so that when the consumer presses the star button she hears daily specials, or can speed-dial directly to a waiting Fresh Chicken Express order taker. An Internet option is also discussed to facilitate on-line ordering capabilities that would electronically recall past coupons and orders and automatically generate a choice of appropriate deals for the consumer. For both of these marketing suggestions, it is the agency's negotiation of the consumer's emotional state that facilitates marketing options through liaisons with phone companies or agency Web site developers.

The discussion then turns to ordering chicken for the planned mom, which generates still another set of marketing options. As an agency account executive states, 'Since her emotional state seeks to please her family, she is open to suggestions about trying additional menu items, or is more likely to try a new item altogether'. He continues, 'Our business opportunity here is to extend our relationship with the customer through dialogue, since she is appreciative of courteous feedback and wants affirmation of her choice'. He then suggests a plan for training the phone-order receiving staff of Fresh Chicken Express to politely engage the customer and 'negotiate deals that optimize her anticipated meal experience'. The trained staff would then recommend to the caller that she add a new menu item, such as a salad, dessert or candy to complete her 'fun dinner occasion'. The idea is to 'leverage' the consumer's consensus-seeking emotional state into purchasing more, by offering positive feedback and additional menu suggestions that align brand values with what marketers perceive as the consumer's desire for 'family fun'. Thus, marketers anticipate making more out of a simple purchase occasion by expanding an embodied notion of 'fun' into an extended food experience.

For the next touch point, waiting for food, the hurried mother's emotional state is considered most time-sensitive. The account team cites data that show while speed of delivery matters once the food is ordered, consumers use the 'wait time' to complete unfinished household chores, such as reading the day's mail or checking the children's schoolwork. For this reason, an account supervisor states: 'Accuracy of quoted delivery time is more important than early arrival, since too early of an arrival can disturb her and be as bothersome as a late arrival'. The client agrees and states, 'Because on-time delivery is so critical to both of our consumers, we should require that our local chicken restaurants place a courtesy call to inform her that the order is on its way'. The agency Web site developer then suggests a way to optimize consumers' wait-time by providing online games for them to engage while waiting. He claims this branded experience would not only direct waiting customers to our 'Family Games Room' site, but also entertain them while they 'build a healthy Fresh Chicken Express appetite'.

For the next touch point, food arrival, the discussion shifts to the physical interaction between consumer and brand. An agency account supervisor warns not to 'pass up this opportunity' since, he claims, 'research shows that parents often encourage their child to interact with the delivery person at the door'. He then points out, 'the difference between our two consumers may be that, while the tension of the day ends on food arrival for the hurried mom, the expectation of the total food experience begins for the planned mother'. He then states that the marketing opportunity is to assure that delivery personnel understand the importance of smiles and courtesy, especially if greeted by a child, 'who is always observed by watching parents'. The executive continues stating that in addition to ensuring that delivery vehicles are clean and presentable, Fresh Chicken Express can target the household child and enhance the level of fun through the delivery person's uniform. To this, he states, 'Let's add a Santa hat for Christmas, an orange and black uniform for Halloween, and Easter bunny ears for Easter'. The client nods his head and smiles. The agency sales representative then pipes in with another marketing opportunity: 'For the hurried mom, a swipe card at the door for automatic debit payment could insure convenience and ease. And for the planned mother, we could deliver her a television guide with a front-page brand promotion: 'Fresh Chicken Express—What's on television tonight', with recommendations for family television viewing, courtesy of Fresh Chicken Express'. Thus, new media channels are developed by the agency to customize the consumer's brand experience, from seasonal employee costumes for entertaining children, and enhanced credit card payment options, to television guide branded circulars.

The next touch point, eating the delivered food, constitutes the primary brand experience for the consumer where the sensory properties of the brand come to the fore. Nonetheless, marketers reinterpret the complexities of consumer sensory involvement with the brand in terms of most likely food consumption locations. According to an agency account executive, 'Hurried mothers can relax as our food fulfills her need to expedite dinner'. He continues, 'Her Fresh Chicken Express decision is now reinforced and future decisions are planted as she unwinds and lets her family reconnect'. He asserts that, 'Eating our chicken allows the planned mom to transition into the family experience and reconnect with her family through shared and spontaneous behaviour'. For the hurried mother, he determines that the kitchen counter or dinner table make for primary eating locations; whereas for the planned mother, watching television, playing family games, or outdoor backyard activities determine the eating location. He then suggests enhancing the 'fun eating experience' in each location by adding branded disposable tablecloths, or emphasizing family interaction with inexpensive games. A product design executive from the agency suggests ways his department can implement this plan and further improve the experience by offering branded side accoutrements of blended spices, hot pepper, seasoned salt, and dipping sauces or by introducing a dessert option to 'expand the entire meal experience'. An agency account executive then claims he can leverage ties with an ice cream and cookie manufacturer, so that by partnering a dessert option to sell customers a complete meal option, Fresh Chicken Express could 'extend the customer's chicken eating experience and increase our corporate revenues'.

The final brand touch point concerns the disposal of the residual packaging items, such as the chicken delivery box and napkins. The agency's packaging design manager comes to the fore and states that branded messages don't need to end with the clean-up of the product: 'The two need states of our target moms call for different ways of handling this issue. The hurried mother is practical and expedient, and wants to move on to other tasks including clean-up. We can respond to her by offering her branded storage options for leftovers'. The discussion then turns to the planned mother and how branded images etched on the delivery box top can create a symbolic reminder for her next order. The agency's package design manager asserts that the delivery box is likely to remain on the table longer for the planned mother and then comes up with an idea to advertise inexpensive hologram images on the chicken box top. He adds, 'The box top is an ideal property for presenting our customers with images that show a family having fun, rather than just giving them plain coupon deals alone'. The idea is to depart from ordinary text coupons and 'engage' the consumer with 'fun' interactive image coupons. He concludes that by branding fun images on delivery box tops as well as on tablecloths, trash bags and wet wipes, and including them in the order, Fresh Chicken Express can 'own the clean-up experience in a branded way'. After the meeting, many of the steps discussed and presented are implemented in forthcoming advertising and marketing plans.

From this example, we note how various agency divisions interpret and direct constructed emotional states and brand experiences of consumers into specific marketing and media responses. By focusing on the marketing and media applications of consumption, marketers construct a sense of consumer experience and emotions in terms of objectified responses that serve their client's brand. Such 'need state' constructions and assumptions about emotional states are ultimately designed to correspond to the capabilities and opportunities which advertising agencies themselves can fulfill. This objectifying process of consumer emotional experience thus provides a functional benefit for the advertising agency relative to its corporate client. In summing up the emotions at stake, the consumer is either anxiously hurried or optimistically planning what to serve her family for dinner, and these emotional constructions form the wealth of material by which an agency shapes the consumer to its client's brand.

Conclusion

The true 'experience economy', and the function of advertising within it, is thus evidenced in the modes and manners of interactions among the consumer, brand and marketer, which are interpreted and reproduced by advertisers as 'emotional', 'experiential', and so forth. Through such interpretations, advertisers market to consumers as well as serve their corporate clients in more creative ways. Hence, the expanded sense of the consumer's emotional interaction with brands and sensory experience with various new media creates, in reality, an expanded opportunity for advertisers to re-create and reproduce the consumer in their own terms. By directing advertisements and media messages to the level of consumer sensations and private emotions, advertisers not only attempt to avoid the public skepticism that limited them in the past, but also provide for themselves the very means to interpret and advise their corporate clients in more value-added ways.

From this study of consumer emotions and sensations in relation to branding, we can also state that embodiment has become the new consumer territory in which advertisers and marketers cultivate the private production and consumption of goods. Embodiment, as a private and individual experience, operates apart from a generalized discourse and the public arena, and for this reason, it reframes the individual consumer into the new imagined subject by which marketers can produce and market ever more customized means of consumption. Indeed, the growing interest in the consumer's sensations and emotions confirms the shift that Howes calls privatization of sensory consumption (2005). What this also means is that, in the world of advertising and marketing, not only is reason 'out' and emotion 'in', but sentiment has become the ultimate consumer target by which new forms of media and brand messaging will shape and recast consumers' sensory and emotional experiences.

References

Appadurai, A. (1996), *Modernity at Large,* Minneapolis and London: University of Minnesota.

Auletta, K. (2005), 'The New Pitch: Do Ads Still Work?', *The New Yorker,* 28 March: 34–39.

Beeman, W. (1986), 'Freedom to Choose: Symbols and Values in American Advertising', in H. Varenne (ed.), *Symbolizing America,* Lincoln and London: University of Nebraska Press.

Boorstin, D. J. (1965), *The Americans: The National Experience,* New York: Random House.

Davidson, M. (1994, 1992), *The Consumerist Manifesto,* London and New York: Routledge.

Douglas, M., and Isherwood, B. (1979), *The World of Goods,* London and New York: Routledge.

Elliot, S. (2005a), 'Advertising: 'In an industry That Has Historically Snubbed Research on Marketing, the Field Is Suddenly in Vogue', *New York Times,* 18 April: C10.

Elliot, S. (2005b), 'Advertisers Want Something Different', *New York Times,* 23 May, <http://www.query.nytimes.com/mem/tnt.html> accessed 20 July 2005.

Gobe, M. (2001), *Emotional Branding,* New York: Allworth Press.

Goldman, R., and Papson, S. (1998), *Nike Culture: Sign of the Swoosh,* London and Thousand Oaks, Calif.: Sage Publications.

Hill, D. (2003), *Body of Truth,* New York: John Wiley & Sons.

Howes, D., ed. (2005), *Empire of the Senses,* Oxford and New York: Berg Publishers.

Jhally, S. (1987), *The Codes of Advertising,* London: Frances Pinter.

Kemper S. (2001), *Buying and Believing: Sri Lankan Advertising and Consumers in a Transnational World,* Chicago: University of Chicago Press.

Klein, N. (2000), *No Logo: Taking Aim at the Brand Bullies,* New York: Picador.

Lash, S., and Urry, J. (1994), *Economies of Signs & Space,* London: Sage Publications.

Levey, R. (2004), 'Emotion Can Make a Difference', in *Direct,* 22(15) 1 March <www.directmag.com>.

Lien, M. (1997), *Marketing and Modernity,* Oxford and New York: Berg Publishers.

Lutz, C. (1998, 1988), *Unnatural Emotions,* Chicago and London: University of Chicago Press.

Malefyt, T. de W. (2003), 'Models, Metaphors and Client Relations', in T. de W. Malefyt and B. Moeran (eds), *Advertising Cultures,* pp. 139–63, Oxford and New York: Berg Publishers.

Malefyt, T. de W., and Moeran, B. (2003), 'Introduction: Advertising Cultures— Advertising, Ethnography and Anthropology', in T. de W. Malefyt and B. Moeran (eds), *Advertising Cultures,* pp. 1–33, Oxford and New York: Berg Publishers.

Marchand, R. (1985), *Advertising the American Dream,* Berkeley: University of California Press.

Mazzarella, W. (2003a), *Shoveling Smoke,* Chapel Hill, N.C.: Duke University Press.

Mazzarella, W. (2003b), 'Critical Publicity/Public Criticism: Reflections on Fieldwork in the Bombay Ad World', in T. de W. Malefyt and B. Moeran (eds), *Advertising Cultures,* pp. 55–74, Oxford and New York: Berg publishers.

McMurtry, J. (2004), 'Building Your Brand through Emotional Connections', *Denver Business Journal,* 15 October.

Moeran, B. (1996), *A Japanese Advertising Agency,* Honolulu: University of Hawaii Press.

Moeran, B. (2005), *The Business of Ethnography,* Oxford and New York: Berg Publishers.

Miller, D. (1997), *Capitalism: An Ethnographic Approach,* Oxford and New York: Berg Publishers.

Muschamp, H. (1999), 'Seductive Objects with a Sly Sting', *New York Times,* 2 July.

O'Barr, W. (1994), *Culture and the Ad,* Boulder, Colo., San Francisco, Oxford: Westview Press.

Ogilvy, D. (1971, 1963), *Confessions of an Advertising Man,* New York: Atheneum.

Ogilvy, D. (1985, 1983), *Ogilvy on Advertising,* New York: Vintage books (Random House).

Perry, N. (1998), *Hyperreality and Global Culture,* London and New York: Routledge.

Pine, J. B., and Gilmore, J. H. (1999), *The Experience Economy,* Boston: Harvard Business School Press.

Postrel, V. (2003), *The Substance of Style,* New York: Harper-Collins Publishers.

Robinette, S., Brand, C., with Lenz, V. (2001), *Emotion Marketing,* New York: McGraw Hill.

Ries, A., and Trout, J. (1986, 1981), *Positioning: The Battle for Your Mind,* New York: Warner Books.

Ryle, G. (2002, 1949), *The Concept of Mind,* Chicago and London: University of Chicago Press.

Schudson, M. (1986), *Advertising, the Uneasy Persuasion,* New York: Basic Books.

Steel, J. (1998), *Truth Lies and Advertising,* New York: John Wiley & Sons.

Synott, A. (1991), 'Puzzling over the Senses: From Plato to Marx', in D. Howes (ed.), *The Varieties of Sensory Experience,* pp. 61–76, Toronto: University of Toronto Press.

Williamson, J. (1978), *Decoding Advertising,* London and New York: Barion Boyars.

Zaltman, G. (2003), *How Consumers Think,* Boston: Harvard Business School Press.

Notes

1. I use the term 'marketing' throughout this paper to refer to all advertising, publicity, sales and promotion efforts on behalf of a corporate client.
2. See Judith Williamson (1978), William O'Barr (1994), Michael Schudson (1986), for scholarly critiques, and Naomi Klein (2000) for popular critiques of marketing and branding.
3. See Malefyt's 'Models, Metaphors and Client Relations' (2003) for a discussion on how consumer and brand models align to create affinity between client and agency.
4. See Moeran (1996: 104–5) for the full account of the variety of needs an agency fulfills for a client.
5. A touch point (itself a tactile term) is considered any tangible contact a consumer makes with a brand as well as intangible thoughts, feelings and brand associations. QSRweb.com uses six similar touch points to describe optimal drive-through service for quick service restaurants.
6. Undisclosed client branding document, 2002.

–22–

Emotional Baggage
The Meaning/Feeling Debate amongst Tourists

Jonathan Skinner

It seems to me that I would always be better off where I am not, and this question of moving is one of those I discuss incessantly with my soul. (Baudelaire 1962: 211)

It has personality, temperament, individuality, uniqueness. A journey is a person in itself; no two are alike. (Steinbeck 1990: 4)

Emotionally, nothing satisfies as much as extravagant or temporarily permitted illicit behaviour. (Turner 1969: 176)

The premise for the *Incredible Hulk* coaster, like many of USIOA's [Universal Studios Island of Adventure] top thrill rides, can be summed up psychologically, as the 'runaway id', with passengers subject to the primal emotions that torment the raging green Hulk. Catapulted from zero to 40 miles per hour in two seconds flat and hurtling through the ride's seven inversions, I find that premise reinforced with gut-wrenching efficiency. (Adam Berger 2002: online)

Introduction—Emotional Locations and Dislocations

Tourism provides us with one of those 'fateful moments' (Giddens 1991: 112), a space and a time for both anxiety and opportunity, a point of transition during which reflexivity and attention to the self and focus upon self-actualization are heightened. It can result in the construction and experimentation in 'travelling identities' (Desforges 2000: 940) such as those found amongst long-haul tourists (portraying youth, experience, independence, self-sufficiency, masculinity), and indeed 'migrants of identity' who are either at home in a world of movement (cf. Rapport and Dawson 1998) or who use the migration experience as a rite of passage, such as boys from Barbados leaving the island to return as men (Thomas-Hope 1992). The tourism 'contact zone'

(Pratt 1992)—colonial or postcolonial but definitely one of transculturation and hence one of stress, dislocation and shock (Ward, Bochner, and Furnham 2001)[1]—affects and influences host identity as much as guest identity: Zarkia (1996: 166) found tourism had fostered a double personality in many girls on the Greek island of Skyros as their behaviour oscillated between the rhythms of peasant life during the winter, and the cosmopolitan tourist summers when they 'forgot' their community feasts, their language, and their religious observances; and Bruner (1991) also attests to the 'transformation of the self in tourism', but, citing a Chambri initiation ceremony in Papua New Guinea in which the language, timing, packaging and marketing have all been changed to suit the tourist, Bruner argues that it is the native self that is changed before a dominant 'Western imaginary consciousness' (244).

For contemporary social theorists, tourism is seen as a modern and largely first-world luxury activity; as 'imperialist nostalgia' (Rosaldo 1989, see also Nash 1977); as 'alienated leisure' (MacCannell 1976) and quest for the authentic and homemade in an increasingly plastic world (cf. Graburn 1976: 3); as constructed 'gaze' (Urry 1990), sacred travel (Graburn 1977) or modern-day pilgrimage (Coleman and Eade 2004); and as an example of our 'neurasthenic attitude' in modern life (Rojek 1997: 64, after Simmel 1907), one which oscillates between the extremes of indifference and over-excitement and stimulation. The tourist space, a physical and ideational 'pleasure periphery' (Turner and Ashe 1975)—is a space for consumption (Urry 1995, Sheller 2003) and performance—real (Coleman and Crang 2002), 'staged' (Desmond 1999) or 'empty' (MacCannell 1992). The Caribbean and the Costa del Sol have become tourism signifiers where tourism has deracinated local culture and imposed a new plantocracy (Patullo 1996) under the guise of seemingly innocuous but emotionally charged tourism advertising (cf. Crick 1989, Laffey 1995, Selwyn 1993) of pleasures from the sun (sunlust) and the sea (Skinner 2004), and the vices of the body (Pruitt 1995, Skinner unpublished) in the former; an expat colony for Brits abroad unhappy, bored and cold from life in the motherland (O'Reilly 2000) in the latter.

It might be argued that the tourists visiting the Caribbean islands, or the expats leading a peripatetic existence in southern Spain, are moving to suit their moods, that they are relocating to realign their inner world with their outer world and thereby live a narrative harmony (cf. Mattingly 1998, Rapport 2000). According to Levy (1984), cultures range between 'hypocognised' (muted) and 'hypercognised' (elaborated) tendencies, depending on what extent particular emotions are recognized. Brits back home, "put on the shelf" because of their age, find themselves included in Spanish society where the pace of life is slower, and the call to express emotions and to relish life greater. Levy developed his theory from ethnographic research on Tahiti where he found an attention and preoccupation with 'fear' and 'shame' emotions. Heelas (1986: 241) extends Levy's hypo/hypercognised dichotomy and applies it cross-culturally: for the hypercognised, Heelas connects 'love' and 'guilt' to 'us' (presumably Heelas is referring to the West), 'pressure' to Rastafarians in the Caribbean, 'passion' to the Ilongot in the Philippines, and 'gentleness' to the Utku

Eskimo in Canada. He admits, later on, that this approach to emotions assumes a typically Western chain of cause and effect, a naturalistic understanding that emotions are a combination of 'internal locus and external aetiology' (1986: 248). It is certainly applied in the main to the indigenous as opposed to the exogenous tourist.

Heelas's approach to the study of emotions is widespread but by no means universal. Sadness, grief, nostalgia, depression, frustration, anger, fear, indignation, disgust, contempt, guilt, anguish, envy, jealousy, love, compassion, pity, embarrassment, shame and anxiety: there are a range of understandings and approaches to the study of these emotions, what Williams (2001: 132) has referred to as a 'moving target', 'unidimensional', a 'complex, multidimensional, multifaceted human compound'. In her review of the study of emotions, Hochschild (1983: 204–22) classically points to the emergence of two key models of emotion: the Organismic—emotion as a biological response, led by instinct and overlaid by feeling (Darwin, James, Freud); and the Interactional—emotion as both managed and experienced, elicited, expressed and created in context (Dewey, Wright, Goffman). Amongst anthropologists, this debate translates into a meaning (cultural)/feeling (biological) (Leavitt 1996) rammie, further problematized by universal/culture-specific extrapolations from ethnography (Wierzbicka 1986): the thesis that emotions have a biological/embodied/physical/internal (even 'ecological') basis implies that emotions are universal (H. Geertz 1974, Milton 2005, Myers 1979, Rosaldo 1984, Schiefflin 1983), whether demonstrated or not, and that, concomitantly, emotions as cultural/discursive suggests that they are culture-specific and thus relative (C. Geertz 1973, Lutz 1988, Appadurai 1990, Abu-Lughod and Lutz 1990; see also Wulff this volume for a comprehensive review).

This diversity of opinion, and the problems surrounding the distinction between 'emotions' and 'feelings' and 'cognition', show how difficult it is to study emotions. Further to these semantic and theoretical differences, Crossley (1998) makes the point that physiological and phenomenological research into sensations/feelings/emotions/ experiences is also complicated by the fact that these states are not easily interpreted, mapped or translated. The physiology of fear is sometimes not that much different from the physiology of fun: compare a person's pounding heart and blood pressure rates during physical attack and whilst enduring a roller coaster ride, for instance.

'[T]he equation of meaning with the particularly cultural and feeling with the universally biological still often forces a biological explanation of the familiar, a cultural interpretation of the strange' (Leavitt 1996: 524). Writing in *American Ethnologist,* John Leavitt proposes three ways around the above meaning/feeling impasse, a dichotomy of emotions as biological or emotions as sociocultural in nature—'biological reductionism' and 'cultural reductionism' in Hinton's mind (1993). In a rereading of the intellectual past of the modern West, Leavitt retraces Vygotsky's meanderings, which eventually took him back to the seventeenth-century philosopher Benedict de Spinoza. Leavitt (1996: 525) draws attention to Vygotsky's thesis that organismic models of emotion which start from the body seem to be explanatory, whereas ideational models of emotion which start from the mind seem to be descriptive and interpretive. These notions of causality are premised upon the mind/body split, emotions as a Cartesian derivative. Spinoza's approach was to view the body as a 'composite of composites' (Wartofsky 1973: 350) such that a change in the experience of an emotion does not *lead* to a change in the body's state because they are one. Leavitt concludes that if this is an approach subscribed to, then:

> We would have to see emotions as primarily neither meanings nor feelings, but as experiences learned and expressed in the body in social interactions through the mediation of systems of signs, verbal and nonverbal. We would have to see them as fundamentally social rather than simply as individual in nature; as generally expressed, rather than as generally ineffable; and as both cultural and situational. But we would equally recognize in theory what we all assume in our everyday lives: that emotions are *felt* in bodily experience, not just known or thought or appraised. (Leavitt 1996: 536, author's emphasis)

Leavitt's other two attempts to resolve the meaning-feeling/mind-body approaches to emotion are psychoanalytical and by translation of experiences.

This critique of Western constructions of emotions by Leavitt is a holistic approach which detours around the semantic and mind-body intellectual crevasses. It blurs the mind/body dualism, the mental/physical divide, the meaning/feeling dichotomy in the anthropology of emotions.[2] It is one which allows us to still engage with the ethnography of emotions, to informants' comments such as Berger's reaction to his roller coaster ride as noted at the start of this chapter. Leavitt's approach to the study of emotions is not dissimilar from tourism scholars' Adler (1989) and Campbell (1987) and their accounts of the rise of modern tourism in the last three centuries, linking developments in travel with developments in Western society—and 'emotionality' (Gillen 2001). They both, for example, link the experience of place with emotion through a shift from rational Enlightenment observation of the environment to that of Romantic aesthetic and personal emotional appreciation. Bored with Rouen, the youthful Flaubert evinces this when he leaves for Egypt to experience local life, love and lore in a compressed few months of manic exhilaration and exultation. Steinbeck, Hemingway, Wordsworth, D. H. Lawrence, Delacroix, Ruskin, Van Gogh, Baudelaire: the artist's restless spirit is at home, is settled and happy, touring in this world of movement. Moreover, more contemporaneously, Hochschild (1983) noted that the air stewardesses she studied, whilst they were trained by their airlines, were being taught how to present a veneer of warmth and synthesized natural feeling—'emotional labour' as commodity, behaviour stemming from these earlier Romantic trends made massive.

Emotions in Tourists and Tourism

The tourist is a person under-theorized in the social sciences, particularly when it comes to the study of emotions. The tourist, a person who spends more than 24 hours away from home for pleasure, a person who moves, who displaces voluntarily and temporarily, is a person who engages in a pleasure/danger complex (Lupton 1990). Tourists deliberately move out of their comfort zone to face difference and risk in a controlled fashion, be it on a package holiday, as 'Rough Guide' traveller or amusement park visitor. In Britain, the tourist destinations are frequently liminal (and liminoid) zones where tourists engage in 'time out' in a ritual fashion: visitors to Blackpool have drunk their way through the town, sat on donkey rides up and down the beach, and promenaded or played amusements on the piers ever since the Wakes weekends organized for factory workers in the 1870s (Walton 1983). Whilst the modern-day tourist vacation is commonly seen and referred to as 'a get-away', a chance for the body and mind—Spinoza's composite of composites, Totton's (2003) 'bodymind'—to 'relax and unwind from it all', it is often a time for the manufacture of emotions in a ritualized and stylized fashion. This can be seen to be surprising in that ritualized activities are sometimes seen to constitute a distance between individuals and their emotional experiences (Maher 1984). Perhaps this accounts for the dearth of literature on tourism and emotions? However, the reverse can equally be claimed, as rituals heighten the senses (Whitehouse 1995; 'emotion is not only conventionally expressed in ritual, it is felt', Kapferer 1979: 3).

In his innovative "Tourism and Leisure" MA thesis, *A Moving Experience? Investigating the Social Significance of Emotion in Tourism,* Sean Gillen (2001) is one of the few to draw a direct connection between tourism and the emotions. His thesis is as follows:

> Tourist sights, it is argued, reflect the emotional needs of individuals whilst providing a suitably affective environment for the expression of these needs ... [T]ourism can and does provide the opportunity to experience a contrasting *emotional* landscape, *where the familiar self can be felt in an unfamiliar way.* (online, author's emphasis)

Modern tourist experiences frequently demand emotional involvement, whether as nature tourism (Rosario tours in Bolivia advertising 'nature, emotion, adventure'), as heritage tourism (Museum of the Jewish Diaspora, which demands 'emotional involvement and identification', Golden 1996: 230), or as disaster tourism (attraction to the sublime wonder of the volcanic crisis on the island of Montserrat, Skinner 2003). Cynically, Gillen (2001: online, author's emphasis) suggests that emotions 'have become a commodity to be circulated and *moved* within and between individuals and cultures'.

This control, packaging and synthesizing of emotions suggests that emotions are in stasis in the individual. And that emotions can be packaged with and for the holiday. They are generated and manipulated by the tourist industry (Gnoth 1997). If emotions are studied in the context of tourism, it is more in keeping with the psychology of motivation and desire than the body and feelings. American academic Plog (1987) exemplifies this approach with his development and naming of a psychographic bell curve model around personality and emotion with allocentrics likely to fly and go on adventurous holidays (South Pacific, Africa), and psychocentrics self-inhibited and likely to prefer local, short weekend tourist breaks (Coney Island, Miami Beach, or Blackpool in the UK). This is matched by Iso-Ahola's (1980) intrinsic motivation–optimal arousal approach which looks at tourist motivation in terms of need for stimulation (from biological disposition and socialization to perceived freedom and leisure needs). And Pearce's (1993) travel career model of ascending tendencies with age (relaxation/bodily needs [Pontins/Butlins] stimulation [activity holiday] relationship [Club 18–30] self-esteem and development [touring—fulfilment—timeshare]). Gillen, in his thesis, draws largely upon sociological writings to connect tourism with emotions rather than rely upon the psychology of push/pull factors.[3]

Gillen draws from Elias and his idea that emotionality is learned as part of a sociality or civilization by acculturation: we need to distinguish our emotions in order to survive, but in a more civilized society we are more free from the uncontrolled emotions of others and so 'life becomes in a sense less dangerous, but also less emotional or pleasurable' (Elias 2000: 375). This 'tempering' (Gillen 2001: online) of social life is counteracted by staged dangers and produced emotions, mimesis through action films, murder books, roller coaster rides, extreme sports and adventure activities. This mimesis of danger, a simulation of risk, is often found in tourism: living this thesis, I write this chapter in my motel room having just returned from a controlled hike on my own in the dangerous sand dunes of Death Valley, pleasurable solitude, piquant risk, and adequate compensation for my anger and disappointment at the closure of Zabriskie Point, a popular viewing point. Gillen looks at these tourism 'moments' (Abercrombie and Longhurst 1998), 'the perceptions of the attraction by the tourists themselves', 'the hyper-sensory and cognitive inducement of physical and mental states' (Gillen 2001: online) as found, for him, on the roller coasters in Blackpool, and at "The Beatles Story" exhibition in Liverpool. To varying degrees, both tourist attractions are involved in sensory manipulation. 'The roller coaster ride made me feel like a child again', explained one informant. This is interpreted by Gillen (2001: online) as an example of how 'the emotional subsumes the sensory as the trauma of the here and now encourages "feeling" to eclipse "thinking"'. Gillen continues to interpret this tourist experience in the sociological/psychoanalytical vein: it was an irrational/hyper-rational response, a 'perverse leisure activity [which] had elicited a "temperate de-control' of emotions, allowing a degree of "socially permitted regression" to a child like irrationality'.

Whilst I don't strictly agree with Gillen's line of analysis, his predominantly psychoanalytical route, for instance, his work is useful for encouraging us to think across disciplines in the study of emotions in tourism. From Gillen, I draw ideas about control and release. From Gillen, I reiterate Leavitt's approach: a collapsing, a 'subsumation', of the meaning/feeling divisions. In the next two sections I should like to present some ethnography on the topic of tourism and emotions. The first is an example from a group of dance tourists to Cuba. The second is from a detailed exploration of one person's dance weekend break in Southport, England (at a Pontins

Camp near Blackpool). I will use both case studies to show that the meaning/feeling debate is a blend rather than a dichotomy, a complexity, that 'composite of composites'. Both examples, to my mind, highlight the tourists' emotional baggage, which does not just accompany them but *is* 'them'.

Group Pleasures and Emotions in a Tourist Group

Cuba has long been known as the 'pleasure island' of the Caribbean (Schwartz 1997). Often known by the epithet 'the Paris of the Antilles', Cuba has had an ambiguous tension between tourism and socialism—between 'relaxation and revolution' (Schwartz 1997: 164)—throughout the twentieth century, first as a 'pleasure island' for Americans escaping prohibition in the 1920s (80,000/year) up until the Great Depression of 1929, second as a post-Second World War destination in the 1950s under Batista until the success of the Cuban Revolution in 1959, and third as a foreign exchange earner from the 1980s under Castro. I was fortunate to be able to research and to track tourist behaviour throughout the course of a 10-day dance holiday on the island in the 1990s. I was able to follow tourists on holiday from start to finish, from airport lounge meeting to sun lounge in Valadero via dance lessons in Havana, and eventual leave-taking back in the return airport's luggage collection facility. The holiday was organized by DanceHolidays, a niche tourism operation which specializes in dance lessons in exotic locations. This time it was jive in the lucrative heartland of salsa.

Jason is a middle-aged lawyer who has come on the holiday to dance, and out of 'future nostalgia'. He is a socialist wanting to see Cuba 'before it changes; before Castro goes and it becomes another tourist playground'. Cassie is a secretary in her twenties who has not danced much but has been getting private lessons from the instructors accompanying us on the holiday. 'Sun, sun, sun and fun' is what she wants, and 'a holiday with a difference—it's not everyday that you get a chance to go to Cuba, is it now?' Jenny is a 42-year-old recently divorced mother of three young children who has left them with her family whilst she has her 'holiday fun in the sun'. Amongst the other ten or so tourists on this dance package are Francis and Mary—wanting 'sun, sand, sea and loads'a sex'—who opt out of the dance classes because they feel that the tourist men are ogling them. Instead, they spend their days by the pool and their evenings in Cuban bars drinking and flirting with the local men. Unsurprisingly, given the cocktail of personalities in the group, at the end of the holiday many of the dancers are not on speaking terms with each other and they consider the holiday to have been a flop: the dancing did not fit with the location which was more attuned to salsa; the numbers of dancers and their various levels made classes and dance evenings difficult; the 'talent' in the party was lacking; and the Cuban setting was so desperately poor in places that it made many of the tourists feel uncomfortable.

All of the tourists had expectations about the vacation. They bought into the brochure's pictures of black and white, male and female models dancing on the beach. Their motivations were to get away, to relax, to have fun, to unburden themselves from the stresses and strains of work—and also the emotional upheavals of relationships.[4] These people, in other words, were using the vacation, their dislocation in the sun, to get away from emotional baggage which had preoccupied them. Unfortunately, the attempt to change or distance themselves from their emotions by dislocating themselves, by changing culture, failed. They carried their emotions with them and took up new ones in this environment of proximity with strangers which soon began to rankle. Jenny longed for her children's company and grew increasingly bitter towards her husband—and many of the men in the dance group—as the holiday wore on. Amongst the others, the dancing brought them brief moments of exhilaration, and the sunbathing relaxed their bodies, but the group nature of the break from the everyday exacerbated what Scheff (1990) refers to as a negative 'emotional contagion' in the tourists. It amplified their affective responses. As their bodies moved to familiar patterns on the dance floor, and they struggled to comprehend new moves from the lessons, their feelings and meanings remained indistinguishable, but the group hates for individuals was very noticeable. There was no clear line between cognition of a new move, and bodily enactment; there was no division between body relaxing by the pool, and mind unwinding differently. If anything, in terms of the cultural meaning/bodily feeling debate, the 'emotions [were] *felt* in bodily experience' (Leavitt 1996: 536). Further to this, the individual—'the ultimate seat of emotion in both evolutionary and psychodynamic approaches' (Lutz and White 1986: 408)—was seen to be a member of an unsettled emotional group rather than a number of isolates. In other words, there was not just a mind-body composite of emotions on this holiday, let alone a collection of 'individuals' (Strathern 1991).

Exhilaration and the Meaning/Feeling Debate in a Tourist

It was Goffman (1967) who introduced the idea of institutionalized 'action places'. These are places where individuals can 'let off steam'. It is there that they feel that they have the licence to behave differently, to act in a fashion which would not normally be tolerated or manageable. The seaside is one such location, where leisure is the local occupation. And at Southport, a second sister to Blackpool, the resort industry continues into the twenty-first century, a tawdry, cheap and tacky location for hen and stag weekends, darts competitions, and very low-budget family breaks. As Urry (1990: 102) points out, such locations are no longer new or desirable. They no longer provide the contrast needed for the industrial worker in a post-industrial age. They are, however, cheap and cheerful locations for massive dance camps—1,000 people dancing in huge halls, like an organized rave for the more educated classes.

I was accompanying Helen (from Belfast) on her first residential dance weekend to Southport. She did not feel that it was a holiday that she was on. There was too much to do: 'I'm here to get better at my dancing, to improve and to gain confidence. This is only partly a vacation.' In terms of how she felt, Helen was nervous. She is 52 years old and conscious of her age and self-conscious of her looks. She doesn't want to be seen to be out of place. Fitting in is important. During the weekend, I interviewed her several times a day, asking about how she felt after the classes, the interactions with other dancers, and the dance nights, as well as the touring aspect to the trip. She was exhausted and exhilarated by all the dancing. Her fears were allayed by all the different people dancing—mixed abilities, classes, ages, and dress senses. As the weekend developed, she became increasingly relaxed and started going off to classes on her own. She fell in love with the tango-jive instructor and grew increasingly jealous of all this dancing available to the mainlanders.

I had known Helen for about a year and we had a close relationship from teaching jive classes together several times a week in Belfast. Though, like myself, she remained slightly (and deliberately) aloof from several of our students who had also come on the weekend, she was open and candid during our interviews. Helen stated her emotions on a number of occasions: happiness and love for the dancing; fear of the unknown, having never done this before; dread of embarrassment on the dance floor keeping up with a more proficient dancer; anxiety and nervousness about asking unknown men to dance with her. Each of these emotions was an indistinguishable mixture of what are traditionally conceived of as the mind and the body. These emotions were also coupled with emotions associated around the tourist phases in this dance weekend: before the holiday, Helen was preoccupied with the brochure, with clothes and packing, and with fantasizing about her time there, the dancing, the venue, and the potential nightmares on the dance floor and in the self-catering apartment's unhygienic bathroom. Before the break, Helen's emotions were continually 'up and down' (happy and sad). These emotional lifts and dips smoothed out during the vacation. When we were there in Southport, we were either dancing, eating or sleeping—all the exaggerated functional stimulations of the tourist. During the vacation proper, the bodymind cruised on autopilot as holiday plans panned out. And finally, upon return, post-tourism, the bodymind collapsed in a heap of muscular/mental memories of carrying cases learning dancing and being danced. These final 'tourist' memories contained emotions based upon experiences, just as the emotions prior to the tourist departure were established through Helen's bodymind history—her past, her background, her age and class, her previous holiday experiences, her Protestant anti-dancing upbringing and ambivalent attitude towards dancing, all of which bundled together emotions such as guilt, shame, fear, envy, jealousy and joy.

Back home, Helen told no one about her dancing. Helen felt that she could not let her family know about her secret nights. The point I am drawing out of this dance tourism ethnography is one of emotional baggage: Helen, like other dance tourists to Southport and those to Cuba, lived her emotions in a context of her lived as well as her live self in her new location. The emotions were not entirely new or arising solely from the cultural contact of the tourist, or their activities whether dancing or joy-riding on the roller coasters—the predisposition towards the emotions are merely coordinated and made manifest through the tourism for the psychocentric self (Helen) and the allocentric self (Berger see above). A more secondary thesis coming out of the ethnography in these two sections is one of emotions during the pre-, during and post-holiday.

An Emotional Break?

This chapter has argued that tourism does not necessarily facilitate an emotional break, and that the emotions manifest in the vacation experience do not belong solely or discretely to the mind, or solely or discretely to the body. The tourist might be a person out of their culture (Jason, Jonathan, Cassie, Jenny). They might even be a person out of their depth (Helen). The tourist might even be a post-tourist, what Urry (1990) considers to be a person savvy to the construction of the tourist gaze, a person who makes their tourism wherever they desire. The tourist is, nevertheless, an emotional tourist, a tourist with emotions in personal and cultural context, a tourist with emotional baggage which they are unable to jettison but are able to influence and have manipulated. Yesterday, turning a corner on my drive over the mountains into Yosemite National Park, I was moved to tears by a vista of mountain, lake and receding snow line. The sight resonated with my experience of the Lake District and the Scottish Highlands back home. My bodymind trembled.

Gillen (2001: online) notes that '[t]ourism ... has provided the ... medium of change in the experience of emotion'. He suggests that it is ritualized social behaviour, a cathartic, mimetic alternative to unrestrained behaviour, 'a "controlled de-control" of emotion'. For Gillen, then, tourism is a licensed space for emotional transgression. As we fateful tourists continually expose ourselves to vacations, we become desensitized and desirous of more emotion-rousing experiences. Perhaps we might argue that the emotional tourist is becoming more and more allocentric? Living in a 'post-emotional society' (Mestrovic 1997) where we recognize that our emotions are constructed and teased along, mechanized and 'open to manipulation by self, others and culture [/tourist] industry' (Mestrovic 1997: xi), our emotions become less Sartre's (1962) transformation of the world, or Myers's (1979) communication with the world, than an exposition of baggage surfacing and resurfacing, courted and cuckolded, lost and found. This future is to be embraced as joyfully 'Disneyesque' (Baudrillard 1988) rather than dispassionately 'totalitarian' (Mestrovic 1997), meaningful as well as full of feelings (Leavitt 1996), and gloriously 'composite' after Spinoza (Wartofsky 1973).

References

Abercrombie, N., and Longhurst, B. (1998), *Audiences,* London: Sage.

Abu-Lughod, L., and Lutz, C. (1990), 'Introduction: Emotion, Discourse, and the Politics of Everyday Life', in C. Lutz and L. Abu-Lughod (eds), *Language and the Politics of Emotion,* pp. 1–23, Cambridge: Cambridge University Press.

Adler, J. (1989), 'Origins of Sightseeing', *Annals of Tourism Research* 16(1): 7–29.

Appadurai, A. (1990), 'Topographies of the Self: Praise and Emotion in Hindu India', in C. Lutz and L. Abu-Lughod (eds), *Language and the Politics of Emotion,* pp. 92–112, Cambridge: Cambridge University Press.

Baudelaire, C. (1962), 'Anywhere Out of This World', *Petits Poemes en Prose,* Paris: Editions Garnier Freres.

Baudrillard, J. (1988), *America,* London: Verso.

Berger, A. (2002), *Not Your Average Tourist: An Attraction Designer Explores Universal Studios Islands of Adventure,* <http://www.themedattraction.com/berger1.htm> accessed 6 June 2005.

Bruner, E. (1991), 'The Transformation of Self in Tourism', *Annals of Tourism Research* 18(2): 238–50.

Campbell, C. (1987), *The Romantic Ethic and the Spirit of Modern Consumerism,* Oxford: Blackwell.

Coleman, S., and Crang, M., eds (2002), *Tourism: Between Place and Performance,* Oxford: Berghahn Books.

Coleman, S., and Eade, J., eds (2004), *Reframing Pilgrimage: Cultures in Motion,* London: Routledge.

Crick, M. (1989), 'Representations of International Tourism in the Social Sciences: Sun, Sex, Sights, Savings, and Servility', *Annual Review of Anthropology* 18: 307–44.

Crossley, N. (1998), 'Emotion and Communicative Action: Habermas, Linguistic Philosophy and Existentialism', in G. Bendelow and S. Williams (eds), *Emotions in Social Life: Critical Themes and Contemporary Issues,* pp. 16–38, London: Routledge.

Desforges, L. (2000), 'Travelling the World: Identity and Travel Biography', *Annals of Tourism Research* 27(4): 926–45.

Desmond, J. (1999), *Staging Tourism: Bodies on Display from Waikiki to Sea World,* Chicago: Chicago University Press.

Elias, N. (2000), *The Civilising Process,* Oxford: Blackwell.

Geertz, C. (1973), *The Interpretation of Cultures,* New York: Basic Books.

Geertz, H. (1974), 'The Vocabulary of Emotions', in R. LeVine (ed.), *Culture and Personality,* pp. 249–69, Chicago: Aldine.

Giddens, A. (1991), *Modernity and Self-Identity: Self and Society in Late-Modernity,* Cambridge: Polity Press.

Gillen, S. (2001), 'A Moving Experience? Investigating the Social Significance of Emotion in Tourism', unpublished MA thesis, University of Lancaster, <http://www.arasite.org/sgma1.htm> accessed 6 June 2005.

Gnoth, J. (1997), 'Tourism Motivation and Expectation Formation', *Annals of Tourism Research* (24)2: 283–304.

Goffman, E. (1967), *Interaction Ritual: Essays on Face-to-Face Behaviour,* New York: Garden City Books.

Golden, D. (1996), 'The Museum of the Jewish Diaspora Tells a Story', in T. Selwyn (ed.), *The Tourist Image Myths and Myth Making in Tourism,* pp. 230–52, Chichester: Wiley.

Graburn, N. (1976), 'Introduction: Arts of the Fourth World', in N. Graburn (ed.), *Ethnic and Tourist Arts: Cultural Expressions from the Fourth World,* pp. 1–32, Berkeley: University of California Press.

Graburn, N. (1977), 'Tourism: The Sacred Journey', in V. Smith (ed.), *Hosts and Guests: The Anthropology of Tourism,* pp. 21–36, Philadelphia: University of Pennsylvania Press.

Heelas, P. (1986), 'Emotion Talk across Cultures', in R. Harré (ed.), *The Social Construction of Emotions,* pp. 234–66, Oxford: Blackwell.

Hinton, A. (1993), 'Prolegomenon to a Processual Approach to the Emotions', *Ethos* 21(4): 417–51.

Hochschild, A. (1983), *The Managed Heart: Commercialisation of Human Feeling,* London: University of California Press.

Iso-Ahola, S. (1980), *The Social Psychology of Leisure and Recreation,* Dubuque, Iowa: William Brown.

Kapferer, B. (1979), 'Emotion and Feeling in Sinhalese Healing Rites', *Social Analysis* 1: 153–76.

Laffey, S., (1995), 'Representing Paradise: Euro-American Desires and Cultural Understandings in Touristic Images of Montserrat, West Indies', unpublished MA Anthropology thesis, Texas University, Austin.

Leavitt, J. (1996), 'Meaning and Feeling in the Anthropology of Emotions', *American Ethnologist* 23(3): 514–39.

Levy, R. (1984), 'Emotion, Knowing and Culture', in R. Shweder and R. LaVine (eds), *Culture Theory: Essays on Mind, Self and Emotion,* pp. 214–37, Cambridge: Cambridge University Press.

Lupton, D. (1990), *Risk,* London: Routledge.

Lutz, C. (1988), *Unnatural Emotions: Everyday Sentiments on a Micronesian Atoll and Their Challenge to Western Theory,* Chicago: University of Chicago Press.

Lutz, C., and White, G. (1986), 'The Anthropology of Emotions', *Annual Review of Anthropology* 15: 405–36.

MacCannell, D. (1976), *The Tourist: A New Theory of the Leisure Class,* New York: Schocken Books.

MacCannell, D. (1992), *Empty Meeting Grounds: The Tourist Papers,* London: Routledge.

Maher, V. (1984), 'Possession and Dispossession: Maternity and Mortality in Morocco', in H. Medick and D. Sabean (eds), *Interest and Emotion,* pp. 103–28, Cambridge: Cambridge University Press.

Mattingly, C. (1998), *Healing Dramas and Clinical Plots: The Narrative Structure of Experience,* Cambridge: Cambridge University Press.

Mestrovic, S. (1997), *Post-Emotional Society,* London: Sage.

Milton, K. (2005), 'Meanings, Feelings and Human Ecology', in K. Milton and M. Svašek (eds), *Mixed Emotions: Anthropological Studies of Feeling,* pp. 25–41, Oxford: Berg.

Myers, F. (1979), 'Emotions and the Self: A Theory of Personhood and Political Order among Pintupi Aborigines', *Ethos* 7(4): 343–70.

Nash, D. (1977), 'Tourism As a Form of Imperialism', in V. Smith (ed.), *Hosts and Guests: The Anthropology of Tourism,* pp. 33–47, Philadelphia: University of Pennsylvania Press.

O'Reilly, K. (2000), *The British on the Costa Del Sol: Transnational Identities and Local Communities,* London: Routledge.

Pattullo, P. (1996), *Last Resorts: The Cost of Tourism in the Caribbean,* London: Cassell.

Pearce, P. (1993), 'Fundamentals of Tourist Motivation', in D. Pearce and R. Butler (eds), *Tourism Research: Critiques and Challenges,* pp. 116–36, London: Routledge.

Plog, S. (1987), 'Understanding Psychographics in Tourism Research', in J. Ritchie and C. Goeldner (eds), *Travel Tourism and Hospitality Research,* pp. 203–14, New York: Wiley.

Pratt, M. (1992), *Imperial Eyes: Travel Writing and Transculturation,* London: Routledge.

Pruitt, D. (1995), 'For Love and Money—Romance Tourism in Jamaica', *Annals of Tourism Research* 22(2): 422–40.

Rapport, N. (2000), 'Narrative', in N. Rapport and J. Overing (eds), *Social and Cultural Anthropology: The Key Concepts,* pp. 283–90, London: Routledge.

Rapport, N., and Dawson, A., eds (1998), *Migrants of Identity: Perceptions of Home in a World of Movement,* Oxford: Berg.

Rojek, C. (1997), 'Indexing, Dragging and the Social Construction of Tourist Sights', in C. Rojek and J. Urry (eds), *Touring Cultures: Transformations of Travel and Theory,* pp. 52–74, London: Routledge.

Rosaldo, M. (1984), 'Toward an Anthropology of Self and Feeling', in R. Shweder and R. LeVine (eds), *Culture Theory: Essays on Mind, Self, and Emotion,* pp. 137–51, Cambridge: Cambridge University Press.

Rosaldo, R. (1989), 'Imperialist Nostalgia', *Representations* 26: 107–22.

Sartre, J.-P. (1962), *The Transcendence of Ego,* New York: Noonday Press.

Scheff, T. (1990), *Microsociology: Discourse, Emotion and Social Structure*, Chicago: University of Chicago Press.

Schiefflin, E. (1983), 'Anger and Shame in the Tropical Forest: On Affect as a Cultural System in Papua New Guinea', *Ethos* 11(3): 181–209.

Schwartz, R. (1997), *Pleasure Island: Tourism & Temptation in Cuba*, London: University of Nebraska Press.

Selwyn, T. (1993), 'Peter Pan in South-East Asia: Views from the brochures', in M. Hitchcock, V. King, and M. Parnwell (eds), pp. 117–37, *Tourism in South-East Asia*, London: Routledge.

Sheller, M. (2003), *Consuming the Caribbean*, London: Routledge.

Simmel, G. (1907), *Philosophy of Money*, London: Routledge.

Skinner, J. (2003), 'Voyeurs, Voyagers and Disaster Tourism from Mount Chance, Montserrat', in D. Macleod (ed.), *Niche Tourism and Anthropology*, pp. 129–44, Glasgow: University of Glasgow Press.

Skinner, J. (2004), *Before the Volcano: Reverberations of Identity on Montserrat*, Kingston, Jamaica: Arawak Publications.

Skinner, J. (unpublished manuscript), 'Packaging and Consuming Niche Tourism: The Case against Ceroc Dance Tourism in Cuba'.

Steinbeck, J. (1990), *Travels with Charley: In Search of America*, London: Mandarin Paperbacks.

Strathern, M. (1991), *Partial Connections*, Savage, Md.: Rowman and Littlefield.

Thomas-Hope, E. (1992), *Explanation in Caribbean Migration*, London: Macmillan.

Totton, C. (2003), *Body Psychotherapy: An Introduction*, Maidenhead: Open University Press.

Turner, V. (1969), *The Ritual Process: Structure and Anti-Structure*, Ithaca, N.Y.: Cornell University Press.

Turner, L., and Ashe, L. (1975), *The Golden Hordes: International Tourism and the Pleasure Periphery*, London: Constable.

Urry, J. (1990), *The Tourist Gaze: Leisure and Travel in Contemporary Societies*, London: Sage Publications.

Urry, J. (1995), *Consuming Places*, London: Routledge.

Walton, J. (1983), *The English Seaside Resort: A Social History 1750—1914*, Leicester: Leicester University Press.

Ward, C., Bochner, S., and Furnham, A. (2001), *The Psychology of Culture Shock*, London: Routledge.

Wartofsky, M. (1973), 'Action and Passion: Spinoza's Construction of a Scientific Psychology', in M. Grene (ed.), *Spinoza: A Collection of Critical Essays*, pp. 329–53, Garden City, N.J.: Doubleday.

Whitehouse, H. (1995), *Inside the Cult: Religious Innovation and Transmission in Papua New Guinea*, Oxford: Oxford University Press.

Wierzbicka, A. (1986), 'Human Emotions: Universal or Culture-Specific?', *American Anthropologist* 88(3): 584–94.

Williams, S. (2001), *Emotions and Social Theory,* London: Sage.

Zarkia, C. (1996), '*Philoxenia:* Receiving Tourists—but Not Guests—on a Greek Island', in J. Boissevain (ed.), *Coping with Tourists: European Reactions to Mass Tourism,* pp. 143–73, Oxford: Berghahn.

Notes

1. In Ward, Bochner and Furnham's (2001: 130) own words: 'Tourism is often represented as being an enjoyable, desirable and pleasurable experience, and most people look forward to and expect their visit abroad to be interesting, relaxing and worthwhile ... Research on tourism, however, has found the reality to be somewhat different. Boredom, bewilderment, rage, disgust, physical and mental illness, excessive alcohol consumption, depression, and antisocial behaviour are as much in evidence as delight and recreation'.

2. Leavitt (1996: 428) also recommends an attention to 'feeling-tones'—to the quality and intensity of emotions, as well as their associations—when we are translating and interpreting them.

3. Gillen also considers work on the psychoanalysis of emotions (Scheff 1990) where negative emotions become blocked in the body and need to discharged. This is best achieved through a ritual activity where internal and external controlling mechanisms are lifted, by tourism for example.

4. Out of the dozen or so dance tourists, there were only two couples in the group.

V
The Emotional Self and Identity

–23–

Person, Time, and Conduct in Bali

Clifford Geertz

The Social Nature of Thought

Human thought is consummately social: social in its origins, social in its functions, social in its forms, social in its applications. At base, thinking is a public activity—its natural habitat is the houseyard, the marketplace, and the town square. The implications of this fact for the anthropological analysis of culture, my concern here, are enormous, subtle, and insufficiently appreciated.

I want to draw out some of these implications by means of what might seem at first glance an excessively special, even a somewhat esoteric inquiry: an examination of the cultural apparatus in terms of which the people of Bali define, perceive, and react to—that is, think about—individual persons. Such an investigation is, however, special and esoteric only in the descriptive sense. The facts, as facts, are of little immediate interest beyond the confines of ethnography, and I shall summarize them as briefly as I can. But when seen against the background of a general theoretical aim—to determine what follows for the analysis of culture from the proposition that human thinking is essentially a social activity—the Balinese data take on a peculiar importance.

Not only are Balinese ideas in this area unusually well developed, but they are, from a Western perspective, odd enough to bring to light some general relationships between different orders of cultural conceptualization that are hidden from us when we look only at our own all-too-familiar framework for the identification, classification and handling of human and quasi-human individuals. In particular, they point up some unobvious connections between the way in which a people perceive themselves and others, the way in which they experience time, and the affective tone of their collective life—connections that have an import not just for the understanding of Balinese society but human society generally.

The Study of Culture

A great deal of recent social scientific theorizing has turned upon an attempt to distinguish and specify two major analytical concepts: culture and social structure.[1] The impetus for this effort has sprung from a desire to take account of ideational factors in social processes without succumbing to either the Hegelian or the Marxist forms of reductionism. In order to avoid having to regard ideas, concepts, values, and expressive forms either as shadows cast by the organization of society upon the hard surfaces of history or as the soul of history whole progress is but a working out of their internal dialectic, it has proved necessary to regard them as independent but not self-sufficient forces—as acting and having their impact only within specific social contexts to which they adapt, by which they are stimulated, but upon which they have, to a greater or lesser degree, a determining influence. "Do you really expect," Marc Bloch wrote in his little book on *The Historian's Craft,* "to know the great merchants of Renaissance Europe, vendors of cloth or spices, monopolists in copper, mercury or alum, bankers of Kings and the Emperor, by knowing their merchandise alone? Bear in mind that they were painted by Holbein, that they read Erasmus and Luther. To understand the attitude of the medieval vassal to his seigneur you must inform yourself about his attitude to his God as well." Both the organization of social activity, its institutional forms, and the systems of ideas which animate it must be understood, as must the nature of the relations obtaining between them. It is to this end that the attempt to clarify the concepts of social structure and of culture has been directed.

There is little doubt, however, that within this two-sided development it has been the cultural side which has proved the more refractory and remains the more retarded. In the very nature of the case, ideas are more difficult to handle scientifically than the economic, political, and social relations among individuals and groups which those ideas inform. And this is all the more true when the ideas involved are not the explicit doctrines of a Luther or an Erasmus, or the articulate images of a Holbein, but the half-formed, taken-for-granted, indifferently systematized notions that guide the normal activities of ordinary men in everyday life. If the scientific study of culture has lagged, bogged down most often in mere descriptivism, it has been in large part because its very subject matter is elusive. The initial problem of any ascience—defining its object of study in such a manner as to render it susceptible of analysis—has here turned out to be unusually hard to solve.

It is at this point that the conception of thinking as basically a social act, taking place in the same public world in which other social acts occur, can play its most constructive role. The view that thought does not consist of mysterious processes located in what Gilbert Ryle has called a secret grotto in the head but of a traffic in significant symbols—objects in experience (rituals and tools; graven idols and water holes; gestures, markings, images, and sounds) upon which men have impressed meaning—makes of the study of culture a positive science like any other.[2] The meanings that symbols, the material vehicles of thought, embody are often elusive, vague, fluctuating, and convoluted, but they are, in principle, as capable of being discovered through systematic empirical investigation—especially if the people who perceive them will cooperate a little—as the atomic weight of hydrogen or the function of the adrenal glands. It is through culture patterns, ordered clusters of significant symbols, that man makes sense of the events through which he lives. The study of culture, the accumulated totality of such patterns, is thus the study of the machinery individuals and groups of individuals employ to orient themselves in a world otherwise opaque.

In any particular society, the number of generally accepted and frequently used culture patterns is extremely large, so that sorting out even the most important ones and tracing whatever relationships they might have to one another is a staggering analytical task. The task is somewhat lightened, however, by the fact that certain sorts of patterns and certain sorts of relationships among patterns recur from society to society, for the simple reason that the orientational requirements they serve are generically human. The problems, being existential, are universal; their solutions, being human, are diverse. It is, however, through the circumstantial understanding of these unique solutions, and in my opinion only in that way, that the nature of the underlying problems to which they are a comparable response can be truly comprehended. Here, as in so many branches of knowledge, the road to the grand abstractions of science winds through a thicket of singular facts.

One of these pervasive orientational necessities is surely the characterization of individual human beings. Peoples everywhere have developed symbolic structures in terms of which persons are perceived not baldly as such, as mere unadorned members of the human race, but as representatives of certain distinct categories of persons, specific sorts of individuals. In any given case, there are inevitably a plurality of such structures. Some, for example kinship terminologies, are ego-centered: that is, they define the status of an individual in terms of his relationship to a specific social actor. Others are centered on one or another subsystem or aspect of society and are invariant with respect to the perspectives of individual actors: noble ranks, age-group statuses, occupational categories. Some—personal names and sobriquets—are informal and particularizing; others—bureaucratic titles and caste designations—are formal and standardizing. The everyday world in which the members of any community move, their taken-for-granted field of social action, is populated not by anybodies, faceless men without qualities, but by somebodies, concrete classes of determinate persons positively characterized and appropriately labeled. And the symbol systems which define these classes are not given in the nature of things—they are historically constructed, socially maintained, and individually applied.

Even a reduction of the task of cultural analysis to a concern only with those patterns having something to do with the characterization of individual persons renders it only slightly less formidable, however. This is because there does not yet exist a perfected theoretical framework within which to carry it out. What is called structural analysis in sociology and social anthropology can ferret out the functional implications for a society of a particular system of person-categories, and at times even predict how such a system might change under the impact of certain social processes; but only if the system—the categories, their meanings, and their logical relationships—can be taken as already known. Personality theory in social-psychology can uncover the motivational dynamics underlying the formation and the use of such systems and can assess their effect upon the character structures of individuals actually employing them; but also only if, in a sense, they are already given, if how the individuals in question see themselves and others has been somehow determined. What is needed is some systematic, rather than merely literary or impressionistic, way to discover what *is* given, what the conceptual structure embodied in the symbolic forms through which persons are perceived actually is. What we want and do not yet have is a developed method of describing and analyzing the meaningful structure of experience (here, the experience of persons) as it is apprehended by representative members of a particular society at a particular point in time—in a word, a scientific phenomenology of culture.

Balinese Orders of Person-Definition

In Bali,[3] there are six sorts of labels which one person can apply to another in order to identify him as a unique individual and which I want to consider against this general conceptual background: (1) personal names; (2) birth order names; (3) kinship terms; (4) teknonyms; (5) status titles (usually called "caste names" in the literature on Bali); and (6) public titles, by which I mean quasi-occupational titles borne by chiefs, rulers, priests, and gods. These various labels are not, in most cases, employed simultaneously, but alternatively, depending upon the situation and sometimes the individual. They are not, also, all the sorts of such labels ever used; but they are the only ones which are generally recognized and regularly applied. And as each sort consists not of a mere collection of useful tags but of a distinct and bounded terminological system, I shall refer to them as "symbolic orders of person-definition" and consider them first serially, only later as a more or less coherent cluster.

Personal Names

The symbolic order defined by personal names is the simplest to describe because it is in formal terms the least complex and in social ones the least important. All Balinese have personal names, but they rarely use them, either to refer to themselves or others or in addressing anyone. (With respect to one's forebears, including one's parents, it is in fact sacrilegious to use them.) Children are more often referred to and on occasion even addressed by their personal names. Such names are therefore sometimes called "child" or "little" names, though once they are ritually bestowed 105 days after birth, they are maintained unchanged through the whole course of a man's life. In general, personal names are seldom heard and play very little public role.

Yet, despite this social marginality, the personal-naming system has some characteristics which, in a rather left-handed way, are extremely significant for an understanding of Balinese ideas of personhood. First, personal names are, at least among the commoners (some 90 percent of the population), arbitrarily coined nonsense syllables. They are not drawn from any established pool of names which might lend to them any secondary significance as being "common" or "unusual," as reflecting someone's being named "after" someone—an ancestor, a friend of the parents, a famous personage—or as being propitious, suitable, characteristic of a group or region, indicating a kinship relation, and so forth.[4] Second, the duplication of personal names within a single community—that is, a politically unified, nucleated settlement—is studiously avoided. Such a settlement (called a *bandjar,* or "hamlet") is the primary face-to-face group outside the purely domestic realm of the family, and in some respects is even more intimate. Usually highly endogamous and always highly corporate, the hamlet is the Balinese world of consociates par excellence; and, within it, every person possesses, however unstressed on the social level, at least the rudiments of a completely unique cultural identity. Third, personal names are monomials, and so do not indicate familial connections, or in fact membership in any sort of group whatsoever. And, finally, there are (a few rare, and in any case only partial, exceptions aside) no nicknames, no epithets of the "Richard-the-Lion-Hearted" or "Ivan-the-Terrible" sort among the nobility, not even any diminutives for children or pet names for lovers, spouses, and so on.

Thus, whatever role the symbolic order of person-definition marked out by the personal-naming system plays in setting Balinese off from one another or in ordering Balinese social relations is essentially residual in nature. One's name is what remains to one when all the other socially much more salient cultural labels attached to one's person are removed. As the virtually religious avoidance of its direct use indicates, a personal name is an intensely private matter. Indeed, toward the end of a man's life, when he is but a step away from being the deity he will become after his death and cremation, only he (or he and a few equally aged friends) may any longer know what in fact it is; when he disappears it disappears with him. In the well-lit world of everyday life, the purely personal part of an individual's cultural definition, that which in the context of the immediate consociate community is most fully and completely his, and his alone, is highly muted. And with it are muted the more idiosyncratic, merely biographical, and, consequently, transient aspects of his existence as a human being (what, in our more egoistic framework, we call his "personality") in favor of some rather more typical, highly conventionalized, and, consequently, enduring ones.

Birth Order Names

The most elementary of such more standardized labels are those automatically bestowed upon a child, even a stillborn one, at the instant of its birth, according to whether it is the first, second, third, fourth, etc., member of a sibling set. There is some local and status-group variation in usage here, but the most common system is to use *Wayan* for the first child, *Njoman* for the second, *Made* (or *Nengah*) for the third, and *Ktut* for the fourth, beginning the cycle over again with Wayan for the fifth, Njoman for the sixth, and so on.

These birth order names are the most frequently used terms of both address and reference within the hamlet for children and for young men and women who have not yet produced offspring. Vocatively, they are almost always used simply, that is, without the addition of the personal name: "Wayan, give me the hoe," and so forth. Referentially, they may be supplemented by the personal name, especially when no other way is convenient to get across which of the dozens of Wayans or Njomans in the hamlet is meant: "No, not Wayan Rugrug, Wayan Kepig," and so on. Parents address their own children and childless siblings address one another almost exclusively by these names, rather than by either personal names or kin terms. For persons who have had children, however, they are never used either inside the family or out, teknonyms being employed, as we shall see, instead, so that, *in cultural terms,* Balinese who grow to maturity without producing children (a small minority) remain themselves children—that is, are symbolically pictured as such—a fact commonly of great shame to them and embarrassment to their consociates, who often attempt to avoid having to use vocatives to them altogether.[5]

The birth order system of person-definition represents, therefore, a kind of *plus ça change* approach to the denomination of individuals. It distinguishes them according to four completely contentless appellations, which neither define genuine classes (for there is no conceptual or social reality whatsoever to the class of all Wayans or all Ktuts in a community), nor express any concrete characteristics of the individuals to whom they are applied (for there is no notion that Wayans have any special psychological or spiritual traits in common against Njomans or Ktuts). These names, which have no literal meaning in themselves (they are not numerals or derivatives of numerals) do not, in fact, even indicate sibling position or rank in any realistic or reliable way.[6] A Wayan may be a fifth (or ninth!) child as well as a first; and, given a traditional peasant demographic structure—great fertility plus a high rate of stillbirths and deaths in infancy and childhood—a Made or a Ktut may actually be the oldest of a long string of siblings and a Wayan the youngest. What they do suggest is that, for all procreating couples, births form a circular succession of Wayans, Njomans, Mades, Ktuts, and once again Wayans, an endless four-stage replication of an imperishable form. Physically men come and go as the ephemerae they are, but socially the *dramatis personae* remain eternally the same as new Wayans and Ktuts emerge from the timeless world of the gods (for infants, too, are but a step away from divinity) to replace those who dissolve once more into it.

Kinship Terms

Formally, Balinese kinship terminology is quite simple in type, being of the variety known technically as "Hawaiian" or "Generational." In this sort of system, an individual classifies his relatives primarily according to the generation they occupy with respect to his own. That is to say, sibling, half-siblings, and cousins (and their spouses' siblings, and so forth) are grouped together under the same term; all uncles and aunts on either side are terminologically classed with mother and father; all children of brothers, sisters, cousins, and so on (that is, nephews of one sort or another) are identified with own children; and so on, downward through the grandchild, great-grandchild, etc., generations, and upward through the grandparent, great-grandparent, etc., ones. For any given actor, the general picture is a layer-cake arrangement of relatives, each layer consisting of a different generation of kin—that of actor's parents or his children, of his grandparents or his grandchildren, and so on, with his own layer, the one from which the calculations are made, located exactly halfway up the cake.[7]

Given the existence of this sort of system, the most significant (and rather unusual) fact about the way it operates in Bali is that the terms it contains are almost never used vocatively, but only referentially, and then not very frequently. With rare exceptions, one does not actually call one's father (or uncle) "father," one's child (or nephew/niece) "child," one's brother (or cousin) "brother," and so on. For relatives genealogically junior to oneself vocative forms do not even exist; for relatives senior they exist but, as with personal names, it is felt to demonstrate a lack of respect for one's elders to use them. In fact, even the referential forms are used only when specifically needed to convey some kinship information as such, almost never as general means of identifying people.

Kinship terms appear in public discourse only in response to some question, or in describing some event which has taken place or is expected to take place, with respect to which the existence of the kin tie is felt to be a relevant piece of information. ("Are you going to Father-of-Regreg's tooth-filling?" "Yes, he is my 'brother.'") Thus, too, modes of address and reference within the family are no more (or not much more) intimate or expressive of kin ties in quality than those within the hamlet generally. As soon as a child is old enough to be capable of doing so (say, six years, though this naturally varies) he calls his mother and father by the same term—a teknonym, status group title, or public title—that everyone else who is acquainted with them uses toward them, and is called in turn Wayan, Ktut, or whatever, by them. And, with even more certainty, he will refer to them, whether in their hearing or outside of it, by this popular, extradomestic term as well.

In short, the Balinese system of kinship terminology defines individuals in a primarily taxonomic, not a face-to-face idiom, as occupants of regions in a social field, not partners in social interaction. It functions almost entirely as a cultural map upon which certain persons can be located and certain others, not features of the landscape mapped, cannot. Of course, some notions of appropriate interpersonal behavior follow once such determinations are made, once a person's place in the structure is ascertained. But the critical point is that, in concrete practice, kin terminology is employed virtually exclusively in service of ascertainment, not behavior, with respect to whose patterning other symbolic appliances are dominant.[8] The social norms associated with kinship, though real enough, are habitually overridden, even within kinship-type groups themselves (families, households, lineages) by culturally better armed norms associated with religion, politics, and, most fundamentally of all, social stratification.

Yet in spite of the rather secondary role it plays in shaping the moment-to-moment flow of social intercourse, the system of kinship terminology, like the personal-naming system, contributes importantly, if indirectly, to the Balinese notion of personhood. For, as a system of significant symbols, it too embodies a conceptual structure under whose agency individuals, one's self as well as others, are apprehended; a conceptual structure which is, moreover, in striking congruence with those embodied in the other, differently constructed and variantly oriented, orders of person-definition. Here, also, the leading motif is the immobilization of time through the iteration of form.

This iteration is accomplished by a feature of Balinese kin terminology I have yet to mention: in the third generation above and below the actor's own, terms become completely reciprocal. That is to say, the term for "great-grandparent" and "great-grandchild" is the same: *kumpi*. The two generations, and the individuals who comprise them, are culturally identified. Symbolically, a man is equated upwardly with the most distant ascendant, downwardly with the most distant descendant, he is ever likely to interact with as a living person.

Actually, this sort of reciprocal terminology proceeds on through the fourth generation, and even beyond. But as it is only extremely rarely that the lives of a man and his great-great-grandparent (or great-great-grandchild) overlap, this continuation is of only theoretical interest, and most people don't even know the terms involved. It is the four-generation span (i.e., the actor's own, plus three ascending or descending) which is considered the attainable ideal, the image, like our three-score-and-ten, of a fully completed life, and around which the kumpi-kumpi terminology puts, as it were, an emphatic cultural parenthesis.

This parenthesis is accentuated further by the rituals surrounding death. At a person's funeral, all his relatives who are generationally junior to him must make homage to his lingering spirit in the Hindu palms-to-forehead fashion, both before his bier and, later, at the graveside. But this virtually absolute obligation, the sacramental heart of the funeral ceremony, stops short with the third descending generation, that of his "grandchildren." His "great-grandchildren" are his kumpi, as he is theirs, and so, the Balinese say, they are not really junior to him at all but rather "the same age." As such, they are not only not required to show homage to his spirit, but they are expressly forbidden to do so. A man prays only to the gods and, what is the same thing, his seniors, not to his equals or juniors.[9]

Balinese kinship terminology thus not only divides human beings into generational layers with respect to a given actor, it bends these layers into a continuous surface which joins the "lowest" with the "highest" so that, rather than a layer-cake image, a cylinder marked off into six parallel bands called "own," "parent," "grandparent," "kumpi," "grandchild," and "child" is perhaps more exact.[10] What at first glance seems a very diachronic formulation, stressing the ceaseless progression of generations, is, in fact, an assertion of the essential unreality—or anyway the unimportance of such a progression. The sense of sequence, of sets of collaterals following one another through time, is an illusion generated by looking at the terminological system as though it were used to formulate the changing quality of face-to-face interactions between a man and his kinsmen as he ages and dies—as indeed many if not most such systems are used. When one looks at it, as the Balinese primarily do as a common-sense taxonomy of the possible types of familial relationships human beings may have, a classification of kinsmen into natural groups, it is clear that what the bands on the cylinder are used to represent is the genealogical order of seniority among living people and nothing more. They depict the spiritual (and what is the same thing, structural) relations among coexisting generations, not the location of successive generations in an unrepeating historical process.

Notes

1. The most systematic and extensive discussions are to be found in T. Parsons and E. Shils, eds., *Toward a General Theory of Action* (Cambridge, Mass., 1959); and T. Parsons, *The Social System* (Glencoe, Ill., 1951). Within anthropology, some of the more notable treatments, not all of them in agreement, include: S. F. Nadel, *Theory of Social Structure* (Glencoe, Ill., 1957); E. Leach, *Political Systems of Highland Burma* (Cambridge, Mass., 1954); E. E. Evans-Pritchard, *Social Anthropology* (Glencoe, Ill., 1951); R. Redfield, *The Primitive World and Its Transformations* (Ithaca, 1953); C. Lévi-Strauss, "Social Structure," in his *Structural Anthropology* (New York, 1963), pp. 277–323; R. Firth, *Elements of Social Organization* (New York, 1951); and M. Singer, "Culture," in *International Encyclopaedia of the Social Sciences,* vol. 3 (New York, 1968), p. 527.

2. G. Ryle, *The Concept of Mind* (New York, 1949). I have dealt with some of the philosophical issues, here passed over in silence, raised by the "extrinsic theory of thought," above, Chapter 3, pp. 55–61, and need now only re-emphasize that this theory does not involve a commitment to behaviorism, in either its methodological or epistemological forms; nor yet again to any disputation of the brute fact that it is individuals, not collectives, who think.

3. In the following discussion, I shall be forced to schematize Balinese practices severely and to represent them as being much more homogeneous and rather more consistent than they really are. In particular, categorical statements, of either a positive or negative variety ("All Balinese"; "No Balinese ...") must be read as having attached to them the implicit qualification "... so far as my knowledge goes," and even sometimes as riding roughshod over exceptions deemed to be "abnormal." Ethnographically fuller presentations of some of the data here summarized can be found in H. and C. Geertz, "Teknonymy in Bali: Parenthood, Age-Grading, and Genealogical Amnesia," *Journal of the Royal Anthropological Institute* 94 (part 2) (1964): 94–108; C. Geertz, "Tihingan: A Balinese Village," *Bijdragen tot de taal-, land- en volkenkunde,* 120 (1964): 1–33; and C. Geertz, "Form and Variation in Balinese Village Structure," *American Anthropologist* 61 (1959): 991–1012.

4. While personal names of commoners are mere inventions, meaningless in themselves, those of the gentry are often drawn from Sanskrit sources and "mean" something, usually something rather high-flown, like "virtuous warrior" or "courageous scholar." But this meaning is ornamental rather than denotative, and in most cases what the meaning of the name is (as opposed to the simple fact that it has one) is not actually known. This contrast between mere babble among the peasantry and empty grandiloquence among the gentry is not without cultural significance, but its significance lies mainly in the area of the expression and perception of social inequality, not of personal identity.

5. This is, of course not to say that such people are reduced in *sociological* (much less psychological) terms to playing the role or a child, for they are accepted as adults, if incomplete ones, by their consociates. The failure to have children is, however, a distinct handicap for anyone desiring much local power or prestige, and I have for my part never known a childless man who carried much weight in hamlet councils, or for that matter who was not socially marginal in general.

6. From a merely etymological point of view, they do have a certain aura of meaning, for they derive from obsolete roots indicating "leading," "medial," and "following"; but these gossamery meanings have no genuine everyday currency and are, if at all, but very peripherally perceived.

7. In point of fact, the Balinese system (or, in all probability, any other system) is not purely generational; but the intent here is merely to convey the general form of the system, not its precise structure. For the full terminological system, see H. and C. Geertz, "Teknonymy in Bali."

8. For a distinction, similar to the one drawn here, between the "ordering" and the "role-designating" aspects of kin terminologies, see D. Schneider and G. Homans, "Kinship Terminology and the American Kinship System," *American Anthropologist,* 57 (1955): 1195–1201.

9. Old men of the same generation as the deceased do not pray to him either, of course, for the same reason.

10. It might seem that the continuation of terms beyond the kumpi level would argue against this view. But in fact it supports it. For, in the rare case where a man has a ("real" or "classificatory") great-great-grandchild *(kelab)* old enough to worship him at his death, the child is, again, forbidden to do so. But here not because he is "the same age" as the deceased but because he is "(a generation) older"—i.e., equivalent to the dead man's "father." Similarly, an old man who lives long enough to have a great-great-grandchild kelab who bas passed infancy then died will worship—alone—at the child's grave, for the child is (one generation) senior to him. In principle, the same pattern holds in more distant generations, when, as the Balinese do not use kin terms to refer to the dead or the unborn, the problem becomes entirely theoretical: "That's what we'd call them and how we would treat them if we had any, which we never do."

–24–

Emotions and the Self
A Theory of Personhood and Political Order
Among Pintupi Aborigines

Fred R. Myers

Between 1973 and 1975 I did field work with the Pintupi at a settlement called Yayayi, 180 miles west of Alice Springs.[1] At this time, the Pintupi were no longer living a traditional hunting-gathering life in the desert; for the past 40 years, the Pintupi have been drifting eastward from the Gibson Desert homeland, although the majority "came in" the 200–400 miles to European missions or settlements between 1954 and 1966. They were living, then, on the Australian equivalent of a "reservation" and not on their *own* land. A few months before I arrived, however, the Pintupi moved from a large government settlement (Papunya) comprising Aborigines of several different language groups to Yayayi, the site of a windmill-driven pump that was their own place ("all Pintupi"), and where about 300 people lived with little more than the windmill, some government-granted tents, and a few vehicles for transport. In theory, they were "governed" by a democratically elected Village Council, a notion introduced by the government.

Emotions

When I use the phrase "concepts of the emotions," I refer to the vocabulary and cultural understandings that bear on a particular sort of feeling, on "symptoms" that "convey and represent information about one's *mode of relationship* as a total individual to the social and nonsocial environment" (Levy 1973: 271). Pain, fatigue, and the like would not be considered as "emotions." What I am arguing here is the Pintupi use of concepts of the emotions frequently does not present an introspective view of a person's feelings.

Indeed, I found it very difficult to elicit private or individual interpretations of experience, as in the matter of a parent's death. Even when the Pintupi are talking about what Levy calls the "private self"—"those aspects of an individual's experience that are related to his body, his feelings, his sense of self, his needs for personal definition and integration, his understanding of what is going on around him as it involves himself" (Levy 1973: xix)—they seem to present it in terms that reflect more about the cultural system than about the individual. The Aboriginal autobiographies I have seen, as well as those I tried to elicit, emphasize the cultural expectations much more than they do the specific experiences and interpretations of the individual; they seem illustrations rather than self-conscious introspections. It was frequently difficult to tell whether a person was genuinely "angry" (feeling anger) or whether the display was a "cultural performance," or finally what sense it made to distinguish these. Pintupi talk of emotion, then, is not necessarily the talk of "raw experience." Just what it is I hope to explain in what follows.

The Moral Order of Walytja

In this light, the key symbol for the Pintupi social order is the concept of *walytja,* which recognizes the relationship of the self to various others. While psychoanalysts have described how these "cathected objects" become part of an individual's self-orientation, the Pintupi have based their culture on the concept of *walytja* as the dominant symbol of shared identity and mutual support. "Official" Pintupi representations of their social life stress that they are "one family" (*walytjatjuta,* also "all related"). For any individual, the Pintupi social universe is divided into two categories: (1) those who are "kin," "relations," or "family" (*walytja*), and (2) those who are not kin, often described as "not men" or "different men" (*munuwati*), that is, those who are in the deepest sense unrelated. The term *walytja* specifies a sense of belonging together, or shared identity. It is used to refer to (1) possessions, (2) "kin," (3) "one's own" (my own), (4) a wider sense of belonging, and (5) "oneself" as "he did it himself" or "she is sitting by herself." The concept asserts a relationship between oneself and persons, objects, or places; it recognizes as fundamental in Pintupi life the identity extended to persons and things beyond the physical individual. In contrast, those who are not truly "relations" are often described as "nothing to do" (a pidgin phrase), "other" (*munuka*) or "not the same," and sometimes with a metaphor of spatial separateness as "outside." All such explanations imply that nonrelations are those with whom one has little or no interaction. Finally, the term as applied to social space has expanding application, depending on whom the speaker is viewing in contrast with "relations."

One's *walytja* are not necessarily actual consanguines; they are those with whom one grows up, those with whom one is familiar, those who have fed and cared for one, those with whom one camps frequently. Strangers, those who are unknown, are likely to be feared or suspected dangerous.

The usual domestic unit of a "camp" of husband, wife (or wives), and small children defines the closest group of *walytja* and the primary food-sharing unit. Beyond this are other family "camps" that may frequently co-reside as parts of the same band. The members of different "camps" may spend significant time with each other, share meat, look after small children, feed them, and lavish attention on them. During the day, infants may be handled by a variety of women and girls, and men will play with or feed a child, although it is rarely permitted out of the mother's sight. These people, who cooperate in economic life as well as in recreation, are also seen as *walytja*. Some attitudes to *walytja* seem highly reminiscent of childhood experience. There is no attempt to discipline a small child and any discomfort perceived is met with attempts to relieve it. The breast is never denied, and the child is encouraged to respond favorably to those who play with him or her, as these are seen as the child's *walytja*. To be brief, the Pintupi child's world is one of support, generosity, familiarity, and warmth. These are precisely the qualities that ideally characterize relations among adult *walytja,* who help each other, do not frustrate each other's wishes, and share food. Thus, we are likely to hear the characterization by informants, *in moments of tranquility,* of the Pintupi as all "one family," a characterization not applied on occasions of dispute. Of course, jealousy, envy, dislike, and greed are enduring parts of Pintupi life, but the "official representation" of themselves is as "family," and acts that indicate contrary feelings are not usually displayed openly.

The concepts of *walytja* can be said to define the moral order of Pintupi society as "family" as opposed to relations with "strangers," which are full of fear, hostility, and suspicion. It is important to keep in mind that such a conception of society as mutual aid and care well fits the actual economic relations among Pintupi where mobility and flexibility of band composition is great and where sharing among band members is a duty. The image of Pintupi society, then, is of a group of closely cooperating kin, each no better than the rest, with all sharing some kind of identification and mutual concern, The Pintupi view of the self and other, then, receives validation from their experience of social life in which kin should and do help each other.

Fragments of the Self

The next set of concepts have what Wittgenstein called "a family resemblance," which the Pintupi recognize in using the term *ngaltutjarra* as the conventionalized expression for any of these feelings. In reference, however, they may be distinguished as indicated here. "Compassion" (*ngaltu*) and "grief" or "sorrow" (*yalurrpa*) both refer to a feeling of sorrow or concern for another, a kind of compassionate empathy, although "grief" ordinarily represents the more extremes of emotionality. The concept I translate as "melancholy" or "pining" (*watjilpa*) seems to convey a similar state of spirit, but one whose original source is oneself. Thus, a man might say *ngaltutjarra, ngayuku, ngurra,"* meaning something like "poor me, my own country." He points to himself, his feelings of melancholy, as one who should be "pitied."

Underlying the concept of compassion is a recognition of "relatedness" or "closeness"—a recognition of shared identity (*walytja*) or empathy between the person who is compassionate and another. This is the source of the other's legitimate claim on one's compassion. Not to have compassion (or not to display it) is seen as "not liking" the other person, that is, not recognizing the link, and this "linking" is a matter of great concern to Pintupi.

As one might expect, such feelings are cultivated and to be a "compassionate" person (and when to be such) is the goal of considerable childhood training, Typically, young children holding an item desired by another who cries for it are told "be compassionate, give it to him" (*ngaltutjarra, yuwara*). Adults frequently play at this with children, who then become accustomed to sharing. Similarly, on hearing of some misfortune which befell another, Pintupi commonly bespeak their compassion: "Oh, the poor fellow" (*ngaltujarra*).

Indeed, without going into too much detail, it seems that the Pintupi live up to their ideal often enough; they are moved to help at the sight of another's pitiful condition. Food is never denied to the hungry, as the story of a prospector, Lassiter, illustrates: lost in the Gibson Desert and without food, he was fed and cared for by the Pintupi's neighbors, the Pitjanytjatjarra. For similar reasons, one should not threaten the weak. "Poor fellow, she is harmless," they may say of a woman whose husband had beaten her viciously.

It is on this basis that the widely-described pressure of relatives on richer kin is brought to bear. It is among kin most appropriately that such considerations are important. One who has something should share with the less fortunate. Jurally, a relative *should* share food, but since it cannot be shared with everyone, whether he or she does share or not is considered to be a manifestation of "affect." One who is not given food is likely to say, "You don't love me." What seems clear is that concepts of affect are the idiom in which relatedness is expressed. Those who do not exhibit such feelings and come through with the goods are felt to be "hard" or "like rocks." Like rocks, they are without emotion, without recognition of shared identity, and perhaps not quite human. I have heard Pintupi threaten those whom they considered to have responded frequently in less than human fashion; one who treats another this way, who denies relatedness, invites physical retribution: "I'm no bullock" (i.e., I'm human).

That the concept of "compassion" is best understood as the notion of being moved by another's wishes or condition is expressed by one man's hope that the doctors would take away his insane wife. They should not, he said, feel sorry for her (*ngalturrinytja wiya*), but should do what *he* wanted (i.e., have compassion on *him*).

In Pintupi life, "compassion" is both a characteristic quality of social relations and a concept commonly alluded to. It has significant implications for decision-making and consensus. Most threats of sending away wrongdoers or sacking individuals from their jobs (no matter how well-intentioned) were followed by a subsequent decision to "give them one more chance." The wrongdoers often prompted this by referring to kinship links or asking, "Don't you trust me?" and thereby alluding to the link between them. They rarely failed to evoke "compassion," as the plaintiffs reflected on the moral ideal. Such a strategy also permits the plaintiff to display publicly his or her "compassion," his or her moral qualities. I say this because, despite their "compassion," leaders do not seem to forget or truly forgive the offense—as private comments after such occasions revealed. "Strangers" (non-relations) are less likely to receive much concern, although the Pintupi are certainly capable of extending their compassion to anyone with a "good case" (including anthropologists).

Indeed, few of the accounts available about Aborigines illustrate cruelty or torture; many are the accounts of their kindness to unfortunate Europeans. "Compassion" or "pity" seems a highly adaptive quality among people whose resources are somewhat unreliable. Men told me they would never send visitors away from their own water-holes in time of drought. Such action was unthinkable: "We would feel compassion for them." The concept clearly phrases the limitations on an individual's autonomy and subjects decisions rather consistently to a shifting push-and-pull, a quality noted by Nancy Williams (n.d.) for the so-called Murngin. The possibility is always there of manipulating others' actions toward one's desired end, because others will feel "compassion," or because one makes the other think that he or she should feel it.

This does not mean that Pintupi are never selfish. Individuals sometimes hide possessions to avoid sharing, and often enough they are goaded into giving by veiled taunts. With possessions such as cigarettes or extra clothing hidden, one may express "compassion" without having to give up anything. This withholding may be rationalized by commenting that the other is "not really *walytja*" or "nothing to do." On the other hand, some individuals are generous in the service of building a kind of informal following. Such an informal leader must be "compassionate" with individuals or lose his following. Those leaders (in the Council) who tried to be "hard," to stick to their decisions, also tried to seek a support base from the white boss or the white community (government employees).

To show "compassion," then, may be a strategy by which individuals hope to gain something else. Perhaps fear of retaliation by the offended party is the motivation. There are, it seems, numerous possibilities, and only knowledge of the individual's history, his or her dispositions or personality would enable us to interpret the motivational basis for his or her acts. By acting with compassion, whatever the motivations, one's act is presented in a favorable light for oneself and for others.

This emotion is a moral ideal, an emotion Pintupi say that people *should have,* just as it is said that one should love his or her spouse and children. Acts are interpreted in light of this theory of motivation. The cultural value placed on such emotions does permit individuals to elaborate and emphasize them, both in their understanding and in comprehending others.

The related concept of "grief" (*yalurrpa*) is seen as generated by loss or threat of loss of some related other, usually a close relative, felt as a loss of part of oneself. Such "grief" is expressed by wailing at the news of a death as well as through the expected self-injury (head-gashing, thigh-stabbing) appropriate for the kind of kin relationship—a kind of imprinting of the body social onto the individual. So is the native cat of mythology said to have split his own head open with "grief" (*yalurrtu yatunu*) at the sight of his dead sons. Another native cat, grief-stricken at seeing the slaughter of his relatives by another group, was moved to revenge.

"Grief" is a powerful emotion, a real shaking of the foundations, an intimation of mortality. As seen by the Pintupi, "sorrow" is a particularly human trait. "Grief" attaches to many situations surrounding death. One should not mention the names of the dead because their relatives will be too "sorry." This may last for years after the death of a close relative; some women will wail for years after a son's death. Because people are "too sorry," they may avoid the place where one of their kin died for several years. For others to approach such a site would bring anger from the deceased relatives, because of disrespect. Abandonment of a place in which death occurs is a cultural convention, a proper way to behave. It need not derive spontaneously from "feelings" of grief, but the display is clearly meant as an expression of one's relatedness to the dead. Similarly, one's claim to "land ownership" is an emotional one, through relationship to one buried at a place. Goodale (1971:100) has reported similar customs for the Tiwi, and it may be worth considering the importance of the accretion of "sorrow" to associated things in the context of the value of sacred sites, sacred objects, and the like. The significance of *place* in Aboriginal thought may derive some emotional force from the displacement of emotional ties with the dead to places associated with them.

In any case, the concept of "sorrow" is clearly attached to ritual paraphernalia and to sacred places of The Dreaming, both considered of extreme value. On sight of these, older men often begin to wail, because they are "sorry." An informant explained this to me with reference to the designs incised on a spearthrower:

> Dead men schooled me, gave it to me. When people see it they get sorry, Give one like this to a man and people will see it and give you a woman. Too much crying (from sorrow) for this one.

While this single context cannot make it fully clear, it seems that ritual and sacred things are associated with the memory of people now dead, who previously handled them and passed them on. This is the source, in part, of their emotional value. Charged with reminders of the dead, they may make one cry with "sorrow," remembering that which binds them to this object.

The Pintupi make this explicit in revealing rituals to the young men. The elders frequently emphasize that "this belonged to dead men, you have to hold it and pass it on." I think we cannot help but regard this theme in male ritual as drawing upon the strongest sentiments of relatedness and continuity juxtaposed with mortality to imbue that which is of universal and transcendent value—The Dreaming—with the most powerful sentiments of identity available. The significance of this binding or "cathecting" of initiates to the transcendent makes sense to us in the light of the other fundamental social implications of "sorrow."

In narrative—and other evidence supports this—"sorrow" or "compassion" was often said to be the reason that revenge expeditions turned back. If they had sufficient time to think about the identity of the one they wanted to kill, they became "sorry." In one reported case, the revenge party threw spears at the guilty man, which he repeatedly and successfully dodged. They became sorry for him and let him go.

On the other hand, it was said that a man who had recently committed a grievous ceremonial offense was recently killed by another group—"no sorrow." This identifies a clear problem for those who want to bring sanctions to bear on offenders against moral law—that is, how to overcome the "feeling" of sorrow or compassion for "relations" that might prevent them from carrying out punishment.[2] In some cases, this is circumvented by asking outsiders to punish relatives who had broken "the Law" (a term used to refer to the moral imperative of The Dreaming). Close relatives might be "too sorry" to carry out punishment, as I described above. (This is certainly the reason why outsiders perform ritual circumcisions.) Although the explanation for such expeditions of punishment is "sorrow," the motivation may be vastly more complex for any individual; one may go out of duty, honor, love, hate, or self-hate. "Grief" seems a convenient way to express complex feelings about a person now lost.

In reference to punishments carried out (such as past killings of wrongdoers) the Pintupi often mention that there was "no sorrow." The Pitjanytjatjarra, they said, would kill anyone who crossed the path of their travelling secret ceremonies—women, children, or whites; they were not moved by "sorrow." Great anger, as at the sight of a heinous moral crime, could move men to "spear anyway" (*wapaltuwakala*); that is, without recognition of the opposing party. This, they say, would be without sorrow, without consideration of the identity of the other person. Drunkenness might produce the same excuse for violence: ignorance of the identity of another. This explains the threats to get revenge "anytime, when I'm drunk."

One might argue that the importance of male initiation and male cult is the way in which a man is re-oriented to a greater value than his relatedness to kin; namely, to the Law, The Dreaming. Those who violate The Law, the Pintupi say, will be killed "without sorrow." I suggest that among other things, male initiation provides a mechanism for assuring conformity to things of transcendental value, assuring that concerns beyond the immediate feelings of relatedness will prevail when vital moral issues are at stake. Pintupi describe sacred objects, songs, and such as "Law" in pidgin, emphasizing the binding power. It seems that in Pimupi theory the binding power of Law over compassion comes from "sorrow"—the very expression of relatedness to others, just as in Freudian theory the superego derives from the id in order to oppose it. How else could Pintupi overcome the tendency to "compassion"? An interesting note is that the men are bound to the higher Law through the same considerations of relatedness and "sorrow" for the dead, and also that they do it as agents of a higher authority and not of their own will, so that they are not "'responsible." The Dreaming is something outside of them to which they truly must conform.

I will mention only briefly the third concept of this "family," *watjilpa*. This is often rendered as "homesick," "pining," "lonely," "worry," or "melancholy." The core of the concept refers to separation from objects or persons of security and familiarity—family and home—places and people among which and whom one grew up and where one feels safe and comfortable. Separation from these is the source of "worrying."

This is the Pintupi version of the sentiment Peterson (1972) referred to as an important factor in local organization. Time and again in the life histories collected, Pintupi talked of their travels and the "homesickness" (*watjilpa*) that made them come back to their home country. One friend (who had not seen his country for a long time) explained to me, "I close my eyes and I can see that place. It's very green. There's a rockhole and a hill where I used to play. My brother pushed me down—it makes me 'homesick.'"

A Moral Order

The self described in Pintupi ideology is not an aggressive, self-contained, egotistic, autonomous individual. Pintupi concepts of the emotions represent a self that recognizes a significant identity with important others, such that these others are represented as part of the self. One is malleable to these others, not "hard." One should be moved, not stolid in willfulness. Autonomy, when it comes, comes from outside the individual and is not a product of private will. Rather, this "autonomy"—the zealousness of upholding the Law "without sorrow"—is a representation within the individual of a socially valued moral imperative.

The ideology of the emotions can be read almost as a moral text against the wrongness of private willfulness. Stanner (1956) describes the "mystery" that the Murbinbata attached to the motivation for such private will in an important myth about the "wrongful turning of life." Acceptance of these emotions as appropriate ways of "articulating experience" can be said to represent the "society's interests," although there is no self-conscious collective representation of the "community welfare." In the traditional situation, "community welfare" was achieved through individual ties or dyadic relations, through the emotional response of individuals to significant others, and through maintenance of a core of collectively accepted traditional regulations to which individuals were also emotionally bound by investing the Law with intimations of others.

Ironically, it is precisely this traditional moral solution to the problems of life in society that now constitutes an obstacle to contemporary political organization.

References

Goodale, J. C. 1971. *Tiwi Wives*. Seattle: University of Washington Press.
Levy, R. I. (ed.). 1973. *Culture, Behavior, and Personality*. Chicago: Aldine.

Myers, F. 1976. To Have and to Hold: A Study of Permanence and Change in Pintupi Social Life. Unpublished Ph.D. dissertation, Bryn Mawr College.

———. n.d. Ideology and Experience: The Cultural Basis of Pintupi Politics. Unpublished paper.

Peterson, N. 1972. Totemism Yesterday: Sentiment and Local Organization among the Australian Aborigines. *Man* 7:12–32.

Stanner, W.E.H. 1956. The Dreaming. Australian Signpost (T.A.G. Hungerford, ed.) Melbourne: F.W. Cheshire.

Williamson, N. n.d. Some Observations Concerning Certain Characteristics of Aboriginal Decision-making (mimeograph).

Notes

1. Field research with the Pimupi was supported by NSF Dissertation Improvement Grant No. GS 37122, an Australian Institute of Aboriginal Studies Living Stipend, and NIMH Fellowship No. 3FOIMH57257–01. Invaluable help in the Pintupi Language was provided by Ken Hansen of the Summer Institute of Linguistics. This paper is based on Chapter 5 of my Ph.D. dissertation (Myers 1976) written at Bryn Mawr College under the direction of Jane C. Goodale. I gratefully acknowledge the helpful suggestions of Bette Clark, Don Brenneis, and Michelle Rosaldo. They are, of course, not responsible for what flaws remain. I would also like to thank Pitzer College for the Faculty Research Grant that helped me to prepare this paper.

2. There seems to be less difficulty in cases of delict, when the aggrieved party is usually more than ready to get even.

–25–

Rachel's Emotional Life
Movement and Identity

Nigel Rapport

Introduction: 'Emotion'

> Psychology has split and shattered the idea of a 'Person', and has shown there is something incalculable in each of us, which may at any moment rise to the surface and destroy our normal balance. We don't know what we are like. We can't know what other people are like ... But in practice we can and do ... For the purpose of living one has to assume that the personality is solid, and the 'self' is an entity, and to ignore all contrary evidence.
>
> E. M. Forster (1972:75–6)

Look at the way Forster reasons in the above sentences. Advances in modern psychology, he explains, have split the atom of personality such that our depths are now recognized as unknowable and incoherent. 'Self' and 'other' alike are surface likenesses only; there is no true identity. But these deductions nevertheless do not accord with practice; there, we continue to live 'as if', and purposively ignore the evidence. Forster's argumentational course involves setting up psychology against practice and then shifting attention from one to another so as to reach his conclusion: a purported *modus vivendi* that is nonrational. This argumentation by way of zigzags I would call an 'emotional' way of reasoning. It relies on movement between positions such that the movement becomes the thing rather than those positions' seeming fixity.

The following essay takes as a case study aspects of the life-course of one Rachel Silberstein in order to offer a consideration of the relationship between emotion and self-identity. Rachel is a new immigrant to Israel from the United States; she is to be found making decisions on who to be in her new country, where to live, how to earn a livelihood, with whom to be friends and politically allied. Like Forster, she reasons emotionally; as with him, it is a source of personal strength (see Rapport 1994).

'Emotion' is approached in the chapter as broadly referring to those aspects of an individual's living that concern fluidity and movement ('emotion' from the Latin *'emovere'*, to stir up, ultimately from *'movere'*, to move). 'Emotion' denotes a stirring up of feeling, an agitation of mind. What can an anthropologist say about such emotion in the constitution and the experience of the individual, in the career of an individual life? What can the anthropologist add to the philosophical debate, current since the exchanges of Hume and Kant, on the question of how the *emotional,* the movemental, relates to both the static, fixing qualities of *intellectual* model-building and the driving qualities of *will* that give onto reasoned behaviour? Emotion I shall consider as the fluid, motile part of an individual's conscious life, identity and decision making.

The chapter offers an analysis largely based on ethnography. It is an account of the way in which Rachel Silberstein accrued experiences in Israel which she found to be 'schizo'—neither absolutely one thing nor another—and of the way in which she found herself—her new Israeli identity—by travelling physically, sentimentally and intellectually between one experiential landmark and another. Rachel, I shall say, settled herself into the Negev town of Mitzpe Ramon, and into Israel more generally, by *emotional* means. The chapter thus builds on the anthropological recognition that movement and identity form a vital relationship (Rapport 1997a: 64–79). Such movement may be imaginative (mental) or physical, or both (see Appadurai 1996; Wulff 1998). Not only does one become at home through movement, but movement as such is home, is where identity resides (see Rapport and Dawson 1998).

Philosophical Echoes: Hume and Nietzsche

Let me allude, briefly, to philosophical voices that have been heard querying the nature of our human reasoning: the relationship between emotion, intellect and will.

In considering the way that we reason, David Hume (2000) famously described human beings as 'slave to their passions'. The mind, he asserted, is initially recipient to impressions which come to it through the senses. Ideas are then derived from these impressions, forming the basis of thought and reflection. But ideas are like copies of originals, and both ideas and the impressions that precede them are subjective constructs; knowledge is thus consequent upon embodiment, our knowing things a derivative of our ideation, which itself is epiphenomenal upon our garnering impressions. How, then, do we come to act in a world we consider to be external to us, stable, and common to others? For the sense organs of different individuals are discrete, and limited to the body, while the impressions they furnish—the sensory atoms of consciousness—are fleeting and shifting. Through our imagination, Hume contended, we fill in the gaps. We associate impressions with others similar in kind or contiguous in our experiencing, and thus come to believe there are no gaps. Sensory atoms are bundled together into structures of feeling: imaginatively extending the nature of our impressions, we construe a sense of consistency over time and place and point of view.

Nevertheless, Hume concluded, permanent and independent objects are a figment, a fiction, a product of our imaginative construction of the world. What we know, the objects of our awareness, cannot be separated from the processes of our consciousness, our being there to experience them. We might not be able to help making these fictions—and believing in them might be a human psychological necessity—but in truth the subjective imagination is subject to no checks of objective rationality. There is only the motility of a lifetime of different impressions, transmuted into ideational forms, imaginatively extended into consistent and coherent models and classificatory schemata. Moreover, attentive introspection assures us of this process; when human beings look inside themselves they never meet 'the self' as such, only particular versions of it; human selves are bundles of different perceptions succeeding one another with great rapidity and in perpetual flux.

The paradoxical consequences—the nonrational conclusion of positing a kind of universal human knowing which derives only from individual consciousness—Hume escaped (equally famously) through playing backgammon. There was both Psychological Truth, he concluded, and there was the Practice of engaging with a world of consistent objects (backgammon sets) in common with others (backgammon opponents); the Practice seemed to transmute the metaphysics of the Psychology into a mere 'artificial mood' which he experienced (cf. Gellner 1998:44). Yet, as with E. M. Forster, Hume kept with his conclusion, resisting the solution of a rational *a priori,* either of a transcendental or a relativistic kind. That is, unlike Kant, Hume did not seek to escape the paradox through a claim that the ideas, concepts and categories which we individually derive from our discrete, subjective acts of sensing—such as notions of cause, substance and unity—and the ways we apply these to experience, are actually universal, necessary and logical (hence, while experience may be individual, knowledge will not be). Nor, unlike Herder or de Maistre, did he claim that cultures planted common Gestalts into the bodily faculties of those socialized together such that individuals' animal sensations were disciplined and domesticated into equivalent structures of interpretation. Hume's reasoning remained 'emotional', as I have employed the term: remained in movement between nonreconciled intellectual positions.

Friedrich Nietzsche, too, rejected *a priori* notions of knowledge or knowing, and claims to independently verifiable, objective truth. Our convictions, he wrote, are 'directed by our instincts', by 'physiological demands' (1979a: 3); 'we have no categories which allow us to separate a "world as thing-in-itself" from a world of appearance. All our *categories of reason* have sensual origin' (1968: 488). Human beings construct the world by way of intellectual models and systems of classification, and this concerns not only how things appear to us (what Kant referred to as the 'phenomenal' nature of things) but also what we take to be things' ultimate reality (their 'noumenal' nature); there is no way to derive the appearance/reality distinction except through ourselves. In other words, Nietzsche contended, human consciousness is not separate from the objects and relations it conceives around it, and what it conceives derives ultimately from its sensory physiology. This, in turn, was neither universal nor necessary in character. Our conceptions, according to Nietzsche, derived neither from socialization nor from God, nor from a transcendental Nature; rather from wills-to-power.

Life, as Darwin had argued, was a struggle to survive in which elements of physical life—from atoms to complex organisms—acted as centres of power—'power-quanta'—and sought ever to aggrandize themselves as means to survival. Human conceptions and convictions were means by which the many and competing power-quanta of which their bodies were physically comprised sought to fulfil their wills for life; our intellectual processes and products were the media through which were expressed the physiological desires of the elements of life which our bodies contained—and contests between these. The conceptions and convictions were not 'true' as such. Even Darwinian notions of 'species' surviving in 'environments' were simply part of one particular conceptual schema produced so as to further the fitness, the strength, of particular power-quanta. There was no 'truth-in-itself' as far as the elements of life were concerned, only models: conceptual environments to be exploited and managed towards the furtherance of particular wills-to-power. Like Hume, however, Nietzsche recognized the ongoing human need for the 'fiction' of objective truth, of things-in-themselves, of cause and effect. These were intellectual habits which afforded us strength, self-belief, practical ways forward—also excuses, compensations, rationalizations for failure.

We cannot offer a critique of our human way of knowing, Nietzsche concluded, and occlude the sensory influences on our conceptions; mind is epiphenomenal upon our sensual embodiment. 'Knowing' this does offer us the potential for a kind of piecemeal escape, however; we are no longer trapped within the net of intellectual habits and languages and schemata *as if they were true.* Careful and sustained introspection can allow us to break free from any particular *habitus,* any one interpretative grid, and put us in a position to experiment with new intellectual presuppositions. And who's to say where deeper and deeper introspection might not lead us? The word 'depth' might defy logic (in the light of Nietzsche's own analysis), but it yet accords with our 'intuitions'; probing deeper into the properties of the self, might we not approach essential depths?

Nietzsche's oeuvre, in its entirety, thus treads a nonrational line: 'I am a nuance', he wrote at one point (1979b: 124). In his (autobiographical) writing he wanted to capture both the complexity of what he knew and its rootedness in bodily experience. Western philosophy to date (Christian philosophy, certainly) had misunderstood the body and the role of desire, of sentiment and will, in knowledge. Whereas, in fact, there were no abstract 'philosophies', only 'philosophers'; philosophical insight is simply desire made abstract. Nietzsche was determined, however, to do justice to his individual being-in-the-world; what he knew was an emanation from his bodily becoming: a complex of sensation, intellection and will. His body was like a community or a state of struggling forces, and only his name, 'Friedrich Wilhelm

Nietzsche', gave the impression (maintained the illusion) of singularity, stasis or self-identity. The forces struggled with one another and with elements of life beyond the body, and all the time the body as an entity changed (ingested, grew, moved, became diseased, died), its mental and physical states changed, and its knowledge and identity changed.

We are approaching my ethnography, and the story of Rachel Silberstein. The point of the above historical-philosophical excursus is to provide a context in which my account will sit. Not only is Rachel in venerable company, I would contend, in her 'emotionalism', her paradoxical nonrationalism, in the way that she reasons between contradictory positions and lives out this paradox. But also, here is a way in which anthropology can enter into a continuing metaphysical debate concerning our knowledge of human consciousness, adding its own kinds of insight into human experience and the science of human nature. Rachel Silberstein, we shall see, lives her life by way of an emotional kind of reasoning wherein 'everything resolves itself, finally, into contradictions' (Soren Kierkegaard 1985).

Rachel's Emotional Reasoning and Her Israeli Immigration

When I came here from the States folks said I must be either crazy or else idealistic. But it was a personal journey ... I was brought up very morally and also as a Jew. And I thought putting the two together would make me complete; it was a road I had to go. But it has just led to more illusions being broken. Though I guess I still have a few, deep inside, about Judaism.

Rachel Silberstein would often use road and travel imagery, and not just to recount her *aliyah* [ascent] to Israel from the United States. She described being 'a ceramist' in America, but of having 'taken it as far as it [would] go': 'it [would] not go much further' for her. Once arrived in Israel, she came to find the idea of engaging with the state's bureaucracy dispiriting; but she told herself that since she had gone this far she may as well go the rest of the way, 'to see the heights at the end', but then she 'never seemed to get there'. At first she had thought that the desert town of Mitzpe Ramon was the perfect place for her, 'a place to grow', but soon she found she had 'gone past that'.

Telling Rachel's story, as her fellow new-immigrant in Israel, is for me to give an account of an experiential journey. She did not profess to know where she would end up, nor what she would pass *en route,* but she felt she knew what made her happy, she trusted her intuitions and her inquisitiveness, she believed in her right, even her duty, to make her life into that journey.

Mitzpe Ramon is an isolated development-town deep in the Negev desert in southern Israel, perched high on the panoramic brim of an enormous wind-gouged crater (Rapport 1998). When I first met Rachel she was checking her mailbox at the post office in the company of her dog, an Afghan hound. 'My dog is called Giacomo, after Puccini', she explained to me when, unannounced, she came calling at my apartment two days later. 'Though I didn't know it at the time: I looked round for ages to "find" his name, you know? Then I discovered he and Puccini were born on the same day'. The deep attachment which Rachel had to Giacomo was readily apparent—it was no mere introductory affectation—and the respect too in which she held him. She had no scruples in buying him mincemeat, for instance, even though she herself professed a staunch vegetarianism (and expected all right-thinking humans to do so too).

Rachel was 49, tall, straight-backed and sturdy, with dark (though greying) hair. She grew up in Boston, Massachusetts, where she also went to university (majoring in political science) and married. From the age of 24 she supported herself financially through the sale of ceramics which she herself cast and fired, developing a name for herself—and for her brand, 'Slithery Snake'—on the American East Coast. When she was 28, Rachel and her husband separated. But it was only some 20 years later that they formally divorced, and it was the monetary sum her ex-husband settled on her which became Rachel's means finally to 'make the break' and emigrate to Israel. Over the years she had made a number of shorter trips to *Ha'Aretz* ('the Land'), her first couple being through an organization called Volunteers for Israel, which involved Rachel roughing it in army barracks for three weeks—not to mention sleeping with Israeli soldiers! Her second trip with Volunteers for Israel Rachel recalled as being less successful than the first—she encountered too many closed, 'Type A' personalities—but it still had not put her off, and finally she had decided to make *aliyah*.

For the first seven months of her immigration Rachel had lived in a government Absorption Center in Upper Nazareth, with other, new Jewish arrivals. Meanwhile she also sought out and visited artist centres, villages and workshops—En Hod, Kibbutz Nachshon—in order to initiate a network of relations with like-minded people. Finally, she struck out on her own and moved south to Beer Sheva, a city she hoped would connect her experientially to the Negev desert—an environment she found thrilling. On one trip into the desert she visited a field school in the small town of Mitzpe Ramon (some 50 kilometres away) and agreed to serve as a volunteer pottery teacher to those teenagers who attended the school as part of their educational trip to the famous crater; she would match her skills to their needs. Indeed, she liked the town so much, and she found the utopian vision of the old man who ran the field school, Uri Hazan, so beguiling, that after only a month in Beer Sheva—where, sadly, she was 'experiencing nothing'—she moved to Mitzpe. As she explained to me that first evening in my apartment:

Rachel: I thought Mitzpe would be a great place for alternative energy.
Nigel: Oh, right ... wind power, solar energy, and that.

Rachel: No. I meant mental energy. [Embarrassed at the misunderstanding, we avoid each other's eyes for some moments] But there are so few people here, I don't know ... Before I left for my trip to the States I spoke with people who are spread throughout Israel but looking for a base; this'd be a great place to caucus. Yoga, meditation, that kinda thing.

When I first met Rachel she had spent a total of five months living in Mitzpe, but she had also just returned from an eight-month trip to the United States. The reason she had gone was that a dog of hers—Giacomo's father—was dying and she had wanted him to have the best care up to the final moments. When he had finally died, aged 13—she had a photo of him the very day he died—she had arranged to come back here.

The sad thing now was that Giacomo himself was not so well; in coming back to Mitzpe, Giacomo's water-on-the-lung had returned too. He was 12 and 1/2 now, and so a fair age, but Rachel felt assured that he was not yet ready to die; all she needed was to give him pills to stop him hurting.

When Rachel took Giacomo to the vet in the local clinic, however, she complained to me:

this Russian guy couldn't understand my concern. 'Yes, its gonna die', he says, 'and I'm gonna die and you're gonna die. So what?' I explained how I wanted the longest and the healthiest life for him that was possible, and also to know exactly when he was gonna go. 'Oh, you Americans! ... ', he says.

It was 'a natural human desire to look after something', Rachel supposed. Even before Giacomo finally died, Rachel had also taken to looking after stray dogs from around town in her apartment, dogs which town officials were trying to kill by putting down strychnine-laced sardines. Having lost a dog to poison once herself (while a Volunteer for Israel at the army camp), Rachel found the deliberate practice 'horrible, and a terrible way to go'. She looked up an old copy of the *Encyclopaedia Britannica* which she had brought to Israel in the hope of finding some information concerning the length of time strychnine might remain potent, but without any luck; she realized she was lost without a pharmacologist. But she thought three days would be a good guess; in any event, she was determined to offset the bad and irresponsible treatment meted out to dogs by many people in Mitzpe, even if it meant a gaggle of strays always following her around town and barking outside her apartment:

My neighbour keeps saying he's gonna get someone to take them away ... I hate him. I spat in his face once, you know, Nigel. Actually spat. Whenever he sees the German shepherd he yells 'Hitler'. He's about 70. Its understandable, but its sad. And yesterday, a policeman who lives in the building told me off too.

In short, Giacomo might have gone but she still had 'those other guys as company', Rachel explained. Moreover, unlike spoilt pups, the strays were grateful for every little attention.

In crisscrossing the Atlantic with (and, to an extent, for reason of) her dogs, in her spending time with them and expending energy insuring their comfort and security—even at the expense of securing easy relations with new human neighbours—Rachel demonstrated her continuing commitment to certain values she held dear. Bringing her dogs with her to Israel, continuing to visit Giacomo's grave to be near him, refusing to accept local practices regarding the poisoning of strays—finding them irresponsible—were ways too of embodying a continuity with a past life. But her behaviour also instantiated something particularly characteristic of her. Her dogs, her values, her behaviour were just how Rachel found they had to be, and she had the sense of right, of self-righteousness too, stubbornly to maintain them, irrespective of consequence. But then Rachel was well aware of their consequence. It became apparent that she deliberately related to local people, and the local milieux in Israel as such, by mediation of her relations with her dogs. She set up an opposition between herself and her dogs on one side and Israelis and their practices on the other, seemingly as a deliberate challenge, even provocation. Not only, I suggest, did Rachel maintain by this means of a sense of self, of who she was in the United States and should continue to be in Israel, but she also gained a sense of moral superiority. Her opposition (dogs versus Israelis) allowed her to test one thing against another, to represent options to herself, and to see which way she should go.

For Rachel was on a personal journey, as I have said. What you took with you were certain values, and setting these in the context of where you happened to be at a particular time—testing how you and others would react to them—you discovered the way to proceed. Not to live one's own individual life, not to grow into one's life by one's journeying through it, Rachel believed to be not merely a waste but a sign of pathology, both social and mental.

Over the months of our meeting—on the streets of Mitzpe, in my apartment or hers, in Hebrew class or the shops—Rachel returned to this theme repeatedly. The tensions involved were painfully obvious in Israel. For here, Rachel discovered many people who were 'literally crazy':

> There is lots of mental illness, Nigel; 'cos people come from repressive traditional societies—the Orientals—where individuality is not allowed and is repressed, and people's real eccentricities don't come out ... All these young people you meet here: they know they're searching for something, but they don't know what. They're really keen to ask you all about the West, America and that—like, someone who actually came here, from there, by choice! 'Cos, I mean, here they are, school, army, 'Look after your Brother!', and all the time there's something individual inside wanting to come out. So they rush here and rush there—all this energy, and aggression—and they dunno for what ... I take it you're not on the Right, Nigel!? [I shake my head and grin]

Sadly for her, Rachel came increasingly to find that she could put her discussions with many (if not most) Israelis to music; she knew exactly where she and they were going to converge and diverge, and it was always the same. What was so depressing was that the Israelis could not put the energy generated by their blind-spot about the Palestinians to better use, to achieving something constructive. 'The place is like a psychic cesspool! Don't you feel that, Nigel?'

Rachel also admitted to me, with a shake of her head and a wry smile, that: 'only a Jew could come here and understand the place—all the mental illness around. A non-Jew would not know what was going on'. Even: 'I get to feel a little mentally ill here myself!' It is as if Rachel domesticates the mental illness she infers, and its accompanying effects, as something of an intra-family trait, something Jews can know about themselves, discuss among themselves, but not expect to overcome. Treated as 'a Jewish issue', mental illness becomes something in Rachel's life to which she grows acculturated, something that—like her attachment to her dogs—just is; something which Rachel expects to represent a certain fixity in her life, and which she might accept as such.

Equally, however, Rachel does not expect what 'just is' to be *a single thing,* alone and uncontested. Her relationship with her dogs was something, I suggested, which Rachel construed simply had to be. But then she also construed this relationship as existing alongside other essential things in her life: her personal journey across the globe, to where her values regarding dogs were contested by her new Israeli neighbours and their contrastive experience of dogs during the Second World War. In the opening quotation from Rachel, likewise, we find her talking about her upbringing in the United States as both 'very moral and also Jewish': here too there appears to be a fundamental contrast, a duality, and an ambivalence which Rachel possessed in regard to that duality. She was Jewish, but not necessarily in terms of her moral foundations, nor in terms of how morality and ethnicity might be squared. In Israel now again, Rachel admitted to her Jewishness but reserved the right to differentiate herself from the 'mental illness' it seemed finally to have spawned. Or again, Rachel admitted to her potential Israeli citizenship but at the same time distanced herself from Israeli 'backwardness': blind-spots, chauvinism, under-education and institutions of state.

In other words, Rachel recognized the ontological nature of certain things—their 'is-ness'—but only 'emotionally': as part of a deliberate process of dialectical reasoning. Certain things just were, but in their 'is-ness' they also thereby contrasted fundamentally with other things. Her recognizing ontological contrasts, contests and oppositions, I would say, was an epistemological and developmental strategy by which Rachel would ascertain who she was at a particular time and place, and could discern how next to proceed. *It was a life-policy of an emotional kind.*

Questions of Jewishness, not surprisingly, arose quite frequently in our exchanges. Part of the reason Rachel had come to Israel was, after all, out of a desire to understand her Jewishness better. And even though the two years since her *aliyah* had disillusioned her, in a way, there was still a deep sense of her own Jewishness to which she held true. And yet, 'what is this Jewishness?', she asked me one day, before answering her own question:

> It's something in me, Nigel. Like I lived in Yeruham [another Negev development-town] for a while and suddenly, at a bus-stop, I chatted to a sixty-year-old Moroccan; and we liked each other. It wasn't sexual, but there was this immediate understanding. So what is that? Are we genetically alike, or do we have the same circuiting in the head, which causes similar behaviour and reactions? 'Cos we have something similar to all the different types in Israel, don't we?

Or again, she would ponder what it was that made being Jewish something special, before answering her own question in Jungian vein: there was perhaps something 'immortal, a divine spark, witnessed on Mount Sinai', which continued to descend the generations and engender ethnic characteristics.

On the other hand, Rachel would also admit that she had only really known religious Judaism before 'as a sentence', not formed it 'as a reality living beside her'. Furthermore, now that she had:

> I don't feel Jewish any more: I feel 'human', you know, Nigel? [I nod agreement.] It was like, in the States I was deprived of Jewishness before I was ready. It was a bit like losing a father: you keep moping after him—even though working for him all his life may not in fact have been better! You know? [We laugh.] But now I've worked Jewishness out of my system; if I went home now, I would take this experience with me.

I found it significant that Rachel spoke so openly of having worked through her Jewishness and of going 'home' to the United States. It was, after all, only some days previously that Rachel had assured me that 'home' was something she carried round in her head. Now, however, she was above all 'pleased to be American':

> Looking back I like the blanket spread lightly over a very diverse society. I like America ... When I first came here I liked the family feel about the place, you know. But not now: people expecting you, as a stranger, to answer personal questions all the time, and them expecting to have the right to keep asking them.

In the United States she found she was 'left alone' in all sorts of ways that made her testy here.

This vacillation or restlessness is something we might associate with Rachel by now. What is perhaps distinctive here is the way Rachel veered between what might be called mystical and practical, or mythopoetic and empirical, poles of meaning. She imagined an alchemical mystery of Jewish archetypes with divine origins, and she recognized a psychological rationale for the hold Jewishness had over her and the difficulties of actually living a myth; and she also admitted the gulf separating the two kinds of reasoning.

In describing Rachel's reaction to the 'mental illness' she found in Israel I proposed that she came to accept it as something of a 'familial' trait: something she could understand, even assume and find in herself, however sad the occurrence. Likewise, the 'is-ness' of her Jewishness was, I would say, something Rachel construed in familial terms. Jewish Israel was like one big family, one she grew to find suffocating. More than this Jewishness itself was 'like a father': a genetic inheritance which engendered you—and was inescapable—but which you might not consciously know as a form of life. But at the same time Rachel did not expect her individual journey through life to be determined by her ethnic origins, nor as necessarily similar to those who began where she did. There was more to her than her Jewishness, her family beginnings and relations, however others might seek to apply such mystical or mythopoetic collective archetypes in her regard.

On another occasion I was interested to hear Rachel reasoning thus:

> I was beaten up as a girl, you know. 'Cos I was more sensitive and apt to cry; and 'cos I was more intelligent than the blockheads around me. And my dad would blame it on anti-Semitism and get very passionate about it. But I knew it wasn't that at all; I didn't tell him though 'cos I didn't have the vocabulary. And he was so passionate about it he wouldn't have heard me even if I'd tried! But I also learned a psychological lesson: that when I finally hit back and beat the bully to a pulp—it took me a few years to build up to that level of violence—the bully immediately wanted to be best friends.

In other words, Jewishness understood as an inherited archetype—something genetic or neurophysiological, something as inescapable as one's family origins and as mystical as a divine spark—was something that Rachel could recognize in others' behaviours; it was even something that she could draw for herself. But she still reserved the right to claim an individual intentionality which was practical, empirical and selective. She set up familial Jewishness against merely human Americanness, tested the experience of one against the other, and—at least while in Israel—chose to be more at home in the latter. However Jewish she might continue to feel, it was by no means all she was, or what she essentially was, and she resented it if others assumed the latter to be the case.

The individuality of her pathway through life was often enunciated by Rachel in terms of her ceramics. When Rachel emigrated to Israel, as we have heard, she thought she had possibly left ceramics behind her; it had taken her as far as it could. Nevertheless, the men she found herself gravitating towards in Israel tended to be artistic (a painter in En Hod, a geologist in Yeruham), and it was as a pottery teacher at the field school that they had 'invented' a job so that she might legitimately settle in Mitzpe. In practice, the pottery-teaching had not amounted to much and she was soon drawing an unemployment dole while she sought out casual employment and considered her options. She cleaned rooms at the field school and at the youth hostel for free food; she did some piecework at the pottery factory in Yeruham. On beginning a relationship with Zvi (a Hungarian Holocaust survivor with four children, whose wife had recently left him), she took to working with him on the town gardens.

Gradually, however, Rachel realized how inspiring she still found the desert, how it kept drawing her in. Furthermore, it felt as if there were a large void in her life which could be filled only by her setting up a potter's wheel and kiln again, and creating her own ceramics. Once she had made her decision, however, she was energized. She fetched her container of personal effects, shipped from the US to the port of Haifa, and she used the plywood packing case to make a flywheel for a potter's wheel; she ordered a kiln kit. Once her wheel was up she began to feel more like herself again.

Rachel had first moved to Mitzpe Ramon from Beer Sheva, we have seen, because she felt spiritually connected to the place; she could imagine Mitzpe as a centre for those like herself seeking an inspirational source of mental energy. It was not long after she and I met, moreover, that she told me that one of Uri Hazan's projects was for pots to be made at the field school clayery which might then be sold to tourists in the gift shop at the new Ramon Crater Visitors' Center. And Rachel could now imagine making and selling something herself:

> Something that captured the *machtesh* [crater] somehow; I'm not sure how yet. Not glazed on the outside, definitely not. Possibly on the inside.

Making pottery in and of the desert would be a way of manifesting and signalling her newly fashioned relationship to the desert town.

Another of Rachel's new ideas was for 'an energy centre'. In the United States, she recounted to me, she and her husband and friends had opened 'a kinda cafe', a coffee shop, for poetry readings, plays and the like. Everyone had contributed $100:

> [W]ell, me and my husband put in $500, and the rest put in $100. Do you want to do the same thing here? Everyone chips in, lets say, 100 shekels and then they get in for free—for performances and refreshments and the rest. And in the end, like in the States, we get our investment repaid. Hopefully! [She laughs.] It would have to be in some central place where people would see it and just drop in, like a store front. And with Americans and Brits and ... Russians coming, it would be a cultural centre. For poetry and art, and gatherings, and getting energy.

At a public meeting of the Mitzpe branch of the 'Anglo-Saxons' immigrant organization, Americans and Canadians in Israel (AACI), Rachel had mooted the plan; but she was met with, at best, a polite indifference from the audience of largely elderly townsfolk. She was thoroughly saddened and disappointed.

Her disappointment, moreover, was to become symptomatic of a change in attitude Rachel soon found herself experiencing with regard to Mitzpe as a place to live. It would be okay, she confided in me, 'if the place took off'; she could even imagine buying one of the scores of empty *cottagim* [villas] for sale at ridiculously low prices if that were to happen. As it was, the place felt deserted and she did not find any community of interests between her and her heterogeneous neighbours. More particularly:

> I'm not surprised more artists don't want to move here ... I guess few people will have the mental energy to live in a place like this. (And in a country of five million people, there aren't gonna be the numbers; they'll wanna be by everyone else.)

In her disillusionment, the place she had once regarded as potential source of alternative energy now seemed a drain on the very energy individuals possessed when they arrived.

Soon, indeed, I was to find Rachel's disappointment in Mitzpe turning to despair, especially when she returned from a visit with friends in Jerusalem or Tel Aviv:

Rachel: Don't you feel a sort of *'hud'* [she drops her shoulders and makes a noise of weary resignation] coming back here to Mitzpe, Nigel? Have I missed anything? [I shrug, and shake my head.] What would I do if I didn't have you to talk to? ... I've been very depressed.

Nigel: Yeah, you haven't seemed your usual self.

Rachel: Oh! Did it show? I'm still depressed; but less so ... I'm a bit schizo about being here. Are you as well, Nigel?

By 'here', it became clear before long, Rachel was including Israel as well as just Mitzpe:

> Living anywhere in Israel leaves you with a *'hud'* after a while.

But then I could also recall how disillusionment had been a recurring theme in Rachel's conversation from the beginning. It had not been long after we had met, after all, that she had confided in me how 'weird' her decision to come to Israel already seemed. She was, she explained, prepared to:

> give the place one-and-a-half years, till my 50th birthday. A year seems like a natural, organic period of time to see if its right for me.

It is not long before Rachel is telling me that she has decided to move away from Mitzpe altogether; she is going to find an apartment in Jerusalem. There she had already met up with a group of radical women affiliated to the Peace Now group, and to civil rights groups and the International Peace Brigade, who liaised with Palestinian counterparts on the West Bank.

But soon there is another new development:

Rachel: I'm in love, Nigel, for the first time since my husband and I split twenty
years ago.
Nigel: Zvi? The gardener?
Rachel: Yeah, Zvi. You'll have to meet him.
Nigel: That's great!
Rachel: I mean I've had relationships, but not with anyone I could see no faults in.
And if I get a flat in Jerusalem, Zvi also said he'd visit.

Leaving my apartment she rushed home to dye her hair.

But then, as her relationship developed with Zvi, so did the confidence with which
Rachel espoused the continuing contradictoriness of her feelings. On the one hand,
she was still 'bored shitless' in Mitzpe and looking forward to going to Jerusalem, if
only to 'check it out' for a few days. On the other hand, she found she was

> still learning here [in Mitzpe]; so I'm not ready to leave. You know, I find more of the
> kind of experiences here that are not clear-cut, they're not one thing or another: they're
> good and bad at the same time.

And this was indicative of something specific Rachel felt she had learned:

> I was surprised to find that my feelings about Israel are shared by people who have been
> living here a while too. They still have reservations about the mentality and are not all
> taken in by the place ... Like this old Rumanian I got speaking to in Beer Sheva who said
> its okay here for the kids—'cos they know no better—but not for the rest of us.

In short, Rachel began to find, in Mitzpe as well as beyond, people with whom she
felt she shared 'similar vibes', as she felt she did with me:

> Hey, Nigel: it's so nice having someone else here who isn't so sure about the place! ...
> We'll have to keep in touch, over the years, see who leaves first. But my life is full at the
> moment. I mean I'm pleased I went to Jerusalem; I couldn't have hacked it here much
> longer. But now I can get into both places. Like, my pottery is coming together here
> now; I made a big wall piece and the hotel said they'd like it. I wanted something that
> had come out of 'the individual-in-the-desert'. So it's this huge wall-ceramic, with pock-
> ets—like, organic protuberances where you can put flower pots. And it would be easy to
> do again—it had no plan, it was just organic—and I could do it anytime, relaxed.

As is characteristic, Rachel divides up her experience of Mitzpe into 'desert' and 'deserted'; she finds herself attracted by the beauty and spiritual potential of the place
and, in seeming equal measure, put off by the narrowness and lack of focus of its

émigré population. Having created the distinction, she knows more where she stands and where she is going. Life becomes full again, a learning curve, by way of new experiences which are grounded in, and consequent upon, a dialectics of agonism and contrariety.

*

In sum, Rachel seemed to settle herself into Mitzpe, and into Israel more generally, by accruing experiences which are 'schizo'—neither absolutely one thing nor another—and between whose poles her reasoning and actions might travel. Her intellectual practice was continually to construe certain essentialized but contrastive aspects of the world—Judaism and morality; mental illness and alternative energy; her relations with her dogs and her movement round the world; the desert and the city; her pottery and her politics—and then to proceed to vacillate between these fixed points. Her vacillation freed her from the overriding influence of any one fixity—whether that influence was of an intellectual kind, or sentimental, or physical, or cultural, or historical, or autobiographical. Her attempts to come to terms with and overcome the contrasts between these fixities, meanwhile, provided a tension, a dialectic, whereby she continued to give her life impetus and direction; her identification of extreme positions—'psychic cesspool', 'bored shitless'—gave onto the comparative moderation which her own journey eventually took. I was impressed by Rachel's willingness and capacity for enunciating her own self-analyses. She knew she felt 'schizo' in Mitzpe and in Israel—also that this mirrored a duality that had brought her here initially—and that she was continuing to find experiences which were not 'clear-cut', not 'one thing or another'. She also knew how a juggling with difference was in her nature, and necessary for her equilibrium; as she put it on one occasion: 'I'm a political animal, Nigel, but I also need to touch the earth for my sanity'.

Rachel's conceptualization of the world around her, the cognitive landmarks she identified in the social and cultural landscapes through which she moved—'morality' versus 'Judaism', 'left-wing' versus 'right-wing', 'desert town' versus 'lively metropolis', 'Jew' versus 'Arab', 'bureaucrat' versus 'artist', and so on—these classifications and evaluations could be said to be hardly particular to her ('a child of the 1960s'). However, what I would define as characteristic is the precise way Rachel dealt with her conceptualizations, navigating around and between extreme positionings as she charted a continuing life-course for herself, conjuring up *her own* dialectics of personal growth, refusing the haven, the stasis and the limitation of any one landmark. She was brief in her habits of identity and professed having an enjoyable fullness to her life chiefly when she provided herself with a novel tension, an opposition, whose dialectical resolution would ultimately lead her further down the road of personal completion—if only by way of further tensions. She moved between essential features of a landscape, but she herself claimed none, adopting a largely affirmative attitude towards the fate that her emotional engagements brought about.

Conclusion: 'Identity'

I have described Rachel's life as an 'emotional' one, causing her to travel between countries, livelihoods, relationships, memories, loyalties, social structures, institutions and habitations. All the time believing she was engaged on the same 'life-project' (Rapport 2003), she reasoned her way between intellectual positions which were contradictory and social attachments which were paradoxical; motility was Rachel's preferred experiential modality. What, finally, does this enable us to say on anthropology's possible contribution to the question of identity and its emotional aspect?

'We set up a word', Nietzsche wrote (1968: 482), 'at the point at which ignorance begins, at which we can see no further': words represent 'the horizon of our knowledge' and not things-in-themselves, singularities or truths. The English word 'identity' derives from the Latin *'identitatis'* and ultimately from *'idem'*, meaning 'the same'. 'Identity' the dictionary defines as when something is 'the same as itself'. To make sense of the concept of something being the same as itself is to consider thingness as intrinsically plural, or at least dual; there must be two or more versions or aspects of a thing so that one can be adjudged the same as the other. We might say that built into the concept of identity is the idea of extension: a thing is intrinsically extensive; thingness is a kind of extension. This extension might be temporal—so that a thing is adjudged to be the same now as before. Or extension might be spatial: a thing is the same here as there. Or again, extension might be situational, with a thing adjudged as being the same in company as by itself, in monologue as in dialogue. Extension, in short, may itself be of different kinds, but the concept of identity makes a claim to sameness between two or more moments of existence at which change might have occurred and difference resulted. 'Identity' becomes an issue of retention and a site of tension.

The people whose voices this chapter has mainly deployed—Forster, Hume, Nietzsche, Rachel Silberstein—and whose reasoning has been described as 'emotional', would also concur, I suggest, that the word 'identity' is an oxymoron; it is illusory to claim that human beings are ever the same as themselves. Individual embodiment—human physiological, sensual, ideational, conceptual processes—has the consequence that 'we' are never the same at different moments: our lives are a becoming, a career. The truth is to be found in the paradox that only change is constant; as Nietzsche put it (1994: 125), 'the real immortality is that of movement'.

But then, Forster, Hume, Nietzsche, and Rachel Silberstein also recognized, I would suggest, the benefits of maintaining the illusion of identity, of taking consolation in the seeming fixity of the concept and the word. However nonrational, they all appreciated both the attractiveness of living the ideology of identity—concerning selfhood (Forster), the customary (Hume), will (Nietzsche), or completion (Silberstein)—*and* that such habitude could exercise a tyranny over the full experience of one's life.

Their 'emotionalism' extended to their willingness, certainly in their own lives, of accepting intellectual positions and engaging in practical activities which were contradictory, which made them patently different to themselves, at the same time as they believed that their personal names ('David Hume', 'Rachel Silberstein', and so on) were words that identified the same people. Their emotionalism allowed them to compass the paradoxical in their lives (see Rapport 1997b).

'Emotion' has been approached in this chapter as pertaining intrinsically to movement, to the motile part of an individual's physical constitution, reasoning and behaviour. Human beings are emotional creatures, I conclude, inasmuch as our consciousnesses are constituted by movements between the sensory and the conceptual, and between different moments and different versions of sensation and of conceptualization. Furthermore, the behaviours to which our consciousnesses give rise may move in recursive, looping, zigzagging and other, nonlinear fashions through the careers of our lives. Finally, admitting this to ourselves—that the movements of our lives may make our identities incoherent, contradictory (however comforting it is on occasion to believe the opposite)—may be a source of insight and strength.

References

Appadurai, A. (1996), *Modernity at Large,* Minneapolis: University of Minnesota Press.

Forster, E. M. (1972), *Two Cheers for Democracy,* Harmondsworth: Penguin.

Gellner, E. (1998), *Language and Solitude,* Cambridge: Cambridge University Press.

Hume, D. (2000), *A Treatise of Human Nature,* Oxford: Oxford University Press.

Kierkegaard, S. (1985), *Fear and Trembling,* Harmondsworth: Penguin.

Nietzsche, F. (1968), *The Will to Power,* New York: Random House.

Nietzsche, F. (1979a), *Beyond Good and Evil,* Harmondsworth: Penguin.

Nietzsche, F. (1979b), *Ecce Homo,* Harmondsworth: Penguin.

Nietzsche, F. (1994), *Human, All Too Human,* Harmondsworth: Penguin.

Rapport, N. (1994), *The Prose and the Passion: Anthropology, Literature and the Writing of E. M. Forster,* Manchester: Manchester University Press.

Rapport, N. (1997a), *Transcendent Individual: Towards a Literary and Liberal Anthropology,* London: Routledge.

Rapport, N. (1997b), 'The "Contrarieties" of Israel. An Essay on the Cognitive Importance and the Creative Promise of Both/And', *Journal of the Royal Anthropological Institute* 3(4), pp. 653–72.

Rapport, N. (1998), 'Coming Home to a Dream: A Study of the Immigrant Discourse of "Anglo-Saxons" in Israel', in N. Rapport and A. Dawson (eds), *Migrants of Identity. Perceptions of Home in a World of Movement,* pp. 61–83, Oxford: Berg.

Rapport, N. (2003), *I Am Dynamite: An Alternative Anthropology of Power,* London and New York: Routledge.

Rapport, N., and Dawson, A., eds (1998), *Migrants of Identity: Perceptions of Home in a World of Movement,* Oxford: Berg.

Wulff, H. (1998), *Ballet across Borders: Career and Culture in the World of Dancers,* Oxford: Berg.

Afterword by Robert A. LeVine

Can anthropology advance our understanding of the emotions in an era when neuroscience is the primary hope for scientific progress in this field? The articles in this collection of selected readings leave little doubt that anthropology can—and has—contributed uniquely to our scientific understanding of the emotions, and they also point to the ways in which those contributions will continue to be important as knowledge of the brain advances. I shall attempt to summarize these ways.

The first is field research and laboratory experiment. The history of the life sciences over the past 150 years shows field research to be an essential and central part of its spectacular progress. Had biology been limited to the laboratory experiments of Mendel, Pasteur, Koch and Morgan, we would have learned a great deal about the mechanisms of heredity and infection at the microscopic level, but it was the naturalistic observations of Darwin that eventually led to the integrated understanding of processes in all living organisms that lies at the basis of the modern life sciences. There was no contradiction between findings in the laboratory and those from the field; their complementarity was the greatest strength of biological science as it surged forward in the twentieth century.

So it could be with the study of emotion. The exciting laboratory experiments of neuroscientists described in Chapter 3 by Morten Kringelbach, revealing areas of the brain involved in emotional activation, do not contradict the findings of anthropology or other social sciences but rather cry out for exploration in the diverse contexts in which humans live. When psychologists gave up the presumption of continuity in psychological process between infrahuman laboratory animals and humans, one major obstacle was removed to a future synthesis of neuroscience and social science. There remain methodological barriers, especially the problem that laboratory scientists tend to count as knowledge only findings that have been established through experiment, but I have hopes that in the area of emotion it will be evident even to the white-coated tribe that contexts beyond the laboratory are critical to their science.

In their ethnographic investigations of emotions in context, anthropologists are natural historians of diversity. Like Darwin studying the Galapagos finches, anthropologists discover patterns of emotion in strange places—among civilians under attack in Northern Ireland and Israel, among headhunters in the Philippines, in the love magic of healers in post-Soviet Russia—and in many other places represented in this volume. Their explorations are necessary to the study of emotions in a human species differentiated by their symbol systems, moral standards and social relations across populations and historical periods.

Second is ethnographic research. The descriptive accounts of emotions in context recorded by anthropologists in their ethnographic reports on diverse human populations are complementary to experimental studies: Ethnography captures emotional experience in naturally occurring situations, rather than the artificially contrived situations of the laboratory, which endows its observations with the ecological validity lacking in controlled experiments. Rather than seeking to isolate the basic elements or universal building blocks of emotional experience, ethnographers seek to uncover and understand that experience *in all its complexity* in a particular setting. An ethnographer, unlike an experimenter, attempts to understand a phenomenon already located in a person's life from the point of view of the person living that life, and anthropologists tend to suspect that the most significant aspects of emotional experience to the person are those that are culture-specific rather than those with clear equivalents in all human cultures. Just as we cannot speak without speaking a particular language (Geertz, 1973, p. 87, quoting Santayana), if we leave out the particular cultural and psychological meanings of emotions by reducing them to their universal elements, we have omitted their functional significance in human communication and experience.

The studies reported and reviewed in this volume illustrate how mistaken it would be to assume that emotions are unproblematically translatable from one culture or historical period to another. It is in the work of 'thick description', that is, attempting to describe the multilayered and culture-specific emotional experience of people in one community to readers in another, that ethnographers identify what it is about that experience that has an impact socially and psychologically. This reconstruction of the actor's point of view is indispensable for understanding how emotions operate in human societies.

Third is the comparative perspective. Ethnographic knowledge of emotions, however focused on the unfamiliar in distant places, eventually comes home to reshape our perceptions, scientific and otherwise, of emotional experience. In examining emotions in diverse human contexts, ethnographers and their readers become aware not only of the many forms and meanings emotions take there—for example, of the unexpected ways in which emotion talk, facial expressions and bodily experience are combined, or the relationship imagined between reason and emotion—but also of the political, economic, social and cultural factors that affect emotional experience. These factors operate, as many of the chapters in this volume emphasize, not only in strange places but also in our own experience of emotions, and even in the assumptions we bring to the scientific study of emotion.

After examining a variety of non-Western cultures, it becomes clear that Western religious and philosophical thought as well as folk concepts predispose us to see emotions in mentalistic terms, that is, as characteristics of a psyche—a rational or irrational faculty and its "inner experience"—rather than as properties of situations, bodies, communities or deities. This "mentalistic" frame for viewing emotion was elaborated during the twentieth century with the emergence of psychiatry and psychology, not only as medical and research disciplines but also as popular frameworks for conceptualizing and evaluating behavior in everyday discourse. There was already a moral discourse for viewing emotions as signs of authenticity, integrity and courage (or their absence), but during the second half of the century concepts of mental health and illness came to prevail, and with it the idea that children and adults are emotionally vulnerable creatures, easily injured by 'adverse' circumstances that had formerly been seen as building moral character.

It seems likely to me (and some of the authors represented in this volume) that Western scientists studying emotions inadvertently take some of their assumptions—for example, concerning the place of emotions in psychological experience or the distinction between rationality and emotion—from the culture-specific perspective of Western mentalism, in its mental health version or other forms, rather than from an empirically grounded view of emotion in the human species. The antidote for this bias is now available in this cultural reader on the emotions.

Reference

Geertz, C. (1973), *The Interpretation of Cultures,* New York: The Free Press.

Contributors

William O. Beeman is Professor and Chair of the Department of Anthropology at the University of Minnesota. A linguistic anthropologist, he specializes in discourse analysis and performance studies. His research has centered on the Middle East, particularly Iran; Japan, South Asia and Europe, where he performed as an opera singer in Germany. Among his publications are *Language, Status and Power in Iran; The "Great Satan" vs. the "Mad Mullas": How the United States and Iran Demonize Each Other;* and *The Third Line: The Opera Performer as Interpreter*, which he wrote with opera stage director Daniel Helfgot.

Billy Ehn is Professor of Ethnology at the Department of Culture and Media, Umeå University. His latest publications, in Swedish, deal with various topics, for example the university as a workplace and the meaning of academic cultures, the use and interpretation of monuments in European countries and new perspectives in cultural analysis.

Don Handelman is Sarah Allen Shaine Professor Emeritus of Anthropology at the Hebrew University of Jerusalem. He is the author of *Models and Mirrors: Towards an Anthropology of Public Events* (1998), *Nationalism and the Israeli State: Bureaucratic Logic in Public Events* (2004), the co-author (with David Shulman) of *God Inside Out: Siva's Game of Dice* (1997) and *Siva in the Forest of Pine: An Essay on Sorcery and Self-Knowledge* (2004) and the co-editor (with Galina Lindquist) of *Ritual in Its Own Right: Exploring the Dynamics of Transformation* and (with Terry Evens) of *The Manchester School: Practice and Ethnographic Praxis in Anthropology*. His research interests include complexity theory; boundaries, borders, and framing; ritual; bureaucratic logic and the state. Current field research is in Israel and South India. He has been a fellow of The Netherlands Institute of Advanced Study, The Swedish Collegium of Advanced Study, Collegium Budapest and The Max-Planck Institute for the History of Science and has served as the Olof H. Palme Visiting Professor of the Swedish Research Council. He is a member of the Israel Academy of Sciences and Humanities.

Signe Howell is Professor of Social Anthropology at the University of Oslo. She obtained both an M.Litt. and D.Phil. from Oxford University and has been a lecturer in the Department of Social Anthropology at the University of Edinburgh. Before studying transnational adoption, her research was in Southeast Asia. She has published widely on various aspects of social organization, religion, ritual, kinship and gender. Her books include *Society and Cosmos: Chewong of Peninsular Malaysia, Chewong Myths and Legends, Societies at Peace: Anthropological Perspectives* (edited with Roy Willis), *For the Sake of Our Future: Sacrificing in Eastern Indonesia, The House in Southeast Asia* (edited with Stephen Sparkes), *The Ethnography of Moralities* and *The Kinning of Foreigners: Transnational Adoption in a Global Perspective*. She has also published a number of articles in books and journals on the topic of transnational adoption.

Morten L. Kringelbach, D. Phil, is Senior Research Fellow in the Department of Psychiatry, Oxford University, and Research Professor at CFIN, Aarhus University, Denmark. Kringelbach's main research interest is in understanding the functional neuroanatomy of human conscious and unconscious processing, in particular aspects related to pleasure, desire, emotion, learning and reward processing. His research has helped to further our understanding of hedonic processing in the human brain as described in many highly cited papers. He received the research prize at the MRC Showcase 2006 'Breakthroughs in Neuroscience and Mental Health' for his pioneering research using new neuroimaging methods to better understand the functional neuroanatomy of the brain. In recognition of his significant contributions to the public understanding of science, he also received the 2006 Danish Science Communication Prize from the Crown Princess Mary.

Robert A. LeVine is Roy Edward Larsen Professor Emeritus of Education and Human Development, Harvard University. His research concerns cultural aspects of parenthood and child development in African, Asian, Latin American and other societies. His most recent research is on the influence of maternal schooling on reproduction and child health care in Nepal. He is examining how women's literacy positively affects their health and that of their children, as well as contributing to children's emerging literacy. Among his books are *Childcare and Culture: Lessons from Africa* (1994), *Human Conditions: The Cultural Basis of Educational Development* (with M. I. White, 1986), *Culture, Behavior, and Personality* (1973) and *Dreams and Deeds: Achievement Motivation in Nigeria* (1966). Robert LeVine has been given several honours including the American Educational Research Association Award for Distinguished Contributions to Educational Research (2001) and Distinguished Career Contributions, Society for Psychological Anthropology (1997). Robert LeVine is a Fellow of the American Academy of Arts and Sciences and a Member of the National Academy of Education.

Galina Lindquist is Associate Professor at the Department of Social Anthropology, Stockholm University. She has done research on ritual, play, healing and multiple medical systems in Scandinavia, Russia and Southern Siberia. Her publications include *Shamanic Performances on the Urban Scene, Conjuring Hope* and *In Search for the Authentic Shaman*, and she co-edited (with Don Handelman) the collection *Ritual in Its Own Right*. Her present research is on Buddhism and shamanism in Southern Siberia.

Orvar Löfgren is Professor of European ethnology at the University of Lund. His research is focused on the cultural analysis of everyday life. Currently he is leading a research project on 'the cultural production of the inconspicuous', focusing on activities like mundane routines and daydreaming. Among his recent publications are *On Holiday. A History of Vacationing* (2000), *Magic, Culture and the New Economy* (edited together with Robert Willim, 2005) and *Off the Edge: Experiments in Cultural Analysis*, edited with Richard Wilk (2006).

Timothy de Waal Malefyt is Vice President and Director of Cultural Discoveries at BBDO Worldwide Advertising in New York and adjunct Professor at Parsons, the New School for Design, in New York. At BBDO, Dr. Malefyt leads a strategic group which uses ethnography across the spectrum of client brands, such as FedEx, Visa, Target, Chrysler, Pepsi and HBO. In particular, his group seeks out rituals of consumption and applies discourse analysis to study products, brands and services in the context of consumer use. He earned his PhD (1997) in Anthropology from Brown University and received Fulbright and National Science Foundation Research Grants to study flamenco in Spain. He is co-editor of *Advertising Cultures* (2003) from Berg, published in the International *Design Dictionary (Wörterbuch Design)* by Birkhäuser Verlag (T. Marshall and M. Erlhoff, eds), and is widely quoted in *Business Week*, the *New York Times* and *USA Today*. He can be reached at timothy. malefyt@bbdo.com.

Kay Milton is Professor of Social Anthropology at Queen's University, Belfast. She has worked in the field of environmental anthropology for many years, conducting fieldwork with conservation groups in Britain and Ireland. This research produced two authored books (*Environmentalism and Cultural Theory*, Routledge, 1996, and *Loving Nature*, Routledge, 2002), several edited volumes (including *Environmentalism: The View from Anthropology*, Routledge, 1993) and numerous book chapters and journal articles. Over the past few years, she has turned her attention to the study of emotions as ecological mechanisms. In 2005 she and Maruška Svašek published the edited volume *Mixed Emotions: Anthropological Studies of Feeling* (Berg). Her current research combines these two strands by examining the emotional aspects of human–animal relations, attachments to landscape and responses to global warming.

Hélène Neveu Kringelbach, PhD, is a Departmental Lecturer in African Studies at Oxford University. For her D.Phil. at the Institute of Social and Cultural Anthropology, Oxford, she carried out research on the relationship between social mobility and performance in urban Senegal. In particular, the research highlighted the ways in which social hierarchies—along the lines of class, 'caste', gender and generation— are renegotiated through both popular and theatrical forms of dance and music in Dakar. Dr Neveu Kringelbach also holds a French Masters degree in Management Studies and has several years of work experience in industry. Her research is therefore always informed by a concern with the political economy of performative and artistic practices in West Africa. She is also developing an interest in migration issues and is currently preparing a new research project on West African artists in the Diaspora.

Nigel Rapport is Professor of Anthropological and Philosophical Studies at the University of St. Andrews. He has also held a Canada Research Chair in Globalisation, Citizenship and Justice, and acted as founding director of the Centre for Cosmopolitan Studies at Concordia University of Montreal. His research interests include: social theory, phenomenology, identity, individuality, consciousness, literary anthropology, humanism and cosmopolitanism. Among his recent publications are *I am Dynamite: An Alternative Anthropology of Power* (2003, Routledge), *The Trouble with Community: Anthropological Reflections on Movement, Identity and Collectivity* (2002, Pluto), and (as editor) *Democracy, Science and The Open Society: A European Legacy?* (2006, Transaction). Currently he is working on a second edition of *Social and Cultural Anthropology: The Key Concepts* (Routlpedge) and a monograph based on his most recent fieldwork as a porter in a Scottish hospital, provisionally entitled *Of Orderlies and Men: Hospital Porters Achieving Wellness at Work.*

Moshe Shokeid received his PhD from the University of Manchester and is currently Professor of Anthropology at Tel Aviv University. Dr Shokeid conducted fieldwork on diverse populations in various locations: Jewish immigrants from the Atlas Mountains in Israeli farming communities, Arabs in Jaffa, Israeli immigrants in the Borough of Queens and gay institutions in New York City. Major publications include *The Dual Heritage* (Manchester, 1971; Transaction, 1985); *The Predicament of Homecoming* (with S. Deshen, Cornell, 1974), *Distant Relations* (with S. Deshen, Praeger, 1982), *Children of Circumstances* (Cornell, 1988) and *A Gay Synagogue in New York* (Columbia, 1995; Pennsylvania, 2003).

Jonathan Skinner, PhD, is a Lecturer in Social Anthropology at Queen's University, Belfast. He has interests in the areas of social dance (jive and salsa), tourism, development, narrative, poetry and post/colonial discourse. He has conducted fieldwork on Montserrat in the Eastern Caribbean (post/colonial discourses) and in the United Kingdom and Northern Ireland (social dancing). He is Editor of the journal *Anthropology in Action* and author of *Before the Volcano:Reverberations of Identity on Montserrat* (Arawak, 2004).

Maruška Svašek is a Lecturer in the School of History and Anthropology, Queen's University, Belfast. Her main research interests are art production, emotional dynamics and migration. Major publications include *Anthropology, Art and Cultural Production* (Pluto, 2007), the edited volume *Postsocialism. Politics and Emotions in Central and Eastern Europe* (Berghahn, 2006) and the co-edited volume (with Kay Milton) *Mixed Emotions: Anthropological Studies of Feeling* (Berg, 2005). Her current research focuses on the emotional dimensions of migrant belonging and non-belonging in Northern Ireland.

Helena Wulff is Associate Professor of Social Anthropology at Stockholm University. Her English-language publications include *Twenty Girls: Growing Up, Ethnicity and Excitement in a South London Microculture* (Almqvist & Wiksell International, 1988), *Ballet across Borders: Career and Culture in the World of Dancers* (Berg, 1998), *Dancing at the Crossroads: Memory and Mobility in Ireland* (Berghahn, 2007) and articles for journals and volumes. She has co-edited the volumes *Youth Cultures: A Cross-Cultural Perspective* (with Vered Amit-Talai, Routledge, 1995) and *New Technologies at Work: People, Screens and Social Virtuality* (with Christina Garsten, Berg, 2003). Her research interests have revolved around youth culture and ethnicity and currently focus on the anthropology of dance, the arts, visual culture, the emotions, writing and Irish literature, new technology and transnationality. She is Editor (with Dorle Dracklé) of *Social Anthropology/Anthropologie Sociale*.

Copyright Permissions

Index

Abu-Lughod, L., 3, 4, 63, 251, 341
academic hatred, 103
academicians, 101–16 passim
actor's point of view, 398
ad agencies, 321, 329
Adams, D., 61, 64
admiration, 8, 104–7, 113–14
adoption, 2, 6
advertisers, 321–36 passim
advertising, 2, 8, 9
age, 6, 312–4
   see also generation characteristics
agency, 154, 162, 164
agent, primary and secondary, 232, 235–6,
   243–4
AIDS epidemic, 302, 312
alcohol consumption, 172
aliyah, 383–4, 387
alliesthesia, 42, 44
allocentric, 343, 348
Amazon, the, 241
Americanness, 389
amygdala, 40–3, 53, 281–5, 297n19
am yisrael, 125
àndal ak sa sago, 251
Anderson, B., 132, 140n16
anger, 4, 5, 6, 11–12, 174–5, 199–203
   passim, 206, 208–11, 213n3, 215n8, 215n9,
   216n13, 216n16, 216n17, 216n19, 370,
   374–5
anxiety, 185, 222
Appadurai, A., 323, 341, 380
Aristotelian divide, 254
Aristotle, 325
artefacts, 6
artificial elation, 84–5
attentional shift, 33
attraction, 303–5, 307, 310, 314
Austin, J., 276, 284
Australia, 369
authenticity, 240, 399
autism, study of, 285
autobiographies, 102, 104–5
autonomy, 373, 376

Bachoriwski, J. A., 12
Bali, 357
Bandura, A., 33
Bateson, G., 278, 298n23
Bauman, R., 277
Bedouin community, 143
Beeman, W. O., 276, 279, 288, 295n1, 297n20,
   298n22
behaviourism, 40
Belfast, 93
Bell, D., 87, 90n8
Berridge, K. C., 43
beta blockers, 39
biology, 1, 12
biophilia hypothesis, 67
birth order names, 361–2
bitterness, 8, 103, 107, 110–12, 114
black gay men, 307–10, 312
Bloch, C., 103, 109
Bloch, M., 358
body
   and brain, 39
   and mind dichotomy, 22, 34, 39, 280, 343,
      347–8
      see also Cartesian dualism; emotion and
         thought; Reason and Passion; nature–
         culture divide
   grooming, 258–9
   micropractises, 115
   parts as objects of art, 235–41
   theory of emotion, 11
Body Worlds, 238
Boorstin, D., 326
Bourdieu, P., 103, 264, 279
brain lesions, 282–3, 285
brain structures, 12, 38–9, 42, 53, 54f3.4
branding, 327, 332, 335–6, 338n2
brands, 321, 323–4, 326–8, 335
Braverman, H., 87, 90n9
Briggs, J., 202–3
Bruner, E., 340
Bulgakov, M., 154, 156
bureaucratic logic, 120–39 passim
byt, 157–9, 164